Suspense Thriller

(GENRE WRITER SERIES)

SUSPENSE THRILLER

HOW TO WRITE CHASE, SPY, LEGAL, MEDICAL, PSYCHOLOGICAL, POLITICAL & TECHNO-THRILLERS

PAUL TOMLINSON

Copyright © 2018 by Paul Tomlinson

All rights reserved. This book may not be reproduced or transmitted, in whole or in part, or used in any manner whatsoever, without the express permission of the copyright owner, except for the use of brief quotations in the context of a book review.

The content of this book is provided for educational purposes. Every effort has been made to ensure the accuracy of the information presented. However, the information is sold without warranty, either express or implied, and the author shall not be liable for any loss or damage caused – directly or indirectly – by its use.

For country of manufacture, please see final page.

To find out more about the *Genre Writer* series and to receive additional free writing advice, sign up to the mailing list: **www.paultomlinson.org/signup**

ISBN: 978-1-717768-71-1

First published July 2018
Publisher: Paul Tomlinson

www.paultomlinson.org/how-to

Cover image and design © 2018 by Paul Tomlinson

Contents

	Introduction	5
1|	Amateur on the Run	11
2|	Professional Secret Agent	39
3|	Conspiracy	83
4|	Suspense	89
5|	What's at Stake?	125
6|	'Expert' Thrillers	134
7|	Espionage Thriller	137
8|	Political Thriller	190
9|	Legal Thriller	230
10|	Medical Thriller	278
11|	Techno-Thriller	305
12|	Psychological Thriller	328
13|	Manhunt – The Chase	384
14|	Bourne, Langdon & Reacher	410
	Bibliography	414
	Index	424

Introduction

Thrillers account for twenty to thirty per cent of all adult fiction sales, making this genre second only to Romance. And between 1995 and 2018, Thriller/Suspense movies accounted for 8% of American cinema revenue – almost $18 billion – putting them in fifth place. There is a big audience looking for new stories from writers who understand the conventions of the genre and can provide something that is 'the same only different.'

What is a thriller? Many genres are defined by their content: a *Romance*, for example, centres on the relationship between two people, and a *Western* is set in the American West during the late 1800s. But the *Thriller* is defined by what it does. It *thrills*. That is, it evokes – and sustains – an emotional response that is exciting and pleasurable. That emotional response is usually described as involving suspense, tension, anxiety, or anticipation. Beyond that, there isn't really a formal definition of what a thriller is.

The *100 Thrills* list produced by the American Film Institute in 2001 included a wide range of movies whose 'adrenaline-inducing impact' created "an experience that engages our bodies as well as our minds." The list includes the obvious crime and mystery stories – but also some horror, science fiction, action-adventure, and war stories. Even if we exclude these outliers, the thriller genre still includes a broad range of subject matter, including crime, espionage, medicine, politics, the law, technology, and human psychology. It would be impossible to cover the full spectrum in a single volume, so I have split coverage of the thriller across two books in this series: *Suspense Thriller* and *Crime Thriller*.

In *Suspense Thriller* I will cover the following sub-genres:

- Amateur-on-the-Run – Hitchcock and beyond
- Spy Thriller & Espionage – James Bond and John Le Carré
- Political Thrillers – conspiracies and cover-ups; assassination; terrorism, and hostage-taking
- Medical Thrillers – conspiracies and outbreaks of deadly diseases
- Legal Thriller – prosecution and defense cases in the courtroom
- Techno-Thriller – technology misused; technology gone wrong, and technology as weapon
- Psychological Thriller – psychoanalysis, amnesia, stolen identity and mistaken identity, woman in jeopardy, and stalker thrillers
- Manhunts and chases

And in Crime Thriller I will cover the following:

- Hardboiled/private detectives
- Gangsters
- Police Procedurals
- Forensic investigation
- Undercover cops
- Psychological profiling and serial killers
- Capers & Heists
- Prison thrillers
- Noir Romance
- Enforcers & Vigilantes

In *Supsense Thriller*, we will also explore the concept of a *conspiracy* and – coming back to the idea of emotional response – we'll look in some detail at theories relating to *suspense* and at techniques you can use to create suspense in your stories.

We'll begin by looking at the two main variations of a thriller plot – those with an amateur hero, such as Hitchcock's thriller *The 39 Steps,* and those with a professional hero, such as the James Bond series. Then we will explore specific sub-genres listed above, before rounding off with a quick look at how popular modern thriller writers have mixed-and-matched different thriller elements in their stories.

I should also point out at this early point that I am only discussing 'full-length' stories – feature films and novels – and not short stories, novellas, or television episodes or series. While many of the ideas in this book could be adapted for shorter or episodic works, that is not my primary focus. I don't particularly distinguish between film and novel in what follows – the basic plot structure of both is very similar, and many of the movies I refer to as examples are adapted from novels. If there are any major differences between the way a story can be presented in a movie or a novel – in terms of point of view, for example – I have noted them, otherwise I assume that techniques are equally applicable between the two. Full-length plays for the stage or the radio are subject to additional restrictions in terms of presentation, but much of what is included in this book could be adapted for use in those media.

In the following pages you will fine twenty-two 'plot templates' for different types of thriller including terrorism plots, legal trials, amnesia thrillers, women in jeopardy, technology-gone-wrong, and disease outbreaks. There are also thirty or so large and small-scale techniques for creating suspense in stories.

Genre Conventions

People choose to read genre fiction because they want books that have certain things in common – but at the same time they want a fresh new story. The trick for the writer is identifying those things that need to remain constant and those areas where originality is required – how can we create something that is 'the same only different?'

In the *Genre Writer* series, I am using a standard set of genre conventions to show what story elements readers expect to find in a particular type of story:

- *Setting:* Where and when the story is set – including physical place, historical period, and 'social milieu.'
- *Iconography:* What objects or props, clothing, or other items appear, and what is their symbolic meaning?
- *Themes:* What human values are defended or opposed? What issues or concepts are explored?
- *Tone:* What is the emotional mood or style of the story?
- Characters: What roles are required and what types of people fill them?
- *Plots:* What is the typical sequence of events and what scenes regularly occur?

In chapter two, I will look at each of these conventions as they relate to the archetypal 'amateur-on-the-run' thriller, and in subsequent chapters I will highlight any differences or additions to these that relate to each of the other sub-genres.

Coming up with definitions for genres and sub-genres (and sub-categories of sub-genres!) can be tricky. I want to have something that is both helpful for writers wanting to create new stories and that can be used to classify existing stories to provide lists of examples. But genres are notoriously slippery things – they don't have *official* names or definitions, people use the same name to mean different things, and individual films or novels can often legitimately be listed in more than one sub-genre. All of which is by way of saying that I've done my best to provide usable definitions and descriptions – but mine may not always match up exactly with those you see elsewhere.

Plot Conventions

Most genre fiction is plot-oriented rather than character-based – character tends to become a function of the plot. That being the case, plot will be my main focus in this series – though I will highlight any genre-specific characters as we go along.

In the *Genre Writer* series, I use a model for analysing and creating plots that is based on the typical 'three-act structure' and the 'eight- sequence' model that is often taught in screenwriting classes. The eight sequence model was originally devised by Frank Daniel for teaching screenwriters at UCLA and has been widely used by writers since then. If you have never come across it before, you can read about it online or in Paul Gulino's book *Screenwriting: The Sequence Approach*. I also wrote about using it for novels and screenplays in my *Plot Basics* book.

By deconstructing typical examples of the different sub-genres, I will reveal the fundamental requirements of suspense thriller plots. The aim is to detail not just *what* features a story in this genre requires, but also to show how to achieve them with the tools and techniques provided. The information presented here draws extensively on what academics have written about the genre. Using theoretical explorations of genre techniques and conventions, and studies of how and why these appeal to readers, I outline practical ways of creating those things that people enjoy most in this type of story.

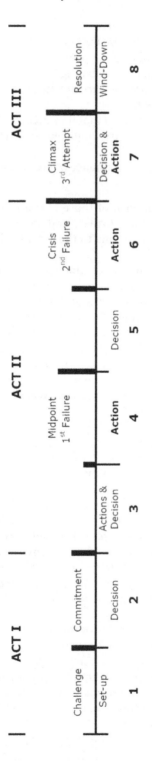

Theory & Practical Application

My research into the suspense thriller genre is based on the structural analysis of novels and movies, looking at the sequence of narrative elements (or 'functions'), in a way pioneered by Vladimir Propp in his *Morphology of the Folktale* (1928), and on academic books and articles in several fields including media, literature, medicine, and the law. There is a lot more in-depth detail here than you might find in a typical 'how to write' guide: I didn't want to regurgitate material you could find in dozens of other places – there is no value in that. But I did want to share some of the things I have discovered as I have learned how to write suspense thrillers. You may find some of the material here a bit dense and as much fun to read as a college textbook – the chapter on suspense, in particular, includes a lot of theoretical detail before exploring how to apply the ideas in practice – but I thought that 'dense' was preferable to superficial in these areas. I have avoided footnotes and references, but have included a thematic list of 'sources,' including URLs where appropriate, at the end.

Most of the chapters are self-contained, but some do build on or reference ideas in earlier chapters. Also, some of the things covered under a particular sub-genre might be equally applicable to others. The best approach might be to read the whole book through once to get an overview, skimming the detail occasionally, and then go back and dip into the relevant sections as you develop your own thriller.

The History of the Thriller Genre

The historical development of some genres is well-covered – the detective mystery or whodunit, for example, has been extensively written about. Coverage of the thriller genre is much patchier – the spy or espionage thriller has been studied in depth, but almost nothing has been written about some of the other sub-genres. In the following pages, I do include some material on the historical development and antecedents of each of the sub-genres, but this is not intended to be a comprehensive history of the suspense thriller genre – my emphasis at all times is the practical application of anything related to the conventions of the genre.

Part of the problem here is that, without a formal definition of what a thriller is or is not, it is difficult to pinpoint the first appearance of something we can point to and say 'that is a thriller.' The genre overlaps with so many other genres and sub-genres that picking out the line of if its development is almost impossible. Jeopardy, suspense, and conspiracy are an integral part of many stories written since ancient times, but which of the earliest ones can we honestly say belong on the thriller's family tree? When does a quest or a chase become a thriller? We could reach as far back as Gilgamesh if we wanted to.

Most genres can be traced back at least as far as the Victorian era when books were mass-produced for the first time. The thriller has been traced as far back as Erskine Childers' *The Riddle of the Sands* (1903), which is hailed as the earliest espionage thriller. John Buchan's *The Thirty-Nine Steps* (1915) then brought us one of the first man-on-the-run thrillers. But look further back than the early 1900s and things get hazier. The genre certainly owes something the

Victorian Gothic and 'Sensation' novels. Although hailed as a pioneer of the mystery genre, several of Wilkie Collins' novels are closer to being thrillers than whodunits.

Another writer from that era who wrote proto-thrillers was Robert Louis Stevenson. His *Strange Case of Dr Jekyll and Mr Hyde* (1886), while often regarded as a horror novel, could fit equally well into the medical or psychological thriller sub-genres. Stevenson's *Kidnapped* (1886) has also been compared to the modern thriller. In his introduction to the Oxford University Press edition of *Kidnapped,* published in 2014, Ian Duncan wrote: "David's island ordeal and the ensuing 'flight in the heather' are the racing heart of *Kidnapped.* With them Robert Louis Stevenson transforms his literary model, the historical romance of Walter Scott, into the modern thriller or adventure story." Duncan refers to one of the sequences of the novel in which "... an innocent man witnesses a murder, he is accused of it, he runs," noting that this is an early example of something that occurs in Alfred Hitchcock's films *North by Northwest* and. He also points out that another Hitchcock movie with a similar scene, *The Thirty-Nine Steps,* includes an element that is in Stevenson's novel but not John Buchan's – the hero goes on the run with a companion, though there is no romance between David Balfour and Alan Breck. Stevenson's account of the chase, along with his descriptions of the countryside location, are something every thriller writer could learn from. Ian Duncan also praises the author's ability to evoke the physical experience of his characters, allowing us to feel how cold, wet, and tired they are.

Robert Louis Stevenson acknowledged Alexandre Dumas, whose *The Count of Monte Cristo* might also be counted as a proto-thriller, and Daniel Defoe as inspirations for his novel. If we wanted to choose three 'ancestors' for our present genre, then Stevenson, Dumas, and Defoe would do quite nicely.

Cut to the Chase

One final thing to bear in mind at all times when devising a thriller plot: thrillers are fast-paced stories. From the moment the hero receives his 'call to adventure' – which should happen no later than the middle of Act I – the pace rarely lets up. The plot is like a chain-reaction or a series of dominoes that continue to fall right up until the climax in Act III. Every scene must move the story forwards, providing new information to the audience and new challenges to the hero. The story will typically take place over a short time frame – hours or days, rather than months – and there will usually be some kind of deadline: the villain's plot involves an event that will take place at a specific time and place, and the clock is ticking. With that in mind, we should move on quickly.

Chapter 13 here is devoted to creating a chase within a story and to creating a story that consists entirely of a chase or 'manhunt.'

1 | Amateur on the Run

The amateur-on-the-run plot forms the basis for all sub-genres of the thriller, so we will use this as our baseline and then explore how other types of thriller adapt it. This sub-genre is also sometimes referred to as a 'man on the run' or 'wrong man' thriller. The plot structure that I describe in this chapter is probably as close to a 'formula' for a full-length thriller novel or screenplay as it is possible to get. I will use the three-act, eight-sequence plot model to show what typically goes where in a thriller, and why these elements occur in this particular order. I will also cover the genre conventions of setting, iconography, themes, tone, and character.

When we think of the suspense thriller, a name that comes instantly to mind is that of director Alfred Hitchcock. His speciality was the film featuring an amateur – though not always completely *innocent* – character who finds him or herself caught up in a conspiracy or other dangerous situation. These films included classic examples of the man on the run, woman in jeopardy, and psychological thrillers. Often referred to as the 'master of suspense,' Hitchcock shared his theories on how to create suspense in the thriller, most notably in a series of in-depth interviews with French film director Francois Truffaut. Many of Hitchcock's best-known movies were based on novels and he planned his screenplays in great detail with his screenwriters. Where a typical Hollywood screenplay consists of 90 to 120 pages (averaging a page per minute of screen time), screenplays for Hitchcock movies run from 140 to over 200 pages, with many of the scenes and images being carefully visualised and set down during the writing stage. If you can find copies of them online, they are well worth a look. But I wouldn't recommend modelling your own thriller screenplay on them – choose a more recent one of fewer than 120 pages as your example.

John Buchan's novel *The Thirty-Nine Steps* (1915), a 'man on the run' thriller set just before the First World War, is an early example of this sub-genre. It centres on a conspiracy by a German spy ring to steal British military plans. It includes (almost) all of the essential ingredients for a thriller – an amateur hero, motivated by patriotism, wrongly accused of murder, who escapes in order to prove his own innocence and to thwart the conspiracy being planned by enemies of his country. Alfred Hitchcock directed two adaptations of the novel, in 1935 and 1959, with the earlier one generally being regarded as the better of the two. Hitchcock and his screenwriter made a number of changes to the story, the most significant one being the addition of a co-protagonist, Pamela, who is handcuffed to the hero against her wishes and is forced to accompany him as he tries to escape his pursuers. She eventually comes to trust him and helps him, and the two form a romantic bond.

There were other thriller novels before 1915, and we'll discuss some of them in later sections, but *The Thirty-Nine Steps* was – and is – successful as both a novel and a movie. Between them, Buchan and Hitchcock created the template for the amateur-on-the-run thriller. The director used the format again in *Saboteur* (1942) and perhaps most famously in *North by Northwest* (1959).

The plot structure that follows is based on *The Thirty-Nine Steps* and *North by Northwest*, but it is the same structure that was used in *Three Days of the Condor* in 1975 and the Will Smith movie *Enemy of the State* in 1998. I've listed a few more examples of amateur-on-the-run films and novels at the end of the chapter.

Basic Structure – Three-Acts, Four Quarters

Before we look in detail at the eight sequences that make up an amateur on the run thriller, let's quickly look at the basic three-act structure. Three-act structure is based on the idea that a story has a beginning, a middle, and an end and that each of those three parts serves a particular function within the story. Screenplay theorist Syd Field expanded on this basic concept and said that Act I consisted of the first quarter of the story; Act II was the second and third quarters, with something significant happening at the midpoint; and Act III was the final quarter. These are intended as approximate proportions only. Acts I and III can be shorter than a quarter of the overall length of a novel or screenplay, and in a fast-paced thriller they often are, so bear in mind that the quarters are just a 'serving suggestion.'

Here is how a typical amateur on the run thriller can be broken down:

Quarter 1: Challenge or 'call to adventure.' The hero accidentally stumbles on some part of the villain's conspiracy, and as a result becomes a threat to the success of the evil plan.

Quarter 2: Escape. The hero runs away from the villain's henchman and/or the heavies. The hero often finds himself accused of a murder committed by the bad guys. And the hero often meets someone who will become his romantic co-protagonist – though initially, their relationship is antagonistic.

Midpoint: Discovery and decision. The hero learns of the true nature of the conspiracy and the threat it poses to society. He decides that he cannot keep trying to run away – he must turn and fight. He changes from pursued victim to pursuer, having decided that he will do whatever it takes to stop the villain's plan.

Quarter 3: Pursuit. The hero now goes after the villain, often using the villain's own methods against him. The hero deliberately or accidentally enters the villain's lair. Often at this point, he is trying to rescue the romantic co-protagonist, who has been captured by the villain.

Quarter 4: Final confrontation. The hero puts a stop to the villain's plan and proves himself innocent of the earlier murder. Equilibrium has been returned to the world of the story, and this is often confirmed by the hero and co-protagonist being in a committed relationship.

If you read or watch thrillers, that basic plot structure should feel familiar to you. And if you look at it, there is a logical progression to it that feels right: each part of it serves a story function that draws the reader or viewer into the action and moves them closer to the finale. In plotting your own thriller, I would advise starting with four quarters plus a midpoint, because they give you major staging-posts that help keep your plot on track. With these, you know at any point where your story is heading. In the next section, we'll look at how these four quarters can be further broken down into eight sequences that, in turn, each have a specific function within the story structure. Again, bear in mind that these 'eighths' are only approximate guides and not mathematical absolutes.

The eight sequences below show what elements of the thriller (typically) need to be introduced at each point of the story. Many of these elements are conventions of the genre, and we'll look at them in more detail later in this chapter. Each sequence, with the exception of the eighth and final one, has its own mini climax – a plot point that sets up the next part of the story.

Remember, the three acts of a story are divided into eight sequences plus a midpoint as follows:

ACT I = Quarter 1 = Sequences 1 & 2
ACT II = Quarters 2 & 3 = Sequences 3 & 4 – Midpoint – Sequences 5 & 6
ACT III = Quarter 4 = Sequences 7 & 8

Amateur on the Run Plot structure

Sequence 1 – Perhaps a prologue featuring the conspirators in action. A crime or pursuit that will soon impact on the hero's life. It may show someone who has the 'MacGuffin' and is trying to escape from the conspirators. This person may be injured during the course of the pursuit. Climax: The catalyst – the hero encounters the pursued man and either assists him, accidentally collides with him, or is given the MacGuffin by him. It is typically a co-incidental encounter that brings the hero into contact with the conspiracy. If there is no MacGuffin as such, the hero may be an unsuspecting witness of a criminal act related to the conspiracy, or he may be mistaken for someone connected with the authorities who oppose the conspirators.

Sequence 2 – The hero may not yet be aware that he has become mixed up in the conspiracy, but the conspirators are aware that he is. They believe he is an accomplice of the man they were pursuing, and they believe that the hero now has the MacGuffin in his possession. Or they believe he has information that they need, or that he has witnessed something that means he is now a danger to them. The hero is now 'locked in' and becomes a target for the conspirators. Often the pursuit begins at this point. It is common for the hero to be accused of a murder that has been committed by the villain or his people. The victim may be the person how handed the hero the MacGuffin, or it may be someone the hero turns to for help. The hero, either by accident or by design, passes a point of no return, and at the end of Act I he is typically pursued by both the conspirators and by the police, who believe him guilty of murder.

Sequence 3 – The hero is drawn into the world of the conspiracy. The conspirators remove his options and support systems – they fight dirty, ensuring that he is cut off from help from authorities, friends, family, or work. The hero becomes aware that he is pursued – he feels threatened. He wants to return to his normal everyday life. He discovers what his pursuers want from him – but he doesn't have it. Or believes that he doesn't. He learns that the villains are prepared to destroy him to get what they want – and about the methods they are prepared to use to do this. It is also during this sequence that we learn about the hero's apparent lack of beliefs or convictions: there appears to be nothing that he cares deeply about, and he avoids commitment to anyone or anything. His life has been humdrum and uneventful, and he has been happy to allow that to continue, even though he may have had feelings of being unfulfilled by it. Climax – the hero learns that he has lost everything and is on his own. His status and reputation, his credibility, have been destroyed. No one can or will help him. He is isolated and in danger. Despite his attempts to lie low, often he is threatened with recognition and exposure in a public place.

Sequence 4 – The hero's low point – it seems that he has lost everything. His comfortable world has fallen apart or is no longer available to him. In fact, it no longer exists: it was a sham all along. He now knows what lies beneath the façade, what the real world is like. At this point he probably becomes hunted by the authorities as well as by the conspirators: he has probably been framed for some crime, usually murder of one of his own friends or colleagues. Family and friends desert him or are taken away. He loses his job. He is betrayed by someone he thought he could rely on, and now believes he can trust no one. He also learns the full extent of what he is up against, and how desperate his situation is. He is now fully aware that the conspiracy threatens not only his life but society at large: the situation affecting him takes on a moral meaning. He tries to run but soon discovers that escape is impossible. Things from his everyday world frequently appear in a new and threatening way – they are no longer a source of reassurance. He is forced to re-evaluate everything and can take nothing for granted.

Midpoint – The hero makes a decision. He cannot carry on running forever – he'll never get away. And if he could, he doesn't want to live in exile, always looking over his shoulder. He will change from being reactive to being proactive. He will turn and take the fight to the villain, using his own methods against him, and beating him at his own game. He may discover he had the MacGuffin or secret knowledge all along, and so decide to use it to defeat the conspirators. Or he may decide to take action and obtain the MacGuffin.

Sequence 5 – Friends will not help him in his quest – they're afraid for their own safety, or they don't believe he's innocent, or are corrupt themselves. The hero may encounter a new ally, usually a female co-protagonist. Initially, they may be thrown together in circumstances that make them antagonistic towards one another. They come to like each other – there may be a brief romantic interlude. She trusts him and believes he's innocent. He is ready to give up and admit defeat. Climax – She helps him to discover his own deeply held beliefs – what he believes is worth fighting for. She convinces him to go on, despite the odds. She will help him defeat the conspirators. He feels able to make a commitment to her and to trying to foil the conspiracy.

Sequence 6 – The hero begins to learn the villain's methods in order to use them against him. He may be taught by a mentor. Or the romance character may act as a mentor. This is an important stage in the hero moving from being a novice/amateur to becoming a warrior/expert. The villain's henchmen and/or the authorities may close in, resuming the chase after the romantic interlude. Climax – the hero's darkest hour. He is captured by the conspirators, or the co-protagonist is taken hostage. Or both. Or she betrays him – or appears to. The hero renews his commitment to foiling the conspiracy. He may be trapped in an enclosed space and have to demonstrate his adaptability in order to escape. Again the hero is unable to rely on things being what they appear to be – evidence he was relying on may disappear; people he thought dead may 'come back to life'; false identities may be revealed; dialogue has double meanings, even between friends.

Sequence 7 – The hero turns the tables on the villain. He has nothing to lose now. He threatens the villain. He has become an expert – uses the villain's own methods against him. Having become self-sufficient, the hero is now able to act alone, out-manoeuvring the villain in a battle of wits. Chaos erupts in one final set-piece.

Sequence 8 – The conspiracy is foiled – the villain is exposed, and defeated when the hero exploits his weakness. Equilibrium is restored, and the hero is able to return to the normal world he has helped to protect. But he is changed – he knows what lies beneath the placid surface of this world. Having changed from an avoider of conflict to a self-sufficient individual, the hero must now face the larger world with heightened vigilance. The hero and the co-protagonist are often reunited, with some threatening situation from earlier being humorously reprised as a fadeout joke.

Genre Conventions

Now that we have established what needs to go where in our amateur on the run thriller, we can look in more detail at some of these basic elements. Based on our standard list of genre conventions, we will look at:

i. hero
ii. villain
iii. conspiracy
iv. MacGuffin
v. romantic co-protagonist
vi. settings
vii. iconography
viii. themes
ix. tone
x. other characters

Suspense is such a major element of the thriller that I will devote a chapter to it.

(i) The Hero
"I have never been interested in making films about professional criminals or detectives. I much prefer to take average men, because I think the audience can get involved more easily." – Alfred Hitchcock

The amateur-on-the-run thriller is normally told from the hero's point of view – we follow him closely as his or her adventure unfolds. However, as we will see later when we come to examine the nature of *suspense*, we as the audience are often given information that the hero does not have.

The hero is usually handsome, smart, and witty – but there is something *lacking* in his life. Rather than living his life, he seems more of a disillusioned observer. He may seem lost, shallow or disconnected – not really *involved* in what he is doing. He may be 'going through the motions' without even knowing it. He may be a cynic, outside of society, and commenting on it, but not really participating. He may be good at his job, but he finds his work unfulfilling. Aloof, ambivalent, supporting no cause, he is morally uncommitted, and may even come across as irresponsible.

There is a similar void and lack of commitment in his romantic life. He may be married – or engaged to – someone he no longer loves, or who is the wrong person for him. This 'wrong person' is probably the embodiment of his shallow, meaningless life. Or the hero may engage in a series of meaningless romances, refusing to commit to anyone because he says that he enjoys his 'freedom' – but secretly he longs to meet someone with whom he can make a real connection. Cary Grant in *North by Northwest* says of himself: "I've got a job, a secretary, a mother, two ex-wives and several bartenders that depend upon me..." and James Stewart in *Rear Window* is afraid of committing to a relationship with Grace Kelly, claiming that his work is too important to him.

This sort of hero has room for growth, or self-discovery, during the story. In fact, he *needs* to grow up and have a proper adult relationship with another person on equal terms. Being accidentally caught up in the villain's conspiracy turns the hero's world on its head. He is forced out of his safety zone and put under pressure, placed in a position where he must make decisions on his own – evaluating options and choosing actions. He is inexperienced, not a professional adventurer, and is challenged and threatened.

This hero's adventures (a) allow him to meet the 'right' person, and (b) allow him to discover what values are important to him – what he is prepared to fight for. The two things are connected: he learns how important life is, in the form of a relationship with someone, and he learns that the villain's evil plan threatens not just his own recently-discovered happiness, but that of every other ordinary person in the world around him. That's why he makes the decision to try and put an end to the villain's conspiracy: to save the romantic co-protagonist's life, and to protect the way of life he has just discovered is important to him. His brush with chaos has made him reassess his beliefs and his lifestyle: he has gone from being a cynical critic of society to being its defender. The hero, unlike the villain, is capable of *redemption*. We will look at redemption again under the heading of *Themes* later.

Positive social values – truth, justice, democracy, whatever – are represented by the hero's romantic relationship with the person he meets while he's trying to escape from the villain in the first half of the story.

The villain represents the opposing values – and threatens the socially approved ones. The villain appears to be a fine, upstanding citizen but is revealed to be a traitor. The hero *is* a fine upstanding citizen, but the villain makes it look like the hero is a murderer and a traitor. In both cases, neither are what they appear to be, and they are like mirror images of each other. Only at the end is the true nature of each revealed.

Having the hero unjustly accused of a crime helps the audience side with him: we all hate to see someone being unjustly or unfairly treated. Alfred Hitchcock: "I think it creates a rooting interest within an audience, because nobody likes to be accused of something that he wasn't responsible for."

The battle the hero engages in requires that he have both physical stamina and intelligence: he must *survive* and *outwit* his opponents. There is an element of the detective in what he must do: he has to discover the nature of the conspiracy: What are the bad guys up to? And he must also figure out the significance of their actions: What threat does their conspiracy pose to society? Like the mystery hero, the thriller hero tries to come up with an understanding of the world by seeking information. But the classical detective is investigating something that has *already taken place*, he is trying to discover something that happened in the past. His aim is to restore balance to the world of the story: this world is known to him and is felt to be worth restoring.

The *thriller* hero is in a different position. The conspiracy that the hero has uncovered is something that is *currently taking place*, and he must take action to prevent the criminals from successfully completing their plot. He needs to be able to turn the tables on them and beat them at their own game. He discovers that the world is *not* as he understood it to be. Things are occurring that ordinary people do not know about. These things take place in a hidden world, a clandestine place, which exists beneath or alongside the ordinary world. And having become aware of this, the hero can never see the world in quite the same way again. The amateur hero is also risks being destroyed by the clandestine world – he doesn't belong there and doesn't have the experience or skills necessary to thrive in it.

But, having become an exile, the hero is able to view the ordinary world from a truly objective viewpoint, and he can see that it is – for the most part – a thing worth protecting. There are values in place that make the ordinary world a *good* place. He can also see that the conspiracy planned by the villain and his men threatens the values of this ordinary world. If the conspiracy succeeds, something important will be lost. As the story approaches its climax, the hero doesn't just want to escape from back to the ordinary world, he may never be able to really go back, but he does want to ensure that the conspirators cannot achieve their aims and seriously damage this ordinary world. The hero has been changed by his experiences in the clandestine world: he has discovered that he is prepared to fight – and if necessary, to die – to protect the ordinary world.

Even if it didn't destroy him, there was a danger that the hero could have become lost in the clandestine world forever. He needed to remain connected to the real world, and the only way he could do that was through contact with real people. That is, people who are not part of the clandestine world. The amateur hero in the thriller is able to do this through the romantic relationship he has with his co-protagonist. This relationship enables him to discover the values that are important to him, while at the same time keeping him grounded in the ordinary world where he belongs, and to which he will – if he survives – be able to return.

The combination of physical endurance and mental capacity required by the thriller leads us to seek a hero who is of a certain type or archetype. Someone who believes in a cause and is prepared to take action to defend or achieve it. We need a *Crusader*.

The Crusader Archetype

In discussing characters, I tend to use the *head, heart* and *gut* model to distinguish between people who are primarily motivated by thought, emotion, and physical (visceral) feelings respectively.

Martin Rubin says that the thriller "… works primarily to evoke such feelings as suspense, fright, mystery, exhilaration, excitement, speed, movement. In other words, it emphasises visceral, gut-level feelings, rather than more sensitive, cerebral, or emotionally heavy feelings…" He also says that the thriller "… stresses *sensations* more than sensitivity. It is a sensational form."

The classical detective – the Sherlock Holmes or Hercule Poirot type – is an example of the *Thinker* archetype. I explored this type of character in depth in *Mystery*. The thriller hero has some of the same qualities as the classical detective – he seeks information in order to make sense of a criminal situation – but he also has other qualities that are drawn from a different archetype. Where the detective lives almost exclusively within his own head, the thriller hero also operates in the external, physical world – though he may do so reluctantly at first – and forms relationships – romantic and otherwise, antagonistic and otherwise – with the people he encounters. He is more of an extrovert than the pure Thinker archetype.

As a person of external action, the thriller hero draws on both head and the physical body, which is symbolised by the *gut,* relating to our 'visceral' selves. This means that the thriller hero shares qualities with the Warrior and Adventurer archetypes. He may wish to believe that he's a Thinker, like the detective, acting purely based on knowledge or evidence; but more often he is trusting to his 'gut instincts' to do what he *feels* is right, seeking to explain or justify his workings only later. He's a much more spur-of-the-moment character. He doesn't need to spend ages planning things in detail, he can improvise on the spot and take immediate action.

I have called the character archetype that combines qualities of *head* and *gut* the *Crusader*: a person who fights for a just cause. It sits between the Thinker and the Warrior.

Obviously James Bond is closer to the Warrior-Adventurer end of the spectrum of this *head-gut* hybrid, while John Le Carré's George Smiley is closer to the Thinker or Classical Detective end – the first two Smiley novels had him in the role of a classical detective investigating murder, rather than as a spymaster; and in the first and third novels of the Karla trilogy we see a Thinker – a strategist – at work.

The hero of a thriller may be a predominantly *thought*-motivated character who must learn the importance of taking action. The Robert Redford character in *Three Days of the Condor* is an example: he needs to get away from his books and live in the real world. Or the hero may be a *gut*-motivated character who needs to apply logical thinking before he acts. With a thought-motivated character, you can explore psychological fears brought out by the character's jeopardy – fears of loss of control and madness: his model of how the world works has been demonstrated to be wrong, does this mean that he is going mad? While a gut-motivated character – like James Bond fears physical disablement and imprisonment; he fears being unable to take action: in his darkest moment in a story he is often a prisoner of the villain, helpless and subjected to torture.

But the hero of a thriller will not be a heart-motivated character. If you put a heart-motivated character into a thriller situation, you either have a romance story, where the thriller elements provide obstacles to the romantic relationship; or you have a 'character-based' story, where the thriller elements are used to explore a character who is totally unsuited to dealing with such a situation. Either way, you don't have a thriller.

This is not to say that a thriller cannot have a romantic subplot – as we will see, a relationship between the hero and his co-protagonist can be an important element in a thriller. But this relationship serves a particular plot function. And it can also be used to add obstacles or increased jeopardy to the story.

(ii) The Villain
"The more successful the villain, the more successful the picture." – Alfred Hitchcock

The villain is the mastermind behind the conspiracy. Initially, the villain may be hidden – his identity a mystery – and we are aware of him only through the actions of his henchman and/or the 'heavies.' When we do see him, he will appear to be wealthy, powerful, respectable and honest. A successful businessman, perhaps.

He will be intelligent, well-spoken, well-dressed, calm and carefully organised. He will often be of the same character-type as the hero, a combination of Thinker and Warrior. Someone who makes plans and puts them into action to achieve goals. He will have his own personal crusade – but rather than being motivated by the good of society, he will be spurred on by a desire for power. Often, he represents a group seeking to seize power. Villains seek power without the responsibility that goes with it; or reward without having earned it; or victory without having to fight for it.

But the villain's point of view and his moral beliefs are at odds with the hero's – he represents 'evil,' or rather he embodies values that conflict with those generally accepted as 'good' by society. He *appears* to be a civilised person, a member of society, but he is a predator who is prepared to betray society to further his own ambitions.

Often, the thriller hero does not see the villain's true self, or recognise the extent of his power, until a turning point in the middle of the story. When he realises how dangerous – how insane – this person really is, the hero knows that he will have to stop him. Somehow.

The villain lacks the hero's capacity for romance. He is cold-hearted; an emotionless Thinker. He lacks empathy and conscience and is able to take action to achieve his desires without giving a thought to the people who may be harmed along the way. There is no line he will not cross to get what he wants. He is prepared to sacrifice anyone, including his own people, if they are weak, a traitor, or incompetent. He has no sympathy for innocent bystanders, and so is not concerned if his actions result in 'collateral damage.' Ruthlessness is a quality found in all the best villains. They will stop at nothing to achieve their goal. Anything or anyone who stands in their way will be removed. They have no mercy, no sense of honour, no fear, no doubt.

The villain's actions are premeditated, planned out and carefully executed. He does not act rashly or emotionally: he is a cold-hearted professional. He often lacks the spontaneity and ingeniousness of the hero. He is 'programmed' to operate in a single way, robotic, bureaucratic. His lack of empathy means he is unable to see things from another person's point of view, so cannot predict the hero's willingness to sacrifice himself for others. Also, he cannot see why his callous treatment of one of his own people might cause that person to turn against him: 'But it was nothing personal – it was for the good of the conspiracy.'

Conspirators, by definition, betray others and it is not unusual for them to betray each other. They also lack trust, are unable to trust, and so they cannot understand those who can and do trust others; nor do they understand the concept of friendship and personal loyalty. Where the hero of a thriller learns that there are people he can trust – symbolised by the co-protagonist – the villain never learns this. He believes that he can trust no one and that people should never trust anyone else. He is quite comfortable sacrificing even the most loyal of his own people if it will further his own ends.

The villain's inability to trust anyone may ultimately manifest itself in feelings of *paranoia.* The villain has spent so long in the clandestine world that it is more real to him than the ordinary world outside. But the clandestine world is a warped and dangerous one, and spending too much time there can damage a person's sanity. A villain who is paranoid is a dark reflection of what the hero may become. If the hero does not remain connected to the real world, to his ordinary world, he risks becoming like the villain. The romance he has with the co-protagonist helps him stay connected to reality. We will look at paranoia again under the heading of *Themes* later.

The villain sees empathy and love as weaknesses to be exploited: he will often kidnap and threaten the romantic co-protagonist, believing this will cause the hero to retreat – to save her and himself. But instead, it helps the hero realise he's prepared to sacrifice himself to rescue the person he loves and the values he has come to believe in. It is the extent of the villain's 'evil' actions, and their escalation, that pushes the hero to greater heroism.

The villain is the person behind the conspiracy – he is the one with the plan. For the first half of the story, he drives the action. His men pursue the hero because he has become a threat to the successful completion of the plan. The second half of the story is driven by the hero's desire to oppose the villain – to prevent his plan from succeeding.

The villain becomes increasingly *selfish* and monomaniacal – focused only on what he wants, and more and more distant from relationships with others.

The hero becomes increasingly *selfless* – he seeks to save the person he loves and then broadens his goal to save the society he and his lover belong to. He becomes closer to society, reintegrated.

Villains lose not because they are 'evil,' but because they are deeply flawed, and are unable to adapt in such a way as to overcome their flaw. Where the hero is able to grow and learn and to redeem himself, the villain is unable to escape his basic 'programming.' He is a tragic character who brings about his own downfall, resulting in a kind of ironic, poetic justice.

(iii) The Conspiracy or Criminal Intent

As we have already seen, a conspiracy is a secret plan by two or more people to do something that is wrong or 'evil.' It involves a betrayal of trust, and the breaking of an accepted code – legal, moral, or ethical. The conspiracy in a thriller typically involves a breach of the accepted code of behaviour in law, business, medicine, religion, or politics. It usually involves people who are already in positions of power, who seek to abuse their status for personal gain, or to further the ends of some secret group that they belong to, at the expense of the people they are meant to serve and respect. Thrillers involve corruption in high places.

The goal of a conspiracy is to either gain (or maintain) power; to acquire material wealth, or to destroy a rival group (from a 'them or us' survival motive, or an 'it's their fault' revenge motive). The conspiracy is a plan carried out in secret. Those involved do not want their identities revealed, as this would jeopardise the success of their plot.

There is usually some sort of deadline that the conspiracists are working towards – this allows for the inclusion of a sense of urgency, a 'ticking clock,' in the plot.

In his book *Thrillers*, Jerry Palmer writes: "... the villain is dispensable: provided there is a conspiracy, it is immaterial what the personal characteristics of the conspirator are. It is the characteristics of the conspiracy that are important. The fundamental characteristics of the conspiracy are mystery and disruption. A conspiracy that presents no serious threat to the order of the normal is inadequate: routine watchfulness and bureaucratic procedures would take care of it. It is only the truly monstrous that can serve as the subject of a thriller. Mystery is equally integral. Devoid of mystery, one is in the presence not of conspiracy but of opposition, or obstacles; the world presented by the story would lose its characteristic opacity, and the nature of the threat would be radically different."

A conspiracy involves two or more people involved in criminal activity, but in some thrillers the innocent protagonist finds him or herself caught up in the scheme of a lone antagonist. Steven Spielberg's 1971 film *Duel* is a great example of an innocent protagonist pursued by a single, largely unseen, truck driver who randomly chooses Dennis Weaver as his victim. The 1981 movie *The Hitcher* is a variation on the same theme. The stalker thriller, which we'll explore in the women-in-jeopardy chapter, also features a single antagonist rather than a conspiratorial cabal.

While the conspiracy is optional, I think a thriller *does* require one or more people involved in criminal activity to oppose the hero. If the antagonist is a monster or supernatural being, we have moved away from the thriller and into the horror genre; and if the hero faces non-human opposition in the form of a natural or man-made catastrophe, then we are talking about the action-adventure or disaster movie (or novel) genres, not the thriller.

(iv) The MacGuffin
"A true MacGuffin will get you where you need to go, but never overshadow what is ultimately there." – Alfred Hitchcock

The 'MacGuffin' is a term popularised by Alfred Hitchcock. It is the thing that everyone in a movie is after – it is a plot device that gives the villains a reason to pursue the hero – something tangible that symbolises the battle between the hero and the villain. Whoever has possession of the MacGuffin at 'zero hour' is the winner. If the villains have it, they will succeed in their evil conspiracy, so the hero must obtain it before they do, or prevent them from taking it from him, or destroy it.

"The MacGuffin is nothing at all," Hitchcock said. "It is that mechanical element that usually crops up in any story. In crook stories it is almost always the necklace and in spy stories it is almost always the papers."

In *Enemy of the State*, the MacGuffin is a computer game disc containing a video of a political assassination. In *North by Northwest* it is a statuette containing a microfilm of secret government documents. And in *The Maltese Falcon*, the 'black bird' that everyone is seeking – and that they are prepared to kill for – is a MacGuffin.

Although Hitchcock's term is now widely accepted, the concept has existed for as long as there have been movies: actress Pearl White, the heroine of such silent movie serials as *The Perils of Pauline*, called it a 'weenie.' And before that, in literature and folklore, it has appeared as a talisman or 'fetish' – the 'Holy Grail,' for example.

The MacGuffin is usually a physical object that is vital to the success of the villain's plan. In a spy story, it is typically secret defence plans or the design for a powerful weapon. The plans are usually in the form of a microfilm because the MacGuffin must be easy to carry and easy to conceal. The MacGuffin could be a piece of evidence that identifies and/or incriminates the conspirators and could expose their plans – a photograph, video, or sound recording, perhaps.

Other examples of a MacGuffin include a map of a secret location; a disc or some other form of data storage for a computer; a key for deciphering a code, or fissional materials for the creation of a nuclear bomb. The MacGuffin can also be a person – the inventor of a weapon; a diplomat about to negotiate an important treaty that the conspirators do not want to see signed; or a secret agent or double agent.

The MacGuffin is a 'thing' that the villain needs – and it either comes into the possession of the hero in Act I or its location is told to the hero. Or the villain *believes* the hero has it or knows where it is. In such cases, in order to save himself and/or prevent the villains getting hold of it, the hero must embark on a quest to obtain the MacGuffin.

Initially, the hero may not know that he is in possession of this valuable thing or knowledge about the thing. Often the innocent hero is drawn into the story because someone gives him the MacGuffin or tells him its location. In its most clichéd form, the MacGuffin is handed to the hero by a dying man.

The object itself is usually of little value, rather it is what it *stands for* that causes people to fight over it. In *North by Northwest*, Cary Grant notes that Eva Marie Saint is holding the MacGuffin (a statue with microfilm hidden inside) and says: "I see you've got the pumpkin."

The MacGuffin as technically optional in a story, you don't actually *need* a physical object to symbolise the conspiracy. But in movies especially it can be useful to have something tangible, a visible object, to represent what is at stake. Who holds the MacGuffin at any point in the story tells us whether the hero or the villain has the advantage at that moment.

(v) The Romantic Co-Protagonist

"Sex on the screen should be suspenseful, I feel. If sex is too blatant or obvious, there's no suspense." – Alfred Hitchcock

The hero meets his co-protagonist when he is on the run, usually before the midpoint of the story. The two of them are thrown together by circumstances and against their wishes. They do not like each other, and they do not trust each other. Their relationship is, initially, antagonistic.

Sometimes the hero holds her prisoner or kidnaps her, because he needs her help to stay alive, or needs to prevent her from alerting the villain or the authorities. She resents his behaviour, and acts against him, providing more obstacles and/or complications for him to deal with.

Occasionally the co-protagonist is attracted to the hero from the start, seemingly turned on by the fact that this apparent criminal has ended the monotony of her humdrum life. But if this happens, he doesn't feel the same way – he does not trust her, he doesn't feel that he can. Even if she professes to believe that he is innocent. And besides, a romantic entanglement would just be a distraction at this point.

Sometimes the hero is attracted to her immediately, but she then doesn't feel the same way, as she regards him as a criminal on the run from justice and someone who is holding her against her will.

The two may initially be a typical movie 'odd couple' – like Humphrey Bogart and Katharine Hepburn in *The African Queen:* they have nothing in common and seem destined to oppose each other until they are separated. Or killed. But the relationship between them gradually thaws. They come to know each other as individuals – and find that they have things in common. Typically, they are both dissatisfied with the lives they have been leading up to this point, and both are – at least to some degree – excited to be involved in this current adventure. At some point, she may even help him evade the authorities who are seeking to rescue her and capture him.

The romantic co-protagonist is usually a link to the everyday world – the society – that the hero has been wrenched out of, and that he has never felt that he has properly belonged to or felt committed to. He has always been something of an outsider, a cynic, but she offers him an opportunity to *belong*. And he offers the same thing to her.

The co-protagonist represents the 'virtue' that opposes the 'vice' embodied by the villain. She shows the hero the importance of the positive value of this virtue to society – which enables him to see the threat that the vice of the conspiracy represents to society. She helps him to see that society's values are worth defending. As a result, he comes to understand that he is not fighting the villain simply to save his own life, but rather he must defeat the conspiracy in order to save a *way* of life.

The romantic co-protagonist also represents *trust* – a value that is important to society, and which the hero has lost faith in. The conspiracy represents *betrayal*, the opposite of trust. Having discovered the conspiracy, and seen that the world is not how he always thought it was, the hero believes he will never be able to trust anyone again. But the co-protagonist demonstrates that she trusts him – and that he can trust her.

She also shows him that he cannot defeat the villain without help – and that he doesn't have to do it alone. She demonstrates how people in a society work together to help each other – for the greater good.

The villain may use the hero's new-found love for this character against the hero. Typically, at the end of Act II, the point that marks the hero's 'darkest hour,' the villain will capture the co-protagonist and threaten to kill her. The villain uses his possession of her to dissuade the hero from opposing him: he will let his captive go *after* the deadline for the successful completion of the conspiracy has passed.

At the climax of the story the hero finds himself isolated again – but now he has someone he wants to be reunited with. But the villain has underestimated the hero and the co-protagonist – not only is each prepared to die for the other, they are both also willing to die if it will mean that their society can be protected from the toxic effects of the villain's conspiracy.

It is the combined love of hero and co-protagonist for each other and for their world that provides them with the determination and courage they need make one final, last-ditch attempt to defeat the villain. They have discovered a commitment that had been missing in their lives, and they are now willing to sacrifice everything to defend it.

Charles Derry, in *The Suspense Thriller*, writes that hero and romantic co-protagonist are together in the final scene and "... the narrative is ended as some earlier threatening situation is humorously reprised as a fade-out joke."

The relationship between hero and co-protagonist does not have to be romantic, it can be the platonic relationship of two 'buddies.'

(vi) Setting

"When making a picture, my ambition is to present a story that never stands still." – Alfred Hitchcock

"I want to make the Hitchcock picture to end all Hitchcock pictures – something that has wit, sophistication, glamour, action and lots of changes of locale." – Ernest Lehman, screenwriter on *North by Northwest*.

The amateur-on-the run thriller, by definition, involves chase and pursuit, and must therefore take place against a moving backdrop. In this type of thriller, the hero is an amateur with no experience of dealing with dangerous situations. He has no special training, and no weapons or other equipment. He is thrust into a series of environments which are new to him, and which present him with obstacles and threats to his safety. He is a fish out of water and must learn to cope with these situations.

Thrillers commonly take place against four kinds of background: the ordinary world, transportation, 'exotic' locations, and the villain's lair. Often all three appear in the same story.

The Ordinary World. This is where we usually first meet the hero. We are able to identify with him and his world – and probably the fact that he is not entirely happy there, or is bored with his life. Once this has been established, something happens to interrupt the equilibrium of the hero's everyday world. He is accidentally pushed or pulled into the villain's conspiracy, to the extent that he unwittingly becomes a threat to the villain. At this point, we remain in the ordinary world, but it begins to take on a new and dangerous aspect.

The aim is to take the hero, who was too comfortable in his everyday life, and test him by stripping away his feeling of safety, to see if he's up to the challenge of a thrilling and dangerous adventure.

Initially, the hero will deny the problem – try to ignore it, fob it off on someone else, or try to pass on the responsibility to the appropriate authorities – just as any of us might do. But the villain doesn't want the authorities involved – he needs to keep his plans secret from them – and so he arranges things such that the hero is cut off from official help, and any help that he might have expected from friends or colleagues. Usually, this is done by making it appear that the hero is a criminal so that he has to go 'on the run' to try and prove his innocence.

Now the hero is a fugitive, and as such the ordinary world is no longer safe and familiar. The sight of a uniformed policeman is no longer comforting. Crowded places are dangerous – any one of the people there might recognise him and raise the alarm. Even surrounded by people, he finds himself isolated.

He used to feel safe out in the daylight, and at risk after dark; but now he associates daylight with the risk of being seen and identified as a fugitive, and feels safer travelling at night.

The hero chooses voluntary exile – (a) to go to a place where the risk of recognition is lower, and (b) because the evidence he needs to prove his innocence is to be found somewhere else.

Transportation. Many thrillers feature scenes set in forms of transportation. Cars, aeroplanes, or boats are used – but more often it is trains (or occasionally buses). Why trains? In *North by Northwest* Cary Grant's character says he's taking the train because there's nowhere to hide on a 'plane. Trains also have the advantage of compartments, where scenes can take place in private. And trains make stops – police officers or the villain's men can come aboard, increasing the risk to the hero. And the search of a long train of carriages can be used to add suspense, as the searchers get closer and closer to where the hero is hiding. The hero can also disembark from a train – either at a station or while the train is moving – and continue his journey some other way.

Trains also move through landscapes, which provide filmmakers with an opportunity to photograph new scenery – once you've seen one 'plane in the clouds, you've seen them all. Trains also move at speed – this can add a sense of urgency and danger, especially if the hero is clambering around outside to avoid his pursuers, or having to fight them on top of the coaches.

Trains, then, offer more opportunities for action while travelling long distances between locations – but they are also confining: they are comparatively cramped spaces, and so add to the feeling that things are closing in on the hero, and that he will soon be trapped.

Having made all of these observations about the benefits of trains as a setting, it is only fair to say that trains in thrillers are now something of a cliché. They are probably best avoided, unless you have some fresh new twist to surprise the audience. Try instead to come up with other forms of transport and use them in ways that filmmakers have used trains in the past. Another thing you can do is have the hero forced to operate some form of transportation he has no previous experience of using – this highlights his status as an amateur, and – perhaps – introduces an element of risk. Or humour.

Exotic Locations. One of the appeals of thrillers is that they take us to strange and exotic locations. Ian Fleming captured the imaginations of British readers who were living in grey post-war austerity by having James Bond visit high-class hotels and casinos, and Jamaican beaches. This was before cheap package holidays allowed ordinary people easy access to such locations. John Buchan took his hero from the streets of London to the windswept wilds of Scotland. While Hitchcock's *North by Northwest* is a journey from crowded Manhattan to the tourist attraction that is Mount Rushmore.

The thriller involves pursuit and escape: if you're going to have people running, you may as well have them running through interesting locations. The trick is not to include locations just for the sake of it – they should have some relevance to the story.

Speaking to Peter Bogdanovich about *The Foreign Correspondent,* Hitchcock said: "When I am given a locale – and this is very important in my mind – it's got to be used, and used dramatically. We're in Holland. What have they got in Holland? Windmills? Tulips? If the picture had been in colour, I would have worked in the shot I've always wanted to do and never have yet. The murder in a tulip field."

One of the reasons to take the hero to a strange location is to increase his sense of isolation – he knows no one there, and doesn't know his way around. He may also risk standing out as not belonging there – the local people might look at him suspiciously just for being a stranger. The hero was at home in the ordinary world and could make his own way, even when that world was 'turned against' him. But out in this exotic or unusual place, he has to use all of his wits and ingenuity to stay ahead of his pursuers.

The hero is forced to travel to new places where he feels physically, emotionally, and psychologically threatened. He is exiled from the safety and comfort of his own environment – and worse, he discovers that the safety he previously felt there was an illusion. The world is not the place he thought it was.

(vii) Iconography

What do audiences expect to *see* in a thriller? The typical image of a spy involves 'cloak and dagger' stuff – the hats, dark glasses and long coats of *Spy vs. Spy* in *MAD Magazine.* We have already mentioned locations and travel, especially by train. Other things that people expect to see in a thriller is things that are not what they *appear* to be. The statue that has microfilm hidden inside it. The briefcase that contains hidden weapons. The umbrella with the tip that injects poison. With the exception of guns, gadgets, and the MacGuffin – which we've already covered – there aren't many iconic objects in thrillers. Most of the things we expect to see are people or events. Here is a brief rundown of some of them.

False Identities and Disguises – People who are not what they seem to be. This can include mistaken identity and stolen identities. As we've said, the villain appears to be charming but is anything but. The hero is made to look like a criminal, even though he isn't. There may also be a character who was believed to be dead, but who 'comes back to life.' Friends and allies may betray the hero, and enemies may turn out to be allies. Almost no one is what they appear to be.

Handcuffs – The hero and co-protagonist are physically or emotionally tied to one another and forced to journey together.

Enclosed Spaces – The hero and/or co-protagonist hide in a small space while someone searches for them. People are in train compartments, locked in the trunks of cars or in closets, rooms with barred windows or prison cells or hospital rooms; they crawl in ventilation pipes or climb in lift shafts. Most of these are clichés now, so try and come up with new enclosed spaces that serve the same function.

Chase/Pursuit – The hero is isolated, pursued by both the enemy and the police. He fears being discovered, exposed, or captured. There must be constant, almost relentless movement in the thriller, with only brief pauses for the hero (and the audience) to catch their breath before the pursuit begins again.

Cliff-hangers and Hairbreadth Escapes – Like the old movie serials, a thriller needs situations where the hero is placed in jeopardy and escape seems impossible. The level of threat increases as the story progresses, as the villain becomes more frustrated at the hero eluding him, and the deadline for successful completion of the conspiracy draws closer. Actions the hero takes may have unfortunate consequences, either immediate or delayed. Pursuers close in on the hero, menacing him.

Watching and Voyeurism – Someone spies on someone else without their knowledge. Hitchcock's *Rear Window* is all about a voyeur – what he sees, and what happens when the villain discovers he's being watched. Modern surveillance techniques have evolved so that we now have mobile phones, computers, and drones that can be used to spy on the unwary.

Assassination – Planned, attempted, or successful killings – especially of the hero's allies, colleagues, or helpers. Sometimes the villain's conspiracy centres on the assassination of some important figured. James Bond is licenced to 'neutralise' enemies who threaten Britain's national security: he is essentially a state-sanctioned assassin.

Kidnapping – The hero is often captured by the villain's men at some point in the story. And the hero is often placed in a situation where he must kidnap the co-protagonist in order to survive or escape capture.

Torture – The hero is interrogated by the villain or his henchman. Sometimes the co-protagonist or another of the hero's allies is tortured, or threatened with torture or a horrible death, in order to force the hero to comply with the villain's demands.

Codes – Messages whose meanings are hidden, and which must be deciphered. This can include dialogue, especially between the hero and co-protagonist, which has double meanings.

Disappearing Proof – In the first half of the amateur-on-the-run thriller, the hero tries to provide proof of his innocence to the authorities; but this proof typically 'disappears' or is publicly discredited – courtesy of the villain – further reducing the credibility of the hero and closing off another avenue of help for him. People who the hero may be relying on for help may also disappear – often they are bumped off by the villain's men – or they may betray the hero to the villain or prove to be part of the conspiracy.

Ticking Clock or Rising Tide – Thrillers almost always include a deadline of some kind. As the climax of the story approaches, the story is often told in what appears to be 'real time,' as the clock ticks down to zero or the waters are about to burst through the dam.

Imprisonment and Escape – The hero is often captured and locked away somewhere so that he cannot rescue the co-protagonist or reach the location where the conspiracy will shortly be concluded. He will need to use his ingenuity to escape.

(viii) Themes

Conspiracy. We've already said that conspiracy or criminal intent lies at the heart of the thriller. A conspiracy involves two or more people with a secret plan to achieve some specific goal that is unlawful or harmful to others or to cover up some wrongful act that has already been committed. In the amateur-on-the-run thriller, an amateur hero accidentally becomes embroiled in the conspiracy, finding himself up against the conspirators with no support from the authorities. In the espionage thriller, a professional agent is given the job of uncovering the conspiracy and preventing it, perhaps by infiltrating the group of conspirators.

The conspiracy often involves *corruption*, being carried out by individuals in 'high places' betraying the trust of the people they are meant to serve. It shows how precarious the stability of our civilised world really is, and how close we are to *chaos* at any time. We are normally unaware of this, but the thriller brings it home to us.

The conspiracy may be an actual crime, something illegal, or it may be something that is *technically* legal, but which we would regard as unethical or immoral. Typically the conspiracy involves the villains seeking personal gain – wealth, power, or revenge – at the expense of an individual, a small group, or society / the world in general.

Any sphere of activity where we expect people to behave ethically is a possible background for a conspiracy: the medical, legal, business and banking, military, policing, and political worlds are all used in thrillers.

The conspiracy must be a *secret* that the villains do not want to be revealed until they are ready to act – and perhaps not even then. Their scheme will be ruined if the secret gets out. They fear *exposure*, and so are prepared to take drastic action – including murder or assassination – to protect the secret and further their plot. This helps to establish what is at stake: the villains are prepared to kill the hero in order to protect their secret and succeed in their conspiracy. Knowing about the plot, or even some small part of it, puts the hero's life in danger: if he also has the MacGuffin that is vital to the success of the plot, or knows its location, then the villains will go to any lengths to capture and interrogate him.

Trust. Conspiracy involves a *betrayal of trust*. Ordinary people are betrayed by those they have placed in positions of power. The thriller shows us that things are not always what they appear, and people are not what they seem. The hero quickly learns that he can trust nothing and no one – not if he wants to stay alive. But betrayal and loss of trust are only half the story in a thriller. In losing everything, his identity and his reputation as well as his comfort and safety, and being an exile from the world he knows, the hero discovers that he can trust in his own personal resources.

The hero of the amateur-on-the-run thriller also needs to learn that there *are* people he can trust: not everyone is corrupt. Key to this is his relationship with the co-protagonist: it begins with antagonism but develops into trust and *romance*. By discovering romance with the co-protagonist, the hero learns to trust again. Not everyone is out to get him. Her faith in him also gives him strength – he feels better able to trust his own moral code and his own abilities when he sees someone else is now depending on him to do the right thing.

Paranoia. The villain trusts no one – he believes that everyone is a potential enemy, and suffers from paranoia as a result. This same fate awaits the hero if he completely loses the ability to trust others. Having been betrayed by people close to him, and finding himself unjustly accused of a crime and pursued by the police, the hero comes to feel that he can trust nothing and no one. His situation looks desperate – how can he possibly survive on his own if the whole of society seems turned against him? He fears for his own sanity as well as his safety. Is all this real, or is he imagining it? The conspiracy undermines the hero's concept of how the world is, and so presents a mental threat as well as a physical one. He is no longer in control of his own life – at least until he makes a stand and determines that he will take charge.

Paranoia involves the belief that someone is out to 'get you.' A paranoid person typically thinks that they are being persecuted in some way, or that there is some sort of conspiracy taking place which is a threat to them. Anxiety and fear are a part of this thought process, as the person believes there is something out there that is dangerous to them personally. They are suspicious of other people and always on their guard.

In extreme cases, a person may suffer from *paranoid personality disorder*. Not to be confused with paranoid schizophrenia, *paranoid personality disorder* is – according to the World Health Organisation – characterised by three or more of the following behaviours:

- excessive sensitivity to setbacks and rebuffs;
- tendency to bear grudges persistently, i.e. refusal to forgive insults and injuries or slights;
- suspiciousness and a pervasive tendency to distort experience by misconstruing the neutral or friendly actions of others as hostile or contemptuous;
- a combative and tenacious sense of personal rights out of keeping with the actual situation;
- recurrent suspicions, without justification, regarding sexual fidelity of spouse or sexual partner;
- tendency to experience excessive self-importance, manifest in a persistent self-referential attitude;
- preoccupation with unsubstantiated 'conspiratorial' explanations of events both immediate to the patient and in the world at large.

Paranoid individuals are keen observers, always seeking signs of danger – but at the same time, they have a tendency to ignore any evidence that says there is no danger. They are suspicious of the motives of others and may interpret another person's actions as hostile and specifically directed at them, when in truth the actions were casual or accidental, and no malice was intended. They may remember these 'slights' for long periods, and come to bear grudges against the 'offender.' In more extreme forms, paranoid behaviour can lead to the *revenge* motive that leads people to scapegoat minority groups and blame them for all of society's ills. These arguments run along the lines of 'I am unhappy/unsuccessful, therefore *they* must be to blame.'

Since everyone is out to get the paranoid person, they obviously believe themselves at the centre of things. This self-importance is a kind of delusion of grandeur: 'Everyone is out to get me, therefore I must be important.' Such people often also have a strong sense of personal right, of being deserving or 'owed' as a result of their persecution. This can be manifested in what is sometimes called 'querulous paranoia' or 'litigious paranoia,' where a person has an obsessive feeling of having been wronged, and so seeks redress through the legal process. This can include people who repeatedly pursue legal actions – often over minor grievances – which are (to the legal system and to almost everyone else) obviously without foundation.

The final item above, regarding a preoccupation with 'conspiratorial' explanations of events, takes us into the realm of conspiracy theories. The television series *The X-Files* had great fun exploring the question: What if the conspiracy theorists are right?

Mystery. Associated with the conspiracy is an element of mystery which arouses the curiosity of the audience. We, and the hero, do not know exactly what the conspirators are trying to achieve, or how they plan to do it. We just know that they're up to something. The nature of the conspiracy is uncovered as the plot develops, as is the method by which the conspirators intend to bring it about. Allied to this is also some mystery about who is behind the conspiracy: often the true identity of the conspirators remains a secret for some time.

Obviously, there is also an element of mystery in the 'main dramatic question' asked at the beginning of the story: Will the hero survive and defeat the villain? The mysteries of what the villain is up to, what the hero has become caught up in, and who is behind it all, are often resolved at the midpoint. At this point, the hero finally finds out what he is really up against, and the audience is aware of the odds he faces. After that, the story concentrates on the main dramatic question.

Commitment. When we first encounter the hero, he demonstrates no beliefs and no commitment. He comes across as a cynical observer of society, rather than an active member of it. He is adrift, aimless, ambivalent and morally ambiguous. He is dissatisfied with his life, but complacency means he lacks the impetus to do anything about it. Having his everyday life, his comfort and security, denied him by the actions of the conspirators, the hero is forced to re-evaluate himself and his life. His adventures provide him with an opportunity for self-discovery – he must draw on personal reserves that he did not know he had. He discovers his own hidden potential.

The hero is given no choice, he *must* take action to ensure his own survival. And this makes him feel more alive than he has ever felt before. As a result of his interactions with the co-protagonist and the villain, the hero makes some important discoveries about himself. In the villain he sees behaviours which he views as immoral and which must be prevented from triumphing. He also sees, in the villain's selfishness and paranoia, something that he himself could become if he took the wrong path. The romance that develops between the hero and the co-protagonist saves him from becoming like the villain. The trust that each of them demonstrates in the other, and their selfless feelings for one another, put them in direct opposition to the villain.

The hero fulfils his true potential, becoming a 'crusader' who defends the values approved of by society. He discovers the importance of commitment and of taking action to defend the things you value most. For the first time, he takes *responsibility* for his actions, unlike the villain who wants power without the responsibility that goes with it, and is prepared to sacrifice himself.

When analysing your thriller idea, ask yourself how facing the conspiracy is going to put the hero in danger, and also how it is going to change him for the better.

Redemption. The amateur hero's development can be classified under the theme of redemption. He begins as naïve and uncommitted or cynical and aloof, and then learns something about himself and the world and goes forward as a changed person.

The amateur hero can never go back to his original state of blissful ignorance – he has learned that the world is a very different place than he assumed it to be. But any disillusionment he suffers is tempered by the discovery of love and trust, and the idealism these have brought out in him.

Redemption is an idea we take from religion. The concept of redemption is found in many world religions: to be redeemed is to be forgiven for past sins, and is typically achieved by proving oneself worthy by making some form of personal sacrifice. The word 'redeem' is also associated with paying off a debt, implying some form of transaction.

Two terms often associated with redemption, and both also taken from theology, are repentance and atonement. To *repent* is to express regret or remorse for something wrong that one has done. It also has the meaning of returning to that which is morally right. We tend to think that *atonement* means making amends for our sins or crimes, but it also has the meaning of 'reconciliation' or coming together, of being accepted back into the relationship, family or group we had rejected or been cast out from as a result of our sins.

Redemption, then, can be seen as a journey that someone makes from vice to virtue; from selfishness to selflessness. There is a strong redemptive path built into the twelve-step programmes of self-help groups, which originated with Alcoholics Anonymous. And in many thriller plots. In literature and the movies, a character is often presented as an anti-hero, or as someone who has 'fallen from grace' – we just can't escape that religious imagery, can we? – and is offered an opportunity to redeem himself. He can pay off the debt of his past sins – or at least some of the accrued interest – by undertaking some selfless mission. He must sacrifice his own desires for the good of others.

The redemption of the amateur hero comes in the form of an unlikely romance. He is thrown together with someone who does not trust him and resents his intrusion in her life. Their relationship begins as antagonistic. But she gradually comes to believe in him and seeks to help him. And in demonstrating this belief, she enables him to (a) see that there are still people in the world he can trust, and (b) that there are things in the world worth fighting for. She also helps him to believe in himself and his own abilities to succeed in preventing the villain's conspiracy from succeeding.

The hero can be redeemed, but the villain cannot. The hero is able, and willing, to sacrifice his own desires – and even his own life – to protect others and to protect the values of the society he lives in. The villain is completely self-obsessed, and could never do this. He trusts no one, loves no one, and sees every situation as a challenge that he must win. Allowing himself to die in defence of a 'greater good' would never occur to him.

The villain is only able to see things from his own point of view, he cannot see things from another person's perspective. As a result, he ascribes his own beliefs to the hero – how often does the villain in a thriller say, 'We are alike, you and I, we want the same thing'?

If I know what you *want* – your goal and your motive for achieving it – I can predict what you will do. I can anticipate your actions and defend against them, even prevent you from succeeding. But, if what you want *changes*, I need to be aware of the change, so I can rethink my predictions. The villain cannot do that, because he cannot put himself in the hero's place. The villain's desires never change, and so he assumes that the hero's remain constant. But the hero's motives *do* change – he goes from wanting to escape back to his old comfortable life (a selfish goal) to wanting to protect an ideology – and if he dies while doing this, he can still *win*. The villain does not understand this, because in his belief system to die is to lose.

Restoration of Order. As in the murder mystery, the hero's actions bring about the restoration of order. But unlike the mystery, things don't go back to the way they were before for the hero – something has changed. He has changed. His eyes have been opened to a new reality – he knows that chaos lies just beneath the surface of the ordinary world. He knows that what we have cannot be taken for granted, because there will always be another villain ready to betray our values and exploit us. We must be prepared to take action and defend our values at any time.

Like the mystery, the thriller assumes that our ordinary world and its values are worth defending. The best thrillers question our values, rather than accepting them blindly, while the worst ones can be xenophobic in their 'us versus them' attitude, where 'foreigners' of whatever kind cannot be trusted.

Ultimately, the hero's battle with the villain is not about physical survival, it is about conflicting belief systems – something along the lines of tyranny versus democracy. During the Cold War, the thriller promoted Western democracy over a despotic form of Communism. Before that, it was Britain versus Germany. More recently, in the so-called 'war on terror,' we have Western democracy versus a corrupted form of Islamic fundamentalism. This will be replaced, in time, with something else.

The stakes do not have to be as large as nations against nations – often the battle is fought on home soil, as in the example of the corrupt politicians seeking power, or corrupt financiers seeking wealth – conspiracies that undermine the values of our society. It should be said that thrillers are typically conservative – that which is, is good and should be protected from destabilisation.

The hero of the amateur-on-the-run thriller does not, initially, appear to possess either physical survival skills or any great sense of moral or political conviction. If he did, the story would simply become a 'good versus bad' melodrama. Instead, we see the hero *learn* the importance of the values of his society, through positive examples by allies – at least one of whom is likely to die to defend these values – and through his relationship with the co-protagonist; and negative examples as demonstrated by the villain, his henchman and his heavies. Having *discovered for himself* the importance of these values, he is then prepared to risk his own life to defend them.

Part of the appeal of amateur-on-the-run thrillers is that they allow us to believe that we too might demonstrate hidden strengths and convictions if faced with similar challenges: our survival instincts would kick in and we would be able to prove ourselves heroes.

The overall theme of an amateur-on-the-run thriller concerns the importance of having something to believe in, and of being prepared to sacrifice everything to defend what you believe in. The amateur hero discovers that he does have deeply held beliefs, they have just never been challenges in such a way before. And he discovers that he does have the physical and mental strength that enable him to fight, and perhaps even die, to defend his beliefs.

Reducing it as far as possible:

Villain = irresponsible; selfish; betrayer
Hero = responsible; selfless; crusader

The Psychology of Suspense – The Appeal of the Thriller
The main appeal of the thriller is that audiences enjoy suspense. Curiosity (or mystery), surprise (or shock), and suspense (or tension) are what give us pleasure in all kinds of stories. We will explore suspense in chapter four.

The chase and escape motifs of the thriller might give us the same thrill as a schoolyard game of 'tag,' but thrillers also remind us of the fun of hide-and-seek. In *The Spy Story,* John G. Cawelti discusses the patterns and psychological appeal of what he calls 'clandestinity,' and highlights some additional themes found in the thriller.

According to Cawelti, clandestine operations are undertaken because someone is deeply committed to achieving a particular goal, and is prepared to go beyond the usual boundaries of action. Or the goal itself may be illegal. Politics and national security are areas where clandestine activities occur: "For example, when those in power feel that public opinion will resist certain courses of action deemed vital for national security, or the success of an administration, there may be a great temptation to resort to secret actions against a foreign power or against an organisation that is felt to be a domestic threat."

Obviously where an agent is operating in a foreign country, his or her actions must remain secret. And the same is true where activists are plotting revolution in their own country.

Outside of politics and national security, covert activities are carried out in other areas – industrial espionage being one example. Crime, by its very nature, must be carried out in secret – or at least in such a way as to avoid leaving conclusive evidence – in order to avoid arrest.

And finally Cawelti notes that illicit love affairs are carried out with many of the same practices as espionage operations – "... secret communications, hidden rendezvous, complicated alibis, and elaborate disguises." He goes on to note that "... such lovers often experience the special closeness of people who share a dangerous bond unknown to others. Not surprisingly, poets have noted the analogy between love and espionage. Shakespeare and Donne both use spy metaphors to express secret love, for example."

It is probably worth noting that people engaged in clandestine activities can come to rely on the thrill it gives them, and feel a need for it when it is no longer necessary. Secret lovers may find that, once they can declare their love openly, they no longer feel the same intense thrill they felt when their relationship was a dangerous secret.

In discussing the psychological appeal of 'clandestinity,' Cawelti highlights three themes: *invisibility, disguises,* and *conspiracy.*

Invisibility, he says, is a "... very powerful fantasy ... a motif whose recurrence in myth, legend, and literature indicates a compelling appeal for many people in many different cultures." The spy is invisible in that he is an unseen observer, listening at doors or spying through peepholes, or employing modern technology to do similar things. The professional spy also belongs to a secret organisation that frees him from the obligations and responsibilities of ordinary people – James Bond, for example, is given a 'licence to kill.' Cawelti: "These aspects of invisibility – voyeurism, self-concealment, and licence – clearly have a powerful attraction quite apart from the purpose they are intended to serve."

Invisibility can also be extended to include the 'unseen world' in which espionage and other clandestine activities take place. The 'criminal underworld' is another such place. Ordinary people rarely enter these worlds and have only a dim awareness of their existence. Being allowed access to hidden worlds is one of the appeals of the thriller – and of other types of stories. It is also the appeal of many real-world activities, from online games to musical subcultures; and is found in some occupations – the military, police and legal systems, medicine – occupations that are often depicted in television and film.

Disguise is another "... fantasy connected with clandestinity," according to Cawelti. This too is found in myth, folktales, and popular literature in many cultures. Cawelti writes that the power of this fascination "... very likely resides in the thrill of trying on other identities – social, racial, sexual, or chronological. Men fantasise themselves as women, whites as blacks, rich men as poor men, young people as aged, and vice versa ... Disguise is a temporary escape from one's own identity; the role of the spy contains the possibility of a controlled but total escape from the constraints of self."

Conspiracy, according to Cawelti, concerns the secret exercise of power: "To imagine becoming part of a secret organisation is a compelling fantasy not only in terms of the exercise of power without its responsibilities and risks, but also as a particularly strong image of belonging. To belong to a clandestine organisation seems to carry with it a profound involvement, a relationship to other members of the organisation deeper than that characteristic of other kinds of organisations because it requires life-and-death loyalty. This particular fantasy of clandestinity is probably especially powerful in modern industrial cultures where people feel relatively alienated from most of the organisations to which they belong."

Cawelti notes that the appeal of *The Godfather*, which concerns a 'clandestine family,' fully exploited this fantasy of belonging and intense loyalty.

(ix) Tone
"For me, suspense doesn't have any value unless it's balanced by humour." – Alfred Hitchcock.

Generally speaking, apart from some banter between the hero and the co-protagonist, the overall tone of the amateur-on-the-run thriller is serious. The suspense relies on the audience believing that the threat to the hero is real. That being said, macabre or gallows humour underlines the seriousness and throws it into relief. That's probably what Hitchcock meant. That and the fact that he knew he could get away with more unpleasantness if it was leavened with humour. When we are afraid, we like to laugh to release the tension.

Any humour arising from an improbable situation in a thriller is usually contrasted by serious or tragic consequences of seemingly ridiculous actions. The flip-side of laughing to relieve tension is laughing at something that seems absurd, then feeling guilty because someone is hurt as a result of the absurd event.

Amateur-on-the-run thrillers are normally optimistic: the hero rises to the occasion and defeats the threat to the established order. But there is an underlying sense of a loss of innocence – the hero will never look at the world in quite the same way again. And, at the end of the story, the newly-restored equilibrium has to be viewed as precarious – it could quite easily be threatened by another conspiracy soon.

The thriller can be parodied – Mel Brooks' *High Anxiety* takes on Alfred Hitchcock – and occasionally a light-hearted thriller such as *Jumpin' Jack Flash* appears. But amateur-on-the-run thrillers are probably best played straight, with any humour coming from the characters rather than the situations.

(x) Secondary Characters
We have already identified and explored three main characters as essential ingredients of the amateur-on-the-run thriller:

- the hero
- the villain

- the co-protagonist

Other characters likely to appear are:

The Henchman. The person who represents the villain until the villain's identity is revealed. The villain's right-hand man.

The Heavies. A couple of thugs or gunmen who work for the villain and whose actions are directed by the henchman. One of these is likely to be killed soon after the midpoint in Act II and one late in Act II.

The Authorities. Typically, the hero finds himself fleeing from both the conspirators and the authorities – the bad guys and the good guys. In amateur-on-the-run thrillers, the police are not seen as corrupt, although a single official may be working for the villain or may be one of the conspirators himself. In *noir*-style hardboiled detective stories, people in the ordinary world of the thriller, including the authorities, are all regarded as corrupt: this is not the case in the thriller. There may be a single 'authority' figure that the hero regards as an ally, but this person might betray him if he is secretly in league with the villain. Or he could be in league with the villain and then see the error of his ways, and seek to help the hero. Either way, he stands a good chance of being killed.

The Betrayer. As the thriller deals with themes of trust and with people and situations that are not what they appear, it is common for there to be a character that the hero believes he can trust but who – at an important and dramatic moment – betrays him. Usually this means that the betrayer is actually working for the villain, but it can also be that the character lets him down in some other way: he may refuse to help the hero in a moment of need; or he may prove to be weak and not the paragon the hero believed him to be; or he may simply turn up dead, often in circumstances that make it look like the hero is the murderer. The betrayer may be someone with whom the hero has been romantically involved, similar to the *femme fatale* in *films noir.*

The Doomed Ally. Another character who often appears is a person who the hero is relying on to help him. This may be someone with special skills or experience or access to information, who can potentially help prove the hero innocent or the conspirators guilty. But before the hero can reach this ally, the villain's men kill him. This serves to increase the tension – cutting off the hero's final vital source of help and completely isolating him. Worse, the situation could be staged to make it *appear* that the hero murdered this ally.

Amateur on the Run Thrillers – 10 Examples

Devising a list of *pure* amateur-on-the-run thrillers is tricky because many novels and movies fit into more than one sub-genre, and many have some but not all of the elements I have described above. Below are novels and films that I think best fit our definition – the ones marked with an asterisk are ones that I think ought to be read or viewed by anyone who wants to write this type of story.

The Thirty-Nine Steps by John Buchan (1915, filmed in 1935, 1959, 1978)*
Manhunt (vt. *Rogue Male*) by Geoffrey Household (1939, filmed in 1941, 1976)
The Ministry of Fear by Graham Greene (1943, filmed in 1944)
North by Northwest (1959)*
The Cypher by Alex Gordon (1961, filmed as *Arabesque* in 1966)
House of Cards by Stanley Ellin (1967, filmed in 1969)
Six Days of the Condor by James Grady (1974, filmed as *Three Days of the Condor* in 1975)*
Absolute Power by David Baldacci (1996, filmed in 1997)
Enemy of the State (1998)*
Eagle Eye (2008)

2 | Professional Secret Agent

The amateur-on-the-run thriller had an *amateur* as its protagonist in part because having a character who is obviously out of their element and out of their depth is a great way of creating dramatic action, and partly because in any area of human endeavour there have to be amateurs before there can be professionals. Experts only come into existence when there is a body of knowledge and skills for them to become expert in. The difference between an amateur thriller hero and a professional one comes down to a combination of experience and intent. The amateur has no experience and becomes involved in his adventure by accident. The professional has experience in the field and deliberately takes on his adventure – or, more likely, since this is his job, he is assigned a mission.

James Bond is probably the most famous and most influential of the professional thriller heroes – other writers have either patterned their hero on him or deliberately tried to create a hero *unlike* him. I'm going to use Ian Fleming's novels, particularly *Dr. No,* and the Bond films as examples for the professional hero thriller. Not all professional heroes are secret agents, but all *are* experienced and all are assigned their missions or choose to take them. There is a hybrid form that we can call the professional-on-the-run thriller which I'll cover later in the book.

To clarify what we're discussing in the present chapter, I want to emphasise that by 'secret agent' I mean a protagonist who is a professional person. As we'll see later, there are other thrillers that take place in particular professional fields – medicine, the law, politics – in which the heroes while being professionally qualified or experienced in their subject area are still amateurs when it comes to being a thriller hero. Our secret agent is a professional hero. And while I have titled this chapter *Secret Agent,* I'm not really talking about spies here. As Kingsley Amis wrote in his book *The James Bond Dossier,* "It's inaccurate ... to describe James Bond as a *spy*, in the strictest sense of one who steals or buys or smuggles secrets from foreign Powers." Bond is, Amis says, more properly a *counter*-spy, "one who operates against the agents of unfriendly powers." Others have described James Bond as an enforcer or even a professional assassin. We will stick with the term 'secret agent' and I will deal with the more 'realistic' type of spy-hero, as typified by the novels of John Le Carré in the chapter on espionage thrillers.

Historical Development

In a 1963 interview, Ian Fleming said that his James Bond stories were probably influenced by stories he read in his childhood and he gives the authors Sax Rohmer and E. Phillips Oppenheim as examples. Oppenheim wrote over one hundred novels between 1887 and 1943, including many of them thrillers of the 'cloak and dagger' variety, featuring secret documents that will determine the fate of the country. His first, *Mysterious Mr. Sabin* was published in 1898. The best-known is *The Great Impersonation* (1920) in which a German discovers he is the doppelganger of an English gentleman and takes on his identity in order to spy on the English in the period leading up to the First World War. Over a million copies of the novel were sold in its first year of publication and it has been filmed three times – in 1921, 1935, and 1942.

William Le Queux (pronounced Kew) was another patriotic Englishman who wrote cloak and dagger stories – in part because he wanted to warn his compatriots about the threat posed by Germany, whose spies – he was convinced – had infiltrated the English establishment. His biographer, N. St. Barbe Sladen, wrote in 1938 that Le Queux invented the 'adventurous spy as a literary type' and that he served in a voluntary capacity for the Secret Service. Le Queux readily mixed fact and fiction in his conspiracy theories, but his fictional account of an invasion of Britain, *The Invasion of 1910*, which was originally serialised in the *Daily Mail* newspaper in 1906, reportedly went on to sell over a million copies in book form.

Oppenheim and Le Queux were among the earliest writers of 'secret agent' novels but their contribution to the genre is regarded as relatively slight in comparison with the next three writers: John Buchan, Sapper, and Dornford Yates.

John Buchan we have already encountered as the author of *The Thirty-Nine Steps* (1915) – this was the first of five novels with Richard Hannay as the protagonist. Published after the start of the First World War, this and the later novels were focused more on the conspiracy faced by the hero than on warning of German aggression.

Sapper (pseudonym of Herman Cyril McNeile) wrote ten novels about hero Bulldog Drummond and the series was continued by other writers after McNeile's death. The first, *Bulldog Drummond,* was published in 1920. Twenty-four Bulldog Drummond films were released between 1922 and 1969. In the early 1930s, Alfred Hitchcock wanted to direct a film featuring the character and a screenplay for *Bulldog Drummond's Baby* was written by Charles Bennett. Unable to obtain the rights to use the character, the story was rewritten to feature a different hero and became the 1934 film *The Man Who Knew Too Much.*

Dornford Yates (pseudonym of Cecil William Mercer) wrote dozens of novels and short story collections, many of them thrillers. Some were stand-alone titles, but the eight 'Chandos books,' beginning with *Blind Corner* (1927), were narrated by the hero Richard Chandos and featured among his colleagues was Jonathan Mansel, who had featured as a character in earlier Yates stories.

Richard Usborne wrote a book-length study on the characters created by the three writers, *Clubland Heroes* published in 1954. Describing these characters, O. F. Snelling has said, "They are all West End clubmen, they all appear to be of independent means and they all conform to a rigid code of honour made up by equal parts of birth, public school, university and the army." The gentlemen's club – later referred to as a *traditional* gentlemen's club to distinguish it from a strip club – was a private, members-only establishment for upper-class English gentlemen. These clubs, notoriously choosy about who they admitted as members and charging significant annual membership fees, flourished from the eighteenth century until the early twentieth and typically contained a formal dining room, a bar, library and reading rooms, and rooms for billiards and other games, including gambling. 'Independent means' refers, of course, to inherited wealth that meant a man didn't have to work for a living – in Jane Austen's novels a gentleman's suitability as a husband is often judged by the annual income he gets from the estate he has inherited.

Alan Bennett referred to the three writers in his 1972 play *Forty Years On*, saying that Sapper, Buchan and Dornford Yates were "practitioners in that school of Snobbery with Violence that runs like a thread of good-class tweed through twentieth-century literature." As well as snobbery and violence, the stories of these three writers – to greater or lesser extent – have been accused of being patriotic to the point of jingoism, racist and anti-Semitic: they are very much a product of their time.

The larger-than-life villain who plans to conquer the world, hold it to ransom, or gain revenge on it, belongs to a much older tradition. Jules Verne gave us Robur in *Robur the Conqueror* (1886) and *Master of the World* (1904) and also Captain Nemo in *20,000 Leagues Under the Sea* (1869-70). Sax Rohmer (pseudonym of Arthur Henry Sarsfield Ward) wrote *The Mystery of Dr. Fu-Manchu* (1912-13) creating a character that would appear in thirteen novels up until the author's death, with the series then being continued by other writers. Fu-Manchu also appeared in a number of British and Hollywood movies. Ian Fleming's villain Dr. No was probably inspired, in part, by Rohmer's villain. After the Second World War, writers also had a real-life tyrant to base their villains upon.

The character of James Bond grew out of this tradition of upper-class British heroes and accounts of the genre usually have it that Ian Fleming's creation is their *direct* descendant. But in an article titled 'The Secret Origins of James Bond,' novelist Jeremy Duns identified another potential source of inspiration: Dennis Wheatley's secret agent novels. Wheatley is today best-known for his occult-themed stories including *The Devil Rides Out* (1934) and *To the Devil... a Daughter* (1953) which were adapted into movies. But he also wrote a number of historical espionage stories, notably the 'Roger Brook' series set during the Napoleonic Wars, and contemporary secret agent stories featuring Gregory Sallust which began with *Contraband* (1936). Beginning in 1940, Wheatley worked for Churchill's War Cabinet, first imaging ways that Britain might be invaded by the Nazis and how the attack might be foiled, and then writing disinformation that could be fed to the enemy. He was one of the few novelists to write about espionage and counter-espionage *before* he became involved in it in real life. Ian Fleming's older brother, Peter, was also involved in counter-espionage while based in India and Wheatley wrote about him in his memoir *The Deception Planners* published after the author's death. Peter Fleming wrote a secret agent novel of his own, *The Sixth Column* (1951), which was a sort of parody of the 'snobbery with violence' thrillers he'd read during his youth that may have been inspired in part by Wheatley's work during the war.

In his article, Jeremy Duns describes the plot of Wheatley's Gregory Sallust novels: "A gentleman adventurer reports to an older man in the secret service, and is given a mission to stop a villainous plot that has international implications; he races through glamorous casinos and hotels at home and abroad, using his fists and firearms against assorted henchmen until he is drugged, struck unconscious and captured by a rich, deformed villain, who interrogates and/or tortures him; after learning the full particulars of the villain's plan (usually from the villain himself), he escapes. Saves the beautiful woman in the cocktail dress he took a fancy to in the first chapter and assures the safety of the realm." This was not an original plot when Wheatley used it in 1936, as Duns notes it had "been the formula of British secret service stories since the nineteenth century," but the tone of his novel and its somewhat ambivalent hero were new. Writing in *The New York Times* in 1968, Richard Boston suggested that Ian Fleming had created James Bond by taking Bulldog Drummond and giving him a sex life, but Fleming wasn't the first to add sex to the previously sexless 'snobbery with violence' thriller – Wheatley's hero was having pre-marital sex in 1940 and the plot of *The Black Baroness* centres on the use of mistresses to seduce and compromise senior military figures. Duns details a number of other instances where Dennis Wheatley's novels may have influenced Fleming's, including *Strange Conflict* (1941) set in Haiti and including voodoo rites and a villain called Doctor Saturday.

How much inspiration Fleming took from the works of Rohmer, Oppenheim, Buchan, Sapper, Yates, or Wheatley it is impossible to say. But we do know that he blended various pre-existing elements together in a way that proved popular with readers and film-goers.

The Creation and Evolution of James Bond
In an interview with *Playboy* magazine, Fleming said that the James Bond stories featured a 'bowdlerised' version of things he'd learned during his own Naval Intelligence experience and from what he had learned from others engaged in secret operations. He also said that while Bond himself was "a sort of amalgam of romantic tough guys, dressed up in twentieth-century clothes," he did feel that the character was true to the modern hero, such as "the commandoes of the last war ... and to some of the secret service men I've met..." He felt that the Bulldog Drummond type of character was 'rather cardboardy' and didn't really have a place in modern fiction.

Interviewed by Geoffrey T. Hellman for *The New Yorker*, Fleming said, "I wanted Bond to be an extremely dull, uninteresting man to whom things happened." And in another interview said, "Exotic things would happen to and around him, but he would be a neutral figure – an anonymous, blunt instrument wielded by a government department." Seeking a name for his new character he took inspiration from a book in his collection, *Birds of the West Indies*, written by the ornithologist James Bond: "I thought, My God, that's the dullest name I've ever heard, so I appropriated it." It was a more suitable name, he thought, than one like the old cloak-and-dagger heroes who had names like 'Peregrine Caruthers.'

"I don't think that he is necessarily a good guy or a bad guy. Who is?" Fleming said in an interview with *Playboy*. "He's got his vices and very few perceptible virtues except patriotism and courage, which are probably not virtues anyway ... I didn't *intend* for him to be a particularly likeable person." And in another interview, "He's not a bad man, but he is ruthless and self-indulgent. He enjoys the fight – he also enjoys the prizes."

When it came to providing a physical description for James Bond, Fleming chose to make him look like an American composer and actor whose appearance was possibly not that well known to the public. In Chapter 5 of *Casino Royale,* Vesper Lynd says of Bond, "He is very good-looking. He reminds me rather of Hoagy Carmichael, but there is something cold and ruthless in his . . ." She doesn't get to finish her sentence because a window is suddenly smashed close by. In Chapter 8 Bond, having been told about the comparison, looks at himself in the mirror:

His grey-blue eyes looked calmly back with a hint of ironical inquiry and the short lock of black hair which would never stay in place slowly subsided to form a thick comma above his right eyebrow. With the thin vertical scar down his right cheek the general effect was faintly piratical. Not much of Hoagy Carmichael there, thought Bond...

In *Moonraker* Fleming again has a female character, Gala Brand this time, make the comparison: "... he was certainly good-looking ... Rather like Hoagy Carmichael in a way. That black hair falling down over the right eyebrow. Much the same bones. But there was something a bit cruel in the mouth, and the eyes were cold."

Umberto Eco has suggested that Fleming chose Hoagy Carmichael because his "face is an improved version of that of Ian Fleming himself..." But I think the 1947 photograph in Carmichael's Wikipedia entry looks more like Fleming's older brother, Peter, than it does Fleming.

When it comes to describing your hero in a thriller, my advice would be to keep it short and keep it simple and get it in early. Readers will begin forming an impression of a character in their mind's eye as soon as that character appears. You should give them a few key details on which to base this image – but you should also give them room to add details of their own, because there is every chance they will form an image of the character that ignores some of what you give them anyway. I think Fleming had enough with the cold blue-grey eyes, the cruel mouth and the dark hair – we didn't need Hoagy Carmichael.

In fact, I would strongly advise against comparing your characters to a particular actress or musician or other well-known person – particularly if you want your novels to have some kind of longevity. In ten or twenty years' time, people may not remember what Justin Bieber looked like or the person you choose may be involved in some Weinstein-like scandal such that you wouldn't want to associate your character with them. It's also cheating your reader. Your job as a reader is to create images with words, not to say go and Google an image of this actress. I am definitely *not* saying do not use actors to help you visualise characters and imagine how they speak and act – all of us probably do that, at least sometimes. But try and have two or three actors in mind so that you can create a Jack Nicholson-*type* of character rather than making your character be Jack Nicholson. If you start writing dialogue in a rhythm that is obviously Nicholsonian, then again you're short-changing your reader. You should be creating new characters for them, not putting together your ideal fantasy film cast. And it goes without saying that you shouldn't use real people or characters from other people's work – unless you're writing some kind of parody or homage.

Sex, Snobbery, and Sadism
Fleming was questioned by Roy Norquist about the 'sex, snobbery and sadism' in his novels and argued that these were 'quite proper ingredients of a thriller,' saying, "Sex, of course, comes into all interesting books and into interesting lives. As to snobbery, I think that's pretty good nonsense, really. In fact, we'd all of us like to eat better, stay in better hotels, wear better clothes, drive faster motor-cars, and so on, and it amuses me that my hero does most of these things. As for sadism, well, I think the old-fashioned way of beating up a spy with a baseball bat has gone out with the last war, and I think it's permissible to give him a rather tougher time than we used to..." When asked about it in the *Playboy* interview, Fleming argued that the Bond stories had to reflect their times and that we were living in violent times, with the horrors of the battlefield and the concentration camps of the Second World War still fresh in people's minds. "I hear it said that I invent fiendish cruelties and tortures to which Bond is subjected. But no one who knows, as I know, the things that were done to captured secret agents in the last war says this. No one says it who knows what went on in Algeria."

On a BBC radio programme, Raymond Chandler asked Fleming why he always included a torture scene, and in answer Fleming said, "I suppose I was brought up on Dr. Fu Manchu and thrillers of that kind and ... even in Bulldog Drummond ... the hero at the end gets in the grips of the villain and he suffers – either he's drugged or something happens to him..."

In that radio interview, Fleming also spoke about the difficulty of creating villains. "I find it extremely difficult to write about villains. Villains are extremely difficult people to put my finger on. You can often find heroes wandering around in life. You meet them... as well as plenty of heroines, of course. But a really good solid villain is a very difficult person to build up, I think ... Of course, the difficulty is to set in oneself – and be able to persuade the reader – that the man is not to be pitied for being a sick man." Fleming's solution, in part, was to create exaggerated, larger-than-life villains, as he told *Playboy:* "It amuses me to have a villain with a great bulbous head, whereas, as you know, they're generally little people with nothing at extraordinary-looking about them."

Fleming spoke about his writing process in the *Playboy* interview. Each year he would go to his house, *Goldeneye*, in Jamaica for January, February, and part of March where he would enjoy the sun and the sea and write the new novel. He would begin at about ten o'clock each morning "... and type about fifteen hundred words straightaway, without looking back on what I wrote the day before. I have more or less thought out what I am going to write and, in any case, even if I make a lot of mistakes, I think, well, hell, when the book's finished I can change it all. I think the main thing is to write fast and cursively in order to get narrative speed." He would then return to the typewriter again in the evening at six o'clock "... doing another five hundred words. I then number the pages, of which by that time there are about seven, put them away in a folder, and have a couple of powerful drinks, then dinner." He would return to England in March with the novel complete, "except for minor revisions."

A feature of Fleming's writing that has often been commented on is his use of specific brand-name items – Fleming referred to them as his 'favourite foods and liquors and scents, and so on.' Bond's cigarettes were the ones Fleming himself smoked. This attention to detail was something Dennis Wheatley had used before Fleming, but it also goes as far back as Sherlock Holmes, whose Baker Street study had been described in such detail that replicas have been created in several parts of the world. There is a purpose in including this sort of detail, as Fleming told *Playboy*. "Exact details of individual private lives are extremely interesting to me ... The more we have of this kind of detailed stuff laid down around a character, the more interested we are in him." This fascination comes partly from Fleming's background as a journalist but it is also explained by the sort of voyeuristic fascination we see in celebrity gossip magazines – it's a combination of interest in wealth and bling combined with a need to know that our heroes are only human after all.

In the same interview, Fleming said that research as something that he generally only did *after* he'd finished the first draft. "I realise that I've been rather vague or thin on some topic or other, and then I go to the right man and try to get the true gen out of him and then rewrite that particular area." This was presumably a lesson he learned after making a mistake in the choice of gun for James Bond.

In a November 1962 *Sunday Times* article 'James Bond's Hardware,' Ian Fleming said that correspondents from all over the world were enthusiastic in writing to point out errors in his books. While some people were critical of the made-up gadgetry – some of which was actually genuine – it was Fleming's inexperience with handguns that drew the most significant criticism. In May 1956 he received a letter from Geoffrey Boothroyd on the subject of Bond's "rather deplorable taste in firearms." He was particularly critical of the fact that "a man who comes into contact with all sorts of formidable people using a .25 Beretta. This sort of gun is really a lady's gun, and not a really nice lady at that." Boothroyd suggested more suitable handguns and went on to become Fleming's official weapons advisor and even became a character in *Dr. No* in which a 'Major Boothroyd' is the armourer who gives Bond the Walther PPK as a replacement for the Beretta. In the movies, Q is sometimes referred to as Major Boothroyd. Richard Chopping's cover illustration for the first edition of *From Russia, with Love* (Jonathan Cape, 1957) has an illustration of a gun – a modified Smith & Wesson .38 Special – loaned to the artist by Boothroyd.

Writer's today have much greater access to online information about weapons and there are several good weapons about the guns that have been used in movies and literature. There are also forums where experts and knowledgeable amateurs share their knowledge and will answer specific questions posted by writers. Many thriller readers know something about guns, so it is vital to do the proper research yourself – don't accept what other authors have written, go to a reputable non-fiction source, and talk to someone with first-hand experience if you can.

How to Write a Bestseller and Make a Lot of Money
Although they sold well, the first novels in Ian Fleming's James Bond series did not immediately become bestsellers. They became a phenomenon as a result of a combination of circumstances that the author had almost no influence over: the publication of the novels in paperback, a newspaper serialisation, the success of the film *Dr. No* in 1962, the casting of Sean Connery as Bond – and a plug by an American president. In a March 1961 *Life* magazine article, 'The President's Voracious Reading Habits,' Ian Fleming's *From Russia with Love* is listed as one of 'Ten Kennedy Favorites.'

Casino Royale, the first of Ian Fleming's James Bond novels, was published in hardcover 1953 but, as Michael Denning points out, "... the moment of Bond does not really begin until the publication of *Casino Royale* in Pan paperback in 1956, and the serialisation of *From Russia, with Love* in the *Daily Express* in 1957; after which the sales of Bond books took off, reaching a peak in 1964 and 1965 in the wake of the release of the first Bond films." Of the first eighteen Pan paperback titles to sell more than a million copies, ten were reported to be James Bond novels.

One thing that Fleming *was* able to do was capitalise on the success that the movies brought him. He stayed with the 'formula' that had proved popular and included in the novels more of those elements that filmgoers enjoyed. When Sean Connery proved that he *was* James Bond, Fleming didn't fight against it, accepting that this was the sort of hero audiences in the 1960s wanted, and making the character in the novels more like the one on the screen.

The trick for writers today is to take the same thriller 'formula' – established by Fleming and *Dr. No* screenwriter Richard Maibaum – and use it with a hero that appeals to *today's* audience.

The Bond 'formula' has been described and analysed by a number of writers, including Umberto Eco in an essay 'The Narrative Structure in Fleming,' in his book *The Bond Affair* (1966); by Arthur Asa Berger in *Popular Culture Genres* (1992); and Ray Morton in his article 'James Bond's Goldenscribes' for *ScriptMag* (November 2012).

We can summarise the typical James Bond plot in terms of our four quarters and a midpoint.

Four Quarters plus Midpoint
Quarter 1: The hero is assigned to investigate the criminal activities of an individual or group.

Quarter 2: The hero disrupts the activities of the villains – and in the process attracts their attention: they now know he's a threat to their plans. The villain's henchman is sent to deal with the hero.

Midpoint: The hero discovers the true nature of the villain's conspiracy – he learns what is at stake for the world at large. The hero decides that he must put an end to the plot.

Quarter 3: Recovering from his encounter with the henchman, the hero takes time to plan how to deal with the conspirators. During this period, he may also spend time with a beautiful woman. His plan involves sneaking into the villain's secret base – but he is captured and tortured by the villain. The countdown to the final launch of the villain's plan begins.

Quarter 4: Time is running out. The hero escapes captivity and fights the villain's henchman one final time, defeating him. The hero improvises an ingenious plan that puts a stop to the conspiracy – usually destroying the secret base and (probably) killing the villain.

If you have ever seen a James Bond movie or read one of the novels, this basic structure should be familiar to you. And even if you haven't, you may recognise it as being the structure used in other thrillers. As I have already said, James Bond is not strictly a spy and others have noted that Bond draws too much attention to himself to truly be regarded as a spy. He is a government-sanctioned enforcer or a professional assassin – he is, after all, 'licenced to kill.' He has also been said to have much in common with a superhero, and the basic plot described above could equally be used for a superhero story.

To examine it in more detail – and compare it to the amateur-on-the-run thriller – we can break the James Bond plot down into eight sequences.

Eight Sequences
Sequence 1 – Either a series of scenes showing the conspirators in action or the results of one of their crimes; or scenes showing the hero in action – unconnected with the main story and demonstrating the hero's professionalism. In the movies, either of these prologues might serve as the pre-credits sequence.

Sequence 2 – The hero is given a mission to investigate the mysterious actions that are the first evidence of the villain's conspiracy. James Bond typically receives a new car and/or some gadgets from Q during this sequence.

Sequence 3 – The hero takes action against the conspirators, perhaps disrupting a crime that is part of their plot. Sometimes this involves humiliating the lead villain in some way – perhaps beating him at cards or some other game or sport. This attracts the attention of the villain and/or the conspirators – and is often done on purpose in order to draw them out so the hero can find out more about them and their plot.

Sequence 4 – The villain's henchman is sent to deal with the hero. The hero is often chased, and his car destroyed. There may be hand-to-hand fighting, and the hero may be injured. The car and his other gadgets may be used and/or lost during this sequence. The hero may also lose an ally – injured, killed, or captured by the conspirators.

Midpoint – The hero discovers the full extent of the conspiracy – and what is at stake. It is a threat to the 'free world' which the hero is employed to protect. The stakes have been raised and he realises that he has got to stop the conspiracy. He also decides that the only way to stop the plot is to get *inside* the villain's secret base. He also learns that there is a countdown to some can of launch, attack, release or other action by the villain.

Sequence 5 – While he is laying low and recovering from his fight with the henchman, the hero may spend time with a beautiful woman. She may be the villain's mistress or assistant. She may be someone working for the conspirators, and who may later betray the hero. The hero may or may not be aware of her allegiance. She could be working for the villain but decide to switch sides and help the villain. She may be the one who provides the hero with details of the conspiracy and the countdown – and/or she may be someone who can help him sneak into the villain's secret lair. Or she may reveal other important information.

Sequence 6 – The hero tries to get into the secret base to destroy the conspiracy. It looks as though he is about to succeed but then – disaster. The hero is captured. The woman who is helping him may also be captured. The hero or the woman (or both) may be tortured by the villain – he wants to find out how much they know about the conspiracy, and who else knows about it. The villain often reveals his own story and motives during this sequence – gloating about his 'foolproof' plan. The villain may try to persuade the hero to join him. The hero refuses and so then faces an unpleasant death. This is the hero's darkest hour – and the conspiracy is only minutes away from succeeding.

Sequence 7 – The climactic battle. The hero escapes captivity – this is usually difficult and painful, requiring him to show courage, strength and ingenuity. He fights the villain's henchman one last time: it is a gruelling fight, but the hero manages to defeat his opponent. The countdown is in its final seconds. The hero comes up with an ingenious improvised plan to destroy the villain's weapon – and this often involves blowing up the secret base as well. The chief villain is usually killed in the process – unless he escapes to fight another day.

Sequence 8 – Usually a brief epilogue. The hero's boss may confirm that the conspiracy has been successfully dealt with – he often approves of the outcome, validating the hero's work, but is critical of the hero's unorthodox methods. This also serves as a reminder that the hero is a professional who is doing a job. The hero often gets to spend some time with the beautiful woman he met earlier, before having to report in for his next assignment. There is often a jokey one-liner from the hero before the fadeout.

Comparing the eight sequences side by side, we can see that the plot for the professional hero story includes many of the same stages as that for the amateur hero story – but there are some key differences in how the similar events are handled. These differences mainly relate to the nature of the hero himself. For the amateur, dealing with the conspiracy is a one-off event – he goes back to normal life afterwards, perhaps a little wiser for his experience, but still an average citizen. If your amateur hero ends up being a series character dealing with other conspiracies, he is likely to become more 'professional' and less 'amateur' as the series progresses.

The professional hero starts off from a position where dealing with conspiracies is his day job. He regularly goes looking for trouble – because that's what the job requires. And he is comfortable working alone in the field because that is in the nature of the work he does.

There are certain parts of the professional hero plot that are virtually identical to those in the amateur hero plot. Almost everything to do with the *villain* and the *conspiracy* remain the same. What the conspirators set out to achieve isn't altered in any way by the fact that the person who discovers their plot is a professional rather than an amateur.

The nature of the hero's *isolation* also remains the same – the fact that the professional is working for an organisation doesn't mean that he can rely on the cavalry riding to the rescue if he gets into trouble. He is often operating in an area where his agency doesn't legally have jurisdiction and his actions may not always be within the bounds of the law and so cannot be officially sanctioned. The professional hero is often told – when he receives his assignment – that if he gets into trouble, he's on his own. And if he's captured, his employers will deny that he works for them. The professional hero may have a professional ally early in the story, or perhaps a mentor or a local guide – but he will quickly lose the support of that person; either because they are killed or captured by the enemy, or because they are a traitor who betrays the hero to the enemy.

Professional hero and amateur hero also have much in common when it comes to their personalities. Both need to be able to learn from experience; able to investigate and solve mysteries; react quickly to unexpected circumstances; have great physical stamina; and come up with ingenious solutions to the problems they encounter. They must be self-motivated and self-reliant.

But it is the *differences* between the amateur hero and the professional hero that give these two different kinds of thriller their unique qualities. We will compare and contrast the two under similar headings to those used in the amateur-on-the-run chapter:

    i.   hero
    ii.   villain
    iii.   conspiracy
    iv.   MacGuffin
    v.   romantic co-protagonist
    vi.   settings
    vii.   iconography
    viii.   themes
    ix.   tone
    x.   other characters

(i) The Hero

Professionals, Bureaucrats & Incompetent Amateurs

How does the hero of a secret agent thriller differ from that of an amateur-on-the-run thriller? We said that our 'innocent' hero was an amateur, but that he possessed qualities of ingenuity and resilience – he had to be able to cope with new situations and improvise solutions to problems he encountered, and he needed physical stamina and determination to enable him to keep going against the odds. The secret agent hero needs the same qualities, but he is not an amateur – he is doing his job. Anyone who deals with something on a daily basis during the course of their work is going to respond to it differently than someone who encounters that same thing for the first time. This is true if the 'thing' in question is a medical, mechanical, or law enforcement issue. And it is true when it comes to dealing with conspiracies. Our amateur hero is going to be surprised and shocked and deeply concerned when he encounters a conspiracy. Our professional hero is likely to be more blasé and even cynical about the whole thing. The professional hero has experience and training to call on – he has dealt with this sort of thing before. To the amateur, the situation is new and unique. Generally speaking, our amateur hero has more learning and adapting to do than our professional.

Jerry Palmer in his book *Thrillers* refers to there being three types of people in the world of the thriller: professionals, bureaucrats and amateurs. Here he uses 'amateurs' to mean ordinary men and women who are not involved in the secret agent 'business.' I will refer to them as *incompetent* amateurs to distinguish them from our competent amateur hero. Palmer's *professionals* and *bureaucrats* are an expansion of one of the 'oppositions' identified by Umberto Eco in the Bond series and listed in his essay 'The Narrative Structure of Ian Fleming.'

The Incompetent Amateur. Like our amateur-on-the-run amateur hero, the incompetent amateur becomes caught up in the action of the conspiracy. But they do not become *actively* involved in dealing with the conspiracy. The incompetent is essentially passive – a victim of circumstance who remains a victim. Palmer says that this type of character is most often seen in the form of "… a girl whom the hero is obliged to rescue. She's unable to save herself…" The reason she is unable to save herself is that she lacks the ability to improvise. Everything is new and strange – she has no experience to draw on and she lacks the ingenuity to make up solutions to problems when she finds herself in a predicament. In Palmer's words, 'she doesn't belong' in this world. In this category of character, we can also include the ordinary, average citizen who is not involved in the conspiracy, except perhaps as a scared witness or bystander.

The Bureaucrat. In some ways, the bureaucrat is the opposite of the incompetent amateur in that he believes that nothing is new and unique and that every situation can be foreseen and planned for. He does not believe that anything is outside his ability to predict and plan for – nothing is outside of his control. Umberto Eco characterises this quality of the bureaucrat as 'planning' or 'programming.' It results in rigidity of thinking and an inability to respond spontaneously. When a new, unexpected situation *does* arise, the bureaucrat is not able to deal with it, because – like the incompetent amateur – he lacks the ability to improvise. He can only operate successfully within the boundaries of his plan or his programming. As an example of this, Palmer quotes from chapter six of *Thunderball* where the villain Blofeld as 'the chairman of the board – outlines the company's plans...' Blofeld's speech includes phrases as 'Plan Omega,' 'Sub-Operator G,' 'the Special Executive,' and 'Area Zeta.' As Palmer says, this is the sort of language used by 'a tetchy senior civil servant, or a particularly unpleasant general.' A villainous bureaucrat might be described as a 'control freak' who believes he is infallible – someone who shuts himself away in an environment which he can manipulate and surrounds himself with people who he can dominate. These are the characteristics of a dictator, and the main villains in virtually all of the Bond novels fit this profile. But while most villains are bureaucrats, not all bureaucrats are villains. Politicians, civil servants, the military, and local law enforcement agencies are often portrayed in the thriller as being bureaucratic and inflexible. And we see that this rigidity of approach causes them to fail in their attempt to deal with the conspiracy. To some extent, they have to be portrayed this way – because we want to see the hero's imaginative and unorthodox methods save the day.

The Professional. We have already mentioned that the professional secret agent has training and experience to draw upon. And we have drawn attention to his physical stamina (see also *Torture and Violence* below) and ability to improvise in the field. Being a professional also requires the ability to plan ahead – in chapter five of *Moonraker* we learn that, "Bond knew what he was doing. Whenever he had a job of work to do he would take infinite pains beforehand and leave as little as possible to chance." In this sense, the villain is professional too – he often makes meticulous plans for every stage of his conspiracy. But Bond does not stick rigidly to his plans – he can't because, especially during the first half or even three-quarters of the story he is responding to the actions of the bad guys and doesn't know the full extent of what they are planning. It is in the nature of the hero – and a requirement for the plotting of a thriller – that his plans are thwarted by the villain so that he is forced to improvise a new plan. He must be able to respond rapidly to whatever the villains throw at him.

In his essay, Umberto Eco contrasts the rigid 'programming' of the villain with the hero's ability to take a risk on a new plan, to gamble or to take a chance. This is something that a bureaucrat would never do: they stick rigidly to The Plan. Without the supporting framework of The Organisation and The Plan, the bureaucrat is unable to function – he is as helpless as the incompetent amateur. This, of course, gives us a clue to the way in which the professional hero can defeat the villain in our thriller.

Unlike either the bureaucrat or the incompetent amateur, our professional hero is completely self-reliant. He can make decisions and take actions based on those decisions, even when he is completely cut-off from the agency he works for. The professional secret agent is able to work in isolation – and this is another important characteristic of our hero, as we will see below.

Insiders and Outsiders

I said in the previous chapter that the amateur hero initially lacks commitment to any cause, but that during the course of his adventure he discovers that there are some values or beliefs that he is prepared to fight to protect. Because he belongs to ordinary society, and wants to return to it, the amateur hero is willing to risk his life to ensure that the conspiracy doesn't destroy that way of life. A professional hero, whether he's a spy or some other form of agent, is *not* part of ordinary society and is unlikely to return to it (see also *Ennui versus Thrills* below). In *Moonraker* we are told what James Bond earns – 'the salary of a Principal Officer in the Civil Service' – and how he spends it, and that "... it was his ambition to leave as little as possible in his banking account when he was killed, as ... he knew he would be, before the statutory age of forty-five." The nature of his professional life also means that the secret agent doesn't engage in normal friendships or in committed romantic relationships, as we will see later.

The villain in a thriller is an outsider because he is carrying out a conspiracy that threatens or preys upon society. The professional hero shares the moral values of society and acts to defend it, but is – as Jerry Palmer writes – "... forced to spend most of his time outside it, in an unpleasant world to which he is professionally adapted, and to behave in a way that is only just tolerable to the community."

Many professionals, whether it be the police, fire service, paramedics, or fighter pilots, have their own communities. They have experiences in common that mean they, to some extent, regard themselves as different to everyone else. They have experience of a world that 'ordinary people' don't really know anything about. This is also true for the professional thriller hero – though he is unlikely to socialise with others of his profession, unless a 'night out' occurs during the course of his work. The professional hero may feel he has little in common with ordinary people in society, and may even speak of them in a condescending manner, but is actually their ordinary way of life that he is risking his life to protect.

Ennui versus Thrills

In chapter eleven of *From Russia, With Love,* Fleming writes: "The blubbery arms of the soft life had Bond round the neck and they were slowly strangling him. He was a man of war and when, for a long period, there was no war, his spirit went into decline." And in *Moonraker* we learn something of what Bond's life is like when he is not on an assignment. This recalls Sherlock Holmes' boredom and frustration when he didn't have an interesting case to solve. As Palmer writes: "While there are problems which demand their capacities, they are somebody; when there are none they are nobody, and bored. Their identity lies in their exclusive capacity for a particular kind of action." Only when our professional hero is working does he feel truly alive. When your work involves such a high degree of risk, ordinary life must seem extraordinarily ordinary. Our professional hero is addicted to the thrill of it.

2 | Professional Secret Agent

Isolation – 'You're On Your Own'
"If a spy is caught he can expect no help from his employers. They will not acknowledge him. He is on his own," writes John Atkins. "A curious result of the sordidness of espionage is that the authorities will not recognise their own involvement." The sordidness he is referring to is the fact that an English gentleman should never engage in the sort of deception that spying requires – it just isn't cricket. He quotes from Valentine Williams 1928 novel *The Crouching Beast* in which the two heroes find themselves in trouble and one says she will go the Embassy for help; the other laughs and says that even though he is 'a properly accredited secret agent ... a salaried servant of the crown...' the Ambassador will not lift a finger to help them: "He's not allowed to. It's one of the rules of the game. When we're on the job, my dear, we're untouchables, pariahs, with every man's hand against us..." In part, this is what we said above about the secret agent being involved in actions that are 'only just tolerable by society.' But it is also a part of the game that is writing a thriller – in order to create the required levels of jeopardy and suspense, we can't have the cavalry riding in to save the hero every time he gets into trouble.

Upper-Class or Classless Hero?
Ian Fleming's original vision of the character of James Bond was as an old-school hero with a background that reflected his own – 'Eton and Sandhurst, inherited money, government service, world travel, social assurance,' as *Playboy* described him. When it came to casting the role for the first James Bond film, Fleming's choices of actor included David Niven, Cary Grant, and James Mason. He was meant to be an elegant English gentleman – because that's how Fleming saw himself. When the producers chose Sean Connery for the role, Fleming was not pleased saying, "He's not what I envisioned," and referred to the actor as an "over-developed stunt-man." Connery also came from a working-class background and was Scottish. But while Fleming was a snob about such things, it turned out that the rest of the world was not. Sean Connery *was* James Bond – and to many people he still is.

By the 1960s, upper-class English heroes were out of vogue and working-class folk like The Beatles were suddenly chic. Connery might have been a 'rough diamond,' but he looked good on screen, he was sexy and had a hint of danger about him that made you think he really could fight the bad guys. With a little mentoring from director Terence Young, Connery was also able to pull off the 'English gentleman' aspect of the character with a hint of sardonic humour. The films recreated James Bond for a new audience and seeing the popularity of the character, Fleming began to reflect this change in the novels.

If you look at many of the most popular characters you will see that there is a sort of classlessness to them – they appeal to people from all walks of life. They're either roguish commoners and thieves who manage to charm the upper classes due their innate charm and dignity – Falstaff, Long John Silver, Robin Hood – or they are gentlemen who aren't quite upper class and who seem at home (or equally distanced) in working class and upper-class environments – Sherlock Holmes, Hercule Poirot, and many of the characters played by Cary

Grant. This (a) helps a character appeal to a much broader audience, and (b) prevents the character from becoming too one-dimensional.

But that isn't to say that audiences want their heroes to be ordinary. We want to spend our reading time or our time in the cinema with *fascinating* and unusual characters. Arthur Asa Berger refers to James Bond as a 'hierarchical elitist': "He is one of a small group of spies who are licensed to kill. He works for an elite organisation dedicated to maintaining the power relations that obtain in the world (including domination by the British and their allies), and he has a decidedly expensive lifestyle – paid for by the British government..." Bond isn't ordinary, but neither is he so different from us that he seems to be from another world. There is a balance to be struck – if you're going to present extraordinary situations, then you need your hero to seem ordinary because an extraordinary person in an extraordinary situation doesn't give the audience anything to hold on to. But in an ordinary situation, you want your character to be the centre of attention without needing to do anything. A character like Connery's Bond that can slip between being ordinary and extraordinary, and can seem at home in ordinary or extraordinary, gives you the best of both worlds. It can also be used to create anticipation – suspense – because even in his quietest moments, you know what this person is *capable* of.

How Do You Create 'Immortal' Characters?
Michael Denning says that James Bond is a character who has "transcended the novels and films which brought him to life, and joined the small group of fictional characters who are known many who never read or saw the 'original' texts – figures like Robinson Crusoe and Sherlock Holmes." Cawelti and Rosenberg use the term 'immortal characters' and ask: What qualities are imperative to the creation of such characters? They look to the creator of Hamlet, Othello, Macbeth, King Lear and Falstaff for an answer – and note that a key quality of such characters is "striking combinations of qualities that we usually think of as contradictory." They quote indirectly from Maurice Morgann's *An Essay on the Dramatic Character of Sir John Falstaff*, in which Morgann said, "... he is a character made up by Shakespeare wholly of incongruities; — a man at once young and old, enterprising and fat, a dupe and a wit, harmless and wicked, weak in principle and resolute by constitution, cowardly in appearance and brave in reality; a knave without malice, a liar without deceit; and a knight, a gentleman, and a soldier without either dignity, decency, or honour..."

Cawelti and Rosenberg also use Charlie Chaplin's character of The Tramp as another example that demonstrates a "... striking linkage of conflicts: the tramp was funny and sad, gentle and sadistic, loving and hating, awkward and graceful, hopelessly incompetent and brilliantly capable."

They admit that Ian Fleming's creation "lacks the universally human conflicts of qualities that characterise Shakespearean characters or Chaplin's tramp," but go on to say that, like Sherlock Holmes, James Bond is "a striking compendium of conflicting cultural themes. Holmes unified in one person the contending cultural forces of poetry and science, the 'two cultures,' which since the mid-nineteenth century have been so ambivalently hostile to each other.

Bond's character and activities bring together a number of the conflicting cultural values of the mid-twentieth century: he is an organisation man who remains a determined individualist; he is cool and detached, yet committed to his country; he is a man of technology yet capable of exercising the brute physical force of a primitive savage; he is a bureaucrat and a killer; he is sexually liberated but capable of romantic love; he is an affluent consumer, yet alienated from a corrupt and decadently materialistic society; he is something of a racist, yet he loves the exotic and is always involved with men and women of other races and cultures."

(ii) The Villain

The nature of the villain does not change as a result of the hero being a professional as opposed to an amateur: the villain does what he wants to do regardless. This means that everything said about the villain in the amateur-on-the-run chapter applies equally here. The villain's main purpose is to be the person behind the conspiracy. In terms of the plot, the conspiracy is more important than the villain: the criminal actions are more important in the thriller than the person who thought them up or the person carrying them out.

The villain of the thriller has much in common with villains in earlier types of story, especially the Victorian Gothic and 'sensation' novels. But in those stories, his actions were usually harming only an individual or small community: in the thriller, the villain's actions are said to be a threat to the world or at the very least to 'Western democracy' or some other large-scale community that a broad international audience will consider itself part of.

The James Bond villains also must owe a debt to Sax Rohmer's Dr. Fu Manchu, the criminal genius who featured in thirteen books between 1913 and 1959. Fu Manchu first appeared on film in a 1923 silent movie and was played four times in the early 1930s by Warner Oland, best known for his portrayal of Charlie Chan. Boris Karloff played the character in *The Mask of Fu Manchu* (1932) a film that was little-seen for many years, in part because of its racism. Sax Rohmer's books reflect the racist attitudes of their time. Christopher Lee played Fu Manchu in five films between 1965 and 1969.

Ian Fleming's villains are almost always described in a way that makes them out to be grotesque and unnatural. This is quite a crude way of encouraging the reader to dislike the hero and it has some pitfalls that you should try to avoid in your own writing. Umberto Eco summarised the various ways Fleming described his villains. Many of the Bond villains have unusually large heads; several have red hair and others are completely bald; and large ears or ears with large lobes are mentioned more than once. Mr. Big in *Live and Let Die* is compared to a 'week-old corpse in the river.' In *Diamonds Are Forever* one of the villains is a hunchback with dry red lips and eyes that look like they came from a taxidermist. In *Moonraker* half of Hugo Drax's face is scarred and his teeth stick out. Rosa Klebb has pale wet lips stained with nicotine and her hair is tied in a tight 'obscene' bun. Dr. No meanwhile is unusually tall, has unusually smooth skin, and metal pincers instead of hands. Goldfinger is only five feet tall and looks 'as if he had been put together with bits of other people's bodies. Nothing seemed to belong.'

Fleming doesn't restrict himself to the physically grotesque. Eco also highlights the fact that the villain is "... as a rule of mixed blood and his origins are complex and obscure; he is asexual or homosexual, or at any rate not sexually normal..." The villains are also not gentlemen – they cheat at sports and games. Fleming uses every trick he can to cause the reader to view the villain as repulsive, prodding at their tendencies towards racism, revulsion at sexual deviancy, and irrational fears of those who are scarred, disabled, or deformed. Pointing a finger at someone who is physically different and saying 'Villain!' is not going to work with modern audiences. You might as well give him a black cloak and a moustache to twirl. You are on much safer ground if you concentrate on personality and motivation: a torturer does not need to be a red-haired hunchback with a glass-eye for the reader to find him repulsive – the fact that he is a cold-hearted torturer should be enough. Audience expectations have changed – a scarred, illegitimate dwarf can be a hero in a top-rated television show, as can a eunuch, though the series does less well with its treatment of homosexual characters. Let your characters be judged by their actions rather than their appearance or their sexuality.

In creating his stories, Ian Fleming knew that James Bond was part-Warrior and that the greatest fear of the Warrior is to be imprisoned and helpless, unable to act. The Warrior hates to be in any situation which makes him feel powerless – he wants to be calling the shots, at least as far as his own life is concerned, and he is a competitor who wants to win. As readers, we want that for our thriller hero too. Bond's darkest hour, usually near the end of Act II, has him captured by the villain, bound and helpless – and then the villain demonstrates that he is in the dominant position, the 'winner,' by subjecting Bond to physical torture. Being injured or suffering illness such that he is physically weakened is another of the great fears of the Warrior archetype.

Cawelti and Rosenberg suggest that there is often also an implied sexual element in the domination of Bond by the villain. In *Casino Royale,* Bond is bound naked and Le Chiffre attacks his testicles with a carpet-beater. In *Dr. No*, when Bond is unconscious, Dr. No pulls down the sheet to examine Bond's upper body.

The grotesque Bond villain is often placed into greater contrast by placing him in an idyllic and exotic location. We will explore these under *Settings* below.

The Henchman
The villain in a Bond story is sometimes a shadowy figure, pulling strings in the background, and sometimes he is a flamboyant figure who takes centre stage from an early point in the story. Either way, he is likely to have a henchman – or, occasionally, a female equivalent. The James Bond series brought us a number of colourful characters in the role of henchman: Oddjob, Jaws, Tee Hee Johnson, Nick Nack, May Day, Red Grant and Rosa Klebb, Irma Bunt and others. The henchman is often a professional assassin and is as experienced and deadly as our professional hero: we want them to be equally matched because we want the fight between them to be a fight worth watching.

The hero usually encounters the henchman on two occasions: around the midpoint, when there is a fight which the hero only narrowly survives; and then at the climax of the story (Sequence 7) where we want to give the impression that the henchman really could beat our hero this time.

The henchman exists to provide *active* opposition to the hero. The main villain – Blofeld, Goldfinger, Dr. No or whoever – may be the brains behind the conspiracy, but he is more of a bureaucrat – a back-room manager rather than operating on the frontline. As two active professionals, there is potential for there to be an interesting relationship between the hero and the henchman, because although they are on opposite sides, as workmen they have much in common. It might be argued, for example, that James Bond is actually a henchman who is employed by M. As two people with similar jobs and similar levels of skill and experience, the hero and the henchman might show respect for one another. This echoes the relationship between the hero Shane and the gunslinger in the black hat – played by Jack Palance in the movie.

(iii) The Conspiracy

I have covered the conspiracy at length in a separate chapter and there is not a great deal to say about it in the context of the James Bond story. As in the amateur-on-the-run thriller, the conspiracy – or rather, actions taken to bring about the object of the conspiracy – serve as the call to action, inciting incident, challenge or whatever you want to call it. These actions are what trigger the action that makes up the rest of the story.

Conspiratorial actions are what give the professional hero a reason to take action. It is a convention in storytelling that is only appropriate to have the hero respond to *prior* aggression – he cannot take pre-emptive action before the conspirators have actually done anything. These conspiratorial actions provide a clear motivation for the actions of the hero and help us to identify with his purpose – he is trying to restore balance to a world that has been disrupted by criminal activity.

(iv) The MacGuffin

MacGuffins such as stolen plans or secret inventions are less common in the professional hero thriller. In an amateur-on-the-run thriller, the MacGuffin typically serves as something that causes the amateur hero to be drawn into the world of the conspiracy – he is given it or is assumed to have it, and the bad guys go after him. The professional hero doesn't need a gimmick to draw him into the story, it's his job to become involved.

In the James Bond stories, it could be argued that the villain takes the place of the MacGuffin – he is what Bond and his organisation are trying to 'get'. Or, in some of the stories, the villain's mistress is the person Bond needs to befriend and/or seduce in order to get to the villain and his lair.

(v) Romantic Co-Protagonist

The relationship between the professional hero and the person with whom he has a romantic liaison is quite different to that between the amateur hero and his co-protagonist. In the amateur-on-the-run thriller, she represents trust: by believing the hero and assisting him, she demonstrates that trust is still possible in their world. She also represents the 'normal, ordinary life' that the amateur hero hopes to return to. The two of them being together in a committed relationship at the end of the story is one of the things that proves the conspiracy has been defeated and validates the hero's actions.

The professional hero does not have this kind of relationship with a romantic co-protagonist. As Palmer phrases it, "... the warm companionship of adult love..." is excluded from the professional hero's life, and that he is "... as alone in this most intimate relationship as in his most antagonistic ones." Professional heroes have sex, but they do not have long-term relationships.

In an amateur-on-the-run thriller, the relationship between the hero and the co-protagonist is typically antagonistic – at least in the beginning. The two are usually forced together by circumstance, and sometimes the hero is forced to kidnap her or hold her prisoner in order to protect himself. She initially believes that he is guilty of whatever crime he has been accused: the police are chasing him, so he must be guilty. Only gradually does she learn what sort of person he is and come to believe him and trust him.

Palmer says that the relationship between the professional hero and the woman he has sex with is also antagonistic, but in a different way and for different reasons. He describes the relationship as *competitive,* in the sense that the woman functions as a temptress – she often turns up naked in the hero's bed – and he has to prove that he has the willpower to resist their temptation. More on this later.

"Both critics and enthusiasts of James Bond focused on his sexual adventures," writes Michael Denning in *Cover Stories,* "they all noted that the Bond tales were the first British thrillers to make sexual encounters central to the plot and to the hero." He also notes that *Casino Royale* and *Playboy* magazine were first published in 1953 and describes them both as "the first mass pornography." By modern 'standards' the December 1953 magazine and the passages regarding sex in the Bond novels both seem fairly tame, so we have to treat them within their historical context. There wasn't hint of sex in John Buchan's *The Thirty-Nine Steps* (1915) and there wasn't any romance either – Hitchcock had to add that in 1935. As Cawelti and Rosenberg write that it was sensible for Fleming to take his cue from American hard-boiled detective writers and use "his central character's unusual sexual attractiveness as a chief sign of his heroic prowess..." because for contemporary readers, "... sexual chastity and restraint are no longer meaningful symbols of manliness and heroism." In terms of historical context, we should also remember that D. H. Lawrence's *Lady Chatterley's Lover* was (unsuccessfully) prosecuted for obscenity in England in 1960.

The 1960s were a time of sexual liberation, resulting from or brought about by changing attitudes to public nudity, pornography, premarital sex, homosexuality, and abortion. Medical developments too played a part with the introduction of the female contraceptive pill and the availability of treatments for sexually transmitted diseases. Sex, the liberationists said, should be celebrated as a normal part of life and not repressed as a result of a morality imposed by the family, religion or the state. Guilt and shame were supposed to become things of the past. You know how that turned out. The sex in Ian Fleming's novels was written at a point where old and new values co-existed, and what he wrote about reflects this.

The presentation of the latest 'Bond girls' to the media was a big part of the promotion of each new movie, at least until the end of Roger Moore's tenure. And they're a big part of the novels too, with tongue-in-cheek names like Tiffany Case, Honeychile Rider, Kissy Suzuki, and Pussy Galore making them sound like either Playboy bunnies or drag queens.

There is an elephant in the room that we must acknowledge: the portrayal of women in the Bond novels is sexist and misogynistic. Fleming wrote things that no modern author should even consider including. I will quote just one example and then move on – this is James Bond in chapter four of *Casino Royale:* "He sighed. Women were for recreation. On a job, they got in the way and fogged things up with sex and hurt feelings and all the emotional baggage they carried around. One had to look out for them and take care of them."

Cawelti and Rosenberg have noted that the sexual encounters in the Bond novels do not simply involve two adults enjoying the physicality of the act – there are always complications. Honeychile Rider is 'a nearly pathological man-hater'; Pussy Galore is a lesbian; Vesper Lynd and Tatiana are enemy agents; and Tracy is a nymphomaniac. These women are also, frequently, doomed: "the mortality rate of Bond heroines is strikingly high." Casual sex alone, it is suggested, isn't enough for the fantasy that is a modern thriller, there needs to be danger and more than a hint of the taboo. Jerry Palmer views this with a cynical eye: "James Bond is good for you, we are to understand: 'curing' girls of frigidity and lesbianism is a common male myth, for it implies that one is more of a man than the others."

Long-term relationships and marriage are part of the 'ordinary world' that the professional hero works to protect, but as we have said he himself does not belong in that world. 'Settling down' does not appeal to this type of character and the risky nature of his work means that he never knows if he will return home alive, so 'planning a future together' with someone is never on the cards.

Femme Fatale
Woman as temptress and betrayer appears in the Bible in the story of Samson and Delilah and one of the most famous real-world spies is Mata Hari, who spied for the Germans during the First World War. In the James Bond stories, the activities of the female spy are never fully explored – there are female agents who try to kill Bond and female agents who sleep with him, and some who attempt both, but they are never explored as characters in their own right.

John Atkins, in *The British Spy Novel*, gives Baroness Orczy's 1934 novel *A Spy of Napoleon* as an example of a novel that does explore this type of character. I will explore the role of the *femme fatale* in more detail in the *Crime Thriller* volume in this series, as she plays a greater role in hardboiled detective stories and 'noir' thrillers than she does in the professional hero type of thriller.

In the Bond series the *femme fatale* really only appears as a plot function. In writing a thriller we always want to keep piling the pressure on the hero, making his situation more dangerous, so that we can increase suspense. One way we can do that is by having someone the hero trusts betray him. It doesn't have to be a romantic co-protagonist that betrays him, but it is best if it is someone close to him: it helps to demonstrate his isolation and need for vigilance and self-reliance.

That being said, not all women in the Bond novels are treacherous temptresses. Arthur Asa Berger notes that, in *Dr. No*, James Bond's 'love interest' Honeychile Rider has a significant role in the novel because she effectively represents the antithesis of the villain, Dr. Julius No. She is a positive character, natural, pure and innocent; whereas Dr. No is negative, a man who is part machine having claws for hands and is associated with 'impurity' such as guano (bird poo) that he mines for money and the 'half-breeds' he employs as slave workers. But as Palmer points out, even when the woman he encounters is not a betrayer, the hero is haunted by the experience of having been betrayed by a lover in the past.

Sex and Pain
Cawelti and Rosenberg write that "... the intensification of romantic feeling through love and death..." is a motif that is implicit in Bond's affairs and that sometimes comes to the surface. Bond must suffer danger and hardship, and frequently physical torture at the hands of the villain, before he is allowed the 'reward' of "... a few brief moments of sexual pleasure..." with the romantic co-protagonist.

Voyeurism
Michael Denning described the James Bond novels and *Playboy* magazine as 'mass pornography,' but that they do not provide depictions of male dominance of women. Instead, they treat women as something to be *looked at* by men. Women are sexualised objects and men are voyeurs or spectators. This is demonstrated, according to Denning, by the fact that "... much of what passes as pornography is not the representation of sexual activities but the representation of women's bodies in various states of undress." This objectification of the female body became a part of the popular culture of the twentieth century and was found, to varying degrees, in fiction, films, advertising, music and art. Only now, towards the end of the second decade of the twenty-first century, is this treatment of women really being challenged.

As an example of James Bond as voyeur, Denning quotes the scene from *Dr. No* where Bond observes the naked Honeychile Rider while she is unaware of him watching her. Denning also points out the irony of the scene in *From Russia, With Love* where Bond returns to his hotel room to find Tatiana Romanova naked in his bed – rather than seeing the sexual encounter from Bond's point of view, Fleming shows it from that of two Russian spies who are watching the couple; "... the cine-cameras whirred softly on and on as the breath rasped out of the open mouths of the two men and the sweat of excitement trickled down their bulging faces into their cheap collars." These being the villains, the scene isn't just voyeuristic – it is *sordidly* voyeuristic. And there is an additional level of irony in that fact that we, the readers, are voyeurs watching the Russian spies voyeuristically watching Bond and Tatiana.

Irony is a great way for a writer – and reader – to have their cake and eat it, especially when it comes to depicting sex or violence.

This voyeurism and commodification of the female body is related to the expansion of the consumerist society in the late 1950s and 1960s – and the concept that 'sex sells' – and Denning also believes it is related to the use of *tourism* in the James Bond novels. We'll explore that further under the 'Setting' heading below.

While the hero looks at the nude female as erotic, the romantic co-protagonist does not look at him in the same way. Jerry Palmer: "The male body is construed entirely differently ... women are not especially turned on by the hero's body: it is his personality, his *presence,* that attracts them." He is talking about Mickey Spillane's novels here, but it seems like a general principle. The male body is not objectified in the same way as the female, at least not in Ian Fleming's day. Except, as we have already mentioned, in the context of the villain's 'unhealthy' interest in Bond's body.

There is one notable voyeuristic moment in *From Russia, With Love* where a male body is the subject of interest, and that concerns the introduction of the henchman Red Grant in the first chapter. The lingering description of him lying naked by the pool is interesting in that it portrays a man who should be physically attractive but isn't, there is an uncomfortable incongruity that isn't resolved until the final paragraph of the chapter when we learn how we are really supposed to regard him.

'Winning' at Sex

We have described our professional hero as a competitive individual, as a voyeur, and also seen that in his world the *femme fatale* is a very real danger. We can put these things together and come up with an explanation of why the hero has to be a 'lone wolf' and behave as he does when it comes to women.

As an agent on assignment, alone in the field, the professional hero cannot afford to trust anyone – even the women he finds attractive. Their interest in him may be designed to trap him. In fact, James Bond often knows that the woman is an enemy agent or that she is the mistress of the villain, so he knows he's in dangerous territory. It is part of the game that, before he sleeps with a woman, the hero has to *prove* that he can resist their charms. He is strong-willed enough to avoid succumbing to their temptation. He may flirt with them, engaging in banter and sexual innuendo, but he will never *ask* them to go to bed with him – if he shows that he *wants* that, he has fallen into the 'honey trap' and may never escape. Or so he fears.

The hero chooses the moment when sex takes place, and he only does this when – to use Jerry Palmer's phrase – the woman has already 'seduced herself.' The hero's personal magnetism is such that the woman betrays her previous allegiance – though perhaps only temporarily – in order to spend the night with him: she has been trapped whereas he has proved that he could walk away any time. He has won the game – and his prize is lying naked in his bed waiting for him. To quote Palmer again, "... there is always the sense that in sex, as in violence, the hero is, in the final analysis, alone."

I should say here that the hero finding a naked woman in his bed happens so frequently in thrillers – not just the Bond series – that it has become a cliché.

The Hero's Ideal Woman

Jerry Palmer has speculated on who would be the ideal mate for a professional hero character. A 'good girl' couldn't offer him the excitement he craves – she would be boring and predictable, there would be no mystery about her. But a 'bad girl' would be too much – he would never be able to trust her. What he really needs is a combination of the two – a good/bad girl – who he can trust but whose unpredictability offers an appropriate level of excitement. This is an unlikely combination, at least within the world of the thriller, and Palmer describes such a woman as an 'unattainable ideal.'

Sexual encounters are not an essential part of the thriller – many successful modern thrillers do without them. But if you do include a sexual or romantic element, the brief encounter is better suited to the thriller than is a committed relationship, because it fits best with the elements of an isolated, competitive hero who is confronted with a conspiracy. Whether you include a physical encounter or not, the *femme fatale* is also an optional ingredient. Jerry Palmer has also pointed out that what we refer to here as 'thriller sex' isn't only found in thrillers – the same kinds of male-female relationships are found in other genres where the lead male character has an element of the Warrior in his make-up.

(vi) Settings

In the amateur-on-the-run thriller, we talked about how an ordinary, everyday setting can become threatening for the amateur hero if he finds himself on the run from the police having been falsely accused of murder or treason or whatever. The same thing doesn't really apply to the professional hero because the ordinary, everyday world isn't his natural habitat.

To place our professional hero in an environment where he will be isolated, it is usually necessary to send him to a foreign country. We can either send him on a covert mission into an enemy country – the USSR during the Cold War, for example. Or to a more neutral country – a sort of political no-mans-land – where agents from two opposing sides can engage one another, or where our hero can take on some form of a freelance conspirator. James Bond's enemies were often either villains working alone – Berger refers to them as 'competitive individualists' – or members of international criminal organisations without allegiance to a particular country.

It has been noted that setting played an important part in the popularity of the James Bond novels: it contributed to the 'thrill' of those thrillers. Ian Fleming set his stories in exotic countries and luxurious casinos and hotels, and he did it at a time when Britain was emerging from a dismal period of post-war austerity and before cheap package holidays were available to the public. He also gave his readers a taste of luxurious living, with detailed descriptions of things like food and alcoholic drinks. There can't be many people who don't know James Bond's favourite cocktail, but as well as his vodka martini Bond also invented a drink of his own that has come to be known as a Vesper (after the character Vesper Lynd in *Casino Royale*): "Three measures of Gordon's [gin], one of vodka, half a measure of Kina Lillet. Shake it very well until it's ice-cold, then add a large thin slice of lemon peel." It should be served in a 'deep champagne goblet.'

Arthur Asa Berger wrote: "A number of commentators have pointed out that Bond's taste is not really sophisticated but only seems to be (to people who do not know much about such things) ... it is really more a middle-class person's idea of what upper-class taste is than upper-class taste."

Jerry Palmer writes: "Bond is either in circumstances of considerable luxury or in circumstances of extreme deprivation: hungry, tired, badly hurt, fighting for his life. He is never in circumstances of modest suburban comfort."

Michael Denning, in his book *Cover Stories,* has argued that the James Bond stories present the world not in terms of an imperialist adventure, but rather in the form of tourism: "Travel and tourism make up much of the interest and action of a Bond thriller," he says. The 'third act' of the novel *From Russia, With Love* takes place on board the Orient Express and in *Goldfinger* the final confrontation occurs on a BOAC airliner. He also notes that the stories have an additional link with tourism in that "almost all of them take place in exotic locales," and that these places are the "settings for sports, elaborate meals, and sexual adventure."

Denning compares Ian Fleming's descriptions of these various locations with the prose of a travel or tour guide and says this lends the novels some of their interest and 'a certain degree of verisimilitude.' In *You Only Live Twice* the setting is Japan. In *From Russia, With Love,* it is Istanbul, though the accuracy of his presentation of Istanbul has been queried.

Denning also writes about the dilemma that we experience as a tourist: we are there "to see, to capture the authenticity of the object in a moment of individual self-development" – but at the same time we are aware that tourism is a "mass spectacle" and that many other tourists have come here for 'the view' and that "other tourists may well be blocking the view and rendering impossible the solitary experience." We want to feel that we are superior to these other tourists, while at the same time recognising that we're really no different. James Bond solves this dilemma for us – at least vicariously: he seems like a tourist, seeing what they see and enjoying similar activities, but he is not there for leisure purposes – he is a lone agent working on an assignment and so is, indeed, superior to the ordinary tourists.

In his (non-fiction) travel book, *Thrilling Cities,* Ian Fleming wrote: "All my life I have been interested in adventure and, abroad, I have enjoyed the *frisson* of leaving the wide, well-lit streets and venturing up back alleys in search of the hidden, authentic pulse of towns." This is the desire of the 'superior' tourist to leave the well-trodden path and explore a more *authentic* version of the local culture offered by the package tour. Denning: "Bond is given a more privileged access than the average tourist. He is taken, by his secret work, into secret worlds – the Harlem of Mr. Big in *Live and Let Die*, the Jamaica of Dr. No, and the Istanbul of Kerim in *From Russia, with Love*."

There are other contradictory feelings associated with tourism. While we want an 'authentic' experience, to see how people in another place or another culture live, we do not necessarily want to have to consider the reality of what we are seeing – that the scene in front of us represents someone's daily life. As an extreme example, consider 'slum tourism' – it began in the 19th century with people visiting the ghettoes of cities such as London and Manhattan, but today takes in places in Africa, India and South America. There is an argument that the money from tourism helps these places develop, but at the same time, they treat the appalling living conditions of local people as an entertainment. Some of the locals will profit from tourism, but there are also those that do not want to be looked at and photographed. Others don't want rich foreigners in their area because they are afraid that their own culture will be lost, swamped by monopolistic Western companies. But all this in turn adds that extra *frisson* that Fleming talked about: there's a thrilling feeling of danger if you're in a place that you feel you are 'not supposed' to be or 'not wanted.'

This danger is part of the appeal of the locations in James Bond too. There is a sense of a hidden, darker side to the idyllic locations he visits. His local guides show him places that visitors usually do not see. In *Live and Let Die*, Felix Leiter warns Bond that people don't visit Harlem like they used to: "Harlem doesn't like being stared at anymore." And later Bond experiences what this means: "They were trespassing. They just weren't wanted."

Denning describes tourism as a new form of colonialism – and while the preferred tourist destinations, including places in the Mediterranean, Caribbean, Philippines, Indonesia and Hong Kong might welcome tourist income, they are still suspicious of the tourists – and rightly so.

Why did Fleming choose exotic locations for his stories and – more importantly for us – do they still appeal to audiences today? Part of the reason why the stories were set abroad rather than in Britain relates to the loss of the Empire – Britain was no longer the centre of the universe and so stories set there had less appeal. This was particularly true if a thriller author or a publisher was seeking to sell into an expanding international market. Another reason for Fleming's own interest might be that his elder brother, Peter, was a successful travel writer.

Tourism allows people to visit new places. Travel writing and fiction including a travel element allow people to experience places that they have not visited – and perhaps never will. In the 1950s when Fleming began writing, Britain was emerging from a period of post-war austerity and people wanted to read about places that they perhaps aspired to travel to, but couldn't yet afford to visit. Today people might wish to experience exotic and even dangerous locations, but don't want to take the 'risk' of leaving their own nations. There are places we are afraid to visit because we associate 'foreign' with 'dangerous' or, more specifically, with 'terrorism.' Where terrorist are active, they are aware of this fear and may seek to target tourists as a soft target that will gain maximum media coverage. And some people, of course, just don't want to travel: only around 36% of people in the US have a passport, compared to 60-75% of people in Canada, the UK and Australia. Vicarious travel in the form of thriller locations will certainly appeal to many readers, but stories set solely in the USA are also likely to have a large readership.

Like sex, exotic locations are not restricted to thrillers – other popular genres make use of them. But if your aim is to isolate your hero in a place where there are hidden threats – and as a thriller writer this *should* be one of your aims – sending him on assignment to a foreign country is an ideal way of doing this.

(vii) Iconography

When it comes to what audiences expect to 'see' in a James Bond thriller, the movie adaptations tend to eclipse the novels. But most of the visual images have their basis in Ian Fleming's stories. Many of these images and symbols have been covered in a previous section in this chapter, so I will mention them only briefly below and in roughly the order they typically appear in a Bond story. There are a couple things we haven't explored fully, and I will cover them in more detail here: the use of *games* and the use of *torture*.

Bond in action. The genre of the story and Bond's professionalism are usually demonstrated in a thrilling pre-credits sequence in the films – a similar scene occurs in some, but not all, of the novels.

Villain in action. We some intriguing, mysterious and disruptive act which either signals the start of the conspiracy or that the conspiracy in progress. We may not see the villain at this stage – he is often a shadowy figure who Bond must identify and track down – but we will see an example of his people at work. We must see that these actions threaten the safety of ordinary society, as this threat is what gives Bond his mission and his actions are legitimised by the fact that he is trying to eliminate the threat.

The Organisation & the Mission. Bond is assigned his mission by his boss, M. Again, this serves to show that he is acting in an official capacity and is not some freelance vigilante. M's secretary, Miss Moneypenny, is often a part of this scene and she represents the good people that Bond protects.

Gadgets and the Car. As part of his initial briefing for the assignment, Bond usually receives several new spy gadgets from Q and a new car that has a few features not found on the standard model. In the films especially, these gadgets are usually just a bit of fun – they may play a small part in the action during the early part of the story, but they do not normally feature in the climactic battle and they should never be the thing that allows Bond to succeed at the climax. Typically, Bond uses up or loses the gadgets earlier in the story – it is one of the ways that we see his increasing isolation and need for self-sufficiency: once his gadgets are gone, he has to rely on his own ingenuity and whatever resources are at hand. The danger with 'off the shelf' gadgets is that they are like magic that can be whisked out to save the hero from a dangerous situation – they effectively become a 'Get Out of Jail Free' card. If you use too many of them in a thriller, you blunt the effect of the suspense you have built up – rather than being a mini climax, the hero's escape causes a groan of anti-climax. Readers and viewers much prefer to see their hero cobble together some kind of makeshift device to help him escape. This resourcefulness is part of what we enjoy about this type of hero. Television shows like *MacGyver* and *The A-Team* recognised the appeal of this quality and made it central to their plots.

Some of the most famous Bond gadgets include the briefcase with various hidden weapons in *From Russia, With Love* and a pen that is a gun and a watch containing a laser in *Never Say Never Again*. There is a *Wikipedia* entry for all of the gadgets used by Bond and his enemies in the films, and it is a very long list! Wristwatches feature a number of times – early on they are Rolex watches, continuing the Ian Fleming fad for premium name products, but in later films there seems to be have been an element of 'product placement' involved in the choice of brands.

The car most often associated with James Bond is the Aston Martin: the DB5 was the classic 'Bond car,' first appearing in *Goldfinger* and then in five other films in the series, including two of the Daniel Craig films. Timothy Dalton got the V8 Vantage Volante in *The Living Daylights* and Daniel Craig has had several of the more recent Aston Martins. Other cars have featured in memorable sequences in the series, but the one non-Aston Martin car most people remember is Roger Moore's Lotus Esprit S1 which was – thanks to the special effects team – able to transform into a submarine.

For a modern audience, gadgets have become pretty commonplace – most of us have all kinds of technology at home, including a few items that might have been inspired by the Bond movies. And because of the Bond movies and their imitators, we all know a bit about 'spy gadgets' such as bugs and bug-detectors. It's more difficult now to put something in a story that seems fresh and realistic, and that won't seem to be outdated within six months. This is another reason by improvised devices are preferable to off-the-shelf tech. If you need inspiration for creating improvised devices for different purposes, there are various 'survival' manuals out there that provide details for creating the things you will need after the apocalypse. Obviously, be aware of the restrictions in your own country with regard to accessing manuals that tell you how to create improvised weapons and explosives.

Made-up gadgets – improvised or otherwise – are an area where you can use your imagination. If you're going to write about cars, do your homework. There are a lot of auto enthusiasts out there for both modern and classic cars – and they're going to know if you haven't done your research properly. You can access all kinds of information about cars online, from the manufacturers, professional reviews, and people who upgrade and tune automobiles. If you're going to have your hero put something in the boot/trunk at the back of a car, for example, make sure that it's a car that doesn't have the engine there.

Weapons. Ian Fleming included details about places and vehicles and leisure activities, including food and drink, to give his stories a sense of verisimilitude. He felt that the more detail he included, the more real the story would seem to readers – and the more likely it was that the reader would believe that he, as the writer, knew what he was talking about. His details might not always have been one-hundred-percent accurate, but he delivered them with confidence and most people never noticed the occasional slip-up. Chances are that if you write about a street in Istanbul and get a detail wrong, most people are not going to spot it. But when it comes to weapons – especially guns – I would advise you to do your research thoroughly: a lot of people know their guns, especially in the USA, and many of them are thriller readers. Again, there's a lot of information online and there are catalogues and reference books that you can consult. If you can, try and find first-hand information about the weapons you want your characters to use – you can often find videos on YouTube about modern and historical weapons, and if you have a specific question you can usually find an online enthusiasts' site or forum where you should be able to make contact with someone who can give you the answer you need. Be careful about using information from other thrillers or from movies – it isn't always accurate.

As writers we're often warned about including chunks of undigested research in our fiction, but details about weaponry seems to be one area where you are allowed to do this – Ian Fleming did it in the 1960s and Lee Childs has done it in recent years: have a look at Childs' second Jack Reacher novel, *Die Trying*, if you want to see how a modern author handles this kind of detail – there is a fair amount of detail on sniper rifles and how to use them, and it is provided in such a way as to avoid holding up the action or diminishing the suspense.

Chase Sequences. Thrillers need chase scenes – they can involve cars, skis or people running. Chases are such a fundamental part of the thriller that I have included a chapter later in the book on creating a chase/manhunt.

Fight Scenes. Physical one-on-one or one-against-many fight scenes occur in most thrillers of this type. Do I need to say that in a one-against-many fight there is a lone hero against multiple assailants? Bear in mind what I said above about the way that the hero uses violence, and his attitude towards it, as compared to that of the villain or henchman: for the hero it is something that he has to do to protect his own life and that of others, a necessary evil; for the villain or henchman it is something done either cold-bloodedly or for pleasure.

Henchman. Henchmen are often bizarre and fascinating characters – villains in adventure stories and horror stories have them, and *Star Wars* gave is Darth Vader. Typically the henchman is 'hired muscle' – an expert in some kind of martial art or a professional assassin. They are the hero's closest 'opposite number' – have equal training and experience, so that they too are a professional. Bond and the henchman are usually equally-matched, with Bond barely managing to survive an early fight with him. This sets up a later confrontation at the climax where the audience or reader should wonder whether the hero will manage to outwit him again. There is more about the henchman character under the *Villain* heading above.

Travel to exotic places. I have covered this under the *Setting* heading here. Remember that the idyllic tourist setting seen early in the story can be used as a sharp contrast with a rugged and inhospitable location that the hero may have to travel through as he approaches – for example – the villain's hidden lair.

Sexual encounters. See *Romantic Co-protagonist* above.

Isolation – including death of the support team. At different points in the story, the professional hero may be helped (or hindered) by various people but as the story approaches the climax he will become increasingly isolated as these people are taken from him. These people can be broadly classified as Law Enforcement, Professional Colleagues, and Local Guides, and we will cover them under the *Other Characters* heading below.

Villain's secret base and capture. If you are familiar with the theory of the 'hero's journey' in the work of Joseph Campbell or from Christopher Vogler's *The Writer's Journey*, you will know that there is a sequence referred to as 'descent to the inner-most cave' or 'descent into the underworld.' The hero has travelled from a safe, luxurious, touristy place through a hazardous and inhospitable no-mans-land, getting closer and closer to the villain's territory. He enters the 'dark cave' which is the most dangerous region of the story. This is the villain's domain, the place where he makes the rules and controls everything. It is the home of a dictator whose rule is absolute. It is filled with people programmed to do the villain's bidding. The hero does not belong here and if he is discovered, he faces a terrible consequence. In terms of the hero's journey, this is the place where the hero faces – and must overcome – the thing that he fears most. It is a dark place psychologically as well as physically – his mental well-being is threatened as well as his physical self.

Entering the villain's lair typically signals the start of Act III and the climax of the story. To refer to the hero's journey again, the hero's 'darkest hour' usually occurs when his infiltration of the secret base is discovered and he is captured. He then faces physical torture at the hands of the villain – I will cover this separately below. There is also a psychological element to this scene with the villain. The villain might try and tell the hero that they are 'very much alike' – the hero's methods, his use of violence, isn't so very different to what the villain has been doing. He may also highlight the fact that they are both outsiders that have no place in the society of ordinary people. And the villain may ask the hero to join him. The hero refuses and takes the opportunity to state his own ideology – why he does what he does and how his attitude to violence and espionage is different from that of the villain: essentially he is selfless, acting on behalf of others, while the villain is selfish, motivated by greed and/or revenge. At which point, the villain condemns the hero to an unpleasant death.

Escaping death and destruction of the villain's lair. The hero manages to survive whatever fate the villain had lined up for him – attack by a deadly squid in *Dr. No!* –using a combination of physical stamina and ingenuity. And then another improvised action sets in motion a sequence of events that will see the villain's secret base destroyed, the conspiracy ended and – usually – the villain killed in some suitably ironic way.

Torture

The threat of torture and actual acts of cruelty have been a part of the thriller genre since its earliest days. Ian Flemings said that he had been inspired to use it by the Fu-Manchu stories he read in his youth and in Geoffrey Household's *Rogue Male* (1939), the hero tells us that his captors tore out his fingernails.

Two things have changed since then. In the old stories, the author would *tell* us what happened to the victim, but in modern stories we are more likely to be *shown*. The same is true in movies in that the camera is now less likely to cut away from what is occurring. Also in the older stories, and in the original James Bond novels, torture is only ever carried out by the bad guys. There is a sense that torture is something that 'we' don't do – it is ungentlemanly.

The truth is that torture has been used by both sides throughout history, and it has been used by 'our' side to a much greater extent and in a much more brutal way than ordinary people could ever have expected. The revelations of the *Committee Study of the Central Intelligence Agency's Detention and Interrogation Program,* released in 2014, make grim reading. Torture is an abuse of human rights. Amnesty International has campaigned since 1961 to put an end to abuses of human rights, including the use of torture. Amnesty and others have highlighted not only the physical harm caused by torture but also the psychological trauma suffered by victims. There is also credible evidence that torture – especially prolonged and repeated torture – does not work: under such circumstances, a victim is likely to tell you whatever they think the torturer wants to hear.

Against this very real background, we have to consider torture in entertainments such as thrillers. John Atkins writes while the appearance of torture in thrillers reflects the extent of its use in the contemporary world, "What is not a truthful reflection ... is the victim's ability to withstand and recover from torture." The heroes of such novels are "fantastically tough ... Bond suffered but never gave in and always recovered." He says this is no more realistic than a "cartoon mouse, embedded in a brick wall without damage to flesh and bone..." Atkins also notes that in the case of some lesser thriller writers "... the description of torture is the major attraction..." and that sometimes it is depicted "...in gruesome detail..."

The purpose of the torture scene in the James Bond stories seems to have been a combination of proving the stamina and resilience of the hero; placing the hero in the worst possible situation so that the reader worries about him; and of weakening him so that he seems less of a superhero, which makes the outcome of the climactic battle that is to come less of a sure-fire victory for the hero.

One of the things that the 2014 *Committee Study* noted was that the methods used were designed to demonstrate the power the torturer held over the victim and that there was often a sexual element to the methods involving physical violation or rape. This happened to male victims as well as female. That is nothing like the sadomasochistic fantasy that the Bond stories present.

Where does all this leave us as thriller writers today? First of all, I think that everyone ought to be aware of the reality of torture and its effect on real-life victims. Whether you think torture is justifiable by 'our' side is a matter for your own conscience – but you should base your opinion on this (as in all things) on evidence rather than a vague gut feeling. Writers have a duty to be truthful within the context of their stories – torture is used in our world, therefore it is not inappropriate for it to be included in thriller stories. If you are aiming for realism in your story, then torture has to be approached realistically

– you can't treat it as a bit of S&M fantasy. And it would be entirely inappropriate to present it in a way to titillate readers.

Bear in mind that extended scenes of brutal physical torture are likely to make a reader turn away – there is a point where people say, I've had enough of this. A catalogue of gruesome acts presented to a reader who is a fly-on-the-wall is likely to be far less effective than a scene where the reader experiences the situation from the point of view of the powerless victim or the cold-blooded torturer. The psychology behind what is going on is more compelling than the butchery itself. Also be honest about the long-term impact of both the physical and psychological damage caused.

Having said that, if it is clear from the outset of your story that you are writing a non-realistic fantasy with elements of sadism and masochism, then your approach may well be different – and the 'abuses' that you subject your characters to will be of a very different kind. This is one area where context really is important.

Games

Games are an important element of the Bond stories in a number of ways: writers have identified that the stories themselves follow a game-like structure; that actual games – including card games and golf – feature in the stories; and that espionage itself is often referred to, in the Bond stories and elsewhere, as a game or even as the 'Great Game.' I'll cover the first two briefly and then spend a little more time on the 'Great Game' as that will help set-up chapter seven which covers what is sometimes referred to as the more 'realistic' type of espionage story, as typified by the novels of John Le Carré.

Game-like Plots. Michael Denning: "Umberto Eco has analysed the James Bond stories as a game, a form where the reader knows the pieces, the rules, and the moves, and watches it unfold, taking pleasure in the game and its minor variations." In his essay 'The Narrative Structure in Fleming,' Eco said that the Bond novel consisted of a "fixed sequence of 'moves' " and listed the eight main ones:

- A. M gives Bond a task.
- B. The Villain appears to Bond (perhaps in alternating forms).
- C. Bond moves to 'check' the Villain or the Villain checks Bond.
- D. The Woman shows herself to Bond.
- E. Bond possesses the Woman or begins her seduction.
- F. The Villain captures Bond (with or without the Woman).
- G. The Villain tortures Bond (with or without the Woman).
- H. Bond conquers the Villain.
- I. Bond convalesces and enjoys the company of the Woman, who he then loses.

These are similar to the eight sequences that I identified earlier. Eco writes that "It is not imperative that the moves should always be in the same sequence." Moves can also be repeated. He identified *Dr. No* as following the A-I sequence exactly. *Goldfinger* has the moves in the following sequence: B.C.D.E.A.C.D.F.G.D.H.E.H.I while the sequence he gives for *From Russia, With*

Love is: B.B.B.B.D.A.(B.B.C.)E.F.G.H.G.H.(I). This more complicated structure accounts for a long prologue set in Russia that introduces the villains and a long interlude in Istanbul, in which a secondary villain figure Krilenku appears.

Eco said that a Fleming novel could be compared "...to a game of football, in which we know beforehand the place, the number and the personalities of the players, the rules of the game, the fact that everything will take place within the area of the great pitch..." but he said that the analogy broke down because, in a game of football, we do not know the outcome and can ask, Who will win? A Bond novel, he said, was more like a basketball game where a small local team take on the Harlem Globe Trotters – we know the better team will win but can sit back and enjoy watching how they play. James Bond, like most thriller heroes, is the better team.

Sports and Games. Michael Denning praises Ian Fleming's ability as a 'sportswriter' based on the "extraordinary amount of space devoted to representing games and sports." In *Goldfinger* Bond plays golf against the villain; in *Casino Royale* he plays baccarat against Le Chiffre; in *Moonraker* it is bridge against Hugo Drax; and in *On Her Majesty's Secret Service* there is a ski chase.

In the pre- and post-First World War spy thrillers the hero was always a 'good sport.' He went to a public school and learned to play cricket like a gentleman. It is difficult to imagine Sean Connery's James Bond playing cricket – he perfectly captured the feeling on Bond being note quite a gentleman. When Hugo Drax cheats at cards or Goldfinger cheats at golf, Bond doesn't seek to expose their ungentlemanly behaviour – he wins by being a better cheat than they are. This is in accordance with Bond's competitive nature. And as well as being licenced to kill, he seems to be licenced to cheat: in *Goldfinger* we are told, "It was Bond's duty to win." Any money he wins from his opponents is handed over to his employers – he doesn't profit personally.

Games are also used to indicate the characters of the opposing sides. In keeping with their nature as bureaucrats following their programming, the Russian villains – such as Kronsteen in *From Russia, With Love* – are shown as chess players who treat people like pawns on a game board; where Bond, representing the British, is shown as a gambler, which again is in tune with his character as an improviser.

Denning also says that the portrayal of sports and games fits with the idea of the Bond stories reflecting modern consumerism and tourism. "The sports represented are not the public school cricket pitch, nor the aristocratic blood sports and yachting, nor the working-class spectator sport of football: they are the consumer sports of golf, skiing, and casino gambling. They have the glamour of being sports of the wealthy, the sports of the holiday on the Continent, yet are relatively free from traditional class connotations." He argues that the novels don't just portray leisure and consumption, the attempt to redeem it by making an ordinary game of golf into something that has consequence in terms of global politics. Fleming coverage of the golf game in *Goldfinger* is three times as long as his account of the robbery on Fort Knox, and Denning says, "this is surely because the detail and attention to the contest the reader can imagine not only prepares him or her for the absurdity of the Fort Knox plot, but is also a more interesting story than the Fort Knox plot."

The Great Game. 'The Great Game' is a term that was originally used to describe the political hostility between the British and Russian empires during most of the nineteenth century. It centred on Afghanistan and neighbouring territories in Central and Southern Asia – Russia was concerned about British commercial and military expansion into Central Asia and Britain was afraid Russia wanted to add India to the Asian part of its empire. Malcolm Yapp has shown that it was originally a French term – 'Le grand jeu' – referring to games of risk, chance and deception, it was probably first used in relation to the Afghanistan situation by diplomats in about 1840. The term was made popular when it was used in Rudyard Kipling's 1901 novel *Kim* in which the title character, among other adventures, becomes a spy for the British. The term has since come to be a general term for international diplomacy and/or espionage. The World War II Soviet spymaster Leopold Tepper titled his memoirs *The Great Game.*

John Atkins says that the appeal of the Great Game is "a love of pitting their wits against the enemy, short of war." He also points out that, "There is a huge contradiction at the heart of the Great Game. It is obviously a most cynical description of activities which were regarded as despicable by many people and yet the players often insisted on a high code of morality."

In the Great Game, 'players' are viewed as cold-hearted – they move people around like pawns on a chessboard and do not feel any remorse when they have to sacrifice one of their own agents. Ian Fleming treated espionage in this way. In *The Spy Who Loved Me,* Bond says: "It's nothing but a complicated game, really. But then so's international politics, diplomacy – all the trappings of nationalism and the power complex that goes on between countries. Nobody will stop playing the game. It's like the hunting instinct."

From the earliest spy novels through to Bond, the basis of the game was simple – there was 'us' and there was 'them.' We were on the side of good, and they were bad. The foreign aggressor was at various times in the history of the British Empire the Germans, the French or the Russians. After the end of the Empire, and during the period of the Cold War, the situation became less straightforward.

It wasn't until the publication of John Le Carré's *The Spy Who Came in from the Cold* in 1963 that the idea of spying being a game was challenged. As we will see in chapter seven, his novel is almost a negative-image of a Bond novel in all respects.

(viii) Themes

Umberto Eco identified a series of juxtaposed vales in the James Bond novels and I've used some of them – though not necessarily his terminology – for some of the sub-headings in this section. Some of these themes have been covered in detail in earlier sections of this chapter.

Manichean Ideology. Eco uses this term because it refers to a conflict between opposites and to a religious system based on a belief in an ancient conflict between light and darkness. The James Bond novels, like the earliest spy novels, present a worldview which says that you're either on 'our' side (good/light) or you are the enemy (bad/darkness). This is represented in terms of the 'Free World' versus the Soviet Union, or as 'Great Britain' versus non-Anglo-Saxon countries. Ian Fleming's adoption of this simplified worldview is one of the things which place his stories closer to the 'romantic heroic fantasy' end of the spectrum than the 'realistic.' Michael Denning: "... the spy thriller transforms an incomprehensible political situation (or a situation the knowledge of which is being repressed) into the ethical categories of masculine romance, the battle between the hero and the villain becoming one between Good and Evil, the forces of light and the forces of darkness."

Selfishness versus Selflessness. This is almost the definition of the *hero* in all genres: someone who is prepared to risk his own physical or emotional well-being in order to defend or rescue others. Someone who puts the needs of others first. The hero is self-sacrificing, but the villain acts out of purely selfish motives, usually a desire for power, greed, or revenge.

Loyalty versus Treachery. Again, this is part of the definition of the hero: he is loyal to his friends and colleagues, to his employer, to his country and to the allies of that country. In the world of the thriller, where trust is a scarce commodity, betrayal is a terrible thing. To earn someone's trust and then to sell them out marks a person out as being an agent of badness/darkness. This relates to Manicheanism, which allows for no shades of grey – you're either with us or against us. Only towards the more 'realistic' end of the espionage story spectrum – which we'll explore in chapter seven – do ideas of loyalty become more complex.

Bureaucracy versus Individual Action. We have covered this in terms of the hero's ability to improvise being in contrast to the villain's more rigid programming. It is a theme that is seen as central to the popularity of the thriller by some studies of the genre. Michael Denning says that it is no surprise that the spy thriller first appeared at the beginning of the twentieth century – it was a response to the situation in the (Western) world at that time. Denning refers to 'rival imperialist states' and a 'capitalist world system' which were responsible for the dominance of "international politics and intrigue, of multinational economic organisations." This was a world in which it was "increasingly difficult to envision the totality of social relations as embodied by any single 'knowable community'." This is an environment where the individual risks feeling lost and insignificant or, at best, as just a small cog in a vast machine. Denning suggests that the spy thriller helped people make sense of their world: "... it kept a fairly traditional plot by making the spy the link between the actions of an individual – often an 'ordinary person' – and the world historical fate of nations and empires. History is displaced to secret conspiracies and secret agents, from politics to ethics. The secret *agent* returns human *agency* to a world which seems less and less the product of human action." The other way in which it helped people make sense of their environment was by transforming an "incomprehensible political situation" into a battle between good and evil – the 'Manichean ideology' mentioned above.

Hedonistic Consumerism versus Self-Sufficiency. We've said that the James Bond novels portray and defend modern consumerism as represented by mass tourism, brand awareness, and the objectification of women in advertising and mass market pornography. We see Bond in luxurious surroundings playing high stakes games and consuming expensive food and drinks. He also has exclusive technological devices and a very nice car. But on the flip-side, we see him gradually stripped of these things and thrust into a harsh environment where he has to rely on only his physical stamina and his wits. His survival rests on his own abilities – he is like Robinson Crusoe washed up on the shores of an inhospitable island. This has a similar appeal to audiences as television shows that show ordinary people or celebrities dropped into an environment where they have to 'survive' without any of the comforts they are accustomed to.

Corruption versus Innocence. We've seen in *Dr. No* that Honeychile Rider represents innocence and purity and that this used in contrast to the corruption, ugliness, perversity and inhuman character of Dr. Julius No. She represents the 'good' that James Bond is fighting to protect from the conspiracy of the villains. This innocence is also represented by characters like Miss Moneypenny. The corruption of the villain extends to his motivations, which we have covered above under *Selfishness versus Selflessness.* Because Bond is not an amateur or an ordinary man caught up in extraordinary circumstances, this type of thriller needs someone to be a symbol of the ordinary, innocent individual. They show us what and who the hero is fighting for.

Cold-blooded versus Necessary Evil. In the amateur-on-the-run thriller, the amateur hero does not engage in acts of violence, unless he is forced to defend himself in a face-to-face confrontation. And even then, he will probably prove to be either incapable of causing injury save by a lucky blow, or he will fight in accordance with the Queensbury rules. The professional hero is more likely to have to engage in more deadly violence and may even, on occasion, have to strike first. In the latter case, the level or type of violence used by the hero is very much like that used by the enemy. It is necessary in the thriller to somehow distinguish between the two.

Jerry Palmer says that descriptions of violence perpetrated by the hero are designed to 'exhilarate' the reader, but descriptions of violence perpetrated by the villain are supposed to 'nauseate' the reader. How do we, as writers, pull off that trick? In part, we can do this by creating a hero that the reader likes and a villain that they despise. The differences between hero and villain mentioned earlier in this chapter contribute to this. In my book *Plot Basics,* I covered a number of general techniques that can be used to create sympathy for and/or empathy with the hero and antipathy for the villain – these can be applied to creating heroes and villains in any genre. As far as the thriller is concerned, the main techniques you can use involve the *motivation* of the villain and hero for using violence and their *attitude* to the violence as it is being used. As Palmer writes, the difference between the two "... is to be found in the cold-bloodedness of the villain."

As an example, Palmer quotes the discussion of torture in chapter 21 of *Thunderball*, in which the villain's "bureaucratic attitude towards suffering is nauseous. It is not the use of torture itself that is intended to arouse our revulsion, but the calm detachment of the man." The villain is *indifferent* towards the people to whom he uses violence – to him they are mere objects, a nuisance to be dealt with or something to squeeze information out of. The villain's use of violence is also casual and frequent – he doesn't have to agonise over whether to use violence or not, he just does it. And he will use it against his own people as easily as against an enemy agent. He also has no qualms about using it against ordinary innocent people. The villain gives almost no thought to what might be an appropriate level of violence given the circumstances – the fact that he is indifferent to the suffering of others means that he is apt to be extremely brutal no matter what the situation. He may also take pride in his skill in inflicting pain, he might celebrate it, and he may even enjoy it. Usually, his enjoyment will come from the thrill he gets from having power over the victim.

By contrast, the hero has to be forced by circumstances to use violence and for him, it is usually only used as a last resort. The hero would never use violence against someone who is on his side – unless rendering them unconscious has to be done to protect them from greater violence or to prevent them from taking an unnecessary risk. And he would never use it against an ordinary innocent person except, perhaps, under the same circumstances. In addition, when considering the use of violence against an enemy, the hero is also aware of the potential risk to innocent bystanders – for him, it is unacceptable for there to by any death or injury from a 'friendly fire' incident or for there to be any 'collateral damage'. Even when it does come to using violence against an enemy, the hero does not feel indifferent towards them – they may be trying to kill him or someone he cares about and 'deserve' the violence, but they are still human beings. And the hero's use of force will always be proportionate – he will only use the level of violence that is required by the current situation. He will never take pleasure in the use of violence and he will never glorify it.

Cynicism versus Commitment. In an earlier chapter, I said that the amateur hero begins with no real commitment to any values but discovers what is important to him as the story progresses. With the professional hero, the situation is different – part of his professionalism is that he is committed to his job. He is loyal to his agency and his country and defends the values that are – broadly speaking – common to the people of that country. In discussing the professional hero, I also said that dealing with conspiracy was part of his day job and that he unlikely to be surprised or shocked by what he sees, because he has experienced it all before. This can lead to him becoming cynical about his work. He may come to feel that 'his side' is not so very different from the 'other side' as people might like to believe. Espionage is not a simple battle between good and bad, rather it is – in John Atkins words – a case of the greater evil being beaten off by the lesser. Where the spies of Buchan and Oppenheim were certain they were protecting the world from barbarism, the modern spy might feel that – especially in a world where torture and violence are routinely used by both sides – barbarians are protecting the world from barbarians. This is an area that John Le Carré chose to explore.

Ian Fleming took a more pragmatic approach, introducing the hero's doubts at the end of the first James Bond novel and getting them out of the way once and for all. In chapter 20 of *Casino Royale,* while he is recovering from his torture at the hands of the villain, Bond gives voice to the idea that he might resign: "... but this country-right-or-wrong business is getting a little out-of-date. Today we are fighting Communism. Okay. If I'd been alive fifty years ago, the brand of Conservatism we have today would have been damn near called Communism and we should have been told to go and fight that. History is moving pretty quickly these days and the heroes and villains keep on changing parts." His French colleague, Mathis, sets him straight: "... about that little problem of yours, this business of not knowing good men from bad men and villains from heroes, and so forth. It is, of course, a difficult problem in the abstract. The secret lies in personal experience ... Surround yourself with human beings, my dear James. They are easier to fight for than principles ... But don't let me down and become human, yourself. We would lose such a wonderful machine." This – coupled with the fact that he is betrayed by the woman he had come to trust and perhaps even love – is enough to set Bond back on his isolated professional track and his conscience is (almost) never troubled again.

Where the amateur hero of our amateur-on-the-run story must discover what values are important and become committed to them, the professional hero is often beset by doubt and must rediscover the values that are important to him and *re*-commit to them. This is what happens to Humphrey Bogart's character Rick in *Casablanca* and it is also an exercise that the hardboiled detective often has to complete.

Poetic Justice. Poetic justice consists of a punishment being given that is suitable for the crime committed and – in story terms – there is often an element of irony involved. In the novel *Dr. No*, the villain, who has treated Bond and everyone else around him like shit, is killed by being buried under tons of bird droppings. In thrillers, this justice is often served by having the villain succumb to a death which mirrors how he intended to kill the hero or how he did kill other victims earlier in the story.

Within the tradition of the 'romantic heroic fantasy', it is generally not permissible for the hero to act as judge, jury and executioner – this makes him too much of a high-handed vigilante and is not consistent with the values of our society. A hero is supposed to detain the villain so that he can be properly processed through our criminal justice system. Poetic justice provides us, as writers and readers, with another way to have our cake and eat it. Our hero cannot push the villain into the jaws of a wood-chipper, but if the villain's *own* criminal or cowardly actions were to cause him to *fall* into the grinding mechanism, that would be just fine.

(ix) Tone

In their book *The Spy Story*, Cawelti and Rosenberg ask, "How then does Fleming make us swallow a formulaic fantasy in which these basic modern tensions are reconciled in a story of heroic adventure? How does a writer like Fleming make us suspend our basic awareness of reality in order to enjoy something we know is not only a fantasy but in many ways an obsolete one?" The answer, they say, lies in Ian Fleming's "special tone and style." He makes sure the reader knows that they are not to take Bond's adventures too seriously. "Almost every page in the Fleming opus has at least one or two sentences which hint at some form of put-on or self-parody. Some of this is conscious, some doubtless unconscious, perhaps most of it."

"Much odium has been incurred by Fleming for his style," Atkins writes. "This is mostly undeserved. It is not his style that is objectionable but his view of life ... it was this that caused later spy writers, such as Le Carré and Deighton, to revolt against him."

Kingsley Amis was a Bond aficionado, he wrote a book about the James Bond novels and under the pseudonym Robert Markham wrote a Bond novel, *Colonel Sun* (1968), after Fleming's death. In an entry for the *Dictionary of National Biography*, Amis said of Fleming, "His style is plain and flexible, serving equally well for fast action, lucid technical exposition, and serious evocation of place and climate; if it falls here and there into cliché or the novelette, it never descends to pretentiousness. The strength of his work lies in its command of pace and its profound latent romanticism." We shall come back to that last point on romanticism.

Fleming knew he was writing old-fashioned adventure stories but presented them with a tone of irony and cynicism that made them palatable for a more sophisticated mid-twentieth-century audience. As I said before, irony lets you have your cake and eat it. Tip a wink to the audience and they will go along with you.

If you plan to write a thriller that fits into the more fantastic and romantic end of the spectrum, then Ian Fleming's 'knowing' style is something you can adapt for your own writing. Irony and humour still appeal to audiences. I wouldn't recommend trying to include those witty one-liners and innuendos that appeared in the Roger Moore movies: there is a fine line there between funny and failure, and readers tend to object to anything that is arch or 'too clever.' These are just suggestions, not rules – if that kind of humour is your natural style and you can pull it off, go for it. A more realistic thriller is going to touch on darker aspects of the field of espionage – cynicism and irony can still work there, but there is going to be a darker edge to the humour too. Or you can play it totally straight, as John Le Carré does.

(x) Other Characters

We have already discussed the villain's henchman under the 'Villain' heading, and there are a couple of other types of secondary character that we need to consider.

Ordinary People. In an amateur-on-the-run thriller, the hero is essentially an ordinary person who is caught up in extraordinary circumstances. His chief objective, once he has thwarted the conspiracy, is to return to his ordinary life. While he is on the run –from the conspirators and the police – ordinary people become a threat to the amateur hero and he must take pains to avoid them: any one of them could recognise him from a photograph in the newspaper or on television and alert the authorities. Part of the amateur hero's isolation is that there is no one he can turn to, no one he can trust.

The professional hero rarely has any interaction with ordinary people. He has no particular reason to fear them, and his attitude towards them may be condescending: they have no idea about what his world is really like and the dangers he faces. His job is to protect their lives and their way of life, without them ever being aware of their need to be protected. The work of a professional hero is an example of the 'benevolent conspiracy' that is mentioned in chapter three.

The only time that a professional hero may encounter an ordinary person is if they are a bungling amateur who starts poking around on the fringes of the conspiracy, putting themselves in danger. Or they are a terrified witness of some criminal act by the conspirators. Or they are innocent bystanders who may be harmed by actions taken by the conspirators or by the hero: the hero may be prevented from taking his preferred course of action because of the risk of 'collateral damage.'

Law Enforcement. Under this heading, we can include any of the 'authorities' that the hero might encounter, either at home or while he is on foreign soil. Generally speaking, the hero will regard these authorities as less competent and less 'professional' than he is. They usually appear as an obstacle or hindrance from the hero's point of view. Some are inexperienced or incompetent. Some are corrupt – either engaged in their own illegal activities or taking bribes from the conspirators the hero is pursuing. And all typically resent the hero's presence on their 'turf.' Even a good and honest official is likely to feel annoyed at the presence of an uninvited, unauthorised, and unregulated foreign agent in their territory.

Sometimes the local authorities take action which prevents the professional hero doing his job. They may slow him down with their bureaucracy or they may imprison him for infringing their laws. They may ban him from entering places or from engaging in activities that are vital to his mission. Or they may make their own attempt to tackle the conspirators, getting in the hero's way and making the situation more dangerous for everyone concerned. Don't underestimate the possibilities of these people for creating obstacles and suspense on your story.

Professional Colleagues. Sometimes the hero is not the only agent who has been sent to the area. Our hero may have been sent to investigate the disappearance of an agent who had been investigating the activities of the conspirators. Or he may have been sent to work with an agent in the field who has already made some progress in investigating the conspiracy. In some cases, the hero may have to liaise with an agent from the country where the conspirators are at work. Or he may have to work with another foreign agent: James Bond, for example, occasionally encountered American agent Felix Leiter.

Although these characters are fellow professionals, they tend to be *less* professional than the hero. They are often injured or captured by the conspirators, meaning the hero has to rescue them.

Professional colleagues include the hero's boss, M in the case of James Bond, and any sort of instructor or mentor who provides him with special skills, knowledge or equipment – Q serves this function in the Bond series. Another of their functions is to highlight the legitimacy of the hero's actions – James Bond isn't just a lone vigilante killing people he doesn't like, he is acting with the tacit official approval – he is 'On Majesty's Secret Service' and *licenced* to kill.

Local Guides. Another type of character found in the James Bond novels serves what Michael Denning (using the terminology of Vladimir Propp) calls 'donors' – the characters who Bond meets while on an assignment and with whom he forms a working alliance. These are often people who serve as local guides, providing our hero with 'insider' knowledge and allowing him access to places that tourists are not normally allowed to see. Kerim is Bond's local contact in Istanbul in *From Russia, With Love;* Quarrel is his man in Jamaica in *Dr. No,* and Felix Leiter is his guide in the Harlem area of Manhattan in *Live and Let Die.*

Given a choice, it's better not to be either a professional colleague or a local guide in a thriller because authors often kill them off in order to highlight the hero's isolation and self-reliance. There is one final type of secondary character to cover, and this one serves as a contrast to the romantic co-protagonist we talked about earlier.

Unattainable Women. In the James Bond novels, and in other similar thrillers, there is often one or more women who exist to represent the ordinary world that the professional hero is fighting to protect. They are often 'unattainable' in the sense that they are not the kind of women to fall for the hero's gruff charms and because they are the kind of women that the hero cannot afford to lose his heart to, because he couldn't promise them that he will 'settle down.' In the Bond novels, she is represented by M's secretary, Miss Moneypenny and – to some extent – by Bond's Scottish housekeeper, May. These are good British women that he wants to protect from the evils of foreign conspiracies. In hard-boiled detective thrillers, this character often appears as the hero's long-suffering secretary or his 'steady' girlfriend – someone who is a 'companion' – a genuine friend – rather than a lover. In the thriller, things become muddled if the professional hero ever tries to form a committed relationship with a woman like this. James Bond was married in *On Her Majesty's Secret Service,* and that did not turn out well. And when he married off Philip Marlowe, Raymond Chandler was unable to complete his next adventure, *Poodle Springs.* The typical professional thriller hero isn't really the marrying kind.

Realism versus Romanticism

How realistic are the events portrayed in a spy thriller? The James Bond novels are usually held to be the *least* realistic with John Le Carré's novels being towards the more realistic end of the spectrum. When it comes to novels about intelligence services and activities, many readers want to feel that they are getting something close to the truth of what really happens – they want to believe that they are getting 'inside information.' For this reason, readers also like to know whether the author of a novel has experience of Intelligence work. A surprising number of them do, including Ian Fleming and John Le Carré. Graham Greene apparently belonged to the same 'subsection' as Kim Philby. And the former Director of MI5, Dame Stella Rimington, has – to date – written ten thrillers featuring Liz Carlyle in a series that began in 2004. On the other hand, respected thriller writer Eric Ambler had no experience in the field. It has also been pointed out that being a former-spy doesn't necessarily mean that you will be a great thriller writer.

There is some question about whether an account of real-life espionage would actually make for a good spy thriller. We have to bear in mind Alfred Hitchcock's observation that drama is 'life with the dull bits cut out.' One imagines that there are a lot of dull bits in real-life espionage and very few exploits that would be suitable for a James Bond novel. It may also be the case that some real-life incidents are too bizarre to make believable fiction: Bulgarian dissident and journalist Georgi Markov was murdered in 1978 when a ricin-filled pellet was injected into his leg by an umbrella wielded by an assassin whose code-name may have been 'Piccadilly.' Alexander Litvinenko was assassinated in 2006 when a radioactive substance, polonium, was placed in his tea. Kim Jong-nam, brother of the North Korean leader, was (probably) assassinated in 2017 when a nerve agent was smeared on his face by two women who said they thought it was a prank for a reality TV show. You can't make this stuff up – and probably shouldn't. Fiction has much stricter rules about what is believable than real life.

Many writers and critics, says Michael Denning, make a distinction between realism and romance, "between 'realistic' spy stories and 'fantastic' thrillers." He writes that these two styles can be seen in 'two literary precursors of the genre,' who wrote novels featuring spies but weren't themselves 'spy novelists' – Rudyard Kipling and Joseph Conrad. "For the heroic romance of adventure, of spying in defence of the Empire, the story of the 'Great Game,' comes from Kipling's *Kim* (1901), and the cynical, realistic story of intrigue, betrayal and double agents was established by Conrad's *The Secret Agent* (1907) and *Under Western Eyes* (1911)."

Denning also notes that there is a sort of chronology of increasing realism: John Buchan wrote stories that were more realistic than the earlier 'cloak-and-dagger' stories of E. Phillips Oppenheim. While W. Somerset Maugham's *Ashenden* (1928) was more realistic than Buchan's tales, as were Eric Ambler, whose first thriller was published in 1936 and Graham Greene's, whose first was *The Confidential Agent* published in 1939.

Ian Fleming did not seek to continue this trend of increasing realism. Instead, he chose to combine elements of the John Buchan thriller with something from the hardboiled fiction writers who had achieved popularity in the USA and then in Britain. Cawelti and Rosenberg have commented on the link between Fleming and Buchan, saying they both "make the spy story into mythic romance with their tales of epic confrontation between noble heroes and diabolical villains…"

We will pick up the theme of 'realistic' espionage fiction in chapter seven. To end this one, we will briefly look at what the James Bond stories have in common with the heroic or mythic romance. By 'romance' we mean what my *Compact Oxford English Dictionary* defines as 'a medieval story dealing with the adventures of knights' rather than the genre romance, which is a 'book or film dealing with love in a sentimental or idealised way.' In what ways are James Bond novels similar to those medieval tales of chivalry? Jerry Palmer has said that "It is often suggested that the thriller hero is no more than the medieval knight in shining armour, minus chastity, plus technology..." but that while both feature heroes we are meant to admire, "... the qualities that arouse admiration have changed in the interim."

The chivalric romance originated in France during the 12th century and includes stories based on stories from Ancient Rome, stories from French history and stories from Britain, most notably the legends of King Arthur. According to the *Oxford Dictionary of Literary Terms*, the stories are said to have an emphasis on 'love and courtly manners' rather than the 'masculine military heroism' found in other forms. The hero of these tales was frequently a knight errant – a wandering or roving knight seeking adventure to prove his chivalric virtues. It is generally believed that there was a 'chivalric code' to which these knights adhered, but there is actually no single document that tells us what that code was. In 1883, Leon Gautier made an attempt to set down 'ten commandments' that might have served as this code – his list looked something like this:

1. Believe all that the Church teaches and observe all its directions.
2. Defend the church.
3. Respect those who are weaker and be a defender of them.
4. Love your own country.
5. Do not recoil from your enemy.
6. Make war against the infidel without cease and without mercy.
7. Scrupulously perform your feudal duties, if they are not contrary to the laws of God.
8. Never lie and remain faithful to your pledged word.
9. Be generous and give largesse to everyone.
10. Be everywhere and always the champion of Right and Good against injustice and Evil.

Gautier's commandments have been criticised for over-emphasising the religious aspect of chivalry, when the original code is believed to have encompassed aspects of the military, nobility, and religion. Others believe that the chivalric code is a poetic ideal that never actually existed, though there was a code of 'noble habits' that were recorded before the 'age of chivalry.' It consisted of the following virtues: loyalty; forbearance, including self-control and mercy; hardihood, meaning boldness or daring; largesse, i.e. generosity to others; protection of the weak and helpless, and opposition to the cruel and unjust; honour – loss of honour was a humiliation worse than death. To these virtues, the chivalric code must have added 'courtly love' by which was meant that a knight should serve his lady, and after her all ladies, and that he should be gentle and gracious towards all women. It is this last that we have come to associate with the idea of chivalry.

It is a bit of a cliché to compare the thriller hero with a white knight riding off to kill the dragon and rescue the damsel, but if we accept that the dragon symbolises the conspiracy that threatens society, we can see that there is some truth in it. Our professional hero – at least in his James Bond guise – also adheres to a code of behaviour that is not so very different from the chivalric code.

Ian Fleming's romanticised view of the work of a spy allowed readers to feel more comfortable with the incongruities and contradictions that frustrated them in their normal lives. It is a feature of popular fiction that it makes us feel comfortable about the status quo and to accept things as they are; whereas more realistic or literary fiction forces to confront the things that trouble us and frustrate us in life and in the world around us.

Not all writers share Fleming's romantic view of the life and work of the spy, as we will see in chapter seven.

3 | Conspiracy

A *conspiracy* is a secret plan by two or more people to do something that is unlawful or harmful. The plan may be to carry out a wrongful act, or to cover-up something that has already occurred. A conspiracy involves a plot to achieve a specific goal. It is most often motivated by a desire to acquire (or maintain) power, usually political. Other possible motives include material profit; the destruction of a rival group, often with an element of either survival (us or them) or revenge (it's their fault).

Originally, I wanted to say that every thriller *must* involve a conspiracy – because that would have made defining the thriller genre easier. But I found that there are a few thrillers that don't involve a conspiracy. Some chase thrillers, such as Steven Spielberg's *Duel,* have jeopardy and suspense, but there is no conspiracy as such. There is no plot involving two or more people. *Duel* has only a nameless and occasionally-glimpsed truck driver with murderous intent. *First Blood* focuses much more on the chase and the psychology of hunter and hunted than it does on a conspiracy – though Sheriff Teasle and his men are technically involved in a conspiracy. So I will say here that a conspiracy is *optional* – though as we will see later, it *is* essential to many sub-genres of the thriller plot.

In his book *Thrillers,* Jerry Palmer points out the importance of the conspiracy: "In the absence of a conspiracy the hero would never do anything – and would therefore never be a hero. It is the conspiracy that kick-starts the plot, and it is this initiative that justifies the hero's response."

The villains take action to achieve their goal, and these actions are outside the accepted moral code of the society of the story. These actions can include murder, kidnapping, attempted genocide, experiments on human subjects, torture, blackmail, illegal business practices, drug trafficking, money laundering, slavery and people trafficking, incitement of civil unrest or even of war, contamination of food or water supplies, assassination, counterfeiting, impersonation, and probably any other illegal activity you can think of.

The hero in a conspiracy-based thriller will typically come into contact with some small part of the action of the conspirators. It has been described as a small thread, which he or she pulls, leading to the eventual unravelling of the whole plot.

The idea of a conspiracy seems to be something that appeals to us as human beings. Conspiracy theories have sprung up around all manner of events, from the 'Roswell Incident,' to the assassination of John F. Kennedy, the death of Princess Diana, and the attack on the World Trade Centre in 2001. The essence of a conspiracy theory is that 'there is something going on that we're not being told about.' A thriller is based on the idea that a central character discovers that there really is a conspiracy underway, and it then explores the consequences of that discovery. To create a conspiracy for a story, it is useful to have an understanding of what conspiracy theories are, how they work, and why they seem to appeal to mass audiences.

To clarify the terminology used below, I should point out that a *conspirator* is someone who is actively involved in a conspiracy (a 'bad guy'), and a *conspiracist* is a person who believes that a conspiracy exists and regards themselves as one of the 'good guys'.

Conspiracy Theories

A *conspiracy theory* is a belief that some secret but influential organisation is responsible for an unexplained event. The term has come to be regarded as derogatory, with conspiracy theorists ridiculed as wearing tin-foil hats and seeing sinister groups as being responsible for every unexplained event or problem in the world. But, as Joseph Heller wrote in *Catch-22*, "Just because you're paranoid doesn't mean they aren't after you." Genuine conspiracies have had a huge impact on human history and will continue to do so.

And a conspiracy theory itself can be a conspiracy. As Chip Berlet writes in the *New Internationalist* article, 'Zog Ate My Brains,' "In the early 1900s, Czar Nicholas II's *Okhranka* (secret police) in Russia promoted a hoax document called the *Protocols of the Learned Elders of Zion* – claimed to be the minutes of a secret 'cabal' of Jews who manipulated world events through the Freemasons and other groups. The *Protocols* were translated into many languages and circulated around the world ... it was used to justify pogroms in Russia and the scapegoating and murder of Jews in Nazi Germany."

In his book *The United States of Paranoia*, Jesse Walker outlined five basic kinds of conspiracy theories:

- *The Enemy Outside* – based on devilish figures mobilizing outside the community and scheming against it.
- *The Enemy Within* – the conspirators lurking inside the nation, indistinguishable from ordinary citizens.
- *The Enemy Above* – powerful people manipulating the system for their own gain.
- *The Enemy Below* – the lower classes ready to break through their constraints and overturn the social order.
- *Benevolent Conspiracies* – 'angelic' forces that work behind the scenes to improve the world and help people.

As I mentioned earlier, in fiction the nature of the conspiracy often defines the sub-genre of the thriller. In real life and in fiction, a conspiracy tends to focus on a significant action, or a series of actions, relating to a particular area of human activity. Examples include:

Assassination. An assassination is a typically the murder of a powerful or influential person, motivated by political rather than personal or financial gain. The murder is planned by a group of people who seek to gain power or to influence the outcome of some situation in which they have a collective stake.

Ethnic, national or minority repression. Here one group seeks to dominate, enslave, supplant, or eradicate another. Including the communist versus imperialist conflict of the post-war period, as well as racist groups, and those who target and try to deny the human rights of minority groups such as homosexuals.

Financial or business conspiracy – corrupt bankers or corporate executives misuse their power to make profits unlawfully, at the expense of ordinary people.

Government conspiracy – politicians who have been 'democratically elected' to serve the people, pursue their own selfish ends at the expense of those who elected them. Watergate is perhaps the most famous example.

Religious or cultist conspiracies – closed religious communities who plan to eradicate one faith in favour of their own. Or religious leaders who, rather than being concerned with the spiritual well-being of their followers, seek instead to exploit them for gain, typically by brain-washing and leading them into closed communities, and inciting them to carry out harmful acts.

The UFO 'cover-up' conspiracy – aliens have contacted mankind, and this has been kept secret from the ordinary public. Usually a subcategory of the government / military conspiracy. Similar to the 'moon landing was faked' conspiracy.

Medical conspiracy – doctors who are meant to care for the health of the public, are exploiting or harming their patients in order to achieve some form of gain for themselves. May involve illegal medical experimentation or testing of drugs; sale of human organs; or others ways of profiting from harming others.

Legal conspiracy – the professionals who are meant to ensure that the legal system operates in a fair and honest manner, misuse their positions for personal or corporate gain, typically by ensuring that justice is *not* properly served.

In films and novels, the story centring on a conspiracy is usually presented as a morality play: evil people act in unethical and/or immoral ways, and virtuous people oppose them, seeking to prevent their conspiracy from succeeding.

The conspirators, the 'villains,' usually belong to one of the following categories:

A secret or ancient society. This includes groups such as Freemasons, Rosicrucians, and the Illuminati, as well as national or ethnic groups, religions and cults. The beliefs and values of the society are passed on from generation to generation and are given an aura of authenticity by being described as ancient or ancestral beliefs.

The society within a society. A hidden 'threat from within' can be much more disturbing than a visible external threat. America's communist 'witch-hunts' arose from just such a fear. Government, legal, and medical conspiracies are carried out by people within our own society: they prey upon ordinary people. In recent years, there has been much controversy surrounding agencies such as the CIA spying on ordinary people.

Criminal organisations. These can be a form of society within a society, but – in these days of multinational corporations – they can also be multinational crime syndicates. Part of the criminal conspiracy is that it involves people at the highest levels – politicians, businessmen, bankers, lawyers and judges, the police, and influential figures in the military and security agencies.

Betrayal of Trust

From all of this, it is clear that a conspiracy is based on a *betrayal of trust*. There are ethical codes that we expect people to respect – including those in medicine, business, law, democratic politics and others – but conspirators ignore, or even exploit, these codes. The villains in a conspiracy thriller believe themselves to be beyond the influence of such codes – while the heroes remain bound by them. The villains are interested only in achieving their goal – in succeeding in the conspiracy. The hero must act within, and seek to protect and reinforce, the moral behaviours that are approved by his society.

Typically, the villains are prepared to go to *any* lengths to achieve their aims. There is no line they will not cross. They will use terror, torture, and murder if it will further their cause. They will amass and utilise power – for them, there is no such thing as 'proportionate' use of force: they will employ whatever violence or weapons they have available.

It isn't possible to list all of the different types of actions conspirators might undertake, but here is a partial list as a starting point:

- assassination
- kidnapping
- attempted genocide
- experiments on human subjects
- blackmail
- planting incriminating 'evidence'
- illegal business or financial practices, including money laundering
- drug-trafficking
- slavery and people trafficking
- incitement to civil unrest or war
- contamination of food or water supplies
- counterfeiting
- impersonation of another person
- suicide bombing
- release of toxins or biological weapons
- obtaining military and defence secrets
- espionage
- obtaining blueprints for weapons, including nuclear devices
- obtaining details of codes or cyphers

The Appeal of Conspiracy Theories

Psychologists and sociologists have considered why conspiracy theories seem to have such a strong appeal. Writing in *The Sociological Review* (2013) about the political significance of anti-Semitic conspiracy theories, Türkay Salim

Nefes said: "Conspiracy theories explain power relations as being secretly manipulated by certain groups or individuals."

In his book *A Culture of Conspiracy,* Michael Barkun argued a similar point, writing that a conspiracy "...purports to locate and identify the true loci of power and thereby illuminate previously hidden decision making. The conspirators, often referred to as a shadow government, operate a concealed political system behind the visible one, whose functionaries are either cyphers or puppets."

In an interview with Chip Berlet for *New Internationalist Magazine,* Barkun explained the threefold appeal of conspiracy theories:

"First, conspiracy theories claim to explain what others can't. They appear to make sense out of a world that is otherwise confusing. Second, they do so in an appealingly simple way, by dividing the world sharply between the forces of light and the forces of darkness. They trace all evil back to a single source, the conspirators and their agents. Finally, conspiracy theories are often presented as special, secret knowledge unknown or unappreciated by others. For conspiracists, the masses are a brainwashed herd, while the conspiracists in the know can congratulate themselves on penetrating the plotters' deceptions."

Barkun also points out a key difference between a legitimate concern that a conspiracy exists and a conspiracy theory based on irrational beliefs or prejudices: "A sure sign that we have gone past the boundaries of rational criticism is the conspiracy theory that's non-falsifiable. Such a theory is a closed system of ideas which 'explains' contradictory evidence by claiming that the conspirators themselves planted it."

'Good' Conspiracy Theories versus 'Bad' Ones

While many conspiracy theories are harmless and are used as a sort of safety valve or coping mechanism, there are instances where a conspiracy theory can become dangerous. In an article about anti-Semitic conspiracy theories, 'Zog Ate My Brains,' Chip Berlet summarised the features of 'destructive conspiracy theories':

- *Dualistic division* – The world is divided into a good 'Us' and a bad 'Them'.
- *Demonizing rhetoric* – Our opponents are evil and subversive... maybe subhuman.
- *Targeting scapegoats* – 'They' are causing all our troubles – we are blameless.
- *Apocalyptic timetable* – Time is running out and we must act immediately to stave off a cataclysmic event.

Michael Barkun: "Conspiracism often gains a mass following in times of social, cultural, economic, or political stress. Immigration, demands for racial or gender equality, gay rights, power struggles between nations, and war can all be viewed through a conspiracist lens. Conspiracism started as a way to defend the status quo, but it spawned a flipside where the conspiracy is perceived as controlling the government."

The human mind has a need for understanding and is uncomfortable when explanations are not forthcoming. It likes to find patterns and connections, and seeks them even when events are random. One of the reasons conspiracy theories appeal to people is that they provide reassurance. They tell us that nothing happens by accident, that every effect has a cause, and that things are connected in some way.

A curious fact about conspiracies is that they tend to feed one another: people engaged in an anti-Semitic conspiracy, for example, often believe their actions are legitimate because they are responding to a conspiracy being masterminded by a secret Jewish cabal. It's easy to see how the whole cycle of conspiracy and counter-conspiracy can get out of control.

4 | Suspense

"There is no terror in the bang, only in the anticipation of it." – Alfred Hitchcock

We are watching a wildlife documentary. On the screen, a river has swollen into a raging torrent, and a herd of wildebeest are desperately trying to cross it. The animals swim against the current, struggling to keep their heads above water, and then when they reach the other side they have to clamber up a steep muddy bank. We see one wildebeest complete the crossing and start up the bank, but the reddish mud crumbles and the creature slips back down into the water. It is in danger of being swept away by the river, or of being trampled by other wildebeest desperate to make their own way up the muddy bank. The fallen wildebeest makes another attempt up the bank, reaching up with its forelegs, scrabbling for grip, hind legs pushing upwards – it seems to be making progress, but then a hind leg slips and it slides towards the water again.

To be continued...

For a few brief moments, we are engaged in the fate of that single wildebeest. We will it on, wanting to see it succeed in climbing the bank. The fate of the wildebeest is in the balance, and we are in a state of suspense until we learn its fate. The documentary may have been filmed months or even years ago, but whilst those images are on the screen, that struggle is happening now, and we have an emotional interest in its outcome. I have deliberately chosen this example of a nameless, genderless wildebeest, and I have been careful not to anthropomorphise it in any way. I will explain why later.

I want to introduce another example before we move on to the theory and mechanics of creating suspense in stories. This one is from the Alfred Hitchcock movie *Strangers on a Train,* and it occurs near the end. The villain, played by Robert Walker, is on his way to frame the hero: he will do this by planting the hero's monogrammed cigarette lighter at the scene of a murder. As he heads for the scene, the villain accidentally drops the lighter down a drain. He pushes his hand through the grate, fingers tantalisingly close to the lighter, not quite able to reach it... Here's the thing: the character we are watching on screen at this moment is the *villain*, a person we *do not like*. He intends to harm the hero, a character that we *do* like. But as he's reaching down, trying to retrieve the incriminating lighter, we experience suspense on two levels. One, we don't want him to reach it, because it will mean curtains for the hero. But two, as his fingers brush the lighter, we are willing him to succeed in retrieving it. We want to see him succeed in the goal he has set himself, in the same way that we would want to succeed if we had dropped one of our own possessions down a drain, even though the consequences of success will mean harm to our hero.

I will come back to these two examples later because I think they demonstrate something about suspense that is often overlooked.

What is Suspense?

"Suspense is the art of making the reader care what happens next." – Marie F. Rodell

We experience suspense when we anticipate the outcome of a situation or event. The outcome may be a pleasant one that we desire and hope for, or it may be an unpleasant one that we dread or fear. And this outcome may be known – we sit in the dentist's office awaiting an experience that we know will be uncomfortable – or the outcome may be uncertain: we wait for the results of a medical test, hoping that they will reveal nothing serious is wrong with us, but fearing that they might.

In any story or film, suspense exists in two areas: there is the suspense that the characters in the story feel as they anticipate the forthcoming outcome of an event; and there is the suspense that the story evokes in the reader or viewer, which is not experienced by the characters.

Anticipation and Dread

Hans J. Wulff writes that the "... experience of suspense essentially lies in equally calculating, expecting, and evaluating a coming event. I want to call this activity *anticipation*." Anticipation, Wulff says, is dependent upon four factors:

i. when information is given it should be regarded as the starting point for future developments
ii. the reader should be able to draw up a scenario of what could happen, based on what the story tells them and what they themselves bring from outside the text
iii. the future situations in the plot are a collection of alternative possibilities which are more or less probable – and it is in the act of anticipation that the degree of probability of a particular outcome is calculated
iv. the reader can evaluate the individual possibilities and come up with ways in which the protagonist might counteract them

We will look at each of these under the headings foreshadowing, audience expectations, danger zone, and reader participation.

Foreshadowing

Wulff writes of the importance of "references to future developments in the plot," which provide the "material from which viewers can extrapolate future developments." He refers to Seymour Chatman's work on foreshadowing in narrative structure. Chatman said that there are key scenes that propel the narrative forward, and there are scenes that prepare the way for these key scenes. Wulff says that these preparation scenes "... can be removed from a narrative without it suffering any major damage – although the text would lose any suspense it had." The preparation scenes have the function of influencing the reader's anticipation of what could happen in the story. They help shape the reader's expectations. Often these scenes 'set-up' an expectation, but the reader's desire to see the action completed in the form of an outcome is not fulfilled: instead, the scene points to an outcome that is delayed until some future point. The reader's expectation is not always fulfilled – the anticipated event may not occur, or the situation may play out in some other way. Preparation scenes open up a number of future possibilities, promising either a happy or unhappy outcome for the character involved in the situation. Future scenes may expand or reduce the possible outcomes, and new information may cause the reader to re-shape the possible trajectories they believe the story might take. These scenes try to control and guide the reader's expectations of what might happen.

Audience Expectations
A lifetime of reading, movie-going, and television viewing means that most people today are 'story literate.' They know the 'rules' of storytelling and the 'laws' or particular genres. When they read a story or watch a movie, one of the things they bring from outside the text is their knowledge of 'the way stories work.' This experience helps them to piece together possible future events in a story based on the clues the writer has placed in the text. Terry Pratchett had fun with one of these story expectations – the 'million-to-one chance that just might work.' He noted that it had become such a cliché in storytelling, that a million-to-one chance was almost a certainty, and he proceeded on that basis.

Bans or interdictions work in the same way: if someone in a story is forbidden to do something, it is almost certain that they will do it. This is such a common story event, as M. Lüthi has pointed out, that the ban actually creates an expectation that the banned action will occur. And the transgression itself also has anticipated consequences.

Audiences also have expectations when it comes to 'planting' within a story. In writing, we refer to the 'rule' of Chekhov's Gun. In 1889 playwright Anton Chekhov said in a letter: "One must not put a loaded rifle on the stage if no one is thinking of firing it." This is a specific example of the unwritten rule that in writing, we don't waste words – anything that is written about must have significance in the story. And this is something else that the story-savvy reader is aware of. If they see an object, piece of information, or skill 'planted' early in the story, they know it will 'pay off' later. The same is true if specific features of a landscape or setting are drawn to the reader's attention. Our story-literate reader will also be aware that weapons and tools can be fashioned from certain things available in a setting or environment. Most of us couldn't wire a plug if someone offered us fifty bucks to do it, but we know that MacGyver or The A-Team could do something with a couple of rusty oil drums and a bag of M&Ms. And we use that story experience when we anticipate what could happen in a story, because we expect our heroes to be adaptable and ingenious. Sometimes writers have to counteract these expectations by making the hero a nebbish who couldn't possibly fashion a weapon from whatever he found under the kitchen sink.

Wulff also notes that the 'moral virtue' that the thematic argument promotes is understood by the reader, such that the reader can anticipate poetic justice being served on anyone – whether a protagonist or an antagonist – whose actions are seen as 'immoral.'

Danger Zone

Hans J. Wulff says that one of the functions of preparation scenes is to allow the reader to see the possible catastrophic outcome of a dangerous situation, but that it is not necessary for the outcome that is hinted at to actually occur. He quotes a much-used example: "... the protagonist is hanging from a rope which is scraping against a cliff edge and could snap. The rope often doesn't snap, but that is not what it is about. The important thing is that viewers can visualise the possibility of an unhappy course of events." Dangers are introduced as possibilities, and the reader is left to consider the probabilities of the range of possible outcomes. The writer will try and guide the reader into believing that some possibilities are more likely to occur than others. And this 'guidance' is likely to be an act of misdirection. As we will see, stories generally try to make the reader believe that a desired/happy outcome is unlikely and that a feared/unhappy outcome is highly likely.

Reader Participation

Readers do not like to be told what to think – they want writers to present them with the evidence so that they can make up their own minds. We need to allow our readers to make their own contribution to the story. This observation is also relevant to our present topic. Readers do not want to be shown the danger that will face the protagonist, they want to receive bits of information that they can piece together in order to come up with their own predictions about the dangers he faces. Hans J. Wulff writes: "The more indirect a depiction is, the more viewer activity is drawn to it and the greater the increase in the experienced involvement." He has also said: "It is not what the film shows, but what it discloses, that is the subject of the analysis of suspense."

Defining Suspense

It has been said that suspense is a combination of intellectual, emotional, and physical anticipation. It occurs because we need to be ready to respond to a situation that we find ourselves in. Suspense evolved as a survival mechanism, a way of successfully dealing with risk. Mentally we try and predict what will happen so that we are prepared with an appropriate reaction – which might be withdrawal, moving forward to attack or defend, or moving toward to embrace or to offer support. There is evidence that the suspense we experience as a result of fictional stories and films, operates according to the same psychological processes as that we experience in real life situations. Stories evoke the same preparedness for action as an actual event.

The terms *suspense* and *tension* are often used interchangeably – we say that a scene in a story is suspenseful, or that the middle part of a story requires 'rising tension.' To *suspend* is to hang something, either from a single point – from a hook in the ceiling, for example – or between two points, as in a suspension bridge. Or it can mean to temporarily halt something. *Tension* means to stretch. When we think of events, both terms imply a time element – a stretching out or pause before the outcome of a situation comes about. There is a period in which we are, to greater or lesser extent, helpless: we can only wait to see how things turn out.

In their paper on the psychology of tension and suspense, Moritz Lehne and Stefan Koelsch define tension and suspense as "... affective [emotional] states that (a) are associated with conflict, dissonance, instability, or uncertainty, (b) create a yearning for resolution, (c) concern events of potential emotional significance, and (d) build on future-directed processes of expectation, anticipation, and prediction." I think this definition is helpful, as it gives us four specific areas to explore (a to d), but is also sufficiently broad as to cover different types of suspense or 'tension phenomena.' Lehne and Koelsch also note that "... tension phenomena usually require time to unfold and thus predominantly reflect time-dependent aspects of affective experience..." For them, suspense and tension are closely related, where "suspense usually involves the anticipation of two clearly opposed outcomes," i.e. the hero destroys the villain or the villain destroys the hero, whereas "tension often denotes a more diffuse state of anticipation, in which anticipated events are less specific."

Moritz Lehne and Stefan Koelsch also write that the 'future-directed processes' of expectation, prediction, and anticipation are important underlying components of tension and suspense. Expectation refers to a specific event that is expected to happen. Anticipation relates to expecting 'something' to happen, without being sure exactly what. And prediction is about trying to evaluate all possible outcomes and, perhaps, settle on the most likely. Prediction is usually regarded as being an intellectual activity, a reasoning process that attempts to discover the likely outcome of a situation. Expectation and anticipation have an emotional component as well as an intellectual one, in that they may relate to outcomes that are either hoped for or feared.

An interesting aside from Lehne and Koelsch: "Being related to both predictive processes and emotion, tension phenomena could provide the 'missing link' that may help bridge the gap between the 'cold' cognitive processes on the one hand and the 'hot' processes of emotion on the other hand."

In their 2014 paper, Brian O'Neill and Mark Riedl write: "Suspense is an affective response, akin to anxiety, that humans frequently feel when being told a story. Expert storytellers who craft narratives for entertainment – films, novels, games, etc. – often structure their narratives to evoke strong affective responses."

Some writers have argued that suspense is dependent on *uncertainty,* that the outcome of the waiting event cannot be known in advance. But clearly this is not true in all situations – someone awaiting the attentions of the dentist or the hangman is in little doubt about what will happen (though in both cases the victim might hope for a reprieve). All that suspense really requires is an unresolved situation, where there is something at stake, and where there is a delay before the outcome of the situation comes about. Suspense is created in the way that the situation is created, not in the uncertainty of the outcome. It is quite possible to experience suspense where the outcome of a situation is known, which is why we are able to enjoy viewing a suspenseful thriller or horror movie more than once.

There are, of course, some suspenseful situations which cannot be repeated. One example is that of the lottery ticket holder who sits waiting for the numbers to be drawn. Once they know that they do or do not hold a winning ticket, the suspense is over and cannot be re-experienced. Re-watching the draw cannot be suspenseful as there is nothing important at stake. Stories – on the page and on the screen – are different in that they draw us in. We become 'lost' in a story, entering an almost hypnotic dream-like state. This is what allows us to 'suspend disbelief' concerning the events of the story, and also enables us to experience the story as it unfolds – in what passes for 'real time' – without looking too far ahead. Even if we have never seen a movie before, we can be fairly certain that the hero played by the big name star is not going to suffer a tragic and depressing fate – at least not in a popular genre movie. As in life, it is not the ultimate destination that matters so much as the journey we experience before we get there. Stories are only one example of an activity where we become 'lost in the moment,' there are many activities – such as driving, sports, or creative pastimes – where we become indifferent to the passing of time. Mihaly Csikszentmihalyi explores this in his book *Flow: The Psychology of Optimal Experience*.

When we consider how stories work, we must remember that reading a story (or watching a movie) is a *subjective* experience and not an objective one. For the duration of the story, if it is a good one, we are 'in' the story, not watching it from outside or from above. It may be too much of a stretch to say that we *become* the hero, but we are certainly standing at his shoulder. As writers, our goal is to craft story situations in which our readers will become lost. The use of cause and effect is one important tool for this, and creating suspense is another, and as we will see, the two are closely related.

How is Suspense Created?

There is no standard definition of suspense, but if we look at studies of suspense in the fields of psychology, narratology, and entertainment theory, we can identify a number of elements that are worth exploring:

1. An unresolved situation and a desire for closure
2. Uncertainty of outcome and paired positive/negative outcomes
3. Probability – a probable negative outcome and/or an improbably positive outcome
4. Delayed outcome
5. Affinity for the protagonist
6. Disparity of knowledge between the protagonist and the reader (dramatic irony)
7. Helplessness
8. High stakes

We will explore each of these in turn.

(1) Unresolved Situations

As human beings, we tend to feel uncomfortable when the equilibrium of our everyday world is upset. A new or changed situation is viewed as potentially threatening, and it puts us on our guard until such time as we know whether something is dangerous or not. This is probably related to an old survival mechanism: Is this thing approaching us food or threat? Individually, we respond to disruptive events with different levels of anxiety, and different people regard different situations as triggers for tension. Phobias relate to a specific object or situation, for example, and sufferers seek to avoid the trigger. Some people – we refer to them as 'thrill seekers' or 'adventurers' or even 'adrenaline junkies' – actively seek out new and challenging situations which will stimulate the 'thrill' emotions. These differences are the reason why, as writers, we ask ourselves: Why does this situation develop into a crisis for this particular character?

Moritz Lehne and Stefan Koelsch have said that events that disturb our equilibrium are usually associated with *conflict, dissonance,* or *instability*. When we encounter such an event, either in real life or in a story, it creates in us a yearning to return to a stable state. We seek some form of closure. In other words, we want the disturbing event to end, and we want to know how things turn out.

Conflict

If the audience sees, or is told, that someone wants to achieve something, then we have created a situation that requires resolution. The viewer will ask: Does the character achieve his goal? We then introduce physical obstacles and opponents, and so increase the odds against the character's success. The audience now asks: Can the character succeed when faced with this level of opposition? Throughout the story, we can use conflict to create suspense. Can the hero avoid capture by the villain? We increase tension by bringing the hero and villain closer and closer together until capture seems inevitable. And then, if the hero is captured, we ask: Can he escape? Or if the hero must fight an opponent, we ask: Can he win?

Conflict does not necessarily require physical action: it can just as easily be someone trying to change another person's mind. Conflict delays or prevents closure, and can therefore create and heighten suspense. The greater the opposition the protagonist faces, the greater the potential for suspense.

Dissonance

Leon Festinger's *A Theory of Cognitive Dissonance* was published in 1957 and is interesting – especially for writers – because it provides explanations for the seemingly inconsistent behaviours people sometimes engage in. His theory was that human beings want all of their 'cognitions' – opinions, attitudes, knowledge, and values – to be consistent. Dissonance occurs when there is conflict between two of these elements, or when a person's behaviour is in contradiction to their cognition. For example, a person smokes (behaviour) but they know that smoking causes health problems (cognition).

Dissonance is a feeling of discomfort or mental stress, and causes people to try and restore their inner balance. Something must change to eliminate the dissonance. This can be achieved in one of four ways:

(i) Change of cognition (opinion, attitude, knowledge, or value) or behaviour. This can be extremely difficult, as deeply held beliefs and long-term behaviours – such as smoking – cannot be changed quickly.
(ii) Gain of new information to support existing cognitions or behaviours. For example, seeking out data on long-term smokers who have lived into old age with no health problems.
(iii) Decrease the importance of elements causing dissonance. This might include *justifying* existing behaviour – e.g. believing that enjoying life in the moment is more important than long-term health risks from smoking.
(iv) Ignoring or denying the conflicting cognition – which may include seeking out others who also deny or reject the cognition, and trying to persuade others to do so. People who deny the reality of global warming are an example.

Research into cognitive dissonance has produced interesting information in three areas:

Decision-Making. When we make a decision between two alternatives – choosing between two models of new car, for example – we often suffer from dissonance, fearing that we've made the wrong choice. The decision was not clear-cut: the model we chose has some negative characteristics, and the model we rejected has some positive characteristics. This type of dissonance is sometimes called 'buyer's remorse.' We may try to overcome it by trying to convince ourselves – and others – of the superiority of our chosen model, and of the inferiority of the model we rejected. We try and increase the attractiveness of our new car.

Effort. If we put a lot of effort into something, and the outcome is disappointing, we experience dissonance because we believe that hard work usually pays off. We try to overcome this by trying to convince ourselves and others of the value of the outcome. We try to justify our effort by exaggerating the desirability of what we have achieved. Alternatively, we may try and downplay the actual effort that was expended.

Forced Compliance. If we are persuaded (by reward) or coerced (by threat of punishment) into doing something that we do not want to do, or which is not in accordance with our values or beliefs, we experience dissonance. We gain something – a reward or avoidance of punishment – but we feel uncomfortable. We may try to overcome this feeling by emphasising the value of what was gained, or by arguing that we were placed in a situation where we 'had no choice.'

Festinger also highlights other situations which cause dissonance:

Expression of disagreement in a group. If someone who is a member of our group, and who is like us and has much in common with us, we will experience dissonance if that person expresses an opinion that is contrary to our own. This can cause splintering of the group, with people taking different sides, or it may cause the group to turn on the dissenter. Or the group might be persuaded by his argument and all side against us. Deciding that someone is not like us after all is one way of dealing with this dissonance.

Exposure to new information. We may have new information forced upon us, or come across it accidentally, and find that it conflicts with what we already know or believe. This creates dissonance that we will try to overcome using one of the four usual methods.

Change of group belief. Dissonance can occur in a large group in the same way that it can occur in an individual. An event may occur which is so compelling as to produce an alteration in the beliefs of everyone. Or it may produce dissonance such that the group decides to engage in wholesale denial or justification behaviours.

Dissonance, like conflict, is an unresolved situation that we would like to see resolved. It is a form of internal cognitive conflict and can be used to create and increase feelings of tension in a similar way.

Instability
We have already said that human beings prefer to exist, for the most part, in a state of equilibrium, and that when the stability of our lives is upset, we desire to return to stability. If we accept that equilibrium is our normal state, then upsetting this creates a situation that is in need of resolution. We see a return to stability as a desirable form of closure. In a story, we upset the equilibrium of our hero's life with an inciting incident – the challenge or 'call to adventure' in Act I – and he is not returned to a stable state until after the climax in Act III. Story situations are inherently unstable and are designed to keep the hero – and the reader – looking forward to a resolution where stability can be regained. Change, we said earlier, is upsetting because it brings with it the potential for danger. An unstable situation is one that is in a constant state of change or one where change can occur at any time without warning. They make prediction of what will happen next almost impossible and mean that nothing and no-one can be relied or depended upon.

(2) Uncertainty of Outcome
When you have been for a job interview, you sit and wait for the 'phone call or the letter, not knowing whether you have been successful in securing the new position. You remain in a state of suspense. There are two possible outcomes, a positive one and a negative one. This type of uncertainty – where the outcome could go either way – is typical of the sort of thing faced by story heroes, to the extent that some theorists believe that uncertainty of outcome is the *only* definition of what suspense is and requires.

Ortony, Clore, and Collins proposed a theory of suspense that is referred to as the 'standard account' by Aaron Smuts: "The standard account holds that suspense is composed of three things: fear, hope, and the 'cognitive state of uncertainty.' Ortony, Clore, and Collins define 'fear' as a feeling of displeasure about the prospect of an undesirable event, and 'hope' as a feeling of pleasure about the prospect of a desirable event. On the standard account, people feel suspense when they fear a bad outcome, hope for a good outcome, and are uncertain about which outcome will come to pass … This account of suspense sounds plausible, but by overemphasizing the role of uncertainty, the standard view runs straight into a problem known as the paradox of suspense."

The Paradox of Suspense
The 'paradox of suspense' can be summarised in three statements:
  i. Suspense requires uncertainty of outcome.
  ii. A repeat viewer or reader knows a story's outcome, so cannot experience uncertainty.
  iii. Repeat viewers or readers do experience suspense.

Individually, each of these statements could be true, but collectively they contain a contradiction. Various attempts have been made to resolve this paradox, the resolutions each showing which of the three statements must be false.

Kendall Walton argues that when viewing a film or reading a text for the second time, we must *imagine* that we do not know the outcome in order to be able to experience suspense. In other words, we behave as if we are uncertain of a story's outcome. Richard J. Gerrig (1993), on the other hand, believes that our brains are used to dealing with unique, non-repeatable experiences, and so treat a repeat reading or viewing as a new experience. This being the case, even a repeat reader or viewer can be said to be uncertain of a story's outcome. Harold Skulsky says that suspense does *not* require uncertainty, but is dependent on the reader or viewer's sympathy for the hero. Robert J. Yanal says that repeat viewers or readers do not experience suspense but rather apprehensiveness about what they know is coming. True suspense is not a repeatable experience. He makes it clear that he is referring to what he calls 'true repeaters,' who retain knowledge of the story, rather than casual repeaters who may forget many of the details of a story, even its eventual outcome. Yanal, referring to an example from Gerrig, also points out that in re-reading or re-watching a story, we may *wish* to see a different outcome than the one we know is coming, but this is not the same as being uncertain about what is going to happen.

While each of these theories has merit, and each is partially correct, none of them completely resolves the paradox. I believe that the problem here is that the first statement about suspense requiring uncertainty is incorrect, or at least incomplete, and that Lehne and Koelsch are correct when they say that suspense arises from situations related to *conflict, dissonance, instability,* or *uncertainty*. If uncertainty is removed, suspense can still arise as a result of one or more of the other three – we still have a desire to see the situation resolved so that we can experience closure. At the same time, I think Christy Mag Uidhir and Robert J. Yanal are correct when they say that what repeat readers or viewers experience is a different kind of suspense than that experienced when they read or viewed the story for the first time.

Linked to uncertainty of outcome is the *probability* of possible outcomes.

(3) Probability of Outcomes

We've said that suspense can be created when there is uncertainty about the outcome of an event or situation and that in any given situation there can be a 'positive' outcome and a 'negative' one. There are two main theories regarding what makes a positive or negative outcome. Noel Carroll believes that positive outcomes are 'moral' and that negative ones are 'evil.' Aaron Smuts, on the other hand, writes that the positive outcome is 'desired' and that the negative outcome is undesired. According to Smuts, suspense arises when an attempt to achieve a desired goal is frustrated – he calls this the *desire-frustration* theory.

Generally speaking, when it comes to genre stories, the outcome that is desired by the protagonist is the one which the audience will also regard as 'moral' – they will approve of what the hero is trying to achieve. One of the ways we create affinity for the hero (see below) is to give him a desire – a goal – of which the audience can approve. As far as creating suspense is concerned – and to avoid complicating our discussions here – we will assume that the hero has chosen the correct/moral goal and that the desired outcome and the moral outcome are essentially the same thing. (In many stories, particularly ones which involve character development, we see the hero initially choose a 'wrong' goal, and in an ironic twist we see that failure to achieve the goal is a positive outcome – or, perhaps, that success in achieving the wrong goal leads to negative, even tragic, consequences.)

Noel Carroll writes that suspense "... arises when a well-structured question – with neatly opposed alternatives – emerges from the narrative and calls forth an answering scene." As an example, he gives an old silent movie cliché: The heroine is tied to the railroad tracks; the locomotive is steaming towards her; will she be rescued or squished? Carroll agrees that there must be "something desired at stake," and that "whatever is at stake has some psychological urgency partly because the outcome is uncertain." He argues that – in the case of film – 'desirability' can be narrowed down to an outcome "... which is morally correct in terms of the values inherent in the film," and that 'uncertainty' can be narrowed down to improbability. He then says that the possible outcomes of a story situation can be classified as follows:

(i) moral and likely
(ii) evil and likely
(iii) moral but unlikely
(iv) evil but unlikely

Suspense, according to Carroll, is created in a story when the alternative outcomes have the qualities of (ii), evil and likely, and (iii), moral but unlikely. The two possible outcomes of a story situation should be *morally correct but un-*

likely and *evil and likely*. Audiences love to root for a protagonist who is an underdog – so as writers we create powerful antagonists who seem sure to win and a protagonist who is outgunned and seems unlikely to succeed.

From their own experiments, Paul Comisky and Jennings Bryant concluded: "Rated suspense was at a maximum when the hero's chances of success/survival were perceived to be about one in 100 and minimal when either success or failure seemed absolutely certain."

In order to create suspense, stories generally focus on the probability of negative outcomes and the improbability of positive ones. We stack the odds against the hero. Dolf Zillmann (1980) notes that the attainment of positive incentives, such as money, glory, and privileges, is "secondary to the creation of apprehensions" about negative outcomes, such as death, mutilation, torture, injury, and social debasement. He writes, "Suspenseful drama features such events as bombs about to explode, dams about to burst, ceilings about to cave in, fires about to rage, ocean liners about to sink, and earthquakes about to rampage. It features people about to be jumped and stabbed, about to walk into an ambush and get shot, and about to be bitten by snakes, tarantulas, and mad dogs. The common denominator in all of this is the likely suffering of the protagonists. It is impending disaster, manifest in anticipated agony, pain, injury, and death. Suspenseful drama, then, appears to thrive on uneasiness and distress about anticipated negative outcomes. In short, it thrives on fear."

Noel Carroll writes that he considers "... things like time-bombs as part of the probability structure of a suspense sequence; each tick make it more likely that an evil will occur." He also believes that *probability* is more important in generating suspense than simply *delaying* the outcome of a situation. Delay on its own is not sufficient for suspense. Addition of something that alters the probability of an outcome has the additional effect of forestalling the outcome, but this is an accidental rather than fundamental purpose of such an event. For example, "... the raised drawbridge that stalls the rescuer, something that one might want to say 'delays' the final outcome of the narrative, but which – more significantly – makes the rescue less likely."

According to Noel Carroll's model, we need to:

a) pose a question that has opposing answers
b) provide morality ratings for the two answers – i.e. which is good and which is evil
c) demonstrate the relative probability ratings of each, such that the evil outcome seems likely to occur and the good outcome seems unlikely.

If the hero faces *almost* overwhelming odds, the suspense will be greater than if he is involved in an even match with the antagonist. However, if the audience becomes *certain* that the hero will fail, then their feelings of suspense disappear, being replaced by disappointment and sadness. Zillmann writes that "... there is reason to believe that the onlooker's certainty about a forthcoming deplorable event will serve a preparatory appraisal function which protects him or her against overly intense noxious arousal in response to the depiction of the event once it materializes." Faced with a tragedy, we will seek to minimise the emotional impact. In other words, to create and sustain suspense, no matter how bad we make things for the hero, there must always remain a glimmer of hope.

(4) Delayed Outcome

Robert J. Yanal writes: "A narrative lays out over time (not all at once) a sequence of events, and because the events of a narrative are not completely told all at once, questions arise for the audience which will be answered only later in the narrative's telling." Suspense, by definition, relies on a time delay between a situation being set-up and the revelation of the outcome of the situation. We prolong the period of uncertainty, milking it for all it is worth. This occurs at different levels within a story. At the macro or overall plot level, a 'story question' is asked in Act I – 'Will the hero succeed? – and this is not answered until the climax in Act III. On the next level down, we have suspense within scenes and sequences of scenes. A scene has a similar sequence of set-up, suspense, outcome: there is a character who is trying to achieve a scene goal; he or she takes action in order to achieve it; they face obstacles or opposition, resulting in conflict; each action or beat within the scene can have a positive or negative outcome, and so we have suspense on the micro level.

A thriller requires lots of suspense at both macro and micro levels. Noel Carroll says that an entire film may be regarded as suspenseful – or as a 'suspense film' – if:

(i) its macro-question (or questions) have a suspenseful structure
(ii) it is made up of a large number of suspenseful scenes or sequences of scenes; or
(iii) its final or climactic scene or sequence involves suspense

Suspense can be heightened when we 'stretch out time' by having two scenes occur at the same time and we cut between them so that the outcome of each is delayed. We should also note here Noel Carroll's comments, under *(3) Probability of Outcome*, that making a desired outcome seem less likely is probably more important in creating suspense than simply delaying the outcome.

(5) Affinity for the Protagonist

If we look back at the two examples I used at the beginning of this chapter, we can see that the audience doesn't need to know much about the protagonist – an anonymous wildebeest – or to have any particular sympathy with his intentions – the villain who tries to retrieve the cigarette lighter. Suspense requires only that we witness an event where the outcome is not achieved immediately and where there is something at stake (more on this below) – but it requires very little else, at least in a short narrative or a section of a longer one. However, in a full-length novel or movie, we need to sustain and increase suspense over a much longer period. One way to do this, promoted by Harold Skulsky and experimentally confirmed by Paul Comisky and Jennings Bryant, is to make the audience *care* about the protagonist.

We feel more intensely if we see trouble befall someone we know than if we see it happen to a stranger. And, generally speaking, we are more likely to feel a connection with someone who is like us – in appearance and beliefs – than someone who is obviously different. The same holds true for the people in stories. As writers, we need to make our readers feel that they know our hero – that they have some form of connection with him. Alfred Hitchcock once said: "I try to put in my films ... what Poe put in his stories: a perfectly unbelievable story recounted to readers with such a hallucinatory logic that one has the impression that this same story can happen to you tomorrow. And that's the rule of the game if one wants the reader or the spectator to subconsciously substitute himself for the hero, because, in truth, people are only interested in themselves or in stories which could affect them."

Sympathy or Empathy?
Definitions first – what is the difference between sympathy and empathy? *Sympathy* is to feel sorry for someone who is unhappy or in difficulty. *Empathy* is the ability to understand and *share* the feelings of another person. It is an important distinction. Sympathy involves seeing what is happening to someone else and having our own emotional reaction to what we see. We may feel angry because someone has suffered an injustice, or we may weep when someone suffers a tragedy. But the sufferer may not be feeling anger or they may not themselves be crying. Empathy, on the other hand, requires us to share the *same* emotional experience as the person on the screen or in the story. Empathy involves us being able to put ourselves in the same situation as the story character and feel what they are feeling.

It has been argued that an audience does not want to see a character have an emotional experience, they want to have the experience themselves. Therefore, we should not show a character weeping, we should make the audience weep by showing a character who suffers and steadfastly refuses to weep. There is another argument that says a writer must create empathy between reader and protagonist – that the reader should experience emotion vicariously through the character. We should ensure that the reader can 'identify with' our character. Dolf Zillmann (1980) believes that empathy is not required and that we can create effective, suspenseful drama if the reader experiences "... the affective reaction of a concerned 'third party' who vehemently deplores impending outcomes." He says that vicarious feelings are not necessary, and "... may in fact be counterproductive." Noel Carroll writes, "... I have studiously avoided any reference to the concept of identification ... I do not believe that we need as elaborate a piece of psychological machinery as identification to account for audience responses to suspense scenes. The idea of moral allegiance will do our work for us ... In film, I contend that what is generally called identification is best explained in terms of an audience's allegiance to a given character on the ground that character exemplifies personal values that the audience has a pro-attitude toward."

I think they are both right, especially when it comes to the suspense thriller. This type of story requires – at least in part – that the reader engage in objective consideration of possible alternative outcomes. We need the reader to be able to judge the protagonist's actions: has he chosen the correct action? And, as we will see below, we often create suspense by giving the reader information that the protagonist does not have. This approach doesn't work if we try and get the reader to put himself 'into' the story in place of the hero. Rather, we need the reader to be there as a sympathetic observer – someone who cares what happens to the hero.

(6) Disparity of Knowledge – Dramatic Irony

Alfred Hitchcock: "... *suspense* consists of inciting a breathless curiosity and in establishing a complicity between the director and the spectator, who knows what is going to happen." Hitchcock, regarded by many as the 'Master of Suspense,' believed that the most effective way to create suspense is by forewarning the audience – by letting them know what is going to happen. "As far as I am concerned," he said, "you have suspense when you let the audience play god."

Hitchcock's most famous and most-quoted example is the 'bomb under the table' example. Here is one of the versions he gave in an American Film Institute Master Seminar – the video clip is available on YouTube:

"Four people are sitting around a table talking about baseball or whatever you like. Five minutes of it. Very dull. Suddenly, a bomb goes off. Blows the people to smithereens. What does the audience have? Ten seconds of shock. Now take the same scene and tell the audience there is a bomb under that table and will go off in five minutes. The whole emotion of the audience is totally different because you've given them that information. In five minutes' time that bomb will go off. Now the conversation about baseball becomes very vital. Because they're saying to you, 'Don't be ridiculous. Stop talking about baseball. There's a bomb under there.' You've got the audience working."

The technique Hitchcock is describing is *dramatic irony*. Dramatic irony occurs when a reader or audience knows or understands something that one or more characters in the story does not know or understand. This is also referred to has putting the audience in a 'superior position' or 'audience omniscience.' Having gained this knowledge or understanding, the dialogue and actions of the characters take on a different meaning for the audience – one that can be the direct opposite of the meaning understood by the characters.

If the audience knows something that a hero doesn't, we have created a situation that requires closure. The audience is wondering *if* the character will find out; they wonder *when* he will find out; they wonder what might happen if he *doesn't* find out; and they wonder what will happen if he *does* find out. All of these things can create or enhance suspense in a scene. Shakespeare often uses dramatic irony – in *Othello,* for example, he has Othello telling Iago how much he trusts his good friend when the audience already knows that Iago is plotting Othello's downfall. A similar speech occurs in *Macbeth* when Duncan says he trusts Macbeth, while we know the latter is planning Duncan's murder.

When characters talk at cross-purposes – often to create humour – the dialogue is based on the fact that one character lacks knowledge or understanding that the audience (and perhaps other characters) already have. An example that is sometimes used in films is when a character is being questioned about a crime (or perhaps about a 'sexual indiscretion'), but thinks he is being asked about something else. *There's Something About Mary* has a scene where the character Ted is being questioned by police about a murder, but he thinks he is being asked about picking up a hitch-hiker. Suspense and humour arise when he says things like 'it's no big deal' and 'I've done it several times before.' Misunderstandings and mistaken identity are other situations that rely on this effect.

Alfred Hitchcock, in a number of interviews, argued that suspense was much more valuable in storytelling than shock or terror. "Suspense is more enjoyable than terror, actually, because it is a continuing experience and attains a peak crescendo fashion; while terror, to be truly effective, must come all at once, like a bolt of lightning, and is more difficult, therefore, to savour." He also said that there was a 'rule' for creating them: "terror by surprise, suspense by forewarning." Best practice in choosing between the two, he said, "...is to play most of the situations for suspense and a few for terror."

When the audience knows something that a character doesn't, and they can see a negative outcome resulting from the character's lack of this knowledge, we feel a desire to help the character. This arises from our ability to empathise and the sympathise – if we can stop someone from having to suffer, we feel that we should. But when we are reading or watching a movie, there is actually nothing that we can do. Our desire to help is frustrated. We are helpless spectators.

(7) Helplessness

Alfred Hitchcock: "The audience is longing to warn the characters on the screen: 'You shouldn't be talking about such trivial matters. There's a bomb beneath you and it's about to explode!'" Moritz Lehne and Stefan Koelsch write that a lack of control, or an inability to influence the course of events, contributes to feelings of suspense. During the waiting period before the outcome of a situation is revealed, the protagonist and the reader is effectively helpless: all they can do is wait. Any action that the protagonist can, or does, take will not influence the course of events.

Wanting to be able to act in order to determine the outcome of a situation is a normal human feeling; being unable to act makes us feel uncomfortable, as we prefer to believe that we can influence our own destinies. Being made to feel helpless is another way of upsetting our equilibrium. Again this may be related to a survival mechanism – suspense keeps us poised and ready to act when the outcome of the situation comes about; being unable to act makes us uncomfortable as it means we can't help someone (the character) that we care about. Here again we must separate the feelings of the story protagonist from those of the reader. Our hero may be frustrated because he is unable to do anything to influence the outcome of his present situation. As readers we are spectators, and so are never able to actually do anything that will affect the story. Our helplessness is even greater. We may wish the hero to take a specific action, but we can do nothing to make this happen.

Skilful storytellers increase our discomfort – and our suspense – by allowing us to become aware of potential threats that the hero remains unaware of. We cannot stop him walking into danger or warn him, and must watch helplessly and wonder what will happen, and try and predict what he will do when he discovers what we already know. This helplessness on the part of the reader may also account, in part, for the fact that we can experience suspense even when we have seen a film or read a story before. We know what happens and can only see the hero make the same moves again. Suspense situations create a strong desire to take action but prevent us from being able to do so.

Aaron Smuts refers to this as the *desire-frustration* theory: "Rather than fear, hope, and uncertainty, the desire-frustration theory holds that suspense results from the frustration of a strong desire to affect the outcome of an imminent event." He quotes Hitchcock's 'bomb under the table' as an example of the audience being given information that the characters do not have and says that the frustration of desire, the suspense, is felt by the *audience,* not the characters. "We feel suspense not simply because we know something that could potentially save the life of a character, but because no matter how strongly we desire to help, we cannot do anything with our knowledge." He continues: "Suspense only arises when our ability to make a difference is radically diminished. Suspenseful situations are those where we want to affect an outcome – that is, where we strongly desire to have a causal impact – but our desire is frustrated." Smuts also highlights the fact that the desire must be a strong one, and that "... the event one cares about must be imminent." Suspense is greater if we know something negative is going to happen soon, rather than some vague future point.

Even when re-watching or re-reading a story, we can still experience this frustration of desire – the fact that we know the outcome does not prevent us desiring a different outcome, or wanting to be able to take action to prevent the outcome we know is coming. The first time we watch, and in subsequent viewings, we are in possession of information that could change the outcome of the situation, but there is nothing we can do with it: we are helpless witnesses to what is about to happen. Smuts argues that the desire-frustration theory means there is no paradox of suspense, "since it does not propose uncertainty as a necessary condition for suspense. Regardless of our knowledge of the outcome, we can be frustrated in our attempts to affect the outcome of a narrative event."

(8) High Stakes
There is a fair bit to be said about the subject of 'what's at stake' in a story, so I will cover that in the next chapter. All I will say here is that Moritz Lehne and Stefan Koelsch say that anticipated events in a story "have to have some emotional significance in order to generate tension or suspense." There must be something at stake for someone – some specific event or outcome that they want to happen (or not to happen). And the more deeply something is desired (or feared), the greater the tension or suspense created. If we want our reader to care, someone in the story has to care. And, ideally, the reader should also care about that someone.

Why Do We Enjoy Suspense?

In his *Conflict, Arousal and Curiosity* (1960), Daniel Berlyne proposed what is now referred to as the 'arousal jag' theory. He argued that people sometimes seek an increase in arousal of emotion because reducing it is then enjoyable. This was an attempt to explain why people sought out such things as roller coaster rides and horror movies. Berlyne suggested that the level of arousal needed to be moderate rather than, say, abject terror, and that the thrill-seeker needed to be certain that relief would follow arousal. Berlyne's theory has been disputed. Dolf Zillmann (1980) has said: "Any model that bases its predictions of the enjoyment of suspense solely on the consideration of relief from aversion is bound to be convincing when truly euphoric reactions are concerned. It would seem that the enjoyment of suspenseful drama derives its affective intensity from something more than the mere reduction of annoyance." Paul J. Silvia in *Exploring the Psychology of Interest* (2006) put it even more bluntly when he compared the theory to 'hit yourself on the head because it feels good when you stop.'

Zillmann argues that we don't seek suspense in drama because it feels good when it stops, but rather because of a fundamental human desire to *maximise pleasure*. High levels of stress, he says, can be transformed into high levels of euphoria. In support of this he quotes the work of S. Z. Klausner, who studied the reactions of skydivers, which Zillmann summarised: "The more frightened the skydivers are at the start of the jump run, the more enthusiastic they become later. Since the level of arousal is fairly constant throughout, it is the jumper's appraisal of the situation and of the task remaining before him that changes from point to point. Under one set of conditions the organism's excitement is experienced as fear, and under other conditions this same energy, arousal, or excitement is experienced as enthusiasm – this is a 'transformation' of fear into enthusiasm." Zillmann concludes that the same process occurs during our enjoyment of fiction: "Distress is accepted not because it produces need-satisfying sensations, but because it is instrumental in achieving intense, euphoric reactions; and the drama enthusiast is willing to live through some initial discomfort because he or she has learned to anticipate the benefits that derive from it. The appeal of suspenseful drama is thus explained on the basis of a fundamental behavioural tendency (i.e., the maximisation of pleasure), and assumptions about new motivational forces such as the sensation-seeking motive are not necessary." Dolf Zillmann's explanation of the enjoyment of suspenseful drama is referred to as the *Excitation-Transfer* theory.

This idea of transforming fear into enthusiasm, suspense into euphoria, seems odd at first glance. But if we look back at the structure for Act III of our story, this is exactly what we are trying to achieve. Act III begins just after the crisis – our hero is at his lowest point – but at the climax of Act III we want to create a complete reversal of these circumstances – we want some form of 'euphoric victory' to be snatched from the jaws of defeat.

Zillmann also quotes from several papers that provide pointers for writers:

First, J. Bryant (1978b), who says that "... the effect of suspense-induced distress on the enjoyment of drama depends greatly on the resolution of suspense." That is, it is not enough to create a suspenseful situation, we also need to show how the protagonist gets out of it.

Second, S. Bergman, who has written that: "The endangerment of a liked protagonist appearing to be utterly incapable of coping with the situation proved to be very effective for creating a high level of suspense." This refers back to the idea of the low probability of a desired outcome occurring and also reinforces our argument about making the hero suffer.

Third, J. Bryant (1978a), who said that a "... story was enjoyed to a greater degree when the protagonist resolved his own dilemma through his own actions." Readers want to see the protagonist solve his own problems – this makes sense because we all like to feel that we are capable of looking out for ourselves. We have already warned against ending your story with the cavalry riding to the rescue or having a deus ex machina: Bryant's research demonstrates that readers don't like such endings. Show the protagonist taking charge of his own life – that's what we expect of our heroes.

A final note from Zillmann: it may not be a desire to experience fear that motivates people to seek suspensive stories, but rather a desire to experience the reassurance that comes once the fear has been overcome: "Even a cursory look at television drama makes it quite clear that suspenseful drama does not merely present the victimisation of liked protagonists and innocent bystanders by hordes of wrongdoers who plague society as they please. Although the display of transgression is undoubtedly an essential part of suspenseful drama, it should not be overlooked that such drama almost always features the triumph of justice. Wrongdoers are caught and duly punished; justice is brought to the situation; society is freed from dangerous elements; rapists, murderers, and kidnappers are 'put away.' Even a hostile environment (e.g., an earthquake, an epidemic) is ultimately brought under control. If anything, suspenseful drama on television distorts reality more toward security than toward danger: It projects too just, and maybe too safe, a world. In real life, bank robbers, rapists, and killers are less frequently and less promptly brought to justice than in the world of television. To the extent that such portrayal of 'crime and punishment' affects the viewer's perception of reality, one should expect the troubled and anxiety-ridden citizen to find comfort and seek refuge in drama that features the clean-up operations of law enforcers, 'private eyes,' and vigilantes. In fact, it may be argued that it is the very projection of a just and safe world that attracts those who are acutely worried more than it attracts those who experience little apprehension."

"It is conceivable, then," Zillmann says, "that anxious people resort to watching much suspenseful drama because it reduces their anxieties."

Catharsis – The Release of Tension

'Catharsis' comes from a Greek word meaning purification or cleansing, and was used by Aristotle in his *Poetics* in relation to the purgation of emotions, particularly pity and fear. Aristotle said that the purpose of tragedy was to arouse fear and pity and thereby effect the catharsis of these emotions. I'm not sure whether he meant that watching tragic plays released these emotions so that spectators left the theatre in a healthier state of mind, or whether he meant that tragic plays should stir up these emotions and then release them before the audience went home. Zillmann's theory gives us a third option: drama stirs up feelings of pity and fear, and then transforms them into a feeling of euphoria. The truth may be some combination of all three.

Most popular genre stories build towards a positive outcome, but the plot is constructed in such a way as to make this outcome seem increasingly unlikely. Tension builds as a negative outcome seems almost certain. And then, as a result of some (hopefully) unforeseen twist, the situation is turned around and the positive outcome is achieved. A happy outcome is all the happier, for protagonist and reader, if events preceding it have been almost exclusively unhappy. The contrast makes for a greater emotional release when the situation is finally resolved.

Techniques for Creating Suspense

Out of all those academic theories, can we now come up with some practical techniques?

Audience Participation

We've said it before, but it bears repeating: reading is not a passive experience – our readers make their own contributions to the story as they read. The more active we can make their participation – the more they have to put into the reading experience – the more they are likely to get out of the story. Part of this participation is the work-out that we give them by evoking emotional responses. Another part is the ongoing act of prediction they undertake as they try to anticipate what is going to happen in the story. Prediction is part intellectual and part gut-instinct and is an ability that has enabled our species to survive and evolve. There is an element of deduction in this, in that the reader has to figure out the relevance of each particular piece of information that the writer discloses, and then has to try and work out how the new information fits in with everything the reader already knows. This is most obviously the case with whodunit detective mysteries, where the reader tries to follow along with the detective and work out the identity of the murderer before the hero does. But in every story there is an element of mystery. Every story begins by asking a 'major dramatic question,' and the answer is not revealed until the climax of the story. As writers we need to drop little hints and plant clues for the reader to find, and these need to appear like natural parts of the narrative or dialogue of a scene. We make it easier for them to find the clues we want them to know – including the 'red herrings' that misdirect their attention – and more difficult to spot the clues that lead in the right direction, though even these we cannot bury completely. We need the reader to be able to recall these things, when they are mentioned later, without highlighting their relevance. There are a number of techniques used by the writers of whodunits that we can adopt including presenting information during an action scene, where its relevance is likely to be overlooked; presenting it as part of a list or description of irrelevant items; mentioning an action, trait, or habit without commenting on it further;

having someone say something a little out of the ordinary, which no one else picks up on; having an item misplaced and then forgotten after a brief search; an unusual reaction by a character to an object, person, or situation, that is not dwelt upon; an unexplained entrance or exit of someone; an effect that seems to have no cause, or a cause that seems to have no effect.

We must remember the words of Alfred Hitchcock here, who said: "I do not believe that puzzling the audience is the essence of suspense." Hitchcock, as we have seen, believed that suspense was best achieved by allowing the viewer or reader to 'play god' – to know things that characters on stage do not know. Remember his example of the bomb hidden under the table? Suspense is created as a result of the audience knowing something, of being able to predict a terrible outcome, but being unable to warn the characters. Mystery, or curiosity, is the opposite in that it concerns information that the reader does not have. It comes from withholding information from them. You can really only create suspense from curiosity when the audience is made aware that there is information that they do not have and that is vital in the story. We need to make them anticipate receiving this information. Curiosity is an intellectual response, and we need to turn it into an emotional one. We have to make them want to gain a piece of information, or want to discover the significance of a piece of information, and then we have to delay satisfying this want. Obviously, the longer we make them wait, the more significant the information must prove to be.

Later in this chapter, we will look at some other ways of creating suspense using the order in which information is presented.

While readers try to figure out what will happen next, they do not want to be correct all of the time. Or even most of the time. If they are, they will dismiss a story as being predictable. For the sake of shock, humour, or to avoid predictability, we must do the opposite of what the reader has been led to expect. Keeping them off-balance by reversing the anticipated action will increase interest and emotional involvement. Keep them guessing.

Anticipation

Suspense is what keeps our reader turning the pages. It is what makes them care what happens next. In order to create suspense, the reader must be able to anticipate what could happen next. We create anticipation by setting up or foreshadowing events that could happen to the characters in the near future. We can also create a mood that causes the reader to anticipate what the course of events will be. And we can plant objects, skills, character traits, or information that will pay-off later in the story. A plant needs to be clear enough that the reader notices it and can predict that it will be important later – but not 'sign-posted' or 'telegraphed' in such a way that the reader can accurately predict exactly how the plant will pay off. There are a few foreshadowing techniques you can use that we haven't mentioned previously:

Dialogue: We've mentioned the obvious 'direct statement' kind of foreshadowing, that includes making appointments – "I'll see you at lunchtime" – or warning of impending arrivals – "Mother will be here in time for dinner" – or making threats – "I'm going to kill him." But you can also use dialogue – including interior monologues or 'thinking aloud' in novels – to increase suspense by having characters talk about something that is going to happen, or that might happen, or have them ask questions: "I wonder what she wanted?" or "What was he doing there after dark?" Or "I wonder if there is anything dangerous down here in this dark cellar?" We can use the predictions of characters within the story about what will happen next to influence those of the reader.

Chapter Headings: You can use intriguing chapter titles to create curiosity and raise questions in the reader's mind: 'Who is Kyser Soze?' or 'A Shocking Discovery' or 'Death of a Witness.' A word of warning though, I would avoid using chapter headings for important dates, or for an important countdown of time: many people skip chapter titles in the same way they skip the 'Chapter 4' text, and so could miss something you want them to know. If it's vital for the reader to know it, make sure it is repeated in the text of the chapter somewhere too.

Character Traits: If a character normally reacts to a particular situation in a particular way, then you can create that situation and guide your reader into expecting a particular outcome. If, for example, you have a character with a short temper, you can create a situation that will provoke it, and your reader will anticipate the explosion. If you also create an outspoken character who voices their opinions without considering the consequences, you can bring this character into a scene with our hot-tempered friend, and then sit back and wait for the fireworks. But as we have said, the reader doesn't always want to be right in their predictions, so occasionally you can surprise them with unpredictable character reactions. The unpredictable reaction must seem reasonable in retrospect, so like any surprise it will need to have been prepared for. Once we have seen that a character can respond to a situation in one of two ways, we have prepared for suspense in the next scene where that situation arises: the reader will try to predict which way the character's reaction will go.

Character Relationships: Someone once said 'Never put two characters in a scene who agree with one another.' They were basically saying that a dramatic scene needs conflict. But there are different ways to create conflict in a scene, and you can use them to create or heighten suspense. Suppose you have two people in a scene who need to work together in order to get out alive. Their situation has suspense inherent in it, but we can increase it through their relationship with one another. Let's say that one of them wants to get out alive while making sure the other – unsuspecting – character doesn't escape. This is one of those situations where the reader knows something the character doesn't and wants to warn him of the impending danger. Or perhaps both characters are afraid that the other will betray them – neither trusts the other, and so their chances of escape are diminished because neither one wants to take the risk of becoming the victim of the other – 'I don't trust you enough to turn my back on you' or 'I don't trust you to pull me to safety with the rope' or 'I don't trust you enough to give you a loaded gun.' Antagonism between characters is common in the early part of many stories, where the protagonist and the co-protagonist don't trust each other – only as their relationship develops do they gain mutual respect. Another time when this technique works is if you have a hero and his opponent trapped and having to work together – the science fiction movie *Enemy Mine* is a good example, as is the movie *Hell in the Pacific*, which may have inspired it. *Assault on Precinct 13*, which was inspired in part by Howard Hawks' Western *Rio Bravo*, had the tagline: "A cop with a war on his hands. His enemy an army of street killers. His only ally a convicted murderer." The 1976 original and the 2005 remake are both very suspenseful films.

Jeopardy

We will explore stakes in the next chapter, so I won't say too much about risk and danger here, other than saying that a good way of creating suspense is to take a character that the reader cares about and place them in a situation where they are at risk of something terrible happening to them. As long as there is impending danger, there will be suspense, and the reader will stay with us to find out how things turn out. Remember that despite what most of the examples in this chapter seem to suggest, the danger that a character faces doesn't have to be the risk of physical violence or injury. If that's the only type of threat the character's face, even in a thriller or an action-adventure, your story will be monotonously melodramatic. Other types of danger that characters can face include loss of someone or something important; risk of failure, of exposure, or loneliness.

In humour the threat is often of exposure: the hero is pretending to be something or someone he isn't, perhaps as a means of impressing a love interest. Or he may have some guilty secret he is trying to keep from her – typically something stupid he has done in the recent past. Or there may be a threat to the hero's dignity – he risks being made to look foolish or small. Think how terrible it would be to have your deepest, most personal fears or wishes revealed – and ridiculed. Imagine how embarrassed you would be. Now do that to your hero.

In a romance, the hero may fear that he will never be with the person he loves, and then when they get together, he fears that he may lose her. And then a situation develops that makes it seem that he is about to lose her. And then he does lose her. And then he decides he'll do anything to try and get her back... there is as much suspense in a romance as there is in an amateur-on-the-run thriller – but the stakes are different.

Putting the hero in jeopardy requires that the audience or reader is aware of the potential danger to the hero. Sometimes the hero isn't aware of the danger himself – we know something he doesn't – and we feel helpless because we can't warn him that he is blithely heading into the jaws of 'the terrible thing.' Unable to lift a finger to help him, all we can do is watch and hope for the best.

Delayed Outcomes

Situations that create suspense require time to unfold. Typically, they will occur in 'real time,' and sometimes it is more effective to 'stretch' time, by slowing down the action, showing the action from multiple viewpoints, or by cutting away from one scene to another and so delaying the outcome of the first scene.

A classic, and oft-quoted, suspense sequence occurs in Chapter 25 of Stephen King's *The Shining*. A young boy, Danny, is drawn to a locked room in the deserted Overlook Hotel. It is a room where something terrible happened in the past. In this chapter, Danny has stolen the key that will let him into the room. But King doesn't have Danny go marching straight into the room: where's the emotional mileage in that? Instead, we have to wait for two pages or more for Danny to work up the courage and step inside. The suspense is heightened. And then when Danny does go inside... well, you'll just have to read it and find out for yourself – you won't be disappointed, King knows how to create a pay-off. Dean R. Koontz, in an essay titled 'Keeping the Reader on the Edge of His Seat,' has said that *The Shining* is "... essentially one long anticipation sequence. In the very beginning of the book, we know that Jack Torrance is sooner or later going to go after his little boy, Danny, with an axe. But King withholds that ultimate scene of terror for more than four hundred pages, building towards it with such care that it is excruciatingly tense when it finally arrives." Unfortunately, Stanley Kubrick's film adaptation doesn't succeed in creating suspense nearly as effectively, so my advice would be to read the book instead.

A film that does make effective use of suspense is *Jaws*, directed by Stephen Spielberg. The 'terrible thing' in the film is the great white shark, but its appearances are brief, often consisting of little more than a shot from the shark's point of view, a dorsal fin, and blood in the water. The shark itself is the payoff, but it is the anticipation of the shark's appearance – heightened by the effective use of John Williams' music – that keeps the audience on the edge of its seat, and that makes the violence so effective when it does occur. *Jaws* establishes the threat right at the start when the girl goes swimming in the opening scenes and we see what the shark is capable of.

Other near-perfect examples of suspense movies include Ridley Scott's *Alien* and John Carpenter's *Halloween*.

A common technique used in horror films is to set-up the threat very early on. We know that something horrible is going to happen to the hero and his girl because they have just arrived at a place where earlier we saw another couple meet a horrible death. The killer lurks in the bushes, watching our hero and heroine, and the suspense grows. What will happen? Will he murder the hero and his girl, or will they escape? Or will they kill him? The suspense is built up as the killer gets closer and closer. Then he makes an attack on them, but it fails. Hero and heroine try to make their escape, but discover the tyres on their car have all been slashed, they are trapped, and the killer is closing in on them again...

Effective use of violence is made early on in Clive Barker's film *Hellraiser*. We are introduced to a character and a mysterious artefact, and then something unpleasant – involving hooks and chains – happens to the character. While there is some suspense in the setting up of this scene, the violence is so sudden and unpleasant that it is more shock than suspense. But Barker does not go on to show even more unpleasant violence after this (not at first), instead he uses this initial shock as a basis for building suspense. He has established a baseline, he has said that the violence in this film is going to be sudden and unpleasantly painful when it comes. Now when he builds suspense sequences, the audience's anticipation and dread are heightened because they know how bad the payoff is likely to be. And they're looking forward to it.

The anticipation of violence is more emotionally involving than violence itself. Violence works when it startles the reader or viewer, but it is almost impossible to sustain effectively: the effect diminishes with repetition. Many filmmakers seem to think that increasing the level of carnage, making each set-piece bigger, is a solution to this problem; but this is only a partial, and unimaginative, solution at best. This is not to say that violence is wrong, cheap, or ineffective. But violence alone is not enough. Violence needs suspense. But suspense also needs a pay-off.

If you threaten a character with danger, the threat must be real. If you create a suspenseful situation, there must be some kind of payoff. It doesn't have to be – and probably shouldn't be – the climax that the reader is expecting, but it should be a climax. Anti-climaxes can be effective if used very occasionally – but use them too often and the reader will feel cheated. The best use of an anti-climax is when it lulls the reader – and the character – into a false sense of security.

Pay-offs in suspense sequences are like punchlines in comedy: the audience must be allowed time to react, to discharge the emotion or expectation that has been built up, and then once they have relaxed, you can build up ready for the next payoff. A story should not be told at peak emotional level – a 'suspense film' is not one long breathless sequence of suspense – there needs to be peaks and troughs. One of the most memorable scenes in Jaws occurs on board the Orca when the hero and his fellow shark-hunters share a quiet drink and trade stories – and we know the shark could attack at any time.

Probable Outcomes

We need the reader to be able to predict more than one possible outcome. Ideally, we want a happy/desired outcome (the hero succeeds) that appears to be extremely unlikely to happen; and an unhappy/undesired outcome (the hero fails) to seem like the most probable outcome. During the course of the story, we want the desired outcome to seem increasingly unlikely, and the undesired outcome to seem almost a certainty. We can achieve this by increasing the odds against the hero – adding obstacles, removing required resources and people, and increasing the strength of the opposition.

Misdirection – Red Herrings

Knowing that the reader is always trying to predict what is going to happen, and that they revise their predictions as the story progresses, we disclose information to them in such a way that we can guide their predictions in a particular direction. We want them to be able to see – quite vividly – how the undesired outcome will come about. At the same time, we make it more difficult for them to visualise how the desired outcome could ever be achieved. As the writer, we know how the desired outcome will be brought about, but we subtly direct the reader's attention away from anything that would reveal how we will achieve it. We still need to use foreshadowing and plants, so that the way we reach the desired outcome seems logical and not a rabbit-out-of-the-hat cheat

– but we don't draw attention to this information. We can use misdirection to lead the audience in one direction, and then surprise them when the true nature of a piece of information is revealed. In Alfred Hitchcock's remake of *The Man Who Knew Too Much* one of the clues is a name – but is it a person or a place? The heroes must find out, and time is running out for them.

Detective mysteries use red herrings to misinform and misdirect readers. A clue may seem to point to the guilt of a particular suspect – until the detective later reveals that the same clue can be seen to have a different meaning. A suspect may seem to be acting suspiciously, even lying to the detective, but then it is later revealed that this person did so to protect another guilty secret – not the murder – or to protect another innocent individual. Or a guilty one. Sometimes the detective may present misinformation to other characters in order to confuse or misdirect the villain – misdirecting the reader at the same time.

Reversing Audience Expectations

Our readers may not understand the techniques of storytelling in the same way that a writer does (or should), but they know how stories work – and they have read enough novels and seen enough movies to know how particular situations are 'meant' to play out. And they are more than capable of spotting a cliché. Having spent decades making thrillers, and having established many genre conventions, Alfred Hitchcock – in his later years – made great efforts to avoid clichés. If something in a screenplay seemed too familiar, he would say to the writer, "No, no, that's how they do it in the movies!" He would make the reader come up with a more original approach. He knew the importance of giving us something that was 'the same only different.' Hitchcock also knew that he could use audience expectation to lead us in one direction, and then pull the rug out from under us by giving us something unexpected. The fate of Janet Leigh's character in *Psycho* is just one obvious example. Audiences like to be surprised, as long as the surprise is logical within the context of the story.

'Don't open that door!' The nervous hero approaches a door and we expect the serial killer to be behind it. The situation is suspenseful because even though we think danger lurks behind the door, we aren't certain what will happen next. The tension peaks as the hero reaches for the door hand and turns it, pulls it open, and reveals... nothing. But if, just as he and the audience are breathing a sigh of relief, we switch the viewpoint and see that the killer is actually standing behind the hero, knife raised, this unexpected twist provides an even greater rush of adrenaline.

Reversing the anticipated payoff can also be used to create humour. A famous example is in Steven Spielberg's *Raiders of the Lost Ark*, where Indiana Jones fights off a bunch of bad guys, and then finds himself facing a big man in black whirling a dangerous-looking scimitar. The audience expects another fight, but the resolution of the scene is both unexpected and amusing; it is both a climax and an anti-climax, and is more effective than another fight sequence would have been. In *Tootsie*, Dustin Hoffman is playing soap actress Dorothy, and is not looking forward to his first onscreen kiss with an actor the other actresses have nicknamed 'the tongue.' This romantic clinch is the climax of the scene

4 / Suspense

and pays off in an unexpected way. But the joke comes in a second payoff, providing the audience with a double-reversal.

In our campaign to outwit the reader – so that we can come up with the unexpected during the story, and top it off with a surprising ending – we can use the reader's story knowledge and expectations against them. We can set up situations that appear to be a standard, even a clichéd, story development – so that we lead the reader to predict the typical ending for such a situation. Having guided them in this direction – but at the same time, having set up a different outcome – we can surprise them with an unexpected twist. In a thriller, the hero is often lured to an isolated location, where the audience expects him to be ambushed and either beaten up, shot at, or kidnapped. Or all of the above. The location he is sent to is typically a dark alley, a deserted underground car park, or a dilapidated building. It is always dark and filled with shadows. It looks menacing. That's how they would do it in the movies. Hitchcock rang the changes on this by sending Cary Grant out to a crossroads in the middle of a featureless prairie in bright sunlight. For around eight minutes he kept us in suspense – what was going to happen? We know the set-up was a trap, but where on earth was the ambush going to come from? Not 'on earth' as it turned out. The same, only different – and a brilliant sequence.

The same thing applies to stock characters and stereotypes, especially in genre fiction. We can lead the reader to believe that a character is what they appear to be so that they will expect them to behave in the typical manner: then we can set-up the unexpected twist. By allowing the reader to jump to conclusions, you aren't cheating them – subverting a cliché is entirely within the rules of the game!

Hitchcock's use of the cool, sophisticated blonde woman in his thrillers was another way he avoided cliché – until it became a cliché in his own work. Traditionally in stories, blonde females were seen to be innocent and virginal, while dark-haired women were earthier and more worldly-wise. Hitchcock liked to take the idea of the pale-haired ice-maiden, and gradually reveal that she was anything but innocent or frigid.

Look for the clichés and stereotypes in any genre that you write in – then think up ways to use what the audience knows about these familiar elements to create something unexpected. See how far you can lead the reader in the expected direction, without cheating, before pulling your switch. Readers enjoy recognising patterns, but they also enjoy seeing something unexpected. It's our 'same only different' rule again.

Spontaneous Suspense

We should not overlook the fact that some situations have suspense inherent in them. A character steps onto a narrow ledge on a cliff or building; or steps onto a tight-rope. Chase sequences – one of Alfred Hitchcock's favourite situations – have suspense built-in, whether the hero is being chased, or is pursuing someone. This can be particularly effective if the hero seems to be outmatched by his pursuer. Remember the relentless robot in *The Terminator*, never giving up – emerging from the burning truck, it's flesh burned away – and never giving poor Linda Hamilton a moment's rest. Or the truck in *Duel* that doesn't seem to have a driver and that keeps on pursuing and victimising poor Dennis Weaver. Or that character I mentioned earlier trying to retrieve the cigarette lighter...

Suspense and Viewpoint

Novels can be written in a first-person viewpoint; in a third-person viewpoint mostly restricted to following a single character, and the 'omniscient' third-person viewpoint, that allows us to follow multiple characters. In a film, the positioning of the camera offers a comparable selection of points of view. Each of these viewpoints offers different opportunities for creating and maintaining suspense.

First-person viewpoint makes use of the 'I' pronoun, as though the viewpoint character is telling the story to us. If we are experiencing everything that the character is experiencing, as it happens, there is almost no opportunity for us to utilise dramatic irony. The reader never gets to know something that the viewpoint character doesn't know. This is a particular issue if the viewpoint character is also the hero. You have slightly more flexibility if your narrator is the hero's ally – Sir Arthur Conan Doyle used this approach with Sherlock Holmes and Doctor Watson. Holmes often knew things that Watson and the reader did not. Conan Doyle also hit on the idea that Watson was slightly slower on the uptake than the reader. This had the double benefit of (a) flattering the reader, and (b) allowing for some instances of dramatic irony, when the reader was able to deduce something that seemed to be beyond Watson.

The other way to have a first-person narrator use dramatic irony and other techniques for creating suspense is to have him behave in the same way as any author, and manipulate the revelation of events for the greatest dramatic effect. As long as this doesn't draw too much attention to the fact that the story is being 'told' after the fact, rather than 'shown' in 'real time,' this can be effective.

A restricted third-person viewpoint is similar to the first-person in that it follows a single character and allows us access to only their thoughts and observations on events. It has similar restrictions to the first-person.

The 'omniscient' third-person viewpoint allows the author to follow any character – or even provide a bird's-eye (or 'god-like') view from above all of the characters. It allows entry to any person's thoughts, and allows switching from character to character as the story demands. We can know the villain's thoughts as well as the hero's, and we can even dip into the head of the ally or the henchman as necessary. This offers the most flexibility in terms of creating suspense, as you can cut from one scene to another at will, and use dramatic irony as much as you like.

To maintain interest in the hero, it is probably best to stick with him as much as possible – he or she is the person we want the reader to care most about. For the same reason, it is probably best to stay away from other character's thoughts, unless absolutely necessary.

Movies, for the most part, offer an omniscient viewpoint that sticks closely to the hero for most of the story, cutting away to other characters and scenes to create dramatic irony and to heighten suspense, and with no access to any character's thoughts. You can use this approach for novels too – readers are familiar with it from the movies – but then you are losing out on one of the features that make novels novels – access to character's thought processes. You can use a character's thoughts to heighten suspense, by allowing the reader to share the character's concerns and fears. You can also share the character's own predictions of what might happen, and so influence the reader's anticipation.

Event Order

One way of creating anticipation is to begin at the end of a scene or sequence – that is, to show the outcome or effect or consequence first. This allows you to grab the reader's attention with a shocking or intriguing action – something unexpected that will have a profound effect on one or more of the characters in the story. This then raises the question: How did this terrible thing come to happen? The story can then backtrack to show events leading up to the shocking action, and all the time the reader is anticipating the event they have already witnessed and, hopefully, is dreading it happening. If the scene is told effectively, the reader will come to know and care about the characters more, so that the inevitable event that is about to happen will be even more undesirable than it seemed to start with. We've already said that this technique has been used effectively in films like *The Usual Suspects* and Quentin Tarantino's *Reservoir Dogs* and *Pulp Fiction,* but it can also be used in novels. Mario Puzo begins one section of *The Godfather* with a shock – the bullet-riddled corpse of Don Corleone's son arriving at the undertakers'. Then the story backtracks to show the sequence of events that climaxed in this violent death. Rather than leading up to a short-lived sudden and unexpected shock, the sequence has a sustained emotional impact as the inevitable death-scene is anticipated.

William F. Brewer and Edward H. Lichtenstein (1982) studied the effect of event order in stories. They note that authors are able to arrange the events in a narrative in any order they wish and that they can also choose to omit "... any of the events in the underlying event sequence..." They take as their example the underlying events in a prototypical murder mystery story – they refer to this as the event structure:

- the murderer develops a motive
- the murderer obtains a weapon
- the victim is murdered
- the body is discovered
- the detective arrives on the scene
- the detective searches for clues
- the detective solves the crime

The chronological sequence of events is presented above, but as Brewer and Lichtenstein point out, this is not the sequence in which they are presented to the reader. A mystery novel often begins at some point after the murder, and the details of what happened earlier are scattered about and are only gradually pieced together by the detective. At least one crucial piece of information – the identity of the murderer, and possibly his or her motive – is kept from the reader until very near the end of the story. The events are re-ordered to achieve the maximum dramatic effect. Brewer and Lichtenstein propose that there are three main 'discourse structures' that account for enjoyment in most stories:

a) Surprise
b) Suspense
c) Curiosity

These are the three main effects we can create to entertain our readers.

Surprise is created when critical information from the beginning of the event structure is omitted, according to Brewer and Lichtenstein. As an example they offer the following: Charles got up from the chair. He walked slowly towards the window. The window broke and Charles fell dead. The sound of a shot echoed in the distance. The death of Charles is a surprise because crucial information from the beginning of the sequence of events has been omitted: namely, the arrival of the murderous gunman outside Charles' window. We did not know that the shot was coming, so were surprised. The scene is resolved when we receive the omitted information – the gunman outside – and reinterpret the event sequence in the light of this final piece of information.

Suspense requires an "initiating event or situation ... which could lead to significant consequences (either good or bad) for one of the characters in the narrative. The event structure must also contain the outcome of the initiating event ... the initiating event occurs early in the discourse... [and] causes the reader to become concerned about the consequences for the relevant character and this produces suspense." Brewer and Lichtenstein note that additional material is usually placed between the initiating event and the outcome event to "encourage the build-up of the suspense." Suspense is resolved when the outcome is presented. As an example they give a variation of their original: The sniper was waiting outside the house. Charles got up from the chair. He walked slowly towards the window. There was the sound of a shot and the window broke. Charles fell dead." Brewer and Lichtenstein point out that suspense is experienced by the reader, the shot is still unexpected from Charles' point of view.

Curiosity. This is similar to 'surprise' in that critical information from the beginning of the event sequence is omitted, but unlike surprise, curiosity requires that the reader be made aware that the critical information is missing. The reader then becomes curious about the missing information. Curiosity is resolved when the reader learns enough information to reconstruct the omitted significant event. This is the sequence that is used in the murder mystery story. The example Brewer and Lichtenstein give is: Charles fell dead. The police came and found the broken glass, etc.

Brewer and Lichtenstein's theory predicts that readers will enjoy stories that succeed in producing surprise and resolution, suspense and resolution, or curiosity and resolution. They also predict that a story that produces and resolves an effect will be enjoyed more than one that simply produces the effect.

Brewer and Lichtenstein then present another 'event structure' for consideration:

1) Butler puts poison in wine
2) Butler carries wine to Lord Higginbotham
3) Lord Higginbotham drinks wine
4) Lord Higginbotham falls over dead

Suspense, they argue, is created at the point when the reader becomes concerned about the outcome of events, so to create suspense from the above events we would need to structure them as follows:

1) Butler puts poison in wine
2) Butler carries wine to Lord Higginbotham
3) Lord Higginbotham drinks wine

The resolution would be the revelation of (4)

Surprise requires that the significant initiating event be omitted, and so the events should be presented as follows:

2) Butler carries wine to Lord Higginbotham
3) Lord Higginbotham drinks wine
4) Lord Higginbotham falls over dead

The resolution would be the revelation of (1)

Curiosity requires that significant initiating events be omitted and that the reader is made aware that the information is missing. The presentation of this would be:

4) Lord Higginbotham falls over dead

Given the mysterious death of Lord H, the reader will be curious about what caused his death; if someone was responsible for it, who they were; and how it was brought about. In other words, they are curious about events (1), (2) and (3) and the resolution would be the revelation of these events.

Brewer and Lichtenstein also note the importance of foreshadowing to either increase the reader's concern for the character or to increase the significance of the outcome.

The examples given above may seem simplistic, but they offer a model for exploring how the chronological sequence of events that underlie a story can be used to generate different responses – surprise, suspense, and curiosity – in the reader. It shows the importance of the sequence of the depiction of events, and also the events in the sequence that should be included and – more importantly – excluded to create a particular effect. Once you have created the sequence of events for your own story, you can use this model to help you structure your scene to create either surprise, suspense, or curiosity. Or if you have a scene that is not creating the effect you require, you can compare it against this model and see if your events have been appropriately utilised.

Running Out of Options

Richard J. Gerrig and Allan B. I. Bernardo discuss another option, "...in which authors make readers feel suspense by leading them to believe that the quantity or quality of paths through the hero's problem space has become diminished." As an example, they use a scene from Ian Fleming's *Casino Royale* in which James Bond is about to bankrupt the villain Le Chiffre at the baccarat table. A man behind him presses a gun into Bond's back and whispers, 'Withdraw your bet before I count to ten. If you call for help I shall fire.' The man begins to count and supplementing the suspense of this 'countdown' we have Bond trying desperately to come up with a way of escaping. As the seconds tick away, he thinks up, evaluates and discards a number of possibilities.

"Bond's initial state," Gerrig and Bernardo write, "is the reality of the gun pressing into his back; Bond's goal state is to be able to let his bet stand without dying. To navigate from the initial to goal states – to 'transform' his dilemma into another triumph – Bond must find a path through an appropriate sequence of intermediate states. The difficulty for him, as the text reveals, is that his solution paths are constrained." Fleming's story has Bond considering different options open to him – including help from casino staff or help from his friend Felix Leiter – and dismissing each one as either unlikely to succeed or too risky to attempt. Gerrig and Bernardo put forward the theory that "... material within a text that appears to restrict a character's range of possible solutions to a problem will lead to greater feelings of suspense."

They tested their theory with an experiment in which people were given two versions of an extract from *Casino Royale* to read. One included mention of a pen that was in Bond's position, but which was taken from him by the villain; the second version had no mention of the pen at all. The version with the pen was judged to be more suspenseful. "All we have done is manipulated the readers' perceptions of the immediate existence of an escape route by providing a possible solution and then pulling it back," Gerrig and Bernardo write, and concluded from observation of reader reactions that "... suspense only increased when a solution was offered and then snatched away ... the removal of Bond's pen caused reports of suspense to be increased – even though readers may not have had a very specific idea of why Bond wanted to retain the pen, its removal had a reliable impact on their feelings."

In another version of the same experiment, this time involving a comb, Gerrig and Bernardo again used two versions of the text – one where the comb was taken away from Bond by the villain, and one where Bond used it to comb his hair before it was taken by the villain. Based on the responses of their test subjects they concluded that: "... we undermined the effect of the removal of an object by letting our readers experience its normal function. Once readers came to think of the comb as just a comb it lost much of its value as a means of escape." I mention this second version of the experiment because it could be used to misdirect a reader from the importance of a clue in a mystery story: if the reader sees an object used for its usual function, they are less likely to think about it in any other terms, e.g. as a murder weapon.

I have some issues about Gerrig and Bernardo's use of a pen and a comb in their two experiments – I think the pen has far more potential as an aid to escape, and it has been used a number of times in various films and television programmes. Bond even had a pen that served as an explosive weapon. But even without such knowledge, a pen would seem a much more obvious choice for stabbing someone than a man's pocket comb. However, as Gerrig and Bernardo point out, there is other evidence that people find difficulty in seeing alternate uses for objects, tending to fixate on their typical functions. Karl Duncker's 'candle problem' (1945) is given as a famous example – have a look at the *Wikipedia* entry for *Candle Problem* for an explanation.

Gerrig and Bernardo offer one final example of how reducing the possible number of solutions can increase suspense, which they call Prior Solution Removed. This example "... specifically alluded to past circumstances in which Bond was Blofeld's prisoner and made it clear that Blofeld had taken pains to eliminate an important component of Bond's past means of escape ... our readers reported reliably more suspense when they had read a scene in which Bond's past solutions were unavailable than when they had no information to that effect ... Our results support the general hypothesis that passages of texts that create the impression that solution paths are being pruned away will lead readers to report more suspense."

In conclusion, Gerrig and Bernardo write, "... these results support our contention that readers experience suspense in parallel to their frustration as problem solvers. There are, of course, other ways in which authors can create suspense. Our data support the claim, however, that one reliable way to create suspense is to prune the readers' perceptions of paths toward solution ... To the extent that readers cannot navigate their way to a solution, they will have an enhanced experience of suspense."

Techniques for Increasing Suspense

Having put the protagonist – or someone the protagonist cares about – in a potentially dangerous situation, and having created suspense by delaying the outcome of the situation, we can increase the level of suspense in a number of ways.

"Time is Running Out, the Timer of the Bomb is Counting Down, and the Water is Rising!"
A countdown or deadline or some other 'time pressure' ups the ante, making life more difficult for the protagonist, and increasing suspense for the reader. The digital timer on the bomb is ticking down to zero; the fuse is burning down towards the barrel of gunpowder; torrential rains and an incoming tide are causing water levels to rise; the pressure is building up behind the weakened dam. Will the train carrying the hero get across the bridge before the villain blows it up? Will the heroine catch her train and make the rendezvous with her lover so they can make one last attempt to save their relationship? Will the hero find the victim before the air in her underground prison runs out?

These are all pretty hoary devices, but they still crop up all the time in tv shows and movies. They're still effective – especially if you can come up with a new variation on the countdown theme. To be effective you need to make sure that there is a clear definition of the time limit or deadline, a bunch of time-consuming obstacles and confrontations, and a way of measuring time and reminding the reader or viewer that it is running out. Examples include the detective who is given twenty-four hours to locate the real murderer before the (possibly) innocent suspect in custody is formally charged. Or the adventurers in the desert who have only two-days' worth of drinking water. Or the submariners with only two hours' worth of oxygen. A time limit and something important at stake. The passing of time makes the chances of success seem less and less certain, as options run out and the deadline approaches. Throw in a near-disaster and a moment of false-victory – when it seems like the problem is solved, but then turns out not to be – and you have the makings of a suspenseful scene or sequence of scenes.

"All Alone in the Dark"
A reader or audience is more likely to worry about a character who is isolated and vulnerable. If the terrible thing is getting closer and closer and we know the hero has nowhere to run, nothing to defend himself with, and no one to help him, our suspense is greater. In Alfred Hitchcock's *Psycho*, Janet Leigh seeks refuge from a storm by checking into an isolated motel. In her room she undresses and steps into the shower, unaware that she is being watched by a psychopath in an A-line skirt... In Steven Spielberg's *Jaws* a young woman undresses and swims out into the sea: she is pale and vulnerable in the dark water... At the end of Ridley Scott's *Alien*, Sigourney Weaver is the sole survivor in the escape ship. Thinking she is alone, she undresses ready to enter the suspended animation chamber, unaware that...

Spot any similarities? Woman. Alone. Undressed. It is one of the simplest ways of showing a vulnerable character on screen. We feel more vulnerable without our clothes. In *Die Hard*, the Bruce Willis character was made more vulnerable simply by having him barefoot: remember all that broken glass? And in Stephen King's *Misery*, author Paul Sheldon is both isolated and vulnerable – and both novel and film are equally effective in achieving suspense.

"There's a Monster Out There – You've Got to Believe Me!"
You don't have to be on your own to be alone. Sometimes you're the only person who knows about the aliens, the monster, or the conspiracy because no one else will believe you. It's another cliché to have the hero as the only person in town who knows that the new owner of the local junk store is really a vampire and to have him unable to convince anyone else of the fact. But it is another way of isolating the hero. And if the vampire knows he knows... It doesn't have to be vampires, of course. It could be a small-town sheriff who believes there's a dangerous shark swimming just offshore. Or an incapacitated photographer who believes the man across the way has murdered his wife.

"It was a Dark and Stormy Night..."
During a quiet scene in a suspense movie, we often hear one of the characters recount some anecdote that has a direct bearing on the present situation. In

Jaws Quint describes what it's like to be in the water in the dark when the sharks are circling. Nancy's mother in *A Nightmare on Elm Street* explains how a child murderer came to be killed. Creepy stories told around the campfire – everyone's heard about the escaped psychopath with a hook for a hand – and urban legends – the choking Doberman, anyone? – are a part of our culture, and a part of our stories. Pick the right story, and you can enhance the suspense in your story. You have to create a new story, but you need to give it the feel of an existing creepy story. Who knows, people may even start telling it to each other as if it was true. Candyman, candyman, candyman.

Anecdotes don't have to be creepy stories – they can just recount the pre-story experiences of one of the characters. In Sequence 5, the hero often unburdens himself, sharing with the co-protagonist the story of how he came to be psychically wounded by some traumatic event in his past. Handled badly, it will sound like cheap pop psychology; handled well it can add dimension to your character and help towards proving the thematic argument of your story. Or when the hero is at the mercy of the villain in Sequence 6, the villain might reveal his own backstory – the reasons why he became a supervillain.

In his book *Making Movies,* Sidney Lumet warned against using this type of material from your character's backstory: "In the early days of television, when the 'kitchen sink' school of realism held sway, we always reached a point where we 'explained' the character. Around two-thirds of the way through, someone articulated the psychological truth that made the character the person he was. [Paddy] Chayefsky and I used to call this the 'rubber-ducky' school of drama: 'Someone once took his rubber ducky away from him, and that's why he's a deranged killer.' That was the fashion then, and with many producers and studios it still is.

"I always try to eliminate the rubber-ducky explanations. A character should be clear from his present actions. And his behaviour as the picture goes on should reveal the psychological motivations. If the writer has to state the reasons, something's wrong in the way the character has been written."

"Leave 'em Hanging..."
In her *Mystery Fiction: Theory and Technique,* first published in 1943, Marie F. Rodell referred to an "... ancient and time-honoured device..." used in old movie serials. "Pauline was left hanging by her fingernails to the edge of a fearful abyss as the lights went up and the serial was over. The book counterpart of this device is to close a chapter with a climactic scene in which the villain has at last cornered the heroine in a deserted house and has her at his mercy, and to leave her there through one or more chapters while you follow the actions of other characters in the book." Cautioning against blatant uses of this technique, Rodell says: "Subtler forms of it are more permissible: the heroine manages to call the hero on the telephone; the reader, seeing the whole story only over the hero's shoulder, hears her agonised plea for help – and then a shot and silence. What has happened? Neither hero nor reader can tell until the hero manages to find out where the heroine is, and get there. This method has at least the grace to provide a reasonable excuse, other than a mere whim of the author, for breaking off in the midst of the heroine's danger."

William G. Tapply, in *The Elements of Mystery Fiction*, notes that many mystery writers recognise that readers tend to stop reading at the end of a chapter, and so end chapters with a cliff-hanger to keep them turning the pages. He cautions against overuse of the cliff-hanger: "If every chapter ends in the middle of the dialogue, or with the unexpected intrusion of a mysterious stranger, or with the ringing of the telephone, or with a gunshot, the reader will begin to feel manipulated." He says that people don't keep reading just to see what happens next – they keep reading because they are 'emotionally invested' in the story.

All that said, cliff-hangers can be effective, and they are still used all the time in novels, movies, and on tv. You create them by setting up a scene and developing the conflict, and then stopping at a point where the reader doesn't expect you to stop – the point at which something is about to be explained; the point at which conflict erupts; just before the moment of victory – or defeat. Cut away and show us a different scene with a different emotional content, different tempo, and different sort of suspense. Then cut back to the original scene at a point where the reader or viewer doesn't expect it. Next time you can give the reader something different by having a scene play out all the way to the climax with no cutting away. Variety helps keep people interested in your story.

Spoiler Alert
In the nature documentary, Oscar Wildebeest does indeed succeed in making it up the muddy bank to safety, though some of his comrades do not make it. And in *Strangers on a Train,* the villain does succeed in retrieving the lighter – and as for the consequences of that action, well, you'll just have to watch the movie and discover that for yourself.

5 | What's at Stake?

The job of the writer is to provide the reader with an emotional experience, and we can do this by making the reader *worry* about what is going to happen to the characters. In other words, writers are professional sadists who are paid to make the reader suffer – to make them squirm, to make them feel tense, uneasy, and afraid! This is true for stories of all genres, but it is particularly true for the thriller genre.

The way that we can achieve this is by creating a hero that the reader likes – or that they at least have an interest in – and then making this character *suffer.* This is true whether you are writing a thriller or a romance. How do you show how ecstatically happy your heroine is when she falls into the arms of her love at the end of the story? By contrasting this with the emotional anguish you put her through during her quest to win the heart of her true love. In real life, we try to avoid unpleasant situations. We have also learned that we should try and avoid creating unpleasant situations for other people. The technique for creating plots for novels and screenplays is exactly the opposite. We have to create unpleasant situations for our characters and our readers to endure. And in real life, if we find ourselves in one, we try and get out of it as quickly and painlessly as possible. But doing this is a story does not make for high drama. Effective stories require that difficult situations must endure and grow. The problem must intensify, becoming more challenging for the hero, before he is able to resolve the situation. If you are offended by bad puns, look away now: The stakes in your story must be well-done and not rare.

Genre and popular stories tend to be goal-oriented. The hero wants to achieve some objective by the end of the story. This goal must be something that is important to the character. But we must bear in mind that the reader could look at this goal and say: *Why should I care?* For our readers to care, we must show that there is something important at stake. What does the hero stand to lose if he fails to achieve his story goal? His car? His job? His lover? His life? For the story goal to be important to the reader, the hero must risk losing something important if he fails to achieve the goal. The greater the degree of risk, the more important the goal will seem to the reader – and the more they will care about the outcome of your story. This applies to both the overall story goal, and to the individual scene-goals that we have mentioned previously. At every stage in the story, we must – as writers – ask ourselves: What is the worst possible thing that could happen now? In every single scene there should be something at stake for at least one of the major characters – honour, love, self-esteem, friendship, wealth, respect, loyalty, authority... whatever.

Jeopardy

As we saw in the last chapter, suspense is created when the reader dreads something terrible happening to the hero or to someone the hero cares about. We must place our characters in *jeopardy*. That is, in situations where there is the threat of pain or failure, or some other undesirable outcome. The anticipation of suffering is usually more dramatic than the suffering itself – as any trip to the dentist will prove. The most emotionally involving horror movies, for example, are those that employ more suspense than shock and gore. You can draw suspense out for pages where a *boo!* is quickly gone and you have to come up with something new. Playing hope against fear creates tension, and that keeps the reader's interest. Place a character in jeopardy, and the reader will want to know how things turn out for him. When a character is threatened with something bad, the reader's attention will be focused on him to see what happens. The more helpless the character and the more terrible the danger, the more importance the reader will attach to the character. I have seen the hero defined as the person who suffers most in a story.

To be effective, the reader must believe that the threat to a character is real – that the suffering that is threatened might actually happen. Often the way to achieve that is to have one or two scenes where a similar sort of suffering does actually happen. It may not happen to one of the major characters, so its impact could be less, but it does make the reader aware that the threat of suffering later in the story isn't an idle threat.

If you are going to threaten your hero with some terrible fate, either at a story level or a scene level, think about utilising something that is feared by a large percentage of your audience. Common fears include rats, spiders, and snakes. Suffocation, enclosed spaces, drowning, being buried alive, or being burned alive. Total paralysis. Falling from a great height. Insanity. Loss of identity. Public humiliation.

When we talk about jeopardy, what sort of situations can that involve? Here are a few examples:

(i) Anticipation of physical harm. Also known as 'Don't open that door!' This is the obvious one. Let the reader know that something terrible awaits the hero – a beating from the villain's henchmen; a sabotaged parachute; or a mad axeman hiding in the closet. Or place the hero in a situation where the slightest slip will bring disaster – such as walking a tightrope, defusing a bomb or climbing a sheer rock face.

(ii) A race against time. Or 'We've just *got* to get there in time!' The timer on the bomb is ticking; the tide is coming in or the rain is falling and the water level is rising; the toxic chemicals are slowly eating through their container; the air is running out; the heroine is stuck in traffic, and she is late for the rendezvous she promised to attend so she and her lover could make one final attempt to salvage their relationship.

(iii) Fear of exposure or discovery. The reader knows that the hero has a secret, and anticipates what will happen when everyone finds out. In any movie where the hero is undercover or in some other way pretending to be something he

isn't, the hero risks exposure. A burglar searching someone's room risks discovery by the room's owner. Any person who is in hiding risks their location being found.

(iv) Threat to the hero's dignity. The hero risks being made to look foolish, perhaps in front of someone he is trying to impress. Think how terrible it would be to have your deepest, most personal wishes or fears revealed and ridiculed; imagine how humiliated you would feel. An old favourite of this type is having the hero lose all of his clothes and have to try to travel some distance without being seen. Or the hero may be deliberately humiliated by someone who has authority over him.

(v) Give the hero an internal conflict. Desire versus duty: the hero wants to go off and win the hand of his true love or achieve sporting success, or whatever, but he has obligations - to family, to work, or some such - which mean he can't just abandon everything to pursue his goal: he is faced with a choice, a *dilemma*. Or, he needs to pursue a course of action in order to achieve his goal, but that course of action will put others - innocent bystanders - at risk. Again, a dilemma, a difficult choice to make.

(vi) *Make the hero choose a course of action.* This is linked to (v) above: the hero comes to a fork in the road, does he go left or right? If he makes the wrong choice, he risks a terrible fate for himself or someone he cares about; but he cannot go back, because not making a choice will also bring about a terrible fate. He must choose a direction, and then accept responsibility for the consequences of that choice. His actions must have consequences, and they will often result in him being left in a worse position with respect to his goal than he was before he made the choice.

There's some overlap here with the creation of suspense, which we have already covered.

Suffering

A character who suffers pain – whether physical or emotional – is likely to evoke a strong emotional reaction in the reader. A character who *inflicts* pain is also going to cause people to have strong feelings. Remember that strong emotional responses are what we *want* to evoke in our readers – it is the kind of experience they are seeking – and so, as writers, we must regard suffering as our friend. [Rubs hands and cackles maniacally]

The level of pain we inflict on characters needs to be carefully judged. If it is a trivial injury – that movie cliché 'just a flesh wound' or the emotional equivalent – then the reader isn't going to care. On the other hand, if we subject a character to unbearable physical or psychological torture, the reader is likely to turn off and refuse to remain engaged in the story. Suffering also loses effectiveness with repetition: the first time a character is whacked over the head, the pain is real and draws sympathy from the reader; by the third or fourth time, the pain has become a joke and the character a comic victim, or the story has lost all sense of credibility. Hard-boiled detectives and James Bond tend to get slugged over the head and endure multiple beatings that no human being could ever really endure, so this is a matter of genre and context, but in all things story repetition tends to diminish an effect. Similarly, with grief and/or loss – the first time it is referred to, the reader is emotionally moved. But keep harping on about this suffering, and the reader begins to feel that the character is whining, and emotional involvement decreases.

The effectiveness of suffering is increased not by describing the injury and loss in greater detail, but rather by showing more of its cause and effect. If you can make us understand how intensely the character loved before losing their loved one, or how deeply they trusted before being betrayed, then the suffering will have greater impact. In terms of effect, we tend to feel more strongly when someone endures pain or grief stoically, refusing to succumb to it. I mentioned this before, but it is an old Hollywood truth – if a character on screen cries, the audience won't usually feel the need to; but if we give the hero a reason to cry, and he doesn't, then the audience will often cry for him.

Sacrifice

The emotional and dramatic impact of suffering increases in proportion to the sufferer's degree of choice. We feel sympathy for someone who suffers because they have no choice in the matter. We tend to feel *more* sympathy for someone who chooses to put themselves in a situation where they must suffer – providing their choice is a moral one rather than a stupid one. For example, we are likely to admire a character who chooses to stand up for a principle, even though he knows he will suffer as a result. Someone who chooses to suffer in order to protect other people is regarded as heroic. Someone who chooses to endure suffering because they feel they must atone for past sins, evokes a strong emotional response in us – whether we feel their actions are correct or not.

Similarly, a character who accidentally injures someone evokes an emotional response from us, but a person who consciously *chooses* to inflict pain on someone else evokes a much stronger response in us. We have much stronger feelings of fear and hate for the torturer than we do for the hit-and-run driver. This is why the sadistic villain is often much more memorable than the goody-goody hero. And that's why we have to make our heroes suffer – so the reader has much stronger emotional reactions to them.

Establishing What's at Stake

We establish the stakes in a story by asking: What terrible fate awaits the hero if he fails to achieve his story-goal? What does he stand to lose? As the story progresses, we will raise the stakes, which we will come on to below, but for now, let's look at how we can establish the stakes to start with. Bear in mind that what is said here about the overall stakes in a story, applies – on a smaller scale – to individual scenes within a story. As writers we need to be able to conjure up 'terrible fates' for our hero – but what does that mean, and how do we do it? A terrible fate should be something that the hero is afraid of suffering, and something that the audience will dread happening to him. At times during a story, the hero doesn't know what danger lurks ahead – but the reader always knows. We need them to be able to look ahead and imagine what could happen.

To do this, we may give the reader information – or allow them to figure out clues or infer consequences – that the hero remains unaware of.

We can explore stakes on two levels – the personal stakes for the hero. That is, what terrible fate awaits him as an individual. And the 'societal' stakes – what terrible fate could befall the hero's family, group, hometown, country, or world.

Personal Stakes

There are effectively three types of personal threat:

(i) Physical threat – risk of injury, threat to health, or risk of death
(ii) Emotional threat – risk of loss of love or friendship
(iii) Threat to mental well-being – risk of insanity; including the threat to dignity that is used in many humorous situations

If we think about characters in terms of archetypes, we can see that these three types of threats can be related to the three hero types. The *Warrior* is a physical type who is motivated by a desire for mastery and power. He fears being weak or exploited, so that risk of physical injury or imprisonment – anything that makes him feel vulnerable – will be seen as the major stakes for this type of person. The *Carer* is an emotional type who is motivated by love and a desire to be nurturing. She wants to experience a loving relationship or help others achieve their greatest potential. She fears losing love or being unable to help others, and so threats to these things will be regarded as major stakes for this type. For the *Thinker,* sanity is at stake: he wants a stable and safe view of the world, and to be free from fear. He desires to understand the world and to be able to safely predict what will happen. Randomness or chaos make him extremely uncomfortable, and he risks great harm if he feels that his grasp on reality is being undermined: if he feels that the model of how the world works that he holds in his head is being threatened. These threats correspond with universal fears: if we can create a specific situation which involves a credible threat of this kind, we can hook the interest of the reader.

Societal Stakes

If the hero of the story fails in his quest, what does society or the world as a whole lose? We often hear the standard cliché used to describe thrillers – *the fate of the free world hangs in the balance* – but it is quite difficult to make the reader feel that this is true. What we're really asking here is: How does the villain's conspiracy threaten society as a whole? Typically, the villain represents the negative side of an ethical argument: his plan goes against some value that our society views as important. The conspiracy will usually threaten national security, or democracy, or justice, or freedom, or some other value of this kind. As we have said, the conspiracy concerns something that is essentially unethical.

In action-adventure movies, the hero's life is often at risk, but these situations often feel empty because there is nothing important underlying the superficial threat. You can create a series of car chases and other action-adventure set-pieces, but they are unlikely to genuinely move the audience unless they can be made to feel that there is something of value at stake. It isn't enough to threaten the hero with injury or death, there needs to be an important ethical or moral value at stake as well. The reader should feel that if the hero fails in his personal quest, we all fail. Damage is done to society as a whole. The hero is our representative and our champion. It is not enough that his life or his happiness is in jeopardy – we should feel that something important to us is threatened too. The aim is to take something specific – the hero's situation – and make it feel universal.

Authorial Stakes

For the reader to care, the author must care. In establishing what is at stake in a story, you must decide – or discover – what is important to you as an individual. What human values do you feel passionate about? If you do not personally *feel* that what is at stake is important, the jeopardy in which you place your hero will feel weak or unconvincing. Write about something that is important to you. Think of some behaviour that you personally find immoral and offensive, some injustice that makes you angry, and then seek to recreate that feeling using a specific situation that your hero must face.

Raising the Stakes

If the threat level in the story remains constant, it will quickly lose its effect on the reader. To keep them turning the pages we must increase the tension by raising the stakes. We must place the hero in greater and greater physical, emotional, and mental jeopardy. Rising tension shouldn't be a linear progression, as this would become monotonous and even boring or unbelievable. The tension in a story should ebb and flow like a great piece of music. There should be moments of calm, lulling the reader, so that the next crescendo stands out in greater relief. But the overall trajectory, from the middle of Act I to the climax in Act III, should be a rising one.

The goal of the writer is to make the protagonist suffer. Being nice to the hero doesn't make for a dramatic story. You should always be thinking: How could his situation be made worse? When is the worst possible moment for it to be made worse? And rather than just threatening the hero with danger, have bad things *actually happen* – a near-miss, a major accident, a small loss – to prove that the dangers he faces are real. "Ask yourself, who is the one ally your protagonist cannot afford to lose? Kill that character," Writes Donald Maass. "What is your protagonist's greatest physical asset? Take it away. What is the one article of faith that for your protagonist is sacred? Undermine it. How much time does your protagonist have to solve his main problem? Shorten it."

There are seven key points in the story at which the stakes are raised. That is, at the turning point at the end of the first seven sequences of the story. In a movie, we keep the audience's attention by raising the stakes every ten to fifteen minutes.

Arthur Sullivant Hoffman, in *Fiction Writing Self-Taught,* offers five ways for increasing the stakes, relating to the value of the protagonist's goal:

1) Increase its intrinsic value;
2) Increase the hero's need for it or his desire for it;
3) Increase the penalty of failure both in size and in number of people affected;
4) Increase the need, desire and penalty in the case of the opposition;
5) Add other issues to be decided by the same struggle.

Hoffman also offers a list of ways for raising the odds against the protagonist:

(i) Increase his physical, mental, emotional and moral handicaps;
(ii) Decrease his abilities, gifts, resources, facilities, influence;
(iii) Increase his limitations as to information, location, position, liberty, weather and general natural conditions;
(iv) Increase his ties and obligations, financial, of blood, friendship, love, good faith, loyalty, honour, morality;
(v) Decrease the number and power of his allies or of aiding factors;
(vi) Make some of these allies and factors a hindrance rather than a help;
(vii) If the final end he seeks, or an end along the way, is a decision by any other actor, prejudice that actor against him;
(viii) Add manufactured handicaps to his real ones by making him the victim of misrepresentation or of misunderstanding;
(ix) Have him miss opportunities that lie open to him, but do not make him a congenital idiot in these failures;
(x) Have him lose assets he had possessed at the start or advantages he has gained;
(xi) Search all circumstances and events for other points to lessen his chances and thereby increase the magnitude and desperation, the stress, of this struggle.

"Another method, plainly," Hoffman writes, "is to do these eleven things, in reverse, to the opposition."

There are other ways in which additional pressure can be brought to bear on the hero:

Increase the Importance of the Goal. You can increase pressure on the hero by making the achievement of the story-goal more important. At the same time, you can increase the penalty for failure. This is linked to increasing the personal and social jeopardy (see below). The goal may become more valuable to the antagonist as well as the hero, making the antagonist intensify his efforts to prevent the hero from succeeding.

Increase Societal Jeopardy. A story may begin by impacting on the hero or the lives of a small group of characters. But as the story goes on, the consequences of the characters' actions may spread out into the world around them, impacting on the lives of others. This will gradually increase the feelings of responsibility in those who take the decisions to act: a choice of action which has consequences for yourself alone is much easier to make than one which might cause danger to dozens of innocent bystanders. The lives of secondary characters may be put at risk, and only the hero can save them.

Increase Personal Jeopardy. Rather than spreading the consequences out to affect the lives of others, the consequences can be made to impact on the intimate relationships and inner lives of the principal characters. The consequences may have an emotional, psychological, physical or moral impact. Dark secrets or fears may be exposed, unspoken secrets which lie behind the public mask.

Symbolic Jeopardy. Outside events can be used to symbolise an increase in tension; they can act as signs and portents. Build the symbolic charge of the story's imagery from the particular to the universal, the specific to the archetypal. Start with actions, locations, and roles that represent only themselves. But as the story progresses, choose images that gather greater and greater meaning, until by the end of the story characters, settings, and events stand for universal ideas.

Sexual Tension. Will they, won't they? If the audience sees a man and a woman and wants them to get together romantically, tension is generated by keeping the two characters apart. Sexual tension is a form of jeopardy, except that it is related to a desire for something to happen, rather than a fear of something bad. If two people meet and become important to each other, the sexual tension increases – especially if we introduce a negative element into their relationship. Rivalry, contempt, anger – the more intense these negative feelings are, the more sexual tension there is. Sexual tension intensifies the audience's involvement with the characters involved. However, as several TV series have discovered to their sorrow, tension dissipates when the characters come together in sexual harmony. It isn't like violence, which establishes the villain's credibility and makes the next round of jeopardy even more powerful. Instead, sexual fulfilment has the same effect on sexual tension that the death of the victim has on jeopardy. For that character, at least, the tension is over.

Take Away the Resources. You can make life more difficult for the hero by taking away the things he is relying on to reach his objective. He may be robbed, or his vehicle may be vandalised or destroyed. He could be cut off from people who can offer him help – his team may be killed, injured, or they may desert him. The same with his mentor or closest ally. A road or path may be washed away. The weather may be too extreme for flying. He may run out of fuel or drinking water. He may lose his local guide or interpreter. In a thriller, the first half of Act II (Sequences 3 & 4) often consists of a series of scenes where every possible source of help the hero could turn to is taken away. We set up the situation so that he cannot go to the police for help, and then we ensure that he cannot even go to colleagues, friends, or family for assistance or moral support.

Reduce the Hero's Authority or Influence. As a result of his own actions or failure to take action, or as a result of the machinations of others, the hero may lose a position of influence, authority, or social standing. He may find himself discredited or undermined. He may even find himself accused of crimes he did not commit. As a result, he may lose support, or have vital resources or sources of information denied him.

Conflicts of Loyalty. If the hero has obligations to others, or has made promises he must honour, he may find his options for action are reduced as a result. He may be prevented from taking a necessary action because it would require him to break an oath or bond. Or he may have some sentimental reason for not taking an action.

Relationship Issues. An ally may betray him. A mentor may refuse to help. He may become estranged from a lover or a family member because of a mistake, a misunderstanding, or because someone has deliberately undermined the relationship. The hero may need a decision or permission from someone, but that person may be prejudiced against the hero for some reason. A long-standing feud with another person or group may become an obstacle to achieving the story-goal.

Raise Doubts. Doubt and uncertainty can cause or intensify danger. Anything that is uncertain, unknown, or untried carries an element of risk. Something that the hero believed to be true – about a person, a place, an object, tool, or weapon – may be thrown into doubt: if his plan depended on this truth, the mission is put in jeopardy. Is he or isn't he? Is it or isn't it? Is there a traitor in the hero's team? Is the so-called expert actually a fake? Has a vehicle or weapon been sabotaged? The aim is to undermine the hero at every opportunity!

Use the Location Against Him. Depending on the circumstances of the story, and the nature of the hero's plan, a setting can provide addition risks: it could be too large or too small; too remote; too open; too public; too light; too dark; inaccessible; too accessible; too remote; too close to other places; lacking in facilities; structurally unsound; contaminated; sacred; too wet; too dry; too hot; too cold... whatever the hero needs the location to be, make it be the opposite. If you can make his actions more difficult and his life more uncomfortable, then do it! Be a sadist.

We have now covered all of the basic tools for creating a thriller. In Chapter 13, I will cover some techniques for creating the kind of chase or manhunt that often features in a suspense thriller. Before that, we will explore some of the major sub-genres of the thriller, beginning with a brief look at the professional fields in which thrillers are often set.

6 | 'Expert' Thrillers

Before we move on to look at specific sub-genres of the thriller, I want to briefly explore a few things that the sub-genres have in common. The sub-genres covered in Chapters 7 through 12 are all based in a particular professional sphere and many of the characters are experts in that specialised field. This has led some academics to refer to them collectively as an identifiable sub-set of the thriller genre, with the legal thriller, medical thriller, techno-thriller etc. all belonging to this subset.

The idea of 'professionally-based' fiction was identified by French researcher Michel Petit – he referred to it as *Fiction à Substrat Professionnel* often abbreviated to *FASP* and translated into English as professionally-based fiction (PBF). I've already used 'professional' to mean a protagonist who is not an amateur, so I have titled this chapter *'Expert' Thrillers* to avoid confusion. I will also note here that while a protagonist is an expert in a particular field – law, medicine, the military, politics, or whatever – that does not necessarily make them a professional hero. A top class lawyer can just as easily find him or herself out of their depth when pursued by the mafia as a person without a law degree.

According to Jean-Pierre Charpy, novels in this category had "... a solid professional basis that reinforced the credibility of the narrative and discursive elements present in the novels..." Charpy also said that "... the fictional representation of doctors, forensic doctors, lawyers or military experts can be equated with clearly-defined specialised genres (medical thrillers, forensic thrillers, legal thrillers, and military techno-thrillers)..." Shaeda Isani has said that the *substrat professionnel* is "the highly specialised professional and/or technical springboard which fuels the plot dynamics of a fictional thriller" and notes the "author's exceptional degree of insider knowledge" as a defining characteristic.

Expert Thriller Authors

In terms of the authors of FASP, Michel Petit makes four observations, with John Grisham and Robin Cook being his primary examples:

(i) They have a personal competence resulting from their initial training, usually demonstrated by a university degree.
(ii) They have a personal competence that results from professional experience, usually demonstrated by a number of years of practice of the profession.
(iii) They are specialists in a particular sub-genre of thriller, demonstrated by the success of these previous works – particularly if they are 'bestsellers'.

(iv) They supplement their own personal competence by calling upon the expertise of professionals in specialized fields – typically listing their contributions on an acknowledgments page.

To point (iv) we might also add the fact that the author may include an appendix of professional journal articles and other texts that he or she consulted when writing the novel – though as Stéphanie Genty has observed we must observe caution in this respect because an author may fabricate the references or misuse the content of real ones.

Michel Petit also notes that the four items above are often used in the promotion of an author or an author's latest novel, with promotional literature emphasising professional expertise and previous bestselling status.

Expert Thriller Story Content

In terms of the content of the novels, Petit writes that they are 'specialised thrillers' which have much in common with other thrillers. In particular, he notes that these are stories where readers desire to know the outcome and that suspense is an essential element. The novels are marketed as 'suspenseful' and as 'page-turners.'

At its most basic, the plot of a FASP novel, according to Petit, "... is essentially based on the personal adventure of a central character who, from an ordinary situation in his professional life, will be confronted with a series of extraordinary situations, endangering his personal security and/or socio-professional status and opening up collective issues of a magnitude and severity that are also extraordinary." (All translations from French by Google Translate)

Petit: "The starting point of the story is usually a case submitted or brought to the attention of the central character in his professional life (lawyer takes on a new legal case, doctor a medical case, etc.). His ordinary work will lead him to investigate the circumstances of this case. In some cases, the starting point may be murder, but the FASP is different from the police thriller (or mystery) in the nature of the resulting investigation and the fact that the investigating character is not a policeman or detective."

The protagonist will conduct the investigation in a manner consistent with his specific professional field – that is, a doctor would investigate using techniques appropriate to medical diagnosis and/or research, whereas a lawyer would investigate using procedures used in his everyday work in a law office and/or courtroom.

The nature of the mystery or conspiracy investigated by the expert-hero will also be related to his field of expertise. There would be little point in having a surgeon-hero caught up in an adventure that didn't centre on a medical conspiracy. And as Petit writes, in FASP space is given to present the people, objects, and procedures that make up the reality of the specialised field in which the thriller is based.

As mentioned above, the author may consult experts as he writes the novel but the protagonist within the story may also seek advice from more seasoned practitioners in his own field. Often the main character is newly qualified and inexperienced and has to ask questions of a more senior character. This device allows the author to include specialist explanations – senior to junior – in dialogue that two experts of equal standing would not normally engage in. To quote the old example, when a character in a movie says 'As you know, professor...' the audience knows they're in for an infodump. This kind of writing is lazy and unconvincing – why would you tell someone something they already know? But having a mentor share something with his protégé is entirely natural.

In the FASP or expert thriller, the reader expects to be fed explanations, details of technical procedures, and explorations of theories in the field – it is part of the reason they seek a particular sub-genre of the thriller in the first place. They want to see what goes on 'behind the scenes' in this field and observe an expert at work. They want to experience what it is like to work as a lawyer, or a surgeon, or the commander of a nuclear submarine. They want to learn about the equipment that is used in day to day activities. They want to see how problems encountered in this field are dealt with – as well as how the protagonist deals with the larger thriller-conspiracy situation.

Specialised vocabulary is a feature of virtually all professions, including technical terms, abbreviations and acronyms. These may be used in what Petit refers to as procedural exchanges such as radio exchanges between military pilots and ground control or the use of legal terminology and phrases in the courtroom. Some of these terms have been used frequently in novels and on film and television screens so are well-known to audiences. As well as formal professional language, there are informal and slang terms used by those in a particular profession and these can be used in fiction to add to the feeling that readers are being allowed a glimpse behind the curtain.

While the use of this type of language, and other aspects drawn from the field, can be used to give a sense of verisimilitude or colour, I should emphasise that the professional field in which a FASP thriller is set is not there simply as a backdrop. Although the plot will normally follow the conventions of the thriller genre, the story will make use of – and at times, depend upon – features of that professional field. Protagonist and antagonist will make use of specialist knowledge and procedures to achieve things – or achieve things in a way – that could not be achieved in a thriller set in another field. Ideally, the protagonist's final solution to the story problem should also be field-specific while also being something that the ordinary reader could see themselves achieving in similar circumstances.

7 | Espionage Thriller

What is an Espionage Thriller?
There are essentially two kinds of espionage or spy thriller – (a) those in which the hero engages with an enemy *outside* of his home nation and (b) those where he faces a representative of the enemy on the *inside* in the form of a traitor. In the language of John Le Carré's novels, the spy who goes off on a mission against the enemy is out 'in the cold' while the spy who searches for a traitor in his own government or intelligence organisation is hunting for a 'mole.' There are variations on these, but they are the two main types.

There is another binary division that we also need to be aware of – the difference between *espionage* and *counter-espionage.* At the most basic level, espionage means spying on the enemy and stealing their secrets, and counter-espionage means preventing the enemy from spying on us and stealing our secrets. Both espionage and counter-espionage can take place either at home or out in the field.

Cawelti and Rosenberg have said that "... more than any other character or occupational type, the spy must have freedom of movement. Arrest, imprisonment, capture, or even revelation of his identity render his mission inoperative and his function in life useless. Thus, the spy of fiction should always be in danger of losing that mobility or in danger of exposure. Fear felt by the empathetic reader imparts the thrill to the thriller."

In the past, the act of 'spying' meant obtaining documents – secret blueprints for a military device, a codebook, plans for a military operation, a list of spies operating in enemy territory, or something of that nature – or less tangible 'intelligence' about the activities of a country's military and espionage activities. While counter-spying involved preventing the enemy from obtaining your secret documents or transmitting intelligence about your activities. But after the end of the Second World War, the work of intelligence agencies expanded, as Cawelti and Rosenberg write in *The Spy Story,* to include "... arranging assassinations, financing revolutions and training the combatants, bribing foreign soldiers to defect with their aircraft or tanks intact, salvaging vessels that have sunk while on classified missions." These additional activities have also found their way into thrillers. There has also been a change in the nature of the enemy – as well as seeking intelligence about other nations, there is also the need to obtain information about terrorist groups that pose a threat to 'our' country.

These developments mean that there are now significant overlaps between the espionage thriller and both the *political thriller* and the *techno-thriller.* The 'assassination thriller' and the 'terrorism thriller' could easily be included in this chapter, but I have chosen to treat them as sub-categories of the *political thriller.*And stories such as Tom Clancy's *The Hunt for Red October* and Craig

Thomas' *Firefox* – which both fit into the extended range of espionage actions Cawelti and Rosenberg listed – I have put into the *techno-thriller* chapter.

What's the Difference Between an Espionage Thriller and a Secret Agent Thriller?
In Chapter 2 I wrote about the James Bond thrillers as examples of the professional secret agent thriller – but aren't they really spy stories? Yes and no. Technically, James Bond is a counter-intelligence agent engaged in missions 'out in the cold.' M says to Bond, Go and find out what the villain is up to, stop him from doing it, and kill him if you have to. He almost always has to, making him a government-sanctioned assassin – that's why he's 'licenced to kill.' While the definition of espionage work has been broadened to include assassination, most agents in the field are not engaged in this sort of work. And most spies are nothing like James Bond.

Stella Rimington, the former Director General of Britain's MI5 has said, "The best and most successful spies are the quiet, apparently boring and dull people who go on doing the same thing in an unostentatious way year after year and the best counter-espionage officers are those who match them for perseverance." W. Somerset Maugham worked in the intelligence service during the First World War and was the first British author to write about his experiences in fictional form. The stories he published in *Ashenden* (1928) show that spies are typically more like civil servants than superheroes and have been described by Michael Denning as "quiet and desperate tales."

The difference between what I'm calling an espionage thriller and a secret agent thriller is the difference between George Smiley and James Bond. The stories about John Le Carré's protagonist are so different from those by Ian Fleming that I felt I had to separate them and treat them in separate chapters. George Smiley seems to be exactly the sort of person Stella Rimington was describing – and the exact opposite of James Bond. For our purposes in this book, then, the espionage thriller is the sort of book John Le Carré writes. Later I will demonstrate some of the things that Le Carré's *The Spy Who Came in from the Cold* has in common with the James Bond 'formula' plot, but to begin with we'll concentrate on those things unique to the espionage thriller.

One difference between a Le Carré novel and an Ian Fleming novel is that the former is regarded as being more 'realistic' than the latter. Le Carré is also said to be a more 'literary' writer than Fleming, but that doesn't really concern us here as we are exploring how their plots are created rather than how their writing styles differ.

What are the Differences Between the Espionage Thriller and Political Thrillers and Murder Mysteries?
I have already said that there are similarities between the espionage thriller and the political thriller, but what is the major difference between them? Both deal with the defence of ideologies or worldviews, assassinations, traitors and infiltrators, but the political thriller is told from the point of view of a character who belongs in the 'real' world as opposed to the 'secret' world. The protagonist of a political thriller discovers that there is a conspiracy going on and either

deliberately or accidentally becomes mixed up in it and ends up trying to expose it or end it. The protagonist of an espionage thriller is part of the secret world that most people don't know about – and part of his job is to keep the secret world secret, even from people in his own country. He is himself part of a 'conspiracy' carried out to protect his country.

Later in this chapter, I will show how the espionage agent's hunt for a traitor in his organisation proceeds on similar lines to the hunt for the murderer in a whodunit, but it is important to be aware of the differences between the two types of plot as well. In the classic murder mystery, the detective's mission is known to all – the suspects know he is searching for the murderer in their midst, as does the murderer, who is one of the suspects; in the spy thriller, the investigation itself must be kept secret for fear of tipping off the traitor and his spymasters. Also in the mystery, the detective is an outsider providing an objective viewpoint, whereas in the spy thriller the investigator is a spy himself – he is part of the organisation that he is investigating.

Also, in the murder mystery, the conspiracy involves the murderer trying to hide his guilt by making it *seem* that a false set of circumstances – which 'prove' his innocence – are true. The equilibrium of the real world is upset until the detective can prove that what *seemed* to have happened was false by showing what *really* happened. Only for a brief period did a disturbing version of reality seem to be true. In the espionage thriller, the reader – and sometimes an innocent hero – discovers that as well as the real world that we know, there is another disturbing world, a clandestine world, that also exists and is *equally real*. Once we and the hero have gained knowledge of this world, we can never be returned to the comfort of knowing that this clandestine world has been proved false.

The Appeal of the Espionage Thriller

These thrillers appeal to emotions that we all share. Although few of us ever engage in espionage as such, there are aspects of our lives that involve similar activities and feelings. Cawelti and Rosenberg say that, "Carrying out a love affair often requires many of the same practices as an espionage mission: secret communications, hidden rendezvous, complicated alibis, and elaborate disguises. Such lovers often experience the special closeness of people who share a dangerous bond unknown to others. Not surprisingly, poets have often noted the analogy between love and espionage. Shakespeare and Donne both use spy metaphors to express secret love, for example."

Other feelings evoked by the espionage thriller include:

Patriotism. Espionage thrillers explore feelings of *patriotism* – either celebrating the actions of someone who is 'doing their duty' for their country; or questioning what patriotism means and exploring whether certain actions are ethical in the service of protecting one's country. Espionage heroes also defend the dominant ideology of their country – they do what they do because they believe it is morally right; their individual actions may be ethically questionable, but they are undertaken for the best of reasons – in defence of human rights and democracy, or because of a strongly-held political or religious doctrine. But as

Sam Goodman has noted, there is a paradox here – spies operate outside the rules of their own state in order to protect that state, and these actions undermine the state they seek to protect. If we spy on them, they spy on us. If we turn their agents into double agents, they do the same to ours.

Paranoia. I discussed paranoia in Chapter 3 and although it may be regarded as an unpleasant or negative feeling, it still accounts for some of the appeal of the espionage thriller because – having experienced it ourselves – we empathise with story characters who are experiencing it. We appreciate the feeling of being followed or watched. Associated with this are feelings of being betrayed or being the betrayer. There is the fear of capture and interrogation – of torture – and of being forced to reveal our secrets. And there is the fear of being taken over and forced to submit to an 'alien' ideology or religion.

Fear of Being Caught or Exposed. Cawelti and Rosenberg have written that the spy thriller appeals to that part of us that fears being caught or exposed. "Espionage fiction is not alone in allowing the reader to concretise repressed conflicts – in the case of spy novels, repressed anxiety – and once concretised as literary symbols, to deal with them safely. Objectified repressed matter can, without being acknowledged, be confronted and thus (as Simon Lesser tells us in *Fiction and the Unconscious*) cathartically relieved." Fear of exposure is linked to the idea that we all have secrets that we don't want the world to know.

Disguise and False Identity. Cawelti and Rosenberg write that "...folktales, myths, and stories indicate the perennial human fascination with disguise, the power of which very likely resides in the thrill of trying on other identities – social, racial, sexual, or chronological." They associate this with the idea of hiding and being unseen or invisible to others, which also features in myth and folktale. Jacques Barzun has suggested that espionage literature may also appeal to other, deeper feelings that people share. In psychological terms, we all have façades – we have a public self and a secret, private self that we share only with people we trust. This knowledge that we are, in our daily lives, an imposter is something we see reflected in spy thrillers and we can – perhaps only a subliminal level – say, 'I have felt like that' and 'I have that fear of being found out.' These feelings also mean that we know other people are presenting a façade and that they too have a secret life. There is a part of us that wants to 'spy' on these people and see what they are *really* like. The idea of presenting a false-self to the world – wearing a disguise – and hiding your true self is also linked to the appeal of the archetype role of the Trickster or outsider (see *alienation* below).

Voyeurism. Alfred Hitchcock in particular exploited our voyeuristic tendencies – and his own – in stories where he set about demolishing the façade of the cool blonde female so that he could show what she was *really* like behind the mask. The modern obsessive interest in celebrity gossip has turned this fascination into an industry with numerous magazines offering to give us a peek into the secret lives of celebrities and royalty. The 'bonkbuster' novels of the 1980s and

90s aimed to satisfy the same interests, taking us behind the scenes and showing us the secret lives of the wealthy and the beautiful.

Alienation. This is the feeling of being a stranger or outsider, not knowing the social rules and trying to fit in. Cawelti and Rosenberg have also noted that the spy thriller also reflects a sense of alienation that many people felt in their own lives during the latter half of the twentieth century. They refer to "the alienation of the individual from the large organisations – corporations, bureaucracies, professions – which dominate our lives," and say they believe that "it is this sense of alienation and the deep feeling of conflict between individual self and social role which it engenders that makes the spy so compelling as a contemporary everyman hero." The spy carries out a mission in 'territory dominated by the enemy' or is 'threatened by betrayal from his own organisation' and this reflects the frustrations of many individuals during that period. Being an outsider or not belonging is not always a negative feeling. We are often attracted by the idea of being a rebel, of not conforming. Being self-reliant and shunning authority is a quality we like to see in fictional characters – James Bond being an obvious example. In literature, the Trickster is the character that causes chaos, upsetting the equilibrium of people's lives and challenging their beliefs, but who also makes people question their assumptions in a healthy way.

Mystery and Puzzles. Espionage thrillers may also have the same appeal as the classic murder mystery, in that there is usually a puzzle to be unravelled – such as the identity of the enemy agent or the double-agent that has infiltrated the home organisation.

Secret Societies. Membership of a group or gang can make people feel special and/or in some way protected. The idea of a 'band of brothers' to whom we remain loyal and who remain loyal to us has a strong appeal in real life and in fiction. Belonging to an outlaw gang that serves as a surrogate family is part of the appeal of the legend of Robin Hood and it is found in movies like *The Warriors,* S. E. Hinton's novels, especially *Rumblefish,* and Mario Puzo's *The Godfather.* Spies belong to a secret club and, interestingly, there is a sort of fellowship between field agents from opposing sides – like the soldier in the battlefield trench the combatants from each side often have more in common with each other than they have with the generals and even the people back home.

Historical Development of the Espionage Thriller
The history of espionage fiction falls into six distinct periods:
- (i) Ancient Antecedents to the Nineteenth Century
- (ii) Premonitions of War & Clubland Heroes (1900 to the 1920s)
- (iii) The Rise of Fascism (1930s)
- (iv) The Second World War (1940s)
- (v) The Cold War (1950s to 1980s)
- (vi) The War on Terror, Cyber-Attacks & Domestic Spying (21st Century)

(i) Ancient Antecedents to the Nineteenth Century

John Gardner has said that "... the spy and the whore both vie for the title of the oldest profession." The oldest example (of a spy) he quotes is Judith in the biblical Apocrypha which dates from before the fifth century BC. Cawelti and Rosenberg add that, "Joshua sent spies into Canaan, and, in one of the most famous biblical stories, the great warrior Samson was brought down by a neat bit of counter-espionage work carried out by history's first recorded female agent." They also note that Judas Iscariot was a spy in the camp of Jesus Christ and ultimately his betrayer, "The legends of espionage are full of the progeny of Delilah and Judas." John M. Caldwell has also reported that Moses also used spies when his people were camped in the wilderness, sending them across the border to see what the Promised Land was like.

Also dating from the fifth century BC is Sun Tzu's *The Art of War*. Sun Tzu said there were five classes of spy:

- Local spies – inhabitants of a district
- Inward spies – officials of the enemy
- Converted spies – taking the enemy's spies and using them for our own purposes
- Doomed spies – giving disinformation to our own spies, such that they believe it is true and will give it to our enemies when they are captured
- Surviving spies – those who bring back information from the enemy's camp

The mention of 'doomed spies' here is interesting as it is an idea that was used to good effect by John Le Carré.

Predating these examples, Homer's *Iliad* and *Odyssey* dating from the eighth century BC, depict the hero spying on his enemies. Gardner also mentions that the 14th Century Chinese text *San Kuo* (*The Romance of the Three Kingdoms*) contains a great deal of 'incidental espionage detail.'

Spies have probably existed for as long as there have been two groups of people brought into conflict by their desire for territory and/or religious beliefs. In the Elizabethan age – Sir Francis Walsingham was the Queen's 'spymaster' – and spies were used during the war for American independence. But the spy has not really featured as the central character in fiction much before the beginning of the 20th Century.

The first spy *novel* is thought to be J. Fenimore Cooper's *The Spy* (1821), inspired by a real-life spy who operated during the American War of Independence. In his introduction to the anthology *To Catch a Spy*, Eric Ambler dismisses Cooper's novel as "...noteworthy only in that it is unreadable." Cawelti and Rosenberg say that despite this, Cooper's novel is significant in that it recognises the spy as existing in 'liminality,' in no-man's-land, and that "... he was able to capture the essential sense of that characteristically 'modern' phenomenon, life on the margins, the borders, the limits of society, the interstices of its structure." In the same introduction, Ambler explores a possible reason for the absence of spy fiction before the 1900s. It is not, he says, because public interest in spying was lacking before the Dreyfus Affair (1894-1906), rather it comes down to the unwritten military code of honour that was in place until the Hague Convention of 1899. This unwritten code indicated what sort of behaviour was acceptable during warfare and what was not. Any form of deceit, including espionage and counter-espionage, was regarded as ungentlemanly and therefore no one who acted as a spy could be regarded as a hero. Military commanders needed the information that spies could provide, but at the same time they could not bring themselves to admit that they employed spies.

Napoleon is believed to have said, "One spy in the right place is worth twenty thousand men." His most celebrated spy was Karl Ludwig Schulmeister, who Ambler describes as "a man of great courage, skill, and loyalty." The intelligence he gathered for Napoleon was invaluable, but as Ambler says, "when it came time to reward Schulmeister for his services, it was the same Napoleon, a stickler for proprieties in some matters, who refused him the Legion of Honour, remarking contemptuously that money was the only suitable reward for a spy." By definition, Ambler argues, a spy is a liar and a thief, and therefore was not suitable material to be the hero of a novel.

The 1871 novella *The Battle of Dorking: Reminiscences of a Volunteer* by George Tomkyns Chesney was propaganda disguised as fiction telling of the invasion of Britain by an unnamed country referred to as The Other Power or The Enemy – though the fact that they spoke German may have been intended as a clue! It is significant in that it inspired future war stories in what would become the genre of science fiction and of adventure stories warning of the threat posed by foreign powers that became espionage fiction. Two such stories were William Le Queux's *The Great War in England in 1897* (1894) and *England's Peril* (1899). Erskine Childers and John Buchan also drew inspiration from this type of story.

(ii) Premonitions of War & Clubland Heroes (1900 to the 1920s)
If ever you are looking for an example of the stereotyped 'cloak and dagger' spy story, William Le Queux is your man. His stories have innocent heroes with high moral values and dark villains, usually foreign, engaged in wicked conspiracies. These stories have clear links with Victorian Gothic novels. Another writer of this period was E. Phillips Oppenheim who published his first spy novel, *Mysterious Mr. Sabin,* in 1898 – though he preferred to say he was writing about the "...shadowy and mysterious world of diplomacy," since 'spying' was still regarded as ungentlemanly – as late as 1920, in *The Great Impersonation,* Oppenheim had one of his ambassadors say, "I detest espionage in every shape and form, even where it is necessary."

Jacques Barzun, writing in 1965, said, "From medieval chivalry to Elizabethan times, the spy was a 'base fellow,' known as such to others and to himself. This notion survived from then to within recent memory: when Henry Stimson, as Secretary of State, was shown the progress of code-breaking, he pushed the documents aside and said curtly: 'Gentlemen do not read each other's mail.'" Stimson was Hoover's Secretary of State from 1929-1933. It has also been noted by Eric Ambler that up until the end of the nineteenth century, soldiers fought in the open and in uniform, never seeking to disguise themselves or to use camouflage and such gentlemanly rules of combat were not fully abandoned until the advent of 'modern' warfare in the trenches of the First World War.

Kim (1901) by Rudyard Kipling, while not a spy novel as such, takes place against the backdrop of the political conflict between Russia and Britain in Central Asia and popularised the 'The Great Game' as a term referring to this conflict. It is also thought that the real-life spy Harold Adrian Russell Philby got his nickname 'Kim' from the novel as he was born and grew up in India.

It wasn't really until the publication of Erskine Childers' *The Riddle of the Sands* in 1903 that the heroes finally decided that it might, in some circumstances, be okay for a gentleman to be a spy. Our heroes want to protect their country from a traitor who has gone over to the Germans saying, "If we can't do it without spying we've a right to spy." Julian Symons in *Bloody Murder* writes, "This is the first adumbration of the double standard by which They are viewed as spies pursuing evil ends, while We are agents countering their wicked designs with good ones ... the moral problem involved in spying was thus easily solved." In the modern world, as Barzun says, "The advantage of being a spy as of being a soldier is that there is always a larger reason – the reason of state – for making any little scruple or nastiness shrink into significance." But even to this day, foreign powers have spies, while 'we' have intelligence officers, counter-intelligence officers, or agents.

The Riddle of the Sands contains extracts from the author's own logbook from sailing trips along the Frisian coast, providing what writer Carol Fowler has called a "mass of verifiable detail that give authenticity to the story," but which a less charitable modern reader might call 'padding.' Though it is said to have influenced the work of John Buchan, this novel is more of an adventure story than a thriller. Oddly, even at this early date, we see Carruthers making fun of the traditional image of the spy in 'sixpenny magazines' – "with a Kodak in his tie-pin, a sketch-book in the lining of his coat, and a selection of disguises in his hand luggage."

Joseph Conrad's *The Secret Agent* (1907) is important for its serious treatment of anarchism, espionage and terrorism, and is based on a real-life attempt to blow up Greenwich Observatory. It also has the dubious honour of being cited as an influence on the Unabomber, Theodore Kaczynski. *The Man Who was Thursday* (1908) by G. K. Chesterton (creator of amateur detective Father Brown) is a wonderfully ironic story telling of a detective who goes undercover to infiltrate an anarchist cell. To say anything more about it would be to spoil it.

The 1920s were also the heyday of what Richard Usborne has christened the 'Clubland Heroes' in his book of that title. These were upper-class gentlemen belonging to exclusive West End clubs who occasionally engaged in a bit of amateur espionage work and their adventures were written by Dornford Yates, John Buchan and Sapper. Buchan's hero, Richard Hannay, we met in Chapter 1 and Dornford Yates' Jonah Mansel and Sapper's Bulldog Drummond were introduced as forefathers of James Bond in Chapter 2. Reviewing Usborne's book, Anthony Hartley said these were men with 'physical strength, ruthlessness, a measure of low cunning, a public-school education and an acquaintance with influential people' fighting for 'country, womenfolk and St. James's Square' and who were sexually adoring but remained unsatisfied. These were adventure stories with a bit of cloak and dagger thrown in and featured the last of the upper-class heroes.

Ashenden: Or the British Agent (1928) by W. Somerset Maugham is a collection of linked stories based partly on the author's experience working for the British Secret Service in Europe during the First World War. Maugham later said, "The work appealed both to my sense of romance and my sense of ridiculous." The stories show the more mundane and bureaucratic nature of the life of a secret agent who never "had the advantage of seeing a completed action." The lack of glamour in these stories influenced John Le Carré, who said that Maugham wrote "about espionage in a mood of disenchantment and almost prosaic reality." Alfred Hitchcock's 1936 film *Secret Agent* features John Gielgud as Ashenden and is based on two of Maugham's stories, 'The Traitor' and 'The Hairless Mexican.'

If Maugham was the first to turn his espionage experiences into fiction, Compton Mackenzie was a close second. His *The Three Couriers* published in 1929 contains three linked stories in which the absurdity of the work is explored in a more light-hearted way. Mackenzie was a Director in the British Intelligence Service during the First World War and published two autobiographical accounts, *Gallipoli Memories* and *Greek Memories*, the second of which was subject to a prosecution under the Official Secrets Act.

The irony and cynicism that Maugham introduced to the espionage story set the tone for the next phase in the sub-genre's history which would be defined by the novels of Graham Greene and Eric Ambler.

(iii) The Depression and the Rise of Fascism (1930s)
The optimism and naiveté of the 1920s were replaced by a much bleaker tone in the 1930s. For the first time, we saw heroes who failed and anti-heroes and villains who were traitors to their own country.

Eric Ambler made an attempt to define the genre in 1964, 'A spy story is a story in which the central character is a secret intelligence agent of one sort or another.' But he said that if you applied that definition, none of his stories were spy stories and some of Graham Greene's would have to be excluded too. Ambler's central character is usually an 'everyman' and a non-heroic one at that. Although they are amateurs, they are not John Buchan gentleman adventurers. Julian Symons wrote that Ambler's protagonist was "... an innocent man mixed up in violent events, who slowly comes to realise that the agents and spies working on both sides are for the most part unpleasant but not important men. They murder casually and without passion, on behalf of some immense corporation or firm of armament manufacturers whose interests are threatened. These, rather than any national group, are the enemy. In his 1936 novel *The Dark Frontier*, partially a parody of the Clubland Hero story, Ambler has one of his characters say, "Wars were made by those who had the power to upset the balance, to tamper with international money and money's worth;

those who, in satisfying their private ends, created the social and economic conditions that bred war."

The word 'fascist' has been misused to such an extent that in 1944, George Orwell noted that to most people it meant the same thing as 'bully.' Fascism originally began after the First World War as a kind of workers' rights movement in Italy in which peasants and workers came together to demand political reform and improved working conditions. This 'strength through unity' principle was turned on its head when Mussolini's government and wealthy industrialists came together to crush opposition, becoming a one-party state with Mussolini as its dictator. Fascism came to be associated with the far-right in politics opposing any form of socialism or true democracy. The Great Depression of the 1930s brought social unrest across the Western world and right-wing political movement sought to exploit this, seeking to blame convenient scapegoats for their nation's economic problems. This was seen most dramatically in Germany with the rise of the Nazis and Hitler's adoption of the Mussolini model of dictatorship.

The influence wielded by wealthy industrialists, even in countries such as Britain and the United States, has continued to be a cause for concern. In his farewell address in 1961, Dwight D. Eisenhower recognised the need for both a strong military and an effective arms industry, but cautioned that the government "must guard against the acquisition of unwarranted influence, whether sought or unsought, by the military-industrial complex." The other issue with wealthy industrialists that came to light during the First World War was that they would put profit before principle by selling goods, including munitions, to the enemy during a time of war. Legislation had to be enacted in Britain and the USA to prevent this – though there is evidence it still occurred even during the Second World War.

The economic depression, the rise of fascism and the build-up to the Second World War make up the background against which the novels of Eric Ambler and Graham Greene were written. This was not a world of gentleman-heroes and unquestioning patriotism. Looking back, there is a sense that the descent into war was inevitable and this resulted in public anxiety on both sides of the Atlantic. At the same time, as Cawelti and Rosenberg observe, there was a 'countertheme' that reflected a dissatisfaction with society was it was as a result of the Depression. "The figure of the corrupt tycoon and the arms merchant so prevalent in these stories raises some questions as to whether the homeland is worth fighting for."

The protagonists in Ambler's stories typically begin with no deeply held political beliefs and only become involved when circumstances cause some conspiracy to impact on their personal or working lives. He discovers that as well as the world he knows, there is a secret, but equally real, world in which espionage and counter-espionage take place. This secret world is not enemy territory, it is the same location he lived and worked in and assumed to be safe – and he is forced to view it in a new light. This secret world is not his world and he wants no part of it, but having become aware of it he can no longer deny its existence – there is no going back. Ambler said that what he wrote about was the loss of innocence. The protagonist then finds himself in a predicament where he is forced to act in order to survive and typically find himself more and more helpless as events unfold. Denning says that the plots are of two types – 'the hunted man and the trapped man.'

Michael Denning describes the typical Eric Ambler hero: "... an educated, middle-class man (a journalist, teacher, engineer) travelling for business or pleasure on the Continent who accidentally gets caught up in a low and sinister game (no longer the Great Game) of spies, informers, and thugs. He is innocent both in the sense of not being guilty and in the sense of being naïve. He is an amateur spy, but not the sort of enthusiastic and willing amateur that Hannay is; rather he is an incompetent and inexperienced amateur in a world of professionals." To which Cawelti and Rosenberg add: "Having neither the strength nor the bravery of the heroic spy, the Ambler-Greene protagonist rarely brought a mission to a triumphant conclusion, saving the homeland from enemy threats. On the contrary, his greatest achievement was to narrowly escape with his life from the conspiracy into which he had been unwittingly implicated. More often than not, this escape was a result of blind luck or, in some cases, depended on the assistance of a more skilful and powerful person who sympathised with the hero's predicament."

In contrast to the creators of the 'Clubland Heroes,' Eric Ambler used the espionage thriller to, in his own words, turn the Buchan hero upside down "and make the heroes left wing and popular front figures." In his novels, a Communist character could be sympathetic and even an enemy spy could become an ally of the protagonist, and a betrayer or perhaps the main villain could be someone from his own side.

Eric Ambler's novels include *The Dark Frontier* (1936), *Epitaph for a Spy* (1938), *The Mask of Dimitrios* (1939), and *Journey into Fear* (1940). He also wrote successful screenplays and the caper novel *The Light of Day* (1962), filmed as *Topkapi*. We will examine his novel *The Levanter* later in the section of terrorism thrillers.

Ambler created hapless heroes who survived rather than triumphed but where the conspiracy was ultimately thwarted by a combination of luck and assistance from unexpected allies. Graham Greene, on the other hand, concentrated more on the idea of the failed hero. In *The Confidential Agent* (1939), 'D' is a spy who comes in from the cold having failed to complete his mission. In *This Gun for Hire* (1936) the central character is an anti-hero, Raven, an assassin with a conscience who is hired by an arms manufacturer to kill the socialist leader of a European country in the hopes of fomenting unrest which will increase the sale of arms. Raven discovers he has been paid with counterfeit bank notes and tracks down those who have betrayed him – with tragic consequences.

Atkins notes that Greene's *The Confidential Agent* is a 'conspiracy novel, if not a spy novel' and that "Philby quoted it with approval in *My Silent War* for the agent's choosing a side, once and for all, and letting history judge," and that it "did highlight, long before it became fashionable, the complete lack of trust that lies at the heart of espionage. This is reiterated again and again. 'The one person that you trusted was yourself.' 'Nobody trusts a confidential agent.' And so on."

Gloria Emerson, writing in *Rolling Stone*, said, "Betrayal — of love, of country, of God, of faith, of self — is a recurring theme with Graham Greene ... But it is never simple treachery, or clear-cut. Most Greene heroes, however doomed or disloyal, however their allegiances conflict, seem to have a faithfulness to someone or something. They lack belief in themselves most of all." Michael Denning has also commented on the way that Greene's religion may have influenced his attitudes towards spies and spying: "Greene, as a Catholic, has always put himself on the outside; and by an analogy of Catholicism and Communism he can justify (in his essay on Philby) Philby in his own terms, comparing Philby with the Elizabethan Catholics who worked for the victory of Catholic Spain." Ideas of guilt, conscience, confession, contrition, and a need for redemption also find their way into Greene's stories, which concentrate more on what is going on inside his characters' heads than in external plot developments. Cawelti and Rosenberg have suggested that, "Graham Greene's burnt-out cases are usually defined by their alienation from God, like the drunken priest in *The Power and the Glory*. Their redemption involves a renewal of their faith which, in turn, enables them to act morally in the world."

Greene's espionage novels also include *The Ministry of Fear* (1943), *The Third Man* (1949), *Our Man in Havana* (1958) and *The Human Factor* (1978). John Gardner says that the best of Greene's novels in this genre is *The Quiet American* (1955), "a brutal and savage assault on the clandestine methods of modern superpowers."

In the novels of Ambler and Greene, the villains are morally grotesque rather than physically monstrous and they come from within the protagonist's own world rather than being an outside enemy power. The hero is forced by circumstance – rather than being given a mission or volunteering – to take action and commit himself to defend what is morally just rather than simply waving a patriotic flag. There is perhaps also a sense that, while the next war – the Second World War – is inevitable, if ordinary people take a moral stance, the greed and corruption of that infects the military-industrial complex might be overcome and future war averted.

Following on from Maugham, Ambler and Greene's novels are regarded as being more *realistic* than those of the earlier generation of thriller writers. Michael Denning has said that this realism exists on two levels, first "a certain view of reality where violence and brutality are fundamental, where the decorums of 'civilised' behaviour are but a thin veil over naked power relations, where nations and empires are less the expression of a civilising mission than the mask for exploitation, and where the ethic of sportsmanship and the game is at best an anachronism and at worst a mystification." And secondly, it "encompasses the formal conventions which produce the effect of this 'reality': the meticulous representation of physical violence, the depiction of the brutality and seediness of ordinary life, a dialogue composed of abrupt, tough slang, and melodramatic plots that dramatise the eruption of the real – the violent – into everyday life." Denning also notes a similarity with the 'realism' of the American hardboiled detective novel on the late 1920s and 1930s celebrated in Raymond Chandler's essay 'The Simple Art of Murder.'

(iv) The Second World War (1940s)
During the years of the Second World War, patriotism became fashionable again in England – in America it had never really gone away – and patriots were encouraged to join the fight against fascism. Film rather than printed fiction is where the spies could be found. The novels of Eric Ambler and Graham Green were adapted for the screen, but their left-leaning, anti-capitalist undertones were toned down or removed. Films included *Background to Danger* (1943), *The Mask of Dimitrios* (1944), *This Gun for Hire* (1942), and *The Ministry of Fear* (1945). Perhaps the most famous story about a cynical, individualistic hero who is persuaded to join the fight against Fascism is the 1943 movie *Casablanca*. Another interesting film of the period was *The House on 92nd Street* (1945) made with the co-operation of the FBI and based on the real-life story of double-agent William G. Sebold and the Duquesne Spy Ring.

Espionage – intelligence gathering and counter-intelligence and subversive activities such as sabotage – is important in a time of war, and there are many real-life stories of people – many of them women – who risked their lives by undertaking these vital tasks. But the stories of these people, and of the secret military operations which went on behind enemy lines, were not revealed until after the war was over. Similarly, the work involved in intercepting and decoding enemy communications went on without ordinary people being aware of it.

While few new spy thrillers were written during the war, other than patriotic pulp magazine tales of derring-do that mixed cloak-and-dagger with hard-boiled action, there were – and are – stories written about the period afterwards. Alan Furst has written a dozen historical spy novels set during the period from Hitler's rise to power to the end of the Second World War, the first being *Night Soldiers* (1988). "I don't want my books to be about the '30s and '40s," he is quoted as saying, "I want them to read as if they had been written then."

Victory over the Nazis was eventually celebrated, but a new conflict arose that would usher in a new type of espionage thriller – this was the era of the Cold War. The detonation of nuclear bombs over Hiroshima and Nagasaki by the United States meant that the deterioration in relations between the atomic super-powers the USA and the USSR brought with it the fear of nuclear destruction.

(v) The Cold War (1950s to 1980s)
The most influential espionage thriller writers during this period are Ian Fleming, John Le Carré, and Len Deighton. The new enemy was the Soviet Union and Communism replaced Fascism as the ideology the West feared. The fact that the two sides in the Cold War both had nuclear arsenals that could virtually wipe out all life on the planet increased the public's sense of unease. It was believed for some time that conventional warfare was now obsolete – but as we will see in the chapter on the techno-thriller, this proved not to be the case. But in the immediate post-war period, it seemed that open physical warfare had been supplanted by a covert war between the intelligence agencies of the two sides. Instead of building up their armies, East and West built up their intelligence agencies. Although Churchill spoke of an 'iron curtain' separating

the two sides, it was concrete poured in 1961 for the Berlin Wall that became the symbol for the division. Guard towers and checkpoints became a part of the landscape in the divided city – and these became part of the iconography of the espionage novel.

In the United States, fear of the 'enemy within' was exploited politically and resulted in the McCarthy era where the search for 'reds under the bed' became a national obsession, with many individuals, both government officials and people in other walks of life, being falsely accused of being communist spies.

The post-war years in Britain were a time of austerity, with wartime rationing only slowly lifted. The horrors of the Second World War – on the battlefield, in the scale and nature of the Jewish Holocaust, and in the aftermath of the nuclear bombs exploded over Japan – also cast a long shadow. Ian Fleming judged the public mood correctly and created his larger-than-life hero who enjoyed the finer things in life – the first James Bond novel, *Casino Royale*, was published in 1953 and he would publish a novel a year after that. We have already explored the popularity of the Bond novels in Chapter 2 and there is nothing to add here.

John Gardner has written that the success of a series like James Bond "automatically brings a backswing," and says that Len Deighton was the first to react against it. *The Ipcress File* (1962) introduced a nameless first-person working-class narrator who would be named Harry Palmer in the 1965 film version and played by Michael Caine. There was absolutely no snobbery there – unless, as Gardner suggests, it is inverted snobbery. Deighton gives the hardboiled narration of Dashiell Hammett and Raymond Chandler and gives it a British twist – ironically achieving what Ian Fleming wanted to do.

Another writer who went against the James Bond-style story was John Le Carré. "I'm not sure that James Bond is a spy," Le Carré said in an early BBC interview. "It seems to me that he's more some kind of international gangster with, as is said, a licence to kill. He's a man with unlimited movement – but he's a man entirely out of the political context. It's of no interest to Bond, for instance, who is the president of the United States." Cawelti and Rosenberg write that "Le Carré may have written his early books at least in part as a corrective to Fleming's extravagant fantasies." They also note that, while he wrote about burnt-out cases like Graham Greene had, "Le Carré's burnt-out cases are ... alienated from their fellow human beings by the dehumanising forces of twentieth-century society. Their redemption is not religious, but humanistic and involves a new growth of trust in the ordinary pleasures of life and in friendship and love with others."

John Le Carré is the pseudonym of David John Moore Cornwell. "I've told so many lies about where I got the name from, but I really don't remember," he says. Perhaps it was from Mathilde Carré, known as 'La Chatte', who was a French Resistance agent during World War II who turned double agent. *Le carré* also means 'the square' in French.

Le Carré's greatest creation is the character of George Smiley. Initially, he appeared to be a variation on the Hercule Poirot type of amateur detective. In Le Carré's first two novels, *Call for the Dead* (1961) and *A Murder of Quality* (1962), George Smiley was a retired espionage agent involved in what were essentially murder mystery stories set against the background of intelligence work. But it was the third novel that brought the author critical acclaim and made him an influential writer in the field. *The Spy Who Came in from the Cold* (1963) was a very different kind of novel to the earlier ones – George Smiley was present, but in a much smaller role, and the story focused on the work of a single field agent. John Gardner describes it as "a brilliant, dark, economically-written book which seemed, almost for the first time, to take us really to the heart of the true clandestine world." It is also one of those books which critics tend to say is too good to be a *genre* novel. It was adapted into a movie in 1965 with Richard Burton in the central role of the burned-out British spy, Alec Leamas. Leamas, like James Bond, is a secret agent with a mission but the tone of the story, the characters, and locations are all much more muted. It is almost as if Le Carré set out to show how unrealistic a Bond story was by rebutting it point by point. Sam Goodman refers to "... Le Carré's depiction of espionage as a bleak landscape devoid of glamour, detailing the pointless and inconsequential sacrifice of individuals for the maintenance of an anachronistic state."

More espionage novels followed, but Le Carré's most significant achievement came with the novels that came to be known as the 'Karla trilogy,' *Tinker, Tailor, Soldier, Spy* (1974), *The Honourable Schoolboy* (1977), and *Smiley's People* (1979). Here we see George Smiley back in his role as a spymaster controlling field agents and dealing with the internal politics and conspiracies of his agency, the Circus. The first in the trilogy concerns the hunt for a traitor in the Circus, a 'mole,' and Smiley's investigation is carried out in a similar way to the hunt for a murderer in a whodunit. The second is a larger scale espionage mission story and closer to a Bond story. The final novel combines elements of both mystery and espionage mission, as an investigation into the murder of a former Soviet general who spied for the British opens up a much more complex plot involving Smiley's opposite number in Russia, a spymaster known as Karla.

Le Carré's *The Spy Who Came in from the Cold* helped to define the 'realistic' espionage mission novel and *Tinker, Tailor, Soldier, Spy* is a classic example of the 'mole hunt' or investigation type of story. Later in the chapter, we will use these two as models to explore the conventions, content, and plots of the two types of espionage thriller, comparing them to the James Bond professional agent story.

To date, Le Carré has written twenty-four novels, most of them espionage thrillers; those written since the end of the Cold War have centred on the Israel–Palestine conflict, the smuggling of drugs and weapons, a Russian money launderer, and the 'war on terror.' There have been more than a dozen film and television adaptations of his books. His first, *Call for the Dead* (1961), was filmed as *The Deadly Affair* (1966), directed by Sidney Lumet with the George Smiley character changed to 'Charles Dobbs' and played by James Mason. *A Murder of Quality* was adapted for television in 1991 with Denholm Elliott in the role of George Smiley. In 2011 Gary Oldman portrayed Smiley in the film adaptation of *Tinker, Tailor, Soldier, Spy* – before that, the actor most closely associated with the role was Alec Guinness, who played George Smiley in the BBC television six-part miniseries *Tinker, Tailor, Soldier, Spy* in 1979 and a similar adaptation of *Smiley's People* in 1982.

The fall of the Berlin Wall in 1989 effectively marked the end of the Cold War and an end for the novels it had inspired. Len Deighton's 'Game, Set, and Match' trilogy (1983–85) is probably the last major work of this era, though Cold War espionage fiction was later resurrected as 'historical' spy fiction.

The period immediately following the reunification of Germany were wilderness years for espionage writers as they sought new contemporary enemies to oppose. The worlds of South American drug cartels and Middle Eastern conflicts served for a while, until the declaration of the 'War on Terror' by George W. Bush in 2001. The election of ex-KGB officer Vladimir Putin as President of Russia in 2000 and his dominance of Russian politics since then has also led to a world situation which has been referred to as Cold War II.

(vi) The War on Terror, Cyber-Attacks & Domestic Spying (21st Century)
In this section I will cover some of the incidents that I believe are significant in terms of the background against which a present-day espionage novel or screenplay would be set and/or which may provide inspiration for stories. I can only skim the surface here, but Wikipedia has articles on all of the subjects below with references and links to much more in-depth information. At the end I will include the names of a few authors writing espionage thrillers with a contemporary background.

On the 11th of September 2001, al-Qaeda terrorists hijacked four passenger planes and used them as weapons to attack targets within the United States of America. Almost 3,000 people were killed and another 6,000 were injured. These attacks came to define the beginning of the 21st century, with President George W. Bush declaring a 'war on terror' on 16th September. Communist spies were no longer a threat – they had been replaced by a new enemy, 'radical Islamists.' Comparisons between the Cold War and the 'war on terror' are inevitable and there are similarities, but there are significant differences too.

Modern intelligence gathering includes satellite and aerial photographs much more detailed than anything available during the Cold War, but with an enemy like ISIS/Daesh, it has proved more difficult to obtain insider information. Writing in 2015, John R. Schindler said that while the infiltration of terror groups "is doable, it's likely to get Americans killed in horrible ways." During the hunt for Osama bin Laden, the CIA discovered the dangers of recruiting spies to work within al-Qaeda with mole turned suicide-bomber Humam Khalil Abu-Mulal al-Balawi.

In the United States, the 'war on terror' included Terrorist Surveillance Program, an electronic surveillance programme implemented by the National Security Agency through which they secretly monitored phone calls made by millions of U.S. citizens. Challenged in 2006 as being unconstitutional and illegal, the programme was replaced by a new one codenamed PRISM.

The 2003 Invasion of Iraq by a United States-led coalition was authorised, in part, because the country was believed to be harbouring al-Qaeda terrorists and also because of Saddam Hussein's possession and development of chemical and biological weapons and Iraq's actively seeking to develop nuclear weapons capability, all of which was deemed to pose a threat to the national security of the United States and to peace and security in the Persian Gulf region. Evidence of Iraq's possession of 'weapons of mass destruction' was contested and the intelligence assessments were ultimately shown to have been flawed. In Britain, the death of the scientist and former weapons inspector David Kelly, who was fact-checking a dossier on the weapons of mass destruction possessed by Iraq and spoke to journalists about his work, caused a great deal of media interest.

In 2010, Chelsea Manning passed almost 740,000 classified and sensitive military documents relating to U.S. military action in the Iraq and Afghanistan, and relating to Guantanamo Bay, along with a video of an airstrike in Baghdad to the Wikileaks website. Manning's motive was stated as being to draw attention to the true nature of modern warfare and to change public attitudes towards it. It was the biggest leak of documents since the Pentagon Papers in 1971.

In June 2013, whistle-blower Edward Snowden leaked between 1.5 and 1.7 million classified documents which indicated that America's NSA and its allies Australia, Canada, New Zealand, the United Kingdom and other European countries were involved in global surveillance programs targeting foreign nationals and U.S. citizens. The disclosures led to the creation of social movements against mass surveillance and reviews of the ways agencies in the named countries collected and shared data.

There seem to be patterns that recur in history that, in turn, influence fiction. The McCarthy 'witch-hunts' of the Cold War period echo the situation in France at the end of the nineteenth and beginning of the twentieth century which led to Captain Alfred Dreyfus being falsely accused of spying for the enemies of France. The crime committed against him was compounded by the fact that the French government engaged in a conspiracy of denial and cover-up that was echoed by the Watergate scandal. The fate of Dreyfus and many of McCarthy's falsely-accused victims has most recently been echoed in the treatment of those wrongly accused of terrorism, including Khalid El-Masri, falsely imprisoned and tortured by the CIA, and a number of Guantanamo Bay detainees. The El-Masri case also shows that the CIA today continue to carry out illegal, and occasionally incompetent, activities on foreign soil.

Public attitudes towards the intelligence communities today are very similar to those of the Cold War era. We want strong and effective intelligence organisations that can protect us from an enemy perceived as a threat to us – then the Soviet Union, now Islamic terrorists – but at the same time we are aware that intelligence organisations have abused their authority both in terms of their treatment of foreign citizens but also in spying on the folks at home. This feeling that we need them but don't like them reflects the age-old opinion that spies are not 'gentlemen' and that they cannot be trusted. Dan Brown's 1998 novel *Digital Fortress* explores the practice and ethics of digital surveillance of private citizens – though the novel was criticised for its inaccurate portrayal of technology and its account of corruption in the Spanish city of Seville.

'Trust no one' still seems to be the golden rule in espionage, where there is no such thing as a friendly intelligence agency – although the United States, Britain, Canada, Australia, and New Zealand are on reasonably friendly terms, they all spy on each other. And they all spy on – and are spied on by – Russia, China, Cuba, and Israel.

Something that did not exist during the Cold War was a publicly accessible internet and wide use of social media. This online or 'cyber' world has become a new battleground for spies and a key element in what some are calling Cold War II. New terms have been coined to cover activities in this area.

Cyber attacks are defined by the U.S. Committee on National Security Systems as: "Any kind of malicious activity that attempts to collect, disrupt, deny, degrade, or destroy information system resources or the information itself." Cyber attacks may be politically or criminally motivated. Individual companies have been the victim of 'denial of service' attacks and there are also concerns in relation to key utilities such as banking and electricity distribution being disrupted as happened in Ukraine in 2017. The 2017 attack is said to have been the work of Russian intelligence agents. In 2007 the whole of Estonia was disrupted by a similar attack and in 2008 Georgia was targeted. Most countries have one or more agencies whose purpose is to protect them from cyber attacks. China has a specialist unit, 'Cyber Blue Team' or 'Blue Army,' whose designated task is cyber-defence and there have been suggestions that it or a similar unit also plans and/or conducts offensive operations.

Cyber espionage or cyber spying includes both online intelligence gathering designed to obtain the secret 'documents' of a country or plans relating to military devices, procedures and deployment, and also the large-scale gathering of data on private individuals such as the recent Facebook / Cambridge Analytica scandal. It has been suggested that 'intelligence gathering' by British and Israeli companies and the application of 'psychographics' methodology to the data obtained was used to try and influence the outcome of the 2016 presidential election in the USA. In January 2017, Director of National Intelligence James R. Clapper testified before a Senate committee that Russia's attempts to affect the outcome of the 2016 presidential campaign went beyond hacking, and included disinformation and the dissemination of fake news, often promoted on social media. Donald Trump denounced this statement itself as being fake news.

Cyber terrorism, like other forms of terrorism, is politically or religiously-motivated action intended to coerce or intimidate a government or civilian population. Mohammad Bin Ahmad As-Sālim's article '39 Ways to Serve and Participate in Jihad' includes discussion of targeted hacks of websites in the West. The villain of the 2012 James Bond Film *Skyfall* Raoul Silva uses cyberterrorism in his plot to gain revenge on his former employer MI6. The multiple-author series *Tom Clancy's Net Force* features a special unit designed to combat crime and cyber terrorism.

Cyber warfare. The definition of 'cyberwar' has been debated for some time, given that there is no obvious point where cyber espionage crosses the line and becomes an act of war, especially given the fact that a war can exist – such as the Cold War or the 'war on terror' – without a formal declaration of war being issued. Cyberwar would probably need to involve a deliberate campaign of cyber attacks by one nation-state against another and/or the use of cyber attacks on the military devices of a nation involved in a conventional physical war. Outside of this, cyber attacks are probably closer to being espionage or terrorism.

In the 21st century, authors seem to be taking one of two approaches. Some have returned to the period of the Cold War or to the Second World War to write 'historical espionage' thrillers. Alan Furst I mentioned above in the Second World War category. Jeremy Duns is the author of 'The Dark Chronicles' featuring double agent Paul Dark. The novels are *Free Agent* (2009), *Song of Treason* (2010), *The Moscow Option* (2012), and *Spy Out The Land* (2016). He has also written non-fiction about Cold War spies (*Dead Drop*, 2013) and about Edward Snowden (*News of Devils*, 2014).

Olen Steinhauer has written a series of five Cold War thrillers 'The Yalta Boulevard sequence,' beginning with *The Bridge of Sighs* (2003), and a trilogy of modern-day espionage stories featuring CIA operative Milo Weaver beginning with *The Tourist* (2009). The trilogy is very much in the tradition of Cold War thrillers and the villain is a Chinese spymaster called Xin Zhu.

Jon Stock has written seven contemporary spy thrillers to date, the first being *The Riot Act* (1997), including the 'Legoland Trilogy' (2010-2012) featuring MI6 agent Daniel Marchant.

Simon Conway is a former British Army officer who worked clearing landmines in conflict-affected countries and has since campaigned against cluster bombs and supported the work of the HALO Trust. His the author of five contemporary spy novels beginning with *A Loyal Spy* (2010).

Stella Rimington was the Director General of MI5 from 1992 to 1996 and has published nine espionage novels featuring MI5 intelligence officer Liz Carlyle, beginning with *At Risk* (2004). She also published her memoir *Open Secret* in 2001.

The Espionage in Espionage Thrillers – Gadgets & Tradecraft

Most of the work carried out by intelligence agencies around the world involves gathering, analysing and passing on information – and the bulk of it is done by people sitting at computers all day. The office equipment may have changed, but the routine isn't very different from the clerical work described by W. Somerset Maugham in 1928. It has even be said that many of these people read spy thrillers to escape the monotony of their daily lives.

How much of what we see in espionage stories is true? Spy stories are often thought to be a bit fanciful, depicting unrealistic and overly-dramatic events. But a look at some relatively recent real-life events proves that fact is sometimes just as strange as fiction. In 1978, Bulgarian defector Georgi Markov was assassinated on a London street when a tiny pellet filled with ricin was fired into his leg from an umbrella thought to have been wielded by someone connected to the Bulgarian Secret Service. In 2006, Russian defector Alexander Litvinenko was poisoned using radioactive polonium thought to have been administered in a pot of tea, having been put there by a Russian spy. Kim Jong-nam, the half-brother of Korean leader Kim Jong-un, was assassinated in 2017 in Malaysia when VX nerve agent was smeared on his face by two women who said they thought they were taking part in a reality TV show.

Many of the gadgets that appeared in James Bond movies and super-spy TV shows can now be bought on the internet for use at home – everything from hollow coins for hiding your microfilm, hidden cameras and listening devices, tracking devices, and detectors for checking whether someone is spying on you. If you want to see some of the devices that have been used by spies in years gone by, check out Kim Zetter's article 'Tools of Tradecraft: The CIA's Historic Spy Kit' on the *Wired.com* website. Or just Google 'spy gadgets.'

'Tradecraft' or spycraft is a term used to refer to the methods and technologies used in espionage work. It covers photography and listening devices, cryptography, weapons, interrogation, surveillance and a lot more besides. The Wikipedia article 'Tradecraft' is a good place to begin a search for information on these things and an internet search will give you a lot more, including various 'manuals' that reveal how secret agents carry out their work. Obviously, much of what you find online will be outdated and declassified – real-life spies don't reveal their current methods and technology.

Many former intelligence agents from various countries have published memoirs and these are another good source for insider-information. But be warned, not everything revealed in these memoirs will be true – spies, after all, are professional liars. Author and ex-spy Ted Allbeury said that he found most non-fiction accounts by ex-intelligence agents unreadable, "If you've been in this business, you recognise all too easily those great patches of bull. Real-life espionage is boring. It has too little action and its victories are mainly from paperwork, not valour." John Gardner has also suggested that some of the autobiographical and other non-fiction accounts about espionage and counter-espionage have been faked by the intelligence services for their own purposes. There's probably a story in that idea...

During the Cold War, a number of rules-of-thumb were developed and used by those working as spies in the Soviet Union, and these came to be known as The Moscow Rules. These are often referred to in espionage stories, but there was never a formal written list of the rules. One version appears on a sign in the International Spy Museum in Washington, D.C. which gives them as:

1. Assume nothing.
2. Never go against your gut.
3. Everyone is potentially under opposition control.
4. Do not look back; you are never completely alone.
5. Go with the flow, blend in.
6. Vary your pattern and stay within your cover.
7. Lull them into a sense of complacency.
8. Do not harass the opposition.
9. Pick the time and place for action.
10. Keep your options open.

Screenwriters might also want to check out 'Tony's Hollywood Moscow Rules' – Tony Mendez is the author of *The Master of Disguise: My Secret Life in the CIA* (1999) and also has experience working in the film and television industry.

Unlike writers of other types of professionally-based thriller, you are unlikely to find anyone currently working in the espionage field to answer your questions. You can conduct desk research into modern technologies and invent your own uses for them – trying to guess how modern field agents might use the devices. You can also use the older sources and extrapolate from them. Methods and gadgets may have moved on since the days of the Cold War spy, but the basic objectives have not: we want to get hold of their secrets; we want to stop them getting hold of ours, and we may want to feed them fake secrets to put them off the scent. You just need to come up with new ways in which these objectives can be achieved. Put a modern spin on them. You might also find useful ideas in up-to-date texts on *industrial* espionage, as methods and technology detailed there might equally be used in international espionage. Also look into other types of crime, such as the ways people in organised crime communicate and handle their finances – similar techniques will be used by terrorist groups.

Computers, cell phones and the internet – including the 'dark web' – are used much more widely today and hardware and software encryption are likely to play a more important role than old-fashioned coded messages. 'Hacking' into another nation's security service or defence computers has been going on – in real-life and in movies like *WarGames* and *Sneakers* – since the early 1980s. This is another area where information dates quickly, but you can extrapolate from the basic objectives found in older material.

As technology has become more difficult to 'crack,' the use of 'social engineering' to persuade people to give you the information or the passwords you need has become much more prevalent. The sort of methods used by online scammers can work just as well for a field agent. Search for websites or books on 'social engineering' to learn about these techniques – knowing about them can also help you protect yourself from becoming a victim of them.

The 'The Fifth Estate' – organisations and individuals who operate in a similar manner to journalists but outside the normal regulations and safeguards imposed on the mainstream media – are another source of information about the work of the intelligence services and a source for the latest conspiracy theories. *Wikileaks* is one example, which has itself been enmeshed in conspiracy theories and has been the subject of a thriller movie, *The Fifth Estate,* starring Benedict Cumberbatch as Julian Assange.

Please be aware that while it is possible to obtain information and technologies of all kinds via the internet, it may be illegal in some countries to access such information or to use such technologies or equipment. If in doubt, check *before* you use it.

The Spy Writer Spy

There is quite a list of writers who were involved in intelligence or espionage work, including William Le Queux, Compton Mackenzie, W. Somerset Maugham, A. E. W. Mason, Dennis Wheatley, G. K. Chesterton, Ian Fleming, John Le Carré, Ted Allbeury, John Buchan, Bernard Newman, Sidney Horler, John Masterman, Phil Atkey ('Barry Perowne'), Francis Warwick ('Warwick Jardine') and Stella Rimington (who was Director General of MI5). American author Charles McCarry was a former undercover operative for the CIA. But not all successful writers of espionage thrillers are former spies – Eric Ambler freely admitted he had no experience in the field.

Graham Greene worked for British Military Intelligence, being posted to Sierra Leone during the Second World War. Kim Philby, later revealed to be a Soviet spy, was his supervisor at MI6.

Genre Conventions
Secret Agents & Double Agents
In their book *The Spy Story*, Cawelti and Rosenberg introduce the 'cycle of clandestinity' to describe the three different phases that a spy might pass through in his career.

Phase 1. An individual or group has a purpose and to achieve it they must engage in clandestine activities. Examples of such a purpose include spying for your country via clandestine activities in another country or engaging in revolutionary activities in your own country. In either case it would be dangerous and/or impossible to carry out these activities openly. A third type of secret activity occurs where the authorities in a country feel that public opinion or national laws would oppose an action deemed to be vital for national security or for the success of the administration – though this sort of thinking can get you into a Watergate situation.

Phase 2. Having formed a secret group or cabal, individual members must now adopt a dual identity, living in both a secret world and carrying on their lives in the ordinary world. This can lead to "psychological tension between conflicting worldviews." Participants in this secret world may become increasingly distanced from the ordinary world and find it difficult to be part of it. The secret world has its own morality and its own language. In his book *An American Life*, Jeb Magruder – who participated in the Watergate cover-up – wrote, "Essentially, we used management terms to discuss a legal problem. Yet we were not dealing with a tidy managerial problem." Cawelti and Rosenberg write that "… the clandestine participant's attitude toward the ordinary world is a mixture of superiority, loneliness, and resentment. He feels that he has a better understanding of reality and therefore is not deluded by the illusions and facile pleasure-seeking of the majority. On the other hand, he feels terribly isolated by his secrets and resents the innocent happiness of those who cannot share his frightening knowledge. As his participation in the clandestine world continues, the spy finds the two roles he must play increasingly difficult to relate to each other…"

Phase 3. Living in the ordinary world and the secret world, an individual may feel unable to commit fully to one or the other and may fear being exposed in both of them. He may also fear that other participants in the secret world are more concerned with achieving their purpose than in protecting their comrades and this may lead him to feel so vulnerable that he trusts no one except himself. Being an outsider to both worlds, and having perhaps come to feel that neither is worth his loyalty, coupled with his desire for self-protection may lead the individual to become a double agent. If he pretends to work for the other side, he may feel that he is protected from harm by them. As well as protection from both sides, he may also receive money from both sides, selling secrets from each side to the other. At this point, Cawelti and Rosenberg write, the double agent has entered "... a state of moral and personal isolation so complete that there is no way out but death, exposure, or total flight. The only purpose that remains to him is that of self-preservation through an increasingly complex improvisation of stories to hide his true position of multiple disloyalty." He has become "... the most isolated human being imaginable, for he must act as if every man's hand is against him ... He must lie to everyone." The longer a spy spends 'out in the cold' in a state of isolation, the more likely it is that he could be 'turned' by the enemy and become a double agent – agencies that don't provide adequate support for agents in the field are more likely to see this happen to their people.

Cawelti and Rosenberg compare the spy's situation to that of the schizophrenic, due to the tension that may arise from living in two different worlds. The secret world becomes more and more real and comes to dominate his existence but he must keep it entirely separate from his life in the ordinary world. He must "... remember the attitudes, perceptions, and words characteristic of both the clandestine world and the world outside, and he must manipulate both consciousnesses effectively enough to shift back and forth between them..." such that it is "... amazing to think of a man who can continue to function in a situation where he must play a slightly different role for everyone he meets and where the penalty for a slight discrepancy in action or story is imprisonment or death."

In the stories of the 'Clubland Heroes' and Ian Fleming's James Bond series, there is no possibility of the central character becoming a double agent – his patriotism is such that he could never betray his homeland. Double agents entered espionage fiction with Maugham's *Ashenden* and became key elements in the stories of Eric Ambler, Graham Greene, John Le Carré, Len Deighton and Adam Hall.

The 'traitor' character gained particular significance in Britain during the 1950s and 60s when there a number of highly publicised defections to the Soviet Union. In more recent times, the leaking of confidential documents by Edward Snowden and Chelsea Manning has renewed interest in the character who finds moral or ideological beliefs in conflict with their national loyalty. 'Home-grown' radical Islamist terrorists fall into a similar category.

(i) The Hero
At the beginning of this chapter, I quoted former head of MI5 Stella Rimington as saying the best spies are "quiet, apparently boring and dull people." In the 'realistic' espionage stories we are studying here, there are two main variations on this type of character – the cynical 'burnt-out case' who is like a hardboiled private eye and is typified by Alec Leamas in *The Spy Who Came in from the Cold* and the unassuming academic who is like a cozy whodunit detective, seen in the character of George Smiley in *Tinker, Tailor, Soldier, Spy*. Of the two, Leamas is closest to James Bond – in terms of taking action, at least – but as we shall see

later, there are significant differences between the stories of John Le Carré and Ian Fleming.

Cawelti and Rosenberg have written that 'ennui' is a factor found at the beginning of many spy thrillers, with the hero expressing either boredom or a wish to retire. *Goldfinger* opens with James Bond suffering from ennui before the action begins; *The Quiller Memorandum* opens with Quiller looking forward to his return to London. *The Spy Who Came in from the Cold* has the hero persuaded to carry out one last job. When we first meet George Smiley he *is* retired and only later is he persuaded back into his old line of work.

Alec Leamas. Leamas is an experienced field agent who knows how to take care of himself if it comes down to a fight. But as the novel opens he is transferred to a desk-job, against his wishes. "I wondered whether you were tired," his boss, Control, says, "Burned out." The 'burnt-out case' is a character that Graham Greene used a number of times in spy stories and Cawelti and Rosenberg make a link between the world-weary spy and Dashiell Hammett's hardboiled detective Sam Spade: "... he faces the world with hostile suspicion and cynicism. His capacity for love has been almost totally blunted by his lifetime experience of corruption and betrayal." But this "hardboiled attitude is a mask which he wears to conceal from others and from himself his true sensitivity to people and events, a sensitivity he has not lost in spite of the horrors and betrayals he has experienced."

This is where Le Carré diverges from Fleming: his hero is not a 'machine' who just gets on with the job that has to be done. A Le Carré hero has doubts. In *A Murder of Quality* (1962) he writes of George Smiley, "It was a peculiarity of Smiley's character that throughout the whole of his clandestine work he had never managed to reconcile the means to the end." Even Leamas' boss seems to feel this way, saying that they can't live 'without sympathy' and that it is impossible to keep up the hardboiled act, "... one can't be out in the cold all the time; one has to come in from the cold." But then Control goes on to exploit Leamas' sensitivity and does send him back out into the cold.

George Smiley. George Smiley doesn't look like a spy. One of his own colleagues in *The Honourable Schoolboy* is surprised to find that Smiley is an experienced field agent, "... this owlish little pedant with the diffident voice and the blinking, apologetic manner had sweated out three years in some benighted German town, holding the threads of a very respectable network, while he waited for the boot through the door panel or the pistol butt across the face that would introduce him to the pleasures of interrogation."

In the same book, another colleague, Peter Guillam, recalls hearing Smiley explain his dilemma: to another colleague: "To be inhuman in defence of our humanity ... harsh in defence of compassion. To be single-minded in defence of our disparity." Guillam thought that "one of two things will happen to George. He'll cease to care, or the paradox will kill him."

"Obscurity was his nature, as well as his profession," Le Carré writes in *A Murder of Quality,* "A man who, like Smiley, has lived and worked for years among his country's enemies learns only one prayer: that he may never, never be noticed."

Interviewed by *The Observer* in 1980, Le Carré said of Smiley, "... he belongs to a generation ... who felt particularly strongly that one must commit oneself one way or another, that there is no middle way. And *faute de mieux* [for lack of something better] he has committed himself to the Establishment cause – although I don't think it's enough for him. He has a sense of decency but he's not sure where to invest it."

John Atkins writes that it is difficult for people such as Smiley to motivate those in a community that has largely lost its faith and who "see doubt as a legitimate philosophical posture... Such people like to think of themselves as being in the middle, performing a skilled and necessary balancing act. Smiley doesn't believe this. In the middle is nowhere. No battle was ever won by spectators and he thinks there's a battle that needs winning." That battle began with the Bolshevik Revolution of 1917 and with Soviet Russia's subsequent betrayal of Socialism. Le Carré believed that it was necessary to combat Soviet Communism and to do so decisively – but he also knew that not all of the 'baddies' were on one side. He said that he detested 'dogma, institutionalised prejudice, even party politics' and these same attitudes were reflected in the character of George Smiley.

George Smiley is, at heart, an academic and not the physical 'enforcer' type – he is about as far from James Bond as it is possible to go. I thought the 2011 adaptation of *Tinker, Tailor, Soldier, Spy* was very well-done and Gary Oldman's performance as George Smiley suited a *film* perfectly, I think Alec Guinness' portrayal in the BBC television adaptation in 1979 comes closer to the character in the novel. Unlike Bond, Smiley doesn't work for the organisation out of a sense of duty to his country; he does what he does because he has – after careful thought – decided that what they are trying to achieve is morally right, even though the methods they have to use may not be so defensible. As Le Carré told *The Observer:* "He accepts, however reluctantly, that you have to resort to very unpleasant means in order to preserve society, though he sometimes wonders how much you can do in the name of that society and feel sure that it is still worth preserving."

When Leamas is asked by the East Germans about the philosophy of the people who work for the Circus, he struggles for an answer, "What do you mean, a philosophy? We're not Marxists, we're nothing, just people." And in *The Observer* interview, Le Carré echoed the argument that George Smiley isn't motivated simply by an opposition to Communism – and that he doesn't adhere to any other opposing political ideology: "His engagement against Communism is really an intellectual one... he feels that to pit yourself against any 'ism' is to strike a posture which is itself ideological, and therefore offensive in terms of practical decency. In practice, almost any political ideology invites you to set aside your humanitarian instincts."

Some of Smiley's team were academics too, including Connie Sachs, the Moscow-gazer and Doc di Salis, the 'Mad Jesuit' and head China-watcher: they gathered in the 'rumpus room' to talk strategy, eat biscuits and drink tea made from a 'Russian-style copper samovar.' These were people committed to their work, and by default their organisation – 'the Circus' – but who were definitely not ex-public school, pro-Empire types. Nor are they bureaucrats – they act to achieve their ends despite the bureaucracy that surrounds them. They are professionals in the sense of being experts in their field, rather than professional adventurers, and their job is to gather intelligence. And where James Bond feels that it is his duty to protect 'ordinary people' who are not like him and who he views with a degree of condescension, Smiley and those around him *are* ordinary people with ordinary lives, and as a result Smiley is, in Le Carré's words, 'very understanding of human fallibility.'

These characters reflect Le Carré's own attitudes: in *The Observer* interview he said that he always voted Socialist, in part because of his experiences in the British public school system. He attended a public school where they "... lived a cultureless existence in beautiful buildings, and ... were heirs to preposterous prejudices." They were taught, he said, to aspire for a career in Rhodesia or Kenya or ruling India. He 'defected from' this school aged 16. After completing university, he taught at Eton, the top public school that – at that time and still – produces many of those who go into politics, the civil service, and government in Britain. It was Le Carré's first real experience of 'the British ruling class' and he said that people "don't know how awful they really are – the way they talk, the way they function. Their prejudices are absolutely stunning."

Public schools and the British class system play an important part in the world of espionage in Le Carré's novels, which in turn reflect their importance in the real-world of spies and spying in Britain during the 1950s and 1960s. We will explore this under the heading *Traitors* below.

(ii) The Villain
An individual villain or an enemy organisation is a vital element in the espionage thriller. This villain may be an exotic super-villain like Fu-Manchu or a more enigmatic opponent such as George Smiley's rival Karla. A strong and organised opposition makes the protagonist seem all the more isolated and vulnerable. The main villain is not normally motivated by greed – he is seeking to assert the superiority of his ideology or worldview and to extinguish that of the nation he opposes. He represents not just a fear of conquest or a threat to physical safety – but the loss of a whole way of life. The 1956 science fiction film *Invasion of the Body Snatchers* was a metaphor for the fear felt in America during the Cold War – people who looked identical to us were going to replace us. Zombie movies today probably express a similar fear of loss of identity.

The Spy Who Came in from the Cold is a Cold War espionage story and as such, the 'enemy' is the Soviet Union and East Germany. But while the East Germans serve as the opposition in the story, the hero is ultimately used and betrayed by his own organisation. Even the double-agent, Hans-Dieter Mundt, that Leamas is sent to deal with, is an assassin who has killed a number of people and even made an attempt on George Smiley's life in an earlier novel. The enemy is effectively the business of espionage itself – or the world that makes espionage necessary.

The world of espionage is such that identifying the enemy isn't always easy. John Atkins has written that spy fiction changed after the Suez Crisis of 1956, which effectively marked the end of the British Empire. Before that point the situation was relatively simple – 'Us' meant the British Empire and we were good; 'Them' was anyone who opposed us and they were bad. This was the world of Le Queux, Oppenheim and John Buchan, but by the time the first James Bond novel was published, the situation was changing – in the late 1950s and early 60s Britain was no longer the major international power it had been. The two super-powers were the USA and the USSR.

This world situation didn't allow for a simple us-versus-them story, particularly if you are telling a story that centres on the British espionage community. In his book *Cover Stories* Michael Denning mapped out the new situation as having four main 'players' which I've summarised below – the brackets indicate the relationship between Britain and the various 'not-Britain' players:

Britain (Good)
Not-Britain/Enemy – Soviet Union & East Germany (Bad)
Not-Britain/Ally – United States and other allies (Uneasy)
Not-Britain/Not-Ally – Colonial and ex-colonial countries (Uneasy/Bad)

As well as the loss of Empire, the other major blow to Britain during this period was the public revelation of 'the enemy within' – traitors who betrayed their own country and spied for the Communists. Guy Burgess and Donald Maclean defected in 1951 and the 'third man' Kim Philby defected in 1963. This meant that the British espionage now found that they couldn't trust their own people and also, crucially, it meant that allies such as the United States felt that they could no longer fully trust Britain.

John Atkins explained what this means in terms of the work of espionage agencies: "Spies have four main targets. The first is the original, the enemy. The object is information. The second is counter-espionage; the object, the spy himself. Then it starts getting complicated and progressively more nasty. The spy spies on his allies ... The final stage comes when the spy spies on his fellow spies. There is a complete absence of trust between administration and field operatives." This is the environment in which John Le Carré's novels – and novels such as Brian Freemantle's *Charlie Muffin* – take place.

Traitors
Sir Walter Raleigh warned Englishmen against becoming traitors and serving the Catholic Spanish King, saying, "...they are only assured to be employed in all desperate enterprises, to be held in scorn and disdain even among those whom they serve." And he warned that no traitor he had ever heard of had ever been trusted or 'advanced' by the Spanish.

In the world of the 'Clubland Heroes' – and even of James Bond – traitors were not common. The villain was always an outsider and not 'one of us.' But in the post-war era in Britain, there were a number of revelations of British agents who had passed secrets to the enemy. As John Atkins notes, the shadows of Kim Philby and others from the 'nest of traitors' that was the Cambridge Spy Ring hang over modern spy fiction.

British spies of the late 1940s and 1950s include Klaus Fuchs, Alan Nunn May, Guy Burgess, Donald Maclean, Kim Philby, Anthony Blunt, and George Blake. Biographies, interviews, and memoirs of these figures provide a great deal of information about their activities, motives, and the espionage organisations of their time – but, almost inevitably, there is also a great deal that remains unexplained. Some of these real-life spies have appeared in novels, plays, films, and television shows, either as characters or in the form of characters based on them. Some of them defected to the Soviet Union; some were arrested and convicted. George Blake was arrested and convicted but escaped from prison and fled to Russia. It was rumoured – another conspiracy theory! – that Blake's escape was assisted by British security personnel, but this was never proved. Before his death in 1980, Alfred Hitchcock had worked on a screenplay based on the George Blake case – titled *The Short Night*, it was adapted in part from a novel of the same title by Ronald Kirkbride and a non-fiction book *The Springing of George Blake* by Sean Bourke. Screenwriters on the project included James Costigan, Ernest Lehman and David Freeman. Freeman published his draft of the screenplay in the book *The Last Days of Alfred Hitchcock*. Sean Bourke was Blake's cellmate in Wormwood Scrubs and after his own release, he helped Blake to escape. Bourke lived in Moscow for eighteen months on a 'pension' given to him by the Russians but returned to Ireland. Bourke and George Blake are character's in Simon Gray's play *Cell Mates*. Bourke died from a stroke in 1982, though an ex-KGB agent alleges he was killed by a Russian agent.

Some writers have shown an interest in the lives of spies after they have defected to the Soviet Union. Alan Bennett's play *The Old Country* explores questions of loyalty, betrayal and what it is to be 'English' and his *An Englishman Abroad* tells of an encounter between Guy Burgess and actress Corale Brown, a chance encounter which did happen in Moscow in 1958. In a third play, *A Question of Attribution*, Bennett writes of Anthony Blunt's role in the Cambridge Spy Ring, including his interrogation by MI5, and his work as art advisor to Queen Elizabeth II. The play was written for television, with Edward Fox playing Blunt and Prunella Scales as the Queen – dialogue between the two hints that she knows he is a spy and that he knows that she knows.

Brian Freemantle in his *Face Me When You Walk Away* (1974) has a female character encounter the British expatriate community in Moscow: "She found them grubby, insecure little men, like junior clerks on a firm's outing to the seaside. Their slang vocabulary was of a decade ago, their conversation meaningless trivia involving nostalgia about favoured restaurants that weren't really very good or plays that had long ceased to run or prompt comment. Most retained their old-school ties, she noticed, and wore suits shiny with grease and over-wear, just because there was a London or New York label inside the jacket. There was not one whom she had met whom she did not feel secretly regretted the activity that had forced them into exile." (Quoted in Atkins)

Motivation
Ideology. When a person's ideology and duty to country are aligned, there is no issue. But if their ideology and duty to country clash, there is a problem. In the late 1940s and early 1950s, many well-educated people were attracted to the ideology of Socialism and believed that the Communism of the Soviet Union was going to be a practical implementation of socialist values. As the old British

Empire gradually faded, they saw a need for something new to take its place and believed Socialism could be that thing. This put them in conflict with the dominant ideology of their own country and led some of those people to betray their country and spy for the Soviets – they put ideology before country.

After the end of the Soviet Union, it was thought that traitorous spies would no longer be motivated by political ideology. Modern traitors were more likely to have character defects that make them targets for blackmailers who coerce them into betraying their country; or to be motivated by money or the lure of power or notoriety. While this was true for some, there are still people who are prepared to betray their country because of their beliefs.

There is a class of modern 'spies' – or 'whistle-blowers' – who are motivated to disclose state secrets when they believe the state is acting in a way which is not in the best interests of the people. There is an element here of 'who watches the watchmen.' These secrets are often released publicly, rather than passed secretly to other states who might benefit from them. The information released usually relates to some form of suspected political conspiracy; to alleged misuse of state apparatus – intelligence services spying on ordinary citizens, for example; or to alleged 'cover-ups' of suspected illegal activity, including human rights abuses – accidental or deliberate – by the military or intelligence operatives overseas.

More recent 'traitors' include Julian Assange, founder of WikiLeaks; Chelsea Manning, and Edward Snowden. While each of them almost certainly acted out of a complex mix of personal motivations, they each believed that their actions were, to use Alan Nunn May's words, "a contribution to the safety of mankind."

Money. Criminals of any kind are often given away by the fact that they suddenly appear to have money to spend on extravagant living, with their expenditure easily outstripping their income. But it is unlikely that anyone ever really became rich from being a spy – at least within the intelligence community. Espionage is a risky business, so people will rarely do it for the money alone, there must be another motive – even if it is only a desire to feel that you have proved yourself more than just a mundane wage-slave.

General Vozdvishensky in *From Russia, with Love* says, "Americans try to do everything with money. Good spies will not work for money alone – only bad ones, of which the Americans have several divisions."

Revenge. If someone has failed in their career or believes that they have not achieved a level of success that they feel they deserve, that person may seek 'revenge' on whoever they feel is responsible for their lack of good fortune. These are the sort of people who believe that some figure or some group within society is involved in a conspiracy and that this is the cause of their personal failure. They want someone to blame. This sort of motivation often lies behind extreme forms of nationalism and the actions of white supremacists and anti-Semites. It has also been a motivation for traitors, who believed that they would be treated with more respect if they worked for the other side. Sometimes just the thought of being 'an agent,' working against 'the conspiracy' at home was enough to make them feel special. In *The Spy Who Sat and Waited,* R. Wright

Campbell describes this sort of person as "...the failures, the malcontents, the whiners, the fools. Those who are easily puffed up with small secrets and empty honours. The childish who long desperately to destroy the father figure. The cynical, the cowardly, the self-seekers, the greedy."

Disillusionment. During the late 1940s and 1950s, as the British Empire breathed its last, there were some who felt betrayed and lost – Britain was no longer 'Great,' it was no longer the world power it had once been. Even among those who didn't mourn the end of the Empire, there were some who felt that standards of decency were on the wane.

In a 1980 interview with *The Observer,* John Le Carré compared his character Bill Haydon to Kim Philby, saying that Philby's motive for betraying his country was not some "... half-cocked pro-Stalin Marxism which could not be seriously sustained after university..." but rather, as Connie Sachs says in *Tinker, Tailor, Soldier, Spy,* he felt he had been betrayed: "Poor loves. Trained to Empire, trained to rule the waves. All gone. All taken away." That sense of having been betrayed seemed a much more believable reason for Philby's behaviour, Le Carré said.

John Atkins suggests that there are two groups of people that might belong under this heading. The first being those from wealthy families – the 'landed gentry' – who were seeing their Empire diminish. The second group were of middle-class origins, from families who made significant sacrifices in order to send their children to public school: they were willing to pay this price because they had been led to believe that a public school education would bring their children much greater opportunities as adults. When these opportunities did not materialise, they felt a sense of betrayal – especially when they learned that going to public school didn't actually provide full membership of the 'old school tie' club: if you were from a middle-class family, you were still regarded as 'second-class' by your wealthier ex-classmates. This was another group who could, potentially, hope for a fairer system under Socialism. Or who just might want to spit in the eye of the snob class.

Rebelliousness. Some people feel a need to thumb their noses at authority – to prove themselves better than the plodding bureaucrats who are seen to control too much of what goes on in life. In W. Somerset Maugham's *Ashenden* the hero wonders why the character Caypor had become a spy: "He did not think that he had become a spy merely for the money ... It might be that he was one of those men who prefer devious ways to straight for some intricate pleasure they get in fooling their fellows; and that he had turned spy, not from hatred of the country that had imprisoned him, not even from love of his wife, but from a desire to score off the big-wigs who never even knew of his existence. It might be that it was vanity that impelled him, a feeling that his talents had not received the recognition they merited, or just a puckish, impish desire to do mischief. He was a crook."

Love. In Vienna, Kim Philby met and fell in love with Litzi Friedmann and after they were married she is believed to have recommended him to Soviet recruiters. Romance – genuine or feigned – can be used to recruit spies or to entrap them: someone who has a relationship with the wrong person can be manipulated or blackmailed into betraying their country. Or the person they love may be held or threatened so that a person is forced to do the captors bidding.

Joseph Fouché, Napoleon's Minister of Police, is credited with coining the expression 'cherchez la femme' – literally 'look for the woman.' It refers to the woman who is responsible for a man's problems and is often used when the police were seeking a motive for a man's crimes.

Misplaced Optimism. Some people genuinely thought that Communism in Soviet Russia would embody all of the ideals of Socialism. John Le Carré said he thought Anthony Blunt was one such person. Given that homosexuality among men was illegal in Britain at that time, gay men were of necessity part of what Le Carré refers to as a 'secret world' of their own and that, for some of them, "There was still enough innocence about Marxism around for people to believe that with political liberation would come sexual liberation."

Moles and Sleepers

In the interview with *The Observer*, Le Carré admitted that much of the jargon he used was made-up because the actual terms used were not nearly as 'pretty.' But there was one term that he had taken from real-life: "*Mole* is ... a KGB word which I flatter myself I dragged out of obscurity..." Le Carré first used the word in *Call for the Dead* (1962). The *Shorter Oxford English Dictionary* defines mole: 'A secret agent who gradually achieves a position deep within the security defences of a country; a trusted person within an organisation etc. who betrays confidential information.'

The plot of *Tinker, Tailor, Soldier, Spy* concerns the search for a mole within 'the Circus' – the intelligence agency where George Smiley used to work.

R. Wright Campbell's *The Spy Who Sat and Waited* (1975) tells of a 'sleeper' agent becomes a British citizen, marries and has a son, but who is all the while a German spy, waiting to be called upon to do his work. The story explores the man's feelings and actions after he is called upon to betray the people he has lived among for so long. The 1988 film *Little Nikita* stars River Phoenix as a teenager who learns that his parents are sleeper agents for the Soviet Union. The tagline for the film was: *He went to bed an all-American kid and woke up the son of Russian spies.*

Double Agents

A double agent is someone employed by a government to obtain secret information about an enemy country, but who is really working for that enemy. They pretend to serve one side while actually serving the other. They are often used in counter-espionage operations to transmit disinformation or to identify other agents. Some of the information fed back to the organisation he is actually spying on has to be true and useful, otherwise it will soon become obvious that he is working for the other side.

A loyal agent may be captured by the enemy and threatened with death, or he may be blackmailed, into becoming a double agent working for the enemy.

There is a problem with double agents. An agent, by definition, is someone who can pretend to be something he isn't, so cannot be entirely trusted. With a double agent, this is compounded. Both of the organisations he works for – the good guys and the enemy – are likely to distrust him. He may himself even end up having difficulty knowing where his true loyalty lies.

The first novel to use a double agent appears to be Joseph Conrad's *Under Western Eyes* (1911).

To make things more confusing, there is also a re-doubled agent – a double agent who is found out and then turned so that he again becomes loyal to his original employer. There is a declassified document on the CIA website called 'Observations on the Double Agent' by F. M. Begoum. It includes pros and cons as well as advice on how to manage double agents.

In Len Deighton's *Funeral in Berlin*, the Russian, Stok, says: 'I make my plans upon the basis of everyone being untrustworthy.' In response, the main character says, 'The moment that you think you know who your friends are is the moment to get another job.'

A *triple agent* works for the intelligence services of three different countries or organisations but is usually actually loyal to only one of them.

(iii) Conspiracy

Espionage stories feature two sets of people who are ideologically opposed to one another: nations in conflict, Germany versus the Allies during the Second World War for example; or 'East versus West' during the Cold War. Each side is trying to infiltrate and disrupt the smooth working of the other, and there is usually a threat – sometimes only implied – of one side conquering the other. Each side represents a cause or belief system – 'Communism' versus 'Western democracy' or 'Islamic Fundamentalism' versus 'Western religious and secular ideologies' or something similar. Such conflicts are not new: Christ is said to have been betrayed by an insider – an agent of the enemy – and in the Elizabethan age Protestants and Catholics spied on each other.

The conspiracy surrounds the actions of one side as it tries to spy on, or disrupt the spying activities, of the other. And the activities of the spies take place without the knowledge of the 'ordinary people' they seek to protect – carried out by a *secret service,* and taking place in a hidden world, where the normal rules of law are suspended 'for the greater good.' The people, the spies argue, are better off not knowing what is done in their name. This double level of secrecy – remaining hidden from their enemies *and* from their own countrymen – is an important aspect of the spy thriller.

In the amateur-on-the-run and the James Bond thriller, the conspiracy is an external threat to the established order – and the status quo is regarded as something worth protecting. In Le Carré's novels, the conspiracy is typically underway at home and even within his own organisation.

(iv) The MacGuffin

"The theft of secret documents was the original MacGuffin." – Alfred Hitchcock

In the espionage novel, the vital commodity is *information* or 'intelligence' which Michael Denning calls "the arcane secrets that are the currency of the spy trade. This knowledge is professional, technical, and fragmentary. It is clearly a relation of power; every reader of spy thrillers knows that the interest is not in the secret information itself – how many missiles, or what secret treaty – but in the distribution of knowledge. Power is knowing what they know without their knowing that you know it. If they know you know, you've lost it. And in fact, if you don't know they know you know it, then they've got the power. And it is that 'simple' relation that is at the heart of many of the spy thrillers of the Le Carré/Greene generation."

Borrowing military terms, intelligence is sometimes divided into two kinds, HUMINT which is information collected and provided by human sources, and SIGINT which comes from the interception of signals, whether communications between people (communications intelligence or COMINT) or from electronic signals not directly used in communication (electronic intelligence or ELINT).

(v) The Romantic Co-Protagonist
In *The Spy Who Came in from the Cold* this role is played by Liz Gold. She is not treated as merely a distraction or a 'reward' when the hero has completed his mission – instead, she is someone with whom the hero genuinely falls in love. She is more like the romantic co-protagonist in the amateur-on-the-run thriller in that she is someone that the hero is able to trust. Despite all of the suffering and betrayal that he has experienced in his professional life, she shows him that there is still something in the world that is good – something to believe in and fight for. When he is with her, he can let the tough-guy mask of cynicism drop.

Le Carré was one of the first espionage writers to give his characters real lives – and real relationships – outside their work. George Smiley's troubled relationship with his wife, Anne, becomes significant to the plot of *Tinker, Tailor, Soldier, Spy*. In the same novel, Le Carré made use of a romantic aspect that had featured in real-life espionage, that of homosexual relationships. It should be remembered that homosexuality between men was a criminal offence in Britain until it was (partially) decriminalised in 1967. This left gay men in all walks of life open to blackmail and intimidation – and therefore vulnerable to enemy agents who were seeking 'weak links' in Britain's diplomatic and security services. That men who could only express their sexuality in a clandestine underworld or in secret relationships became caught up in the clandestine world of espionage is somewhat ironic.

Denning points out that the work relationships versus personal relationships and love (loyalty to another) versus loyalty to organisation/country are key themes in Le Carré's work.

(vi) Settings
Whether protagonist is searching for a mole at home or is out in the cold in another country, the setting of the story is the world of international political relations. Operating in another country without the permission of the authorities there is a situation with built-in tension, but 'enemy territory' could just as easily exist on home soil. Although the world in the story is presented in a realistic manner, the claustrophobia and shadows are typically exaggerated such

that it is reminiscent, as Cawelti and Rosenberg write, "of the Gothic castle with its hidden passages, secret panels, and lurking conspirators."

John Atkins on *The Spy Who Came in from the Cold*: "Le Carré gives a depressing picture of post-war Berlin. It is not a tourist's picture, it is the one that lies behind the political exterior." There are other foreign locations used in the 'Karla Trilogy' but here too he avoids the 'guidebook' approach that characterised Ian Fleming's use of exotic locations.

The locations in Le Carré's stories are often cold, dark and barren. There are few if any natural settings – neither the exotic foreign settings of Bond nor the rugged settings of the British countryside. We are shown seedy hotels, boarding houses, apartments, restaurants, casinos, and porn theatres. Stairwells frequently appear in films, especially circular ones that suggest a spiralling upwards or downwards into danger. The sky is grey and overcast. Or we are taken to checkpoints or border crossings where the landscape is man-made – concrete walls – and the dangers are man-made – barbed-wire, deep shadows and the fear of the sudden bright artificial light of a search-light. Sirens followed by gunfire. And it is often cold, with men huddled in overcoats, a physical manifestation of a spy being 'out in the cold.' The ground on either side of a border crossing is equally bleak: Is there much difference on one side or the other? Streets are dark and the cobblestones are wet. These locations owe something to the prisoner of war story and to the 1949 Graham Greene / Orson Welles film *The Third Man,* directed by Carol Reed. If you are seeking to create the off-kilter world of espionage, that film is a must-see.

In espionage stories, meetings often take place in isolated locations, away from any possible witnesses. Or in public parks or town squares when the crowds have all gone home. There is often snow and perhaps even fog in the air, to emphasise the curtain of secrecy that surrounds the meeting or the murkiness of the story situation.

Travel and transportation feature in spy stories and so conversations are likely to occur in cars or train compartments. Until the 1960s, when air travel became more common, passenger ships and trains were used for long-distance travel. Trains were ideal for espionage stories as they were enclosed spaces with few hiding places and no exits when the train was travelling at speed. They were also stopped at border crossings and were boarded by guards who would check travel documents.

Another location often used is the 'safe-house' a concept that suggests an island of security in a dangerous environment – that will only remain safe as long as its location is not discovered. Although there are often several characters in a scene in a safe-house, there is still a sense of isolation. It symbolises ideas of hiding and secrecy, as well as emphasising the claustrophobia that is often associated with espionage stories. And it has links with the idea of hiding in 'priest-holes' during the persecution of Catholics during the reign of Elizabeth I. The risk of a hidden character 'being found' is one way to create suspense in a scene. To emphasise that the safe house is not really a home, there is often a sense of it being impersonal temporary accommodation, like a hotel room. It is also typically occupied only by males, some of who are 'guards' – there for protection and to prevent escape. It may also be a place where work is carried out

– an extension of the bureaucrat's office, or it may be a place where questioning or interrogation occurs.

As well as physical locations, there is also the milieu of the espionage story – what Cawelti and Rosenberg call the 'clandestine world.' This is a world where even the best of the good guys is a deceiver. A world where openness and honesty are not seen as virtues but can instead lead to death. And it is a world where trust is a rare commodity and where even those closest to you, whether lovers or people in your own organisation, can betray you – either deliberately or through incompetence. Spending your working day in this kind of environment – and not being able to drop the façade when you have done your work for the day – has an impact on professional espionage agents. It can affect their sense of who they really are, particularly if they are living the role of another person, as deep-cover or sleeper agents must do. Any agent abroad is likely to be pretending to be someone else, often an employee of a commercial company with legitimate links to the country, and he must stay 'in character.' And having to be able to look into the eye of an enemy, a friend, or a colleague and lie to them must have an effect on how you perceive the world and the honesty of others.

Spies coming in from the cold are likely to require similar support from their organisations as soldiers returning from the battlefield. They will need help to readjust to civilian life. Some may even be 'addicted' to the high-adrenaline lifestyle and fear returning to a mundane existence or a desk-job – as Leamas did.

(vii) Iconography
What sort of images or symbols do we 'see' in espionage novels? Anything that might appear in the amateur-on-the-run or the James Bond-style thriller can be used in these stories. We have already mentioned the different characters that might appear – a few more are coved under *Other Characters* below – and the kinds of settings that might be used. If you look at the covers for spy novels during the past fifty years you will see the usual images of handguns and knives, men in big hats with their overcoat collars turned up, and men leaping from moving trains. Chess pieces have also featured, symbolising the 'Great Game'. Shadows and silhouettes crop up frequently, as does fog; lone figures in cobbled streets or empty town squares – perhaps trying to echo films such as *The Third Man*, are also found. Images of 'top secret' documents with sections blacked out by censors can also be found on a number of covers. Russian Dolls were famously used during the opening sequence of the BBC television adaptation of *Tinker, Tailor, Soldier, Spy* and on the cover of a US edition of the book.

Images relating to covert listening and recording, including things like microphones with parabolic dishes, can be used to symbolise espionage information gathering. Francis Ford Coppola's film *The Conversation* is a thriller about a surveillance expert and the dilemma he faces in relation to material he has recorded. The main character, played by Gene Hackman, is a man obsessed with his own privacy and security. The film is not an espionage thriller as such but explores themes that are relevant to the genre.

Covert watching, photographing and filming are also surveillance activities which can be used to portray the idea of espionage. Binoculars, telescopes and cameras can all be used.

Included below are several other ways in which espionage activity might be shown.

Disguises and Assumed Identities. 'Dressing up' is not used to the extent that it was in the earliest 'cloak and dagger' spy novels, but it still makes an appearance occasionally. Le Carré has a character change from a light coat to a dark one almost mid-stride to make it more difficult for anyone to follow him. Changing vehicles is another variation of this. A 'disguise' in a modern espionage story is more likely to be a complete assumed identity or 'cover story.' Rather than fake hair and moustache, the agent adopts a whole new life, including – as necessary – a fake career and home life. Le Carré uses the term 'legend' for this, borrowing an old KGB term. Assumed identities work well in thrillers because they have built into them the risk of exposure – the slightest slip 'out of character' leaves the agent open to discovery.

Tailing. Following an enemy agent or avoiding being followed himself is a bit of 'tradecraft' that a spy has to learn. To add verisimilitude to their stories, writers often include specific details about how tailing or 'losing a tail' can be accomplished. In *The Honourable Schoolboy*, the character of Jerry Westerby shares this information with the reader, recalling what he was taught at Sarratt, Le Carré's version of spy-school.

Top Secret Files. Files stamped 'Top Secret' or messages headed 'For Your Eyes Only' are a bit of a spy story cliché now, but they are one way of symbolising the information that is gathered as a result of espionage activities. The thickness of a file used to indicate how much data was held about a person or thing, but in these days of computer files everything can be held on a thumb-drive (though USB sticks are fast becoming obsolete and CD-ROMs are already gone) or in an e-mail. Perhaps ironically, paper files are now sometimes used because they are harder to copy and transmit electronically. We even hear stories of actors in the latest blockbuster movies receiving their scripts printed on dark red paper so that they cannot be easily copied, and the plot secrets leaked on the internet. Data can be hidden in electronic files – steganography (literally 'concealed writing') is a method of hiding one file, message, image, or video within another file, message, image, or video. Sounds too can be used to carry secret information. Microdots are still sometimes used – in the third *Mission: Impossible* film in 2006 a microdot on the back of a postage stamp contained a video file.

Cyphers and Codes have not featured to any great extent in spy fiction since the 1950s. But codenames and codewords are still used. The real-life spies all had at least one codename. Codewords or phrases are still used in fiction. In Len Deighton's *Funeral in Berlin*, for example, when the hero phoned his organisation, "I gave the operator the week's code. 'I want the latest cricket scores.'" He must then respond correctly to the question she asked. You may have experienced something similar when you have phoned your bank or a government department – sometimes fiction struggles to keep up with reality. The more modern use of cryptography is in the encryption of computer data files and communication. Security agencies in Britain and the USA have tried to 'encourage' cell phone manufacturers to introduce a secret 'backdoor' that would allow the agencies to obtain data from the mobile devices of criminals and terrorists. There have also been dark mutterings from the same agencies about the availability of encrypted messaging apps and access to the 'dark web.' It's a sad fact that – particularly in Britain – the government has demonstrated their typical incompetence when it comes to the uses and abuses of modern technology: the fact that a Secretary of State couldn't understand why ordinary people might ever need to encrypt their data or communications, and that IT services in hospitals could be paralysed are just two examples. And revelations about security agencies routinely spying on innocent citizens seems proof enough that we still need to watch our watchmen and take precautions to protect our privacy.

(viii) Themes

Betrayal and Traitors. The characters in an espionage novel must decide where their loyalties lie. Is it to their homeland, their country? Is it to the organisation that employs them? To their fellow spies? To their own moral values? Their own ideology or religion? Or do they no longer believe in anything, such that they are prepared to sell secrets to both sides? In Elizabethan England, Catholics found their religious beliefs in conflict with their loyalty to their country. In the 1950s there was a clash between patriotism and belief in a communist ideology. In modern-day England and elsewhere Muslims find their national loyalty questioned because of their religious beliefs. Whatever a person chooses, he or she is going to find them accused of betraying somebody and branded a traitor. In contemporary fiction, an individual's moral dilemma is probably more effective story material than a clash of opposing ideologies. Modern day 'traitors' who leak classified information are more likely to be motivated by moral issues than by a choice between capitalism or communism.

Cynicism. In the James Bond-style thriller we saw that while the hero may have occasional bouts of doubt and cynicism about the value of his work, he eventually recommits to the values of his country and his organisation. In Le Carré's novels, cynicism is a much more significant part of the hero's character. Leamas in *The Spy Who Came in from the Cold* chapter 25 says, "I don't believe in anything, don't you see – not even destruction or anarchy. I'm sick, sick of killing..." The spies don't preach ideology, he says, "They're the poor sods who try to keep the preachers from blowing each other sky high."

Action versus Thought. Some people act without thinking, others think without acting – both can be equally dangerous. James Bond tends to act, doing what he has been told to do, without spending a great deal of time pondering the rights and wrongs of it. And an agent in the field has to respond to situations as they arise and improvise a response. John Le Carré contrasts this with bureaucrats – the politicians and controllers – who seem unable to make a decision, caught up in their deliberations as they try to reconcile the unreconcilable and come up with an ideal solution. Or bureaucrats who make a decision to act without considering the consequences for the agents in the field – or are aware of the consequences and consider the sacrifice acceptable.

Denning writes that Le Carré's stories are more concerned with information – 'what do I know?' – than with action – 'what happens?' and that "They are closer to the detective or mystery paradigm, retracing an already completed action to discover its agency, than to the adventure paradigm, a series of actions united by a hero (the paradigm that dominates the James Bond stories)."

Information is the key resource in these stories, as Denning points out, with the hero acting like a traditional detective: "Smiley accumulates this information by visiting the betrayed and exiled characters and exchanges his trust and love for their knowledge; this culminates in Smiley's recognition of the mole, as well as his own and others' complicity." Smiley discovers who the 'villain' is, the identity of the traitor, but instead of exonerating the innocent, he discovers that they are all – including himself – guilty. Denning says that, in terms of his investigation, "Smiley's knowledge is amateur, humane, and totalising ... Smiley collects his information from a position outside the Circus and his profession. He becomes the advocate for the faithful but dismissed servants: Connie, Sam Max, Jerry, Jim." Like the classical detective, Smiley is an outsider given access to the 'inside' in the hopes that he can restore equilibrium to that closed world.

John Atkins writes about why Smiley believes his particular brand of professionalism is necessary – why he does what he does – and it has little or nothing to do with playing the 'Great Game': "The purpose and task of the Intelligence service ... was not to play chess games but to deliver intelligence to its customers. If it failed to do this, those customers would resort to other, less scrupulous sellers or, worse, indulge in amateurish self-help."

The 'Great Game'. Le Carré opposed the concept of espionage being a 'game' – in *The Spy Who Came in from the Cold* Leamas complains that a double-agent and sometime assassin is 'a savage little bastard' and is told 'Espionage is not a cricket game.' In Le Carré's stories, we are shown that the actions of spies – both 'ours' and 'theirs' – has consequences: people are betrayed, people are hurt, and people die. And that these events have an impact both on those who knew the victims*and* – sometimes – on those who ordered the actions and/or carried them out. The victims are not faceless pieces on a chessboard. Espionage, we learn, is not a game played by gentlemen – it is work done by people who believe that the only thing that matters is success in the field; the ends justify the means. This returns to the old idea that spying is not an occupation for honourable men.

Ironic Failure. James Bond, like the 'Clubland Heroes' before him, succeeds in his mission as a result of his own actions. We can call this a positive outcome.

In Eric Ambler's stories, the outcome is also positive but often *despite* the protagonist's actions – success comes by accident or through outside help, and we might call this an ironically positive outcome. The purely negative or tragic outcome is less common in genre fiction of any kind, but we do see it in Graham Greene's stories. John Le Carré tends more towards the ironic failure in which, as Cawelti and Rosenberg write, "the protagonists succeed only at the cost of becoming as dehumanised, as distorted in their conception of ends and means as their adversaries. In the modern world of clandestine bureaucracies and Cold War, the only choice open to a decent individual seems to be complicity, like Smiley, or destruction, like Leamas..."

Ethics of Spying. Control, Leamas' boss in *The Spy Who Came in from the Cold*, says "... we do disagreeable things, but we are *defensive*. That, I think, is still fair. We do disagreeable things so that ordinary people here and elsewhere can sleep safely in their beds at night. Is that too romantic? Of course, we occasionally do very wicked things." The argument tends to go something like: The ends justify the means – it's a dirty job, but someone has to do it – at least we're not as bad as 'they' are – and we're doing it to protect our country. Nicholas Berdon, a spy during the reign of Elizabeth I made the same argument: 'Though I am a spy (which is a profession odious though necessary) I prosecute the same not for gain but for the safety of my country."

Atkins quotes President Eisenhower speaking in 1960 when he described intelligence-gathering activities as "... a distasteful but vital necessity," and said that the Americans would prefer to work in a different way, but the nature of their enemy – the 'secrecy of the Soviet Union' – made this impossible. Speaking about the nature of these activities, Eisenhower said: "These have a special and secret character. They are, so to speak, 'below the surface' activities. They are secret because they must circumvent measures designed by other countries to protect the secrecy of military preparations. They are divorced from the regular visible agencies of government ... These activities have their own rules and methods of concealment which seek to mislead and obscure." The text can be found on the www.CIA.gov website.

'Patriotism' can be a thorny subject today – in Britain more than in the United States – and so rather than say that our intelligence agents are working 'for Queen and country' we are more likely to say that they are working to protect 'democracy' and the 'security of our nation.' In 1984, John Atkins wrote, "The spy always flies to the security aspect to gain respectability." He was writing before the end of the Cold War, but his words remain true today – as I write this – in the face of the 'war on terror' and deteriorating relations between Russia and the West.

In *The World of Espionage*, Bernard Newman writes: "A spy *must* be a man of integrity and yet must be prepared to be a criminal. A man with scruples is useless in our business."

Fellowship of Spies. John Atkins: "... once the enemy has been established there is a powerful tendency to admire and respect and, finally, even to love him. People who are paid to hate and kill others, that is to say, professionals, have a way of getting on the best terms with those they are supposed to hate and kill. After all, they understand each other. They do the same job. They resemble the eighteenth-century generals who used to mess together before and after they set to work to eliminate each other."

Because the professional spy is an outsider and does not belong to the society he is employed to protect and because – in Le Carré's world – he cannot even trust his own organisation not to betray him, his most 'trusted' friend might be the agent on the opposite side: at least he knows where he stands with that person! The best-known example of this sort of mutual respect and even friendship is that between George Smiley and his Russian equivalent, Karla. The relationship is an important thread that is woven through the three novels – *Tinker, Tailor, Soldier, Spy; The Honourable Schoolboy*, and *Smiley's People* – such that they are known collectively as the 'Karla trilogy' and have been published in an omnibus titled *The Quest for Karla* or *Smiley versus Karla*.

The Public School Spy. 'He hasn't had the advantages of a public school education. His ideas of playing the game are not quite the same as yours,' says R, the spymaster, of a Mexican agent in W. Somerset Maugham's *Ashenden*. If you are ex-public school, you're assumed to be a gentleman and a 'good sport' – someone who plays by the rules, either of cricket or of the Marquis of Queensbury. In the more 'realistic' type of spy novel, we see that it isn't just the enemy who play dirty – no one plays by the rules, and you can't even trust your own teammates.

Writing in 1984, John Atkins said, "It has surprised some people that the postwar British spies have nearly all been ex-public schoolboys yet there could be few better training grounds for espionage than the hothouse games-playing atmosphere of the public school." He also notes that "Recruiting spies from Cambridge (which until recently meant in effect from the public schools) is a tradition that goes back to Elizabethan times."

Before the Burgess and Maclean defections in 1951, MI5 had received information – from the USA and probably elsewhere – that there were suspicions about the activities of the two men – especially Maclean. Investigations after the defections showed that MI5 was slow to react to this information, in part because, as John Atkins says, "the Oxbridge types in MI5 ... could not believe that two Cambridge men had committed treason." The 'Old Boy Network' extended throughout MI5, MI6, the whole of government including the Foreign Office, the Admiralty and the Defence ministry. This was a community that did not want to believe that the country had been betrayed by one of 'their own.' In fact, it had been betrayed by quite a few of them. The extent of the network and the embarrassment caused by the defections naturally led to accusations of cover-up and collusion when many of the traitors escaped justice and fled to Russia. Though you have to wonder whether Le Carré is closer to the truth when he suggests that the bureaucracy of these organisations didn't have the competence to carry out an effective conspiracy of this kind.

John Vassall was a British civil servant who spied for the Russians between 1952 and 1962. He had worked at the British embassy in Moscow and been introduced to the homosexual scene in Moscow by another embassy employee.

Homosexuality was illegal in both Britain and Moscow at the time, and compromising photographs of him with other gay men were used to blackmail him into becoming a spy. Vassall was another ex-public schoolboy, and during a House of Commons debate following his arrest, Harold Wilson said: "Were our authorities too easily reassured by the school the man went to, the fact that he came from a good family ... the fact that he was personable, had a good accent and manner, and was a member of the Conservative and Bath clubs, as Vassall was? I wonder if the positive vetting of Vassall would have been so casual if he had been a boilermaker's son and gone to an elementary school."

Incompetent Bureaucracy. In a 1980 interview with *The Observer,* John Le Carré said that it was "extremely difficult to dramatise ... the persistent quality of human incompetence – particularly in British administration." Given a choice between 'conspiracy or cock-up' he would choose cock-up every time, but for the fact that "in writing, one has to tread a very fine line between the reality of incompetence and the reader's very human wish to visit a world where logic and action have a reasonable relationship to each other." George Smiley, he said, operated 'in defiance' of bureaucratic incompetence. If this sounds like unfair criticism of the British intelligence organisation, Kim Philby believed that one of the reasons he was never unmasked was because the 'secret service' was amateurish and incompetent, and even when they did find out about him, they didn't want to make his actions public because it would reveal their own shortcomings.

Mistrust of Allies. Relations between the American and British intelligence communities was at a low ebb as a result of the revelations about British spies during the late 1940s and 1950s. The Americans began to feel that British agents could not be trusted and represented a security risk; the British resented the fact that information about suspected spies was not always passed by the Americans – though to be fair, when it *was* passed on, the British did not always believe it or act on it. Defections to the 'other side' do not occur in the same way today, but as we have seen allies still feel it necessary to spy on one another.

Isolation. In the amateur-on-the-run and the James Bond thriller, we saw that isolation was a way in which we could demonstrate our hero's self-reliance – he proved that he was up to the job. In Le Carré, being alone and out in the cold makes things much bleaker for characters. As John Atkins says, "The agent may not only be deserted, he may even be betrayed by his own side."

After his assignment is completed, James Bond can spend some time with a beautiful woman, if only briefly. George Smiley goes home to an empty house because it is his wife who is having a night out.

(ix) Tone

Paranoia arising from a fear of discovery is a key part of these stories. Secrets must be kept, real identities and feelings hidden. Places, people, and objects may not be what they seem – nothing and no one can be trusted.

The tone of John Le Carré's novels is both serious and ironic. Under *Themes* above, I mentioned the idea of 'ironic failure' and the fact that there is no triumphant celebration of success: even when George Smiley achieves his goal, there is a sense of loss, a sense that someone somewhere loses something of significance. This almost gentle sense of tragedy is one of the things that had led critics to classify the novels as 'proper literature' rather than genre fiction.

A distinctive part of Le Carré's storytelling is his use of espionage slang or jargon – some of it is based on terms he encountered in his own intelligence work but much of it is made up. Either way, it allows the reader to feel that they are seeing behind the scenes of the espionage profession and being given access to classified information. The Wikipedia entry for *The Honourable Schoolboy* contains a table of 'tradecraft' terms and their definitions and includes burrowers, ferrets, housekeepers, janitors, lamplighters, mothers, pavement artists, scalp-hunters, shoemakers, babysitters and wranglers. Other writers have also created their own jargon – Len Deighton used the phrase 'expedient demise' as a euphemism for murder or assassination, with the abbreviation *XPD* becoming the title of his novel. Other writers have treated the use of jargon less seriously.

John Atkins also noted that "Le Carré adopts a stance that is unusual among spy writers. He writes as if the case is known, is even historical, only he is clearing up some of its darker corners. He corrects false impressions, refers to public anxieties. 'Certain people do still ask why...' "

(x) Other Characters

Smiley's People. Whether operating as an outside investigator or in the role of head of the Circus, George Smiley had a small circle of people who he felt he could trust. His right-hand man was Peter Guillam, a long-time colleague in various posts and a so-called 'scalp-hunters' – that is, someone sent in to "to handle the hit-and-run jobs that were too dirty or too risky" for agents resident abroad, of whom it was said, "they weren't gentle". Guillam is effectively Smiley's own field agent or 'cup-bearer.' And then there was Connie Sachs, a retired expert in the politics and policies of the Soviet Union. Forced out of a job she loved, she is presented as an alcoholic but with an incredible memory – saving Smiley the trouble of having to access files in the Circus. In *The Honourable Schoolboy*, she is brought back to work for the Circus under Smiley. The character is said to have been based, in part, on Milicent Bagot, a British intelligence officer who was the first to warn MI5 that Kim Philby was working for the Soviets.

These characters, a few like them in smaller roles, are significant because they show the hero, Smiley, working with a trusted team. These characters are not taken away from him – they are not captured or killed – as a device to make him appear more isolated. To a certain degree, Guillam is Watson and Connie is Mycroft to Smiley's Sherlock Holmes.

Control. The chief of what is now MI6 (or the 'Secret Intelligence Service') in Britain has been referred to as 'C' since about 1911 and a number of people have held the position. The original C was Captain Sir Mansfield George Smith

Cumming who seems to have been a suitably colourful character; according to his Wikipedia entry, "In 1914, he was involved in a serious road accident in France, in which his son was killed. Legend has it that in order to escape the car wreck he was forced to amputate his own leg using a penknife. Hospital records have shown however that while both his legs were broken, his left foot was only amputated the day after the accident. Later he often told all sorts of fantastic stories as to how he lost his leg, and would shock people by interrupting meetings in his office by suddenly stabbing his artificial leg with a knife, letter opener or fountain pen." One of Cumming's main agents was Sidney Reilly aka the 'Ace of Spies.'

Spy writers have taken C as their model for creating the heads of their own fictional espionage agencies – W. Somerset Maugham had R, Ian Fleming used M, while Le Carré named his 'Control.' In Le Carré's world, different factions with an organisation conspire to get 'their' man into the top job, hoping to see their own careers flourish. The head of a fictional spy organisation nominally reports to 'the Minister' or some other government overseer, but there seems to be a great deal that is kept from him 'for his own good.'

Writing about MI5, Henry Chapman Pincher in *Their Trade is Treachery* said, "the organisation was totally independent. Its staff was paid in cash, and paid no tax, and salaries could be at the whim of the director general. There was an independent auditor to ensure against embezzlement, but no detailed returns were made to the government and recently retired officers can remember how the directors general of both MI5 and the secret service [MI6] had hoards of gold sovereigns, which they could hand out for special operations. That situation ended when Sillitoe demanded that MI5 be expanded. The Treasury agreed but only on condition that it could impose controls."

The Minister. In the earliest days of British spy fiction, either 'the Minister' or 'the Ambassador' might be referred to as the higher authority above the head of a secret intelligence organisation. Since the 1950s it is more likely to be a Minister. In spy fiction, Ministers tend to be seen as distant and incompetent figures who don't really have an understanding of what goes on in the 'real world' of espionage. They either complain that they are being kept in the dark by their own intelligence services, or they say that it is 'better if I don't know' what agents and their controllers are up to. This relates back to the idea that spying was always regarded as 'ungentlemanly' and something that is only done as a last resort, and that no one in authority really wants to admit that spying is taking place. It probably also has something to do with the fact that ministers and senior civil servants never really want to take the risk of admitting responsibility for any decision taken, in case something goes horribly wrong. If you are unfamiliar with the workings of British Cabinet ministers, the BBC comedy series *Yes, Minister* from the early 1980s is – even now – probably much closer to the truth than anyone would want to admit.

In *Tinker, Tailor, Soldier, Spy* the role is played by an intermediary, Oliver Lacon, a senior advisor from the Cabinet Office and a 'watchdog of intelligence' or as Peter Guillam puts it, he's 'Whitehall's head prefect.' It is Lacon who recruits Smiley to investigate when it is suspected that there is a mole inside the Circus.

Field Agents. James Bond is a field agent and so is Leamas in *The Spy Who Came in from the Cold*. But in the 'Karla Trilogy' featuring George Smiley, field agents play a more peripheral role. It could even be said that the second book, *The Honourable Schoolboy* is almost a James Bond story told from the point of view of M, with Smiley being M. In *Tinker, Tailor, Soldier, Spy* the character of Jim Prideaux is a field agent who was injured during an assignment in Czechoslovakia and is now working as a teacher. His relationship with the Philby-Maclean character Bill Haydon is a key part of the plot, but he is an outsider and an enigmatic character throughout much of the story. In the same book, Ricki Tarr is another field agent, a man with personal secrets of his own but who uncovers evidence of there being a 'mole' in the Circus. Like Guillam, he has been a colleague of Smiley's for some time. In *The Honourable Schoolboy*, newspaper journalist and some-time Circus operative Jerry Westerby is called in to be the man in the field when Smiley begins to investigate a case that was deliberately suppressed by the former head of the Circus.

In Le Carré's stories, field agents are not the main protagonist but nor are they pawns in a 'game' played by their spymasters. As mentioned previously, George Smiley is a man with a conscience and is aware that the decisions he makes have consequences in the lives of his agents – people are hurt, physically and psychologically, relationships are destroyed, and sometimes people die. To Smiley, this is very much *not* a game.

Local Rivals. Only 'God and the KGB know how many organisations in Britain are concerned with the gathering of intelligence,' according to John Atkins, writing in 1984. Have a look at the Wikipedia entries for 'MI5' and 'British Intelligence Agencies' today and you will begin to see what he is referring to. Broadly speaking, the Foreign Office oversees MI6, which is concerned with espionage, officially intelligence gathering, and operates abroad. The Home Office oversees domestic security and so manages MI5, which is concerned with counter-espionage, and the Counter Terrorist Command (formed from the old Anti-Terrorist Branch and Special Branch) which is a part of London's Metropolitan Police Service. It is impossible to know with any certainty how well real-life, modern-day agencies co-operate with one another, but in fiction there is often a great deal of mistrust and rivalry. We are also led to believe that similar rivalry exists between the FBI and the CIA in the United States.

Writers of spy novels have felt free to create all manner of security organisations of their own – in John Le Carré's novels we have 'the Circus, for example.

The Americans. As was mentioned above, relations between Britain and the United States deteriorated following the revelations about high-level spying within the British secret services and the defections of many of those responsible. The American intelligence services, understandably, felt that the British could not be trusted. Britain had also lost its position as a major world power with the gradual decline of the old Empire. On the world stage, it was really only a bit-player. Le Carré had to deliberately side-line the Americans – having his characters refer to them as unpopular and unhelpful – so he could concentrate on the British.

Espionage Thriller Plots
In their book *The Spy Story,* Cawelti and Rosenberg list five types of espionage thriller plot:

- The Spy Goes Over
- The Big Job
- The Hero as Victim
- Journey Into Fear
- To Catch a Spy

The Spy Goes Over is referred to as the 'most natural' plot for an espionage story and involves a spy who is spying in enemy territory. They use Adam Hall's *Quiller Memorandum* as their example. The most important element in the story is the agent's secret mission. John Buchan's *Greenmantle*, Graham Greene's *Confidential Agent*, and John Le Carré's *The Spy Who Came in from the Cold* are also examples. This is a variation on the professional secret agent's 'mission plot' that we looked at in Chapter 2, but there sufficient differences that I will compare Le Carré's novel with the James Bond 'formula' below.

The Big Job is also the 'mission plot' from Chapter 2. Cawelti and Rosenberg give as examples Eric Ambler's *A Kind of Anger, The Schirmer Inheritance* and *The Mask of Dimitrios*. The plot is centred on a task which may be to accomplish a specific action or the *prevent* an action. In this category are included Frederick Forsyth's *The Day of the Jackal* (which I cover under 'assassination thrillers' in the *political thriller* chapter) and Thomas Harris's *Black Sunday* and Eric Ambler's *The Levanter* (both of which I cover under 'terrorism thrillers' in the same chapter).

The Hero as Victim is the amateur-on-the-run plot I introduced in Chapter 1. Eric Ambler's *Background to Danger* is another example, as is Len Deighton's *The Ipcress File.* The people who are pursuing the protagonist do not have to be enemy agents, they could be people from his own country or even his own agency. James Grady's *Six Days of the Condor* is an example and so too are Joseph Hone's *Sixth Directorate,* Robert Duncan's *Dragons at the Gate* and – in part – Graham Greene's *The Human Factor* which is also a 'to catch a spy' story.

The Journey into Fear is described as a variation on the hero as victim plot "... in which he must reach a destination at a certain time or with a particular cargo intact. Often that cargo is human, and the hero functions as a bodyguard." Examples include Eric Ambler's *The Journey Into Fear,* Helen MacInnes' *Snare of the Hunter,* Gavin Lyall's *Midnight Plus One,* and Owen Sela's *The Bearer Plot.*

To Catch a Spy, as we have already said, is similar to the murder mystery except that a spy rather than a murderer is sought. John Le Carré's *Tinker, Tailor,*

Soldier, Spy is one of the best known, and best, examples. Other examples include Len Deighton's *The Ipcress File* and *Department K* by Hartley Howard (filmed as *Assignment K*). Graham Greene's *The Human Factor* is a variation on this plot.

As can be seen from the examples given by Cawelti and Rosenberg, there is some overlap between the different categories. In summary, I will say that the different *'Big Job'* plots are covered in Chapter 2 and Chapter 8. The *'Hero as Victim'* has been covered in Chapter 1 and this can be combined with the *'Catch a Spy'* plot which we will look at below. *Journey into Fear* can, I think, be either a mission plot involving a deadline or a combination of mission-with-deadline and hero-on-the-run. The plot where a protagonist acts as bodyguard or escort for an innocent or guilty person is one that I will examine in more detail in the *Crime Thriller* volume in this series because that variation on the 'buddy movie' is popular in that sub-genre.

In this chapter, then, I will outline what I believe are the two main espionage thriller plot templates:

(i) *Mission Out in the Cold.* A spy goes into enemy territory to carry out a secret mission – an act of sabotage; theft of secret information or an important object; rescue of another agent or extraction of a defector; or the assassination of a person important to the enemy, perhaps even their leader.

(ii) *To Catch a Spy.* An investigation to uncover a 'mole' within a country's own secret service or to track down an enemy agent within a country's own territory – a Nazi war criminal, for example, a 'sleeper agent,' an assassin, or a former torturer.

For the first type, I will analyse John Le Carré's *The Spy Who Came in from the Cold* and explore the similarities and differences between it and the 'James Bond formula' from Chapter 2. For the second I will examine Le Carré's *Tinker, Tailor, Soldier, Spy* comparing it with both the 'James Bond formula' and the murder mystery plot that I dissected in my book *Mystery*.

The Spy Who Came in from the Cold

If we break this novel down into eight sequences, we get something like this:

Sequence 1: The main character, Leamas, is introduced, in the middle of a field assignment: a defector is trying to cross the border from East Germany. The mission does not conclude successfully. Returning to Britain and the headquarters of the Circus, Leamas meets with his boss, Control. Control asks him to undertake one more mission before he 'comes in from the cold.' The mission will involve him pretending to that he holds a grudge against the Circus and that he is ready to betray them. The Communists should then recruit him and take him to East Berlin, where he will be able to complete his mission: to kill one of their agents, Mundt, who is a threat to Fiedler, one of the Circus' undercover agents in East Germany. Leamas then appears to go into a rapid decline and he suddenly leaves the desk job he had been assigned in Britain: rumour circulates that he is 'burnt out' and is suspected of some banking irregularity while in his most recent post.

Sequence 2: Leams gets an ordinary job in a library, where he meets and falls in love with co-worker Liz Gold, who is a member of the Communist Party in Britain. His decline continues, to the point where he assaults a grocer who will not give him credit in his store. Leamas is arrested and sent to prison. In prison, Leamas demonstrates his ability to protect himself. On his release, he is contacted by a low-level agent of the East Germans. After the meeting, Leamas demonstrates his tradecraft by taking care to ensure that he has not been followed – and then goes to a meeting with Control. The reader learns that all of the events of Leamas' decline, including the attack on the grocer and being sent to prison, were part of the larger plan. Leamas agrees to carry on but makes it clear that he wants Liz Gold kept out of it from this point on. Again he is told that after this assignment, he can 'come in from the cold.'

Sequence 3: Leamas is taken to meet a more senior Soviet agent in Britain who tells him that they will pay him £15,000 if he provides them with 'reminiscences' of his intelligence work in Berlin. Leamas is then passed on to an even more senior Soviet agent, who offers Leamas a new life 'behind the curtain,' but Leamas refuses this offer. He is asked some questions about the man who tried to defect from East Berlin in the opening sequence.

Sequence 4: Leamas is questioned about his more recent work in the banking section. He tells of an operation called 'Rolling Stone' used to pay a secret source of intelligence – Leamas tries to persuade the Soviets agent that this source couldn't *possibly* have been in East Berlin, though this is part of the plan to, ultimately, convince the Soviets that there *is* a traitor in East Berlin – Mundt, the agent Leamas has been told to kill in order to protect their real east Berlin source, Fiedler. Leamas muses about the life he will have after the mission – maybe he will settle down with Liz. But then the Soviet agent tells Leamas that he is now a wanted man in London – he will never be able to go back. This wasn't part of the plot he hatched with Control – has he been set-up? Leamas 'reluctantly' agrees to go East with the Soviet agent. Elsewhere, George Smiley appears and – unknown to Leamas – pays off Leamas' debts and ensures that Liz is taken care of financially.

Midpoint: Leamas is taken to East Germany. He is handed over to Fiedler, who interrogates him about 'Rolling Stone' and the possible East Berlin spy reporting back to London. As previously agreed with Control, Leamas continues to deny they have a mole in East Berlin, knowing this will only convince them that there *is* a mole.

Sequence 5: Fiedler continues to question Leamas about the Circus. He also gets Leamas to write letters to the banks used to pay the 'Rolling Stone' money – if they can discover where the money was withdrawn, they can see which East German agents were in that location and so identify their mole. Fiedler mentions Leamas' relationship with Liz Gold – this makes Leamas angry: he doesn't want her involved. Fiedler warns that it may be too late to prevent this. Fiedler asks about the work done by Mundt in London, and Leamas answers the questions in such a way that it appears Mundt may have been working for the British. Fiedler says there is other evidence against Mundt – he has killed several enemy agents before they could be interrogated: perhaps he did this to protect himself. Perhaps Mundt was 'turned' in London? Leamas denies this, but Fiedler is not convinced by the denial. Back in Britain, Liz has been invited by the local Communist Party to pay a visit to East Germany – she accepts. In a final twist in this sequence, Fiedler is arrested and Leamas finds himself the prisoner of Mundt.

Sequence 6: Leamas learns that Fiedler has been arrested on suspicion of being a traitor – he is to be put on trial. Mundt wants Leamas to confess that he was conspiring with Fiedler – Leams himself may then be treated more leniently. Then, in another twist, Mundt's interrogation of Leamas is interrupted. Fiedler tells Leamas that Mundt has been arrested as an 'enemy of the people' and will be put on trial. If found guilty, he will be shot. Leamas thinks he has succeeded in the mission originally given to him by Control: kill Mundt. Mundt's trial begins and it is revealed that the 'Rolling Stone' money was taken out at a place and time where Mundt was present – he must be the traitor. He was turned while in London and allowed to escape. Leamas is called to testify – continues to deny Mundt was working for the Circus. Fiedler claims that Mundt was passing on intelligence via the agent killed in the opening sequence. This man was killed by Mundt, who was afraid the agent would be captured by the Soviets and reveal Mundt's treason.

Sequence 7: Leamas is cross-examined by Mundt's defender – he asks about the 'wealthy friends' who have paid his debts in England. And asks why he assaulted a grocer over a refusal of credit if he knew he had money coming to him. This was all George Smiley's doing – Leamas knew nothing about it, it wasn't part of the plan. He begins to feel that things are unravelling. The situation becomes worse when Liz is called as a witness – she explains about Leamas' debts being paid and about being given financial help herself. She also says that Leamas said goodbye to her *before* he assaulted the grocer. Mundt's defender argues that the whole situation has been set up to incriminate Mundt, that it was a plot by the British. Leamas thinks he must try and defend Liz and Fiedler, who is the mole he is supposed to be protecting. He tries to take on the blame for everything, admitting the plot but arguing that Fiedler was just an unlucky dupe who fell for the plot. But by defending Fiedler, Leamas is ultimately condemning him. And it is only at this point that Leamas realises *he* has been the dupe.

Sequence 8: Liz and Leamas are provided with an opportunity to escape by the *real* mole, who tells them that Fiedler had to be sacrificed to protect his identity. Fiedler had learned too much and needed to be publicly discredited. Leamas realises that Control had used both him and Liz right from the start – their meeting had not been a coincidence. The real mole is an unpleasant man, a former Nazi and an assassin responsible for the deaths of London agents, but he is useful to the Circus, so he gets to live. That is the nature of their work.

When Liz and Leamas try to get over the Berlin wall, George Smiley is on the Western side, urging Leams to jump – but the mission does not end successfully.

Is this story a 'negative' version or a 'rebuttal' of the James Bond story, as some have suggested?

Bond Plot
(1) 'Pre-credits sequence' – conspirators in action or James Bond in action proving his professionalism.
(2) Bond is given a mission by M.
(3) Bond takes some action that draws the attention of the conspirators.
(4) Villain's henchman sent to deal with Bond – a close fight. Perhaps an ally is lost.
Midpoint: The hero discovers the extent of the conspiracy. Stakes raised. Hero commits himself to end the conspiracy – by entering the villain's lair.
(5) Bond spends time with a beautiful woman. She may be working for the conspirators. Or she may reveal important information that will allow Bond to enter the lair of the villain.
(6) Bond breaks into the villain's lair – but is captured and tortured/interrogated and then faces a horrible death.
(7) Climactic battle – Bond escapes captivity, defeats the henchman, destroys the villain and his lair.
(8) Brief epilogue – Bond and the beautiful woman. Confirmation that the conspiracy has ended.

Leamas Plot
(1) 'Pre-credits sequence' – Leamas in action, helping a defector from East Germany. The mission ends in failure. Leamas is given a mission by Control.
(2) Leamas takes action that draws him to the attention of the Soviets. This includes meeting a beautiful woman and (genuinely) falling in love with her – and then giving her up.
(3) Agents of the Soviets question Leamas – testing him.
(4) More testing of Leamas. He thinks about retiring after the mission. Control puts into motion parts of the plan that Leamas doesn't know about – the beautiful woman is unwittingly a part of this.
Midpoint: Leamas suspects the plan may not be going exactly as planned with Control. Agrees to go to East Germany.
(5) Leamas questioned – given a task by the enemy to prove himself to them and to further their own actions. The beautiful woman – again unwittingly – is drawn to East Germany. A twist – the good guys arrested.
(6) Leamas in the hands of the 'villain,' Mundt. Interrogation – but this is interrupted: the villain is arrested. Apparent success of Leamas' mission if Mundt is executed as a spy. First part of the trial of Mundt – things look bad for the villain.
(7) Second part of Mundt's trial – the defence. Climax. Leamas' story – and his understanding of the mission itself – is undermined. Mundt will win and the man Leamas was told to protect will die. Leamas tries to sacrifice himself to

save this man and the beautiful woman – but fails. Then Leamas realises he has been set up.

(8) Epilogue – explanations and an opportunity for Leamas and the beautiful woman to escape – this ends in failure.

Although the different actions do not fall in exactly the same places, I think there is – at this very broad level of description – a lot of similarity in the way these two plots unfold. An important difference between Leamas and Bond is that while Bond is in control of his own actions and making the decisions that move the story forward; Leamas only *believes* that he is in control, but later discovers that he has been used by his own boss. While both stories concern the carrying out of a mission, Le Carré's story has an element of the caper or heist story where the reader – and sometimes the hero – are not aware of the whole plot.

Other key differences between the two occur because the Fleming story is essentially a 'comedy' – it has a happy ending – but the Le Carré is a 'tragedy,' with an ironically downbeat ending. In any plot, the situation at the end of Sequence 6 is usually the opposite – from the hero's point of view – of the final outcome at the end of Sequence 7. In a story with a positive ending, Sequence 6 ends with what we often refer to as the hero's 'darkest hour' – he appears to have lost or to have no way of winning. In a story with a negative ending, Sequence 6 will actually make it appear that the hero has succeeded – in this case, it appears Mundt will be shot as a traitor. *The Spy Who Came in from the Cold* has an 'ironic failure' at the end because while Leamas appears to have failed – the man he was sent to protect will die as a traitor – this is actually a success, because his boss really wanted another man protected. There is tragic irony also in the fact that although Leamas doesn't get to come in from the cold, he does choose – in a sense – to be with the woman he loves forever.

Tinker, Tailor, Soldier, Spy

The Spy Who Came in from the Cold is a story about a mission to protect one of 'our' moles who has infiltrated the enemy's organisation; *Tinker, Tailor, Soldier, Spy,* on the other hand, is a story about a hunt for an enemy mole within 'our own' organisation. How does the plot for a 'mole hunt' compare with a typical James Bond adventure?

Smiley Plot

(1) Prologue: Mysterious new teacher with a physical disability arrives at a school. This is Prideaux – his actions will be a subplot that is woven into the main smiley plot, the two not coming together until Sequence 7; though Prideaux is often spoken about in the main plot. Smiley, a retired intelligence agent, and his world are introduced. Smiley meets Lacon, a Cabinet Office advisor.

(2) Lacon has an Australian agent tell Smiley what he has discovered. There is a 'mole' in the Circus. Nobody there can be trusted, so Lacon wants Smiley, as an 'outsider,' to conduct the investigation and find the identity of the traitor.

(3) Smiley gathers people he trusts – his right-hand man, Peter Guillam, and his old friend, also a retired agent, Connie Sachs. Sets up HQ in a hotel. Smiley expresses an interest in the case of Prideaux.

(4) Introducing the opponents – the new 'Control' is Alleline, who got the position when he came in with a major new source of intelligence, codenamed Merlin. There were factions in the Circus – Smiley and Connie were loyal to the old Control, and so were forced into retirement. Alleline's people are Bland, Esterhase and Haydon – any one of these four could be the mole. Smiley learns that the Circus is operating a new safehouse somewhere. Guillam sneaks a file on Prideaux out from the Circus.

Midpoint: Smiley deduces that Merlin is not one Soviet source but several.

(5) Alleline questions Guillam who lies and says he's had no contact with Smiley. Smiley tells Guillam about the Russian spymaster, Karla, and how they once met in Delhi – where Smiley tried, unsuccessfully, to persuade him to defect. This is the man they are really up against. Smiley identifies a Russian diplomat, Polyakov, as the go-between for the mole and the Russians. Smiley warns Lacon that the government shouldn't share Merlin's intelligence with Americans – and that anything the Americans share with them will be sent to the Russians by the mole. Lacon has information that Prideaux and Bill Haydon had a relationship at university.

(6) Smiley interviews the agent, now retired, who was Duty Officer on the night Prideaux was shot and captured in Czechoslovakia. Smiley deduces that Haydon was at Smiley's home on that night, and that he was having an affair with Smiley's wife. He also learns that the Russians were warned about Prideaux's mission the night before, so were in place ready to stop him. These facts were subsequently hidden by Esterhase.

(7) Smiley meets Prideaux. Prideaux doesn't know about all of the changes that have taken place in the Circus. He says that when he was questioned following his capture, the Russians knew everything already. Smiley says he doesn't believe Alleline was the mole, but that his ambitiousness was used by the mole. Smiley questions Esterhase and learns the location of the safehouse among other details.

(8) The safehouse – everyone is gathered together. Haydon is captured as the mole. Smiley plays the tapes that prove everything. In an epilogue, Smiley visits Haydon in his 'cell' – there are secrets Haydon won't reveal, but he drops hints – Control had been close to exposing him as the mole, so the Czech mission was set up to discredit Control. Prideaux, because he had loved Haydon, had warned him. Prideaux was brought back, at the cost of the lives of several Czech agents, to keep things quiet. When Smiley has gone, Prideaux shoots Haydon.

The plot of *Tinker, Tailor, Soldier, Spy* has very little in common with the James Bond-style secret agent story. Smiley receives a mission from a civil servant, but beyond that, it is difficult to make the pieces fit. The reason for this is that

Le Carré has returned to the sort of plot he used in two earlier George Smiley books – he has used the basic structure of a murder mystery story. If we switch murderer for 'mole,' it becomes more obvious. I explored the classic murder mystery plot in the *Mystery* volume in this series, so will outline the eight sequences of what I have called the 'Act I Murder Plot' only briefly here:

Murder Mystery

(1) A body is discovered. Introduce the detective and the world of the story.

(2) Suspects and witnesses, including the murderer, are introduced. Detective's first impressions of the crime scene and the first gathering of clues.

(3) Questioning the suspects. Establishing who was where at the time of the murder and the relationship of each suspect to the victim. Witnesses who are not suspects may be interviewed here or in Sequence 4. Revelation of backstory – from what the suspects and witnesses say about the victim. Detective begins to assess who had the means, motive, and opportunity to commit the murder.

(4) Detective's first attempt to piece together what he has learned. Statements and clues usually taken at face value – though they may be re-evaluated later. Guilty secrets may be revealed – the detective has to decide which are connected to the murder and which are 'red herrings.' Suspects may destroy evidence or obstruct the investigation to hide their own secrets. The detective may form a first hypothesis or be about to speak to a witness with vital information.

Midpoint: Often a second murder – the victim is usually either the person the detective believed was guilty or the vital witness he was about to speak to.

(5) Re-evaluation of what has gone before in light of the second murder. Nothing can be taken for granted. Perhaps an assumption has been made that can't be trusted. Alibis are retested. Suspects re-interviewed. A previously unknown relationship may be discovered between two characters. Previous events may take on new meaning or significance. A new and vital clue is uncovered.

(6) Typically the detective's second attempt to form a hypothesis which accounts for all of the facts. Sometimes this is a 'straw man' that the hero sets up and then pulls apart or proves incorrect – this is what *could* have happened. The failure of this hypothesis may seem like a failure to the reader, but it usually puts the detective in a position where he can say, 'I now know whodunit.'

(7) Often the 'drawing room scene' or its equivalent. The detective draws all the suspects together and looks at each, in turn, explaining how they could have been the murderer, and why, but how evidence shows that they are not. By a process of elimination, the murderer is identified. He is then arrested or commits suicide.

(8) A brief sequence with the detective explaining a few final thoughts. Often something is shown that proves that equilibrium has been restored to the world now that the murderer has been dealt with.

Tinker, Tailor, Soldier, Spy does not follow this plot structure exactly, but it does have much in common with it. The identity of the mole is a mystery. Smiley, as the detective, must interview witnesses – but, interestingly, he cannot interview the main suspects, Percy Alleline and his closest allies. To do this would tip-off the mole that his presence was suspected. Smiley must gather evidence and build his case without their direct input. This absence of contact means that the main suspects are not asked to 'account for their whereabouts at the time of the crime' so alibis are not obtained and tested, so more emphasis is placed on who knew what and when, and what actions were taken when intelligence was received and – more crucially – when was action *not* taken even though intelligence had been received. This may make Le Carré's novel seem less like a mystery, but in fact there are many classic murder mystery stories where the main suspects are not interviewed directly – this includes examples where the detective reinvestigates a 'cold case' from years ago and works from evidence gathered at the time, or historical mysteries concerning events which took place even further back in time, and where only documentary evidence is available. Many 'armchair detectives' also work from evidence gathered by others and solve a mystery without ever leaving their sitting rooms.

It could also be argued that *Tinker, Tailor, Soldier, Spy* is a cross between a murder mystery and a police procedural story, because Smiley works with a team of trusted assistants and reports to a 'superior officer.' The structure of a police procedural novel is one of those that I explore in more detail in *Crime Thriller*. Either way, we can see that this particular novel – and the find-the-mole story generally – is more the investigation of a crime than the planning and execution of a mission.

8 | Political Thriller

"This is no place for you. You're halfway decent. You don't belong here." – Mr. Smith Goes to Washington

What is a Political Thriller?
Robert Silberman writes that a political thriller "... may represent a thriller with a political setting, a thriller with a political purpose, or both." It takes the conventions of the thriller genre – notably suspense and/or conspiracy – and uses them in a story that centres on national or international politics. By 'politics' we mean the activities related to the governing of a country (or part of a country) and the relations between different countries. In a broader sense, we often use the term politics to refer to activities aimed at gaining power in any group or organisation. This brings us to the negative image of politics, the idea of 'playing politics' with issues for personal gain rather than the benefit of others.

Silberman suggests that there are three broad categories of political thriller:

(i) The Hitchcock thriller where politics and the 'deadly struggle for power' are really only the MacGuffin – "... what matters is not the exact nationality of the villain or the political situation as a whole, but the fact that there are villains, that they are sinister, nasty, and dangerous, and that they are chasing the hero." *Foreign Correspondent* (1940) is an example.

(ii) The "overtly ideological and polemic film, identified most closely with Costa-Gavras. Thus *Z* (1967), based on the assassination of a liberal Greek deputy, is a kind of snazzy *policier*, but with a moralistic political argument..."

(iii) The 'paranoid' political thriller where "... the threat comes from within – from corporations, from the CIA, from the police ... in the post-Kennedy assassination world, Kafka becomes the guiding spirit: there's no telling the good guys from the bad guys anymore."

The thing that politicians ought to be concerned with – the thing that is at *stake* – is *democracy*. Democracy is a form of government in which individuals can vote for representatives who will govern a country (or an area within a country) on their behalf and in their name. 'Democracy' comes from two Greek words which literally mean 'people-power,' and it is based on the principle that every individual citizen is equal and can cast one vote – and that he agrees to abide by the majority decision. Realistically speaking, a democracy is an ideal – a goal to strive for – rather than something that actually exists: democratic processes are flawed because people are flawed and the best we can hope for is to maintain a political stability in which no individual or group gains total power over the majority.

A political thriller, then, concerns a conspiracy in which the conspirators attempt to gain – or maintain – power by subverting the democratic process: power is more important to them than principle and they do not respect the votes given by individual members of society. There are different ways for conspirators to try and achieve their aims and this gives rise to different sub-categories of political thriller. I am going to explore these under four headings:

(i) *political conspiracy/cover-up* – lying to the public or concealing information in such a way as to prevent them from being able to make an informed choice, either in an election or in evaluating the activities of their government, e.g. the Watergate conspiracy

(ii) *assassination* – the politically motivated murder of a democratically elected politician or of a candidate standing for office in a democratic election, e.g. the assassination of John F. Kennedy

(iii) *terrorism* – the use of violence, or intimidation by the threat of violence, against civilians to achieve political aims, e.g. the 9/11 attacks

(iv) *hostage-taking* – the capture and detention of individuals or small groups for use as bargaining chips to achieve political aims, e.g. the hijacking of TWA Flight 847; the Iranian Embassy siege

As with all sub-genres, there is some degree of overlap between these types and there are stories which are a hybrid of two or more of them. There is also cross-over with the espionage and war story genres.

It is probably worth noting here that the political thriller sub-genre, like most genre fiction, is fairly conservative. It tends to assume that Western democracy – and the political status quo in the United States in particular – is near-optimal and must be preserved from attack. Nations without a Western-style democracy are at best suspect and at worst seen as dictatorships.

The terrorism sub-category of the thriller – at least in the US – originally focused on the Arab-Israeli conflict, though in the UK there were also thrillers set during the 'troubles' in Northern Ireland. More recently, terrorists have tended to be 'Islamic extremists' or 'Jihadists.'

Other forms of terrorism include cyber-terrorism and eco-terrorism, though neither has featured greatly in thrillers. Where the eco-terrorist has appeared, he has tended to be a mad James Bond villain threatening to destroy mankind in order to save the planet. There is the potential there for much better stories.

Historical Context

Where the espionage thriller reflected the situation in Great Britain during the first half of the twentieth century, the political thriller is much more an American product and is the result of the turbulent post-Second World War period. Political thrillers reflect the times in which they are written, so an understanding of context is vital when looking at the development of this sub-genre. If you are familiar with post-World War II United States history, you can safely skip ahead to the next section.

The Japanese attack on Pearl Harbor in 1941 had shocked the nation and the detonation of nuclear weapons over Hiroshima and Nagasaki changed the world forever. After that came the conflict in Korea and then the Vietnam War, with the United States and the Soviet Union supporting opposing sides in both cases. The post-war period was also the era of the 'second Red scare,' with a campaign of fear being used to justify political repression in the USA. Senator Joseph McCarthy oversaw this witch-hunt, with people in politics and the media being accused – based on little or no evidence – of subversion or treason. The Cold War between the USA and the USSR also led to a nuclear arms race that came to a head with the Cuban Missile Crisis of October 1962, probably the closest the world came to nuclear war. Placement of Soviet nuclear missiles in Cuba had come about as a result of the failed Bay of Pigs Invasion of 1961, which had been backed by the American CIA.

John F. Kennedy became President in 1961 – he was assassinated in November 1963. An investigation by the FBI and a report by the Warren Commission concluded that he had been shot by Lee Harvey Oswald, a lone assassin, but this official conclusion has been doubted by a number of people and various conspiracy theories have grown up around events of that day.

Richard Nixon – who had been defeated by Kennedy in 1960 – was elected President and took office in 1969. Nixon wanted to be remembered as a peacemaker, opening dialogue with the Soviet Union which eventually brought about the signing of the Anti-Ballistic Missile Treaty. He was also the first president to visit the People's Republic of China and his seven-day visit in 1972 marked a major breakthrough in relations between the two countries. Nixon also presided over the end of American involvement in the Vietnam War, with the Paris Peace Accords being signed at the beginning of 1973. Nixon really did seem to be a peacemaker. But all was not what it appeared.

After the election of a Marxist President in Chile in 1970, Nixon authorised a covert operation against the new leader and it is alleged that the CIA supported the coup that overthrew Allende in 1973. In the Middle East, arms sales to Israel, Iran, and Saudi Arabia were increased. When a Soviet-backed Arab coalition of Egypt and Syria attacked Israel in 1973, the USA airlifted supplies to Israel. Early attempts at a truce only served to sour relations between the USA and the Soviet Union, to the point where Nixon ordered the US military to DEFCON3, the closest point to nuclear war since the Cuban Missile Crisis. America's support for Israel led the Arab oil-producing nations to place an embargo on sales to the USA, leading to an oil crisis there in 1973.

Closer to home, Nixon's Vice President Spiro Agnew was investigated on suspicion of conspiracy, bribery, extortion and tax fraud – he denied it all for months but finally resigned in 1973 pleading guilty to a single charge of tax evasion.

In 1972, *The New York Times* published extracts from the 'Pentagon Papers,' the Department of Defense's official history of the United States' political and military involvement in Vietnam. These showed that the Lyndon B. Johnson administration had lied to the public and to Congress and had secretly expanded its actions during the Vietnam War to include bombings of Cambodia and Laos. The papers were not particularly damaging to Nixon, but he tried to prevent their publication and the man who leaked them was accused of conspiracy, espionage, and theft of government property.

Richard Nixon had never had a happy relationship with the media. When he ran for governor of California in 1962 and was defeated, he blamed the media for favouring his opponent and famously told reporters "you don't have Nixon to kick around anymore..." In 1969 Nixon asked the FBI to tap the phones of five journalists and in 1971 when *Newsday* wrote about the financial dealings of one of Nixon's friends, the White House retaliated by requesting an audit of the tax return of the editor. To those within the media, it felt as though the First Amendment, the right to freedom of speech and the freedom of the press, was under threat. Nixon is reported to have had a list of 200 'enemies' within the USA that he asked the Internal Revenue Service to investigate.

Nixon's paranoia extended beyond the news media. He routinely tape-recorded all that occurred in the Oval Office, the Cabinet Room and his private office. These tapes would eventually contribute to Nixon's downfall. After his resignation in 1974, the *New York Times* published an article that said the CIA under Nixon had an "elaborate secret domestic" operation to illegally tap phones and read mail, and that CIA intelligence files were kept on "at least 10,000 American citizens". During the years of the Nixon administration, the government saw the press and 'leftist' individuals and organisations as 'the enemy' engaged in conspiracies at home. And the newspapers saw conspiracy within government, as the facts about secret policies, executive corruption and lies, and widespread illegal surveillance were gradually revealed. Conspiracy was in the air, no matter what your political leanings. It was also a period when the investigative journalist became a hero figure – the 'independent voice' that provided the facts for the people.

The Watergate scandal, as presented in the book *All the President's Men* by Carl Bernstein and Bob Woodward, reads like a political thriller. In its condensed, fictionalised form in the 1976 movie, it is even more thriller-like – to the extent that we can look at it as a model for a political thriller plot.

If all of this political history and intrigue leaves you cold, this sub-genre is probably not for you – the Kennedy assassination and the Watergate scandal were the inspiration for most political thrillers until the declaration of the 'war on terror' by George W. Bush in 2001.

Is There Still an Audience?

In his review of *The Interpreter*, Erik Lundegaard said that there was currently no audience for the political thriller film: "Let's face it: the great unwashed love explosions but don't vote, while the cognoscenti are intrigued by politics but can't be bothered with genre films." Lundegaard was writing in 2005 and was concerned only with films, but I think his comments apply as much to political thriller novels as they do to movies. If you plan to write a political thriller, look very carefully at the market and see what kinds of story are selling and make sure you include enough of the thriller genre elements that readers expect.

While politics hasn't been popular at the cinema for a while, there has been an audience for it on television. The mini-series *Washington: Behind Closed Doors* from 1977 was based on John Ehrlichman's book *The Company*. Ehrlichman was counsel and Assistant to President Nixon and *The Company* – which is a nickname for the CIA – uses fictional characters to present events loosely based on the lead up to the Watergate coverup, centring on the Nixon administration's attempts to cover up its own illegal activity and that of the CIA dating back to the Kennedy administration. Like Ehrlichman's book, NBC's *The West Wing* was political drama rather than a thriller, but it's inside look at the running of the White House proved popular and the show ran for seven seasons from 1999 to 2006. The Fox network series *24*, featuring Kiefer Sutherland as counter-terrorist agent Jack Bauer ran for nine seasons between 2001 and 2014 – it combined elements of the spy thriller and political thriller. *House of Cards*, a novel by Michael Dobbs first published in 1989, has been described as both political drama and thriller. The novel's main character is Francis Urquhart, a Machiavellian schemer who wants to become leader of the Conservative Party and Prime Minister of the United Kingdom. The novel was adapted for television by the BBC in 1990 and a US version was produced by Netflix in 2013. The 2016 ABC television series *Designated Survivor* also centred on a political conspiracy following the assassination of the President of the United States.

All of that being said, the number of *genuine* political thriller films and novels is actually quite small. More common is the thriller that uses a political conspiracy as a MacGuffin – an excuse for the usual thriller action: the 1998 film *Enemy of the State* is a typical example that uses the amateur-on-the-run plot.

Historical Development of the Genre

There have been political conspiracies for as long as there have been leaders governing people that live in social groups. Shakespeare's *Julius Caesar*, *Coriolanus* and *Antony and Cleopatra* all have themes of power-seeking and betrayal running through them, and Michael Dobbs *House of Cards* has been compared to both *Macbeth* and *Richard III*. Alexandre Dumas' *The Three Musketeers* (published in 1844 but set during the 1620s) is set against the political background of pre-Revolution France and Baroness Orczy's *The Scarlet Pimpernel* (1905) takes place during the Reign of Terror following the start of the French Revolution.

There is some overlap between the political thriller and the spy thriller: Joseph Conrad's 1907 novel *The Secret Agent* falls into both categories. It is set in 1886, a period when terrorist activity was on the increase: the novel is based in part on an incident in 1894 when a French anarchist was killed in Greenwich Park in London when the explosives he carried detonated prematurely. There had been several bomb attacks in both Europe and the US, as well as political assassinations.

The President Vanishes (1934) is a novel originally published anonymously by Rex Stout, creator of the detective Nero Wolfe. Set during the build-up to what would become the Second World War, it tells of a president who is facing a major political crisis and possible impeachment by a Congress controlled by wealthy industrialists and financiers, who disappears and is presumed to have been kidnapped. A film based on the novel was released in 1934. Rob Edelman identifies a number of other films from the 1930s with similar themes: "In the satire *The Dark Horse* (1932), the title character, a dolt who happens to be running for governor, is guided in his campaign by a man who has just been freed from jail. *Washington Merry-Go-Round* (1932) is the saga of an upright young congressman who goes off to the Capitol and encounters corruption and graft. *Politics* (1931) chronicles the efforts of an outspoken widow running for mayor against an incumbent entangled with gangsters. *The Washington Masquerade* (1932) is the story of cutthroat lobbyists who pressure senators. In *Bullets or Ballots* (1936), gangsters openly conspire with elected officials. In *Louisiana Purchase* (1941), local politicians try to frame a senator who is bent on investigating them..."

Robert Penn Warren's *All the King's Men* (1946), a Pulitzer Prize-winning novel, was an account of the political career of fictional southern governor Willie Stark during the 1930s, as seen by a political reporter who becomes Stark's right-hand man. It was inspired by the story of real-life Louisiana Governor, Huey Long. The book is not a thriller, but as a study of an amoral politician's actions and their consequences, it is essential reading for anyone who wants to write about a quest for political power. *All the King's Men* has been filmed twice – the 1949 version won the Academy Award for Best Picture, but the 2006 version was not as well received. Another non-thriller item worth a look is the 1972 'political comedy-drama' film *The Candidate* starring Robert Redford: the screenplay was by Jeremy Larner who had been a speechwriter during Senator Eugene J. McCarthy's campaign for the 1968 Democratic presidential nomination. Redford's character Bill McKay runs for the Senate against a seemingly unbeatable opponent: feeling that he has nothing to lose, McKay decides to be open and honest – and this wins him a lot of support. As the election approaches he actually has a chance of winning – if he can win over enough 'undecided' voters. As the story progresses we see how his campaign advisor tries to persuade McKay to play the part of an 'electable' politician. Larner won an Academy Award for his screenplay.

But while there have been stories about political intrigue and assassinations for centuries, the political thriller as a sub-genre is much more recent. As mentioned above, it came out of the post-World War II situation in American politics and its 'golden age' seems to have been from the early 1960s through to the end of the 1970s.

Genre Conventions

The political thriller shares many of the conventions of the amateur-on-the-run thriller from Chapter 1 and the espionage thriller from Chapter 7. The assassination thriller, terrorism thriller and hostage thriller can all be considered specialised examples of the 'professional agent' thriller covered in Chapter 2. Below I will list some of the major *themes* found in political thrillers and briefly cover iconic elements often found in this type of story.

Themes

In his book *The Suspense Thriller*, Charles Derry identifies seven 'thematic ideas' that are found in the political thriller:

(i) Power corrupts
(ii) Politics is inescapable
(iii) Moral necessity to question government institutions
(iv) Conspiratorial nature of repressive government
(v) Distinction between the apparent and the actual
(vi) People's trust in investigators, journalists and politicians with integrity who try to serve the people rather than to acquire power for themselves
(vii) Potential for the individual to bring about political and social change

Iconography

What sort of things do we typically see in a political thriller? What images are associated with them? Many of the images and situations mentioned below have become clichés through over-use in television shows like *The X-Files* which itself used them in an ironic manner. The model for the 'look' of the political thriller is *All the President's Men* with additional elements being provided by assassination thrillers such as *The Day of the Jackal*. Even though much of this imagery is hackneyed, and my treatment of it below is a little off-hand, it is what we have – if you plan to write a political thriller, you have to come up with original ways of using these things.

If the story is set in the USA, there will be an image of the Capitol Building – it'll be on the cover of a novel and in a movie, there will be a stock shot looking up at the building or a slow fly-past from above. How else are you supposed to indicate that the story is about politics? A shot of the White House could be used, but it's usually the Capitol. If it's set in the UK, a shot of the Houses of Westminster can be substituted.

Although the political thriller is supposedly concerned with the lawful running of government institutions and the legislative process, the 'politics' we see is typically restricted to election campaigning – included rallies and speeches – and the ticker-tape parades that follow a successful election. Both of these situations are ideal for the assassination of a major political figure. Occasionally we will also see a political demonstration – and sometimes this will be brutally repressed by either the authorities or by 'counter-protestors' who are really working for the government. A protest rally is also a great place for an assassination. All other politicking tends to go on behind closed doors in offices – including the Oval office – or in committee rooms with long tables and subdued lighting.

Politicians are either handsome, idealistic men-of-the-people who are assassinated and become martyrs for the cause of democracy, or they are sleazy, self-serving, power-hungry, hypocritical crooks who secretly ordered the assassination of their opponent.

In order to add to the realism of the situations presented, films and novels will often use real locations and have titles/captions that give location and time. Political thrillers can also include actual historical figures or characters who are thinly-veiled representations of those figures. Stories will often have a prologue that sets out the historical context of the story about to be presented, or an epilogue that covers its political and/or historical implications.

Surveillance often plays a part in these stories: people are followed; their telephones and their homes are bugged; they are photographed or filmed; their homes are searched while they are absent. In the present day, mobile phones and computers are 'hacked' into; CCTV cameras can be used to spy on people, as can drones and spy satellites that can provide live images to rival Google Earth. This surveillance is often carried out by the security services illegally and constitutes an invasion of privacy.

Newspaper reporters and photographers are usually shown to be fine examples of the 'free press' at work, objectively pursuing the facts of the story and great personal risk. These are field reporters, not studio-bound puppets with a fake tan, a suit and an expensive haircut. They are hard-drinkers, womanisers, insubordinate mavericks, and usually male. They defend their rights under the First Amendment and will always protect the identity of their sources, no matter what. One of their sources is usually a 'deep throat' or 'smoking man' figure – an insider who secretly tells the reporter what is going on 'behind closed doors.' Reporters usually meet their secret contacts in dark underground garages where they cannot be spied upon. These journalists always write front-page exposés of the wrong-doing of political figures. Government organisations may seek to prevent publication of these stories, denying the rights of the free press for reasons of 'national security' which are never fully explained.

Security services, usually the CIA or a close facsimile, will typically ignore the constitutional rights of citizens and engage in activities such as kidnapping, false imprisonment, interrogation, and acts of physical or psychological torture. The ends always justify the means.

The assassin is usually symbolised by a high-powered rifle fitted with a scope that provides a close-up image of the intended victim over vast distances. The assassin is either a cold-blooded professional killer who wears sunglasses or he's a geeky patsy modelled on Lee Harvey Oswald – or he may have been brain-washed or hypnotised. The assassin's victim is usually presented as a martyr, representing all that is good about western democracy.

Model Plots

The most significant element of a political thriller is the political conspiracy – they all contain a conspiracy, a group of conspirators, and a protagonist who becomes a victim of it or becomes aware of the conspiracy and seeks to do something about it. This being the case, a political thriller can use the structure of any of the conspiracy-based thrillers described in this book.

For each of the four types of political thriller I have included a list of examples, and from these I have selected some stories which I think provide the sort of plot that could be adapted for use in your own political thrillers. For the assassination thriller I have looked at *The Day of the Jackal* and the Clint Eastwood movie *In the Line of Fire.* When it comes to the political conspiracy/cover-up story we have to consider Watergate, so I have broken down the plot of the film version of *All the President's Men* and also *The Parallax View*. For the terrorism thriller I'm going to use Thomas Harris' novel *Black Sunday* and alongside that I'll look at the Eric Ambler novel *The Levanter*. And finally, as examples of the hostage thriller I'll use *Raid on Entebbe, Who Dares Wins* and the classic thriller film *Die Hard*.

Under 'Genre Conventions' I mentioned that these stories share elements with other types of thriller and it should also be noted that the assassination thriller and the terrorism thriller are quite similar in terms of plot in that they both split the story between the actions of the criminal – terrorist or assassin – and the authorities trying to prevent them carrying out their plan. It can also be argued that the hostage thriller is also a specialised form of the terrorism thriller. This potential for hybridisation makes choosing 'pure' examples of each type of thriller quite difficult and in the lists below you may find some films or novels that include elements of two (or even more) of the different political thrillers – I have listed them under the heading that seemed most appropriate to me.

(i) Assassination Thriller

When we talk of assassinations, we tend to think of the killing of John F. Kennedy, Robert F. Kennedy, and Martin Luther King in the 1960s as these helped define a particular moment in history. 'Assassination' is usually defined as murder carried out for political or religious reasons, though law enforcement agencies in the United States extend the scope of the term to include some non-political public figures targeted for non-political reasons. A useful summary of information on real-life cases is provided by Robert A. Fein and Bryan Vossekuil in their paper 'Assassination in the United States,' which covers eighty-three cases of assassinations or attempted assassination in the US between 1949 and 1996.

Motivation of Assassins

Fein and Vossekuil identifya number of motives behind the actions of real-life assassins and would-be assassins:

- to achieve fame or notoriety
- to achieve a 'special relationship' with the target victim
- to avenge a perceived wrong
- to be killed by law enforcement officers (suicide)
- to make money
- to bring national attention to a perceived problem
- to save the country or the world
- to bring about political change

The first four of these take us into the realm of the *stalker*, which I will cover separately in the section on *Psychological Thrillers*. A financial motive covers those assassins who have no personal motive to kill the target victim – they are paid by someone else to carry out the 'hit.' The Jackal in *The Day of the Jackal* is a professional assassin of this type. The final three motives in the above list – particularly the final one – are what we tend to think if as 'politically motivated,' and those are the ones we are concentrating on in this section. We're also only looking at 'lone gunman' type killers here, rather than groups as I think groups really fall under the *terrorist* heading. In terms of real-life statistics, the proportion of assassins falling into this distinct category is very small, so they are in no way typical. But that's okay because as writers we're more interested in dramatic exceptions rather than stories about the commonplace or most realistic types of assassin.

Unlike in the traditional murder mystery or detective thriller, the victim and the murderer do not normally have a personal relationship of any kind. The victim represents a group, nation, or political viewpoint to which those behind the assassination plot are opposed. The assassin (or the person hiring the assassin) may also have a personal reason for wanting the target victim dead, but this will be in addition to the political motive.

One final caveat before I move on: When I refer to *professional* assassins in this chapter, I mean those hired to kill political figures on behalf of groups with political motives, rather than contract killings carried out by criminal hitmen for criminal individuals or gangs – we will explore those separately in the *Crime Thriller* volume in this series.

Fundamentals of the Political Assassination Thriller
The assassination thriller requires an assassin, a target victim, and someone who is trying to protect the target and prevent the assassination from taking place. If an assassination has already taken place the 'preventer' will be replaced by an investigator who is trying to identify and apprehend the assassin and/or the people who hired him. For the sake of simplicity, I will refer to these three roles as assassin, target, and protector.

If we're being totally honest, when writing a thriller, the target and the political motive for wanting the target dead are the MacGuffin. You could change both, and the structure of the story would be essentially unchanged. They exist to give us a reason for portraying the actions of the assassin and the protector. Of course, we will do our best to hide this fact from the reader or audience by making the target victim someone they want to see survive and the perpetrator's motivation one which the audience will object to, but in plot terms, they're just a device.

Typically, in the political assassination thriller we will see events from two perspectives – that of the assassin and that of the protector. Both characters have a mission to complete – to assassinate or to prevent assassination – and they are effectively each the protagonist of their own storyline and the antagonist of the other's storyline. Usually one of the two will receive more 'screen time' than the other: in the movie *In the Line of Fire*, Clint Eastwood's character Frank is a Secret Service agent trying to protect the president, and he gets the most screen time – but we still see a lot of the assassin's work as he prepares for his mission. The opposite is true in *The Day of the Jackal*, where we see more of the assassin at work and less of the detective's attempt to prevent him carrying out his mission. 'The Jackal' (played by Edward Fox) is not the hero – we are not intended to approve of his mission or hope that he succeeds – but it is his actions that we follow most closely and his successes and failures along the way are what provide the interest and suspense.

This twin point of view approach means the plot consists of an investigation thread – protector trying to identify, locate and stop the assassin – and a James Bond-like mission thread in which the assassin tries to get to the target victim and kill him. Like a secret agent, the assassin is likely to use disguises and to have some kind of bespoke weapon – which he may have designed and built himself and which will need to be assembled when he gets to the sight of the assassination attempt.

Whether you decide to give your protector the most attention, or your assassin, or you give them an equal share of the limelight, the basic structure is more or less the same. The template below is primarily based on an analysis of the plots of the movie *In the Line of Fire* and Frederick Forsyth's novel *The Day of the Jackal*. Forsyth's novel has been adapted for the screen twice – the 1973 film is much better (and closer to the novel) than the 1997 Bruce Willis film *The Jackal*.

In both of these examples, the assassin is the 'bad guy' because his target is a democratically elected political leader: if an assassin's target is a dictator opposed by revolutionaries seeking to establish a democracy, then the assassin might be portrayed as one of the 'good guys.' There have been several biographies and autobiographies of American military snipers including *American Sniper* (2012) by Chris Kyle, filmed in 2014 by Clint Eastwood. The 2007 film *Shooter* is a conspiracy thriller involving a sniper, based on the 1993 novel *Point of Impact* by Stephen Hunter. James Bond has also been referred to as a government-licenced assassin. The 1995 thriller *Nick of Time* starring Johnny Depp depicts an innocent hero who is blackmailed into assassinating a political figure.

Real-life professional assassin 'Carlos the Jackal' – real name Ilich Ramírez Sánchez – got his nickname because a reporter from *The Guardian* newspaper spotted a copy of the Forsyth novel in a room he had occupied, and it was subsequently assumed he must have been a fan of the story. There is no evidence that he had read or was inspired by the novel, but later writers have been inspired by his life as an assassin.

The Assassination Thriller Plot

Sequence 1. American political thrillers almost always begin with images of the Capitol building and/or the White House and an assassination thriller may also add in the Lincoln Memorial, given President Lincoln's fate at the hands of assassin John Wilkes Booth. *The Day of the Jackal* opens with a prologue that shows a failed assassination attempt on the French president and the death by firing squad of the would-be assassin. *In the Line of Fire* also opens with a prologue that introduces the Clint Eastwood character, Frank Horrigan, establishing him as an undercover Secret Service agent working with partner Al d'Andrea (Dylan McDermott). We see a mentor-student sort of relationship between the two characters. Frank describes the work of a Secret Service agent as throwing yourself in front of a bullet, hoping it hits you instead of the guy you're protecting. Frank is the main character of this story so we spend something like eight or nine minutes with him before we are introduced to the assassin, Leary (John Malkovich). Frank goes to check out a report about a man who has an unhealthy interest in assassinations of the past and who may be about to target the current president. Frank sees Leary's empty apartment, but the audience also sees Leary across the road with binoculars, watching the search. In the early scenes in which Leary appears, we do not see his face clearly – the shots are framed so that we only see a part of his face or see him from behind.

The Day of the Jackal introduces the main character of the assassin, The Jackal (Edward Fox), when he is recruited by the OAS – Organisation Armée Secrète – a right-wing paramilitary organization that operated during the Algerian War (1954–62). The OAS then commit bank robberies in order to be able to pay the Jackal's fee. The opposition – the police – are introduced initially as they keep OAS members under surveillance. The Jackal begins his preparations for the assassination – he is effectively involved in a 'mission' plot, similar to that of a James Bond-style agent. Focus shifts between the activities of the Jack and the OAS, and the police who are investigating – at this stage – just the OAS. Towards the end of sequence one, the OAS: the police do not become aware of the assassination plot until the end of sequence three, beginning of sequence four.

The two separate story threads in *The Day of the Jackal* – the police operations and the activities of the assassin – continue in parallel throughout and only converge towards the end of the story. There is almost no interaction between the two and information that each learns about the other comes from third-party sources. The assassin and the protector characters from *In the Line of Fire* begin a relationship towards the end of sequence one. Leary has recognised Frank Horrigan as one of the Secret Service agents who was on duty beside the limousine when President Kennedy was assassinated. Leary calls Frank, almost in the manner of a stalker calling a celebrity, and says 'I'm planning to kill the president.' He also establishes the situation as being a contest between himself as the assassin and Frank as the protector: 'Going up against you raises the game to a much higher level.' He also taunts Frank by telling him how ironic it will be for him to have been 'intimately involved with the assassinations of two presidents.' As well as presenting the challenge, Leary is also establishing backstory and stakes for Frank – Frank has something personal at stake: he doesn't want to allow another president to die.

These two example stories show the two ways that the two different viewpoints on the action can be presented: as the separate strands of two opposing missions that intersect occasionally throughout or as two separate missions with an added element of personal competition between the lead characters who are the 'protagonist' or mission leader of the separate strands.

Sequence 2. The Jackal's preparations continue and he checks out the scene for the assassination. On the opposite side, the authorities set a trap to capture a key member of the OAS. As we cut between the two viewpoints we see that every forward move by one side is balanced by progress made by the other.

This pattern will continue throughout the story right up until the final moments. This maintains suspense as we don't know which side will win in the end.

The French authorities at this stage are investigating the OAS – they are not aware of the Jackal's mission. Only at the midpoint of the story do they learn of the assassination plot and assign their best detective to the case, Claude Lebel. Even then, we do not learn much about Lebel and the Jackal remains the most engaging character in the story. We do not *like* the Jackal or approve oh his actions or motivation – he kills people for money – but because we are aware of what he is trying to achieve and the risks he faces, and because we are allowed to see his preparations as they progress, we are drawn into the story and want to find out if his mission is successful – even though we know that there was never a successful assassination attempt against President Charles de Gaulle!

In both stories, the assassin uses a fake identity having obtained a passport and/or driver's licence using the birth certificate of someone who died in childhood. This has almost become a cliché in thrillers.

Sequence two of *In the Line of Fire* sees Frank begin his investigation into Leary and also sees him requesting to be assigned to the president's protection detail. We see Frank clash with younger Secret Service agents and we see him struggling to jog alongside the presidential limousine – he's too old for this job. He also refers to himself as a 'borderline burn-out with questionable social skills.' This helps to establish audience sympathy for his character, makes him the sort of anti-authoritarian rebel that people tend to like, and also makes it clear that he's a vulnerable human being and not a muscle-bound superhero whose victory is never in doubt: Frank could well fail here and another president could die. His weakness is also exploited by Leary who telephones him and taunts him about failing to save Kennedy – Why did he not react and step in the way of the second bullet? He also refers to Frank's life after the assassination – his drinking and the fact that his wife and daughter left him. Leary also reveals that he has continued to spy on Frank like a stalker. On the Secret Service side, it seems that they have scored a victory when they successfully trace Leary's phone call, but he is one step ahead of them and leads them to an embarrassing failure.

In this sequence we also see Leary preparing parts for something in his workshop. Are they for some sort of plastic model – or for something else?

We also see the Secret Service take an obvious step – answering the audience question of 'why didn't they just...?' – by asking the president's aide to cancel the president's public engagements so that he is in less danger from a potential assassin. Of course, the aide refuses, saying that if the Secret Service do their jobs properly, the president will be fine. The engagement passes off without a hitch and also provides Frank with an opportunity to flirt with a female agent.

Sequence 3. In this sequence we see the stakes raised – we have passed a point of no return and things begin to get serious. The focus is more on the actions of the assassin – we see him prove his ruthless nature by killing a minor character, we see more preparations for his mission, and we see him obtain or create some sort of bespoke weapon. The weapon is a clue as to how he intends to successfully carry out his mission, but we can't really work out what his plan is from it. We also see the authorities make a significant step forward in their investigations.

In the Line of Fire shows us Leary's face in full for the first time and we see him contributing to the president's re-election fund – we know this is significant, but we don't yet know how. We also see him kill a bank cashier who asked questions about him that he thought might put his mission at risk. Now we know how dangerous he can be. And we see him assembling the parts he has been creating – it is some sort of plastic gun. Frank continues his relationship with the female agent. Leary again calls Frank – telling him that they are both willing to trade their lives for that of the president – meaning he is prepared to risk his own life to complete his mission – and that they have both been 'betrayed by those we trusted.' His implication is that they have both been betrayed in some way by government agencies. This time the phone trace shows Leary was close by – Frank runs out and spots Leary, gives chase. Leary escapes but leaves behind fingerprints. The FBI identify the fingerprint – but the information about the identity of Leary is highly classified, so they tell Frank there was no match. The audience now knows something that Frank doesn't – but just who is Leary and why is his file classified information?

In *The Day of the Jackal,* the OAS arrange for a young woman, Denise, to become the mistress of St. Clair, an advisor to the president: she will obtain inside information from their pillow talk and pass it to the OAS. The Jackal makes more preparations and scouts locations for his mission. He picks up his bespoke weapon and a new passport – and kills the forger when he tries to extort money from him. The authorities, meanwhile, capture one of the OAS members and interrogate him.

Sequence 4 & Midpoint. This sequence leads up to the midpoint incident or revelation, which is typically a major setback for the main character in an assassination thriller.

In the Line of Fire's president is now on the campaign trail, touring the country in Air Force One. Frank is on the protection detail and we see him at work during one of the rallies. Leary, meanwhile, arrives in Los Angeles which the president will visit later in his tour. Lear has established a fake company in an empty office and again we see him contributing to the president's re-election campaign. Why would he give money to a man he plans to kill? Frank and the female agent continue their relationship. At another rally, Frank mistakes the popping of a balloon for gunfire and everyone rushes to protect the president. We see that Leary was responsible for the bursting of the balloon. Because of the embarrassment caused to the president, Frank is thrown off the security team. This is humiliating for him and a major setback in his efforts to stop the assassination.

In *The Day of the Jackal,* the police have the OAS member's confession – he died during his interrogation but revealed that a professional assassin has been hired to kill President de Gaulle and that the assassin is a fair-haired foreigner. They could not obtain the killer's name, but they did get the word 'Jackal.' The president is warned of the danger and he says that he has no intention of going into hiding. The authorities appoint their top detective, Claude Lebel, to investigate – he must learn the identity of 'the Jackal' without tipping off the assassin. This is a major setback for the Jackal, but he is completely unaware of it. He practices with his new weapon, firing at a watermelon with a human face drawn on it. Things are not going entirely in favour of the police: Denise is sleeping with the president's aide and learns that the authorities know about the OAS plot to kill the president.

The structure of *The Day of the Jackal* differs from other plots we've looked at in that the whole of the first half – sequences one to four – seems to be set-up: all beginning and no middle. This often happens in stories with complicated or multi-viewpoint plots. Here the writer is essentially setting up two stories – the Jackal's mission to assassinate the president and the authorities' investigation into the activities of the OAS. Incidents that we would normally identify as 'middle material' is interwoven with the extended set-up – the Jackal's preparations, for example. These are presented as a series of vignettes or montages: we see the Jackal at work, he is efficient and ruthless, a professional, but we do not get close to him as a person – he is always somewhat enigmatic, which is exactly what he needs to be.

Sequence 5. In this sequence we see the investigation by the authorities making progress as they uncover important information about the assassin. This will involve either the name that the assassin is currently using or, more likely and more dramatic, a photograph of him. This is usually gained as a result of typical police investigation. With this information now in the hands of the authorities, the odds against the assassin succeeding seem to be increasing: the authorities now know who they are looking for.

Sequence five of *The Day of the Jackal* begins with a minor victory for the OAS – the mistress Denis passes on information she has gained from the president's aide. But after that, everything seems to favour the police. They have a list of possible suspects from Interpol and then hear that the police in England are investigating a likely suspect. The detective, Lebel, receives a photograph of this man and the police begin their search for him.

The fifth sequence of *In the Line of Fire* begins with Frank in a negative place having been removed from the president's security detail. Leary again phones to needle him – he was witness to Frank's failure. But then the tide turns and things start going Frank's way. One lead takes he and his partner Al to another until they finally have the assassin's name and a photograph. They check out Leary's last known address and there encounter a CIA agent who admits that Leary is a former CIA assassin – and he was a very good one. Frank's partner is having a crisis of confidence and says he wants to quit: Franks talks him into staying. We see Leary testing out his plastic gun – and again demonstrating his ruthless nature. When Leary next calls him, Frank reveals that he knows his identity – and that he has seen evidence of some of his handiwork. Leary says that he has done some horrible things for his country: 'I don't even remember who I was before they sunk their claws into me.' He says that the president will leave California in a box. The president has a rendezvous with death – and Leary thinks that he does too. And so does Frank, if he gets too close.

Sequence 6. At the end of sequence six, we would typically expect our protagonist to face his 'darkest hour,' which would then set-up the final climactic confrontation. In this dual-viewpoint sort of story we would expect to see one side in the 'contest' in a positive position and the other in a negative position. Usually, it will be the side the audience wants to see victorious being in the negative situation.

Sequence six of *In the Line of Fire* sees Frank locate Leary and engage in a rooftop chase. For the first time the two men are face-to-face. Frank slips and hangs off the edge of a building – he has the opportunity to kill Leary, but it will mean that he also falls to his own death. When Frank doesn't shoot, Leary taunts him: is Frank's life more important to him than the president's? Is that why he didn't save Kennedy? As Frank scrambles to safety and Leary makes his mistake, Frank's partner is shot.

In Leary's hotel room, the only clue left behind is a piece of paper with some letters on that appears to be a name. Frank investigates but cannot locate anyone of that name. Meanwhile, the president's motorcade arrives in Los Angeles, California. This is where Leary has said he will assassinate the president. Preparations for the president's arrival are intercut with Leary's preparations. At the end of six and into sequence seven we Frank again make a mistake in public, tackling a member of hotel staff who turns out to be entirely innocent. This will ultimately result in him being sent away to a location where he will not be on-hand to protect the president. At the same time, we see Leary arriving at the hotel in the guise of a wealthy businessman.

In *The Day of the Jackal,* things grow increasingly dangerous for the Jackal. The police have more information about the identity he has been using and details of his recent movements. They know he has crossed the border into France and are checking with hotels to see where he is registered. The Jackal speaks with his OAS contact and learns that the police know of the assassination plot: he decides that he will continue with the mission anyway. The Jackal meets a wealthy woman, Colette, who is attracted to him and instead of staying at a hotel, he spends the night with her. The police continue their investigation and eventually discover the hotel that the Jackal is registered in: they are getting closer to him.

Sequence 7. As in many thrillers, a climax at the end of sequence six and beginning of sequence seven is followed by a build-up to a second and bigger climax at the end of seven and into sequence eight.

In this sequence of *In the Line of Fire* we finally learn more about Leary's plan for getting close to the president – his donations to the re-election campaign mean that he is invited to a campaign dinner and his seat will only be a 'stone's throw' from the president's table. There is a close call when Frank stands behind Leary, but he is not recognised. After that, the danger is lessened when Frank is sent away on an errand so that he can't embarrass the president again. At the airport, ready to leave town, Frank finally uncovers the meaning of the words on the slip of paper from Leary's hotel room, and this leads him to the bank where Leary has his fake business account – the bank whose cashier Lear murdered earlier. As Frank races back, knowing that Leary is in the president's hotel, Leary passes through the metal detector with the parts of his plastic gun undetected. Frank compares a list of bank customers registered by the dead cashier with a list of guests for the president's dinner – finds a match. Leary is only minutes away from contact with the president.

In *The Day of the Jackal*, the police arrive at the Jackal's hotel, but he has already left. The Jackal has changed the number plates on his car and will later change its colour. He is stopped by a police car and there is a tense moment, but it is a false alarm. Instead of going to his hotel, the Jackal drives to the home of the wealthy woman, Colette. She accidentally sees the parts of his rifle and so he has to kill her. He then boards a train for Paris – the location of the assassination. After the close call at the end of sequence six, it now appears that the Jackal has the upper hand.

Sequence 8. Now we come to the moment of the assassination attempt and the final confrontation between the assassin and those who seek to protect the president.

In the Line of Fire shows Leary recognising Frank as he enters the dining room. Frank looks at the seating plan, trying to locate Leary's fake name. Leary has assembled the parts of his gun and is ready to fire. The president is in the room. Frank spots Leary and shouts, 'Gun!' He puts himself in front of the president as Leary fires and the bullet hits Frank. Chaos ensues and the president is hurried out. Leary uses Frank as a shield, gun to his head, and drags him into an elevator. He is impressed that Leary took the bullet for the president, even with a bullet-proof vest. As they fight in the lift Leary falls and ends up hanging over a long drop – a reverse of the situation he and Frank were in earlier. Franks tries to save him, but Leary allows himself to fall – his rendezvous with death. When Frank eventually gets home he finds a message on his answering machine, left by Leary before his death – 'I wonder, Frank, did you kill me? Who won our game?' Frank plans to retire from the Secret Service and begin a new life with the female agent, disproving Leary's theory that Frank will live a lonely life.

In *The Day of the Jackal*, the police discover Colette's body. Now that they are investigating a murder, they no longer have to keep their manhunt secret. They know the Jackal has travelled to Paris and they begin searching the hotels for him. But the Jackal predicts this and avoids the hotels, picking up a man at a Turkish bath and going home with him. The authorities discover the 'mole' in their midst and the president's aide admits he's shared information with his mistress. She is arrested. The authorities also realise that the assassin intends to target the president on Liberation Day – in two days' time. Again, the odds against the Jackal have been raised – his inside source of information is gone and his picture has been broadcast on television in relation to the murder. The Jackal has to kill the gay man after he recognises him from the television. Liberation Day arrives and extensive security measures are in place. It will be almost impossible for the assassin to get close to his target. But the Jackal has anticipated this – he is disguised as a one-legged man and we finally understand why his rifle was constructed as it was: the pieces have been disguised as parts of his crutch. The police allow him to pass through their cordon. The president's motorcade arrives. Learning of the one-legged man, the detective Lebel becomes suspicious and goes in search of him. As President de Gaulle awards medals in an open-air ceremony, the Jackal has him in his sights – squeezes the trigger. Before he can fire again, Lebel enters and the two face each other for the first and final time.

Examples: Assassination Thrillers
The Tall Target (film, 1951) – A New York police sergeant uncovers a plot to assassinate Abraham Lincoln on the way to his inauguration and seeks to prevent it. Based on real-life events known as the 'Baltimore Plot.'
Suddenly (film 1954, story 'Active Duty' by Richard Sale, 1943) – Hired killers, led by Frank Sinatra's character, take over a family home, aiming to assassinate the president when he passes through the town.
Intent to Kill (film 1958, novel by Brian Moore writing as Michael Bryan, 1957) – The president of an unnamed South American country (played by Herbert Lom) travels to Canada for medical treatment. Political opponents hire assassins to kill him in Montreal.
The Manchurian Candidate (film 1962, novel by Richard Condon, 1959. Second film adaptation 2004) – During the Korean War, a group of American soldiers are captured by the Soviets and taken to Manchuria, China, to be brainwashed. On their release they return to America, unaware that they have been programmed to become assassins.
Nine Hours to Rama (film 1963, novel by Stanley Wolpert, 1962) – Follows the assassin during the nine hours leading up to the killing of Mohandas Gandhi and the efforts of a police superintendent who tries to find the killer before it is too late.
Z (film 1969, novel by Vassilis Vassilikos, 1966) – Fictional account of events surrounding the assassination in 1963 of Greek politician Grigoris Lambrakis. Dark satire criticising the military dictatorship in Greece at the time of filming.
The Day of the Jackal (film 1973, novel by Frederick Forsyth, 1971) – A professional assassin is hired by a French dissident group, Organisation Armée Secrète, to kill the President of France, Charles de Gaulle. Inspired by a real-life attempt on de Gaulle's life. The 1997 film *The Jackal* has little in common with this film or the original novel.
The Day of the Dolphin (film 1976, novel by Robert Merle, 1967) – Dolphins trained to speak to humans are stolen as part of an assassination conspiracy that involves them attaching magnetic limpet mines to the hull of the yacht of the President of the United States.
Winter Kills (film 1979, novel by Richard Condon, 1974) – Years after the assassination of a fictional American president, the hero witnesses the deathbed confession of a man claiming to be part of the 'hit squad' who carried out the killing. The ensuing investigation leads the hero through the various groups and people that have been mentioned in conspiracy theories related to the JFK assassination. A black comedy by the author of *The Manchurian Candidate*.

JFK (film 1991, based on the non-fiction books *On the Trail of the Assassins* (1988) by Jim Garrison and *Crossfire: The Plot That Killed Kennedy* (1993) by Jim Marrs) – New Orleans District Attorney Jim Garrison investigates Kennedy's assassination after spotting what he believes to be multiple inaccuracies in the Warren Commission report. Directed by Oliver Stone. Not a thriller as such, but this one had to be included.

In the Line of Fire (film 1993) – Clint Eastwood plays the last active Secret Service agent remaining from the group who were guarding John F. Kennedy. He is assigned to protect the present-day president and ends up playing a 'game' against the man who plans to assassinate him.

The Interpreter (film 2005) – An interpreter working at the United Nations in New York overhears a plot to assassinate the president of an African republic. Agents are brought in to protect the president and the interpreter, but it soon becomes clear that the assassination plot is not all that it appears.

(ii) Political Conspiracy / Cover-up Thriller

Watergate has become almost the definition of a political conspiracy, to the extent that any sort of conspiracy or cover-up reported by in the news ends up being called *something*-gate. The investigation of the Watergate break-in by *Washington Post* journalists Bob Woodward and Carl Bernstein developed in such a way that the book they wrote about it, *All the President's Men*, has been described as a non-fiction thriller and was adapted into a movie starring Robert Redford and Dustin Hoffman. We can't look at the political conspiracy thriller without considering *All the President's Men*, but as an example it does offer some problems in terms of plot structure. I'm going to refer to William Goldman's screen adaptation because he took the true-life events and presented them in the most dramatic way possible – but as we'll see, there were limits on how dramatic he could actually make them while remaining true to the facts.

Any account of a real-life situation begins with *what* happened because the visible external actions and their visible consequences are the most obvious evidence we have about the situation. This happened and then this happened and then this happened. The problem with this is that it is by nature episodic – a sequence of things happening without there always being an obvious connection between the events. A sequence of unconnected events doesn't make for a good story – and in fact, bad stories are often criticised for being 'episodic.' E. M. Forster famously said that 'The King died and then the Queen died' is not a story. At the very least we need to see some sort of cause and effect – this happened and because of that this then happened. But even that is only part of what makes for a dramatic story. What we, as readers, really want to know is *why* a certain person took a certain action that led to a certain consequence. What was their motivation? 'The King died and then the Queen died *of grief*' gives us a story. It tells us something about the people involved and their relationship.

Another problem with real-life stories is that there is often no visible and active opposition as such. In storytelling, the antagonist or villain or opponent is a convention – he or she is a symbol that allows the writer to personalise the forces of opposition that the hero faces. We don't write about 'the Nazis' we focus attention on a single brutal Nazi officer or a monstrous Nazi doctor. Telling a story within the confines of a two-hour movie or a 300-page novel means we need to concentrate our ingredients, boiling them down to their essence, to give our readers or viewers the strongest possible emotional flavours. A vague or diffuse opposition works against that. I think that is the biggest weakness in *All the President's Men* if we want to consider it as a model for a thriller – the opposition remains as a vague background threat. At the end of sequence six we see Woodward feeling jumpy as he leaves the dark garage after his meeting with Deep Throat, and in a made-up story there would be some real danger there – but it didn't happen in real life, so Goldman couldn't make it happen in the screenplay: he did the best he could with the facts available. At the climax of the story Deep Throat tells Woodward, 'Your lives are in danger.' Woodward goes back to Bernstein's apartment, afraid to talk because the place might be bugged, but again there is no real sense that their lives are actually in danger.

Related to this is the fact that Woodward and Bernstein are not a lone thriller hero but more like the duo in a 'buddy' movie. They always have each other for support. Apart from a slightly prickly beginning to their relationship, there isn't the 'dark romance' aspect that thrillers typically have when there are two central characters. Added to that is the fact that the two characters have the support of their newspaper editors, who may occasionally challenge them but who essentially act as protectors and mentors. Woodward and Bernstein are not *personally* isolated or in danger – it is their newspaper that is at risk. Again, this diffuses rather than concentrates the emotional impact of the story.

Finally, the Watergate story is a bit like *Titanic* – we know how it ends. We know the identity of the main 'villain' and we know what happens to him. This is a handicap that doesn't apply to most thriller writers.

I don't say these things to criticise William Goldman, who is a master screenwriter, or the finished movie – which is a great movie that perfectly captures one of the defining moments of its era – but rather to highlight how events in a thriller are presented in an (artificial) manner to maximise suspense. *All the President's Men* does not pretend to be a thriller – the movie poster described it as 'The most devastating detective story of this century,' and in terms of plot structure, it *is* closer to the investigation in a classic whodunit mystery than it is to a conspiracy thriller. But the political background to the story means it belongs in this chapter, as does the fact that imagery from the movie has influenced the thriller genre (and other genres) greatly. *The X-Files* is an obvious example, but the clandestine meeting between shadowy figures in a dark concrete car park has become a movie and television cliché.

I will break down the plot of the movie version of *All the President's Men* (1976) as a separate item here: the structure can easily be used as the basis for a fictional thriller, provided that stronger elements of danger, isolation and a more focused opposition or villain are introduced and utilised in a more 'thriller-like' way.

All the President's Men Plot
Sequence 1. There is a break-in at the offices of the national headquarters of the Democratic Party. Rookie reporter Bob Woodward is assigned to cover the

arraignment of the burglars. His suspicions are aroused when the burglars have an expensive attorney and at least one of them is ex-CIA. Later it appears that two of the burglars have links to high-level White House officials. When he calls the White House, a spokesman denies that they had any connection to the Watergate break-in – *before* Woodward even mentions the burglary. There is obviously a story here.

Sequence 2. The newspaper's managing editor wants to replace Woodward with an experienced political writer but eventually agrees he can stay on it if he works with the more experienced Carl Bernstein. Woodward is initially annoyed when Bernstein starts rewriting his copy but eventually admits Bernstein's is better. They can work together, but their relationship is antagonistic at this early stage. The two discover some minor evidence that Richard Nixon's legal advisor had been conducting investigations into at least one Democratic politician – they write their story but the Executive Editor puts the red pen through some of it, telling them they need to get hard facts next time. Although this seems harsh, he is effectively acting as their mentor.

Sequence 3. Woodward phones one of his Washington sources who refuses to talk about Watergate, but the source won't talk about it. The source – who will come to be known as Deep Throat – contacts Woodward later and puts in place a system for them to be able to meet in secret. The man refuses to be named on the record and will not volunteer information in case it can be traced back to him, but he is prepared to verify things that Woodward learns from third parties. Deep Throat's main advice to Woodward is, 'Follow the money.' He says that the myths about the White House are not true, they're actually not very bright guys and the situation has gotten out of hand.

Following the money, the reporters discover that a cheque for $25,000 given to the Campaign to Re-elect the President (CREEP) was paid into the bank account of one of the burglars. There is a link between Nixon supporters and the burglars. The story appears at the bottom of the front page of the newspaper.

In this sequence we see the stakes raised – the extreme measures Deep Throat takes to protect himself are an indication that something big is going on and it could be dangerous. The burglars were apparently hired by political supporters of the president. And the reporters get their first front page by-line.

Sequence 4. The newspaper begins to feel pressure from the White House and is isolated in that other newspapers are not reprinting their stories. There is a risk here that Woodward and Bernstein could get it wrong and they are relying on unnamed sources. There are some at the newspaper who want to drop the investigation. Under pressure to get more sources to talk – preferably on the record – Woodward and Bernstein obtain a list of CREEP employees and try to get someone involved in the campaign's finance team to talk to them about the money that went to the burglars. They know there was a big slush fund but can't discover who was responsible for making payments from it. Most CREEP employees just slam the door on the reporters and one seems extremely nervous, as if she has been threatened. No one will talk to them – the story has stalled.

Midpoint. Richard Nixon is re-nominated as presidential candidate for the Republican Party. The midpoint is also a low point for the two reporters in terms of their investigation.

Sequence 5. Blake Snyder calls this part of the story 'Bad Guys Close In' and, acknowledging the absence of an actual villain in this movie, suggests instead that Woodward and Bernstein themselves take a 'dark turn.' In *Save the Cat Goes to the Movies*, he says that the desire to get the story overwhelms the reporters' 'sense of fair play' and they resort to tricking sources into going on the record. "You'll have to trick her or threaten her," Bernstein says of one reluctant witness. They manipulate the bookkeeper into revealing the names of some of the men who controlled the CREEP slush fund. They also try to convince the beleaguered CREEP treasurer that their investigation will be to his benefit: he knows their motive is not altruistic but shares some information with them anyway.

Sequence 6. So far Woodward and Bernstein have identified three of the five men who controlled the CREEP slush fund – and they know the duns was over $1 million. Their boss wants all five names and is annoyed that none of their sources is prepared to go on the record. The *Washington Post* runs a front-page story revealing that Nixon's former Attorney General, now his campaign manager, controlled the CREEP fund and that it was used to get information on the Democrats. The White House accuses the paper of biased reporting but doesn't specifically deny the story.

Bernstein gets a tipoff about a group of lawyers who were recruited to sabotage the campaigns of Democratic candidates. And these CREEP-funded activities began a whole year before the Watergate break-in – the break-in and bugging of the Democrat's HQ was only part of a much bigger conspiracy to undermine them.

In this sequence, we see the stakes raised again: the conspiracy is bigger than anticipated and the reporters learn that someone high up ordered the FBI and the Justice Department not to pursue the Watergate investigation. Woodward asks Deep Throat how high up the conspiracy goes but Deep Throat says he'll have to find that out for himself. And he warns Woodward not to get distracted by the small stuff or he'll miss the big picture. The end of sequence six isn't marked by a 'darkest hour' for the heroes, but it does involve a significant increase in tension. At this point, Woodward begins to feel nervous and a little paranoid – are the conspirators watching him too? This is only a minor crisis – in true thriller style the story will build to a bigger crisis at the end of sequence seven.

Sequence 7. Woodward and Bernstein's investigation is getting closer and closer to proving that the conspiracy against the Democrats was controlled by a senior White House official. If they can discover who, they have cracked the whole story wide open. But no one will name the individual. They have hints and suspicions that point to the White House Chief of Staff but nothing concrete. Their boss says the story 'still feels thin' and with a publication deadline looming tells them he wants corroboration from another source before he'll okay the story. Bernstein makes a phone call to a Justice Department contact and obtains what he believes is a tacit corroboration of the story. He presents this to his boss as being more than it was and, trusting his reporters, the Executive Editor runs the story on the front page.

But they have miscalculated. A key fact they have reported is proved wrong, the White House press secretary attacks the *Washington Post* publicly, denying any links between the White House and the Watergate break-in, and there are threats of legal action against the newspaper. *This* is the 'darkest hour' for the reporters, who need to figure out what went wrong and how to retrieve the situation. Their FBI source will no longer talk to them and Deep Throat is annoyed because they ran the story without sufficient proof, allowing the guilty parties to deny it all – they moved too soon and have set the investigation back months. In this climactic confrontation, Woodward demands that Deep Throat reveal everything he knows. Deep Throat relents and tells Woodward that the whole of the intelligence community – FBI, CIA, Justice Department – were involved in covert operations against the Republican Party. The cover-up wasn't about Watergate, it was about keeping these covert operations from being discovered. Deep Throat warns that knowing what they know, Woodward and Bernstein's lives are in danger.

Sequence 8. Afraid that they are under surveillance and their homes bugged, Woodward and Bernstein talk with their Executive Editor in a secure location, telling him what they have learned: 'Everyone is involved.' Including President Nixon. Their boss emphasises what is at stake now: the First Amendment, freedom of the press, and possibly the future of the country. He tells them to write the story and not to fuck up this time. We see the two reporters writing up their story as Richard Nixon is sworn in for a second term as President of the United States – the words of his oath are ironically set against the story that we know they are writing. An epilogue shows a teletype machine hammering out the headlines revealing how events unfolded after the publication of the story in the *Washington Post.*

All the President's Men combines elements of the thriller and the whodunit. The Watergate break-in is a first clue that will ultimately lead to the unravelling of a much bigger conspiracy. The CREEP-funded operations to undermine Republican candidates was the conspiracy, but the story of Watergate is really about the White House cover-up of that conspiracy – it was a conspiracy to hide a conspiracy. Woodward and Bernstein acted as detectives, unearthing clues and interviewing witnesses, trying to piece together the whole picture. They move from *what* happened to trying to understand *why* these things happened – Snyder calls the movie a *whydunit* – to ultimately revealing who was responsible for the actions. The difficulty of their investigation increases – and the suspense rises – as they get closer and closer to the White House. In part, that

8 / Political Thriller

suspense is created because we as the audience already know what they do not: that the identity of the villain is [REDACTED].

Two classic political thrillers are *Three Days of the Condor* (1975) based on the 1974 novel *Six Days of the Condor* by James Grady and *The Parallax View* (1974) based on the 1970 novel by Loren Singer. *Three Days of the Condor* is an example of an amateur-on-the-run story and follows that plot structure almost to the letter, so I will refer you to Chapter 1 if you want to write a similar political thriller. *The Parallax View*, published before the Watergate break-in, centres on a newspaper reporter who investigates a conspiracy surrounding the mysterious deaths of witnesses to a political assassination. In the novel, the assassination resembles that of President John F. Kennedy but in the film adaptation, the assassination is based on that of Robert F. Kennedy in 1968. The film also adds a more downbeat ending. The movie version of *The Parallax View* was directed by Alan Pakula and is referred to as the middle part of his 'paranoia trilogy' – the other two films being *Klute* (1971) and *All the President's Men* (1976).

Like *All the President's Men*, *The Parallax View* combines elements of a detective-style investigation with the suspense and conspiracy of a thriller. The plot breakdown below is based primarily on the movie version of the story.

The Parallax View Plot

Sequence 1. Senator Carroll is assassinated at the top of the Space Needle in Seattle in front of a number of witnesses, including TV news reporter Lee Carter and journalist Joe Frady. There were two assassins – one falls to his death and the other disappears. Cut to a courtroom where the outcome of the senator's death is announced: he was killed by a lone assassin motivated by misguided patriotism and a psychotic desire for public recognition. There was no evidence of a wider conspiracy. Cut to three years later when we are introduced to reporter Joe Frady at work. He outwits and humiliates the police vice squad who are trying to identify one of his sources. He is a maverick with little respect for authority and is described by his editor as 'creatively irresponsible.' Of course we like him.

Sequence 2. Frady is visited by another of the assassination witnesses, Lee Carter, who is obviously distressed. She says that six witnesses to the assassination have died in suspicious circumstances and she is afraid that she is next. Frady is sceptical – but then Lee Carter is found dead, an apparent suicide. He decides to investigate and visits an ex-FBI friend to ask about the best way to obtain a fake ID.

Sequence 3. Frady goes to a small town where one of the assassination witnesses died in a 'fishing accident.' A seemingly helpful sheriff sets Frady up such that he too is almost drowned. Searching the sheriff's home afterwards, Frady discovers papers including a questionnaire from the Parallax Corporation. The sheriff's deputy discovers Frady, who escapes in a stolen police car. There is a chase, but our hero gets away.

Sequence 4. Frady's editor isn't convinced by the story of a conspiracy to systematically eliminate witnesses to the assassination. Frady wants to dig deeper. He takes the Parallax Corporation questionnaire to a psychology researcher who says it looks like it is intended to identify psychopaths – he gives Frady the answers that a psychopath would be most likely to give. Frady then goes to question Senator Carroll's former aide – the man is in fear for his life, but shows Frady photographs that prove there were *two* assassins, not a lone gunman as the official inquiry concluded.

Midpoint: The aide's yacht explodes with him on it – Frady is thrown overboard.

Sequence 5. Frady is thought to have died in the yacht explosion, so his editor is surprised to see him alive. Frady wants to stay officially dead so that he can continue his investigation. He thinks that someone is recruiting assassins and, using his fake ID and the questionnaire responses he got from the psychology lab, he will apply. His editor is the only person who knows he is going to do this. Later, Frady is visited by a Parallax Corporation recruiter – they liked his questionnaire answers – and he is taken to their HQ for further testing. He is subjected to tests that monitor his emotional responses to both positive and disturbing visual stimuli.

Sequence 6. As he is leaving the Parallax Corporation building, Frady spots the second gunman from the Carroll assassination. He follows the man and boards the same plane. A little way into the flight he finds that the assassin is not on board and realises that he must have planted a bomb and then disembarked. He tips off the stewardess anonymously and the plane returns to the ground. The passengers, who include an important political figure, leave the plane – only moments before it explodes. A close call.

Sequence 7. Frady is offered a job by the Parallax Corporation. He records the conversation he has with the recruiter and passes the tape to his editor. The next morning the editor is dead and the tape is gone. Frady has a narrow escape when he discovers his first job for Parallax is going to partner him with a man who can blow his cover.

Sequence 8. Frady again follows the second Carroll assassin – this time to a convention centre where rehearsals for a political rally are underway. The political candidate is shot by the assassin – someone spots Frady in hiding and assumes he is the killer. Frady tries to escape – but fails. Cut to the courtroom again, where the inquiry into the assassination concludes that Frady was a lone gunman who acted alone – there is no evidence of a conspiracy...

I think this sequence of events works incredibly well for a political conspiracy thriller. It mirrors the amateur-on-the-run thriller in many ways – the hero is isolated and finds himself entering the villain's den – and also some parts of the James Bond-style mission plot: the hero adopts a fake identity and *deliberately* gets himself involved in the conspiracy in order to discover the truth of what is going on. But unlike a James Bond story, we never actually see the villain who is behind it all – we encounter only the henchmen in the form of the other assassins in the Parallax program. If I was writing this type of thriller today, I would probably choose to reveal the villain (or villains) at the end – or at least give some clue as to who they were – and I probably wouldn't dispose of my hero. It's hard to write a sequel or a series if you kill off your hero.

Examples: Political Conspiracy / Cover-up Thrillers
Seven Days in May (film 1964, novel by Fletcher Knebel and Charles W. Bailey II, 1962. Screenplay by Rod Serling) – Military and political officials conspire to overthrow the president following the signing of a disarmament treaty with the Soviet Union. Inspired by events early in John F. Kennedy's presidency. The novel's authors were political journalists.
Executive Action (film 1973) – Portrays the assassination of John F. Kennedy as having been planned by American intelligence agents, politicians, and businessmen, and carried out by professional assassins.
Capricorn One (film 1977) – When the first manned mission to Mars has to be halted due to equipment malfunction, the government broadcasts fake footage of the successful mission. When the return spacecraft is destroyed om re-entry, the astronauts realise they won't be released alive and so try to escape.
The China Syndrome (film 1979) – A television reporter and her cameraman are present during an emergency shutdown at a nuclear power plant and uncover what appear to be serious safety issues and an official cover-up. The film was released twelve days before the Three Mile Island nuclear accident.
Missing (film 1982, based on the 1978 non-fiction book *The Execution of Charles Horman: An American Sacrifice*) – An American journalist goes missing in the aftermath of an American-backed coup in an unnamed South American country. The man's wife and father go to the country in search of him and discover the journalist witnessed the violence perpetrated by the American-backed junta and died as a result. Based on the Chilean coup of 1973 and the real-life disappearance of US journalist Charles Horman.
Silkwood (film 1983) – Based on the life of Karen Silkwood, a union activist and whistle-blower who raised concerns about breaches of safety practices at a nuclear fuel fabrication plant from which plutonium had been stolen. In the film, she investigates and assembles evidence, and then at the point she is about to talk to a *New York Times* journalist, she is killed in a suspicious car accident.
Under Fire (film 1983) – Towards the end of the Nicaraguan Revolution, a US journalist is shot dead by a government soldier and his death is captured in pictures by a US photographer. Inspired by the murder of ABC reporter Bill Stewart and his translator Juan Espinoza by National Guard forces in Nicaragua in June 1979.
Power (film 1986) – A political campaign organiser is hired to help a right-wing industrialist win a seat in the Senate. He becomes disillusioned as he and a journalist uncover the extent of the candidate's corruption – but he then finds himself targeted by another ruthless spin-doctor.
Snowden (film 2016, based on the 2014 non-fiction book *The Snowden Files* by Luke Harding and the (then unpublished) novel *Time of the Octopus* (2017) by Anatoly Kucherena) – Dramatised account of events surrounding Edward

Snowden's release of classified information which revealed illegal mass surveillance conducted by the US National Security Agency (NSA). Directed by Oliver Stone. Again, not strictly a thriller, but as a recent example it had to be included.

(iii) Terrorism Thriller

There are two variations on the terrorism thriller plot that I'm going to explore here. The first is where the terrorists plan to commit an attack of some kind and an external protagonist – either alone or as part of a group – seeks to uncover and prevent the plot before it takes place: *Black Sunday* is an example of this sort of plot. The second centres on an innocent protagonist who becomes caught up in a terrorist conspiracy and seeks a way to escape from them and prevent the act itself: Eric Ambler's novel *The Levanter* is an example.

In both sorts of plot, the terrorists are engaged in a mission – they are essentially involved in the bad-guy equivalent of a James Bond plot. The protagonist in both cases, to greater or lesser extent, is an investigator trying to find out the details of this mission – who, when, what, where, how – and then *his* mission becomes preventing the terrorist mission from succeeding.

The Terrorists versus Protagonist Plot

Thomas Harris is best known as the creator of serial killer Hannibal Lecter and author of *The Silence of the Lambs* (1988), which was adapted into a successful film in 1991. His 1975 novel *Black Sunday*, about a terrorist attack on mainland America, was filmed in 1977. The story features a group of Palestinian terrorists, Black September, who are assisted in their latest plot by a disenfranchised and unstable Vietnam veteran. Opposing them are Mossad agent David Kabakov and FBI agent Sam Corley. The plot outline below is based on the original novel by Thomas Harris.

Sequence 1. Introduce the terrorists – who they are and their political agenda. Backstory of the group and the history of their fight. Introduce their plan – to target a public event on U.S. soil with the aim of killing and injuring thousands, including the American president.

In the opening scenes, security forces move in on the terrorists – there is a shoot-out and/or explosion. Most of the terrorists are killed, but one or two escape. One of those who gets away, perhaps their leader, is injured in the attack. The remaining terrorists swear to get revenge on their attackers and to continue their mission – or die trying.

Introduce the protagonist, a security agent who is determined to stop the terrorists. He may have been part of the attack on the group in the opening scenes. He knows that some have escaped and will try to complete their mission – but at this stage, he does not know what their target is going to be.

The terrorists take delivery of explosives, weapons, and/or other equipment. They visit or discuss their target – the audience now knows what is at stake but the protagonist does not.

Sequence 2. We learn more about the surviving terrorists – and see more of their preparations. We see that the nature of the leader's injury is such that he is unlikely to recover quickly, and this may put the mission in jeopardy. As a result, they may have to recruit a new team member. The risk is that this new person could be unreliable or not committed to their cause. The person they recruit will need to have special skills – as a pilot, getaway driver, pilot, scuba diver or whatever – and as a result, we learn something about the nature of the attack that the terrorists are planning. We now know that their attack is going to be something spectacular – on a scale that will shock and possibly demoralise the American people and which will publicise the terrorist's cause. Recruiting a 'newbie' or outsider gives the terrorist characters an excuse to explain things that the author wants the reader to know but which the terrorists would not realistically mention if they were all old hands.

During their preparations there is a near miss as they are accidentally discovered by someone, recognised from a 'wanted poster,' or stopped by a policeman as part of a routine check (e.g. they have a defective tail light on the van that is filled with explosive) – this person is killed by the terrorists. The incident shows that they are at risk of discovery – but it also demonstrates their ruthlessness.

Sequence 3. We learn more about the protagonist. He investigates a scene which has been used as part of the terrorists' activities – perhaps an old storage facility that weapons or explosives have been moved from; perhaps a former hideout, recently abandoned; perhaps the place where the witness in sequence two was killed or their body hidden. When the body is found, the protagonist will wonder why this individual was killed. What did they see or know that made the terrorists eliminate them as a risk?

The protagonist may visit a potential source of information – but this person will be found dead – or he/she may be shot or their home or business blown up in front of the protagonist. Again the protagonist knows that the dead person knew something important – but what? The explosive or weapon used show that the terrorists were responsible for the killing – and they may leave a message or a warning: his opponents want him to know the extent of their information network and their reach. The terrorists may see the protagonist and recognise him as responsible for the deaths of their comrades in sequence one – and they will vow to kill him in revenge.

Sequences two and three establish the pattern of alternating viewpoints – terrorists and protagonist – that will continue through the rest of the story. At this point, the terrorists seem to be in the dominant position, with the protagonist trying to catch up. The 'advantage' will shift from one side to the other, like a tennis match, as the story progresses.

Sequence 4 & Midpoint. Motivated by feelings of revenge, and putting personal emotions ahead of the safety of the mission, one of the terrorists attempts to kill the protagonist. He is injured but not killed – and he saw his attacker. The protagonist is able to identify him and find his photograph on file or is able to work with an artist to create an 'identikit' image or sketch. This is circulated to law enforcement agencies. This is a blow to the terrorists – presenting a risk to their mission – and a minor success for the protagonist. At the *midpoint* the terrorists may be forced into deeper cover, abandoning their hideout and perhaps even going on the run. Someone may identify the terrorist from the identikit image – police surround their hideout and they make a narrow escape, perhaps having to leave something important behind or suffering some other setback, such as re-opening the leader's wound. At this point, the protagonist may also discover a clue that leads him to identify the terrorist's intended target and the date of the attack – but not the exact nature that the attack will take.

Sequence 5. The viewpoint shifts back to the protagonist and we see him perhaps recovering from the attack by the terrorist in sequence four. If there is a relationship with a romantic co-protagonist or 'buddy', it will be explored here. The protagonist will discuss what he has learned so far about the terrorists and their plot. And what he doesn't know. He also continues his investigation, perhaps trying to get information about a vehicle that the terrorists have used or have taken and/or trying to discover where the weapons or explosives were taken and hidden.

Meanwhile, the terrorists test their weapons or explosives in some out of the way and interesting location where they won't attract attention. This is a small-scale demonstration of the destruction that their plan will cause if put into effect – perhaps a truck or a building destroyed or a visual representation of what it would look like if a crowd of people were hit.

Sequence 6. The protagonist identifies a criminal who has done business with the terrorists – a weapons supplier, ship captain, doctor, engineer or whatever. The protagonist goes to interview this person – either in his role as a law enforcement officer 'leaning' on the crook to get information, or disguised as a criminal looking to do some business of his own – perhaps saying the crook was recommended to him by the terrorists. As a result, he discovers some clue about the terrorist plot – something unusual, the significance of which he doesn't understand until later.

Usually, there will be some reminder about the event the terrorists plan to attack – a report that good weather is expected, so there will be a large turnout. Perhaps news about the president attending with his wife. Security forces will be seen putting measures in place to ensure everyone's safety, but they are anticipating a typical attack – a suicide bomber on foot or in a vehicle, a hidden bomb, a sniper – but the terrorists are planning something spectacularly unconventional and these precautions won't protect people.

The injured terrorist leader is vital to the mission – but his condition worsens. Perhaps his wound reopened when they had to escape at the midpoint. Perhaps his wound has become infected. He needs urgent medical attention. Perhaps they take him to a doctor and hold the doctor hostage – or kidnap a paramedic. The condition of this man puts the mission at risk – do they need to find someone to replace him? Is that even possible for a suicide mission? Do they call the mission off? This marks the terrorists' 'darkest hour.'

Sequence 7. The terrorists come up with a Plan B. A smaller scale version or a less spectacular version of their original plan. A bomb in an ambulance, for example, rather than a bomb in an aircraft. They complete preparations on their weapon or explosive. At the same time, they care for their injured comrade, hoping he will recover in time for the attack.

The protagonist makes a major breakthrough – he discovers some information that leads him to guess what the terrorists' Plan B involves. He thinks this is their main plan, not realising that they have another plan that is much grander and will cause much more devastation – if their leader recovers sufficiently to carry out his part in it. The protagonist has measures put in place to protect against Plan B – and to watch locations associated with it. As soon as the terrorists appear, they will be arrested or shot. Perhaps a minor player in the terrorist plan is arrested and questions, but reveals nothing about Plan A. The protagonist believes he has the upper hand at this point.

The terrorist leader recovers – he will be able to carry out Plan A. The protagonist doesn't know this – but it is effectively his 'darkest hour' as he's trying to stop the wrong plan.

Sequence 8. The security forces concentrate all their efforts defending against and trying to prevent Plan B. The clock ticks down to the moment of attack. The crowds arrive and so does the president – all the potential victims are in place. The terrorists load their weapons or explosives into the delivery vehicle and move them to the location.

The protagonist spots something, makes a deduction and/or has a hunch – he realises they're in the wrong place watching the wrong thing. He works out what the terrorists are *really* planning. A fight or a chase – as the final seconds tick away.

An explosive climax – the terrorists are defeated in a way that is ironic and has an element of poetic justice. The people are saved.

The Innocent Trapped in a Terrorist Conspiracy Plot

Eric Ambler was a novelist and screenwriter who is perhaps best known for the novels *The Mask of Dimitrios* (1939) which was filmed in 1944 and *The Light of Day* (1962) which was adapted for the screen as *Topkapi* (1964). His 1972 novel *The Levanter* is one of the few examples I've come across where the innocent protagonist becomes embroiled in a terrorist plot and spends most of the story inside of the terrorist group. This plot, as you will see, has some things in common with the amateur-on-the-run plot, though the hero may find himself on the run with a bunch of terrorists rather than being on the run alone. But after the midpoint he does find himself increasingly isolated and having to depend on his own wits.

Sequence 1. Introduce the terrorist leader and his cause. Backstory, including the nature of and history of the conflict. Introduce the protagonist and his situation – an innocent man who is useful to the terrorists in some way. Include a first mention of how the protagonist accidentally or unwittingly comes into contact with the terrorist group.

Sequence 2. Protagonist discovers the terrorists are using his company's buildings, vehicles, supplies or whatever. The terrorist activities probably involve the manufacturing of explosives or illegal arms shipments. The protagonist encounters the terrorist leader for the first time – either when he confronts the terrorists or is confronted by them.

Sequence 3. The terrorist leader tells the protagonist about an attack that his group are planning – an attack on a scale that will demoralise his enemy and bring publicity to his group and the cause he is fighting for. We see the terrorist leader's moral point of view, justifying his actions for a greater cause. He will also outline the 'crimes' of his enemy. When challenged on a plan that will cause harm to innocent civilians, he will say that in a war of this kind there is no such thing as an innocent bystander or something to that effect.

The protagonist doesn't know whether to take the terrorist leader seriously at first. He finds him arrogant with an over-inflated sense of his own importance and that of his relatively small terrorist group. The group has probably splintered from a better-known group following the terrorist leader's falling out with the commanders of the larger group.

To ensure the protagonist's co-operation, the terrorist leader 'recruits' him into the terrorist group, effectively saying 'You are now one of us.' Evidence is manufactured that will prove the protagonist's guilt if he betrays the group – perhaps fake proof that he was involved in earlier terrorist activity which would condemn him if it was released to the authorities. Or he may be blackmailed into joining with someone he cares about being threatened or kidnapped. Or perhaps he is tortured or mutilated and forced to join for fear of further injury.

A theme here is whether the hero is a coward for joining the terrorist group. Is he betraying his own principles and signing the death warrants of hundreds of innocent people? At this stage, he doesn't know exactly what he is signing up for – he knows what the target is but not the nature of the attack. He may also hope that he can get out of his current situation before he has to be involved in any terrorist act.

Sequence 4 & Midpoint. The protagonist works for, assists, hides, and/or funds the terrorists. He helps them obtain or transport weapons, explosives or chemicals and parts for the manufacture of bombs. He may try to slow down the group's activities, disrupt them, or encourage them to move to another location by causing 'inconveniences' or other semi-passive forms of resistance that cannot be traced to him directly. But these activities make the terrorist leader suspicious – 'I will be watching you.'

The terrorist leader increases the involvement and incrimination of the protagonist – and increases his demands on the protagonist's resources. Eventually, he demands something on a much larger scale – a truck, a ship, or an aircraft. The protagonist seriously thinks of trying to escape – but there must be genuine reasons why he can't run.

At the *midpoint,* he learns the exact target and nature of the attack planned by the terrorists. It is much bigger and more devastating than anything he imagined. And the scope of it proves that the terrorist leader isn't a pathetic windbag after all.

Sequence 5. If the protagonist has a 'buddy' or romantic co-protagonist, we will see their relationship develop here. This character may be another innocent, trapped like the hero, or they may be one of the terrorists. If they are both trapped by the terrorists' plot, they will discuss their options. Neither the protagonist nor his buddy / co-protagonist will want to be responsible – directly or indirectly – for the sort of killing the terrorists are planning. The protagonist will believe that he must *appear* to be co-operating. He may be asked *why* he is doing the terrorist leader's bidding – shouldn't he be sabotaging the plot? He will argue that he is prepared to risk himself to sabotage the plot – but only if he can be sure that the risk is worth taking, that he is assured of success. The risks he faces are great and he doesn't want to throw his life away.

Another question to tackle here is why the protagonist doesn't take what he knows to the security services. He will argue that he doesn't yet have enough information to be useful to the authorities. They know where and possibly what is planned, but don't have precise details of how the attack will be achieved and when it will be launched. If he took what he currently knows, the security services would send him back to find out more. He may as well stay where he is until he knows more.

The protagonist may also be worried about saving his business and/or his reputation at this point. Stopping the terrorists hasn't yet become his only priority – he's still hoping for a magic bullet or an easy option that will allow him to have everything he wants.

As well as developing the relationship with a co-protagonist – or perhaps instead of this – we see a development of the relationship between the protagonist and the terrorist leader. The protagonist engages in another bit of subtle, indirect sabotage that inconveniences the terrorists – perhaps hoping that their plot will be exposed and that the police will move in, taking the responsibility for action away from him. But he fails to achieve this aim. He may find himself being accused of insubordination or being insufficiently committed to 'the cause,' and so find himself subject to punishment. Or he may see another 'traitor' punished as an example. The protagonist is probably too important to the mission to be killed – at this stage, but the threat should be there. This concentrates his thoughts and he works harder to appease the terrorist leader. At the same time, he is getting deeper and deeper into the conspiracy – committing illegal acts and becoming indirectly responsible for harm caused to innocent people. He's passed a point of no return and can no longer justify himself by saying he's biding his time.

Sequence 6. Having learned something more about the terrorist plot and made some deductions from what he has learned, the protagonist feels that now is the time to alert the security services. This is risky for him, but the benefit is that he can pass all responsibility on to them. Or so he thinks. He suggests ways for the security services to thwart the terrorists' plan – ways which involve little or no action from or risk to him – but his ideas are seen as naïve and impractical. But there are still important parts of the plan that he doesn't know or curious bits of evidence that he cannot explain – so, as he feared before, the security services send him back to fill in the missing pieces. A way is arranged for him to be able to communicate secretly with the security services. These are such that they restrict how often he can communicate with them and how much information he can pass on.

Back with the terrorists, the protagonist continues to assist them and then does something that proves his 'loyalty' and – at least temporarily – allays the terrorist leader's suspicions. The terrorist leader then shares more details of the plot with the protagonist. Thinking he now knows everything, the protagonist passes the details on to the security services who then begin a counter-operation.

But the protagonist then discovers that the terrorist plan is even bigger and more devastating than anything he imagined – he has underestimated the terrorists hugely. He tries to warn the security services, but his line of communication has been cut – perhaps his local contact has been killed. Or he is assigned a round the clock guard to prevent him from contacting anyone, or he is kept close to the terrorist leader, or removed to an isolated location. He manages to get a cryptic message out by some source and can only hope that the security services understand its meaning. The protagonist is further isolated when his romantic co-protagonist or 'buddy' is taken from him – either held hostage to ensure his co-operation, or they escape, or they betray him.

An attempt may be made by the security services to stop the mission – based on the protagonists incomplete or accurate information, this attempt fails and people on both sides are killed. A plan the protagonist had to escape is foiled. We have reached the protagonist's 'darkest hour' – and probably also that of the terrorists and the security services.

Sequence 7. The terrorists' mission begins. Men and equipment are assembled. They set off – there is no turning back and no way for the protagonist to escape. From inside the group, the protagonist tries to delay or sabotage the mission – hoping the security services will appear to rescue him. But they don't.
The terrorist leader is already planning his victory celebration, his speech, and ways to capitalise on the publicity the attack will gain for him.

Zero-hour approaches. The protagonist has no outside support. It is up to him to do something to save thousands of innocent lives. He considers blowing himself and the terrorists up – but there is some reason why he can't or doesn't. Perhaps his buddy or romantic co-protagonist is part of the convoy. Or other innocent people might be present. Or perhaps blowing up himself and the people he is with wouldn't guarantee that the mission failed or was aborted. He doesn't want to sacrifice himself unless he can be sure that he has stopped the attack completely. By this stage, he has given up all other concerns, including saving his own life, and his only priority is preventing the attack.

The terrorist leader reveals to the protagonist and his group the full details of the attack. The protagonist may have worked it out beforehand or he may be taken by surprise when he learns the full scale and nastiness of it – he thought it was going to be Plan A or Plan B, but it is going to be A, B, and perhaps even C as well. The clock is ticking down.

Sequence 8. In desperation, the protagonist takes action – in secret. He may risk breaking radio silence and contact the security services – and they may ask him to do something that he cannot do or which he thinks is the wrong thing. His act of sabotage fails or he is caught in the middle of his secret communication. He is challenged by the terrorist leader and forced at gunpoint to complete some act, a final part of the plan, that will mean he is party to the deaths of thousands of innocent people. Their blood will be on his hands. The terrorist leader gloats about this.

Finally, the protagonist manages to turn the tables and defeats the terrorist leader who dies in some way that has an element of irony or poetic justice about it. The means of his death should have been set-up at an earlier point in the story – perhaps he threatened the protagonist or co-protagonist with just such an 'accident.' The protagonist also manages, with perhaps a little external help from the security services who *did* understand his message, to cancel or deflect the terrorists' attack.

The security services arrive to help mop up and all loose ends are tied.

You will probably notice that these 'terrorism plots' have things in common with both the 'assassin plots' and the 'hostage plots' since these too are forms of terrorist activity. Ideas from all of these plots can be mixed and matched.

Examples: Terrorism Thrillers
The Levanter (1972) – Novel by Eric Ambler. A businessman in Syria in 1970 becomes caught up in the activities of the Palestine Action Force who want to use his factories to manufacture bombs to use against the Israelis.
Black Sunday (film 1977, novel by Thomas Harris, 1975) – Terrorists plan to commit mass-murder at the Super Bowl using a Goodyear blimp, while the authorities race to stop them.
The Outsider (1979) – An disillusioned Irish-American Vietnam War veteran travels to Northern Ireland to join the IRA but discovers the truth behind his grandfather's romantic tales of the conflict. Based on the novel *The Heritage of Michael Flaherty* by Colin Leinster.
Under Siege (TV movie 1986, NBC) – Co-written by Bob Woodward. On US soil, Arab terrorists blow up an army base, three domestic airliners, and a shopping centre. The director of the FBI wants them brought to justice; the director of the CIA and a presidential aide don't want the terrorists to have a platform for their views and so want them dealt with by an assassination team.
Rendition (film 2007) – Following a suicide bomb-attack in North Africa, an Egyptian-born man is abducted and sent to a secret detention facility where he is interrogated and tortured. A CIA operative supervising the questioning doubts the man's guilt and ultimately feels compelled to help him escape. Based in part on the case of Khalid El-Masri, who was mistaken for Khalid al-Masri, a man suspected of helping recruit two of the 9/11 terrorists. El-Masri was, according to the European Court of Human Rights, tortured while held by CIA agents.

Unthinkable (2010) – A terrorist who has threatened to detonate nuclear bombs in three US cities is captured and interrogated.

Eye in the Sky (2015) – A British military operation to destroy a building containing three terrorist leaders and two suicide bombers hangs in the balance when a young girl enters the target zone. Explores the use of drones in the 'war on terror' and the risk of 'collateral damage.'

(iv) Hostage Thriller

The structure of the hostage or hijack thriller is dependent on the point at which you want the actual hijack or hostage-taking to take place. It can occur in the first quarter of the story or at the midpoint. In the examples I have looked at, *Raid on Entebbe* and *Die Hard* have the hostage situation begin early (sequence one or two), but *Who Dares Wins* has the terrorist's mission begin just after the midpoint and through sequence five into sequence six. In both cases, the same set of key story points appear, but in the case of *Die Hard* and similar stories, the story points are spread across all four quarters, while in *Who Dares Wins* these story points are concentrated in the second half of the story.

Holding back the actual hijacking or hostage-taking event until the midpoint of the story allows more time to introduce characters and situations. In *Who Dares Wins*, the first half of the story concentrates on introducing the protagonist and the methods used by the SAS (Special Air Service), and on establishing a relationship between the protagonist and the female terrorist leader. This early part of the story uses elements of the 'undercover agent' or 'behind enemy lines' story. The protagonist is pretending to sympathise with the terrorist cause in order to infiltrate their organisation.

Other examples of the hostage thriller include *Olympus Has Fallen*, *White House Down*, *Under Siege*, *Air Force One* and *6 Days*. The majority of them use the *Die Hard* plot model, having the hostage situation begin in Act I.

We'll look at the Act I hostage situation first and then at how the midpoint hostage situation differs from it.

The Act I Hostage Situation Thriller Plot

Sequence 1. Typically, this will be used to introduce the protagonist, the terrorists, and/or the (potential) hostages. If there is a romantic co-protagonist, she may also be introduced here – perhaps as one of the hostages. The location for the hijacking or hostage situation may also be introduced. Any of those not introduced in sequence one will be included in sequence two. Sequence one of *Die Hard* has Bruce Willis as McClane (protagonist) arrive at the office building (location) where his wife (romantic co-protagonist) works and where a Christmas party is underway for her work colleagues (hostages).

Raid on Entebbe does not have a single protagonist as such, but the Martin Balsam character Daniel Cooper serves as a stand-in, acting as witness to events and representative of the hostages. Sequence one opens at the airport and we see the passengers (hostages) board the plane. This has elements in common with the 'disaster movie' genre in that we meet a group of people who will become victims of a situation and these characters are humanised in a series of vignettes during the first two sequences. The plane itself serves as the first location, but it will be replaced by the airport in Entebbe in sequence two. The hijackers are also introduced, as are the Israeli government, who will ultimately decide the fate of the hostages in this story. The terrorist leaders are also introduced – though Idi Amin, another key player in the situation, does not appear until sequence three.

Sequence 2. Elements not introduced in sequence one are included here. In *Die Hard* the terrorists arrive at the beginning of sequence two – they deal ruthlessly with on-site security. We see more of the relationship between McClane and his wife and we see the terrorists taking control of the location and begin wiring explosives. The terrorists contain all of the hostages, with the exception of the protagonist who hides and considers his options. The plane in *Raid on Entebbe* reaches its final destination and the passengers enter the airport building. We learn more about them and about the hijackers. The hijackers make their demands known – what they want in exchange for release of the hostages. Israeli politicians debate the situation – a military solution is considered, but it is agreed to try negotiation first.

Sequence 3. Faced with the hostage situation, the protagonist now tries the obvious first things that anyone would do to try and find a solution. These options have to be tried or discounted first in any story situation. John McClane, in *Die Hard,* sets off a fire alarm, hoping the fire-service will attend and discover what is happening in the office building; and when that fails he uses a radio to send an emergency call. In *Raid on Entebbe,* the Israeli government contacts other governments who have passengers on the plane and who have prisoners that the terrorists want to be released. This sequence also sees the first appearance of Idi Amin, President of Uganda, who is using the hostage situation for his own propaganda purposes: he arrives with a film crew and treats the whole thing as a photo-opportunity. Amin will serve partly as a spokesman for the terrorists and partly in the role of external negotiator.

Sequence 4 & Midpoint. First attempts at a solution having failed, a new approach is required. In *Die Hard* the protagonist finally manages to make a police officer finally aware of the situation so that he calls for back-up. A television crew also learns what is happening and sends a truck to the scene. As a result of McClane's actions, the terrorist leader knows he is loose in the building – and that he could pose a threat to their plan: getting to McClane becomes a priority for his men. By the midpoint the terrorists appear to be in a strong position – the building is locked down – and those outside decide that direct action is required.

Idi Amin, in *Raid on Entebbe,* seizes the limelight again, saying he has negotiated an extension to the terrorists' deadline and that he has also arranged for the release of non-Israeli prisoners. The Israelis try to negotiate with Idi Amin, but by the midpoint, it is apparent that diplomacy has failed to resolve the situation.

By the end of sequence four, the situation has reached some sort of stalemate, such that dramatic action is required to make progress of any sort.

Sequence 5. This sequence sees either the would-be rescuers or the hostages themselves taking some action towards a solution. *Die Hard* has the Deputy Chief of Police send a SWAT team to enter the building: they come under attack and the protagonist ends up having to help them escape. It wasn't much of a rescue – and it was all filmed for television. Meanwhile, the hostages are communicating with the terrorist leader about getting water, access to toilets, etc.

In *Raid on Entebbe*, the Israelis still debate military action and in the meantime the military begins preparations for the mission if it is approved. The hostages in Entebbe are encouraged by Idi Amin to write a letter to their government, asking them to give the terrorists what they want in exchange for the hostages' lives.

Sequence 6. Here we see a rapid escalation of the situation and/or a downward spiral in the fortunes of the protagonist. McClane, in *Die Hard*, finds that there is an 'enemy within' when one of the hostages decides to try and out-manoeuvre the terrorist leader. The man gives the leader useful information but ends up being killed. Outside the building, people argue about the best way to deal with the situation. The terrorists make their demands known (though in this story they are a smokescreen) and the stakes are raised when the FBI takes charge – and are revealed to be a couple of Johnsons.

In *Raid on Entebbe* the debate concludes and, having no other options, the military assault on Entebbe is authorised.

Sequence 7. The situation for *Die Hard's* John McClane becomes more desperate as the terrorists move closer to achieving their goal – and closer to killing the hostages and him. Outside the building, the FBI have ordered helicopter gunships to head for the building – not knowing what is waiting for them on the roof of the building. McClane realises the terrorists' plan and tries to warn the police below but is prevented from completing his message. He also learns that the terrorist leader now has his wife. The hostages are moved to a place where they will be killed.

In *Raid on Entebbe*, the military fly to Uganda – touch-down occurs in the middle of this sequence and their assault on the airport begins. Quietly.

Sequence 8. The final battle – gunfire and explosions. Terrorists are killed and their leader outwitted, probably in a final confrontation with the protagonist. The hostages are released safely.

The Midpoint Hostage Situation Thriller
As stated previously, much of what appears in the eight sequences outlined above is compressed into the final four sequences of a hostage thriller where the hostage situation takes place at the midpoint rather than at the beginning.

Sequence 1 of *Who Dares Wins* begins by introducing the terrorists – and showing how they deal with someone who has infiltrated their group and is acting as an informant for the police. Then we meet the protagonist, SAS Captain Peter Skellen, and see the sort of situations SAS soldiers are trained to deal with. The authorities know that the terrorists are planning something big, but they don't

8 | Political Thriller

know what it is, where it will occur, or exactly when it will happen. Skellen is set up so that he can join the terrorist group, with a secret contact/mentor to support him.

Sequence 2 introduces the romantic co-protagonist, Skellen's wife. And also, a romance develops between Skellen and the female terrorist leader. We learn more about the terrorists and see them training with weapons.

Sequence 3 focuses on the suspicions the terrorists have about Skellen and the measures they take to investigate him: they check into his background and follow him. To strengthen his credibility as an *ex*-SAS officer, Skellen is beaten up by some of his 'former' colleagues. At the end of the sequence, we learn that the terrorists' target is likely to be a group of American dignitaries who have just arrived in the country.

Sequence 4 sees Skellen's situation become more dangerous. He is followed and photographed with his supposedly former-wife. It is looking as though he could be another infiltrator. Only the terrorist leader's feelings for him save him from instant death. Skellen's contact has also been followed – and, at the *midpoint*, is killed by one of the terrorists. The protagonist is now alone and has no support from or contact with his employers.

Sequence 5. From this point onwards, the plot picks up the normal sequence of events for a hostage thriller. The terrorists complete their preparations. The authorities still do not know where the terrorists intend to strike – and do not know if Skellen is still alive. The terrorist leader tells her group that their target will be the American ambassador's residence. A bus carrying a military dance band is hijacked – the band members are taken off and the terrorists take their places. In order to ensure Skellen's compliance, the terrorist leader tells him that his wife and daughter have been taken hostage. The terrorist's mission begins.

Sequence 6 shows the American dignitaries being taken hostage. The terrorist leader announces their demands and sets a deadline for compliance. In dialogue between the American Secretary of State and the terrorist leader, we see the terrorist's point of view contrasted with that of mainstream politics. A police commander and his crew set-up outside the ambassador's residence and try to negotiate with the terrorist leader – they gain some concessions, but on the deadline, she is inflexible.

Sequence 7. Television news reports the hostage situation. The negotiator tries to gain more time, but this is refused. Skellen manages to communicate with his boss outside – setting a time for the SAS assault so that he can cause a distraction inside the ambassador's house. A hostage is killed, and this prompts authorisation for the SAS assault to begin. Helicopters lift off and a signal is given to Skellen.

Sequence 8. SAS assault – gunfire, explosions, hostages freed – with Skellen providing support from the inside. A separate group of SAS soldiers rescue Skellen's wife and daughter.

Examples: Hostage & Hijacking Thrillers
The most famous hostage thriller of all isn't technically a political thriller, but it is impossible to talk about the hostage thriller without mentioning the 1988 film *Die Hard.* The screenplay was based on the 1979 novel *Nothing Lasts Forever* by Roderick Thorp, which does feature more of a political theme. *Die Hard* – thanks to a decent script and an entertaining performance from Bruce Willis – was a surprise hit with audiences and many subsequent movies were either inspired by it or compared to it: *Under Siege* (1992) was '*Die Hard* on a battleship'; *Speed* (1994) was '*Die Hard* on a bus'; and *Olympus Has Fallen* (2013) was criticised for being a poor *Die Hard* rip-off: it was one of two films that year dealing with a terrorist attack on the White House, the other being *White House Down,* which was less popular with audiences. In a similar vein was the 1997 film *Air Force One,* in which American president Harrison Ford has to rescue everyone when terrorists hijack the presidential plane.

Aeroplanes were a popular target for terrorists in the 1970s until changes in airport security made it much more difficult to get weapons onto a plane. Probably the most famous of these terrorist incidents was the 1976 hijacking of a passenger plane by Palestinian terrorists and the mission by Israeli commandoes to free the hostages at Entebbe Airport in Uganda. It has been the subject of numerous non-fiction accounts and several movies, the best-known of which is probably *Raid on Entebbe* (1977) a television film from NBC starring Charles Bronson that received a cinema release in Europe.

Embassy buildings have always been a target for terrorists for both bombings and hostage-taking. The Iranian Embassy siege in London in 1980 served as inspiration for *Who Dares Wins* (1982), in which a British SAS Captain infiltrates a radical political group who are plotting an attack against visiting American dignitaries. The location changed to a US Embassy in order to improve the film's chances of success in America and rather than Iranian extremists, the terrorists were anti-nuclear protestors. The story synopsis is said to have been written in a week by George Markstein and it was then written as a novel by James Follett – published as *The Tiptoe Boys* – with Reginald Rose adapting it into a screenplay as the novel was completed. The live television footage of the six-day siege had been so dramatic that the producers wanted to get their movie out before anyone else used the idea. The 2017 film *6 Days,* based on Rusty Firmin and Will Pearson's non-fiction book *Go! Go! Go!* (2011), is a more faithful account of the same events: Firmin was 'SAS Blue Team – back door Assault Team Leader' during the rescue of the hostages.

The Iran hostage crisis (1979-1981) saw the US Embassy in Tehran taken over and fifty-two diplomats and civilians held hostage for 444 days; there was an ill-fated attempt at a military solution, Operation Eagle Claw, in April 1980 and the hostages were finally released in January 1981 following a period of negotiation. Six diplomats who had not been in the embassy at the time of the siege were rescued by a joint CIA and Canadian mission – the 'Canadian Caper' – in January 1980: these events inspired the 2012 film *Argo*.

The Lebanon hostage crisis (1982-1992) occurred during the Lebanese Civil War and involved the kidnapping of 104 people from 21 countries. Among them were Terry Waite, Special Envoy of the Archbishop of Canterbury, who wrote of his captivity in the books *Taken on Trust* (1993) and *Footfalls in Memory* (1995); Irish academic Brian Keenan, who wrote *An Evil Cradling* (1991) and the English journalist John McCarthy, who with Jill Morrell wrote *Some Other Rainbow* (1993): the McCarthy and Keenan accounts formed the basis of the 2003 film *Blind Flight*.

Foreign hostages have also been taken in Afghanistan, Iraq, Nigeria, Pakistan and Somalia. Freelance photographer Daniel Rye was captured in Syria by ISIS in 2013 and spent thirteen months in captivity along with 18 other hostages: his story is told in the book *The ISIS Hostage* (2016) by Puk Damsgård.

In my research I didn't come across many political thrillers featuring individual hostages – but an interesting example of this type of story is the film *Five Fingers* (2006) in which a Dutch pianist working for a charity in Morocco is kidnapped by terrorists who try and extract information from him about where the funding for the charity came from: only at the end is the true nature of the terrorist plot revealed.

9 | Legal Thriller

What is a Legal Thriller?
The legal thriller takes the conventions of the thriller genre – notably suspense and/or conspiracy – and uses them in a story that centres on the legal system. The legal practices and procedures are not just a backdrop against which the story is set – the law is a key part of the working of the plot. There are several types of story that can be included under the heading 'legal thriller,' and they can broadly be classed as whodunits, chases, and courtroom thrillers.

The 'whodunit' legal thriller typically features a lawyer in the role of detective – the Perry Mason series is probably the best-known example. I have covered the whodunit genre in the book *Mystery*. The 'chase' legal thriller is a variation on the 'manhunt' or amateur-on-the-run story that I cover elsewhere in this book: it features a hero who has to deal with some sort of illegal conspiracy and who takes action, for the most part, outside the procedures of the legal system to bring an end to the conspiracy. John Grisham's *The Firm* is a good example of this type of story. The type of story I want to explore in this chapter is the 'courtroom' legal thriller. These stories feature a criminal trial as a significant part of the plot, with the climax of the plot usually focusing on the final verdict of the jury.

A traditional detective story typically ends with the culprit being taken away to 'face justice.' The legal thriller is concerned more with what comes after – the preparation for the trial and the court proceedings. In the traditional murder mystery, we see witnesses interviewed, clues gathered, and then the Great Detective gathers everyone together in the drawing room and explains the two possible versions of the story – the one that the murderer wants people to believe, that is, what *seems* to have happened, and then what *really* happened. Both versions seek to explain the facts of the situation, but only one of them is true. The courtroom drama is very similar to this 'drawing room scene' but instead of the detective explaining both stories, opposing lawyers each present their version – one tells how the evidence shows that the defendant is innocent, the other tells how the evidence shows the defendant is guilty. The jury must then decide whether the case against the defendant has been *proven* to be the truth.

In the legal *thriller*, there is usually very little *mystery* as such – we typically know the identity of the accused and often know whether or not they are guilty of the crime, or we learn this sometime before the climax. But there is *suspense* inherent in the structure of legal proceedings, as the reader or viewer – along with the characters – awaits the final verdict. Even when they know whether the defendant is innocent or guilty, they do not know which way the jury will decide. The verdict can be one of four outcomes:

(i) an innocent person is found innocent
(ii) a guilty person is found guilty
(iii) an innocent person is found guilty
(iv) a guilty person is found innocent

The first two are what we would expect to happen – they are the 'correct' outcome and show that the legal system has delivered *justice* in the manner it is meant to. The second two are – on the face of it – examples of injustice. Legal thrillers often use (iii) and (iv) to demonstrate that the operation of the legal system is in some way flawed. And if (i) and (ii) are used, they may be used in an ironic manner – as in Scott Turow's *Presumed Innocent* – and again serve as criticism of some aspect of the legal process.

The guilt or innocence of a defendant is not the main concern of the legal thriller – it is not a person who is on trial in these stories but rather the law itself or (more often) the legal system. Legal thrillers raise two important questions: Does the legal system deliver justice? And, What does it mean if it can't? The answer to these questions come at the *climax* of the story, when the verdict of the jury is revealed, and in the *resolution* that comes after.

As we will see later, the courtroom battle is typically an uneven match with the 'good guys' consisting of a lone lawyer or small team, and the 'bad guys' being a big team from a big evil law firm. These two sides represent the two sides of the issue the author wishes to explore in terms of 'What's wrong with our legal system?'

I should note here that the plot structures and themes I discuss below apply to legal thrillers in novels and films, but that things can be very different in television. In TV shows, big law firms may have one or two flawed characters – because they're the best kind of characters to write about – but the firm itself isn't usually portrayed as inherently 'evil.'

A quick note on spelling and terminology. I use 'British' English spellings for most of the text in this book, but because the legal thriller is a predominantly American genre and most of the examples discussed are American movies and novels, I'm going to use 'American' English spellings in this chapter for words like *defense*. And to avoid confusion with terminology – attorney, barrister, solicitor – I'm going to use the term 'lawyer' as far as possible.

The Appeal of the Legal Thriller

We all want to believe that our legal system delivers justice – that the guilty are found guilty and the innocent are found innocent, and that justice is dispensed within the spirit of the law and not just the letter of the law. We also want to believe that the justice system applies the law equally to all, and that wealthy people and big businesses can't buy an innocent verdict if they are in fact guilty. We want to believe that if we were to find ourselves in the courtroom, we would get a fair trial. We *want* to believe these things. But we have these nagging doubts – some irrational and some based on stories we see in the media. Like all thrillers, the legal thriller plays on our fears.

But legal thrillers also *reassure* us. They tell us that problems do have solutions. These stories have an internal logic, cause and effect, that makes sense to us in a way that real life often does not. As Paul Gewirtz says, "It is the sustained process of imposing legal order on criminal violence that reaffirms life's disorder can be controlled." It tells us that even if big evil law firms conspire to prevent justice being done, there will always be heroic lone lawyers who will work tirelessly to thwart the conspiracy, and that no matter what the odds, they will succeed. Part of the appeal of the legal thriller is seeing the little man standing before the faceless, emotionless edifice of big business and not being afraid to hold them to account. We like stories of underdogs who face impossible odds. David vs. Goliath. The lawyer-hero is often compared to the lone gunslinger who rides into a Western town and is not afraid to take on the corrupt officials that run the place.

The courtroom itself also has a particular appeal to readers. The proceedings are formal and structured, almost ritualistic, and the people involved have defined roles to play. Rituals – such as the marriage ceremony – mark important life changes, and a legal trial has a similar impact. Fred R. Shapiro and Jane Garry write that the "... law court is the forum in which intensely private actions and motives are subjected to public scrutiny; it is a stage upon which past deeds enacted in the grip of fear, sexual passion, or rage – or just in cold blood – are reconstructed in order to arrive at a truth of what happened and to ensure that justice is done." Legal thriller writer and former trial lawyer Jeremiah Healy says, "... it is ultimately this interweaving of the public aspects of the law with the impact they have on people's private lives ... that gives the legal thriller sub-genre its extraordinary capacity to captivate both readers and writers."

The adversarial nature of the legal thriller also has an inbuilt appeal. Larry A. Winters, author of the Jessie Black legal thrillers, compares it to a game or a sport, "It is a competition, played by one lawyer against another, governed by rules, and at the end, one side has decisively won ... We root for the players in the courtroom in the same way we root for the athletes in a nail-bitingly close game."

Readers and audiences tend to prefer stories where the *stakes* are high and where it is fairly obvious what is at stake. In the legal thriller and the courtroom drama the stakes relate to what the defendant could lose if found guilty – he might lose money if he is fined; he might lose his freedom, if he is imprisoned; he might lose his family or his job; and in the case of murder, he might lose his life. There is also something else at stake – *justice*. People tend to respond very strongly when they become aware of an injustice – they are aware that something is wrong, and they have a strong desire to see it put right. If you can suggest, during the course of your story, that an injustice is being committed and that those responsible are about to get away with it, you are likely to arouse strong feelings in your reader. And the reader is likely to keep turning the pages to discover if justice prevails. They will be willing the good guys on to victory, happy to know that in a post-Watergate world of cynicism, corruption, and the rise of the faceless, unfeeling corporation, there are still individuals out there prepared to risk all in the pursuit of fairness and honesty.

Another reason why courtroom thrillers appeal to both readers and writers is that the structure of a criminal trial – which we will explore in more detail later – is very much like the structure of a story. Within that overall structure, it also features two lawyers who tell a story to the jury and to the reader. In the film *Amistad*, John Quincy Adams (played by Anthony Hopkins) says, "I realized, after much trial and error, that in the courtroom, whoever tells the best story wins. In un-lawyerlike fashion, I give you that scrap of wisdom free of charge."

Some people, especially those in the legal profession, have criticised the legal thriller because it is critical of the law and the legal system and because it portrays lawyers who are unethical or criminal. But the truth is, a nice lawyer achieving justice for a nice client against a gentlemanly opposing counsel does not make for a dramatic story. In the thriller especially, you need good guys and bad guys; you need dastardly deeds – exaggerated ones, and you need high stakes. Legal thrillers may sometimes seem unrealistic because they make everything much larger-than-life, but their authors do this deliberately to make the issue at the heart of the story more obvious and more clear-cut than it is in reality, bringing the issue out of the shadows and raising awareness of it.

Historical Development of the Legal Thriller

Stories about the legal system have been around for as long as there has been a legal system. Plato and Xenophon wrote contemporary accounts of Socrates' trial for impiety and corruption in 399 BC and William Shakespeare's *The Merchant of Venice* (1597) is one of the earliest courtroom dramas and it introduces the first (unlicensed) female lawyer in the character of Portia. But as with all fiction genres, the legal thriller grew out of late nineteenth-century popular fiction and gradually developed during the first half of the twentieth century. Scott Turow's *Presumed Innocent* (1987) is often identified as the first fully-fledged modern legal thriller. A number of writers contributed to the development of this sub-genre and there are several key works, including plays and movies, that helped define it – I've included some of those highlights below.

Wilkie Collins' novel *The Woman in White* is referred to as an early example of the detective mystery, but it is closer to a thriller that includes some elements of detective work. In her article 'Collins to Grisham: A Brief History of the Legal Thriller,' Marlyn Robinson says Collins "… was the first to bring together the innocent person, a conspiracy, suspense, the detective, the legal system, [in] what was known at the time as the 'sensation novel,' in short, a legal thriller."

Collins studied law and was called to the bar in 1851, though he did not practice. He met Charles Dickens in 1851 and became a writer for Dickens' *Household Words* magazine. His first work drawing on his legal experience was 'The Lawyer's Story of a Stolen Letter,' published in 1954 and perhaps inspired by Edgar Allan Poe's 'The Purloined Letter.' The hero is a lawyer who agrees to recover a letter being used to blackmail a young couple. Collins' novel *The Woman in White* first appeared in instalments in another Dickens magazine, *All the Year Round*, beginning at the end of November 1859. It centres on a conspiracy to cheat a young woman out of her inheritance and is critical of the failure of the law, at that time, to protect a woman's rights in such cases. The story is told from the points of view of four characters, one of them a family solicitor who has failed to protect the young woman's interests, and it is presented – as the author himself notes at the beginning – in the form of testimony as it would be presented before a judge.

Marlyn Robinson writes that Collins used legal themes in many of his stories: "*No Name* deals with the legal rights of illegitimate children; *Armadale* focuses on the societal views of prostitution and abortion; *Heart and Science* is based on the true story of a man who was tried and acquitted under the Vivisection Act; *Evil Genius* details divorce and child custody law." *The Moonstone,* perhaps Collins' best-known work, was based on a real-life trial. Collins also explored issues arising from marriage laws in Britain in his time, notably in *The Law and the Lady* and in *Man and Wife,* which Robinson describes as 'a thriller, rather than a detective story' and also "a carefully crafted mystery which leads us through a rabbit warren of bigamy, death, wild night rides, disappearances, and mistaken identities, all of which comes to a neat conclusion wherein justice wins out, in spite of the legal system."

Melville Davisson Post wrote three collections of stories about lawyer Randolph Mason beginning in 1896. Initially, Mason was an amoral anti-hero who used his knowledge of loopholes and technicalities to help his clients avoid justice for crimes up to and including murder. Criticised for these stories, Post argued that he was drawing the public's attention to weaknesses in the law that ought to be remedied.

Erle Stanley Gardner probably did more than any other writer to develop the image of lawyers in fiction. He wrote his first Perry Mason story, *The Case of the Velvet Claws*, in 1933 and around eighty more followed until the author's death in 1970. Perry Mason appeared in radio and film adaptations but was best known from the television portrayal by Raymond Burr. Gardner's novels were mysteries rather than thrillers. In his book *Perry Mason: The Authorship and Reproduction of a Popular Hero,* Dennis Bounds summarised their plots: "What if an innocent man or woman, who has every reason in the world to commit a murder, has little more than a flimsy alibi to prove to the police that he or she did not, is implicated and arrested for that murder, and gets attorney Perry Mason to defend him or her? ... the plot continues in a trajectory toward the climactic moment – usually at a hearing or trail – where the actual murderer is revealed." Perry Mason's courtroom performances are dramatic and occasionally questionable, but his argument is, "If the District Attorney would be fair, then I could be fair."

In his study of the legal thriller, Lars Ole Sauerberg writes that in the "... postwar decades three strong novels featuring the American courtroom were written – Herman Wouk's *The Caine Mutiny* (1951), Robert Traver's *Anatomy of a Murder* (1958), and Harper Lee's *To Kill a Mockingbird* (1960)." The three novels he lists are essential reading for anyone interested in writing in this subgenre.

Herman Wouk's novel *The Caine Mutiny* (1951) spent 122 weeks on *The New York Times* bestseller list and was awarded the Pulitzer Prize. It was inspired by Wouk's own experiences aboard a destroyer-minesweeper in the Pacific during World War II. A film adaptation featuring Humphrey Bogart was released in 1954. It tells of a first officer in the U.S. Navy who becomes concerned that his captain, Queeg, is showing signs of mental instability. As a typhoon approaches and he fears that Queeg's erratic behaviour will jeopardise the ship and crew, the first officer relieves the captain of command. As a result, he faces a court-martial and this trial provides the climax of the plot. The story explores the moral and ethical decisions faced by captains at sea and also the issue of 'battle fatigue' and how this can affect decision-making. Scherr and Farber write that *The Caine Mutiny* film "... contains a series of excellent scenes involving client interviewing and counseling, as well as some classic trial scenes focused on effective direct and cross and closely-calibrated trial strategy."

When *Robert Traver* (John D. Voelker) began writing *Anatomy of a Murder*, he had been a successful prosecutor and a defense lawyer and wanted to write an authentic courtroom drama. As he says in his 1982 introduction, "... I had a small ax of my own to grind. For a long time I had seen too many movies and read too many books and plays about trials that were almost comically phony and overdone, mostly in their extravagant efforts to overdramatise an already inherently dramatic human situation. I longed to try my hand at telling about a criminal trial the way it really was ... I felt equally strongly that a great part of the tension and drama of any major felony trial lay in its very understatement, its pent and almost stifled quality, not in the usually portrayed shoutings and stompings and assorted finger-waggings that almost inevitably accompanied the sudden appearance and subsequent grilling of that monotonously dependable last-minute witness..."

In the novel, a small-town lawyer defends a US Army Lieutenant, Manny Manion, charged with murdering a local barkeeper. The barkeeper, a violent and bigoted man, allegedly raped Manion's wife. There is no doubt that Manion fired the fatal shot, but was it cold-blooded murder? Much of the story focuses on the trial, during which the local lawyer tries to out-argue a bigshot prosecutor brought in from out of town. Voelker injected another note of realism into the story by giving each of his characters their own motivations and moral standpoint, rather than simply having them serve a function in the plot. There is a degree of witness coaching – which violates legal ethics – on both sides, effectively showing the commission of a crime as part of the process of seeking justice.

Anatomy of a Murder was published at the beginning of 1958. It was listed on *The New York Times* Bestseller list for 62 weeks. A film adaptation directed by Otto Preminger was released by Columbia Pictures in 1959. According to Marlyn Robinson, "Voelker's careful attention to correct legal procedure and the cynical finale raised a new standard for future legal thrillers."

Harper Lee's novel *To Kill a Mockingbird* (1960) spent 88 weeks on the bestseller lists, won the Pulitzer Prize and is estimated to have sold more than 40 million copies since its publication. The 1962 film adaptation featured Gregory Peck. Set in a small Alabama town during the 1930s, the story tells of a white lawyer, Atticus Finch, who defends a black man accused of raping a young white woman. Despite a convincing defence argument and a passionate closing speech, the all-white jury finds the man guilty. In revenge for exposing her own guilt in court, the young woman's father attacks Atticus Finch's children. The novel explores issues of racial prejudice, class, and the loss of innocence. Its approach to legal issues and its depiction of the lawyer as hero have been widely discussed in legal journals.

One final author to consider as influencing the subsequent development of the legal thriller is *Barry Reed*. Reed was an attorney who specialised in medical malpractice, personal injury, and civil litigation cases. His 1980 novel *The Verdict* tells the story of a near-bankrupt lawyer who takes on a medical malpractice case against two doctors after a pregnant woman goes into a persistent vegetative state. The odds are against him since he is up against the Catholic church, the hospital, a hostile judge, and one of the city's most successful attorneys. The hero is offered an easy way out, and enough money to solve his financial problems, when the hospital offers a substantial out of court settlement, but rather than sell out the victim he decides to see real justice for her by taking the case to trial. A film adaptation was scripted by David Mamet and directed by Sidney Lumet, with Paul Newman in the lead role.

The two biggest names in the modern legal thriller genre are Scott Turow, whose novel *Presumed Innocent* was the first bestselling legal thriller and sparked off the popularity of the genre, and John Grisham, who has published a bestselling legal thriller almost every year since the appearance of *The Firm* in 1988.

Scott Turow received his degree from Harvard Law School in 1978 and then became an Assistant U.S. Attorney in Chicago. His first legal thriller *Presumed Innocent* was published in 1987. The novel spent 45 weeks on *The New York Times* bestseller list. The movie adaptation starring Harrison Ford and directed by Sydney Pollack was released in 1990. In June 1990, *Time* magazine featured Turow on the cover and described him as 'Bard of the Litigious Age.' He also wrote the non-fiction work *Ultimate Punishment: A Lawyer's Reflections on Dealing with the Death Penalty* (2003).

John Grisham graduated from the University of Mississippi School of Law in 1981 and practised criminal law for almost a decade, specialising in criminal defence and personal injury litigation. His first novel, *A Time to Kill*, was published in 1988 and garnered little attention. His second novel, *The Firm* (1991), spent forty-seven weeks on *The New York Times* bestseller list and was turned into a successful movie starring Tom Cruise. Eight of Grisham's novels have been made into films.

The Law in Legal Thrillers

Legal thrillers are concerned with the *law*, its application within the *legal system*, and whether or not this results in *justice* being served. It is important to understand the difference between these three things – and the relationships between them. The law is an implement (a tool); the legal system applies that tool (like a workman), and justice should be the final product. As in all areas of human endeavour, the tool and the workman may both be flawed, but together they can still produce incredible pieces of craftsmanship. The same is true for justice.

I should make it clear here – if it isn't clear already! – that I don't hold a law degree. In this chapter, I am trying to present the broad theories of the law and the legal system as they relate to thriller-writing. If you are going to write a legal thriller, you will need to research the detail relating to laws and legal procedures in the jurisdiction within which your story is set.

Justice is one of the 'virtues' that have come down to us from the ancient Greeks and Romans. It relates to moderation and to having no more and no less than your fair share. For our purposes here, it relates to the way in which *fairness* is administered. There are two approaches to the administration of justice. Retributive justice is concerned with punishment for wrongdoing and is directed at the perpetrator. Restorative justice – or 'reparative justice' – focuses on restoring what is good, a return to balance, and focuses on the needs of both victims and offenders.

Justice is often represented by an image or statue of the Roman goddess Justitia (or 'Lady Justice'). She is typically depicted as holding a sword and balance scales, and she may or may not wear a blindfold. The sword is a symbol of authority and it has also been suggested that it denotes the fact that justice can be swift and final. The balance scales represent the weighing of evidence. The blindfold is intended to show impartiality, that justice should be applied without regard to wealth, power, or other status. The blindfold was not used in Roman depictions of the goddess but was added towards the end of the 15th century.

The Law. In order for people to live together in social groups, it is necessary to have agreement on what is, and is not, acceptable behaviour. The rules governing behaviour – and any disputes arising from them – would originally have been decided by either a single leader or a group of elders. As social groups became larger and relationships within and between them became more complex, the system of rules governing behaviour also grew in complexity. We now refer to this system of rules as 'law.' The word comes from Old Norse and means 'something laid down or fixed.'

In the modern world, law can be created in the form of formal *statutes* set down by a legislative body (referred to as 'civil law' or 'statutory law') or they can be established through *precedent*, whereby a judge rules on a specific instance and that ruling is then applied to any subsequent instances of a similar situation (referred to as 'common law' or 'case law'). Laws may also be influenced by a constitution, written or implicit, and the rights set down within it. John Grisham, in his Author's Note in *The Last Juror* (2004) notes that "Very few laws remain the same. Once enacted, they are likely to be studied, modified, amended, then often repealed altogether. This constant tinkering by judges and lawmakers is usually a good thing. Bad laws are weeded out. Weak laws are improved. Good laws are fine-tuned."

In England and the United States, there are effectively two branches of the law: *criminal law* relates to conduct that is considered harmful to social order and *civil law* (not to be confused with statutory law above) which involves the resolution of disputes between individuals or organizations. Legal thrillers usually feature stories centred on criminal law cases. Because legal thrillers typically take place – at least in part – in the courtroom, they are more likely to be set in countries with a tradition of common law (or case law), where the courtroom has a more prominent role.

The Legal System. The procedures followed by courts and the different parties involved in legal cases are controlled by procedural law and influenced by tradition. The United States Constitution and the United States Bill of Rights contain a number of provisions relating to the law of criminal procedure. Other sources of procedural law are federal and state statutes and rules, with each state having its own rules applying to proceedings in court. In England and Wales procedure is covered by a number of Acts of parliament.

In this chapter, we are mainly concerned with stories about the law and the legal system in the United States because that is where most published legal thrillers are set. The law in England and Wales is very similar (Scotland is a separate jurisdiction), but comparatively few legal thrillers have been written in the UK. I have seen little coverage of legal thrillers written in other countries, other than British-based author Vish Dhamija who writes about the Indian legal system and Gianluca Arrighi who has written several novels set within the Italian legal world.

Courtroom procedure within the common or case law tradition is by nature adversarial. Two sides, the prosecution and the defense, present their cases with an omnipotent and neutral judge – often regarded as a 'lawgiver' – presiding over a contest that has been compared to a battle or gladiatorial contest, a game, or a medieval joust. This adversarial system is used, according to Judith A. McMorrow, because it "... envisions that we will come closest to the truth if each side is provided an opportunity to present his or her best case, with a neutral decision-maker examining the best facts and analysis of each side." The neutral decision-maker is typically a jury of the accused's peers whose function is to test the facts and decide whether the case against the accused is proved with no shadow of a doubt. The courtroom requires playing by the rules – failure to do so can lead to losing the game, irrespective of the rights and wrongs of the case. Generally speaking, if the laws and rules regarding procedures are not followed, then a mistrial may be declared or – in the event of proceedings having been completed and a judgment rendered – the defendant may appeal the conviction.

An important element of this system is that a defendant in a criminal case is *presumed innocent* such that the prosecution has a legal obligation to *prove* the defendant guilty – this is referred to as the 'burden of proof.' If a defendant is guilty, but the prosecution cannot prove his guilt, then the defendant must be set free. The goal is *not* to determine right and wrong, the goal is to *prove the case* within the rules of the system. This is an issue that non-lawyers often have an issue with and is an area where the popular concept of justice does not necessarily accord with the *legal* concept of justice. Lawyers are often viewed as perpetrating an 'injustice' by getting their client off on a legal 'technicality.' But from the point of view of legal professionals and the law, it is better that ten guilty men go free than for one innocent man to be punished. The public tends to reject this – unless they find themselves in the position of the one innocent man. This conflict between 'popular justice' and 'legal justice' is often explored in legal thrillers. Author and lawyer, Paul Levine, is critical of those who complain about legal protections such as the "Fourth Amendment's ban on unreasonable searches and seizures..." as being mere technicalities.

Related to the operation of the legal system are issues of legal ethics, particularly in relation to the behaviour of members of the legal profession: we will explore these issues under *Themes* below.

Everything I Know About the Law I Learned from the Movies

How accurate is the depiction of the law that we see in legal thriller movies and books? There has been a great deal of criticism about the way courtroom scenes are depicted in films, often focusing on behaviour that would not be permitted in a real courtroom. Members of the legal profession often complain that the only information the public gains about the law and the legal system comes from the media – that is, from movies, television shows, novels and news reports of the more sensational trials such as the O. J. Simpson case. This causes laypeople to have a distorted understanding of how the system works.

Author Jeremiah Healy believes that it is only right that citizens in a democratic society should have an interest in the legal system. "However, it's pretty hard even for an intelligent layperson to pick up a scholarly treatise on some aspect of legal doctrine and try to stay awake ... The beauty of the legal thriller is that the author writing the novel must also orient the reader on the law driving the plot." It is not only legal thriller writers who believe there is merit in what the popular media shows us about the legal system. Alex Scherr and Hillary Farber in an article titled 'Popular Culture as Lens in Legal Professionalism,' argue that movies and other media can also be helpful in teaching law students about issues within their chosen field, because they "... do not just report the events but also provide contextual information that may be useful to one's analysis, such as relationships between the parties, personal motivations, social status, the importance of this conflict in the actor's life, and sometimes even the origin of the dilemma ... By their very nature, stories encourage the audience to identify with the actors involved and to feel a personal stake or investment in reaching a particular resolution." And Steven O. Rosen in a paper aimed at lawyers titled 'Ethical Lesson from Courtroom Lawyers in the Movies,' shows how scenes from films can help teach lawyers about specific aspects of their role: "Films can show us how to argue motions, tell a compelling story in an opening statement, prepare witnesses for trial testimony, examine and cross-examine witnesses, and deliver a closing argument. Courtroom scenes in movies also illustrate ethical issues that trial lawyers regularly encounter, and possible strategies for success."

Where lawyers *do* have legitimate cause for complaint is in the sometimes inaccurate depiction of courtroom proceedings and in the depiction of unethical lawyers, both of which we will explore in more detail later in this chapter.

The Lawyer-Author

A large proportion of legal thriller authors have legal qualifications and have practised in some professional role. Does this mean that you are required to have a law degree to be able to write a legal thriller? No. But you do need to have access to reliable information about the law and legal processes – ideally from both desk research and discussions with qualified legal practitioners – and you should probably have someone with professional experience read through those sections of your story that rely of aspects of the law and on legal procedures.

There are advantages to having legal qualifications and experience. "Why do readers hunger for legal fiction written by lawyers?" Mary Beth Pringle asks. "For the thrill of knowing that an insider is telling the story, presenting details that give the novel an authentic feel."

Writing Legal Arguments
There are a number of resources – published in print and online – aimed at lawyers who have to prepare written legal arguments and/or present arguments in court. The techniques described are based on the principles of logic and rhetoric originally set down by the Ancient Greeks, which you may remember from school – particularly if you took part in any form of debate. I think it is helpful for writers in all genres to have a familiarity with these principles because we can adapt the formal structure of an argument and use it when we come to have our characters express their own point of view on a central issue in our story.

Genre Conventions

David Ray Papke writes that just as the fictional courtroom is common across works, so are the 'dramatis personae' who appear there. "Characters march into ... courtrooms full of fear, anger, confusion, and determination. They also arrive in one predictable category or another. Readers and viewers can immediately place and process them under the rubrics of judge, jury, prosecutor, defense counsel, and defendant." Christine Alice Corcos drills down to provide more detail about the 'archetypal characters' found in the courtroom – "the ambitious defense lawyer who stops at nothing to obtain an acquittal; the honorable and idealistic lawyer fighting a lone battle to protect a downtrodden and innocent defendant; the cynical and crooked district attorney prepared to railroad an innocent defendant for the sake of his career; the underpaid and overworked prosecutor protecting society from serial killers and uncaring corporate polluters; the bribe-taking judge unfairly overruling the desperate defense attorney's objections; or the courageous jurist suffering with her family through bomb threats and anonymous letters because of a controversial case."

Papke notes that the "... defendants and litigants in the courtroom trial ... play a surprisingly limited role ... the attorneys tend to be the most developed characters. Often they are involved personally, moralistically, or politically with the defendant or at least with the cause or issue represented by the case."

The Lawyer-Hero

Terry White in his introduction to *Justice Denoted* says that protagonists can be "... judges, jurors, legal investigators, paralegals or various minions of some lawyer like private eyes," but that they are predominantly lawyers. More specifically, the lawyer-hero is usually young and idealistic with a strong moral and ethical code of their own. They are young – and often newly qualified – because this allows the author to show that they have not yet been 'corrupted' by a big evil law firm. Such a character also gives us, as writers, an opportunity to have older, more experienced characters explaining aspects of the law and the legal system to their new colleague, without making the explanations look like unnatural info-dumps aimed solely at the reader.

The lawyer-hero also tends to be some sort of 'outsider.' As Jason Bainbridge points out, while the hero remains a part of the legal system, he must often operate outside the usual scope of his role as a lawyer – and sometimes he must act in direct contravention of the system to achieve justice for his client. "Indeed, this has become a narrative expectation for legal thriller writers." Or as Mary Beth Pringle puts it, the hero's "rebellion takes place within the system." Terry Kay Diggs compares John Grisham's outsider heroes to characters from a Frank Capra film, saying that they "emerge from outside the metropolis, only to face the ridicule of the power elite." This is one of the ways in which writers in all genres help to create sympathy for and/or empathy with their hero characters. It is not necessary for the hero to come from an 'outside' place – often he chooses to put himself on the outside. In *To Kill a Mockingbird,* Atticus Finch placed himself outside his own community when he chose to defend the rights of Tom Robinson to the extent that the safety of his own children was put at risk. And at the end of the story, we see him operate outside the legal system, effectively engaging in a 'cover-up', to ensure that justice, as he sees it, can be served.

What makes the lawyer-hero heroic? Author Larry A. Winters believes lawyers make good heroes because they are a "champion of other people" and we "admire people who fight for others." The lawyer-hero is "usually portrayed as a defender of the underdog or a seeker of justice, with a single-minded and selfless drive to help his or her client or society in general ... [they] often single-handedly engaged in an epic showdown between good and evil, fighting on behalf of someone in need. Who wouldn't root for a hero like that?" Carrie Menkel-Meadow has said that "... today's hero must be effective and must act; it is not enough to be idealistic and to care about justice or good causes." She also recognises the sort of lawyer-hero who has 'the courage to keep representing unpopular clients.' (see 'Defending the Indefensible' below). Terry White adds that the heroic lawyer "... must put herself at risk. She or he must be able to risk more than the social embarrassment of misconstruing a legal technicality in front of a veteran trial judge."

The Lawyer-Villain
A hero needs a worthy opponent and to achieve high levels of drama and suspense, a writer has to create a villain who seems much more powerful than the hero. We like our heroes to face overwhelming odds. The lawyer who opposes our hero in the courtroom is usually an expert with years of experience. He is older and projects an image of authority. He is also an accomplished storyteller

– he has appeared in front of juries many times before – and he is a skilled performer. All of this lends him an air of confidence that he uses to draw the jury members in – I'm an expert, you can trust me to do my job right, I'm telling you the truth. Readers like to see an expert at work – this is one of the appeals of the traditional murder mystery, where we see the detective methodically working his way through the problem and arriving at the solution.

But readers also like to see the underdog succeed – especially if his opponent is someone who is wealthier and/or more powerful than him. Ordinary people often dislike arrogant, smarmy lawyers. The expert may make the young lawyer on the opposite side look shabby and amateurish, but this can work in the underdog lawyer's favour because we are typically more like him than the expert. We admire the expert, but we have more sympathy for and empathy with the underdog who appears to be out-gunned.

In the legal thriller, the lawyer-villain serves as the physical representative of two things. He is the public face, the defender and apologist, for some faceless big-business corporation that has committed wrongdoing and is seeking to escape punishment for their crime. And he is a prime example of what Bergman and Asimow describe as "greedy and unethical big-firm lawyers who think nothing of cheating and have the resources to drag out disputes until their opponents are exhausted." The big bad law firm is a major theme in this sub-genre – more on this later.

A good example of the lawyer-villain is the character of Ed Concannon in *The Verdict*, played by James Mason in the film adaptation. He engages in virtually all of the unethical practices we explore in this chapter – and a few more besides. One character in David Mamet's screenplay describes Concannon as "the Prince of Fuckin' Darkness." During a scene that marks a key turning point in the story, Concannon briefly relates a story from his early days as a lawyer which allows him to present his own personal philosophy, saying that "They [the clients] don't pay you to do your best. They pay you to *win*." For him – and for all lawyer-villains – there is no interest in the truth or in justice, all that matters is winning. And getting paid for it.

In the legal thriller greed – for money and perhaps power – is usually the primary motivation for the villain, but there may also be an element of vanity or egotism involved. The powerful lawyer-villain can be arrogant – so sure of his own abilities to win the case that he may make the mistake of underestimating the opposition. He may even mock or humiliate the lawyer-hero, increasing reader sympathy for the hero and increasing our dislike for the villain.

Conspiracy

The conspiracy in a legal thriller usually involves unethical behaviour by lawyers, who are using the law and the legal system for their own ends – or the purposes of their client – rather than for the good of society. The conspiracy is designed to ensure that justice is not served. This misuse of law and legal system typically takes place in the context of a trial in a courtroom, but there are legal thrillers which don't feature a courtroom sequence. It is also possible to have a courtroom drama where there is no conspiracy, in which case the plot becomes a 'mission' to prepare for the court case and try to ensure the desired outcome for the client. But the absence of a conspiracy can limit the opportunity a writer has for including thriller elements.

The Romantic Co-Protagonist

The romantic co-protagonist in a legal thriller can be similar to the one from an amateur-on-the-run thriller but it is more likely that this character will be someone connected with the trial. Most commonly, as in *Jagged Edge,* there is a romantic relationship between lawyer and client. This works well for dramatic purposes but is a breach of the lawyer's professional ethics. Or the romance could develop between lawyers or other officials on the same side in the trial or – again dramatically but unethically – between lawyers on opposing sides in the trial. The conflict of interests that can arise as a result of inappropriate romantic relationships is covered in more detail under *Legal Ethics and Lawyers* below.

In a story like *The Rainmaker,* the romance occurs in a separate subplot that serves to force the protagonist to decide whether or not he can remain in the legal profession. And in *Presumed Innocent,* the role of romantic co-protagonist is – ironically – split between the murder victim and the protagonist's wife.

An early example of a story where a lawyer falls in love with a client is *The Paradine Case,* a 1947 Alfred Hitchcock film based on Robert Hichens' 1933 novel. Hitchcock described it as "... a love story embedded in the emotional quicksand of a murder trial." The film is not among the director's best and doesn't serve as a useful model for a legal thriller – the script is the weakest element – but the relationship between the accused woman and her lawyer makes it worth watching.

Settings

Locations used in legal thrillers can include lawyers' offices, police stations and cells, prisons, law libraries, law schools, and hospitals. Locations are also often used to highlight inequalities – between the offices of a small law firm and a big law firm, for example, or between the homes of a wealthy client and their much poorer opponent. Being a sub-genre of the thriller, the legal thriller can also make use of any locations found in the broader category. But the location most closely associated with the legal thriller is the courtroom.

Not every legal thriller features a courtroom scene, but a majority do. The courtroom is the place where the contest between the opposing counsels – between what is 'good and true' and what is 'evil and deceitful' – is decided. The courtroom has aspects of the field where a game is played, an arena where a gladiatorial fight takes place, and a debating hall where a rhetorical argument is presented. The courtroom, like the church and the hospital, is a special place. It is a place where important debates occur and where important decisions are made. Decisions that affect people's lives. It is a place where objectivity, experience, and wisdom are applied to situations which were extremely subjective and emotional. And it is a place that is important to the functioning of a democracy – in the courtroom, the decisions and actions of our politicians can be challenged; the rules and laws of our country can be challenged, and every single human being (in theory) is equal in the face of the law.

In fiction, whether novels, television or film, this location has become almost a cliché. David Ray Papke, in his article 'Conventional Wisdom: The Courtroom Trial in American Popular Culture,' nails down the description for us: "The courtroom itself is most commonly wood-paneled and well upholstered, one comparable to a courtroom in an older federal courthouse but a far cry from the peeling paint and hard plastic chairs found in many urban courtrooms. In the background are huge doors (sometimes used for dramatic entries and exits), decorative lights mounted on the walls, local and especially national flags, and most certainly stern-faced men in uniform. The judge's bench stands like an altar at the exact center-front and rises above, suggesting something higher and truer. Defense and prosecution tables are symmetrically stationed, and the jury box and rows of seats behind the bar, respectively, are the balcony and orchestra seating."

It is no coincidence that Papke's description makes the courtroom seem like a theatre set – the courtroom has frequently been compared to a stage where performances are given by the opposing lawyers. As long ago as 1966, John E. Simonett wrote an article for the *American Bar Association Journal* titled 'The Trial as One of the Performing Arts,' in which he said that "... counsel may profitably borrow from the playwright to make the dry legal bones come alive, to sharpen interest and focus attention on the issues by using the dramatic devices of exposition, complication, suspense, conflict, crisis and climax."

While the two opposing lawyers are usually familiar with the location, the courtroom is unknown territory for the client, even though he might welcome his day in court. It is also a strange new environment for most witnesses who appear, and the formal setting can have a dramatic impact on their behaviour, demeanour, and even their testimony. It is important to bear this in mind when writing courtroom scenes. Valerie Blum and Alexandra Rudolph wrote an article on the impact of the setting: "For most people, courtrooms are unfamiliar and intimidating theatres where they feel judged – and, in fact, they are." They noted some significant changes in witnesses including:

- use of more rigid formal language, technical terms, and adoption of 'legalese';
- becoming defensive and less responsive, answering questions tersely; or becoming nervous and overly responsive, providing too much information;
- 'role player' – e.g. performing in the manner of 'The Expert' or 'The CEO' or some other role they felt was expected of them;
- exhibiting a fear of public speaking (in front of the 'audience' of the jury) or of speaking in front of an authority figure (such as the imposing opposing lawyer or the judge)

As Blum and Rudolph point out, all of these things mean that the witness appears less likeable and less sympathetic to the jury – and playing a 'role' means they come across as less authentic. A nervous witness who has not been adequately prepared for the ordeal of examination and cross-examination may even say something in the courtroom that is 'worlds apart' from what they said when being questioned in a lawyer's office – this can be disastrous in the real courtroom, but quite dramatic in the fictional one!

Another location we often see is the corridor outside the courtroom itself or the steps in front of the courthouse. These are the places where unofficial business is discussed, where off-the-record conversations take place. Sometimes it is on the way out from the courtroom, and we witness the reaction to what has just happened in front of judge and jury; sometimes it is on the way in, and we have a frantic last-moment discussion – perhaps a discovery or revelation – that is going to have an impact on what goes on in the courtroom. The court steps are also where the victorious lawyer and his client will appear to give their final speech to the press. Sometimes, unscrupulous lawyers may even stop and talk to the press here while the case is still going on.

Iconography

The most iconic element, the courtroom, we have already mentioned. In it we find the judge, usually in robes and bearing a gavel – he sits alone, something between a headmaster behind his desk and a king on his throne, ready to decide the fate of a defendant. There are the witness stand and the Bible – indicating the importance of the person appearing there and the importance of them telling the truth while on the stand. Then there is the witness – perhaps nervous and sweating, or cocky and sarcastic, but in either case probably a little afraid. There is the jury of twelve honest men and women (anger optional), representing the ordinary people of the world, the defendant's peers.

Then we have the two opposing teams – the lawyers for the defense and the prosecution. Typically, we'll see a David versus Goliath situation: on one side several smartly dressed lawyers with expensive suits and expensive haircuts, supported by boxes and files of information and looking like they are well-prepared and ready for anything. On the opposite side is a lone lawyer or a lawyer and one supporter, looking a little dishevelled or very young (or both), and having little in front of him except a battered legal pad.

Also present will be police officers in uniform, representing the officers of the law who operate outside the court and bring people inside to be tried. These police officers are a part of the legal system, and at the same time are subject to it – they must do their daily work within the bounds set down by the law: if they do not, they might be the cause of justice being obstructed. Associated with these officers are the cells that represent the defendant's possible fate – a visual symbol of a person's freedom being taken away in punishment for their crimes.

Being a sub-genre of the thriller, the legal thriller can also feature any of the visuals from that broader category.

Other Characters

The Cynical Mentor. This is usually an older colleague or a retired lawyer or judge who fills the idealistic young hero in on what it is *really* like out on the battlefield. This is someone who used to have the same energy and idealism as the hero, but who has been ground down by the working of the legal system and, perhaps, even found himself corrupted by it. This sort of character challenges the hero, forcing him to examine his own beliefs and perhaps restate or confirm them. The cynical mentor also serves to show the hero – and the reader – what the stakes are, how difficult it is to fight against 'the system.' This mentor is effectively a hero who failed – this is who the hero could become if things go badly.

The Judge. In the United States, federal judges are appointed by the President and confirmed by the Senate and they retain the role for life. State court judges may be appointed locally or elected – in some jurisdictions elections for judges run alongside those for politicians and in others elections for judges take place every six to ten years. While it is argued that elected judges are more accountable to the people they serve, it can be argued that there are some risks inherent in a system which mixes law and politics in this way. In England, judges are selected by an independent body, the Judicial Appointments Commission.

The judge usually sits in an elevated position – 'the bench' – and his status is usually indicated by a black robe. In England judges in different courts wear either black or red robes and (sometimes) wigs according to somewhat complicated rules (see www.judiciary.gov.uk). The judge is meant to be an impartial 'referee' overseeing the opposing arguments of prosecution and defense lawyers.

In legal thrillers and films, as Bergman and Asimow note, "Judges are often biased, crooked, or incompetent..." They may be involved in the conspiracy being perpetrated by the lawyer-villain and/or his client, or the judge's behaviour may be influenced by interests of his own, such as re-election to (or retention of) office. Or they may simply be biased in favour of lawyers and clients who belong to their own social group.

The Jury. The jury is often depicted as a group of people with a role to perform, and only rarely do we see them characterised as individuals. Carol J. Clover has said that the reason the jury remains largely unseen in movies is that the film audience itself is positioned as the jury. There are a small number of exceptions to this: in the movie *Suspect*, one of the jurors (played by Dennis Quaid) is a central character; and in John Grisham's *The Runaway Jury*, the focus of the story is the jury as unscrupulous lawyers try to bribe, compromise, or blackmail them. The film *12 Angry Men* also deals almost exclusively with the deliberations of the jury during a trial.

Christine Alice Corcos also writes that the selection and/or actions of the jury can serve an important function in a story: "The author may elaborate on his critique of the legal system either by showing the actual questioning of the jury [during selection] or by showing the jury's deliberations. The scenes may be amusing or serious, but they often serve to communicate the impression that 'a jury of one's peers' may be neither possible nor desirable." Stories also sometimes explore to what extent the 'jury of one's peers' actually consists of people who are peers – in terms of age, status, background or ability – of the defendant.

We will also look at 'jury tampering' when we discuss legal ethics later.

Themes

Legal thrillers explore the theme of justice versus injustice, and their main thematic question is: Can justice be achieved despite the flaws inherent in the law and the legal system? They also explore the fact that there is sometimes a conflict between what people regard as 'justice' and what the law is able to deliver as a just outcome. These stories combine entertainment and social commentary to challenge readers and audiences to reconsider their assumptions about guilt versus innocence, as Corcos writes, "... by forcing him to confront the conflict between sympathy for the lawbreaker and a desire to maintain order in society." Or they ask us whether it is okay, as Judith A. McMorrow puts it, for a lawyer to "... stretch, bend or violate a rule for a good cause."

The basic format of the story typically has a lawyer-villain from a big law firm who uses unethical – and occasionally illegal – methods to manipulate the legal process in order to achieve the verdict his client wants and ensure that justice is not served. The lawyer-villain is motivated to do this by greed – his client is paying high fees for the required verdict. The lone lawyer-hero seeks to oppose the lawyer-villain and his client and must occasionally work outside the legal system to ensure that justice is served. There are other stories where the idealistic lawyer-hero is manipulated by his own client in order to guarantee the outcome that the client desires.

The lawyer-hero is motivated by his own moral code to seek the truth and try to ensure justice for his client. There are a number of thematic ideas that we can tease out of this.

- Flawed legal system – the letter of the law vs. the spirit of the law
- David vs. Goliath
- Unethical behaviour by lawyers
- Greed and the evil of big law firms

A Flawed Legal System – The Letter of the Law vs. the Spirit of the Law
Ask anyone 'What is wrong with our legal system?' and they will probably come up with a list that looks something like this: too often guilty people escape justice; sometimes innocent people are convicted; some lawyers and judges behave unethically, exploiting the weaknesses of the system; some criminals learn how to scam the system and exploit its weaknesses; and, perhaps the biggest issue of all, the legal system doesn't treat people equally and doesn't take account of the fact that society in general doesn't treat people equally. But ask people *why* these problems exist and how they might be tackled, and they will struggle to provide answers.

The law and the legal system have to try and strike a balance between punishing the guilty, helping victims, and protecting the innocent. Checks and balances have to be put in place. Constitutional rights have to be protected. And the law has to keep pace with changing social values – to take an extreme example, we no longer prosecute 'witches.'

But even if we did ever arrive at a perfect set of laws and a carefully monitored system for applying them, it would still be flawed because human beings are flawed. Our legal system relies on the evidence that is presented by flawed human beings. Eyewitnesses are unreliable and human memories are fallible. The police are not always objective in their investigations. Innocent people sometimes confess to crimes. Innocent people sometimes plead guilty because it is less risky than going to trial. Evidence – including fingerprints, forensic evidence and DNA – cannot always be trusted. Prosecutors don't always play by the rules. Juries don't always follow the instructions they have been given.

To further complicate things, even if a crime has been committed, there may be 'extenuating circumstances' that mean we have to decide whether a crime was premeditated and cold-blooded or committed in the heat of the moment and during a moment of madness. Or whether an illegal act was committed for selfish gain, as an act of vigilantism, or as a morally justifiable action.

Bearing all of this in mind, the best we can hope for is a system that dispenses justice to the best of its abilities, and to try and ensure that – as a society – we watch our watchmen and raise complaints when we feel they are straying from what we believe to be fair and just decisions and actions. But as authors, of course, we should exploit all of the weaknesses of the system to create the most dramatic stories possible. Almost every legal thriller is based around some failure in the legal system. Typically the lawyer-villain exploits some weakness in the system such that the lawyer-hero cannot obtain justice for his client by simply telling the truth. To win against a powerful and unethical opponent, the hero often has to try and redress the balance through cunning – and this may involve him taking some action outside the courtroom which is 'not quite ethical' in order to prevent the lawyer-villain succeeding with some 'massively unethical' action. In popular justice an element of 'the ends justify the means' and the 'lesser of two evils' tends to be accepted by the audience, where the legal system itself might take a very different view.

David vs. Goliath
In most legal thrillers the hero works alone or for a small law company and the opposing lawyer works for a large company with vast resources at their disposal. This works for a story in a similar way to the amateur-on-the-run – the reader or audience roots for the underdog who is battling against overwhelming odds. It is often said that, in the courtroom, the person with the best lawyer wins – and that the person with the most money can afford the best lawyer. That usually means an older, more experienced lawyer from a big law firm. As we'll see later, big law firms and their lawyers are almost always the bad guys in legal thrillers and they use all sorts of unethical practices to ensure that the hero-lawyer can't possibly win.

Legal Ethics and Lawyers
Every profession has ethical standards of behaviour to which practitioners are expected to adhere. In the United States, a good place to find information on ethical behaviour is the American Bar Association's *Model Rules of Professional Conduct*. For England and Wales, the Law Society promotes the Solicitors Regulation Authority *Code of Conduct*. A lawyer has to balance a number of interests – the public interest in the administration of justice; the client's interest; and their own interests and those of the firm that employs them. As a result,

the lawyer – according to ethical guidelines – has specific duties in respect of the *client*, the *court*, and the *legal profession*.

Duties to the Client

A lawyer has a duty to provide a proper standard of service to clients and act in their best interests, within the bounds of the law, including the protection of their money and other assets. Lawyers must also run their business, or carry out their role within a business, in a professional and competent manner, and in a way that demonstrates equality of opportunity and respect for diversity. Areas covered by these duties include:

Confidentiality – the lawyer has a duty to respect the confidentiality of their client's affairs and may not use any information about the client for the benefit of anyone else, unless authorised by the client. 'Legal professional privilege' – often referred to in stories as lawyer-client privilege – is a specific instance, or 'subset', of the duty of confidentiality.

Conflict of interest – the lawyer must avoid any situation where professional judgment or actions regarding one individual or organisation will be unduly influenced by the duty owed to a second individual or organisation. This includes avoiding situations where the lawyer's own personal interests (or those of close relations, colleagues or friends) may conflict with the duty to a client. In legal thrillers and movies, this issue often arises when a lawyer is in a relationship with someone else connected with the case, often their own client. The American Bar Association issued a *Formal Opinion* on Sexual Relationships with Clients (1992) which states that the roles of lawyer and lover "... are potentially conflicting ones as the emotional involvement that is fostered by a sexual relationship has the potential to undercut the objective detachment that is often demanded for adequate representation." Haddad also writes that such a relationship, "... may create a conflict of interest ... it may also create danger regarding attorney-client confidences." Examples include *Body of Evidence, Jagged Edge, And Justice for All,* and *Suspicion*.

Due diligence and competence – this includes the duty of a prosecutor to ensure that the rights of the (accused) defendant are respected, and the requirement to turn over any evidence that might demonstrate the defendant's innocence. A lawyer must also not commit, or encourage a client to commit, any action which impedes the due process of the law. It is in comedy films where lawyers generally appear at their least competent.

Commingling – Lawyers are absolutely prohibited from commingling a client's funds with their own, due to fact that embezzlement of such funds would be easy to commit and difficult to detect.

Self-dealing – this is a form of conflict of interest, in which the lawyer takes advantage of his position and acts for his own interests rather than those of the client. The lawyer is prohibited from misusing a client's assets or opportunities.

Effective assistance of counsel – the US Constitution guarantees the defendant the right to assistance of counsel, and this right is taken to mean representation by a *competent* attorney. The lawyer must perform to an acceptable level, such that his/her performance cannot be said to prejudice the outcome of a trial. He must also be a 'zealous advocate on behalf of a client' within the bounds of the law. McMorrow writes, "Lawyers who push the limits of the law are often seen as overzealous, but this is much less clear, for one can argue strongly that the lawyer's role includes the duty to explore the limits of the law."

Fee splitting – this is another form of conflict of interest. The lawyer is prohibited from paying a commission to a referrer for the purposes of ensuring that the referrer always directs potential clients to the lawyer.

Duties to the Court

A lawyer is required to uphold the rule of law and the proper administration of justice and to comply with legal and regulatory obligations. These duties include:

Perjury – giving a false statement under oath is an offense; it is also an offense for a lawyer to obtain, or permit a client or witness to give, an untrue statement under oath – this also includes false or misleading statements, hiding evidence, and failing to disclose all relevant facts.

Adverse authority – A lawyer has an obligation to quote the law – including precedent – in a manner which does not mislead the court. If a lawyer states that the law is X and suppresses a legal authority that says the law is not X but Y, then he is misleading the court. The lawyer has a duty to draw the court's attention to legal authorities that do not support his case.

Duties to the Profession

A lawyer has a duty to behave in a way that maintains the trust the public places in their profession and in the legal system as a whole. Areas relating to this include:

Limits on advertising – advertising by lawyers is legal in the United States but is subject to ethical rules set down by state bar associations.

Reporting misconduct – with some exceptions, a lawyer who becomes aware that another legal professional (lawyer or judge) has committed an act in violation of the rules of ethical conduct has an obligation to report the violation. Failure to report such acts is itself a violation of ethical conduct and can lead to disciplinary action.

The hero of a legal thriller will normally respect both the wording and the spirit of such ethical guidelines, while the villain and/or conspirators will violate one or more of them.

Unethical Behaviour by Lawyers

There are a number of unethical behaviours that crop up regularly in legal thrillers. Here we are thinking about *deliberate* acts, as opposed to 'errors' committed by fictional lawyers – which frequently occur and may be passed off as 'poetic licence.'

Jury tampering – sometimes referred to as 'jury nobbling' in the UK – is the crime of attempting to influence the vote, opinion, decision or other action of one or more jurors during the course of a trial through means other than the presentation of evidence in court. Attempted influence may take the form of conversations or information offered about the case outside of court, offering bribes, making threats, or approaching relatives or friends of the juror. Jury tampering can also be used to undermine the credibility of proceedings in order to argue for a mistrial. John Grisham's novel *The Runaway Jury* (1996, film version 2003) is a legal thriller based on the concept of jury tampering.

'Jury tampering' has also been used to refer to attempts to influence the composition of a jury before a trial, such as attempting to discredit potential jurors so that they will not be selected for duty. This goes beyond the normal practice of the lawyers on both sides to have input into the make-up of a jury. In England and the United States, lawyers on both sides are permitted to reject a certain number of jurors without stating a reason through *peremptory challenge* – the idea being that if both parties have contributed to the make-up of a jury, they are more likely to accept its verdict. Potential jurors may also be challenged for a reason, such as being ineligible or disqualified from serving, or being reasonably suspected of bias. In the United States, there is also the process of *voir dire* by which lawyers can question potential jurors to test whether their backgrounds or biases might prevent them deciding a case based solely on the evidence presented.

The practice of investigating the backgrounds of potential jurors – by looking at their social media profiles, for example – has been questioned, but is now generally regarded as being part of the role of a competent lawyer exercising due diligence. There are companies that carry out this sort of investigation for law companies. Ethical guidelines currently suggest that it is okay to look at what is publicly available, but that it is not permissible to request information – by sending a 'friend' request, for example – as this is regarded as communication with a (potential) juror.

Investigating all of those in a pool of jurors in order to influence the selection to obtain a jury that will be sympathetic to a client's situation can be achieved in this manner. In theory, both sides have equal opportunity to do this, so the jury selected should remain unbiased, but this is another area where access to resources and information can tip the balance in favour of a wealthy client and/or a large law firm.

Witness Intimidation. Witness intimidation occurs when an attempt is made to threaten or persuade a witness not to give evidence to the police or courts, or to give evidence in a way that is favourable to a defendant. In most cases, it is carried out by either the defendant or family or friends of the defendant. It may involve the threat of violence or an actual attack, and in extreme cases, it may include kidnapping – of the witness or someone close to the witness – or murder.

Coaching witnesses. In England the Solicitor's Code of Conduct states that, "A barrister must not ... rehearse practise or coach a witness in relation to his evidence." They may tell the witness about the process of giving evidence in court, but they may not tell them what to say. The aim is to avoid tainting evidence or encouraging a witness to make a false statement, misrepresent statistical evidence or leave out vital details. In the United States, the situation is not quite so clear-cut, in that witness 'preparation' is seen as a duty of a competent lawyer. The American Bar Association has laid down guidelines for the ethical preparation of witnesses, which serve to provide similar protection to the English rules.

War of attrition. Motions and *discovery* requests are an important part of the legal process and an important part of legal thriller stories which feature trials. Other than a 'motion to dismiss' the case, the motions typically seen in legal thrillers are motions *in limine* or moves to include, exclude, or preclude something from the trial. As an example, this might be evidence of a prior conviction long ago that might prove prejudicial in the current case. They can also be used to try and establish what is, and is not, relevant in the current case. Motions are often made in writing and include examples of case law to back up the request. Opposing counsel must read the motion and prepare a written opposition to the motion.

Discovery is a pre-trial procedure in which either party can obtain evidence from the other part by means of a request for answers to interrogatories, a request for production of documents, request for admissions and depositions. If a request is objected to, the requestor may file a motion seeking the court to compel discovery. From the client's point of view, every discovery request or motion the lawyer has to respond too is a cost burden – either in terms of an hourly fee or in terms of the lawyer spending time on that rather than preparing the client's own case. Wealthy clients who employ law firms with vast staff resources and experience can swamp a one-man operation or a small law firm with paperwork. And this can be done deliberately to get a client to abandon the case or to settle out of court in a way that is much more beneficial to the wealthy client.

Disclosure of evidence. In a criminal case, the prosecution has a legal obligation to pass on any and all evidence that might help prove the accused person's innocence. The defence is not under the same obligation to reveal its evidence, as the legal onus is on the prosecution to *prove* guilt. Innocence is assumed until they do. In legal thrillers, there are often attempts to conceal evidence by failing to provide documents, providing incomplete documents, or trying to bury the documents amid a mass of other, less relevant, papers.

Over-billing. In *The Firm,* the hero is told that he should bill the client for all of his time, even if he finds himself thinking about the case in the shower. In *The*

Verdict, the villain Concannon includes as many staff as he can in preparations for the case so that he can bill the client for their time. Over-billing has been described as the profession's dirty little secret. There is more about how and why it happens below.

Legal Technicalities and Loopholes. These are not – technically – unethical, but they come into arguments about the 'letter of the law versus the spirit of the law.' The legal profession and the public do not always agree on whether application of technicalities and loopholes actually constitutes 'justice.' Here's an example taken from the film *To Live and Die in L.A.:* "A client got busted smuggling fifty pounds of cocaine. I should be able to get him off, though. The search warrant's weak ... The color of the house is listed as brown on the warrant, when in fact it's beige and yellow."

Big Law Firms are Evil

The majority of lawyers today practice in firms. These firms range in size from two lawyers in partnership to multi-national companies with thousands of employees. Michael Asimow has noted that both among the general public and in their portrayal in feature films, law firms have a negative reputation. Some have argued that films have, at least in part, been the cause of the real-life reputation of law firms; others say that movies only exaggerate popular beliefs that are already held.

Some commentators have said that the public reputation of lawyers has steadily decreased over the decades. In the 1930s, lawyers were often portrayed as professional men and decent human beings. Atticus Finch in *To Kill a Mockingbird* is regarded as the archetypal good-guy lawyer, the ideal, and lawyers especially have complained that this type of lawyer is rarely portrayed in films today. But Asimow has pointed out that, even in the 1930s, this type of character was only found when the lawyer practised law alone: "Once movie lawyers join together into law firms ... they are portrayed quite negatively, regardless of the era."

Asimow gives a summary of this type of organisation: "Big firms are money machines run by greedy old men that eat their young and are horrible places to work if you're a half-way decent human being. In conducting litigation, big firms always deploy their superior resources to unfairly thwart righteous claims brought by their adversaries. Big firms are always on the wrong side – generally that of the vicious corporation rather than the deserving plaintiff." Examples from John Grisham's novels include the firm who represents the tobacco industry in *The Runaway Jury;* the firm that evicts poor people in *The Street Lawyer;* the crooked law firm in *The Partner;* and the greedy probate lawyers in *The Testament*.

There are two reasons why this type of law firm appears in his novels, as John Grisham told Allen Pusey: "There are a lot of small-town lawyers who are honest and hardworking. They do their jobs and serve their community – writing wills, teaching Sunday school, serving in the local legislature. But nobody wants to read about that. They want to read about the lawyer that lies to his client, steals all the money, fakes his own death and flies to Brazil. They want to read about a hard-working young lawyer who gets an offer at a law firm that on the surface is respectable, but turns out to be controlled by the mob." The second reason is down to the actions of some lawyers: "They're polluting their own profession. Just watch the TV ads, the lawyers who talk to the press during trials, and the lawyers that are just behaving badly."

Profession vs. Business

Lawyers are regarded as members of the legal *profession*, distinguishing their work from other types of trade. But they can also be thought of as a 'profit-maximising *business*' in a highly-competitive field. But what *is* the difference between a *profession* and a *business*?

As Andy Rutledge has noted, finding a reliable definition of a profession is more difficult than it should be. One from 1917 by Sidney and Beatrice Webb is often quoted: "A profession is a vocation founded upon specialised educational training, the purpose of which is to supply disinterested counsel and service to others, for a direct and definite compensation, wholly apart from expectation of other business gain."

Cruess, Johnston and Cruess have devised a modern equivalent: "An occupation whose core element is work based upon the mastery of a complex body of knowledge and skills. It is a vocation in which knowledge of some department of science or learning or the practice of an art founded upon it is used in the service of others. Its members are governed by codes of ethics and profess a commitment to competence, integrity and morality, altruism, and the promotion of the public good within their domain. These commitments form the basis of a social contract between a profession and society, which in return grants the profession a monopoly over the use of its knowledge base, the right to considerable autonomy in practice and the privilege of self-regulation. Professions and their members are accountable to those served and to society."

I think a key point to note from this definition is that a profession is effectively granted a monopoly in exchange for accepting certain responsibilities towards the public. A business, on the other hand, has no monopoly and has no public responsibilities beyond adherence to the law.

The modern law firm seems to fall somewhere between the two, and the fact that it has features of both can sometimes lead to problems – not least in terms of public perception. The perception is that law firms, particularly in the United States, have increasingly moved away from the 'professional' model and towards the 'profit-maximising business' model.

The Rise of Big Business

During the 1970s American corporations began to grow in size. These larger corporations became subject to increasing government regulation and the threat of lawsuits from employees or customers. They also faced the threat of hostile takeover by a competitor or larger corporation. The result was that they needed lawyers, and lots of them. They needed specialists in different areas of the law, and large law firms started to appear to meet these needs. The big law firms that were formed tended towards the 'profit-maximising business' model – because that was the model their corporate clients used. As Michael Asimow has said, "Money plus power usually equates to evil in the movies, and big business has plenty of each." Big law firms are themselves large profit-making businesses and their main role is to represent other big businesses. If the public views big business as bad, anyone who champions their cause or acts as their apologist is equally bad. The lawyer standing in the courtroom representing them is a much easier target than the faceless corporation itself. In legal thrillers, the 'evil' big firm lawyer typically has the role of symbolising all that the public see as wrong with big business. But this reputation also comes from some of the practices they are perceived to engage in. Scott Turow, quoted on *FiveBooks.com*, has said: "Lawyers were supposed to be the paragons and the reality that they weren't always that way came with Watergate in the seventies." I would also seek to submit the McCarthy communist witch-hunts as a second exhibit.

Scorched Earth Tactics
This is Michael Asimow's term for the litigation tactics big law firms used during the 'mammoth fights between corporations' from the 1970s onwards. "Such tactics," he says, "include unnecessarily protracted discovery and discovery abuse, frivolous and endless motions, and various delaying tactics." And he also notes that there was a "steady slide toward incivility and distrust of other lawyers."

When two behemoth-sized law firms, on opposing sides in a legal battle, behave in this way towards one another we can at least say that it is a fair fight – each side can give as good as it gets. But when a large firm uses these tactics against a much smaller law firm, or against an individual complainant, then most people would see it as an unfair fight and probably an unethical one. This is a situation which often crops up in legal thrillers such as *The Rainmaker*.

'Justice' to the Highest Bidder, No Questions Asked – and No Freebies
Can a client buy the verdict he wants if he has enough money? And if someone has no money, does that mean they will be denied justice? In both cases we want the answer to be a resounding *No!* But we have our doubts – and legal thriller writers are happy to tell us our doubts are justified. The 'profit-maximising business' model does not recognise the importance of public service or pro bono work. If someone wants justice, they have to be able to afford it – and he who has the best lawyer wins. As Terry White writes, "... nothing infuriates the common citizen more than to see the rich get away with their crimes."

In the definition of a profession quoted earlier, there was a reference to the *autonomy* of practitioners. Michael Asimow has said that this ought to apply in respect of a lawyer's relationship with his client, allowing the lawyer to play a 'mediating role.' By this he means that a professional lawyer should advise his client against taking any action that might be detrimental to the client's long-term interests, and even that a lawyer might advise clients to adopt more socially acceptable or morally acceptable behaviour. This is in line with the profession's duties to the public, but the legal profession's move closer to the 'business' model means that this kind of 'mediation' is less likely to occur. Few lawyers would risk antagonising a client by criticising either their objective or their method for achieving it – unless it involved violation of the law. Clients switch law firms much more now than they did in the past and there's always another big firm ready to come and tempt a client away. The lawyer is effectively a 'gun for hire,' paid to do what the client wants him to do and is unlikely to turn work away because it conflicts with his personal values. This is another area where the hero in the legal thriller shows himself to be an outsider – he, like the hardboiled private detective, *does* have a personal moral code and sticks to it.

Law Firm Sweatshops
There are economic benefits for large law firms, as there are for any business, allowing for the investment in resources including technology and support staff to assist the specialists in their work. Large firms are also better able to increase the return on their assets, including their staff. For example, associates and paralegals are paid an hourly wage, but those hours are billed to the client at a higher rate, generating a surplus that contributes towards the profits of the partners in the firm. The more staff a firm has billing hours in this way, the more money is generated for the partners. Associates are recruited from the best law schools and work at this hourly rate because they believe they will receive high levels of training and mentoring from partners and other experienced staff, and because they hope they will become partners themselves at some future point.

In movies and novels, big law firms are depicted as what Asimow calls 'dehumanising sweatshops.' And notes that there is evidence that in the real world, big firm associates do work 'inhuman hours, often performing chores of indescribable tedium.' They carry on because they need the money to pay off student debt, and after that they have become accustomed to a certain level of income. There is evidence that many associates are dissatisfied with their work and that there is a high attrition rate. Complaints include a lack of autonomy and poor levels of communication between associates and partners, but the main issue is the long hours. Associates are expected to bill 2,000 (or more) hours per year, and to achieve that requires close to 3,000 hours in the office. Another major complaint relates to the process for achieving partnership, with the 'rules' within a firm being criticised for being obscure and unfair, with many never achieving the partnership they had dreamed of.

Do Big Law Firms Deserve Their Negative Reputation?
Do big law firms really deserve this reputation? Michael Asimow compared examples of bad behaviour in the movies with an admittedly unscientific sampling of data from within law firms. The verdicts are in.

On the charge of operating law firms that are like sweatshops, Asimow finds big law firms guilty: the depictions of the lives of associates in firms in films like *The Firm, The Devil's Advocate, Class Action,* or *From the Hip* are 'not so very far wrong.'

On the charge of engaging in 'scorched earth' litigation tactics designed to exhaust their opponents, Asimow found these practices 'accurately portrayed' – Guilty.

On the charge of overbilling clients, doing unnecessary work which increases the number of hours billed to the client, and engaging in delaying tactics that increase the costs of the opposition, based on the evidence presented by Asimow, the verdict is guilty. "Days in which lawyers bill more than twenty-four hours are no longer rare..."

On the charge of uncivility and engaging in rude and bullying designed to intimidate other lawyers and witnesses: Guilty.

While many of the behaviours described here would be regarded as unethical or immoral by many non-lawyers, most tend to lie on the ethical side of lines drawn by the Model Rules for Professional Conduct. Based on the evidence he has seen, Asimow is inclined to believe that big law firms have little need to commit 'clear-cut ethical violations' – such as destroying critical documents or lying to the court – and stand to lose too much if they did ever engage in them. Not guilty.

The Behaviour of Small Law Firms
If big law firms are bad, what can we say of the portrayal of small law firms in films and legal thrillers? In his overview, Michael Asimow found that in films of the 1930s and 1940s lawyers in solo practice were good guys and that those who operated within small law firms were portrayed negatively, noting that the argument seemed to be that "Honest lawyers can be corrupted once they join other lawyers and start a firm." Big law firms didn't really start appearing in movies until the 1970s, at which point the small law firm was – comparatively – portrayed more positively. But even then, the small law firm's ethics were sometimes dubious and the only truly good lawyer was one who practised alone. This hierarchy – big law firms bad, small law firms better, solo lawyers best – applies to most films and legal thrillers today, with the only exceptions tending to be in television series about law firms and some films based on true stories.

Michael Asimow looked at the kinds of misbehaviour that caused lawyers from small firms to be disbarred. He said that small law firms are more likely to run into 'cash flow problems' which can lead them to steal from client trust funds. Competition for clients among small firms is also strong, which may lead them to take on "marginal cases or dubious clients and feel they have to cheat to survive financially." The same motivation lies behind the kinds of behaviour that gets some small law firms classified as ambulance-chasers. Aside from financial pressures, the other main reason for malpractice seems to be drug or alcohol addiction – in a larger law firm, a substance abuse problem is more likely to be recognised before it leads to unethical behaviour; in a small firm a lawyer may not be around colleagues who are able to recognise the problem quickly enough.

Redemption
If one of the thematic ideas is that big law firms corrupt those who work in them, there is a related theme that suggests those who give in to temptation or cynicism can redeem themselves. Mitch McDeere in *The Firm* is one character who does that, Frank Garvin in *The Verdict* is another. Many characters, in John

Grisham's novels especially, find that they have to leave the legal profession in order to live according to their own moral values, for example, Michael Brock in *The Street Lawyer*.

Defending the Indefensible

The Sixth Amendment to the United States Constitution says that when faced with a criminal prosecution, "the accused shall enjoy the right ... to have the assistance of counsel for his defence." Everyone has this right. But lawyers are sometimes criticised for defending those whom public opinion judges to be undeserving of counsel. Worse still, the defense counsel is sometimes successful and secures the accused person's release, even when the public feels certain he was guilty. The court of public opinion doesn't recognise the presumption of innocence and doesn't require that the case against the accused be proved.

The American Bar Association's Model Rules of Professional Conduct are clear on this issue: "History is replete with instances of distinguished and sacrificial services by lawyers who have represented unpopular clients and causes. Regardless of his personal feelings, a lawyer should not decline representation because a client or a cause is unpopular or community reaction is adverse." Stephen Gillers in an article titled 'Can a Good Lawyer Be a Bad Person?' points out that defense counsel serves to protect the constitutional rights of everyone from state or federal government abuse: "The criminal defense lawyer monitors the government while it pursues those it most eagerly wants to convict. The more outrageous the alleged crime, the greater may be the state's temptation to ignore rights, and so the greater the need for the defense lawyer's special knowledge. Prosecutorial excesses are hardly unknown."

Judith A. McMorrow says that "If lawyers serve an important social role in representing unpopular clients, it is only logical that lawyers should not be seen as evil or bad for providing representation to unpopular points of view. Indeed, many times we should treat those lawyers as courageous heroes."

Scapegoating

We know that an innocent man being found guilty or a guilty man being found innocent is an example of injustice, but there is a third form that is slightly less clear-cut, and that is scapegoating. Scapegoating occurs when an organisation – a corporation or the military, for example – seeks to 'pin the blame' for a crime on an individual, rather than risk having to accept responsibility as an organisation. If an innocent man is found guilty, it is obvious that an injustice has been committed. To be accused, tried and convicted for another man's crimes is a nightmarish situation. It is a less obvious, but equally frightening and unjust, situation when someone is accused of being solely responsible for a crime or crimes that were committed by a group of people. Often the accused is guilty of being involved in the commission or cover-up of the crime, but his or her role was often a minor one. The lonely defendant finds himself up against both the might of his own organisation and the organisation's big, expensive law company. These are the sorts of odds that work well in a thriller. If the defendant was a 'whistle-blower' of some kind, he or she may find themselves falsely accused of a crime, because the organisation is seeking to discredit them or gain revenge.

Bergman and Asimow in *Reel Justice* write that "Scapegoating is a frequent theme of military justice movies, such as *Breaker Morant* and *Paths of Glory*."

Legal Thriller Plots

There are two sides in any courtroom trial, the prosecution and the defense. In exploring how the plots of legal thrillers work, I am going to use one example where the protagonist is on the side of the defense and one where the protagonist is on the side of the prosecution. In both cases, I will be concentrating on the structure of the story as opposed to legal details. I will also look at what proportion of the movie or novel is taken up by the courtroom scenes. The main examples I have studied are the novel and film versions of *Presumed Innocent* and *The Rainmaker* and the film *Jagged Edge*.

The basic structure of a courtroom trial is the same in each case, so I will outline that first and then look at how the different stories use the various stages of the trial process.

The Structure of a (Fictional) Courtroom Trial

David Ray Papke has outlined the basic structure of a fiction trial as having "... two opening statements, a stretch of examinations and cross-examinations, two closing statements, and a jury verdict."

Christine Alice Corcos points out that a major difference between a fictional trial and a real trial is that in the real world the amount of information that any person has access to is limited. No one person knows *everything* that happens, no one sees every relevant event and hears every significant conversation. The reader or audience of a legal thriller or courtroom drama often has access to everything. Another difference is that in a real-world trial, nothing that happens outside the courtroom can be considered by the jury – who may not even be aware of it – and some of what occurs *inside* the courtroom can be excluded on the instruction of the judge.

Whether or not an author reveals *everything* to the reader as the story goes along depends to some extent on the effect he or she wishes to achieve. Sometimes the author will allow the reader to believe that they have *all* of the evidence to be able to decide the 'proper' outcome of the trial, only to learn at the climax of the story that vital evidence has been withheld by the author. Corcos gives the films *Witness for the Prosecution* and *Jagged Edge* as examples and says that if a story contains such a surprise twist, "... the ultimate fate of the guilty party must be morally satisfying; otherwise the author's trickery leaves the observer feeling betrayed."

Discussions about fictional trials often assume that the lawyer-hero is *defending* his client – perhaps because defending another person is regarded as more 'heroic' than prosecuting them. But as we mentioned right at the beginning, the hero may either be defending someone who is (usually) wrongly accused and innocent, *or* they are prosecuting a faceless 'evil giant corporation' on behalf of their very human client. In either case, the structure of a trial is the same and can be broken down into nine stages.

1. Pretrial

This encompasses anything that occurs before the formal trial preparation begins. How much material is included here is determined by the needs of the story. In a purely linear story, this section could include the crime itself or discovery of the crime; the questioning of a suspect; the interrogation, arrest, and formal charging of the suspect; and the suspect being committed for trial. But some or all of this material could be included during the trial itself – described by witnesses or shown in flashback. It depends how much of the case against the defendant and how much of the defendant's version of events you want to reveal at this early stage. You may want to limit it to the client and the lawyer meeting and the charge against the client being explained. You might also include some information about the lawyer they will be up against and also what is at stake for the client/defendant.

It is important that the reader or audience learns very early on who has been accused of a crime, what their crime is, and what fate awaits them if they are found guilty. It is up to the author whether or not to reveal the guilt or innocence of the accused at this early stage. A great deal of suspense can be generated if we know someone is innocent and events will lead us to fear that they will be wrongly convicted. Similarly, if we know the evil corporation is guilty, strong feelings can be generated if we feel that he will use his money and/or power to get away with is crimes.

Another issue that can be explored here is that of pretrial publicity and whether or not this jeopardises the chances of the defendant getting a fair trial. 'Trial by media' has been an issue in many high-profile cases. Ethically, media services should not present stories in a manner that might prejudice the outcome of a trial, and they should not publish 'evidence' before that evidence has been presented in court and subjected to objective scrutiny. In England and many other jurisdictions, the concept of *sub judice* – meaning that matters are under judicial consideration and therefore prohibited from public discussion – is fairly clear-cut, but in the United States there are potentially First Amendment concerns about the right of free speech. An oft-quoted example is the case of Sheppard v. Maxwell (1966) in which Sheppard challenged his conviction on the grounds that he, in the words of the appeal judge, "was deprived of a fair trial in his state conviction for the second-degree murder of his wife because of the trial judge's failure to protect Sheppard sufficiently from the massive, pervasive and prejudicial publicity that attended his persecution." His appeal was successful.

2. Preparation for Trial

Everything that occurs in this stage, and the stages which follow, is subject to the rules relating to trial procedure and the ethical guidelines relating to lawyer behaviour.

Discovery is one aspect of trial preparation. Discovery is a procedure by which the lawyers on each side can seek to obtain evidence from the other side and from third parties. This may take the form of requesting answers to *inter-*

rogatories (formal questions designed to clarify the other side's legal and factual claims), requests for production of documents, requests for admissions (declarative statements that one side sends which the other side must then admit, deny, or explain why they can neither admit nor deny the truth of), and depositions (a sworn statement taken out of court that gives the oral testimony of a witness that may then be submitted as a transcript for later use in court). Information from third parties can be demanded via a subpoena. If a discovery request is refused, the requesting party can file a *motion* asking the court to compel discovery.

Steven O. Rosen notes that the pre-trial discovery motion is the 'rarest of all courtroom scenes in the movies.' He quotes as an example an excerpt from *Class Action* (1991) – in which Ward (Gene Hackman) refers to the '... discovery motion compelling the defendant to supply the names, job descriptions, current addresses of all Argo employees,' saying: "Plaintiff's counsel begins by succinctly telling the judge what he wants ... The skilled trial lawyer figures out the goals before entering the courtroom and is prepared to state them succinctly." When the opposing counsel argues that the request is too difficult to achieve, Ward has a counter-argument ready: he's already found out that the information is readily available. As Rosen says, "... keep a derivative argument or fact in reserve for rebuttal."

We have already explored the topic of *witness preparation* in the section on professional ethics – the lawyer may prepare a witness for a court appearance, but should not *tell* him or her what to say; they should not suggest new 'facts' to the witness, and they should never advise the witness or client to testify to anything other than the truth as they know it.

3. Trial
An early part of trial proceedings in which the lawyers for both sides participate in the *voir dire* process. The author can use the selection of jurors to comment on the effectiveness of the jury system, by showing the members selected to be impartial and genuine *peers* of the defendant, or by showing them to be biased and from a social group vastly different from the defendant. We have already looked at out the *voir dire* process can be manipulated by lawyers to try and get a panel that will be sympathetic to their client. As examples of this process, Corcos gives the films *Adam's Rib, Inherit the Wind,* and *Twelve Angry Men,* and we can add John Grisham's *The Runaway Jury* to the list.

Another key player in the trial process is the judge. He may have been introduced during the trial preparation, deciding on motions brought by both parties, or we may see him for the first time when the trial begins. In both cases, we have probably learned something of his reputation in comments from the lawyers of both sides – particularly if he is likely to be sympathetic to one side or the other, or if he is suspected of being corrupt.

The relationship between lawyer and client is an important part of any trial, and an important part of that relationship concerns how the lawyer responds to instructions from his or her client. The Model Rules of Professional Conduct say that a lawyer must abide by the client's decisions regarding the objectives of the representation and must consult with the client as to the means by which the objectives are pursued. The lawyer must, for example, abide by a client's decision to accept or reject an offer of settlement in civil cases or to plead 'innocent' or 'guilty' in criminal cases. It is recognised that client and lawyer may disagree about the means to accomplish a client's objectives – clients would normally be expected to defer to the lawyer in respect of technical, legal and tactical matters and lawyers would usually defer to the client in matters concerning a third person who might be adversely affected. As long as the lawyer feels he can diligently represent his client, he can *choose* to follow his client's wishes on most things.

Another matter to consider is when, or if, a lawyer should *withdraw counsel*. There are circumstances when a lawyer *must* withdraw, including where 'representation will result in violation of the rules of professional conduct.' As we saw in the section on ethical behaviour, avoiding conflict of interest is – or a should be – an important issue for lawyers. There are other situations where a lawyer *may* withdraw from representing a client, such as when the client 'insists upon taking action that the lawyer considers repugnant or with which the lawyer has fundamental disagreement.' Guidance in this area warns that lawyers should not withdraw during a trial if such action would 'materially prejudice' client's defense. A defendant should not be left without competent and zealous counsel, and nor should they be left in a position where it looks as though the lawyer has withdrawn because he has decided that the client is guilty.

4. Opening Statements

Both Papke and Clover suggest that the prosecutor's opening statement is usually more effective than that of the defense. Clover writes that, "Even at this early point, the story of guilt is likely to have the upper hand: it is more coherent, seems more explanatory of the rudimentary facts, and is braced by our *prima facie* assumption that the state must have a powerful case in order to bring it to court." Papke also says that the prosecutor's opening remarks are 'coherent and convincing' and that, "... the prosecutor often bursts with confidence and bravado." In contrast, he says, the defense's opening statement "... is often more tentative, revealing uncertainties and creating doubt that the defense has any chance at all."

The opening and closing statements by the lawyers serve to 'bookend' the trial. The opposing counsels tell two versions of a story and attempt to account for the evidence that is presented during the trial. There is an old bit of advice to speechmakers – which may or may not have been inspired by Aristotle: "First tell them what you're going to tell them; then tell them, and then tell them that you've told them." That pretty much sums up the presentation by each side in the trial: opening statement – the prosecution (or defense) will demonstrate that etc. etc.; the witnesses and other evidence; closing statement – the prosecution (or defense) have shown that...

As we'll see below, the opening and closing statements are the most structured pieces of 'storytelling' during the trial. The presentation of witnesses and other evidence is less structured and potentially more confusing for the jury and the reader. The opening statement is an attempt by each lawyer to predispose the jury to fit the evidence to the version of the truth that he has provided in the opening statement.

Steven O. Rosen has advice on opening statements that applies to authors as much as it does to lawyers: "Nothing works as consistently well in an opening statement as telling a story from your client's point of view. The master lawyer uses explicit facts to give the story substance and holds the listener's interest along the way." Rosen quotes the prosecutor's opening statement from *My Cousin Vinny* as a good example. Rosen also notes that the actor, Lane Smith, delivers he speech in a 'visually compelling manner,' holding up a photograph of the scene, pointing at the defendants to identify them, varying the speed and volume of his voice, moving about the courtroom, and maintaining eye contact with the jury; finally he tells the jury, very clearly, what he wants them to decide.

Tonja Haddad points out that opening statements portrayed in films and on television are almost always 'unrealistic and unethical' in order to have a dramatic effect on the audience. Real opening statements, she says, are often monotonous and not at all entertaining. Haddad quotes as an example the film *Suspect,* in which the prosecutor's opening statement includes the observation that "I have prosecuted forty-three murder cases. It's always a horror, always senseless. But of all those murder cases – this is the most horrible, the most senseless, the most indefensible." This statement is highly prejudicial, as Bergman and Asimow say in *Reel Justice*, because not only does the speaker "... inject his personal experience and credibility as a prosecutor directly into the case, but also he invites the jurors to compare Anderson [the defendant] to forty-three other murderers." As well as being a useful guide to legal movies, *Reel Justice* is helpful in that it points out where the behaviour of legal professionals in the movies is good or bad.

Haddad also says that the film *And Justice for All* contains "... the most dramatic, and unethical, opening statement to ever hit the silver screen." While Richard Brust, writing in the *ABA Journal,* says the title character in *My Cousin Vinny* delivers "... cinema's briefest opening argument."

5. Witnesses and Evidence
Carol J. Clover writes that there is an 'abrupt shift of gears' when the trial enters the examination phase. The structured storytelling of the opening statements and the presentation to the audience "... collapses into a jumble of physical items and arrested moments: weapons, carpet fibers, testimony about drug reactions, behaviour at the funeral..." or whatever other evidence is presented. Clover emphasises that this presentation seems disordered and confusing. Each piece of evidence is presented and one lawyer will try and persuade the jury – and the reader – that this evidence shows that a particular fact is true; the opposing lawyer will then contest this, offering an alternate and (possibly) equally plausible account of what the evidence demonstrates – or they will attempt to show that the evidence proves nothing, or that it cannot be trusted to mean one thing or another. Jury and audience must try and keep track of all of these pieces of evidence and the different explanations attached to them.

The lawyer for each side will *examine* his own witnesses and *cross-examine* the witnesses put forward by the other side. Rosen argues that direct examination of witnesses is actually more difficult than cross-examination. He quotes from *Judgement at Nuremberg* – a scene where the prosecutor, played by Richard Widmark, questions Dr. Wieck – as a good example of 'effective direct examination,' saying that it allows the witness to be the 'star' with the lawyer and his questions fading into the background. Rosen's advice to trial lawyers is equally helpful to writers of trial scenes: "To maintain the jury's interest during direct examination, shift back and forth between permissible leading questions and non-leading questions." He also says that a lawyer must 'thoroughly investigate' his own witnesses: he must know what the witness is going to say in answer to his own questions and in answer to any that the opposing counsel might ask. Rosen notes that opposing counsel doesn't always properly investigate their own witnesses and that this is something that can be taken advantage of in cross-examination. He quotes a scene from *My Cousin Vinny*, where a witness is questioned about what he could actually see from his viewpoint: "The prosecutor failed to thoroughly investigate his own witness and thus failed to prepare for the coming attack."

Asking difficult and challenging questions of a witness with whom the jury – and the audience – has sympathy can be tricky. A widower who lost her husband as a result of some action of a corporation or a mother who has lost a child, have to be treated carefully by the lawyers on both sides. Rosen uses the example of the cross-examination of Sarah Tobias (played by Jodie Foster) in the film *The Accused:* "The key is his soft, restrained voice and the respectful manner in which he asks the questions. Second, he opens the door to reasonable doubt, asking 'Is it possible...' His soft style and simple questions increase the attorney's likelihood of obtaining the answer he wants ... [and he] ... uses leading questions to keep Ms. Tobias's answers short and under his control."

Rosen offers one final piece of advice about questioning witnesses: "After obtaining the answer you want, stop."

Anyone who appears on the witness stand swears that they will tell the truth and they are made aware that lying 'under oath' in a courtroom is a crime that has penalties. But as Clover points out, between absolute truth and barefaced lie there is a lot of flexibility. Added to that is the fact that some people who take the oath *will* lie. Lawyers try to catch witnesses in a lie during cross-examination if it is in the interests of their client to do so, but it is ultimately up to the jury to decide who they believe. Corcos also points out that even though a witness swears to tell the truth, he or she may not be given the opportunity to do so, since the lawyer will direct his questions such that he carefully controls the story being told. Lawyers carefully phrase their questions with the aim of drawing the desired response, and often the actual words, out of the witness that are favourable to his client. Objections are used to try and ensure that unfavourable responses are not allowed to stand as part of the court record.

The *rules of evidence* governing what can and cannot be presented as evidence in the courtroom *are* difficult for non-lawyers to appreciate because they seem to prevent the inclusion of things which seem to demonstrate 'the truth.' In the United States, the *Federal Rules of Evidence* (1975) set down the law that applies in federal courts and these same rules (or variations on them) have been adopted by many states. They cover such areas as what evidence is relevant; privileges, including attorney-client confidentiality and confidentiality of information known to spouses, mental health professionals, clergy, and protection for those with knowledge of state secrets. There is guidance on the protection of police informants; and protection of Fifth Amendment privileges, including the protection of 'sources' by journalists. The rules also cover witnesses, opinions, hearsay, expert testimony, authentication of documents, and use of recordings and photographs. The searchable text of the Rules is available at www.rulesofevidence.org

A lawyer cannot just enter the courtroom with a document, a gun, or a video recording and say, 'You honor, I would like this entered into evidence as Defense Exhibit A.' The request for it to be admitted would need to be made long before the trial got underway. The veracity of the item would need to be tested and there is a requirement to demonstrate a 'chain of custody' that shows that from the moment an item was discovered it has been properly handled and not been subject to tampering. Before it can be admitted, it can be subject to objections raised by opposing counsel – usually relating to the Rules of Evidence – and after that, it has to be accepted by the judge. As BrettMW writes, "Numerous cases hinge on one side's ability, or inability, to get their evidence admitted."

When it comes to physical evidence, Clover points out that just as this can be separately collected, "... it can be separately suppressed, destroyed, tainted, fabricated, delayed, planted, altered, and so on, and although official accounts of the legal system remind us that evidence meddling is illegal, the fact is that it *does* happen..." There is a lot of scope for having fun with physical evidence in a legal thriller. In *Presumed Innocent* a drinking glass is an important piece of evidence right up to the end of the story.

This middle section of the trial, the examination stage, takes place in what Carol J. Clover calls 'a strict schedule of turn-taking.' A lawyer examines a witness and then the opposition counsel cross-examines them. As mentioned above, at the beginning of the trial, the prosecution seems to have the advantage, being better prepared to present what appears to be a stronger case. This situation arises because the prosecution is burdened with *proving* the case against the accused. They *must* have a strong case, whereas the defense has the presumption of innocence on its side and its main task is demonstrating that there is some element of doubt associated with as many of the prosecution's pieces of evidence as possible. The job of the defense is to discredit enough of the prosecution's case to cause the jury to decide that it has not been proved beyond reasonable doubt. Introducing doubt is as far as the defense really has to go.

As the defense begins to cross-examine the prosecution's witnesses, the prosecution's initial advantage is typically eroded as the defense 'scores points' against them. Eventually we – the reader and the jury – reach a point where we have sufficient doubt that we feel that the cases of both sides have equal merit. This moment, around the middle of the trial, is described by Clover as "... the most charged moment of the proceedings, one that, once negotiated, delivers us into the most characteristic experience of the adversarial trial: of being pulled rhythmically back and forth, in the almost machine-like alternation of direct examination with cross-examination, between the two positions."

This trial structure, as we have already said, is a great way of creating and sustaining suspense. As the advantage passes from one side to the other, we can gradually increase the strength or size of each victory and each defeat, raising the stakes as we get closer and closer to the climax. It is up to individual authors how evenly-matched they want this courtroom battle to be. Standard storytelling practice suggests that you increase the odds against your lawyer-hero, making his successes seem smaller and his defeats seem greater so that the lawyer-villain seems almost certain to win. Alternatively, you can have the hero seeming to be doing really well, and then have the villain pull a nasty surprise out of the bag. However you do it, you want to have a situation where it seems that there will be a major injustice – the audience will then be willing the hero on and dreading the villain succeeding. And all the while, the reader will probably know something that the hero and the others in the courtroom do not know – the villain has been involved in underhand practices and has a nasty surprise waiting for the hero meaning that some part of the lawyer-hero's case is about to come crashing down.

6. Closing Statements
With the examination stage over, we move back into a more straightforward storytelling phase where the opposing lawyers again tell their version of the truth. Their task here is to play the part of the Great Detective who gathers all of the suspects together in the drawing room and explain to them what all of the clues and witness statements finally amount to. They show how all of the pieces fit together, they explain which clues were red-herrings, and which witnesses were either mistaken or lying. And at the same time, they will try and evoke an emotional response from the jury. Closing statements are often described as 'impassioned.' Each lawyer wants to make every individual juror feel that a terrible injustice will be done if they do not make the 'correct' decision. In their closing statements, the lawyers will try to appeal to logic and reason, to gut instinct, and to emotion – they will try and humanise their client and seek to make the jurors put themselves in his or her position – 'If this was happening to you, how would you feel?' This is another area where fictional lawyers are allowed more leeway than real ones.

The example that is almost always quoted as a model closing statement is that by Atticus Finch in *To Kill a Mockingbird*. As Steven O. Rosen points out, Finch addresses the most difficult issue in the case up front – whether a white jury will believe a black man's testimony. Finch also refers to the 'cynical confidence' of the prosecution witnesses that they would be believed because they are white. Rosen also praises Finch's delivery: "He takes his time, speaking slowly. He pauses for effect. He varies the pitch of his voice, and he moves around the courtroom, even facing away from the jury to give them a bit of relief from his argument. He impresses upon the jurors their duty and gives the jury the opportunity to abandon social mores and render a decision that is right, even if unpopular."

Another good example occurs in the film *Presumed Innocent* where Harrison Ford's character delivers an effective closing statement in a child abuse case.

7. Jury Deliberation

In many stories, the deliberations of the jurors occur offstage and the action of the trial pauses. As the prosecution and defense anxiously await the verdict, they may hold discussions in hushed tones. Where jury deliberation *is* shown, it allows the audience to that what jurors discuss during their deliberations contrasts with what they have been instructed by the judge to consider. Where these differences do occur, it is usually because the author wishes to show the gap between what the formal legal process regards as justice and what ordinary people – as represented by the jury – see as being fair and just. They may rely on their own moral views or 'gut feeling' as to what the defendant 'deserves,' as opposed to objectively deciding whether the case against him has been proved beyond reasonable doubt.

The film *Twelve Angry Men* is the most famous example of a story that depicts the deliberations of a trial jury – almost the entire film takes place in the jury room as their verdict is debated. Christine Alice Corcos writes that through "... an examination of each juror's prejudices the author presents the strengths and weaknesses of the jury system." Initially, the jury sees a guilty verdict as the obvious outcome, but a lone dissenter (played by Henry Fonda) "... insists that the jury re-examine the evidence presented with a critical eye, mulling over the stories told by prosecution and defense and questioning whether they are: (1) coherent and (2) believable – that is, whether they correspond with what the jurors know about the world. Each juror has a different type of expertise necessary to examine the evidence, and Fonda guides each toward the 'right' (that is, the just) decision..."

If the jury plays a major part in a legal thriller, it will probably be because the story includes attempts to illegally influence the decision of the jury. 'Jury tampering' has already been covered in the section on unethical behaviour above.

8. Verdict and Sentencing

Eventually, the jurors shuffle back into the courtroom and resume their places. The jury will have elected a chair, and that person is responsible for delivering their verdict. Papke describes the way this typically plays out in films and on television: "Its chairperson hands the judge a mysterious piece of paper. What's on that paper anyway? The judge looks at the paper, returns it to the chairperson, and the latter reads the verdict. People in the courtroom swoon and exult. They hug and cry. Sometimes the judge must ask for calm before confirming the verdict and pounding the gavel one last time."

The delivery of the verdict provides a natural climax and the story often cuts away at this point. Showing anything other than the immediate reaction to the verdict risks diminishing the scene. The sentence imposed to the guilty party may be mentioned in passing, here or in a later scene, or it may have been mentioned in earlier scenes, so that the audience can be left to assume the guilty person's fate. In a small number of stories, the sentence is important – it allows the author to express some judgment on the jury's verdict – particularly if it is much harsher or more lenient than the jury (and perhaps the audience) anticipated. *Inherit the Wind* is an example of where this occurs.

9. Post-Trial
If the verdict in the trial provided the outcome that the lawyer-hero and the audience wanted, then the post-trial scene or scenes are likely to be brief and restricted to validating the verdict, showing that justice has been achieved, and showing a return to the equilibrium in the world that was upset by the events that led to the trial.

If the verdict was the 'wrong' outcome, and the lawyer-hero and the audience believe that justice has *not* been served, there may be more things to show in the post-trial scenes, perhaps leading up to a second – and more powerful, emotional, or ironic – climax. Sometimes the author's message is that the legal system is not able to deliver justice in such cases, and that it is then up to someone to take action outside the legal system to deliver justice. Idealistic young lawyer-heroes in thrillers often take this course. Or it may be that the author may want to show 'fate' or 'nature' intervening to provide the justice that the man-made court was unable to achieve. In either case, the guilty party's punishment is likely to take the form of some sort of 'poetic justice' – suffering that fits the nature of the crime and may even have been brought about by the guilty party's own actions. In an ironic ending, the guilty person may 'win' the trial, the letter of the law, but lose something even more important to him – his job, his reputation, a relationship with someone he cares about. Conversely, the opposing side may lose the court case but find themselves rewarded with something more important than a favourable verdict. It's important to remember that punishing the guilty is only half the story and that restoring what the other side has lost as a result of the crime can be equally important.

Generally speaking, it's probably true to say that having someone wrongly convicted or wrongly acquitted makes for a stronger and more dramatic climax to a court case than a 'correct' verdict, and that 'post-trial justice' achieved by the action of the lawyer-hero is stronger than an act of fate or coincidence.

Alternatives to the Formal Trial
Criminal trials and courts-martial are formal proceedings that take place within the bounds of the law, but there are other quasi- or pseudo-courts that can be used in stories. An example is Agatha Christie's *Murder on the Orient Express* in which a sort of informal jury passes its verdict.

There are tribunals that imitate formal courts, following formal rules in order to reach fair outcomes, but there are also 'kangaroo courts' that have no official standing and proceed with only a pretence of delivering justice. Illegitimate 'star chambers' and dubious 'drumhead courts-martial' are other possibilities. Some nations have also conducted 'show trials' where the guilt of a defendant had already been determined and the trial is shown in order to dissuade others from engaging in actions against the government. Show trials are usually conducted for political and propaganda purposes. The ultimate form of verdict delivered without legitimate trial is probably the public lynch mob.

How Accurate is the Depiction of Fictional Trials?
The first thing to say is that only about ten per cent of criminal charges ever get to trial – the majority are either plea-bargained or dropped. Statistics show that in trials the jury is more likely to convict than acquit.

Courtroom proceedings as depicted on screen and in novels employ a fair amount of poetic licence. Real trials are much longer than those depicted – often taking many weeks or even months to complete – and they are less dramatic. The judge exercises a much greater degree of control over lawyers, witnesses, and other persons in the court. Author Paul Levine says, "In 17 years as a trial lawyer, I never saw a judge bang a gavel or shout 'Order in court!'"

Papke writes that "Dramatic revelations from witnesses or defendants on the stand are rare, and lawyers rarely break down a witness the way the lawyer played by Tom Cruise did with Jack Nicholson's Colonel Nathan Jessep in *A Few Good Men*."

In fictional trials, lawyers say a lot more during the examination phase than they do in real life. It is important to note that long statements by the lawyers have no place in this section of the trial. While examining his own witnesses, the lawyer is only permitted to extract factual statements from the witness – he must not put forward any opinions of his own or try to ask questions that imply any fact that has not yet been put forward by the witness. Under examination, it is not permitted to ask a *leading question,* that is, a question that prompts or encourages the answer that is wanted by the lawyer. There is more leeway under cross-examination for the opposing counsel to ask leading questions.

In real life trials, the defendant is often advised against taking the stand. The Fifth Amendment right against self-incrimination means the defendant does not have to say anything which might make him appear to be guilty of the crime of which he is accused. But if he voluntarily takes the stand, he waives this right and must answer not only the questions asked him by his own lawyer, but also those asked by the opposing lawyer. He then risks making an answer which might be used by the opposition to make him appear guilty. If the defendant chooses not to take the stand, the jury (in the United States) is prohibited from drawing any inference from this fact – they cannot assume that he has 'something to hide.' But there is a danger that, despite this prohibition, the jury *will* make that assumption. This is a dilemma that the hero of Scott Turow's *Presumed Innocent* faces and he argues with his lawyer, wanting to take the stand and show that he doesn't have anything to hide.

"*Objection, your Honor!*" How many times do we hear that phrase in a drama? A lawyer cannot raise an objection to something simply because it is detrimental to his client's case – there has to be a sound legal reason for the objection. And they must *state* what that reason is. Even if the judge does know why the objection is being raised, the jury and the audience do not. Objections normally relate to the Rules of Evidence. There is a list of 'Common Objections at Trial' on the *International Bridges to Justice – Criminal Defense Wiki* which includes Irrelevant, Immaterial, Conclusion, Hearsay, Leading, Repetitive. A judge can *overrule* or *sustain* an objection – the other responses that we often see in movies – 'Let's see where this is going,' 'Make your point counselor,' and

'I'll allow it – for now' – are usually an indication that the writer is employing artistic licence rather than following real court procedure.

"May we request a recess, your Honor?" Again, we're in the realms of artistic licence here. Courts have a huge workload and every hour that a trial takes involves a financial cost: time cannot be wasted. Lawyers are meant to be prepared in advance of the trial and it is not reasonable for them to ask for a pause so that they can go and do research or hold conversations which should have taken place before. If something unexpected comes up during the trial, they have to deal with it on the fly. Only under extreme circumstances – the sudden illness of a participant, for example – would the judge grant a recess or continuation.

The Legal Defence Thriller – Presumed Innocent & Jagged Edge

In terms of where the different trial stages fit within the eight sequences of the plot, *Presumed Innocent* (film version) looks something like this:

1. Pre-trial events
2. Pre-trial events
3. Pre-trial events
4. Pre-trial events and arrest at the midpoint
5. Trial preparation and beginning of the trial
6. Witnesses & evidence
7. Witnesses & evidence and outcome of the trial
8. Post-trial events

Scott Turow's novel is written in the first person by the protagonist, Rusty Sabich, but still manages to avoid revealing to the reader whether or not Sabich is actually guilty until very late in the story. The film adaptation doesn't go to quite the same lengths to keep the facts from the audience.

Scott Turow, quoted by Charles Champlin in the *Los Angeles Times,* spoke about the difficulties of adapting the novel into a screenplay: "There were three narrative problems to solve. Point of view, getting around the first-person narrative; time sequence, it's all flashback and Hollywood doesn't like that; and then just an awful lot of plot." Turow's novel doesn't exactly fit the eight-sequence model as it is divided into thirds, but the protagonist's arrest occurs closer to the end of Sequence 3 and Sequence 4 then becomes trial preparation with the midpoint being either the first scene in the courtroom or the first day of the trial.

In terms of where the different trial stages fit within the eight sequences of the plot, *Jagged Edge* (film) looks something like this:

1. Pre-trial events – ending with arrest and arraignment
2. Pre-trial events – reluctant hero-lawyer
3. Pre-trial events and trial preparation
4. Pre-trial events and first day in court – opening statements and first witnesses
5. Witnesses & evidence
6. Witnesses & evidence plus investigations

7. Witnesses & evidence and verdict
8. Post-trial events

The Legal Prosecution Thriller – The Rainmaker

In terms of where the different trial stages fit within the eight sequences of the plot, *The Rainmaker* (film version) looks something like this:

1. Pre-trial events
2. Pre-trial events
3. Pre-trial events and trial preparation/motions
4. Trial preparation
5. Trial preparation
6. Beginning of the trial and witnesses & evidence
7. Witnesses & evidence
8. End of the trial, closing statements, verdict and epilogue

I will include a more detailed summary of the plots of these three stories below. If you intend to write a story with a courtroom scene I would advise watching all three of them in their film versions – and if you plan to write a novel, read *The Rainmaker* and *Presumed Innocent* – ideally *before* you see the films. Some of the classic examples I mentioned earlier – both thrillers and non-thrillers – should also be among your study material. The summaries below are based on the films – I have made a few comments about the novel versus the film where appropriate, but a full exploration of how novels are adapted into screenplays is beyond the scope of this book. After the summaries, I have included a few general notes on structure and the use of witnesses in courtroom scenes.

Presumed Innocent

Sequence 1. The protagonist, Rusty Sabich, with his family. He's currently helping his boss run for re-election as prosecuting attorney – if Horgan doesn't get the votes, Rusty is out of a job too. Horgan is up against Della Guardia. Rusty's colleague Carolyn Polhemus was murdered last night – tied up, raped, and strangled. Evidence includes a glass with fingerprints. Horgan asks Rusty to investigate – it looks bad for the campaign to have one of his own people murdered, they need a quick arrest. Rusty wants his investigator, Lipranzer, on the case. Rusty discovers Carolyn was looking into a bribery case – not her usual area as she usually worked on sex crimes. We learn that Rusty had an affair with Carolyn.

Sequence 2. The election is in ten days – they need results before then. Ticking clock. Horgan gives Rusty the file for the bribery case when he asks about it. A man called Leon bribed someone in the prosecutor's office to drop the 'indecency' case against him. Rusty hears about tests on Carolyn – semen was from someone with blood type A, apparently infertile. No hair or skin under fingernails. She was tied up after she was killed. They need to chase fingerprint analysis of glass. Rusty's own home phone number is on Carolyn's phone records – he asks Lipranzer to 'let it go.' Rusty angry because the evidence is being passed to Della Guardia's side.

Sequence 3. Della Guardia slightly ahead in the polls. Rusty learns that Horgan also had an affair with Carolyn – thought he wouldn't run for office again and wanted him to recommend her for it. Horgan talks as if he's already lost the election. Flashback of Rusty and Carolyn working together, winning a case, and becoming lovers.

Sequence 4. Horgan loses the election. Della Guardia and his team take over – including Carolyn's murder investigation. Rusty is to be charged with murder – he needs a lawyer, so goes to Sandy Stern, a good defense lawyer who has opposed Rusty in court. Search of Rusty's house – fibre samples from carpet etc. Don't search for the weapon – they would have to admit it wasn't found. More flashback of Rusty and Carolyn – she wanted him to run for Horgan's post so she could be his deputy, but he wasn't that ambitious. She leaves him – he's no use to her, but he is still infatuated. Stern wants Rusty to plead the fifth and not testify in front of the Grand Jury. *Midpoint:* Rusty is arrested.

Sequence 5. Evidence disclosed by prosecution – physical evidence but motive is weak: Rusty was an obsessed jilted lover. Stern warns they must be discreet in their own investigations – don't lead the prosecution to evidence they don't already have. Horgan will testify against Rusty – will say Rusty asked for the investigation into Carolyn's death and that he had to be chased to make progress on it. Rusty tells Stern about the bribery case – the prosecutor taking bribes was Della Guardia's right-hand man, Molto. Meeting with the Judge – motions filed. Media interest in the case. Trial begins – jury shown photographs of Carolyn's body. The jury will want someone to pay for the crime. Tomorrow Horgan will testify against Rusty, and all the evidence points to him – things do not look good.

Sequence 6. Horgan on the stand. Later, Stern tells the judge that he suspects Della Guardia and Molto are trying to frame Rusty. Stern thinks the missing bribery file is vital evidence – Rusty has asked Lipranzer to find it. Rusty wants to testify – says juries don't like it if the defendant doesn't, but Stern isn't keen on this – he could be tricked into saying something incriminating. And so far there is only rumour that Rusty had a relationship with Carolyn – reasonable doubt exists – on the stand he'd be asked and would have to answer. The glass with the fingerprints has gone missing – prosecution needs to find it, defense needs to prove by precedence that the fingerprint evidence is inadmissible if it isn't found. Lipranzer has located Leon.

Sequence 7. Rusty and Lipranzer speak to Leon – the man he paid off wasn't Della Guardia's man, Molto, it was the Judge in Rusty's case. Back in court, the glass is still missing. The Judge will admit the fingerprint evidence, but tells the jury they may treat the absence of the glass as a reasonable ground for acquitting Rusty. Stern cross-examines coroner – shows there are problems with his evidence, effectively discounting it. Prosecution rests. Stern will move for a dismissal – if that fails, they will have to mount a defense. Does Rusty still want to testify? If he does, he will give the prosecution proof of motive that they currently lack. The Judge dismisses the case – there is no evidence of Rusty's guilt.

Sequence 8. Stern effectively blackmailed the judge because of the bribery file. He tells Rusty the Judge's backstory. Lipranzer had the glass all along – but nobody asked him for it. Rusty discovers the identity of the real murderer – explanation of how the murder was carried out and why.

Jagged Edge

Sequence 1. The murder of Paige Forrester by a masked intruder at the Forresters' beach house – multiple stab wounds and the word 'Bitch' smeared on the wall in blood. After a period of investigation, the District Attorney, Krasny, find a witness who says the husband Jack Forrester had a knife like the murder weapon. Jack is arrested on suspicion of murder – arraignment hearing, bailed.

Sequence 2. Jack doesn't want an expensive out of town lawyer – wants someone from his corporate law firm. They have one ex-prosecutor, Teddy Barnes, who gave up criminal law for a good reason. She is offered a partnership to tempt her into taking Jack's case. She used to work with Krasny – bad blood between them. She is upset when she learns that Henry Styles, a man she and Krasny convicted, has killed himself in prison. She feels guilty – needs to make amends. She agrees to take the case, as long as Jack promises never to lie to her. As she begins preparing for the case, we see that she is good at her job.

Sequence 3. When Teddy sees Krasny she says she doesn't want any problem with discovery – she's not going to let it happen again – referring to the Styles case. Visit to the beach house with Jack – from his reaction, Teddy feels sure he is innocent. Polygraph and psych-evaluation suggest Jack is innocent too. Sam, Teddy's investigator, has the evidence disclosed by the prosecution – it is weak, so he thinks they must be holding something back. Sam thinks Jack could be guilty. Teddy and Jack together – begin flirting. 'You like playing games don't you,' Teddy says. 'I don't play games with my clients.' She asks him about some of the evidence Krasny has gathered – Jack doesn't seem too concerned. Teddy and Krasny meet with the Judge – Teddy says she suspects the Prosecution has not revealed all of its evidence, but can't prove it. She just knows from experience that Krasny has withheld evidence from the defense before. Krasny challenges her to go public about the Styles case – she prosecuted it with him.

Sequence 4. Teddy spends time with Jack – they become lovers. Sam warns Teddy that Jack wants her to like him so she'll work harder to defend him: she says she knows this. First mention of the anonymous letters that say Jack is innocent – written on a 1942 Corona typewriter with a slightly raised letter 't'. First day in court. Opening statements. First witness is Paige's brother – she had all the money; Jack inherits it all; she was happy with Jack's work at the family business; unaware of any problems in their personal relationship. Second witness is Ginny Howell – she says Paige knew Jack didn't love her and she was thinking of getting a divorce. Teddy has evidence that Ginny tried to seduce Jack – and that Ginny and Paige fell out because of this, because Jack told her about it. Having discredited Ginny, the *midpoint* is effectively a mini-victory for Teddy.

Sequence 5. Preparing for the next day. Sam thinks Krasny has a surprise witness – a tennis pro from the club Paige and Jack both attended, Bobby Slade. But the next witness called is Eileen, a woman Jack had an affair with. Teddy knew nothing about it – she is shocked and disappointed. Eileen says Jack wanted to divorce his wife but couldn't because he would lose everything.

Bobby Slade is then called. He had an affair with Paige – and says Paige new Jack was seeing someone. Jack took his lover riding – it was like foreplay. This strikes a nerve with Teddy, as Jack had taken her riding before they went to bed. Teddy is angry with Jack for having lied to her – thinks he's used her. She wants to drop the case. Another of the anonymous letters – and Sam has the 'dirt' on Bobby Slade.

Sequence 6. Bobby Slade is discredited when it is revealed that he was fired from his last job for selling sexual favours. He had sex with Paige, including at the beach house where she was killed. Teddy asked if he ever tied her up – Slade calls Teddy a bitch. The next witness is a janitor who says he saw a knife like the murder weapon in Jack's locker at the club. Prosecution rests its case. Teddy then calls an ex-club member who had a hunting knife in his locker – like the murder weapon. Teddy produces it in court. Recalled and questioned, the janitor admits he could have been mistaken about the locker number. His evidence is effectively discredited. Teddy receives another anonymous note – this time with a date and a name.

Sequence 7. Teddy calls Julie Jensen, a woman who was attacked in a similar way to Paige but who survived. Her attack is very similar – the attacker's mask, the knife, and the word 'Bitch' in blood on the wall. The woman also says she revealed all of this to the Assistant District Attorney but was told it wasn't relevant to the present case. Krasny has deliberately withheld this evidence – he admits this in the Judge's chambers. Krasny says Jack must have attacked Julie Jensen as well – to get himself off the hook and point the finger at Bobby Slade, who also played tennis with Julie. 'He planned this for eighteen months!' The Judge will not allow Jack to be accused of the attack on Julie – he is not accused of that crime. Jury retires to consider their verdict – they find Jack not guilty. Jack celebrates. Teddy makes a statement to the press, admitting her part in the conviction of Henry Styles and revealing that Krasny withheld evidence in that case that would have proved him innocent – Krasny's career is now effectively over.

Sequence 8. Teddy goes to Jack's house and spends the night – but in the morning, she discovers a typewriter. Is it *the* typewriter? If so, she has just helped a guilty man escape justice. She must know the truth – and then she must find a way to put things right. That night, a masked man comes after her – is it Jack or Bobby Slade?

The Rainmaker
Sequence 1. Introduces the hero, Rudy – his backstory in v.o., he's poor, underdog, morally decent. Gets a job with a questionable law firm run by 'Bruiser'

Stone. He brings with him two cases he picked up while working in a law workshop as a student – an insurance case and a rich old lady's will. Meets cynical 'mentor' Deck Shiflett. Introduction of the main case against an insurance company that refused to pay up for a bone-marrow transplant for a leukaemia sufferer. We see the patient, Donny-Ray – he has nosebleeds, leukaemia is real this isn't just about legal theory.

Sequence 2. Rudy gets advice on legal ethics from Deck. Bruiser is being investigated by the FBI. Rudy is studying for the bar exam. He demonstrates that he interested in people as individuals – both the wealthy old lady and Donny-Ray's family – not just as clients. He meets the romantic co-protagonist, Kelly – she is the victim of an abusive husband. Rudy passes the bar exam.

Sequence 3. Bruiser's offices are raided by the FBI. Rudy and Deck set up their own law firm in seedy offices with no money. Rudy has to handle the filing of motions in the case against the insurance company alone – against the big evil law firm. First court appearance – the judge and lawyer-villain Drummond. Drummond tries to buy Rudy off with a meagre settlement for Donny-Ray's family – the judge advises him to take it. Deck advises him to take it. Donny-Ray and his family turn it down. The original judge dies and is replaced by a new one who dislikes big insurance firms – the odds of Rudy winning have just increased.

Sequence 4. Rudy and Deck are broke having spent all they have setting up their new office. The leukaemia-sufferer, Donny-Ray, is near death – his deposition is filmed. Rudy goes to depose key witnesses at the insurance company – but they are no longer there, one having resigned and the other having been 'downsized.' 'Do you even remember when you first sold out?' Rudy asks Drummond. *Midpoint:* Rudy swears he'll get justice for Donny-Ray.

Sequence 5. Rudy goes to help Kelly after she has been beaten by her husband again. Gets her to sign the divorce papers. Donny-Ray's funeral. Big evil law firm has bugged Rudy's phones – he uses this to his advantage. Acting on the disinformation they have been fed, Drummond looks bad during the jury selection process in court.

Sequence 6. Beginning of the trial. Later, Rudy takes Kelly to get her things from home – they are surprised by her husband who attacks them both. The husband is killed.

Sequence 7. The trial – one of the 'missing' witnesses is found and gives damning testimony against the insurance company.

Sequence 8. An objection to the use of stolen evidence raised by the big evil law firm is overruled when Bruiser gives advice to Deck. End of case, closing statements. Verdict. Epilogue.

When I began looking at the plot structures for legal thrillers, I was curious to know what proportion of the stories actually took place in the courtroom. The examples I have studied seem to indicate that three sequences is typical for the trial sequence but with some overlap into a fourth sequence. Sequences 6 and 7 seem to be universally courtroom sequences, with the rest of the courtroom scenes in one or more sequences on either side of these. In most of the stories, the hero-lawyer is assisted by an investigator of some kind and this person continues the detective work even after the trial has begun. This allows the writer to break-up the courtroom scenes and also gives the hero-lawyer someone to talk to outside of the trial. It also allows for the addition of a suspense element in the form of 'we must find X before the end of the presentation of our prosecution/defense case.' X could be a piece of information, a document, or a missing (or reluctant) witness.

Another key question I had was, How many witnesses are included in the trial sequences? There is an issue with examining and cross-examining witnesses in that it can become a bit monotonous if you fill the pages or the screen with 'talking heads.' You can mix things up a bit with scenes relating to the ongoing investigation as mentioned above or with a subplot, usually a romantic one. But there is a still a limit to the number of witnesses you can realistically handle. A similar issue arises in the murder mystery where including too many main suspects for the detective to interview slows the story down – there I found that six major suspects plus two or three minor witnesses were about the upper end. The difference with a courtroom trial is that both prosecution and defense lawyers get to question the witness, not just a detective. In effect, the same witness is being questioned about the same events from two different perspectives – one where the defendant is guilty and one where he, she or they are innocent. In films, three to five main witnesses seems about average with an additional two or three minor witnesses who get only a small amount of screen time. In novels, you have a little more space, but even there four or five main witnesses plus five or six minor ones would seem to be the limit.

There are a couple of techniques that can be used to vary the monotony of witness interview scenes in the court. The first is to include a 'comedy witness' who serves to make the hero-lawyer look good and/or the lawyer-villain look bad. This is often done by having a 'down to earth' witness who speaks the truth bluntly and is not at all fazed by the solemn rituals of the court. The second way is to have a witness say something unexpected, catching the lawyer asking the questions by surprise. A lawyer should have questioned 'their' witness thoroughly beforehand so that there are no surprises, but for dramatic purposes this doesn't always happen in stories. The witness may say the opposite of what they had been expected to say or they may suddenly reveal some fact that has never been mentioned before. The lawyer on the receiving end of this shock could be the hero or the villain, depending on what dramatic turn you need to make at this point in the story.

The prosecution will introduce their witnesses first and question them in a way that elicits information that seems to prove the defendant is guilty. The defense will then cross-examine these witnesses and seek to introduce either an element of *reasonable doubt* – is it possible that this alternative interpretation of events may also be true? – or they will seek to find logical 'holes' in what a witness has said, undermining their evidence, or they will seek to discredit the witness as a person by revealing them to be an unreliable or corrupt person. Catching a witness in one small lie can undermine the whole of their testimony.

Prosecution witnesses should always have been revealed to the defense before the trail as part of the discovery process – but in fiction, the prosecution often springs surprise witnesses for dramatic effect and the judge always allows it. The defense does not have to reveal their witnesses beforehand – they are not under the same obligation to *prove* their case – and so surprise witnesses for the defense are perfectly in order: if the prosecution didn't find a witness, it means they didn't prepare their case properly. Obviously how you deal with the prosecution versus defense issue with regard to witnesses will depend in part on whether your hero is a defense lawyer or a prosecution one, and in part on whether you want to advance or undermine the hero's progress at a particular moment in the story.

10 | Medical Thriller

What is a Medical Thriller?

The medical thriller takes the conventions of the thriller genre – notably suspense and/or conspiracy – and uses them within the world of medical practice or medical research. The healthcare system is not just a backdrop against which a story is set – the medicine is a key part of the working of the plot. Typically, there is either a conspiracy related to the violation of medical ethics, or there is a problem that requires medical expertise to discover a solution. Jasmine Fernandez and Amarjeet Nayak describe the medical thriller as "a mixture of technical details, medical facts, ethical issues, cultural clashes and suspense."

There is some overlap between the medical thriller and the legal, business or financial thriller. The medical thriller also has things in common with the traditional mystery story and the detective thriller. Stories that centre on some form of medical crisis can also feature elements of the disaster story. And when it comes to the area of cutting-edge medical research, there are some links with the techno-thriller and science fiction.

In order to explore how medical thriller plots work, I am going to say that there are two main types:

(i) Medical professionals deal with a medical crisis, such as the outbreak of a deadly disease, e.g. *The Andromeda Strain* and *Contagion*.
(ii) Medical professionals are involved in a conspiracy that is discovered by an outsider, e.g. *Coma*.

A third form which might be included under this heading is the forensic investigation story featuring a pathologist or medical examiner, but I will deal with those as a form of 'police procedural' story in *Crime Thriller*. Here we will concentrate on the 'outbreak' and 'medical conspiracy' forms.

The Appeal of the Medical Thriller

Robin Cook, in an interview with Gail Jennes, said, "I can't think of anything more fearsome than hospitals. When people smell the alcohol and see the equipment, their pupils dilate. They go into a sweat. I need to evoke that atavistic fear of dying." And he told Jay McDonald why he thought this type of thriller is popular: "The main reason is, we all realize we're at risk. We're all going to be patients at some time. You can write about great white sharks or haunted houses, and you can say I'm not going in the ocean or I'm not going in haunted houses, but you can't say you're not going to go in a hospital."

Medical thrillers play on our fears of illness, injury, and death but also on our unease regarding medical practitioners and procedures. The surgeon cuts into us and accesses parts of our body which we ourselves have never seen – and he does it while we are helpless and unconscious. Pharmaceutical researchers combine chemicals to produce drugs which may cure what ails us, but we fear that the pills and potions will have side-effects that may permanently harm us. We put our trust in medical professionals – but we do it because we have little choice. Medicine is a complex field requiring many years of study and practice. It is also a closed and mysterious world – you are either a physician or you are an outsider. Any of us can research medical information – real and bogus – online, but few outsiders can claim to have mastered the magical art. Doctors hold in their hands the gift of improved health and even of continued life. We think of them as miracle-workers and saviours – because we would rather not think of them as ordinary, fallible human beings. And we certainly do not wish to think of a tiny percentage of them being crooks and even murderers.

Except, of course, that we do. We like to confront the things that make us afraid. And in some part of our unconscious minds, we still regard doctors as saw-bones, bloodletters with leeches, body snatchers and vivisectionists. And medical thriller writers exploit those fears for our amusement.

Jasmine Fernandez and Amarjeet Nayak have referred to our "need to have a private self that is separate and hidden from others" which includes, for most of us, a need to cover up our bodies – but the hospital and the operating theatre force us to expose this hidden self. And they also force us to confront our fear of death. In *Coma*, Robin Cook shows us this from the patient's point of view – "the cruel, detached environment of the hospital ... made her acutely aware of her mortality, and that was something she rarely liked to face."

Even death isn't the end of it – we have concerns about what might happen to our bodies after death. We tend to regard the human body as more than simply a vessel or machine that carries our consciousness. We require that dead people be treated with appropriate respect – even those of us without strong religious beliefs. The human body is regarded differently from that of other animals – it is not simply a source of meat or 'spare parts' to be butchered for the benefit of others. That is why organ donation has been such a difficult issue for people to face – and why 'organ harvesting' has been the subject of a number of medical thrillers.

The medical thriller – and the depiction of doctors in literature and other media – appears to be a subject that has been studied more by those in the medical field than by writers in the areas of literature or the social sciences. M. Faith McLellan has written several articles on 'literature and medicine' for *The Lancet*, including one on 'Physician-Writers.' Jean-Pierre Charpy's article 'Medical Thrillers: Doctored Fiction for Future Doctors?' was published in the *Journal of Medical Humanities*; in it he said: "Although it is true that most medical thrillers share the same characteristics as thrillers – namely, fast-paced action, intensity of emotions, tension and excitement – they also have their own specific features, which are closely related to the medical knowledge or expertise of their authors and the professional environment in which they are embedded. Thus, the backdrop, the verbal exchanges and the procedures that are to be found in medical thrillers are often professionally-based."

The Historical Development of the Medical Thriller

In ancient Greece, there were physicians who created literary works and we can safely assume that even before that tribal 'healers' were also storytellers. A *Wikipedia* entry for 'Physician Writer' provides hundreds of names. The list includes Tobias Smollett (1721-1771), whose novel *Roderick Random* includes details of what it was like to be a surgeon's mate on a ship in the 1740s as well exploring themes of deceit and corruption. Also listed is Anton Chekhov (1860-1904) who, in a letter to A. S. Suvorin in September 1888, said, "Medicine is my lawful wife and literature is my mistress. When I get tired of one I spend the night with the other. Though it's disorderly, it's not so dull, and besides neither of them loses anything from my infidelity. If I did not have my medical work I doubt if I could have given my leisure and my spare thoughts to literature."

The medical thriller is a relatively modern sub-genre, but its ancestors include Mary Shelley's *Frankenstein* (1818) and Robert Louis Stevenson's *Strange Case of Dr. Jekyll and Mr. Hyde* (1886). It also has links with the traditional detective mystery – Sherlock Holmes, who first appeared in 1887, was modelled in part on the surgeon Joseph Bell and his creator, Sir Arthur Conan Doyle, was a physician himself. Doyle's contemporary R. Austin Freeman was also a doctor and created a doctor-detective, the forensic investigator Dr. Thorndyke who first appeared in 1907. Josephine Bell, pseudonym of Doris Bell Collier, was another physician who wrote over forty mystery novels, including six featuring Dr. David Wintringham, a junior assistant physician at a London research hospital which were published between 1937 and 1940.

Frank G. Slaughter earned his medical degree at Johns Hopkins University and was a surgeon before becoming a full-time writer. A best-selling author, his fifty-six books are estimated to have sold 60 million copies around the world. He wrote contemporary stories, his first being *That None Should Die* (1941), about a young doctor whose views on socialised medicine bring him into conflict with the health care system; and he wrote historical novels set during the American Civil War and Revolution, the Renaissance, Roman, and Biblical times, often exploring the medical training and practices of the period. In a review of his 1965 novel *Constantine: The Miracle of the Flaming Cross,* the *New York Times* said, "Like all of Dr. Slaughter's books, this one brims with violent action, with intrigue, battles, hairbreadth escapes." There was also a romantic subplot in many of his novels – Slaughter obviously knew what appealed to audiences and has to be seen as a forerunner of modern medical thriller writers.

Emma Lathen (economist Mary Jane Latsis and attorney Martha Henissart) wrote mystery novels set against the background of New York and Washington, DC politics, business and banking and her 1968 novel *A Stitch in Time* features a banker who uncovers a conspiracy involving doctors prescribing overpriced drugs for their own profit. The same two authors, under the pen name R. B. Dominic, also wrote *The Attending Physician* (1980) in which a congressman investigates Medicaid fraud and murder.

Michael Crichton received his medical degree at Harvard and wrote several novels set in the world of medicine and medical research, including *The*

Andromeda Strain (1969) and *The Terminal Man* (1972), both of which were adapted into movies.

Robin Cook graduated from Wesleyan University and trained at Massachusetts General Hospital. Robin Cook is generally credited with establishing the medical thriller as a successful sub-genre: his *Coma* (1977) reached number six on the *New York Times* bestseller list and included as one of the NYT's 'Outstanding Books of the Year.' He has since written more than thirty novels, most in the medical thriller sub-genre, and they are reported to have sold almost 400 million copies worldwide. *Coma* was adapted into a successful film, directed by Michael Crichton who also wrote the screenplay. A number of Cook's novels have been adapted for television, including a 2012 miniseries based on *Coma*.

Michael Palmer, like Robin Cook, graduated from Wesleyan University and trained at Massachusetts General Hospital. His first medical thriller was *The Sisterhood*(1982) and twenty more followed, including *Extreme Measures,* which was adapted into a feature film starring Hugh Grant and Gene Hackman.

Leonard S. Goldberg was educated at the Medical University of South Carolina and became a consulting physician at UCLA in rheumatology and immunology. His first medical thriller was *Transplant* (1980) and he is the author of the Joanna Blalock series.

Tess Gerritsen received her medical degree from University of California, San Francisco and practised in Hawaii. Her first bestselling medical thriller was *Harvest* (1996) and several more followed. She has also written more than a dozen crime thrillers featuring police detective Jane Rizzoli and medical examiner Dr. Maura Isles. The series was adapted for television, running for seven seasons from 2010 to 2016.

C. J. Lyons is a paediatrician who attended medical school at the University of Florida; she is the *New York Times* bestselling author of thirty novels which she describes as 'thrillers with heart.'

The Medicine in Medical Thrillers

Are the medicine and medical procedures depicted in these thrillers realistic? And if so, to what extent? Robin Cook, in his author note in *Seizure*, said: "I think of my novels as 'faction,' a coined word meaning that the facts and fiction are so mixed that the dividing line between the two is often hard to discern."

In his article, Jean-Pierre Charpy said that, "From a practical viewpoint, most of the medical scenes represented in the novels offer realistic views of the ER, the OR, or the ICU to the lay reader ... Pathologies and procedures are usually described with accuracy, and the terminology that is used is likely to be globally understood by the non-specialist..." He quotes a passage from Tess Gerritsen's *The Surgeon* and says, "... the atmosphere of the emergency procedure depicted ... is particularly realistic ... it also portrays professional values by highlighting the tense interpersonal relationships that are brought into play in this kind of situation." Charpy also comments on the accuracy of medical terminology used in such thrillers, saying: "Some definitions are just as good as the ones provided by medical dictionaries..." and gives as an example a piece on lupus from Leah Ruth Robinson's *Blood Run*. Readers can, he believes, gain a better understanding of the meaning of medical terms because they are "presented in context and can often be understood thanks to inference ... [and] to clarify obscure medical words or expressions, the authors of medical thrillers often resort to rephrasing." He gives this example from Michael Palmer's *The Patient:* "But we've got to be especially careful operating around what's called Wernicke's area. That's the centre that controls speech and language." Charpy also notes the importance of metaphor in helping non-specialised readers understand complex medical situations.

Medical language is complex and uses terminology that removes emotional and psychological 'baggage' that might otherwise be attached to procedures. Cutting an organ out of one body for transplant into another is referred to as a 'donation' or a 'gift.' Wounds are not sewn up, they are sutured. Simple and often quite brutal actions are given neutral-sounding names. The human body is a machine to be repaired and it is filled with components with complex scientific names. Then there is the private language used between medical staff – the slang terms, the hostile or insulting references to patients or colleagues, the black humour – all part of a defensive system that allows them to dehumanise the situation and dissipate any psychological or emotional responses that might otherwise get in the way of them doing their jobs effectively.

One mistake that some medical thriller writers make, as Tess Gerritsen told Gale Scott, is "... to go on and on with dry medical details ... That isn't interesting to readers..." She advises that writers concentrate on characters first. Speaking to Doug P. Lyle, Gerritsen explained one way she gets around the problem of 'too much information': "If a technical detail is really interesting to me, or if I can somehow give it a grotesque or creepy spin, then I'll put it in the story. For instance, in *Gravity*, I had to tell the reader about the backup mechanisms that a space walking astronaut has for getting safely back into the spacecraft. If I'd merely described the devices (tether, jet pack, etc.) it would have been boring. Instead, I focused on what happens if the devices fail — what is it like to die in space? What would that death feel like? It was those gruesome details that added urgency to the information."

In his '6 Rules for Writing a Medical Thriller,' Chuck Sambuchino says, "Remember: you're writing a medical thriller, not giving a lecture to a bunch of medical students. Resist the urge to over-explain beyond what is necessary for your story."

Gerritsen acknowledges that handling medical terminology can be tricky, but she wants her "...professionals to sound like professionals, so I want them to use the correct terms. I don't want my physicians to tell each other "Mrs. Jones had a heart attack." I want them to say, 'She had an inferior M.I.' I don't always stop to define the terms, but I try to introduce them in such a way that the reader understands that 'V fib' is a very bad thing."

According to Charpy, it is not only the medical procedures and terminology that are accurately represented – medical thrillers also reflect professional values and ethical issues. In his Author Note in *The Fifth Vial*, Michael Palmer says, "My goal in writing suspense is first and foremost to entertain my readers and to transport them, however transiently, from the stresses and cares of their lives to the highly stylized world of the novel. My secondary goals are to inform and to present, without resolution, issues of social and ethical importance." We will look at medical ethics under the *Themes* heading below.

While generally praising the accuracy of the medicine used in these thrillers, Jean-Pierre Charpy does warn that, while they are 'fairly realistic', they do offer a 'rather selective image of the intricate world of medicine' and "focus on the sensational and/or romantic, which may induce bias and an alteration or manipulation of medical reality." But in his final analysis, he says, "Despite ... a growing tendency to focus on the sensational rather than everyday medical practice, medical suspense novels still dominantly reflect the discourse, the practices, the procedures, and the socio-cultural ways of the medical community. Although the representation(s) of medicine they offer may sometimes be flawed or sensational, they usually provide useful insights into patients' conditions, doctor-patient relationships, medical practices and professional values."

As we saw above, many of the authors of medical thrillers have first-hand experience of working in a medical environment and this enables them to create a world in their novels that feels genuine. In her article on physician-writers, M. Faith McLellan said, "The clinical gaze [has] much in common with the artist's eye," and that it is "through their privileged and intimate contact with those moments of greatest human drama (birth, illness, injury, suffering, disease, death) that physicians are in a unique position to observe, record and create the stories that make us human." Janet Seggie, editor of the *South African Medical Journal* also commented on this: "Doctors' success as writers is a reflection of their dealing with patients' narratives, repeating these in the course of case presentations and documenting consultations, histories and physical examinations, to which all apply analysis and interpretation." Michael Palmer told Gale Scott, "Doctors have two of the three things a writer needs: a love of people and discipline..." but that they also need a love of words. Tess Gerritsen said to the same interviewer, "I'm not sure doctors have an edge, because they are trained to be so objective."

Does all of this mean that you *have* to be a physician to write a medical thriller? No. But you do need access to reliable medical knowledge – probably from a combination of desk research and talking to doctors and scientists – and should ideally have someone with medical experience as one of your beta readers.

The Non-Fiction Medical Thriller
In his book *The American Thriller,* Paul Cobley refers to the 'non-fiction thriller,' using the example of *All the President's Men,* Woodward and Bernstein's account of the Watergate Scandal. There are also examples in the medical sub-genre, including Richard Preston's *The Hot Zone,* an exploration of the origins, nature and risks relating to Ebola-like diseases, and William T. Close's autobiographical *Ebola: A Novel of the First Outbreak by a Doctor Who Was There.* Preston also wrote the thriller *The Cobra Event,* concerning attempted bio-terrorism, and completed the novel *Micro* after Michael Crichton's death in 2008.

Writing the Medical Thriller

Gail Jennes quotes Robin Cook as saying, "Learning to write a bestseller is like teaching yourself to wire a house." He explained his own method of learning in an interview with Geraldine Fabrikant: "I studied how the reader was manipulated by the writer. I came up with a list of techniques that I wrote down on index cards. And I used every one of them in *Coma*." In some interviews Cook says he did this after reading 200 best-sellers. In an interview with Eric J. Topol, Cook said, "I decided to pick two projects to study in-depth: *Jaws* and *Love Story*." He said that trying to approach the story as if it was a movie also helped. One of the techniques Cook adopted was to make sure that each chapter ended in such a way that the reader had to go on to the next chapter. Cook also told Topol, "I did not want *Coma* to be 'horror in the hospital.' That was not the message, and it could have been distorted in that way very easily."

Speaking to Gale Scott, Tess Gerritsen said: "You have to find a medical concept or ethical dilemma that is new and fresh. You can't keep writing about evil viruses and evil drug companies. You have to get down to the human side, write about people. I try to think of things that would really scare me."

Genre Conventions

Conspiracy

The conspiracy in a medical thriller is, unsurprisingly, related to medical practice or medical research methods. Although medical malpractice is covered by the legal system, the actions of doctors are more often judged against a system of medical ethics as symbolised by a medical oath. This oath is designed to protect the patient and to ensure that the doctor behaves in a professional manner at all times. The conspirators in a medical thriller behave in a way that puts their own interests before those of the patient, effectively breaking one or more terms of their oath. Medical ethics and the doctors' oath are covered under *Themes* below.

Characters

Hierarchical social groups work particularly well in fiction – whether it is king and queen and knight and peasant, or godfather and consigliere and capo and soldier. The hospital – and also the pharmaceutical company – is another example. There is potential for internal politics and power struggles, and for relationships between people at different levels in the structure. If you are going to write about a hospital, you need to have a clear picture of this structure and know who is beholden to whom.

Medical thrillers, and stories in other genres that use a medical setting, utilise a number of relationships that occur in the hospital hierarchy: doctor-patient, doctor-nurse, doctor-administrator, doctor-trustee/chairman. These can be explored in a work context, often in terms of which has the more 'powerful' position, or in terms of friendships and romantic affairs. The expressively emotional patient (or relative of a patient) is often contrasted with the calm objectivity of the doctor. But outside the hospital setting, we may then see the emotional side of the doctor in a family setting, giving us a different sort of contrast.

Showing the same person acting and speaking in different situations like this can be a way of deepening character, by showing different aspects of the personality; or of confirming the character traits – if someone demonstrates the same behaviour at work and at home, we can see that it is an intrinsic part of his character.

Locations
The medical thriller typically has a hospital or research laboratory as one of its primary locations. Operating theatres, wards, emergency rooms, morgues, and conference rooms often appear. Seminar rooms and lecture theatres in medical schools are also used, as are nursing homes and psychiatric clinics. The back of an ambulance is also a popular location to use, as it provides an enclosed environment combined with a sense of urgency and movement. An oak-panelled boardroom, where the top tier of management meet, can be used to present a feeling of being in an 'ivory tower' or an oasis of calm, depending on the needs of the story.

These settings are all familiar to us from television shows and films, which means there is a danger that we will create a location that is based on what we have seen on television. The risk here is that the scene will seem generic and lifeless. Writers who have professional experience of such places can include specific details that make these places seem much more real to the reader. Those of us who haven't worked in such places have to find other ways of creating original and specific details. This may mean reading autobiographies of people who do work in such situations – books of medical humour by ex-doctors are often a good source – or it may mean concentrating on the people in the scene and their behaviour, rather than the physical environment itself.

Fernandez and Nayak compare the structures of the hospitals in *Coma* and other medical thrillers with the "gothic castles and palaces of medieval times," with an "endless number of rooms and unknown spaces," and to the hospital as being a 'gothic claustrophobic' space. The Boston Memorial Hospital in *Coma* is referred to as a labyrinth that is home to the "mysteries of birth, death and rebirth." And it is a place where we become "vulnerable and exposed to the ... surgeon's knives."

Being a sub-genre of the Thriller, the Medical Thriller can also feature any of the locations from that, so dimly lit underground car parks and meetings in neutral locations such as parks can also be found.

Iconography
Even if we have never been into hospital ourselves, we have seen the surgical masks and gloves, the clothing referred to as 'scrubs', and trays of equipment including scalpels and syringes. We recognise the biohazard symbol and with the Rod of Asclepius or Staff of Asclepius – a staff with a snake entwined around it – or, more commonly used in the USA, the *caduceus* – a staff carried by Hermes and shown as a short staff with wings on top and two snakes entwined around it. Medicine, particularly out 'in the field,' is often associated with the symbols of the Red Cross, Red Crescent, or Red Crystal which belong to the private humanitarian institution, the International Committee of the Red Cross.

Being a sub-genre of the Thriller, the Medical Thriller can also feature any of the visuals from that.

Themes

Medical Ethics and the Hippocratic Oath

Medical thrillers often refer to the fact that a doctor swears an oath and people generally believe that this is a reference to the Hippocratic Oath, set down by Hippocrates sometime between the third and fifth centuries BC. The Oath is the earliest expression of medical ethics in the Western world. In fact, in US medical schools a number of different oaths are used: the Hippocratic Oath or a modified version of it; the Osteopathic Oath; the Oath of Maimonides; the original or a modified form of the Declaration of Geneva; or an oath authored by students and or faculty. Many people also believe that the phrase 'First do no harm' is part of the Hippocratic oath, but these specific words do not appear in the text.

For our purposes, the best summary of modern medical ethics is that set down in *The Declaration of Geneva,* as published by the World Medical Association, which in its 2017 revision reads:

As a member of the medical profession:

- I solemnly pledge to dedicate my life to the service of humanity;
- The health and well-being of my patient will be my first consideration;
- I will respect the autonomy and dignity of my patient;
- I will maintain the utmost respect for human life;
- I will not permit considerations of age, disease or disability, creed, ethnic origin, gender, nationality, political affiliation, race, sexual orientation, social standing or any other factor to intervene between my duty and my patient;
- I will respect the secrets that are confided in me, even after the patient has died;
- I will practise my profession with conscience and dignity and in accordance with good medical practice;
- I will foster the honour and noble traditions of the medical profession;
- I will give to my teachers, colleagues, and students the respect and gratitude that is their due;
- I will share my medical knowledge for the benefit of the patient and the advancement of healthcare;
- I will attend to my own health, well-being, and abilities in order to provide care of the highest standard;
- I will not use my medical knowledge to violate human rights and civil liberties, even under threat;
- I make these promises solemnly, freely and upon my honour.

The hero of a medical thriller will respect the wording and the spirit of this pledge, while the villain and/or conspirators will violate one or more of ethical guidelines it contains.

You can read more about medical ethics and good practice on the websites of the *American Medical Association* or the British *General Medical Council.*

In her book *Robin Cook: A Critical Companion,* Lorena Laura Stookey says, "Within Cook's novels, the villains who ruthlessly exploit others are invariably motivated by vanity or greed."

Vanity – Medicine versus the 'God Complex'
To save a life, repair an injury, cure a disease, and even to revive someone who has 'died' – these are incredible achievements which some part of our brains may see as requiring god-like abilities. But we require our doctors to demonstrate humility – they are helping others selflessly – and not to see themselves as something more than human. But as Lorena Laura Stookey writes, medicine's "traditional status as a privileged profession presents special temptations for the vain." Robin Cook portrays such men as villains whose "arrogance born of their special calling leads [them] to set their personal goals above the interests of other people. Working in secrecy, these characters do not stop at murder in their singular support of their private ambitions and desires."

Robin Cook, quoted in *Contemporary Authors,* 120, has said: "Researchers feel they're doing something so important that they don't have to be held to the same guidelines that other people are. In a way that's one of the general problems in medicine, researchers feeling that they're doing the most important thing of all and that gives them a sort of licence to do what they think is right. They start making minor or major ethical decisions on their own... The ethical problems of dealing with this kind of thing are horrendous."

Presenting such characters in their stories allows authors to explore the consequences of this arrogance and egotism, and to the ethical issues that arise as a result of their actions. They are modern-day versions of Mary Shelley's Victor Frankenstein, H. P. Lovecraft's Herbert West, or Robert Louis Stevenson's Dr. Henry Jekyll, and only a small step away from the graverobbers and vivisectionists of the era of Burke and Hare.

Even when a senior doctor is not the villain of the piece, he may be presented as a prima donna with an inflated sense of entitlement and prone to temper tantrums. This sort of person is attracted to the power and prestige associated with the position of a successful physician.

Greed – Medicine versus Business
In an ideal world, medical treatment and aftercare would be provided solely on the basis of need. The sick would be healed. Those beyond cure would receive whatever palliative care was required. But we do not live in such a world. We have to have in place a system which meets the costs of medical care and adequately rewards those who spend years of their lives learning to provide that care. But when there is a system which involves money, there will be people seeking to make a profit – and for some of them, profit will be the only goal. And, as Fernandez and Nayak note, doctors too are affected by this culture: "Founded and sustained on highly economic incentives and cultural values, the philanthropic element diminishes and a career-oriented, ambitious and competitive world comes into being."

Writing about the work of Robin Cook, Lorena Laura Stookey says that the field of medicine's "gradual transformation into a form of business enterprise leaves it vulnerable to the manipulations of people too strongly motivated by economic considerations," and this is a topic that the author seeks to highlight in his novels. There are people who will put their own interests above the needs of patients. "Part of Cook's purpose in writing thrilling tales of intrigue and suspense is to demonstrate for readers just where those interests lie. Thus, in exaggerating their dangers through his use of a conspiracy motif, he is able to inform his reading audience ... [that as patients, they too] ... necessarily have a strong interest in understanding developments within the medical profession."

The 'Democratization' of Medical Knowledge
Reviewing *Vital Signs* in *Publishers Weekly,* Sybil Steinberg noted that Robin Cook's novels are "designed, in part, to keep the public aware of both the technological possibilities of modern medicine and the ensuing ethical problems." A number of medical thriller writers have said that entertaining readers is only one of their goals – they also want to make people aware of developments and issues in the field of medicine.

Robin Cook: "not only can fiction gain a much larger audience than, say, if you wrote a serious essay about these problems, but you also get people to experience the emotional aspects of the problems and reach an understanding which they couldn't have otherwise, short of actually participating themselves." (*Contemporary Authors,* 120)

Lorena Laura Stookey: "All of Cook's major themes, his visions of entrapment and the victimisation of innocent people, his scenarios of secrecy in research and the deadly secrecy of conspiracy, can be linked together by the recognition that in knowledge resides a power to confront the designs of special interests that do not serve the public good."

The Medical Conspiracy Thriller Plot

Writing in *Physician's Weekly,* Gale Scott said: "Medical thrillers are formulaic. Writers take an aspect of medicine and make it frightening. Robotics, resistant organisms, genetic manipulation, and organ transplantation have been used to effect. The protagonist is almost always a sympathetic physician – often a woman – whose story involves romantic relationships, a threatened career, and critical choices involving medical ethics." We have already seen that conspirators who break their medical oath are usually motivated by either greed or an egocentric form of vanity. To discover the common plot elements of this type of thriller, I looked at two stories in depth – Robin Cook's *Coma* (1977) and Michael Palmer's *Extreme Measures* (1991). Both of were adapted as movies, in 1978 and 1996 respectively.

The plot of a medical conspiracy thriller is very similar to that of the amateur-on-the-run thriller. Our 'innocent' in this case is usually a young medical professional who accidentally stumbles upon the conspiracy.

Sequence 1

The first sequence typically consists of two parts: (a) introducing the hero, and (b) introducing an intriguing medical situation. In *Coma* we get (a) then (b); in *Extreme Measures* we get (b) then (a).

The hero (or heroine) and their world. Usually the hero is a young professional doctor or a trainee, working in a busy hospital, dealing with life-saving or other important medical procedures. As well as seeing them at work, we may learn something about their home life and/or relationships.

An intriguing medical situation. This will be related to the medical conspiracy – it is the first clue that something is wrong. It is the thing that draws the hero's attention and leads him to stumble onto the conspiracy. In *Coma*, a woman undergoing routine surgery fails to come out of anaesthesia and suffers brain death, lapsing into a coma that she will never come out of. In *Extreme Measures*, two naked men who are obviously sick escape from some sort of facility, trying to elude their pursuers – one ends up in the hero's emergency room where he has a seizure and dies, but not before uttering some cryptic words.

In this sequence there may also be a hint, or even a direct reference, to the main theme of the story – the ethical issue that the story explores. In *Coma* it is 'profit before people' and in *Extreme Measures* it is 'medical progress requires sacrifices.' In both cases there are questions about whether one life has more value than another and whether doctors should be allowed to decide who lives and who dies.

Sequence 2

The hero investigates the death of the patient. He or she is unhappy about the 'official' cause of death, feeling that it doesn't adequately explain how the patient came to die. By requesting information about the mysterious death, and by continuing to investigate, the hero draws the attention of the villain.

Suspicious tests. One clue that the hero often discovers is that unnecessary tests were performed on the patient – bloodwork or tissue-typing that would not normally be requested for the sort of medical treatment that they received. This is often (unconvincingly) explained away as a clerical error or random sampling for quality checking. In *Coma* this clue is discovered in Sequence 2; in *Extreme Measures* it appears in Sequence 3.

Meet the villain. The person masterminding the conspiracy is typically a doctor with years of experience who has achieved a position of power and prestige. We may learn immediately that he is the villain (*Extreme Measures*) or he may be someone that the hero trusts and respects until much later in the story (*Coma*). The audience may learn the identity of the villain before the hero does – this places them in a 'superior' position (they know something the hero doesn't) which can be useful in creating suspense. ('Don't trust him – he's a psychopath!') Whatever the hero knows, the villain is almost always aware of who the hero is and what he is doing – and recognises that the hero is a threat to him and to the continuing success of the conspiracy.

Meet the henchmen. The villain, a respectable medical professional, often has a henchman or a couple of thugs to do the dirty work for him. The villain in *Extreme Measures* has a police detective and an FBI agent working for him –

they appear briefly in Sequence 1, pursuing the escaped men, and are introduced properly in Sequence 2. In *Coma*, the villain has a henchman-killer who is introduced in Sequence 4. He also has other people working for him that we don't learn about until later. By its nature, a conspiracy involves more than one person working alone. Having several opposition characters helps to show that the odds are stacked against the hero, helping demonstrate how big the stakes are, and building suspense, because the audience knows the hero is getting into something more dangerous than he suspects.

Drop the investigation 1. There may be an early attempt to try and persuade the hero to drop the investigation – perhaps a warning that it would not be good for his career to be seen to be spending time on something like this. This first warning may be given by someone who genuinely cares about the hero's well-being – often a co-worker. The hero is told that the patient's death is not as unusual as he seems to think it is – and that time and other resources are not available to look into every situation that someone has a 'bad feeling' about.

Additional Evidence. The hero discovers that there have been more mysterious deaths like the one he witnessed – and/or more disappearing dead patients. The heroine of *Coma* discovers this in Sequence 2; the hero of *Extreme Measures* finds out in Sequence 3.

Sequence 3

In the third sequence, the hero's investigation becomes more serious. Against the advice of friends, colleagues, and/or superiors, he digs deeper.

Missing evidence and misinformation. Aware of the hero's investigation, the villain may arrange for an important piece of evidence – perhaps even a body – to go missing. Or he may arrange for a piece of misinformation to be found – a plausible solution to some or all of the mystery. These are further attempts to get the hero to voluntarily give up his quest for the truth.

Drop the investigation 2. When gentle persuasion fails, the stakes are raised and the hero is *ordered* by his boss to drop the investigation – and there will be some implied threat that the hero's career is at stake if he disobeys. There is usually also an implication that this directive has come from someone higher up the management chain – pressure has been put on the boss to tell the hero to drop it. The hero's boss may be presented as a sympathetic character and/or a mentor – often so that the writer can have this person betray the hero later (*Coma*) or have the mentor taken away – injured or killed! – after the midpoint, when the hero's situation gradually gets worse and worse. Or the boss may act suspiciously, causing the audience – and the hero – to think he is part of the conspiracy (*Extreme Measures*).

Red herrings. Often the writer plants a red herring in Sequence 3 so that the audience – and the hero – comes to suspect someone who is not actually guilty. In keeping the identity of the villain secret, *Coma* leads us to suspect that another character is responsible for the conspiracy, the Head of Anaesthesiology. In *Extreme Measures*, as mentioned above, we come to suspect the hero's boss.

Pathology. Another source that the hero may approach for information about the mysterious death (s) is the pathologist. There is often an element of disrespectful or gallows humour in these scenes – pathologists and morgue attendants deal with dead bodies on a daily basis and so tend to be more blasé about the whole thing. Doctors too often have a nice line in grisly humour. Whether the pathologist is openly helpful or obstructive, the hero will usually come away with some useful clue. In *Extreme Measures* the hero learns that his hospital has a reputation for losing bodies – both alive and dead. The heroine in *Coma* asks a couple of pathologists how they might deliberately induce a coma in a patient and accepting this as a challenge to devise the 'perfect murder,' they suggest giving the patient carbon monoxide instead of oxygen so that the brain dies. But, since all of the dead people had different surgeons and anaesthetists, they couldn't have been murdered – unless the conspiracy involves every anaesthetist in the hospital. This again directs the audience's attention toward the red herring, the Head of Anaesthesiology.

More clues. In Sequence 3, the heroine of *Coma* also learns that comatose patients are normally moved to a chronic care facility, the Jefferson Institute. And, as mentioned under Sequence 2, there are other things that can be included in 3. In *Extreme Measures*, this is where the hero discovers the clue about the unnecessary bloodwork.

Patient records. In both of our sample stories, the main character accesses confidential medical records about patients. The hero of *Extreme Measures* learns that both of the men we saw in Sequence 1 had previously been patients of the hospital and undergone minor treatments – this was when the unnecessary bloodwork was ordered. He also comes to suspect that some computer records have been wiped and goes in search of paper copies – but is caught by his boss before he can find what he wants. In *Coma*, the heroine's access to these records is split between Sequence 2, where she is denied access to them, and Sequence 5, where she sneaks in and looks at them. In both cases, the main character is lectured about the importance of patient privacy and how unauthorised access to such records is illegal – this lecture may be given by someone who genuinely cares about medical ethics and the main character, or it may be given by someone who is guilty of even greater breaches of medical ethics who just wants to keep the main character away from the papers.

Another patient death. Coma ups the ante by having a second patient suffer brain death while undergoing routine surgery. In *Extreme Measures*, the second victim – the second man who escaped from the facility in Sequence 1 – doesn't appear again until Sequence 5.

Sequence 4
As the hero's investigation continues, he becomes more of a threat to the villain – and the villain's responses to the threat will become more extreme. How quickly you escalate these responses depends on the pacing you are trying to achieve in your story. *Coma* takes a 'slow burn' approach. In Sequence 4, the heroine suspects that someone is following her (it is the villain's henchman), but this is the only overt threat and can be shrugged off as paranoia. During the rest of the sequence she continues her investigation.

Hero under attack. Extreme Measures uses an approach more typical of the thriller and shows things rapidly turning bad for the hero. We learn why the villain's two heavies are prepared to do his bidding – no matter how extreme the request: they both believe that the villain's unorthodox medical research will benefit a close relative. Knowing what is at stake for the two henchmen, we realise how much danger the hero is in: they will do anything. The two men break into the hero's apartment and plant incriminating evidence. The hero is arrested and suspended from his job. He accuses his boss of being part of the conspiracy. And then he has to do the 'walk of shame' as he is escorted from hospital premises. A rapid decline in the hero's situation occurs in many stories, not just thrillers, and usually occurs after the midpoint. In *Extreme Measures* the decline starts earlier – and goes on longer: thriller writers like to make their heroes suffer! What we're seeing here is a variation on the amateur-on-the-run thriller, where the hero gradually loses all support and finds himself on the run from both the villains and the police.

A dead end. The heroine of *Coma* knows that two of the coma patients were operated on in the same operating room. Could that be what links all of the victims? She checks out the operating room but can see nothing amiss. And she knows that other operations were carried out in the same room, before and after the patient lapsed into a coma, so it can't be the room that is to blame.

A new location. On a romantic weekend away, the heroine of *Coma* takes a side-trip to check out the Jefferson Institute. She is denied entry but offered a tour at another time. In *Extreme Measures* there is also the appearance of a new location – 'The Room' where the second escapee from Sequence 1 may be hiding. In both stories, this introduction of a new location – which has been mentioned previously but never seen – more or less marks the midpoint of the story.

Sequence 5

Sequences 5 and 6 represent a 'descent' for the hero – his situation grows worse and worse, until he faces his 'darkest hour' at the end of Sequence 6 In both of our examples, the hero or heroine *literally* descends into a dark place in Sequence 5 – and the descent marks a new stage in their ongoing investigation. The heroine in *Coma* goes down into the basement area below the hospital, while the hero of *Extreme Measures* descends into a hidden world below the railway station where homeless people have created their own safe haven. In both cases, their subsequent return to the surface brings them into direct confrontation with the villain's henchman/men.

Death of a vital witness. In *Coma* the heroine arranges to meet a maintenance man who says he knows how the coma deaths are being caused. When she goes down into the basement, she finds the man has been killed and his death has been made to look like an accident. In *Extreme Measures,* the hero also loses a key witness – the second escapee – who dies in a more direct way: this happens in Sequence 6.

An important discovery. The heroine in *Coma* discovers where the carbon monoxide is introduced into the hospital's system; climbing up out of the dark basement, she follows the pipe which leads to the operating theatre where two of the coma deaths occurred. She also discovers the mechanism which is used to turn it on and off. She then tricks her way into the office of the Head of Anaesthesiology and looks at the records of the ten other coma patients – all had surgery in the same operating room. In *Extreme Measures,* the hero descends deep underground. Initially suspicious of him, the people who live there threaten him – but when they learn he is a doctor, they allow him to examine the second escapee (from Sequence 1) who is now very sick. The hero learns that someone has conducted experimental surgery on the man's spine. He needs to get the man up to a hospital or he will die – so he and two of the underground dwellers begin the ascent, carrying the sick man between them.

Attack of the henchmen. In *Coma,* the heroine is stalked through the darkened teaching rooms of the hospital by the henchman who killed the maintenance man – she escapes, but only just. The hero of *Extreme Measures* is attacked by the villain's henchmen in Sequence 6.

Sequence 6

Sequence 6 in any story typically takes the hero or heroine to their darkest hour and it sets up the action for the last two sequences of the story, the climax and resolution. Again, the pacing of our two sample stories differs, with *Coma* relying on suspense and a growing sense of unease and *Extreme Measures* moving into an action sequence much sooner.

Attack of the henchmen. The hero of *Extreme Measures* reaches the surface with the two underground dwellers and the injured escapee. The villain's two henchmen are waiting with guns: the two men and the sick escapee are killed – a vital witness lost. The hero is also shot but manages to get away.

Betrayal. In both cases, the hero or heroine is betrayed by someone they trusted – with *Coma* again throwing the audience a red herring when it comes to the betrayer. The heroine tells her partner everything that she has discovered, but then hears him making a telephone call. She thinks that he has betrayed her, so she runs and hides out at a hotel. When she calls the hospital the next day to pick up her messages, they try to get her to reveal her location. She is now at the point where she can't trust anyone. After he is shot, the hero of *Extreme Measures* needs medical attention and goes to the home of a nurse he believes he can trust – but she betrays him and he is knocked unconscious.

The villain's lair. The heroine of *Coma* goes to the Jefferson Institute and takes the official tour. She sneaks away from the group so she can examine areas not included in the tour. She finally discovers the grisly secret that the villain has been hiding – the way in which the conspirators are making money from the bodies of the coma victims. This is a dark and shocking moment which serves in place of the normal 'hero's darkest hour' because in *Coma* that moment doesn't actually take place until the beginning of Sequence 8. Having been knocked unconscious, the hero of *Extreme Measures* wakes to find himself a prisoner in the villain's lair – in this case, a private medical facility and research lab whose name has been mentioned several times during the story, but the location of which was unknown to the hero.

The hero's darkest hour. What is the worst possible thing that can happen to the hero of a medical thriller? To find himself lying in a bed or on an operating table at the mercy of the 'mad doctor' who is the villain of the story. This is what happens to the hero of *Extreme Measures* and it occurs in the traditional end of Act II/end of Sequence 6 position. In *Coma*, as mentioned above, the same situation does not occur until the beginning of Sequence 8, where it is used as the climax of the story.

Sequence 7

Sequence 7 builds up to the climax of the story. The hero reacts to the crisis situation that ended Sequence 6 and must decide what move to make next.

Hero escapes the villain's clutches. The end of Sequence 6 in *Extreme Measures* was typical of many thrillers, including the James Bond stories: the hero had been captured and was at the mercy of the villain. In this case, there was a 'medical' twist to the situation and a real 'Oh, no!' moment. Instead of physical torture, the hero is subjected to psychological torture by the villain, who tells him he has been paralysed by his injuries. Help comes from an unexpected quarter – the nurse who betrayed him helps the hero get free.

Hunt/chase. Still suffering the effects of his bullet wound, the hero of *Extreme Measures* tries to escape from the villain's lair. He is spotted on a security monitor and the hunt/chase begins – he must not be allowed to escape alive. After the heroine of *Coma* has discovered the grim purpose of the institute, she tries to escape but is spotted on a security monitor. The hunt/chase begins – she cannot be allowed to escape alive.

The villain's speech. At some point before the climax of the story, the villain explains things as he sees them. A similar speech occurs in the James Bond stories when the villain explains 'this is why I do what I do.' It demonstrates his worldview, his psychology, and is – as he sees it – a justification of his actions. In the Bond movies, this speech often takes place when the hero is captured and/or when he is being tortured. In *Coma* it takes place at the end of Sequence 7. In *Extreme Measures* it takes place at the climax of the story in Sequence 8 – though there is a sort of preamble in Sequence 7 where the villain tries to explain to the hero why he has 'tortured' him and tries to persuade the hero to join his team. The villain's speech is his side of an ethical debate and is, from the point of view of the audience and the hero, the wrong side. It typically suggests that doctors and medical researchers are special people and the normal rules should not apply to them – the medical outcomes they achieve justify the means they use to achieve them. It is okay for a few people to suffer and die if it means that hundreds will benefit – the sacrifice is worth it. It is evidence that the villain has, at some point, lost the fundamental idea of what it is to be a doctor – 'first, do no harm' may not be part of a doctor's oath, but it should be a guiding principle.

Outcome of the first battle. The injured hero of *Extreme Measures* engages in a desperate fight with the villain's henchman in an elevator. He eventually manages to overcome his opponent. The heroine of *Coma* manages to outwit her pursuers and escapes from the institute on the roof of an ambulance.

Face to face with the villain. The hero of *Extreme Measures* staggers out of the elevator, battered and bloody – and finds himself face to face with the villain. In *Coma*, the heroine goes back to the hospital and tells the Head of Surgery everything she has learned, believing that the Head of Anaesthesiology is behind it all. Too late, she realises the Head of Surgery is the villain – and he has drugged her drink. He performs his 'villain's speech' as the drug slowly takes effect on her.

Sequence 8

Sequence 8 provides the outcome of the final, climactic battle plus the resolution which validates the ending. The pattern here is: hero and villain engage in final conflict, hero wins (or not), and the world of the story is restored to equilibrium – life returns to normal. Here I will look at how each of our example stories handles that sequence of events.

Coma. The almost-unconscious and helpless heroine is wheeled down to surgery. Staff are told that she has a burst appendix and that she is very fortunate because the Head of Surgery is going to carry out the operation himself. This is her equivalent of the 'darkest hour' that we saw at the end of Sequence 6. Luckily for her, her partner turns out not to be a betrayer after all, and he becomes suspicious when the Head of Surgery *insists* on using the operating room that was used for all of the coma patients. In a race against time, he races off and retraces the journey the heroine took, following the pipes carrying the carbon monoxide, and manages to turn it off just in time. Police are waiting outside the operating room to arrest the surgeon – a sign that order is being restored to the world.

I'm always a little disappointed when the heroine of a story gets herself into trouble and has to be rescued by a man. Perhaps it's just me, but I feel this short-changes the heroine. Isn't this just the same as the hero of *Extreme Measures* being rescued by the nurse in Sequence 7? I don't think so, because the nurse doesn't complete the climactic action of the story – the hero goes on to do that at the end of Sequence 7 and into Sequence 8. I can see *why* it was done in *Coma* – having the heroine helpless in the operating room makes for a very tense climax. And having the male character essentially repeating an action she has already taken almost makes her responsible for the climactic action. But still...

To overcome this weakness, I would probably have had the male character *fail* to get to the carbon monoxide switch in time – and then discover that the heroine has already disabled it, effectively saving herself. But, as I said, maybe it's just me.

Extreme Measures. Hero and villain stand face-to-face in the reception area of the villain's lair. It is like a showdown in the main street in a Western, but the hero is the only one with a gun – he took it from the henchman who lies unconscious in the elevator behind him. The climactic action – after the elevator fight – is almost all verbal. The villain delivers his speech, saying that a few street people will suffer and die, but millions of people will benefit from the research done on them – meaning that those street people are heroes. In his rebuttal, the hero says this is morally/ethically wrong, because those people did not *choose* to be heroes – doctors cannot be allowed to make the choice for them. Their lives have the same value as any other. This echoes a scene in Sequence 1 where the hero had to decide who got to go into the only available operating room – a criminal or a cop. There is a final tussle with the henchman, which ultimately decides the villain's fate. In a final scene, we see the hero back in a professional role – planning to conduct medical research in an ethical manner. The world has been restored to balance.

Extreme Measures has been criticised for being too thriller-like and over the top, particularly in the sequences after the midpoint. Too much 'thriller' and not enough 'medical' for some people. There is always a danger in any thriller sub-genre that the generic thriller elements will overwhelm the unique sub-genre elements. Personally, I think this film manages the balance very well and the ethical argument – the villain's speech and the hero's rebuttal – are stronger than the equivalent arguments in *Coma*. If I have one criticism of *Extreme Measures* it is that the villain's climactic speech is diluted slightly by the fact that there was a lot of talking by the villain over his lair's loudspeakers during the chase and fight before the final confrontation.

One final observation on the medical conspiracy thriller, which you may have already spotted: usually it is the dark places in a story that are associated with fear and corruption, with hell or the underworld, and with the darkest corners of the human mind. But in these medical thrillers, good people dwell in dark places, they are protective caves, and it is in the brightly-lit and antiseptic operating rooms that evil exists. It is a nice twist.

Now relax, breath normally, and count backwards from 100...

The 'Outbreak' Thriller Plot

A story about the outbreak of a deadly disease can be approached as a horror story, science fiction, or thriller. The 'infectious organism from space' has been done as all three in the *Quatermass Experiment* (1953) by Nigel Kneale, *Plague from Space* (1965) by Harry Harrison, and *The Andromeda Strain* (1969) by Michael Crichton. Films of this type have also been described as 'disaster movies,' but I think there is a distinction to be drawn here – generally speaking, in a disaster movie (or novel) there is a group of people who are trying to survive the occurrence and/or aftermath of a calamitous situation; in the outbreak thriller, we have a group of people who are concerned with trying to *prevent* the disaster that the infectious disease could become.

In seeking the common plot elements for the outbreak thriller, I picked three different films as examples for this sub-category of the medical thriller – they have many things in common, but also provide different approaches to the outbreak thriller. *The Andromeda Strain*, like the other two stories, opens with a small town being infected by an unknown virus. But it differs from them in that from Sequence 3 onwards, the action is almost entirely confined to the underground laboratory used by the hero and his team. *Outbreak* tells of a virus that affects two discrete areas which can be cordoned off from the rest of the world. *Contagion* deals with an infection which crosses international borders and becomes a world-wide problem very quickly.

The plot of an outbreak thriller is similar to a James Bond 'mission' plot, with the disease taking the place of the villain's doomsday device. There may or may not be a conspiracy – often we learn that the virus is stored as, or is wanted so that it can become, a biological weapon. The role of villain is usually played by some powerful figure in the military, politics, or business who has selfish motives for opposing the hero who is trying to overcome the threat of the virus. The villain's motive, as in the medical conspiracy, is usually greed or a desire for prestige and power.

The Andromeda Strain gives us the basic structure for this type of 'mission' story: first, there is an outbreak of a new disease, usually a virus. Then there are three stages of the work of the medical researchers – find and obtain a sample of the virus; learn what it is and how it works; how to contain and eradicate it, that is, find a cure and/or a vaccine.

The Andromeda Strain (1971), based on the novel by Michael Crichton, has elements of science fiction and could also be classified as a technothriller. *Outbreak*(1995), an original screenplay by Scott Z. Burns, has the most thriller-like plot and includes elements that wouldn't be out of place in a James Bond movie. *Contagion*(2011) is the most realistic of the three and is based on the 'non-fiction thriller' *The Hot Zone* by Richard Preston. Let's pull them all apart and see what an outbreak thriller plot looks like.

Sequence 1
First infections. The first outbreak of a previously unknown virus and a fairly graphic depiction of its effects on human victims. This helps to establish the stakes of the story – what the hero will be up against and what will happen if he doesn't succeed.

Introduce the hero and his team. We typically see these people in action, demonstrating their professional skills. Their roles are often indicated by having them appear in hazmat suits of some kind. We may see them at the site of the first infection or involved in some other sort of related situation. They are usually received by local people with a combination of relief (thank God, the experts are here) and fear (they're only here because something terrible is happening).

Show normal family life and/or relationships. This may involve the hero or someone in his team, a survivor of the first outbreak, or people who will be affected by the outbreak later in the story. The aim here is to show the ordinary people and way of life that the hero and his team will be battling to protect. Again, we are establishing what is at stake in the story – bad things could happen to these nice people. People who are like us.

Destruction of the site of the first outbreak. If the site of the first outbreak is small and remote, the town or village may be bombed or burned to remove the threat of the virus spreading. This happens in *Outbreak* and it is requested, but not carried out, in *The Andromeda Strain*. Because of the international scope of *Contagion*, this sort of attempt at containment cannot be used. The decision to destroy the site may be taken by the scientists, by the military, or by politicians.

Sequence 2
Visiting the site of the first outbreak. If the hero and his team did not visit the site of the first infections in Sequence 1, they may go there in Sequence 2 (and destruction of the site may occur at the end of this sequence instead). Samples

of the unknown virus will be collected and the survivors (if any) will be placed in quarantine in case they have been infected or are carrying the virus.

The lab and biosafety. Samples and survivors are taken back to the team's research laboratory. At this point, the audience will be told about the different levels of biosafety used in the labs – BSL-1 to BSL-4. A disease such as Ebola – which makes an effective model for any fictional virus – has to be handled at the highest level, BSL-4. This level requires the use of 'positive pressure personnel suits', the features of which will also be shown to the audience. These levels of safety are usually established in Sequence 1 or 2 and may be explained in more detail in a later sequence, to emphasise how serious the threat of the virus is to those working on it. They are portrayed in both *Outbreak* and *Contagion*. *The Andromeda Strain* shows similar levels, and they make up most of Sequence 3, but they're treated in a more science fictional way.

Investigation. The investigation will be a combination of scientific/biomedical lab research and old-fashioned detective work as one or more agents in the field try to piece together the chain of infection – who was infected by whom – tracing it back to an 'index case' or 'patient zero,' the first human to receive the virus from the host animal, the point at which the virus crossed from animal to human. This person may or may not become symptomatic – they may carry the virus and not become ill, passing it on to others unknowingly. 'Typhoid Mary,' for example, was identified as the first person in the USA to carry the bacteria responsible for typhoid fever. The investigators may also try to locate the original host animal, as they do in *Outbreak*.

Conspiracy. If there is a conspiracy subplot in the story, the first reference to it will usually appear in Sequence 2 or 3 – it may be a direct statement or just a hint. The conspiracy often involves the military or a corporation wanting the virus for a biological weapon. In *Contagion*, the conspiracy subplot follows a conspiracy theorist and blogger (played by Jude Law) – he tries to convince people that there *is* a political/military conspiracy when there isn't one – undermining the efforts of the experts at various points in the story.

Chain of infection. Our sample stories deal with the chain of infection in different ways. In *The Andromeda Strain* there is no chain of infection to follow – the source of the outbreak is known from the outset: it comes from a crashed satellite. In *Outbreak* the audience gets to follow the host animal – a Colobus monkey – from the point it is trapped in Zaire, to its journey across the sea in a freighter, and finally to the USA where it infects two humans. The characters in the story only learn all of this later in the story as their investigations progress. In *Contagion* we see the first infected person carry the virus into the USA, but we only learn the pattern of infection as it is pieced together very gradually by the characters, almost working backwards like a traditional detective investigating 'whodunit' – the final piece of the puzzle, 'Day 1', is the last one we see.

What shall we tell the public? This scene may occur as early as Sequence 2, or it may not come in until much later in the story. The experts and their superiors and/or politicians discuss whether to use the media to alert the public to the danger posed by the virus. In *Outbreak* it occurs in Sequence 2 and a media blackout is imposed by the military. In *Contagion* it takes place in Sequence 3.

But in *The Andromeda Strain* the whole 'Wildfire' operation is top secret, so the question doesn't really arise.

Sequence 3
In this sequence, the experts begin their detailed work on the virus. At this point, the team has no treatment for those already infected and no vaccine to protect the uninfected from the virus.

First questions. As the experts begin working on the virus, a number of questions will be raised – things they will have to discover answers to as their investigation goes on. These questions include: How is the virus communicated? What is the infection rate – what percentage of people who are exposed to the virus become sick? What is the incubation period – how much time passes before an infected person shows symptoms? What are the first symptoms? What is the mortality rate – what percentage of those who become sick will die? They also need to work out the 'basic reproduction number' or $R0$ (r-nought) – that is, how many new people are infected by each sick person.

Initial problem. There may be some issue that the researchers must overcome before they can begin work on developing a vaccine. In *Contagion* the problem is being unable to grow the virus in such a way that will allow them to experiment on it – it kills every type of cell they introduce it to without reproducing. Only when a maverick scientist makes a breakthrough and is able to reproduce the virus is this problem solved. But even then, the researchers know that any vaccine is still months away.

Statistics and projections. Several times during an outbreak thriller we will be given the number of cases of people infected. This number will rise as the story progresses – it is a continual reminder of what is at stake: people's lives. Predictions will also be made – usually shown by an infographic based on a world map – of the rate at which the virus will spread. The predictions will be made based on the r-nought and the infection rate. At some point in every outbreak thriller, there will be a reference to the 'Spanish Flu' pandemic of 1918 which killed between three and five per cent of the world's population.

Initial responses to local outbreak. If the first infections are confined to one or two specific areas, we may see these areas being quarantined and cordoned off from the rest of the world. In *Outbreak*, we see the military isolate the town that has been infected and this occurs in Sequence 3. In *Contagion*, where the infections occur on a much wider scale, we see cities being cordoned off as the number of infections increases, and this occurs in Sequence 5.

More conspiracy. There may also be another development in the conspiracy subplot. In *Outbreak*, the military has an antiserum for the virus but do not want to reveal that they have it – they will use 'standard containment measures' instead – meaning they want to destroy the infected town. In *Contagion*, a conspirator seeks to make profit from the situation by advertising a fake cure on his blog.

Sequence 4
In the fourth sequence, we typically see work on the virus in the science lab contrasted with the effects of the virus – or the situation caused by the presence

of the virus – on ordinary people. This sequence leads up to some sort of revelation or discovery at the midpoint.

Ordinary people. These can be represented in the story in various ways. It may be in terms of romantic or family relationships involving members of the investigating team. Family members may be separated, some in the quarantine zone and some not; some infected and some (apparently) not. It may be shown in the growing anger and/or panic of the people trapped in the quarantine zone – which may, in turn, lead to some people trying to escape. Or it may be a reminder from one of the doctors that the patients – those that are sick and/or those that are immune – are human beings and not guinea pigs. It is becoming obvious that normal life is breaking down.

More people infected. There will be a reminder of – and raising of – the stakes as new figures come in showing that the number of people infected has risen dramatically. Medical reception centres may have to be set up to isolate and treat large numbers of victims. Decisions also have to be made about what to do with the bodies of those who die – it is not safe for morticians to handle them and it may be inadvisable to bury them.

It's horrible! There may be a graphic reminder of the effects of the virus on a victim. This may come in the form of ordinary people seeing the full effects for the first time.

One of our own. Another way to humanise the effects of the virus is to have one of the members of the hero's own team become infected. This shows that no one is exempt. This can also be used to create suspense, as the hero waits to see whether this colleague develops symptoms. It may also be used to add time pressure – can they develop a 'cure' before their friend dies? Infection of a member of the hero's team can be an effective midpoint development in the story – it is used this way in *Contagion.*

The virus mutates. In contrast to all of the 'human stuff' above, the work in the highly-secure lab goes on, for the most part, cut off from the outside world. Their progress is frustratingly slow and they have very little to show for all of the time and effort that they are putting in. And on top of that, a new development makes things worse. The virus mutates. It may, for example, change from something that is transmitted by direct physical contact to something airborne that can be passed on like the 'flu. The change will usually be something that makes the virus deadlier and allows it to be transmitted more quickly. Predictions about how quickly the virus will spread countrywide or worldwide will have to be revised. This is another example of raising the stakes – putting more pressure on the researchers by giving them less time to develop a vaccine.

Sequence 4 ends at the midpoint of the story. The midpoint event for *Contagion* has already been mentioned. In *The Andromeda Strain* the midpoint is, I think, where the scientists discover the green 'space virus' on the tiny meteorite, and in *Outbreak* it is the moment when the White House is asked to approve the 'Cleansweep' bombing of the infected town.

Sequence 5

The fifth sequence typically includes a reaction to, or escalation of, whatever happened at the midpoint, plus a further development in the conspiracy subplot.

Funeral pyres and mass graves. A visual representation of the scale of the infection is often given in a series of images of bodies being zipped into body bags, thrown into the back of a military lorry, and then stacked to be burned or buried in a mass grave.

Social breakdown. The disruption to normal life and routines may be quite advanced by this point, with borders being closed and large areas being quarantined. Characters the audience cares about may find themselves trapped in one of the infected areas. There may be violent clashes as people confront the authorities or fight over dwindling fuel, food, or water supplies. Martial law may be declared in certain areas or across the whole country. The president and other senior officials will have been moved to a secure 'undisclosed location.'

Doctors under siege. The medical experts and investigators may find themselves at odds with the military – restricted in terms of the work they are trying to carry out, or the information they are trying to gather or to broadcast. They may also find themselves attacked or criticised by ordinary people, perhaps spurred on by media reports. The military, politicians, and other officials may seem increasingly aloof and uncaring – and the medical experts will find themselves associated in the minds of the people with this group of 'them.'

The virus is coming! The threat of infection spreading may be symbolised by an infected person or animal approaching a place that has so far been unaffected.

One of our own 2. The member of the hero's team who was infected may begin showing symptoms or they may succumb to the virus completely and die – this brings the suffering of the people outside closer to home for the experts.

Conspiracy confirmed. The conspiracy subplot, if there is one, may be advanced by having the hero discover evidence that the military or some other organisation has, or wants, the virus for a biological weapon. In *Outbreak*, the hero discovers that the military had both the original virus and an antiserum. The antiserum could have been used to treat the first outbreak, but now that the virus has mutated, it is virtually useless. In *Contagion*, the conspiracy subplot involves rumours being spread online suggesting that the government already has the vaccine but isn't sharing it with ordinary people. The media then picks up these rumours. The blogger is also promoting a fake 'natural cure' for the virus. As one character says, the spread of these rumours and misinformation is as dangerous as the spread of the virus.

After the midpoint, the pace of a thriller plot usually increases, gathering speed as it heads towards the climax. One way of achieving this is to include some kind of deadline or other time pressure. In *Outbreak* we learn that a bomb will be dropped on the infected town, destroying it and everyone in it, at 20:00 hours.

Another way to increase the pressure on the hero and his team is to show how rapidly the virus is spreading – giving a projection of when the whole country – or the world – will be infected. This is another way of saying that the clock is ticking. In *Contagion*, at the beginning of Sequence 6 we – and the hero's team – learn that the virus has mutated and is now spreading more quickly, reducing the amount of time available to find a vaccine.

Sequence 6
This sequence in a thriller typically leads to the hero's 'darkest hour.' We need to pile the pressure on the hero, and this is often done by allowing him a piece of good news, a glimmer of hope, and then quickly following it up with a piece of terrible news.

Frustration. Among the experts and investigators, there will be growing frustration at the limited progress they have made to date. They have gathered a lot of information but have not been able to piece it together in a way that gives them any sort of solution. This is similar to the situation in a traditional murder mystery where, in Sequence 6, the detective has all sorts of clues and statements from witnesses and suspects, but can't yet put them together and explain whodunit. The team are feeling low and believe that things can't possibly get any worse – but they will, and soon.

Darkest hour. In *Contagion* almost the whole of Sequence 6 seems to be a darkest hour. It ends with a character saying that even if they had a vaccine today, it would still take months to carry out human trials, get FDA approval, and manufacture and distribute it. And more people would die during those months of delay. In *Outbreak*, the hero is allowed a glimmer of hope before his darkest hour: a breakthrough is made – they learn that the first victim was infected by a monkey. This host animal is not sick and so will have antibodies to the virus that could be used to create an antiserum. A search begins, and the monkey is located. The hero now knows the full chain of infection – and there is hope that an antiserum can be developed. This is immediately followed by the darkest hour: the bomber takes off, ready to destroy the town. In *The Andromeda Strain*, the darkest hour occurs when the team learn that the infected town has *not* been bombed and that someone else, a pilot, has been infected.

Sequence 7
The seventh sequence is made up of a reaction to the darkest hour and then the set-up for the climax of our thriller. How do our three 'model' stories handle these plot developments?

The hero of *Outbreak* is helped by an ally who buys him some time by delaying the bombing run. The hero retrieves the monkey that is host to the virus. Sequence 7 then mainly consists of a helicopter chase where the villain tries to stop the hero returning with a potential 'cure' for the victims of the virus.

A monkey also plays a key part in Sequence 7 of *Contagion*. One of the experimental vaccines that the team has been trying out in the lab appears to have 'cured' a monkey infected with the virus – its symptoms have vanished. To avoid a long human trials process, one of the researchers injects herself with the vaccine and then deliberately exposes herself to the virus to see if the vaccine is effective. After that, things move quickly – the vaccine is approved and manufacture begins. The question then becomes: Who among the population should get it first? The conspiracy subplot reaches its climax with questions such as: Who is making profits from the vaccine? Is it safe? What about long-term side-effects? This echoes public fears such as those surrounding the discredited claim that the MMR vaccine caused autism in children.

In *The Andromeda Strain*, the darkest hour at the end of Sequence 6 came when the team learned that the bomb had not be dropped on the infected town. In Sequence 7 they learn new things about the virus – including the fact that a bomb won't destroy it but will, in fact, help it to grow and spread. They have to halt the bombing run. They then run a 'worst case scenario' simulation showing the spread of the virus. And at the same time, they see proof that the conspiracy theory was correct – the military did want to use the virus as a weapon. Then an alarm goes off – the biosafety system in one of the labs has been breached and one of the team is infected. One of his colleagues has a theory about the immunity of the survivors from the original infection, and they successfully test it out on their infected colleague. Then comes something that looks a bit like *deus ex machina*: the virus mutates into something that is no longer infectious. They may as well have said that a wizard fixed it by magic. The virus that gives the story its title is suddenly side-lined and attention is turned to something else. It feels like a cop-out and a let-down, even though it is true to the final message of the story: We got lucky this time, but what about next time? Problems in stories should be resolved by the efforts of the characters, not fixed by coincidence or happy accident – your readers deserve better than that. Again, maybe this is just me. The ending of *The Andromeda Strain* is not a bad ending – it just disappoints me in this one respect.

Sequence 8

The eighth sequence provides the *climax* of the story and then a short *resolution* which validates the outcome of the climactic action. Our three examples between them demonstrate two different ways of handling the climax of an outbreak thriller. *Contagion* is the more realistic of the three and concentrates on the development and distribution of the vaccine. *Outbreak* and *The Andromeda Strain* take more of a James Bond movie approach.

The Andromeda Strain. The biosafety breach in the lab triggers the automatic self-destruct sequence: the hero has five minutes in which to manually disable it. He does so with only seconds to spare. The problem of the virus itself is dealt with by seeding clouds to cause 'alkaline rain.' The crisis has been averted. This time.

The Andromeda Strain is a classic movie and it remains a popular one. It was originally released in 1971 and since then many of its original ideas have been appropriated by other films and television series. I think it is safe to say that the 'countdown to self-destruct' is now a cliché – you shouldn't use it, unless you can come up with a new and dramatic variation of it. Or an amusing way of dealing with it.

Outbreak. The antiserum is produced and tested on an infected team member. The climax involves the hero trying to prevent the crew of the aeroplane from dropping its bomb on the infected town – he tries to convince them to abort using a combination of direct action, logic, ethics, and emotional blackmail. As this approach succeeds, the conspiracy subplot reaches a climax with the arrest of the villain. Later we see normality returning to the infected town as the antiserum is administered and people recover. The return to ordinary family life is represented by the hero's relationship with his ex-wife.

Contagion. The climax has things in common with *Outbreak*, but they occur on a much larger scale. Inoculations with the vaccine begin, but it will take a long time to vaccinate everyone. With the crisis over, a sample of the virus is filed away alongside SARS and H1N1. We see the lives of ordinary people returning to normal in small but significant ways – represented by one girl's 'prom' dance with her boyfriend. As a sort of epilogue, we also see the last pieces of the chain of infection slotted together – how a virus that combined pig and bat components was accidentally created, and how the first human came to be infected with it.

In all three of our examples, the crisis is averted but there is a sense that we were lucky this time. We need to be better prepared for next time. There is also a suggestion that 'we brought it on ourselves' – either because someone wanted a virus for a biological weapon or because mankind is continually encroaching on the habitats of other species and bringing together elements that would never have encountered each other naturally.

Now, please wash your hands.

11 | Techno-Thriller

What is a Techno-thriller?
The two best-known writers of techno-thrillers are Tom Clancy and Michael Crichton. If we take an obvious definition of this sub-genre and say that the techno-thriller takes the conventions of the thriller genre – notably suspense and/or conspiracy – and uses them in a story that centres on some form of technology, then we can say that Tom Clancy's novels are centred on *military* technology and that Michael Crichton's focus on various kinds of non-military science and technology. In both cases, the technology is not just a backdrop against which the story is set, it is a key part of the working of the plot.

The techno-thriller has elements in common with the science fiction, espionage, action and war genres. You will occasionally see stories that mix science fiction and spying referred to as spy-fi, but I would strongly advise against using that to describe your subgenre.

Techno-thrillers fall into five main categories:

(i) The McGuffin: a piece of technology or the design for the technology is used as the excuse for an amateur-on-the-run thriller.
(ii) Technology Misused: a technological object or development (such as a nerve agent or biological weapon) is used to threaten a society to achieve the villain's goal.
(iii) Technology Gone Wrong: a seemingly innocuous or helpful technology gets out of hand and becomes a threat. *Westworld, Jurassic Park* and *Demon Seed* are examples, with *Frankenstein* as their granddaddy.
(iv) Technology as Weapon: there is a new technology and whoever controls it (or uses it the most effectively) will be the dominant superpower – 'our' side must get to it first, keep 'them' from getting it, or steal it from them. *Firefox* and *The Hunt for Red October* are examples. These are effectively 'military techno-thrillers.' Stories that are only about the secret plans for the device, rather than the device itself, fall into the McGuffin category.
(v) Technology is the solution. Perhaps the rarest of all is the story where *real* science enables the hero to resolve the story problem.

We encountered the 'McGuffin' in an earlier chapter, but as a reminder, here's how *The Encyclopedia of Science Fiction* describes it: "... an object whose loss – or rumours of whose existence – triggers the cast of a thriller or detective film into searching for it, or fighting for it, or running from it, but which has in fact no intrinsic meaning once the dust has settled." In the techno-thriller, then, the technological object is sometimes only an excuse to create a thriller plot – it could easily be replaced by some other object. These stories are usually variations on the amateur-on-the-run thriller and we have covered that sort of plot in detail already.

Technology misused stories can either pit a James Bond-style hero against a villain who threatens the world with some form of super-weapon, or they can use a terrorist plot like the one on *Black Sunday*. Again, we have already covered these plots.

'Technology is the solution' stories are not at all common and so there is not really a typical plot pattern for us to look at. The contagious disease thrillers we looked at in the Medical Thriller chapter are examples of this type of story, where real-life medical technology is used to produce a vaccine or antidote. The only other recent example I can think of is Andy Weir's 2011 novel *The Martian*, filmed in 2015 with Matt Damon in the lead role, and that is really a science fiction novel rather than a thriller. Stories about the positive uses of science are more likely to be found in science fiction than in thrillers.

In this chapter I will concentrate on the 'technology gone wrong' and the 'technology as weapon' plots – and the latter I will refer to as the *military techno-thriller*.

The Appeal of the Technology Gone Wrong Thriller

People like stories where things go wrong – we like to see how characters deal with adversity and we like to imagine ourselves successfully dealing with similar situations. You can't have thrills without the threat of something going horribly wrong on either a personal or global scale. In a thriller, you ideally have both. Nobody wants to read stories about the village of the happy people – I'm not sure who first said that, but when it comes to stories it is a golden rule. Interesting stories about utopias are almost impossible to write. This being the case, a thriller about technology needs to have that technology go wrong. This is not true in science fiction, where stories can treat technology in many different ways – we'll talk about that a little bit more under *Themes* below – but in the thriller we want our technology to turn against us.

This type of thriller has things in common with those 1970s disaster movies like *The Towering Inferno* in that they show how people respond when disaster strikes. In the techno-thriller, the 'disaster' is man-made technology.

Since the industrial revolution, humans have had an uneasy relationship with technology. The Luddites of the early nineteenth century who feared that weaving machines would put them out of work are not that different to those today who express fears about industrial robots or artificial intelligence. Fears about genetic engineering and 'designer babies' are not so very far from the concerns that led Mary Shelley to write *Frankenstein*. As we will see under the *Themes* heading, techno-thrillers are often accused of being *anti*-science, but I don't think that we read them because we believe technological developments are wrong and should be stopped. We read them for the same reason that we ride rollercoasters – we find facing our fears in a controlled environment exhilarating. Thrilling. Rollercoasters are a *technology* specifically designed to make us feel both uncomfortable and then delighted at having 'survived' the ordeal. Technology gone wrong thrillers have the same appeal.

The difficult thing about writing stories about gadgets – or other forms of scientific development – is making a dramatic sequence of events out of them. You introduce a fantastic new machine or process and the people who created it or use it – and then what? In the early days of science fiction, when everything was still shiny and new, it was enough to write about gadgets and just marvel at them for their own sake. They relied on a child-like 'sense of wonder' and discovery. Those stories were written by 'technocrats' who thought that science and technology would bring a utopian future for humankind. Those stories seem rather naïve now. They were written before Hiroshima. If you watch the original 1954 film of *Godzilla* as a pre-teen, it is a slightly hokey but thrilling monster movie; watch it as an adult and it is a desperately sad story about the devastation of the nuclear bomb. We can no longer view technology with that pre-war sense of wonder because we know what technology can be used for. And in these days when almost everyone has small computer/television/communication device in their pocket, it takes a lot to *wow* us. So we need our technology to *do* something. In our stories, we need it to go wrong. Big time.

The technology gone wrong thriller allows us to have our cake and eat it. It appeals to both sides of our ambivalent relationship with technology. In the first half of the story we are introduced to the wow-factor of new technology – Look, real live dinosaurs! We see them up close in a theme park and we learn about the 'magical' science that recreated them. And then in the second half of the story our interest is goosed by having the dinosaurs escape and eat people. Disaster! And then we have the pleasure of seeing how people respond to this problem and resolve it.

The Appeal of the Military Techno-Thriller

"I'm interested in all sorts of technology because, like a lot of Americans, I'm fascinated with gadgets," Tom Clancy said in an interview with Martin H. Greenberg, "The military happen to have the best toys."

This is part of the appeal of this sub-genre of the thriller. Not everyone is fascinated with military technology, but most of us have more than a passing interest in some sort of technology because we use it every day. But the 'gadgets' are only part of the appeal. Something that is often forgotten when discussing techno-thrillers is the fact that they are not only concerned with the technology itself. As well as the hardware, the chemistry, or whatever, techno-thrillers depict how the technology is deployed and the people who use it. In this respect, it is another example of the 'professional fiction' or expert thriller that we discussed earlier. While Tom Clancy's novels include specific details of various items of military hardware – fighter planes, submarines, helicopters, missiles, guns and all the rest – he also spent an equal or greater amount of time covering the people who use that technology, including their personal lives and professional career achievements, and on the tactics used by military and political leaders to deploy the men and equipment. Like all 'expert thrillers,' part of the appeal of the techno-thriller is seeing behind the scenes and learning how professional people do their jobs. The use of specific hardware names, acronyms, and other jargon are part of the 'iconography' of this type of story – it provides verisimilitude, even if the reader doesn't always fully understand what it means. We like to believe that our techno-thriller writer knows what he is talking about. More on that later.

Another bit of 'insider info' that readers enjoy in this type of story – as in all 'expert thrillers' – is the use of insider anecdotes. These are the sort of things that you can't pick up from doing research in textbooks and manufacturer websites – they are stories told by people who have actually used the technology in question. These tend to make the technology more realistic from a human point of view. Autobiographies are one source of this type of anecdote – real-life experiences can be adapted into fictional ones – but most techno-authors will gather this kind of material by talking to actual practitioners in the field. Tom Clancy spoke to technicians who had worked on nuclear submarines, for example, and had many friends and acquaintances with military backgrounds, so he knew how these people spoke and he knew the kind of stories they told about their experiences. Before he became an author, Tom Clancy himself worked in the insurance and had no military experience.

Military strategy inspired by wargaming is an important element of military techno-thrillers. This is another example of the 'expert at work' – we see experienced military tacticians and intelligence analysts working behind the scenes to plan military operations. It is not just the technology that readers want to see but also how it is deployed. This is similar to the 'spymaster' in the espionage thriller controlling his agents as if they are pieces on a chessboard, but here the men in charge are politicians, intelligence officials, and military top brass and they are playing something like a wargame. Think more in terms of those World War II movies where men in an underground 'war room' move little wooden ships and aircraft around a table with a map painted on it. In a military techno-thriller, both the good guys and the bad guys have an operations room where they monitor and plan the action going on 'out in the field.'

Tom Clancy used the wargame *Harpoon* as inspiration for parts of *The Hunt for Red October* (1984) and co-wrote *Red Storm Rising* (1986) with the game's creator Larry Bond: the novel is based on a scenario developed using the rules from the game. *Red Storm Rising* came to define the techno-thriller during the late 1980s and early 1990s, with a vast number of World War III novels following in its wake. Marc A. Cerasini points out that before this, most novels about World War III tended to be "... apocalyptic in theme. A superpower confrontation in our post-Hiroshima age was consistently envisioned as a short exchange that would destroy most, if not all, life on Earth." But there were those – Tom Clancy and Ronald Reagan amongst them – who believed that conventional, non-nuclear, battles were still a possibility. Cerasini writes that Clancy and his peers paved the way for Desert Storm: "The shift in public opinion regarding the use of the military can be traced in part to the popularity of the techno-thriller genre, which educated us about weapons, strategies, and the very nature of modern warfare."

Modern war stories fall outside the scope of this book as the conventions of stories about military battles are very different from those of the thriller genre. I include *The Hunt for Red October* and *Firefox* in this chapter because they do use elements of the thriller – especially the espionage thriller – but *Red Storm*

Rising is more of a war story. Tom Clancy's later novels brought him back closer to our current genre: *Patriot Games* (1987), is a 'prequel' thriller featuring hero Jack Ryan in which he foils a terrorist plot, and *The Cardinal of the Kremlin* (1988) is a traditional espionage novel that centres on the 'MacGuffin' of SDI (the Strategic Defense Initiative – Ronald Reagan's 'Star Wars' anti-missile project).

Tom Clancy was a conservative and a Republican who strongly supported the political direction taken by Ronald Reagan. He was pro-military, pro-CIA, pro-gun, and strongly pro-America. His type of conservatism was also popular in Great Britain, where Margaret Thatcher shared many of Reagan's views and had just fought a military campaign over the Falkland Islands. Attitudes towards political leaders, intelligence services, and the military were moving away from the suspicion and distrust that had marked the post-Watergate years. Many people wanted to put memories of Vietnam behind them and read about America as a successful military power. These feelings brought Reagan to power and were reflected in Clancy's novels – they were a big part of his appeal. I've mentioned before that most genre fiction is conservative at heart – it tends to believe that the status quo is worth defending. Clancy took this to an extreme that reflected views at that time. But, as we will see under *Themes* below, he also reflected other values that appealed to conservatives whose political beliefs were not quite so right-wing.

While Tom Clancy's political views are still those of many readers in America and elsewhere, the glory days of Reagan Republicanism are long gone. George W. Bush's 'War on Terror' tried to revive this style of politics, but the tragedy of 9/11 affected the country greatly – people felt they were no longer safe at home. The 'police actions' undertaken overseas suddenly seemed more dangerous than previously thought: they had consequences close to home. People wanted to rethink what military actions the country became involved in. There was, to some extent, a return to the suspicion and paranoia of the 1970s with the role of the Soviets being taken by 'radical Islamists.' And the CIA again became a shady organisation – involved in the 'rendition' of foreign prisoners and also spying on ordinary Americans at home. Added to this was the fact that communication of the news was no longer under the control of a select few – the internet, depending on your point of view, was either the ultimate example of democratisation or the unleashing of anarchy. The world of 2017, in which Donald Trump was elected President of the USA, was very different from the one which Reagan presided over – and modern techno-thrillers have to reflect that change.

Techno-thrillers don't all deal with military technology and contemporary politics. The term 'technology' covers a broad spectrum – military, medical, computing, genetics, communication, robotics, artificial intelligence, nanotechnology, and a host of other areas – and so the subject matter for techno-thrillers is equally broad. During the Cold War years when the threat of World War III loomed over us, military technology was the favourite subject. A lot of money was pumped into research for new weapons and protection systems. After the Cold War ended there was a shift and more money was invested in 'home computing' and computer games, and then into other forms of entertainment and mobile phones. Food manufacturing too moved into the controversial area of genetically-modified crops. Medical technology expanded rapidly. Technology now exists in almost every area of our lives – and the techno-thriller is on hand to exploit our fears of that technology.

The Technology in the Techno-thriller

The technology in this sub-genre is usually either something that currently exists or is some plausible near-future technology extrapolated from something that currently exists. Many techno-thrillers centre on military technology, but the sub-genre isn't exclusively militaristic. These thrillers usually feature a fair amount of technical detail explaining the inner-workings of the technology. Readers of this sub-genre are much more forgiving of long 'info-dumps' and this sort of detail is one of the things they find appealing. This interest in 'how things work' extends to other areas of the story and explanations of the mechanics of martial arts moves, espionage procedures, military strategy and political machinations all feature.

The Encyclopedia of Science Fiction definition quoted earlier said that the techno-thriller treated technology in one of two ways – it is either worshipped in a fetishistic way or it is regarded as threatening. In the first camp we have people who love gadgets, cars and military technology and in the second we have people who compare any new technology with the atomic bomb and fear that it will bring about the end of humankind. The two groups are not mutually exclusive – we can be fascinated by the things we are afraid of.

Much has been written about how accurate (or otherwise) the science and technology is in techno-thrillers. Tom Clancy has been accused of portraying military hardware as being much more reliable than it is in real-life.

Michael Crichton's presentation of the science relating to global warming in *State of Fear* brought a fair amount of criticism – see, for example, Gavin Schmidt's 'Michael Crichton's State of Confusion' article on the RealClimate.org website. The science of *Prey* was subjected to similar analysis by Chris Phoenix in 'Don't let Crichton's *Prey* scare you – the science isn't real,' on the nanotech-now.com website. Amy Rogers at ScienceThrillers.com is less critical of *The Andromeda Strain* in her 'Mythbusting Thriller Science: Space Bacteria' blog posts. And there have been whole books devoted to the subject: *The Science of Michael Crichton: An Unauthorized Exploration into the Real Science Behind the Fictional Worlds of Michael Crichton* (Science of Pop Culture series), edited by Kevin R. Grazier and *The Science of Jurassic Park and the Lost World* by Rob DeSalle and David Lindley.

The Historical Development of the Techno-thriller

Tom Clancy's *The Hunt for Red October* (1984) is often said to be the first techno-thriller but while it is certainly a prime-example and served to put the sub-genre on the bestseller charts – with the help of Ronald Reagan's endorsement – it was not the first example. Interestingly, Clancy himself was unhappy that his novels were even labelled techno-thrillers. "I reject the title of techno-thriller and the claim that I invented it," he told Martin H. Greenberg. "Actually

I argue that if there is a such a genre, [or] subgenre, as that it was probably invented by Michael Crichton with *The Andromeda Strain*..."

As we've already seen, tracing the lineage of the thriller is tricky, and while Crichton's 1969 novel *The Andromeda Strain* is an early example of the subgenre and helped to establish it, it is probably not the first techno-thriller. Mention here should be made of Scottish author Alistair MacLean who wrote a number of novels that are precursors of the techno-thriller. In *The Satan Bug* (1962) two germ warfare agents are stolen from a research lab by a mysterious bio-terrorist who threatens to release them on the country's population unless the research lab is completely destroyed, though the hero later discovers that the villain's real plot is far from altruistic. A film based on the novel was released in 1965. MacLean also wrote war stories, including *The Guns of Navarone* and *Where Eagles Dare*; Cold War and espionage thrillers including *Ice Station Zebra, Circus,* and *The Dark Crusader* (*The Black Shrike* in the USA); and 'terrorism' thrillers that featured techno-thriller elements. His 1976 novel *The Golden Gate* includes a terrorist plot that involves a Presidential motorcade being halted on the Golden Gate Bridge which has been wired to explode, though again the conspirators' plot is not quite what it seems. The structure of the plot is similar to that of the 1988 film *Die Hard* (which was based on Roderick Thorp's 1979 novel *Nothing Lasts Forever*). Other MacLean novels include *Goodbye California* (1977) where terrorists attack a nuclear power plant and threaten to set off atomic bombs on California fault-lines to cause earthquakes; *Athabasca* in which an Alaskan oil pipeline is sabotaged; and *Floodgate* (1983) where terrorists set off an explosion destroying a dike and flooding Amsterdam's Schiphol Airport and then threaten similar attacks throughout the Netherlands.

I have already mentioned Mary Shelley's *Frankenstein* (1818) as an early prototype of the techno-thriller. Its full title is *Frankenstein; or, the Modern Prometheus* referencing the Greek myth in which a human, Prometheus, steals the secret of fire from the gods and must suffer the consequences. Robert Louis Stevenson's 1886 short novel *Strange Case of Dr Jekyll and Mr Hyde* is also a precursor, though it uses a scientific 'potion' as a MacGuffin to explore the theme of the duality of man. Tom Clancy cites Jules Verne's *Twenty Thousand Leagues Under the Sea* (1869-70, English translation 1873) as one of the inspirations for *The Hunt for Red October* along with Frank Herbert's 1976 submarine novel *Under Pressure*.

H. G. Wells wrote a number of stories that might be regarded as inspiring military techno-thrillers, including 'The Land Ironclads' (1903), which predicted the use of armoured vehicles in combat; *The War in the Air* (1908), predicting the use of aircraft in warfare; and *The World Set Free* (1914) which predicted nuclear bombs, though on a smaller scale than those eventually developed. Wells' *The Invisible Man* (1897) and *The Island of Doctor Moreau* (1896) belong on the list of titles that inspired non-military techno-thrillers.

Erskine Childers' *The Riddle of the Sands* (1903) has already been mentioned in the chapter on spyfiction as an early example of a novel predicting the First World War. The first novel predicting modern warfare was the novella *The Bat-*

tle of Dorking (1871) by George Tomkyns Chesney, in which a German-speaking nation – referred to only as The Other Power or The Enemy – invades England. It was the earliest example of what became known as 'invasion literature' or the 'invasion novel.' Between 1871 and the beginning of the First World War, hundreds of invasion stories were published, written by people who were concerned about the development of technology that might be used in warfare – such as the hot air balloon and the railway – and sometimes included in publications that wished to increase their circulation in particular areas and so staged invasion stories there. William Le Queux wrote *The Great War in England in 1897*, published in 1894, in which England is invaded by a French-Russian coalition; but better-known is his 1906 novel *The Invasion of 1910* which sees Germany as the aggressor and includes claims that Germany had thousands of spies in Britain. Journalist and naval historian H. W. Wilson wrote the sections of the book dealing with the navy. Like Childers' novel, this and many other invasion stories were written with a political agenda in mind – to try and persuade people that the government should be more prepared for the threat of invasion. Marc A. Cerasini has noted that with the novel *Red Storm Rising*, "Tom Clancy actually brought the techno-thriller back to its roots in a turn-of-the-century invasion fiction by writing the modern equivalents of Le Queux's prophetic tales."

Meticulous research and detailed descriptions of the behind-the-scenes workings of things were the hallmark of author Arthur Hailey, who wrote eight bestselling novels between 1965 and 1997. The first of these, *Hotel*, explored the running of a large independent hotel and told the stories of various of its residents. Better-known is the second, the 1968 novel *Airport* – the film adaptation of which helped launch the 'disaster movie' genre. Other Hailey novels explored the automobile industry (*Wheels*, 1971), the banking industry (*The Moneychangers*, 1975), the electricity industry (*Overload*, 1979), the pharmaceutical industry (*Strong Medicine*, 1984), terrorists holding a TV network to ransom (*The Evening News*, 1990) and a hunt for a serial killer (*Detective*, 1997). Hailey spent a year researching each of his novels before sitting down and planning how he could then tell a story, or a series of connected stories, that would allow him to present the world of the story to the reader. This 'background as foreground' technique is used in other 'world-building' genres including science fiction, fantasy, and some historical fiction. Dan Brown and other thriller writers also make use of the technique to present their research and theories to the reader. Tom Clancy used it too, to present his research on nuclear submarines in the form of a Cold War thriller plot.

Many of Michael Crichton's novels fall into the 'technology gone wrong or misused' techno-thriller category. The poster for his 1973 movie *Westworld* had the tagline 'Where nothing can possibly go *worng!*' Crichton's *The Andromeda Strain* has already been discussed in the 'Medical Thriller' chapter, but it could equally be described as a techno-thriller. *Binary* (1972) tells of a plot to assassinate the US president using a nerve agent. *The Terminal Man* (1972) tells of a man who has electrodes implanted in his bread to control violent seizures, with unexpected side-effects. *Jurassic Park* (1990) is another 'technology out of control' story – with dinosaurs! *Airframe* (1996) is an account of an air-accident investigation. *Prey* (2002) explores the dangers of experiments with nanotechnology. *State of Fear* (2004) tells of eco-terrorists plotting mass murder to publicize the danger of global warming. Crichton uses a number of different thriller plots in his novels – *Binary* and *State of Fear* draw on the assassination and terrorism plots we have explored previously. *Prey* is similar to *The Andromeda Strain* and *The Terminal Man* in that it has elements of a virus and an experimental scientific/medical procedure. *Airframe* combines a detective story-like investigation with political/business thriller intrigue and an investigative reporter who, for a change, isn't the 'good guy.' *Jurassic Park* is a variation on the *Frankenstein* story with a strong element of manhunt, with the humans at real risk of becoming the prey.

Welsh author Craig Thomas' novel *Firefox* was published in 1977 and a film adaptation featuring Clint Eastwood was released in 1982. A sequel, *Firefox Down* was published in 1983. *Firefox* features a Vietnam veteran suffering a form of post-traumatic stress who is brought out of retirement to sneak into the Soviet Union and steal the prototype of a MiG-31 fighter aircraft. The first (part) of the novel is traditional Cold War espionage involving clandestine meetings, disguises, and avoiding the authorities, so that the hero can reach the base where the prototype is being tested. Once the hero is in the cockpit of the 'Firefox' the story switches to aerial combat and escape. Some less than stunning special effects of the plane – full-size and miniature – and heavy-handedness in dealing with the backstory and PTSD mean that the film is disappointing – the novel is much better.

Other modern practitioners of the military-style techno-thriller sub-genre include Dale Brown, who has written a number of standalone thrillers and also twenty-one novels (up to 2017) in the Patrick McClanahan series; a former United States Air Force officer, Brown's stories are mainly aviation-related. Joe Buff writes naval/submarine thrillers in the Jeffrey Fuller series, beginning with *Deep Sound Channel* (2000); he includes non-fiction information and links on his www.joebuff.com website. Stephen Coonts' first novel *The Flight of the Intruder* (1986), based in part on his experiences as a pilot during the Vietnam War, introduced series character Jake Grafton who has appeared in eighteen novels up to 2017; his thrillers include aviation, naval, and CIA/terrorism stories. David Poyer is a former naval officer and author of a series of naval thrillers featuring U.S. Navy officer Dan Lenson, the first of which was *The Med* (1988). Patrick Robinson has written a number of naval thrillers, beginning with *Nimitz Class* (1997).

Themes: 'Technology Gone Wrong' Thrillers

There has been some discussion about the fundamental difference between the techno-thriller and science fiction – here's what *The Encyclopedia of Science Fiction* says about techno-thrillers: "...they differ from SF in two respects: first, like the unknown in horror novels, science in the technothriller is either inherently threatening or worshipfully (and fetishistically) exploited; second, a typical technothriller plot evokes a technological scenario whose world-transforming implications are left unexamined or evaded, often through the use of McGuffin plots."

In terms of the attitude towards technology, science fiction tends to take a new technology – either current, extrapolated from current, or wildly imaginative – and then explores the implications or consequences of the existence of that technology. SF doesn't judge technology as being 'good' or 'evil,' and it almost never suggests that there is knowledge that humankind should not have – it accepts that the technology exists, that it could be used for good or bad purposes by different individuals, but – as will nuclear fission – the genie can never be put back into the bottle.

The techno-thriller, on the other hand, is more likely to treat the technology in question as something to be feared – technology 'gone wrong' or allowed to get out of hand and technology misused are common themes. The response to technology in the techno-thriller is often compared to Mary Shelley's novel *Frankenstein,* where a man uses science to create something that he doesn't fully understand and which escapes his control, going on to cause misery and chaos. But as I mentioned above, I don't think techno-thrillers are deliberately or necessarily anti-science but they are pro-fear.

An argument often made in favour of the technology gone wrong thriller is that they draw attention to the dangers of hubris. They are cautionary tales. Humankind has the intelligence to develop all manner of technological wonders – but doesn't necessarily have the wisdom to use them wisely. No matter how altruistic our scientists, there is always someone – usually a politician, a soldier, or a businessman – motivated by a desire for power or wealth (or both) who will exploit the technology in a way that does not benefit humankind. As writers, I think it is useful to have this argument in reserve – to justify our stories – but secretly we know that we're writing a techno-thriller because we want to scare the crap out of people.

Themes: Military Techno-Thrillers

In these thrillers, the technology is a weapon and there is either a race to make sure that 'our' side has the advantage of it before 'they' do, or the author sets out to prove that even though both sides have equal technology, 'our' military tactics and training are better than 'theirs.' Back when this sub-genre was young, 'us' was the United States of America, helped out by its allies, and 'them' was the Soviet Union. Modern political developments in Russia and Eastern Europe have made that enemy almost obsolete but, as J. William Gibson points out, "the genre can readily *shift enemies.*" Later military techno-thrillers had Colombian drug lords and rogue American intelligence officials as enemies before the new enemy became radical Islamic terrorists.

The military techno-thriller shares themes with the espionage thriller, particularly the James Bond-style spy adventure, but where spy novels primarily dealt with the post-World War 2 Cold War situation in Great Britain, the techno-thriller focuses on the post-Vietnam situation in the United States. Or rather the post-post-Vietnam situation – the 1980s reaction to the post-Vietnam culture of the 1970s. In his paper titled 'Redeeming Vietnam: Techno-Thriller Novels of the 1980s,' J. William Gibson wrote: "The genre performs a 'recuperative' or healing function; it attempts to restore the military to its former (or pre-Vietnam War) position of prestige and power. It further promises that by increasing the military's economic resources and political autonomy, the United States can once again become the world's dominant power."

Marc A. Cerasini has said that Tom Clancy's popularity was the result of a "... deeply held personal and political philosophy, which is reflected in his novels, and the fact that the author prefers to emphasise positives over negatives." Cerasini suggests four factors that account for the appeal of Clancy's novels:

(i) his positive portrayal of the USA and its political system
(ii) the positive portrayal of the American military and intelligence agencies
(iii) his belief that political and military might can be used for the good of humanity
(iv) his presentation of positive male role-models

While the appeal of the first three is reasonably obvious, particularly if you share Clancy's political outlook, the fourth factor is worth exploring as it possibly accounts for Clancy's appeal beyond the obvious 'Republican' target audience.

Jack Ryan is Clancy's main protagonist in most of his novels and is, by the author's own admission, effectively his alter ego. The creation of this character reveals a great deal about Clancy's personal philosophy. Like many thriller authors, Clancy began from a position of wanting to create a character that wasn't like James Bond, instead – as he told Martin H. Greenberg – he wanted Ryan to be "... a normal guy with a wife and kids that he cared about." He wanted his hero to be someone who was just doing the best that he could in his everyday job, because "... if you look at the Central Intelligence Agency or any security agency, the great majority of the people there are normal, everyday married folks who take their kids to Little League games and fill out their taxes the first week of April just like everybody else." Jack Ryan embodies two things that are important to Clancy: (i) he takes responsibility and gets the job done, and (ii) he is a family man.

"In the real world," Clancy says, "... somebody has to get the job done. If there's an auto accident, somebody's lying in the street bleeding – someone has to stop the bleeding and stabilise the patient long enough to get them to hospital... Somebody has to take responsibility for what's going on in the world. And Jack Ryan keeps getting stuck with that." This takes us back to the difference between the amateur hero and the professional. In the amateur-on-the-run thriller, we said that the protagonist begins without any commitment to a cause and only gains one when he decides, close to the middle of the story, that he will no longer be a victim of circumstance and will take action to resolve the situation. The professional hero – whether he's James Bond or Jack Ryan – doesn't have this lack of commitment; his job means that he takes responsibility for his own actions and 'gets the job done.' Clancy believed that the people who held society together were those who were willing to "... protect and preserve and restore things that are broken." These people are, he says, "... romantics because they're people who believe in the rules..." This is a conservative view – what we have is good and worth fighting to protect – but, as we've said, it is a view common to virtually all genre fiction. It's a popular view so you'd expect to find it in popular fiction.

The 'hero as family man' is less common. In the same interview, Tom Clancy said that "... the family is the building block of society, period. From my perspective, family is the beginning and end of everything we're supposed to be working for. I mean if you don't take care of your kids, what the hell good are you?" The importance of family appears in *The Hunt for Red October*, but comes through much more strongly in *Patriot Games*, a novel that Clancy had drafted before writing *The Hunt for Red October* – this gave Clancy a character, Jack Ryan, who was 'completely fleshed out' when he appeared in the author's first published novel. In *Patriot Games*, we see that while Jack Ryan is fighting to defend American values and the rule of law, he would be prepared to act outside the rules in order to defend his family – and the 'extended family' that is his country. The argument is that he can trust his conscience not to step too far outside the boundaries of the law – and that as long as he is able to look his wife or child in the eye, he has not strayed beyond the acceptable. Clancy has referred to this as the 'Warrior code' – the strong protect the weak.

Any hero who takes action to defend his family is going to have the sympathy of the reader – even if that hero acts outside the law to do so. Where there is more room for argument is if you extend that and say that 'good' men can step beyond the law to protect their country as long as they trust their own consciences. Evidence suggests that some of those 'ordinary folk' at the CIA were party to some pretty unconscionable actions.

J. William Gibson writes about the appeal of the Jack Ryan-type hero: "Techno-thrillers are for *men.* They affirm martial power as the essential male characteristic in ways that are accessible to middle-class men. Techno-thriller heroes are educated professionals: they fight with their minds and with the most advanced technology science can develop. Yet their victories are just as much the harvest as masculine power as are Rambo's; middle-class men are reassured that they too 'have what it takes' to fight and defeat the enemy." And on the subject of 'hero as father,' Gibson says that this type of fiction "... contends that the crucial task in social reproduction is not giving birth and raising a family but is instead the totally male-dominated process of *transforming boys into men through warfare.* Men are responsible for defending the boundaries of society against the enemy. Only when adult men successfully reproduce new warriors and succeed in defending the external boundaries of society can women give birth and raise children inside society."

Military techno-thrillers are essentially patriarchal – father knows best. And this patriarchal attitude extends to the perceived role of the United States in the world: it should accept the responsibility for being the positive father-figure, promoting western democracy and 'family values', setting the rules, making threats and 'reluctantly' doling out punishments for transgressions.

Techno-Thriller Plot 1: The Military Techno-Thriller

My two examples here are Craig Thomas' 1977 novel *Firefox*, which was adapted into a movie in 1982 with Clint Eastwood in the lead role, and Tom Clancy's *The Hunt for Red October* (1984) which was filmed in 1990 with Alec

Baldwin and Sean Connery playing the main characters. These are generally regarded as two of the earliest and best examples of the sub-genre, establishing many of its conventions.

Firefox begins like a John Le Carré espionage novel featuring Cold War spies with a hint of *First Blood*'s John Rambo in its American Vietnam vet hero, Mitchell Gant. As the story gets closer to the midpoint it becomes more James Bond-like and then the second half of the story is more about wargames and aerial combat with the bit more Bond-ish action on an ice-floe.

The Hunt for Red October also has hints of the British espionage novel early on, but hero Jack Ryan works for the CIA so this part of the story is based more on American intelligence gathering and analysis procedures. Again, the story becomes more of an action-adventure after the midpoint with the much-anticipated submarine versus submarine action occurring in the last act.

Sequence 1
As a minimum, we need to introduce three things in this sequence: the hero, the villain or forces of opposition, and the military technology.

The hero represents the 'good guys,' typically the United States; the villain represents the 'bad guys' – in the Cold War years of the 1970s and 1980s that was the Soviet Union but today it is more likely to be a group of terrorists or a rogue Middle East country, probably fictional. Typically the villains have the new form of military technology, it is seen as a threat to the USA – or the 'free world' in general – and the good guys decide they need to take it from the bad guys. The technology must be something *specific* that represents an obvious threat as a weapon. It is not merely a MacGuffin around which a standard thriller plot is woven – it must be integral to the action. In *Firefox* it is a prototype Soviet aircraft with thought-controlled weapons and a design that makes it invisible to radar. In *The Hunt for Red October* is a prototype nuclear submarine with a silent drive mechanism that is 'invisible' to sonar. The fact that both machines here are prototypes is significant because it means that the enemy has the technology but it is not sufficiently advanced to give them military superiority – though the potential is there. This gives the good guys a chance to 'catch up' by stealing the technology.

Also in the first sequence, we see the beginning of the hero's mission. At this stage, he is either finding out about the technology, making plans to steal it and/or setting out on a journey to obtain it. The mission aspect of this type of story means that it has elements in common with the James Bond type of spy story.

Firefox is a straightforward lone hero, single plotline version of the 'technology as weapon' story. The novel is something like 93,000 words in length. The hero, Mitchell Gant, is the main viewpoint character, but the point of view switches to the Soviets and the allied support team at various points. The antagonists are a KGB colonel responsible for the security around the aeroplane project and his assistant; a Soviet police inspector; the First Secretary; and finally the pilot of a second prototype plane. The hero's mission is to sneak into a secret Russian base and steal a prototype of the Mig-31 (or 'Firefox') fighter plane.

The Hunt for Red October is over 160,000 words in length and has a more complex structure in that there are two parallel protagonist plotlines that do not converge until late in the story. In order to break down the plot into eight sequences I've used the novel and the screenplay from the film adaptation. The two heroes are Jack Ryan, a CIA operative who wants to obtain the Red October submarine for the USA, and Captain Ramius who wants to defect from the Soviet Union and bring the submarine with him in order to 'punish' a country he holds responsible for his wife's death. The two are introduced in their separate storylines and information about the submarine is spread between both of them. The Soviet antagonists are revealed in the form of the 'political officer' on the Red October who will later be supplemented or replaced by an undercover KGB agent, the captain of another Soviet submarine, and the Soviet ambassador to Washington.

Sequence 2
Here we establish the stakes, building on what has already been revealed about the technology of the weapon, but also showing what is at stake for different characters – both the good guys and the bad guys, and some of the supporting characters. There is usually one or more killings here – or at the very least an injury or near-miss. We need to show that as well as the high-level 'fate of the free world' threat, there is personal danger for individual characters.

In *Firefox,* at the end of sequence one, the group in Moscow helping the hero kill one of their own people in order that the mission can proceed undetected. During the second sequence, the hero is followed by KGB agents and must make his way through several security checks. At one point he makes the mistake of killing a KGB agent, believing himself to be in danger, and this puts the whole mission in jeopardy. The hero also learns that the Soviet dissidents helping him are prepared to die to ensure that his mission succeeds.

In *The Hunt for Red October,* we see Captain Ramius kill the political officer on board the submarine and substitute fake orders for their real ones. We also learn of other threats that will pay off later in the story: there is another Russian submarine that is supposed to rendezvous with the Red October for a military exercise and one of the crew of Red October may be an undercover KGB agent. We also learn of the threat that the Red October presents when a demonstration of its silent propulsion system shows that it could sneak towards the USA and launch nuclear missiles without anyone knowing it was there.

Sequence two – and/or sequence three – is where we can also 'plant' other elements that we want to use later in the story. In *The Hunt for Red October,* a rescue submarine is introduced that will be used in sequence seven.

Sequence 3
By the end of sequence two, actions have been taken that commit the protagonist (or one of them) to going on with their mission – there can be no turning back. The third sequence emphasises that we have entered a strange, and dangerous, new world. The bad guys have now become aware of the protagonist's plan or are at least aware that *something* is going on. They begin to investigate and this raises the stakes for the hero and anyone associated with him. The fact

that the hero has a mission means that there is also something at stake for one or more of the bad guys – they must stop the hero at any cost.

In *Firefox*, the Soviet authorities make progress in their investigation, bringing them closer to identifying the hero. The hero has completed his journey and made contact with dissidents who work on the fighter plane project and who will help him gain access to the site. But one of the men who has helped him is killed and others have been arrested and brutally interrogated.

In *The Hunt for Red October,* the Soviets become aware of Ramius' plan to defect and send a fleet of ships and submarines to find and destroy the Red October. The Americans learn from their spies that the Red October has gone missing and discuss whether the captain has 'gone rogue' and intends to attack the USA. The American hero, Jack Ryan, believes Ramius intends to defect – he is given three days to discover if this is true. Although Ryan has been actively gathering intelligence since the start of the story, his actual mission as a CIA agent doesn't begin until sequence three.

Both stories show a sort of 'war room' being used in this sequence, with strategies discussed and events in the field monitored.

Sequence 4 and Midpoint
The fourth sequence builds to a midpoint revelation or significant action.

In *Firefox* the midpoint sees the protagonist stealing the prototype fighter plane. Events leading up to this include going over the plans for the theft and then the protagonist getting into the project site in disguise. The stakes are raised as the Soviet authorities identify the hero and realise that rather than gaining information about the plane or sabotaging it, he plans to steal it. This raises the stake for them and they increase security at the site. Meanwhile, the dissidents working at the site prepare to launch a 'distraction' – knowing they are likely to be killed. The hero then kills the Russian pilot and takes his place.

In *The Hunt for Red October,* the Soviets locate Red October and, at the midpoint, try to destroy it. The build-up to this sees Ryan flying to a U. S. aircraft carrier close to the Red October's location – and at the same time trying to come up with a plan that would allow the Americans to keep the prototype submarine without the Soviets knowing that they have taken it. In the novel this plan is devised by a secondary character rather than Ryan.

The first three sequences included quite a lot of espionage or intelligence gathering work, but in both of our example stories the fourth sequence features an increase in the amount of physical action involving the hero. Whereas the first sequences involved planning and preparation, we now see the plan being put into operation. Also, by the midpoint all of the significant characters and situations will have been introduced. The emphasis shifts at the midpoint from show-and-tell to show-and-do. The midpoint in both of our example stories is a *climax* – a fighter plane is stolen, missiles are fired at the stolen submarine – and we're only at the halfway mark. Plotting a story like this means having to have enough in reserve to create an even bigger climax at the end of the second half of the story. Luckily with the military techno-thriller we can have espionage-style – or 'caper' plot – action in the first half and then switch to a more action-adventure mode for the second. Having stolen the military technology the good guys now have to fight to keep it and the bad guys have to chase them to get it back.

A significant difference between *Firefox* and *The Hunt for Red October* is that during the first half of the latter, a great deal more background information is given about each of the named characters as they appear – we learn something about their personal lives and, more significantly, about their experiences and achievements during their military careers. As a writer of any other type of story, you might create detailed background information so that you can get to know your characters, but apart from a few brief references this information does not find its way into the final story; in a military techno-thriller, more of this background information may be of interest to the reader and so mini character dossiers can be included when each first appears.

Sequence 5
The fifth sequence begins with reactions to events at the midpoint. Having lost an important piece of military hardware – and not wanting their opponents to have use of it – the bad guys take steps to destroy the weapon.

In *Firefox*, having stolen the fighter plane, the hero must now get away with it – out of Soviet airspace to a friendly location. And along the way he's going to have to stop somewhere and refuel. The Soviets know he'll need to do this and try to predict where he'll land. Initially the hero manages to trick them into looking for him in the wrong place – but the enemy soon realises their error. Fighters are sent to intercept the stolen plane and heat-seeking missiles are fired at it. The hero realises that (a) the enemy are prepared to destroy the plane rather than let him escape with it, and (b) that despite the plane's advanced technology, he is still vulnerable to heat-seeking missiles and infrared scans. Also, the reader learns that the second prototype aircraft is being prepared – setting up the climactic battle of the story.

When we left the Red October at the midpoint, a Soviet submarine had fired missiles at her. Ramius and his crew manage to survive the attack. The Soviets, desperate to avoid the Americans capturing the Red October, tell the White House that Ramius has suffered a mental breakdown and plans to launch missiles at the USA. They ask the Americans to help them locate and destroy the Red October. This obviously raises the stakes for Ramius as he now has the navies of two superpowers pursuing him.

Sequence 6
The sixth sequence begins with reactions to events at the end of sequence five, where the bad guys planned some action which seemed assured of success. Here we see the balance shift again so that success seems to belong to the good guys. The balance will shift from one side to the other several more times before the end of the story.

At the end of sequence five in *Firefox*, a Soviet plane had fired on the hero; here he manages to escape the missiles and destroy the other aircraft. In the operations rooms of both sides, no one is sure if it is the stolen fighter plane that has been shot down or the pursuing one. The hero is late for his rendezvous with the refuelling vessel – is he dead? If not, he is desperately short of fuel. And just ahead of him is a Soviet missile cruiser and two submarines. These attack, but the hero manages to escape and approaches the refuelling location.

In *The Hunt for Red October,* Ryan learns that American ships and submarines have been given orders to destroy Red October before it gets in range of the U.S. mainland. He tries to persuade the captain of the nearest submarine to give him a chance to communicate with Ramius before opening fire. Ramius' actions seem to indicate that he wants to communicate, so Ryan gets his chance. He warns Ramius of the danger he faces from the Soviets and the US – and then Ryan says he has a plan.

Sequence 7
Following directly on from events in sequence six, here we will see the balance shift back in favour of the bad guys. The good guys will think that their plan is working – and the early stages may go off without a hitch – but then disaster strikes. And this time it will appear that victory for the bad guys seems almost certain.

In both of our example stories, sequences seven and eight form an almost unbroken flow of actions scenes, each leading rapidly into the next. The novel *Firefox* appears to have a short sequence seven followed by a long final sequence; in *The Hunt for Red October* the opposite is true. But in both cases, the action is effectively continuous.

The hero of *Firefox* manages to land his plane at the refuelling site. Local circumstances mean that taking off again will be delayed and it is a race against time to clear a suitable runway as the Soviet fleet is closing in on their location. This overlaps with the beginning of sequence eight where the Soviets pinpoint the refuelling location and send the second prototype aircraft to intercept the first.

In *The Hunt for Red October,* Ramius puts Ryan's plan into operation – if it is successful, the Red October's crew can be taken to safety and the Americans will be able to keep the submarine. But a Soviet submarine locates the Red October and the two captains play a classic underwater cat and mouse game. Events in the novel are more complex than those in the movie adaptation, with Captain Ramius having a plan of his own involving a radiation leak and Ryan's plan involving a decoy submarine, but it gets the story to more or less the same place.

Sequence 8
This is the final battle of the story – a confrontation we have been expecting since the first act. In *Firefox* it is an aerial dogfight between the two equally-matched prototype fighter planes. The sequence and the novel ends with the victor flying back to his people. In *The Hunt for Red October,* the crew of the Red October survive an external attack only to have to face a fight with an undercover KGB agent who tries to blow up the submarine from the inside. The story has a brief epilogue in which Ryan returns home to his own people – and then to his own family, which represents the 'free world' that he has just saved.

Techno-Thriller Plot 2: Technology Gone Wrong Thriller

I'm using the films *Westworld* and *Jurassic Park* here because I think they are two of the best examples of Michael Crichton's techno-thrillers. *Westworld* formed the basis of a successful television series beginning in 2016, but here I am referring only to the 1973 film. Both films take place in theme park settings but this is a coincidence and is not a significant part of the structure of this type of thriller. Laboratories and computer control rooms tend to feature in most of these stories, but beyond that, they can use locations of any kind – these days technology is everywhere.

Sequence 1

In the first sequence we need to accomplish a few things: establish the world of the story; introduce the main characters; tease the technology, but don't reveal it yet; issue a challenge to the main character; and, hint at the trouble that is to come.

Both example films open with a prologue that introduces the world. *Jurassic Park* shows a workman being attacked by an unseen velociraptor. *Westworld* has tourists just returning from the theme park being interviewed for a Delos promotional video in which they say that the robots are extremely human-like.

Jurassic Park then introduces us to palaeontologists Grant and Ellie, showing us that they are romantically involved and that Grant is not comfortable around children. 'Teasing the technology' and 'hints of trouble' come together in the form of the velociraptor attack in the prologue; Grant talking about the deadly hunting skills of the velociraptor and showing the fossil of its wicked claw, and in the scene where Nedry agrees to steal viable dinosaur embryos. We also see the mine where amber is being extracted, setting up the source of the recovered dinosaur DNA. The challenge comes when John Hammond says to Grant and Ellie come to my dinosaur theme park and endorse it. *Jurassic Park* features an ensemble cast – more characters are introduced in sequences two and three – making it more like a 'disaster movie' than a lone hero on the run thriller.

Westworld has a lone hero, though he has a partner during the early parts of the story. Peter is a newbie who has never visited the theme park before – he is excited but unsure as the story opens; he is accompanied by John who already has experience of the *Westworld* park. As in other types of story, having a new guy arrive in a location gives the author an excuse/opportunity to explain things to the reader without having the 'infodump' seem too contrived. We also see two other characters – one who will become the Medieval Knight and a banker who will become a sheriff – and see the cowboys getting their costumes and weapons. 'Teasing the technology' includes a discussion about six-shooters and part of an orientation video for the tourists explaining that there are three sections of the resort: Western world, Medieval world, and Roman world. The hero, Peter, asks if the woman who greets them at the resort is a robot – she looks human. John tells him that the robots look exactly like people except that the hands aren't perfect. We also see the control room that runs things behind the scenes – and here we get the first hint of trouble to come when a glitch causes someone to say 'I'll do it manually.' The challenge issued to Peter by the Delos theme park is to 'indulge your every whim' and the visitors are (ironically) told 'nothing can go wrong.'

The cross-over from sequence one to sequence two occurs in both stories when the heroes arrive into the theme park.

Sequence 2
The second sequence is pretty much all about the technology – this is where we see how cool it is and observe the first reactions of the visitors who are seeing it for the first time. The checklist of things to include in this sequence looks something like this: first sight of the main location; first reactions to the location; first face-to-face encounter with the technology; more about the characters; explanation of the science; more hints of trouble to come; enjoying the technology. There is some overlap between these items and more than one can be achieved in a single scene. The sequence in which they unfold is more or less the order in which they are listed above, though learning more about the characters and introducing new characters can occur at any point in sequence two.

Ellie and Grant in *Jurassic Park* fly to the island and see the 'Jurassic Park' theme park logo on the Jeeps that collect them from the helipad. We're still teasing here – dinosaurs are promised but we don't see them yet. First reactions at this stage are curiosity from Ellie and Grant; the lawyer representing investors is threatening to shut the park down if he doesn't see that it is safe; and 'rock star mathematician' Malcolm is introduced and worries about the theoretical dangers inherent in a project like this. The first encounter with 'real' dinosaurs comes about 19 minutes into the film. We see huge 'veggiesauruses' – this is more tease, we're saving the meat eaters until later. And we see the reaction of the visitors to the live dinosaurs – Ellie and Grant experience that 'sense of wonder' that we only usually get as children when much of the world is new to us. CGI creatures are pretty old-hat these days, but on the cinema screen in 1993 they looked pretty impressive. After that everyone goes inside the theme park and we get an explanation of how dinosaur DNA was obtained from mosquitoes trapped in amber and then sequenced with frog DNA to fill in the gaps. We also learn that all of the dinosaurs are female to make sure that they can't reproduce in the 'wild.' Hints of trouble to come occur throughout the sequence – some are more subtle than others. There are huge electrified fences; the tyrannosaurus rex is first mentioned; we see feeding time at the velociraptor pen – but not the meat-eaters themselves; we learn that the boat off the island leaves shortly, and Malcolm warns that no matter what precautions are put in place 'life finds a way.' Finally, 'enjoyment of the technology' climaxes in the birth of a baby dinosaur – a 'cute' velociraptor hatches from an egg in front of our eyes.

In *Westworld* we get our first glimpse of the town that is straight out of the old west. It looks just like a town from a Western movie. Peter's initial reaction is to be underwhelmed by his 'authentic 1800s' hotel room – he's paying $1,000 a day for this? He's also not yet really into the swing of things, saying 'I feel silly.' In the bar Peter tries to order his usual cocktail, not yet 'in character,' and says that some of the other bar patrons look a bit rough. John is more relaxed and playing his part already – and assures Peter that despite its looks this is still a resort and perfectly safe. Famous last words. In his room, the banker practices quick draws like a kid. The first face-to-face encounter with technology occurs when Peter shoots the Gunslinger – this occurs about 17 minutes into the film. Explanations of the science is limited here since people have seen fake robots before – but we do learn that the six-shooters have a sensor in them that ensures that 'cold' robots can be shot but not warm-blooded humans. Yul Brynner as the Gunslinger is a hint of trouble to come – imagine if his gun *could* shoot people... Peter and John enjoy the technology by visiting Miss Carrie's bordello where they meet a couple of lovely robot girls.

Sequence 3
The third sequence features more enjoyment of, or teasing of, the technology – but with more hints of trouble to come. Elements to consider including here are second reactions to the technology and the location; behind the scenes; setting things up for later; more enjoyment of the technology; character development.

In *Jurassic Park* the characters have had a chance to get beyond their astonishment at seeing live dinosaurs and are thinking about the implications of what they have witnessed. The lawyer is now excited about the amount of money they can make from the park. Grant and Ellie are concerned because there's no way of knowing whether they can keep control of the project or of knowing how dinosaurs and humans will interact, since they were separated by millions of years of evolution. Malcolm says it is worse than he feared – the scientists have created these things without ever asking if they *should.* Hammond is just frustrated that no one will endorse his park. Behind the scenes, we see the computer control room that runs everything semi-autonomously. Hints of trouble come when we learn there are glitches in the millions of lines of code that control the park's systems and that it was built on the cheap – by Nedry, who is still planning to steal dinosaur embryos. Setting things up for later includes a weather report of an approaching storm; mentions of the t-rex and poison-spitting dinosaurs, and Nedry's plan which will exploit 'limitations' of the computer network. We see the potential for character development when Grant encounters Hammond's grandchildren. Enjoyment of the technology is set up as the tour of the theme park begins – but there is disappointment when the poisonous dinosaurs and the t-rex don't show up on cue. Setting out into the park sees the main characters entering a 'new world' and the threats of an approaching storm and behind the scenes shenanigans by Nedry raise the stakes – and now the lives of two children are at stake too.

Second reactions and character development are combined in *Westworld* with Peter becoming more relaxed and more confident – "... this place is really fun!" Behind the scenes and while the guests sleep, crews clean up the 'dead' robots and take them to be repaired ready for the next day. It's a well-organised operation with a smart repair shop – but a hint of trouble to come is given when the technicians discuss an increasing number of breakdowns. The robots are complex machines and some of them were designed by other machines, so the human technicians don't know exactly how they work. When Peter is in bed with the robot girl he doesn't see her eyes momentarily go dead and metallic, but the audience sees it and hears on the soundtrack that even the sex robots might be dangerous. This sequence also features the 'plant' or set-up for something that will be used in sequence seven – the robot repair lab has a table with bottles of chemicals on it, including acids.

Sequence 4 and Midpoint

Here things start to get much more serious. The fourth sequence sets up expectations of good things to come, but then something bad happens. A series of minor glitches lead up to the technology *really* going wrong at the midpoint.

In *Jurassic Park* the official tour has been a disappointment so Grant gets out of the Jeep and the others follow. Finally they get to see a real dinosaur up close – another veggiesaurus, but it's a triceratops which is pretty cool but she is sick. Nedry puts his plan to steal the dinosaur embryos into effect, using the computer to shut down cameras and other security measures so he can get what he wants and head off to get on the ship before it leaves for the mainland. Phones, door locks, and electric fences start to go offline. At the same time, the storm is heading for the island, meaning that the tour of the park needs to be cut short. Power to the Jeeps is cut stranding them – right beside the paddock that holds the tyrannosaurus rex. At the midpoint, the electric fence fails and the t-rex breaks free.

In *Westworld* Peter has a second encounter with the Gunslinger – it seems more dangerous this time, seeking them out, but Peter is more confident with his gun, fanning it when he 'kills' the robot. The banker is having a good time too – he wakes up in bed with an attractive robot girl and later he gets to become the new sheriff. In the control room the technicians note that it is the last day at the resort of the guest playing the Medieval Knight and they determine to make his last experience of it a 'lulu.' Before that, Peter is arrested for shooting the Gunslinger and John has to break him out of jail. The two of them ride out of town – desperados! Their excitement turns to concern at the midpoint when John is attacked and bitten by a robotic snake. 'That's not supposed to happen!'

By the end of sequence four, in both example stories, the heroes have stepped beyond the safe bounds of the theme park experience – the cowboys have ridden out of town into the wilder west and the dino-tourists have been stranded in the open. Away from everyone else, they are now more vulnerable when the technology goes wrong.

Sequence 5

The fifth sequence, as always, includes responses to the events of the midpoint and the beginnings of the descent into chaos that will take us to the climax of the story. More things go wrong and the situation gets worse and worse. The speed and scale of this descent depend on the story – in *Westworld* it is more gradual and on a much smaller scale than in *Jurassic Park*. It depends on what you have lined up for your climax – one man versus one robot or a 'family' facing off against multiple deadly dinosaurs including three velociraptors and a tyrannosaurus rex.

In *Jurassic Park* the t-rex attacks – the lawyer gets eaten and Malcolm is injured; the others climb over the edge to escape. Hammond asks his park ranger to go out and rescue his grandchildren. Meanwhile, the technician is unable to bring the park's systems back online – he needs Nedry's help. But Nedry encounters a poison-spitting dinosaur and won't be able to help anyone. Grant rescues the children and takes care of them, but the three of them are out in the open with no vehicle, no weapons, with a t-rex on the loose somewhere behind them.

The technicians in *Westworld* respond to the attack by the snake. There is a boardroom meeting where they discuss shutting down the park, but decide this would be an overreaction. They're certain they can ensure the safety of their guests. Then another robot acts against her programming, resisting the Medieval Knight's amorous attentions. The technicians bring her in for repair but cannot find anything wrong with her. Finally there is a barroom fight, after which the Gunfighter is brought in for repairs and – setting up the confrontation to come – receives upgrades to his eyesight and hearing, making him an even more formidable opponent.

Sequence 6

In this sequence we have the technology attacking the humans. In both of our examples, there is a self-contained series of events that build to a climax and a second series of scenes that set up sequence seven.

In *Jurassic Park* the injured Malcolm is rescued by Ellie and the park ranger – they can see that the others have escaped on foot but have to flee themselves when the t-rex appears and chases them. These action scenes are contrasted with a quieter scene where Grant bonds with the two children and they have an encounter with a non-threatening brachiosaurus. Hammond still hasn't learned his lesson and talks about what he'll do differently next time – Ellie challenges him on this and tells him the only thing that matters now is rescuing the people they love who are currently out there where people are dying. They try to bring the park's computer system back online by turning it off and then back on again – it seems to work, but someone needs to go to the other end of the compound to reset the circuit-breakers. Ellie and the park ranger go – and discover that the velociraptors have escaped from their enclosure...

As part of his exciting last day in *Westworld,* the Medieval Knight must fight the robotic Black Knight. When the Medieval Knight is injured, the control room tries to shut the Black Knight down – but he kills the guest. Then the Gunslinger confronts Peter and John again – and shoots John dead. Peter is now alone against the Gunslinger – he runs and the robot pursues him, first on foot and then on horseback. In the control room the technicians discover they no longer have any control over the robots and, worse for them, they are locked in an airtight room and will suffocate if they can't get the system controlling the doors back online.

Sequence 7
The seventh sequence builds to a crisis and climax which seems to provide the heroes with a victory – but it is a false victory as they still have another confrontation to come.

In *Jurassic Park* Ellie takes responsibility for re-setting the park's circuit-breakers. She is unaware that Grant and the two children have just started climbing one of the deactivated fences in order to escape from the t-rex. Spielberg cuts back and forth between the two locations to build the suspense. Then, just as we breathe a sigh of relief, the velociraptors attack. A series of narrow escapes sees the 'family' of main characters reunited and it looks as though everything will be okay. But then the children find themselves having to hide in the kitchen as the velociraptors come looking for a meal.

Peter, in *Westworld*, cannot expect any help from the control room technicians as they are suffocating. He manages to stay ahead of the Gunslinger and crosses the border into Roman World. He has been told by a technician that he doesn't stand a chance against the Gunslinger – it is an advanced model and only an attack using acid might disable it. Peter finds his way down a shaft into the underground part of the Delos resort – but it is a maze of corridors. The Gunslinger follows him down there. Using his ingenuity, Peter manages to elude discovery and takes acid from the robot repair shop – he throws it into the Gunslinger's face. It looks as though Peter has won – but after the robot's face melts it pursues its human prey again.

Sequence 8
The final confrontation and resolution of the story.

In *Jurassic Park* the 'family' are reunited in the control room. The velociraptors attack and our heroes flee – and receive a little help from an unexpected source. This might seem like a bit of a cheat except for the fact that Spielberg has had this 'character' make a couple of unexpected appearances before this point. The survivors escape in a helicopter and we see that Grant is now comfortable around children.

In *Westworld* Peter enters the medieval banqueting hall. The Gunslinger stalks him. Peter sets fire to him and exits thinking he's finally succeeded in dispatching his enemy. Peter 'saves' a robot, thinking she's a real girl – and then the Gunslinger appears, charred and scary. Finally it falls and explodes in a shower of sparks and smoke. Peter rests, it's over, and the film ends with the words of the Delos ad 'Boy have we got a vacation for you!'

12 | Psychological Thriller

What is a Psychological Thriller
Many films are mislabelled as 'psychological thrillers'– often by filmmakers who want people to believe that their movie is something more than an exploitative 'slasher' movie. Others feel that any movie in which a character is made to feel afraid – or which exploits the audience's fears – is a 'psychological' thriller. For our purposes here, I am going to say that a psychological thriller has to have a definite psychological element that is central to the plot.

Sticking with the format I've used in other chapters, we could say that a psychological thriller takes the conventions of the thriller genre – notably suspense and/or conspiracy – and uses them in a story that centres on human psychology. That is all right as far as it goes, but 'human psychology' is a much broader subject than, say, the legal system or the medical system. All stories, to greater or lesser extent, deal with human psychology, don't they? Even if I say that a psychological thriller concerns an internal conflict symbolised by external conflicts in thriller form, we're still not much closer to having something workable.

The word 'psychological' gives us a clue that this type of thriller is concerned with the risk of psychological harm rather than physical harm – though, of course, psychological harm can be caused by the threat of – or actual – physical harm. Mental cruelty is much more subtle – and can be much more frightening. The *Oxford English Dictionary* defines *psychology* as the 'scientific study of the nature, functioning, and development of the human mind...' – so we can say that what goes on in one or more character's head is likely to be as important as any external action. As we will see under *Themes* below, psychological thrillers typically centre on a character's perceptions of the world around them or on perceptions of identity – either their own or another person's.

Before we leave dictionary definitions, we can say that the psychological thriller is also a form of *psychodrama*, which the *OED* says is a 'play, film, novel, etc., in which psychological elements are the main interest.'

In this chapter, I'm going to say that there are five main sub-categories of the psychological thriller sub-genre:

(i) The *psychoanalysis* or 'psycho-traumatic' thriller
(ii) The *amnesia* thriller
(iii) The *stolen identity* thriller (including mistaken identity)
(iv) The *'woman in jeopardy'* thriller
(v) The *stalker* thriller

I am not including serial killers here – psychopaths and their psychological profiling fit better in the forensic criminal investigation sub-genre, so I will cover them in the *Crime Thriller* volume in this series. I have also written about them in my book on character creation.

From the sub-categories listed above, it is obvious that as well as overlap with the crime thriller sub-genre, the psychological thriller is also related to the psychological horror novel. The 'woman in jeopardy' and 'stalker' thrillers also have elements in common with romance – particularly Gothic romance.

The Conspiracy

The conspiracy in these stories, if there is one, usually involves an attempt to frighten someone, or to make them doubt their own sanity, in order for the villain to achieve some goal. That goal may simply be the complete psychological domination of the victim, but there is often some more tangible goal to be attained, such as an inheritance. In the psychological thriller, the villain usually tries to convince the victim that the world or the situation around them is something other than it really is, or that the villain or the victim is someone other than the victim believes.

There are also psychological thrillers in which the protagonist of the story may already *believe* that the world is something other than it really is and try to convince others that his or her version of reality is the 'rational' one. This can be done quite subtly by introducing the protagonist in a way that makes them initially seem stable and sympathetic, and then gradually revealing more erratic behaviours or disturbing beliefs. In this kind of story, it is the protagonist – as 'unreliable narrator' – and/or the author who is playing mind-games with the reader.

We've already explored the role that paranoia plays in thrillers generally, but in the psychological thriller things are taken to a new level with the main character – and perhaps even the reader – doubting whether they can trust their own perceptions about anything.

Themes

Central to the psychological thriller is the potential mismatch between external objective reality and what a person subjectively *believes* to be real. This is typically explored in terms of a character's perception of the world around them or a particular situation; or in terms of identity – either their own or that of another character. The psychological thriller is concerned with whether the world is the way that this person thinks it is and or whether a person is who they think they are or claim to be. It also exploits the paranoia that arises when a person comes to doubt their own perception of reality. At the same time, a good writer will also exploit an audience's own fears about the perception of reality.

As we will see in the different sub-categories below, the protagonist of a psychological thriller can be either someone whose own mind is disordered or they may be the victim of a character whose perceptions are impaired.

The Psychology in the Psychological Thriller

The science of psychology is a relatively recent development, having been around for only 150 years or so. Prior to that discussion of the human mind tended to be more philosophical than scientific. As recently as the 1960s and

70s, Thomas Kuhn wrote that psychology had not yet developed a single predominant paradigm that all psychologists could subscribe to and was therefore only in a pre-science stage of development.

One of the main problems with the study of the human mind is that it is difficult to conduct objective observations and experiments from which to develop and test theories. In observing one or more human minds external to himself, the psychologist has to contend with the fact that his own internal mind may affect his observations. For an author, sympathy and empathy for others are great tools, for psychologists, not so much.

In psychological thrillers of the 1940s – especially those of Alfred Hitchcock – the Freudian models of psychology and psychoanalysis were predominant. Their popularity was perhaps due to the fact that a psychoanalytic investigation seemed similar to the investigation in a whodunit. Question the patient and piece together the clues and you could eventually discover the correct answer to 'whatdunit' – the traumatic incident which had been repressed and was the root cause of all of the patient's psychological problems. It's a nice theory, but very much a simplification of Freud's thinking and not the sort of investigation that could really be conducted as quickly and easily as movies suggest. Explanations based on such a cut-down version of Freud's theory are now dismissed as being unrealistic and referred to as 'pop psychology.' Perhaps another reason for Hitchcock's interest in the Freudian model was that it tended to suggest that all repressed traumatic experiences were somehow sexual. But, as Freud apparently never said, 'Sometimes a cigar is just a cigar.'

Carl Jung's theories – particularly those relating to the interpretation of dreams – became more popular with storytellers after the publication of Joseph Campbell's *The Hero with a Thousand Faces* in 1949. *Star Wars* creator George Lucas was heavily influenced by Campbell and discussed this in the 1988 documentary *The Power of Myth*. Screenwriter Christopher Vogler, created a seven-page memo, 'A Practical Guide to *The Hero with a Thousand Faces*,' while working at Disney and he later expanded this into a book, *The Writer's Journey: Mythic Structure for Writers* (1992), which has become a standard screenwriting textbook.

Campbell's 'monomyth' or hero's journey shows how stories that have been told in different cultures across thousands of years contain common elements that are related to experiences and relationships that humans have throughout the course of their lives. This draws on the idea of a 'collective unconscious' that is the source of our instincts or innate behaviours and features a series of universally recognised symbols or archetypes such as the 'wise old man' or the 'tree of life.' The shared nature of this unconscious is very different from Freud's use of a unique personal unconscious.

Modern psychological thrillers tend to avoid the straightforward Freudian investigation, recognising that psychoanalysis is a much more long-term process with no guarantee of a 'Eureka!' moment that solves a person's problems. Dream interpretation – whether Freudian or Jungian – is also used less directly than it was in a film like Hitchcock's *Spellbound*. Filmmakers tend to use visual symbols in a much subtler way, *implying* their significance rather than placing it before the audience and/or characters in the form of a puzzle to be solved.

There is also less emphasis on finding a solution to an individual character's psychological issues, and more of an emphasis on exploiting psychological weaknesses or doubts.

As I mentioned above, the 'Freudian psychoanalysis' story has much of the appeal of a whodunit, but that appeal is – to an extent – an intellectual appeal. We watch as someone attempts to locate the solution to a puzzle. While there is pleasure to be gained from watching an expert, or even an amateur, at work in such an investigation, there is a certain distance between reader and characters that prevents our full immersion in the story. As observers, we feel a level of detachment. People come to the thriller genre for a much more exciting reading experience and want to feel their own emotions and fears rather than simply see someone else's. For this reason, the modern psychological thriller is just as likely to play 'head games' with the reader as it is with the main character. Our own doubts and fears and paranoia are evoked by the story so that we can enjoy 'participating' rather than just observing.

We'll begin by looking at the workings of the more traditional psychoanalysis story as they were an important part of the development of the genre, but I would advise against trying to write this type of story today.

The Psychoanalysis Thriller

Charles Derry, in his book *The Suspense Thriller*, devotes a chapter to what he calls the 'psycho-traumatic thriller,' and writes that this type of story centres on the psychological effects of a traumatic event in the protagonist's past on a current relationship – usually a romantic one.

This type of thriller is based on the theories of Sigmund Freud and the process of psychoanalysis. The *OED* defines *psychoanalysis* as a method for 'treating mental disorders by investigating the interaction of conscious and unconscious elements in the patient's mind and bringing repressed fears and conflicts into the conscious mind, using techniques such as dream interpretation and free association.' For deep-rooted traumatic memories, long periods of psychoanalysis are required, involving two to five sessions per week over a period of several years. Briefer 'dynamic' treatments can be used for some specific, less deep-rooted problems. But the recovery of characters in films involving a few short flashbacks over a period of (at most) several days is unrealistic. Hitchcock recognised this, saying in his films that shortcuts were being taken and that proper treatment would require 'six months to a year' – but his approach was that drama depicted 'life with the dull bits taken out.'

Hitchcock's first 'psychoanalysis thriller' was *Spellbound* in 1945 – it effectively introduced cinema audiences to the subject with the opening text:

Our story deals with psychoanalysis, the method by which modern science treats the emotional problems of the sane.

The analyst seeks only to induce the patient to talk about his hidden problems, to open the locked doors of the mind.

Once the complexes that have been disturbing the patient are uncovered and interpreted, the illness and confusion disappear – and the devils of unreason are driven from the human soul.

'Psychiatric Advisor' on the film was May E. Romm, M.D., who was producer David O. Selznick's own analyst. It has been reported that Hitchcock did not always accept her technical advice, saying to her at one point, "My dear, it's only a movie."

The psychoanalysis thriller typically features some external criminal or other intrigue involving the protagonist. The villains are seeking to take advantage of the protagonist's vulnerability for their own purposes, often trying to intensify the protagonist's feelings of 'masochistic guilt' relating to the repressed memory of the traumatic event. The protagonist is subconsciously punishing him or herself for the event that they are trying not to remember – and the bad guys try and exploit this. The protagonist is a victim of the villains – but may be a criminal him or herself. Or may *believe* that he/she is a victim, feeling that the traumatic incident was a crime for which they were responsible.

The protagonist typically demonstrates external behaviours which reflect his or her inner psychological trauma. The behaviours are an attempt to protect themselves from the pain – real, emotional or psychological – related to the traumatic event. These behaviours often involve an abnormal relationship with one or more objects, either something the protagonist becomes unusually attached to – a 'fetish object' as Derry calls it – or an object which the protagonist has a terrible fear of and takes extraordinary measures to avoid. Only by facing the fear arising from the traumatic incident and bringing this fear out into the open can the protagonist recognise it and deal with it, integrating it into his or her life in a healthy way – they must move from avoidance to acceptance. From an internal fantasy of safety to an external embrace of reality, usually supported by the romantic co-protagonist.

To solve the protagonist's problem situation, an investigation is necessary. This might involve a third person, often the protagonist's romantic co-protagonist who acts as a surrogate therapist, or the investigation may be carried out by the protagonist him or herself. Or the story itself may be in the form of the investigation which unfolds without conscious input from the protagonist or co-protagonist. The nature of the investigation will be that of a Freudian psychoanalysis and the timing and nature of the traumatic event provide the story with a sense of mystery.

As well as the whodunit-style mystery, the psycho-traumatic thriller has some elements of the amateur-on-the-run thriller – but the danger the protagonist is fleeing from is *internal* rather than external. In addition to providing the threat of physical danger, the villains are an external representation of the protagonist's inner fear.

Themes

In these stories, the theme is that to avoid unpleasant truths about ourselves is unhealthy but to accept and integrate them is healthy. Avoiding these unpleasant truths leads to feelings of guilt which can lead us to masochistically punish ourselves and to allow others to (sadistically) exploit us. There is also a suggestion that every personal issue, however painful, has a solution if we are prepared to seek and confront its cause.

Iconography
Things typically 'seen' in this type of story include psychoanalysis including the psychoanalyst's couch and possibly the use of hypnotism to access repressed memories; Freudian 'slips' and symbolism (usually sexual); psychological disorders such as kleptomania, frigidity, acrophobia, vertigo, a 'death wish', self-harm or excessive risk-taking. Images relating to other phobias – rats, spiders, snakes, confined spaces – also appear, as these help to unsettle the audience as well as the characters. Images related to an 'insane asylum' – such as beds with restraints, straitjackets, padded rooms, barred windows, and electro-convulsive therapy apparatus also feature. Dream sequences and flashbacks are sometimes used – and sometimes a dream within a dream, when the protagonist believes they have woken up but haven't. Often father-figures – sometimes in the form of a romantic co-protagonist, therapist or doctor – or step-mothers (or their symbolic representation) are used. Human-like but featureless figures can also appear in dream sequences. Dreams in which the protagonist tries to run away but doesn't make any progress, corridors with many doors, and attempts to follow and speak to a mysterious figure – often an unhappy child – can also be used.

Plot Structure of the Psychoanalysis Thriller
Alfred Hitchcock directed several films that used the 'psychoanalysis thriller' plot. The first was *Spellbound* (1945), with *Vertigo* (1958) being the best example, and *Marnie* (1964), featuring the last appearance of a 'Hitchcock blonde,' perhaps being the most controversial. We can take apart the structures of these three films to get a model for this type of thriller.

Sequence 1
Introduction of the victim-protagonist along with some external evidence of their 'psychological trauma.' In *Spellbound* we see 'Dr. Edwardes' reacting oddly to shapes drawn on a tablecloth by the times of a fork. In *Vertigo*, Scottie leaves the police force because of his acrophobia and vertigo. And in *Marnie*, the title character is disturbed by the sight of red gladioli. Each case introduces an element of mystery – Why is the character disturbed by that object? Or, in the case of *Vertigo* – Will the protagonist be able to overcome that phobia?

The first sequence also introduces the character who will provide a challenge or opportunity for the protagonist, usually in the form of a new romantic relationship. The romantic co-protagonist in these stories will often act as either an investigator/analyst (*Spellbound, Marnie*) or as a catalyst who triggers the protagonist's own investigation/analysis (*Vertigo*).

Finally, we are introduced to the antagonist. This is either someone seeking to exploit the protagonist's psychological vulnerability (*Spellbound, Vertigo*) or someone responsible for, or involved in, the traumatic experience which triggered the protagonist's 'guilt complex' (*Marnie*).

Both *Spellbound* and *Marnie* feature a victim-protagonist suffering from partial amnesia because of a traumatic incident that they do not want to remember. The circumstances of this incident are the subject of the investigation/analysis. The story concentrates on finding the original cause of the 'guilt complex' suffered by the protagonist – and once this has been unearthed, they are essentially 'cured.'

In *Vertigo* there is no search for the cause of the phobia, instead the protagonist seeks to overcome it. The investigation element arises when the protagonist is asked to look into a psychological mystery – the apparent 'possession' of Madeline – which is later revealed to be part of a conspiracy. The plot of *Vertigo* is very similar to that of a traditional 'hardboiled' or private detective story. *Marnie* also features the investigation of a crime, but in this case, Marnie is the criminal and the romantic co-protagonist investigates, and a similar situation occurs in *Spellbound* where the protagonist *believes* he may be guilty of murder and the romantic co-protagonist sets out to prove that he isn't.

One of the first three sequences usually provides the audience with information about the psychological problem faced by the victim-protagonist and how it may be cured. This effectively serves as a plant, setting up events later in the story. Sometimes the information is given in relation to another character or patient with a similar problem. In sequence two of *Spellbound*, psychiatrists discuss the origins, nature, and 'cure' of a guilt complex, the problem that Gregory Peck's character JB will later be shown to have. Mark begins his 'analysis' of the protagonist in sequence three of *Marnie* but doesn't discuss theories about her illness until much later (sequence six). *Vertigo* includes a discussion of Scottie's phobia in sequence one, in which he states his belief that he can overcome his situation gradually – which idea he seems to disprove almost immediately – while a friend says a doctor told her that it might only be cured by 'another emotional shock.' We will explore the 'second shock' theory a little more in the amnesia thriller section.

Sequence 2

Having been presented with a challenge or opportunity in the first sequence, we now see the protagonist's increasing involvement or entanglement in the situation. By the end of the second sequence, he or she should have reached a point where they are thoroughly committed (or trapped) by the situation so that there is no going back.

Scottie, the protagonist of *Vertigo*, reluctantly agreed to investigate the alleged 'possession' of Madeline by a woman from a previous era. Scottie was sceptical at the beginning, but during sequence two he discovers things that make him wonder if what he has been told may be true. He then commits himself to the investigation, partly because he's intrigued by it and partly because he is attracted to the woman he is following. The investigation also gives him a purpose, replacing the police career he's had to give up.

The heroine of Marnie also arrives in a new town with the aim of committing a new crime. Again we see her disturbed by the colour red. She meets romantic co-protagonist Mark Rutland for the first time (the audience saw him in sequence one) and he is attracted to her and intrigued by her. We also know that Mark is a potential threat to her because he has a connection with the company she robbed in sequence one. He comforts her when she is disturbed by a thunderstorm, kisses her – but she does not respond. Marnie dismisses her behaviour as a simple fear of thunder and lightning.

In *Spellbound*, the relationship between Constance and 'Dr. Edwardes' intensifies and they enjoy their first kiss. We also see that there may be something not quite right about 'Dr. Edwardes' and that he has had a bad time with his nerves lately.

There is often some further development or reminder of the conspiracy in this sequence. In *Spellbound*, 'Dr. Edwardes' receives a telephone call from someone he doesn't know. In *Marnie*, the heroine carefully watches her new work colleagues, planning her next robbery – while Mark watches her, hatching a plan of his own. The first five sequences of *Vertigo* are almost entirely conspiracy-related.

Sequence 3
Having passed a point where they can no longer turn back, the protagonist – and the audience – begins to see that the situation he or she has entered is filled with unexpected dangers. The sequence usually contains some dramatic action that provides a whole new level of interest and complexity to the story – effectively showing why this is going to be a full-length film or novel rather than a short.

Scottie's investigations in *Vertigo* unearth important facts and he discusses them with his client, who fills in more pieces of the puzzle. The sequence builds to Scottie's first direct meeting with the woman, Madeline, who he has been following – he saves her from drowning. There is a mutual attraction and this marks the beginning of their relationship. It is also an important turning point in the conspiracy plotline.

Mark's relationship with the protagonist in *Marnie* develops to the point where he invites her to his family home. This development prompts Marnie to put her plans for the robbery into immediate effect – it is time for her to take the money and run. There is also another instance of her being disturbed by the colour red. Another reason for accelerating her plans occurs when a man recognises her, calling her by one of her former aliases – his presence is a threat to her current plan.

In *Spellbound*, 'Dr. Edwardes' suffers a breakdown – which is coolly watched by the antagonist. Constance cares for 'Edwardes' and he tells her that he is an impostor. He has amnesia and doesn't know who he really is – his only clue is a cigarette case with the initials 'JB.' The nature of amnesia is discussed. He believes he may have killed the real Dr. Edwardes and taken his place – Constance thinks not, saying it is a delusion caused by his 'guilt complex'. And she will help him overcome it. When 'JB' flees, the antagonist says it is because he is a murderer. The police search for him and Constance goes after him too, determined to try and help him.

The story situation in all three of our examples develops to the point where the main character *has* to take dramatic action – save a life, rob a safe, go after a man who is on the run.

Sequence three often also sees a new threat introduced. *Marnie* has Mark's curious sister-in-law Lily, who is intrigued by – and jealous of – Marnie. In *Vertigo,* we have the attempted suicide and the continuing threat that Madeline will try and kill herself while under the influence of the dead woman, Carlotta. While in *Spellbound*, we have the possibility that JB is a murderer; that he may kill himself; and that the police are pursuing him. Sequence three is obviously a key place for raising the stakes.

Sequence 4

This sequence typically involves an intensification of the protagonist's psychological suffering – often linked to a confrontation with the romantic co-protagonist – and either a denial by the protagonist that there *is* a problem, or an argument by the protagonist that they *deserve* their suffering. Either way, they seem more afraid of confronting the real problem and resolving it than they are of the suffering it is causing them. Sequence four also builds to a significant midpoint revelation, decision, or action.

Madeline and Scottie in *Vertigo* go on a romantic day trip together. She tells him of her recurring dream and that if she ever reaches the darkness at the end of the dream corridor, she will die. He says that he wants to help her discover the reason for her obsession/possession – she says the answer is that she is mad. She seems resigned to her fate. At the midpoint, their romantic feelings for each other are recognised in their first kiss.

In *Marnie,* Mark has discovered the crime and tracked Marnie down. He is angry with her but also remains intrigued. She tells him her story, but again and again, he challenges her for lying. He has also realised that she was responsible for the robbery in sequence one. Mark feels responsible for her and says that he wants to help her. Marnie argues that she doesn't need his help – that she doesn't need any man and never has. She says she feels like an animal he has trapped and caught – and he seems to like the analogy, saying he's going to keep her. And plans to marry her. At the midpoint, Marnie is trapped and doesn't know what to do.

Constance, in *Spellbound,* locates JB in New York. He doesn't want her to jeopardise her career by helping a criminal, but she insists. Together they will unlock his memories. He is still convinced that he killed Dr. Edwardes and took his place. She disagrees, sure that this is something he imagines because of a deep-seated guilt complex. Before they can make any progress, she is forced by circumstance – at the midpoint – to go on the run with him.

By the midpoint of the story, the situation has been set-up and explored, and the two main characters have committed themselves to each other – whatever happens now, they will face it together. We – and sometimes they – are also aware that the victim-protagonist's *internal* mystery – the source of their psychological suffering – is linked to an external conspiracy and/or a traumatic experience. The memory of the trauma needs to be retrieved, confronted, and understood. By this point in the story, the victim-protagonist has reached a point where they admit they have a psychological problem – and has asked for, reluctantly accepted, or resigned him or herself to accepting the romantic co-protagonist's help.

Sequence 5

This sequence typically concentrates on the relationship between the protagonist and romantic co-protagonist – and often features them going away together. This trip will be a combination of running away and romantic holiday. The journey will include several narrow escapes with romantic interludes.

Constance and JB, in *Spellbound*, escape from the city by train and go to visit her former mentor, Dr. Brulov. She and JB pretend to be newly-weds. During the journey, JB recovers some of his memories. But the closer he comes to the truth – to the painful memories he's hiding from – the more angry and unpredictable JB's behaviour becomes. When it seems that JB could become a threat to them, Dr. Brulov wants to call the police, but Constance pleads for more time to help him. She is prepared to risk her own life for him now.

In *Vertigo*, Scottie and Madeline drive to a historical tourist attraction – and again she seems to fall under the influence of the mysterious Carlotta. When Madeline climbs the stairs in a church bell tower, Scottie's acrophobia and vertigo prevent him following. He can only watch as Madeline jumps to her death.

Sequence five of *Marnie* shows the protagonist and romantic co-protagonist on their honeymoon. Here Mark learns the full extent of Marnie's fear of men. He thinks she needs a psychiatrist. Failing that, he will help her as much as she can. There is a montage of happy honeymoon moments. After this, Mark forces himself on her – and as a result, she tries to drown herself in a swimming pool. Mark pulls her out of the water. This sequence in *Marnie* has been controversial since the beginning: screenwriter Evan Hunter left the project because of it – he, and many others subsequently, felt that the rape scene removed all sympathy for the character of Mark, but Hitchcock didn't agree. It makes for uncomfortable viewing, despite the fact that the camera pans away from the act itself.

Sequence 6

In most stories, as we have seen before, sequence six typically consists of an unravelling or a downward spiral – ending at some sort of crisis point that sets up the climax of the story. Given that we are talking about psychological thrillers here, the downhill journey will be a mental one. External circumstances may also deteriorate – but this will usually occur in a way that symbolises the unravelling of the victim-protagonist's mental state.

This sequence in *Spellbound* concentrates on the interpretation of JB's dream and features on-screen images designed by Salvador Dali. Brulov explains to JB – and the audience – the importance of dream interpretation in psychoanalysis. Having understood some of the disturbing imagery of the dream, Constance and JB know where they have to go next – the place where Dr. Edwardes was killed.

In *Vertigo* there is an inquest into Madeline's death, which is ruled to be suicide, but Scottie's inability to prevent it weighs heavily on his mind. He loved her but he couldn't save her. Scottie suffers a breakdown, symbolised by a bizarre dream that includes his own death by falling, and he ends up in a psychiatric facility. He is in a trance-like state and his doctor says recovery could take six to twelve months. When he is finally released, Scottie is a broken man

– wandering around places he associates with Madeline. Then he sees a woman who bears a striking resemblance to Madeline – and he becomes obsessed with her.

Sequence six in *Marnie* sees her and Mark return to the family home. Mark's former sister-in-law, Lily, suspects that something isn't right between them. She eavesdrops on a conversation in which they talk about covering up a crime in order to avoid jail and then she overhears Marnie making a telephone call to a mother she claimed was dead. Mark, meanwhile, has a detective checking into Marnie's past – and learns that someone died and there was a trial: he wants to know more. Marnie is suffering from nightmares, but when Mark tries to unravel their meaning, she mocks him: 'You Freud, me Jane?' Her opinions about men and women are quite revealing – indicating some deep trauma. But she is also perceptive enough to know that Mark's interest in her isn't entirely healthy. Another episode involving the colour red ends with her crying out for someone to help her.

Sequence 7

This sequence builds to – and sometimes provides – the climax of the story. Typically we see external threats closing in on the protagonist and romantic co-protagonist – either the villain, the police, a third-party investigator, or perhaps all of the above. Past actions will also catch up with our characters, with delayed consequences finally paying off in a dramatic way.

This being a psychological thriller, we often find the writer or director playing 'mind games' with the audience. They seek to 'pull the rug out from under us,' so that we come to doubt the reality and/or meaning of events we have witnessed so far. This may involve a 'false' climax and solution before the real one, in a similar way to the mystery story showing us what *seemed* to have happened before revealing what *really* happened.

Marnie builds to a second crisis situation. Traumatic events during a hunt – including Marnie apparently seeing her own fate in that of a quarry attacked by a pack of hounds – leads her to try and carry out another robbery and flee to a new life. But she cannot make herself go through with it and the sequence ends with Mark telling her that they are going to visit Marnie's mother.

Spellbound has Constance and JB going to the ski resort where Dr. Edwardes was killed. In a tense skiing sequence, Constance wonders if JB will remember that he is innocent or if he will attack her in the same way he may have done to Dr. Edwardes. JB does recover his memories and we seem set for a happy ending involving a marriage – but then it seems that JB may be guilty of murder after all.

Finally, *Vertigo* pulls the biggest switch of all. Hitchcock reveals to the audience the nature of the conspiracy against Scottie, and we are left to wonder if he will discover the truth before it is too late. The rest of the sequence shows him unaware of the danger, becoming increasingly obsessed as he tries to transform his new friend Judy into the spitting image of Madeline.

In two of our examples, an important truth is revealed in sequence seven – one we've been waiting for since the beginning of the story – and then we learn that it doesn't explain everything. There is still more than we need to know.

Marnie is slightly more straightforward in that the truth *isn't* revealed – it is held off until sequence eight: sequence seven serves to build tension and increase our desire to know the solution to the mystery that is Marnie.

Sequence 8
In *Marnie*, the events responsible for her 'psychological trauma' are finally revealed, in a combination of dialogue and flashback. The antagonistic relationship between mother and daughter is demonstrated and explained. We finally learn why Marnie hates men, is afraid of thunderstorms, and can't bear the sight of the colour red. It isn't a happy ending for Marnie, there is still much healing to be done, but it does offer some hope for the future.

Constance, in *Spellbound*, refuses to give up on JB, despite all of the evidence against him. Triggered by one final clue, she is able to discover the meaning behind the last unexplained images in JB's dream. In scenes reminiscent of the final explanation in a murder mystery, Constance explains whodunit and traps the real villain of the piece. Finally, she and JB can have the happy ending they hoped for.

Vertigo shows Scottie taking Judy to the place where Madeline died. He tells her that she is his 'second chance.' In a dramatic climb up the stairs in the bell tower, Scottie finally faces and overcomes his phobia, and in an ironic ending at the top of the tower, he learns what *really* happened the night Madeline died.

The Amnesia Thriller

The Appeal of the Amnesia Thriller
The amnesia thriller has built into it several advantages for a storyteller: a mystery – What can't the hero remember and why? Suspense – Will he recover his memories before it's too late? And a reason for characters to explain things to each other without it seeming contrived – the hero is effectively a 'new guy' and the reader learns about his world as he does. At the heart of every amnesia thriller is an *investigation*. It usually begins with someone – typically a doctor – questioning the hero to discover the extent of his memory loss (and to demonstrate it to the reader or viewer). Then it usually has the hero himself take up the role of detective as he talks to people – family members, friends, work colleagues – to see what they can tell him about himself. Other clues may be presented in the form of photographs, objects, or significant locations. Gradually the hero – and the audience – piece together the missing information and try to understand the meaning of it all.

Often an early 'witness' in the hero's investigation will be a doctor or psychiatrist who provides an explanation of the nature and – possibly – the cause of the hero's amnesia. The doctor may also 'set up' later developments in the story by suggesting ways that the hero might try and recover his memories. It is usually at this point when we discover whether the hero's amnesia has a physical (blow to the head) or psychological (traumatic experience) cause.

Another advantage of this type of story is that the amnesiac hero also has jeopardy built in – with no memory, he can't trust himself and must rely on others – but some of them cannot be trusted to act in his best interests, and the dangerous ones aren't always the obvious 'bad' characters. Even his own doctor or psychiatrist may prove to be inept, cynical, or criminal. Self-preservation is as much of an issue for him as self-discovery. There is also some risk involved in discovering his 'old self' – he may find himself responsible for actions he cannot remember and/or may discover that he was actually a pretty nasty and untrustworthy character himself.

Self-discovery and self-reliance are topics that appeal to readers and moviegoers – by observing someone else piece together their own identity, we hope to learn about ourselves. These stories also feature a hero who is taking responsibility for his own future: whatever he learns about himself and his past, he will incorporate it into his present and decide how to respond as well as choosing which parts of his old life he will take forwards and which he will abandon. The idea of a fresh start or a 'do over' is an appealing one to many people.

The amnesiac hero typically suffers from a particular type of amnesia – a form of retrograde or dissociative amnesia – that offers the most dramatic opportunities to a writer. This involves a loss of long-term memories, including the hero's own name. But there is no damage to his ability to form new memories and no impairment in his ability to perform tasks such as speaking, driving a car or playing the piano. As the story progresses, the hero may even surprise himself by demonstrating special skills that he did not know he possessed. This is broadly in accordance with the accepted theory that the way people create and store memories of their own past differs from 'procedural' memory related to the performing of tasks. As we will see below, not everything that is portrayed in amnesia thrillers accurately reflects medical understanding of the condition.

Historical Development

The word *amnesia* comes from a Greek word meaning 'not-remembering'. Mnemosyne was the goddess of memory and the word *mnēmē* is where we also get the word mnemonic. The Ancient Greeks, from about the 7th century BC, also wrote about Lethe, the river of forgetfulness, said to be one of the five rivers flowing through the underworld. Anyone who drank its waters experienced complete oblivion, losing all their memories and previous identity such that they were ready for reincarnation. Another early story about amnesia is a classical Indian play *The Recognition of Shakuntala* by Kālidāsa, based on a story from the Mahabharata, and dating from the period 1BC to 4 AD – it tells of a young woman whose is forgotten by her husband King Dushyanta.

In 2007, Professor of Psychiatry H. G. Pope and his co-authors conducted a survey to identify any cases of 'dissociative amnesia for a traumatic event' documented in fiction or non-fiction published before 1800. Based on the results of the survey, their conclusion was that 'it appears that dissociative amnesia is not a natural neuropsychological phenomenon, but instead a culture-bound syndrome, dating from the nineteenth century.' This conclusion was challenged within the field and a couple of pre-1800 examples were identified – *Nina, ou La Folle par Amour (Nina, or The Woman Crazed with Love)*, a one-act *opéra-comique* composed by Nicolas Dalayrac with a libretto by Benoît-Joseph

Marsollier, first performed in 1786; and the case of Presidente de Tourvel's brief period of amnesia in Choderos de Laclos' *Les Liaisons Dangereuses* (1782).

As Pope suggested, there are more examples in fiction after 1800. Examples include the characters of Stéphanie de Vandières in Balzac's short story 'Adieu' (1830); Dr. Manette in Dickens' *A Tale of Two Cities* (1859) and the preacher Penn in Kipling's *Captains Courageous* (1896). Perhaps the closest to a modern-day amnesia thriller was Grant Allen's *Recalled to Life* (1891), in which a young woman loses her memory after the murder of her father and investigates the circumstances leading up to his death. Also of note from this period is Wilkie Collins' *The Moonstone* (1868) which features an amnesia sufferer who investigates the theft of a fabulous diamond after he is suspected of being the thief.

Dieguez and Annoni have suggested that the development of the neurological and psychiatric sciences during the second half of the 19th century, coupled with the publication of case reports of amnesiac patients, meant that "literary characters began displaying amnesia in a more clinical than mythological context."

There was a renewed public awareness and interest in amnesia following the First World War, particularly in France. Photographs were published under the headline 'Les Morts Vivants' (The Living Dead) of soldiers who 'having become insane during the war, could not be identified.' These men were amnesiacs unable to recall their own identities. The best-known of the ten men was Anthelme Mangin, whose identity was much-debated after many families claimed him as a lost relative, and who was the inspiration Jean Anouilh's 1937 play *Le Voyageur sans Baggage (The Traveller without Luggage)*. Jean Giraudoux's 1922 novel *Siegfried et le Limousin* (adapted by the author into a play, *Siegfried* 1928) also features an amnesiac soldier, as do *Le Fou* (1926) by Abel Moreau; *Les Veuves Blanches (The White Windows,* 1926) by Marcel Priollet; *Le Pêcheur d'Ombres (The Grayling Fisher,* 1921) by Jean Sarment; and *Le Revenant (The Ghost,* 1932) by Jean Bommart. Luigi Pirandello's play *Come Tu Mi Vuoi* (1929) was inspired by another amnesiac, Mario Bruneri, who was misidentified as the husband of Giulia Canella. Professor Giulio Canella had been reported missing in action in 1916. Pirandello made the central character female, referred to as 'the unknown woman.' A film adaptation, *As You Desire Me*, starring Greta Garbo was released in 1932.

Baxendale notes that there were ten silent films dealing with amnesia before 1926, including *Garden of Lies* (1915), *The Right of Way* (1915), and *The Victory of Conscience* (1916).

More recent explorations of the amnesia theme include *Mine Own Executioner* (1945) by Nigel Balchin, filmed in 1947; David Goodis' *Nightfall* (1947); *The Long Wait* (1951) by Mickey Spillane; Patrick Modiano's *Missing Person* (1978); Anne Perry's series about detective William Monk, beginning with *The Face of a Stranger*(1990); *The Man Who Walked Away* (2013) by Maud Casey; and Dan Brown's *Inferno* (2013) which was filmed in 2016.

The Amnesia in Amnesia Thrillers
Amnesia is the loss of memory caused by physical damage to the brain or by disease (together known as 'organic' amnesia) or by psychological trauma.

Temporary amnesia can also be caused by some types of drugs. There are two main types of amnesia: *retrograde*, in which the sufferer is unable to retrieve memories before a particular time – often the date of an accident or operation; and *anterograde* where the sufferer is unable to transfer new memories from short-term to longer-term memory. The 2000 film *Memento* and Steven J. Watson's novel *Before I Go to Sleep* (2011) are rare examples of the use of anterograde amnesia in a story. Most 'amnesia thrillers' use retrograde amnesia, usually induced by an accident or a severe psychological trauma – or a combination of the two.

Dieguez and Annoni have noted that most real-life cases of amnesia would make for poor entertainment but also that some real-life cases are so incredible that readers of fiction would reject them as implausible. As storytellers, we need to strike the right balance between plausibility and medical accuracy, so it is helpful to have an awareness of the criticisms levelled against this type of story.

In her *British Medical Journal* article 'Memories Aren't Made of This: Amnesia at the Movies,' Sallie Baxendale highlights the 'myths' relating to amnesia as portrayed in the movies. Drawing together her observations and those from Richard Pérez-Peña's article in *The New York Times* we can see the main issues:

(i) Many films make no distinction between amnesia caused by psychological trauma and that caused by physical injury, often resulting in a 'mix and match' approach where physical injury causes the symptoms normally associated with psychological trauma or where amnesia with a psychological basis is 'cured' by a blow to the head. In the real world cause, symptoms, and treatment are not mixed-up in this way. Also, in reality, long-term memory loss caused by physical injury to the brain is likely to be accompanied by other obvious factors such as impaired intelligence or physical control.

(ii) In movies a blow to the head typically causes retrograde amnesia – a loss of long-term memories and personal identity – which is extremely unlikely in reality. In real life, physical damage to the brain, even a concussion, can result in memory impairment – but the memory loss is usually restricted to a few minutes, hours or days before the accident. A person hurt in a car accident, for example, often cannot remember the accident itself and perhaps what happened immediately prior to it. This is caused by an interruption in the process that turns short-term memory into long-term memory.

(iii) In films and television, particularly comedies, where amnesia is caused by a blow to the head, it is often 'cured' by a second blow to the head. In real life, it is extremely unlikely to find that two head injuries are better than one, or that a second somehow 'cancels out' the first.

(iv) Memory loss in fiction is usually only temporary and recovery of the inaccessible memories can be brought about 'via various unlikely means.' Again we have the mix and match problem. Recovery of memories blocked due to psychological trauma is entirely possible, whereas long-term memory loss caused by physical injury to the head is much less likely.

Accepting all of this, then technically we 'can't have' the sort of amnesia that makes for the most dramatic story situations – the combination of physical injury cause and psychological injury effects and cure. But as Dieguez and Annoni have pointed out, it is not the purpose of fiction to depict medical knowledge accurately. Nor is a story required to deal with a 'typical case' since fiction often deals with the unique and extraordinary. Stories are 'thought-experiments' where amnesia performs a function in the plot and allows the author to explore a theme. They also say that because "... we still do not fully understand the mechanisms of these different phenomena, it seems premature at this stage to criticise or condemn literary works as inaccurate regarding their portrayal of memory disorders." I don't think we should take this as permission to do whatever we like in amnesia thrillers – we should at least demonstrate some understanding of the different types of amnesia, and their causes and potential treatments. Obviously, if you are writing a story set in a particular time period, you will need to be aware of what theories and terminology were in use at that time. Many historical textbooks and general encyclopedias from past decades are available online for this type of research. Included below are some of the terms that may be useful as starting points for reading up on amnesia.

Amnesia caused by psychological trauma – referred to as 'dissociative amnesia' – includes repressed memory, where details of a hugely stressful event such as a violent attack or disaster are not recalled by the sufferer. The memory exists but cannot be accessed as a result of a sort of defence mechanism. This kind of repression was referred to as 'psychogenic amnesia' in the past.

Popular in fiction, but rare in reality, is the dissociative fugue – previously referred to as psychogenic fugue and also called a 'fugue state'. It is caused by psychological trauma and is often temporary, but it can recur. A sufferer cannot recall or is confused about his or her own identity and may travel away from familiar locations in order to discover their identity or to create a new one.

'Confabulatory amnesia' is a form rarely tackled in fiction. Confabulation is a disturbance of memory that results in the creation of fabricated, distorted, or misinterpreted memories without the conscious intention to deceive. It is commonly associated with Korsakoff's syndrome.

Another form of amnesia is post-hypnotic amnesia, where a person cannot recall events which occurred while they were under hypnosis because it was suggested to them that they should not remember them when they awoke. Hypnosis can also be used to cause past memories to be forgotten or for new 'memories' to be implanted.

One thing often seen in amnesia thrillers, especially movies, is the vivid flashback indicating a fragment of recovered memory. Similar flashes have been reported in real-life amnesiacs.

It is also common for the amnesia sufferer in these stories to recover their memories suddenly and completely – as if a dam has been breached – usually triggered by some evocative image or incident which results in a strong emotional response. Balzac's short story 'Adieu' (1830) is an early and dramatic example in fiction. In Priollet's *The White Windows* (1926) the heroine manages to unblock her fiancé's memories by restaging the situation which led to their first kiss. This form of recovery has been criticised for being contrived and too convenient, but there are recorded examples.

If you want a more 'scientific' method of memory recovery, the drugs sodium amytal, sodium pentothal, and lorazepam have been used in modern times with a certain degree of success. I would suggest researching their use in amnesia cases before including them in your story.

Themes

Dieguez and Annoni wrote that amnesia gives writers the opportunity to explore themes such as identity, the possibility of rebirth, social relatedness, personal freedom, guilt, or the 'capability to look forwards.'

Identity. John Locke in *An Essay Concerning Human Understanding* (1689) proposed what has become known as the 'memory theory of personal identity,' which says that our conscious memories are a vital component of our identity – we are who we remember being. Our past life provides context for our present life and we cannot really know ourselves – and other people cannot really know us – without understanding something of our past.

Rebirth. In fiction, the idea of starting over as a 'new person' is a common theme. In some stories, such as *The Crooked Way* (1949), the hero's amnesia is permanent, and he cannot go back to being the man he was, even if he wanted to. In others, e.g. *Somewhere in the Night* (1946) and *The Third Day* (1965), the hero discovers that he doesn't like the man he used to be and resolves to be someone better. Dieguez and Annoni describe the amnesiac as possessing 'purity and innocence' in the sense that a lifetime's social conditioning, prejudices, and other 'baggage' have been lost, allowing the character to experience a new objectivity and honesty.

Social Relatedness. As well as issues of personal identity, stories about amnesia explore 'social identity' – who other people believe the amnesiac to be based on their own memories of the character. In fiction the amnesiac often goes 'home' in the hope that other people will be able to fill in the blanks in his or her memory – and often the hero discovers that the people he encounters there are unreliable, either deliberately or accidentally. In real life too, other people often want the amnesiac to be someone other than he is. When an amnesiac is discovered, more than one family may come forward to claim him or her as their lost relative – this happened with the living 'unknown soldiers' in France after the First World War. Jean Giraudoux used this in his novel and play *Siegfried* (1922 and 1928), in which a soldier with no memory is found on the battlefield and taken back to Germany where he takes up a successful life in society – only to discover much later that he had, in fact, been a French soldier fighting on the opposite side in the war. Giraudoux used his character to demonstrate that human conflict based on learned notions such as national identity were absurd and that all human beings had more commonalities than differences. Abel Moreau's novel *Le Fou* (1926) approaches this from the angle of asking what happens to the amnesiac when he discovers that everyone he knew has, effectively, also forgotten about him.

Personal Freedom. Stories about memory loss also suggest that if we have lost who we used to be, then we can choose who we will become. We do not have to be who we were and we do not have to be who other people want us to be (or have been). This is also related to the ideas of rebirth and social connectedness. The real-life case of Mario Bruneri in the late 1920s is an example – found as an unknown amnesiac he was wrongly identified as Giulio Canella and 'went back' to his life with Mrs. Canella. When the error was finally confirmed, and even suspected to be a fraud on his part, Mrs. Canella decided to stay with her 'husband.'

Dieguez and Annoni write that amnesia can be used to "illustrate the notion that identity should not be confused with fate." Losing all memory of the past may be a terrible thing, but it can also have a freeing effect in that the sufferer is no longer bound by old ways of thinking – such stories can "illustrate the destructive power of habit, tradition, and memory, all narrowing forces of the human potential for freedom."

Guilt. In amnesia thrillers especially, the amnesiac often suspects that they may be guilty of some terrible crime – usually murder – or someone tells them that they are guilty. The hero has no memory of the event, so cannot know whether or not he is guilty. This idea is typically explored in one of two ways – either the amnesia exists because the hero is blocking out the fact that he is (or believes himself to be guilty) or the amnesia is exploited by someone who wants to frame the hero for a crime of which he is not guilty. In either case, the story follows the hero tries to discover whether or not he is guilty – usually he is not, but just occasionally he is.

The idea that the hero thinks that he *could* be guilty of a crime is linked to what was mentioned earlier under *Identity* about the hero discovering or suspecting that his 'old self' wasn't a good man. The hero often experiences a sense of shame or regret regarding his previous behaviours and beliefs as he examines them with his new-found objectivity.

In terms of people suspecting or assuming the hero's guilt, there is also the idea that other characters will (want to) believe that the hero is faking his amnesia because it is convenient for him to not remember. Even sympathetic characters may require that the hero *proves* that his amnesia is real, often testing him in subtle or unsubtle ways.

Plot Structure of the Amnesia Thriller

This 'model structure' was created by comparing the eight sequence breakdowns for the movies *Hysteria* (1965), *Shattered* (1991), *The Crooked Way* (1949), *The Third Day* (1965), *Mirage* (1965), and *Somewhere in the Night* (1946).

Many amnesia thrillers centre on the hero's investigation of his own past life but also have a second plotline – usually a parallel investigation involving some kind of MacGuffin. Typically this is an investigation into a murder which the hero may have witnessed or may have committed. *Mirage* features both a traumatic death and a 'secret formula,' and the investigations into these intersect with the hero's search for his own identity.

The structure below contains the various elements that can be included in an amnesia thriller plot. As with any model structure of this kind, individual events may actually occur in a different order and even in different one of the eight sequences that make up a plot. The outline here is designed to be a starting point and source of inspiration. It can also be used to explore the plot structure of other existing amnesia thrillers.

Sequence 1
Introduce the hero. Perhaps begin with the accident or other traumatic event which is the cause of his amnesia – though this can be revealed in exposition of flashback later. Often we see the hero in hospital or just leaving hospital, any physical injuries healed but suffering from amnesia. There will usually be a scene with a doctor or psychiatrist who explains to the hero (and the reader) the nature of the hero's amnesia, its possible cause, and any actions the hero is advised to take to try and overcome it.

The hero will usually travel back to his hometown or city. People he meets may act strangely around him or be suspicious of him. But he isn't sure whether this is significant or simply a manifestation of his own fears or paranoia. There is typically an early clue that his 'old self' wasn't a particularly nice person or that he may have been a criminal of some kind. His reappearance in town and the fact that he is asking questions – in an attempt to recover his memories – draws attention to him. He is quite naïve at this point and doesn't realise that what he is doing could be dangerous.

He may meet someone who claims to know him and who says that they want to help him rediscover his past – but are they the selfless helper they appear? This helper may be the romantic co-protagonist or a femme fatale working for the villain – or she could be both. She, like many the hero meets at this early stage, may not believe that he has amnesia. People think he is faking memory loss to avoid taking responsibility for some crime or other immoral action he was, or may have been, responsible for in the past. Even non-threatening characters may not reveal to him everything they know – they may assume he knows things he doesn't, or they may seek to 'protect' him from memories that will be painful to him, or they may have their own reasons for keeping quiet.

At some point in this sequence there may be a flashback – perhaps only a very brief image relating to the accident/traumatic event – usually triggered by the herp seeing an object, a place, a person, or a particular event, or perhaps hearing a sound or piece of music. This establishes the fact that his memories are likely to return to him in fragments and also hints at the possibility of a full recovery at some future point.

There will also be some mention or hint of the MacGuffin that is at the centre of the external investigation plotline – usually it is something that the villain wants that he believes the hero has. Or it is a piece of knowledge he fears that the hero has that makes him a threat to the villain. Or both. This MacGuffin may or may not be directly related to the accident/incident that caused the hero's amnesia.

Sequence 2
This is where relationships with the other main characters are established and/or developed. The audience along with the hero learn who his allies and who his potential enemies are – but, this being a thriller, none of them can be trusted to be who they first appear to be.

Often a meeting is arranged for the hero so that he can learn something about his 'old' life. But the meeting is a set-up and he finds himself being beaten/interrogated by the villain or his henchmen. The hero may learn something about his relationship to the villain – they may have been friends or partners, or the hero may have worked for the villain. Or he may have been a rival – perhaps a defeated one. Whatever the hero learns may or may not be true – he has no memory, so no way of verifying the truth at this point. The hero may discover evidence or hear information from someone which seems to be true but is actually designed to make him believe a false story that is to someone else's advantage. The villain – or perhaps the police – may tell the hero that he's got twenty-four hours to leave town – he's not welcome here.

There may be another flashback – vivid, but infuriatingly vague in terms of meaning. It is a fragment that makes little sense out of context.

If the hero had been in a relationship with the romantic co-protagonist before his memory loss, he may now enjoy one of the few benefits of his amnesia – falling in love with her as if for the first time. She may be wary of this – she still has all of her old memories and this may seem too good to be true – but she likes this 'new version' of the hero: he is kinder, more innocent, less arrogant. He's also vulnerable. After he has been interrogated/beaten, the hero is often patched up by the romantic co-protagonist – or perhaps the femme fatale.

The hero may learn, from the romantic co-protagonist or someone else, more of the unpleasant nature of his 'old self' – he treated friends/colleagues badly; treated the romantic co-protagonist badly; and may even hear a list of his previous crimes and misdemeanours. He may have had an affair – perhaps with the femme fatale, if she is not the same character as the romantic co-protagonist. The romantic co-protagonist may also have had an affair or another lover. Or perhaps someone *claims* to have been the hero's mistress – but is she telling the truth? This mistress or someone else may also say that the romantic co-protagonist had another lover, though this may not actually be true.

The alleged mistress or another character may suggest to the hero that his accident was not an accident – and that the romantic co-protagonist may have been behind it. And that she may try to kill him again. This sows a seed of doubt – can he trust her? This may be enough to trigger another flashback relating to the accident or to their relationship.

There is often a police detective, district attorney, newspaper reporter or someone else who is investigating the hero or the accident/incident he was involved in – or perhaps some crime that took place prior to the accident which the hero may have been involved in. This investigator will be sceptical of the hero's amnesia, thinking it is an attempt to avoid responsibility for his crimes.

Sequence 3
His initial blundering around asking questions has earned the hero a beating, threats, and very few concrete answers about his former life. He needs to begin a more systematic investigation. And he knows this is likely to cause more friction with the villain.

Sometimes the hero hires a private eye – 'I want you to find out who I am.' Or he may conduct the investigation himself with the help of the romantic co-protagonist. In either case, his investigative partner's first advice will be 'leave it alone' because he might not like what he discovers. But the hero argues that he *needs* to remember – a person isn't anything without their memories. If he hires a private eye, the hero may also ask him to find out something about the villain, the romantic co-protagonist, and/or the femme fatale.

The hero may have another flashback. Or he may see some evidence that makes him doubt his own beliefs and/or sanity. He may see something that, on closer inspection, turns out not to be there. Or may not at first see something that is there. Is someone trying to mess with his mind? Or is he seeing things the way they used to be before his amnesia? If so, is this change between then and now significant? If someone is trying to unbalance him, what is their motive? Are they trying to trick him into confessing? Or leaving? Or dropping his investigation?

The police detective/district attorney investigating the old crime may threaten the hero – 'I'm going to prove you did it and put you away.' This helps establish the stakes – if the hero can't regain his memory and prove his innocence, he'll end up on death row. And there is always that shadow of a doubt – that he may actually be guilty of the crime.

A place, an object, some music or other sound may trigger another flashback – perhaps something that makes the hero think he *could* be guilty. But while he begins to doubt himself, the private eye or the romantic co-protagonist will encourage him and perhaps even uncover some clue that he is innocent.

Sequence 4
The hero's relationship with the romantic co-protagonist deepens. She may try to test his amnesia before being satisfied that it is genuine. If the romantic co-protagonist and femme fatale are separate characters, there may be some friction or conflict between them – or between the romantic co-protagonist and the hero because of the femme fatale. The femme fatale/mistress may again warn the hero that it was the romantic co-protagonist who was behind his 'accident' – and she may even have some sort of proof.

The private eye or the hero uncovers proof that someone has been lying to him. The romantic co-protagonist? It may begin to look as though his accident really *wasn't* an accident. Or the private eye may have discovered a clue that suggests the hero is being set-up to take the blame for the earlier crime that the police detective/district attorney is looking into. The stakes have been raised – this often occurs at the midpoint of the story.

The romantic co-protagonist, especially if she is also the femme fatale, may be under pressure to betray the hero to the villain – or to send him into a trap.

She may warn the hero that the villain is planning to harm him or frame him – she will urge the hero to leave and become angry/upset when he refuses. The hero may be disappointed to learn that she has been working for, or has some other connection with, the villain – and when the villain's thugs then come for him or try to kill him, he may think that she has betrayed him after all.

At the midpoint, the hero may find himself accused of murder and have to go on the run – from both the police and the villain's thugs.

Sequence 5
Everything in this sequence is likely to take place in the context of the hero being on the run – lots of chasing, hiding, and narrow escapes.

This sequence may feature a false version of events – something that has been set-up to make the hero or his pursuers (or both) believe that what they are seeing is the truth. This may be in the form of evidence that shows the hero is guilty of murder – either for a recent killing or one that took place in the past that he cannot remember. Or both. This 'false reality' may be presented in Sequence 6 instead and lead up to the crisis and the hero's darkest hour.

Or the hero may be seeking someone he believes has answers that he needs – but this person does not exist, or was the assumed identity of someone else, or is dead, or is not the person the hero thought they were. Or the hero may find the person, but not realise that they are a fake – the real person having been kidnapped or killed.

This sequence also typically includes an attempt on the hero's life.

The hero may believe that he was betrayed by the romantic co-protagonist or femme fatale at the midpoint – and he may behave accordingly. She will argue that she didn't do it – she loves him – and she wants to be with this 'new' version of the hero. She may or may not be telling the truth. The hero appears to believe her – though he could just be playing along for his own reasons. The romantic co-protagonist/femme fatale may say that she needs the hero's help to change sides. If they haven't kissed before, their first kiss may occur here.

The hero will probably experience another flashback – he has another piece of the puzzle, but still not enough to make sense of it all. The private eye or another character – perhaps his psychiatrist/doctor – may accuse him of not wanting to remember – the amnesia is too comfortable or convenient for him. The hero denies this – but suspects it could be true. Is he afraid to know the truth? What if he really is a killer?

Sequence 6
In this sequence, things go rapidly downhill for the hero – the end of the sequence is a crisis point, the hero's 'darkest hour.'

Some incident will separate the hero from the romantic co-protagonist – either she betrays him, is shot, is kidnapped, or leaves him for some other reason – e.g. she claims he doesn't trust her or she believes he is too good for her. Another form of betrayal can occur if the romantic co-protagonist/femme fatale tells the hero 'what really happened' before his amnesia. This can occur if the 'false version of events' mention under Sequence 5 occurs here instead. She tells the hero that he is guilty of murder (or some other crime) and that she helped cover for him. She kept it from him because she wanted to protect him from the unpleasant memory. In her role as 'protector' she may have killed a witness at the time of the original crime – or she may have killed someone recently because she was afraid they had figured out the truth. But this 'truth' that she is sharing with him is just another attempt to manipulate and control him.

If the hero had employed a private eye or some other helper, he loses that person too – often they are killed, and the hero may be found standing over the body with a smoking gun or bloody knife.

Meanwhile... the police and the villain's men are closing in on the hero. A showdown of some kind is imminent. If the hero was operating to some kind of deadline or countdown, time is running out. The hero cannot run for much longer and the time has come for him to try and put an end to this – but before he can put his cunning plan into action, some terrible event occurs that makes it appear that he has lost. Often he finds himself at the mercy of the villain or the police or held at gunpoint by someone else – perhaps someone out for revenge because of the crime they believe the hero committed before his amnesia. In a face-to-face moment with this person or with the police detective/district attorney, the hero will say that he is prepared to accept the punishment for any crime that he has committed, but that he needs to be able to remember it first.

The hero may gain an important clue or be on the point of gaining one – he may have located a witness to the original crime who can tell him who actually committed it. But before the hero can ask 'Did I do it?' this person will be taken away from him – usually killed or perhaps discovered to be an imposter. The hero doesn't receive the answer that he so desperately needs.

The hero may have another, more significant flashback – recovering some vitally important memory. Ideally (from a dramatic point of view), this memory will be something that makes his situation seem even worse.

The hero must now react to this low point in his circumstances, coming up with a plan which will allow him to find out who was responsible for the crime of which he has been accused, and which will also deal with the villain.

Sequence 7

This is where everything comes together – the hero, the villain and his henchmen, and the police are often all in one location for the first time – or heading towards it. This will probably be a situation that has been deliberately engineered by the hero – the result of a series of 'mistakes' that he has appeared to make.

The final fragments of the hero's memory will also fall into place, allowing him to see the complete picture – he will know the details of the original crime and the part – if any – that he played in it. And he will know the nature and whereabouts of whatever the villain has been trying to get from him.

Like the detective in a whodunit, the hero may explain what *really* happened – contrasting this with the version of events that someone tried to make them believe. This explanation often happens in front of the police and the villain. The hero may even trick the villain into confessing all or part of it.

The hero may have put in place a situation that mimics the original crime, or that initially appears to prove the version of events that the villain claims to be true. It may seem that the hero is accepting his own guilt.

There are two objectives at stake here, the MacGuffin, which is typically an item of monetary value that the villain wants to possess; and the truth about a crime or conspiracy involving one or more murders that the villain does not want to be revealed. Ultimately, the villain may decide that hiding the truth is more important to him than money – he may try to bribe the hero into keeping quiet by allowing him to escape with the valuable object. Or he may decide to silence the hero permanently by killing him, even if this means never recovering the valuable object.

As the hero's memory returns he changes from being a potential threat to the villain to an actual threat. Hero and villain may fight – there may be a gunfight that gets the villain's henchmen out of the way so that finally hero and villain have to slug it out hand-to-hand. The villain may gain the upper hand, offering to give up the wanted hero to the police in exchange for being allowed to escape himself.

Sequence 8
Final outcome of the fight – the villain is defeated. The truth is revealed. The hero is exonerated in the eyes of the law. The hero and the romantic co-protagonist can finally be together. The villain's demise will usually involve an element of 'poetic justice,' will him being responsible for his own death rather than having the hero kill him.

The Stolen Identity Thriller

In many thrillers disguise, an assumed identity, or mistaken identity plays a part but here we are looking at those stories which are constructed around an assumed or stolen identity. In this sub-subgenre, the protagonist is often an anti-hero. The themes explored tend to be more pessimistic and there is usually an ironic (perhaps even tragic) rather than a happy ending. For these reasons, this type of thriller tends to be less popular than other types of thriller.

In these thrillers, the protagonist tries to escape from his or her 'old life' by assuming a new identity. They may be seeking to escape justice having committed a crime – usually murder or sometimes theft – or they may simply be trying to escape from an existence that they find too dull or too claustrophobic. The identity they assume may be made up, or they may pretend to be some other living person, or – quite often – they may steal the identity of a dead person. The dead person may be someone they themselves have killed, found dead, or found injured and allowed to die. The protagonist does not find the escape and happiness he wished for and generally – in some sort of poetic justice – ends up paying for his crimes and his deceit.

Assumed identities have often been used in comedy – obvious examples include *Tootsie, Mrs. Doubtfire, Sister Act* and William Shakespeare's *Twelfth Night, The Comedy of Errors* and *As You Like It* – but even when played for laughs, there is a certain suspense inherent in the story – a fear of being 'found out' or exposed as a fraud. This is a common human fear – often referred to as 'imposter syndrome' – which may explain, in part, why people appreciate stories about this type of character.

Rogues, impostors, mistaken identity and persons in disguise have been elements of drama for as long as stories have been told – the 'trickster' character is found in many cultures. Examples of full-length works in which one character takes over the identity of another (or assumes a fake identity) include: Molière's *Tartuffe, or The Impostor* (1664) which tells of a fraud and hypocrite who enters the home of a wealthy man and pretends to dispense spiritual guidance in order to get his hands on his patron's wealth. *The Government Inspector* (1836) by Nikolai Gogol portrays a stranger who arrives in a town and is mistaken for a government official whose arrival is expected. In Alexandre Dumas' *The Count of Monte Cristo* (1844), the protagonist is falsely accused of treason; escaping from prison he assumes the (fake) identity of the Count of Monte Cristo and sets out to avenge himself on the three men who conspired against him. *The Prince and the Pauper* (1881) by Mark Twain tells of two identical though unrelated boys in Tudor England who briefly exchange places and learn how it is to live as their social opposite. *The Prisoner of Zenda* (1894) by Anthony Hope tells of an Englishman called on to impersonate the King of Ruritania in order to save the kingdom from political upheaval.

There are similarities between the stolen identity thriller and the amateur-on-the-run thriller. Although the protagonist commits a crime by stealing someone's identity (or by creating a fake one), like the genuine innocent who becomes caught up in a conspiracy, the protagonist here – as a result of assuming a new identity – also finds himself caught up in a conspiracy. His stolen identity has – or quickly assumes – a life of its own, with all sorts of actions attributed to it. Some of these may have occurred before the protagonist assumed the identity or they may have occurred afterwards and through a combination of coincidence, mistaken identity, or circumstantial evidence been attributed to the person the protagonist is pretending to be.

The stolen identity thriller is also related to the double agent in espionage fiction, and to the undercover cop and the crime caper or confidence game story – which I will cover in depth in *Crime Thriller*. Assumed or mistaken identities also feature in mystery stories, often in terms of either inheritance swindles or the return of a 'lost relative' – in these stories, unlike the stolen identity thriller, the hero is usually someone investigating whether an individual is who they claim to be, rather than the person doing the impersonating.

There is also a variation on the stolen identity thriller where the hero is the person who is being impersonated and has to investigate the impersonator and try and prove that he is the genuine 'owner' of the identity. This is the plot of the 2011 film *Unknown* starring Liam Neeson, based on the novel *Out of My Head* (*Hors de Moi*, 2003) by Didier Van Cauwelaert. Another variation has the protagonist discover that his wife (or her husband) has apparently been replaced by an impostor. In Robert Thomas' 1960 play *Piège pour un Homme Seul* (*Trap for a Lonely Man*, 1964) a man reports his wife missing and when she is 'found,' the woman is a stranger to him: is he losing his mind or is there a conspiracy against him? The play was adapted for television as *Honeymoon with a Stranger* in 1969. Both the 'that's not me' and 'that's not my wife' thrillers have a structure that combines the amateur-on-the-run plot with a mystery-investigation.

There is one more variation that has been used a number of times.

The Forced Identity Change Thriller

In the stolen identity thriller, the hero chooses a new identity for himself but there are other thrillers where the main character finds him or herself forced into assuming a different identity. These thrillers are often closely-related to the political thriller.

The film *The Groundstar Conspiracy* (1972), loosely based on L. P. Davies' 1968 novel *The Alien*, combines elements of political thriller, assumed identity, and the amnesia thriller and has a plot that is impossible to describe without major spoilers. *The Domino Principle* (vt. *The Domino Killings*, 1977) was adapted for the screen by Adam Kennedy from his own 1975 novel; in it, a Vietnam veteran in prison for murder is offered his freedom if he takes on a new life as a government assassin. These stories reflect the post-Watergate distrust of government which, in Charles Derry's words, "...is immoral precisely because it robs us of our identity and forces us to become something we are not." Luc Besson's 1990 film *La Femme Nikita* is a more recent take on a similar theme. Jason Bourne in *The Bourne Identity* is the protagonist in a similar sort of story with added elements from the amnesia thriller: we will come back to him in a later chapter.

Themes

Charles Derry refers to this type of story as the 'thriller of acquired identity' and says its main themes are "... the existential search for a better life," and "the inability to escape what is central to one's character."

The protagonist in such a story tends to be a 'lost soul' – cynical and world-weary, they have not managed to create for themselves a life that they find fulfilling. Instead, they are a drifter who has no commitments to anyone or anything. Unhappy in their present life, they always think that there is something better out there that they are missing, and they tend to resent the unhappiness of others. The protagonist exists day to day in a state of ennui. As the story opens, something has brought this to some sort of crisis point or the protagonist becomes aware of an opportunity to do something to change his situation. This 'something' will involve assuming another identity in order to escape his own dissatisfying existence.

But changing his name and external appearance, pretending to be someone else, does not 'fix' the protagonist's inner lack – it is an attempt to cover-up the problem rather than deal with its root cause. Generally speaking, in fiction characters are rewarded if they discover their own true nature and act according to their own deeply-held beliefs. The protagonist with a stolen identity is not doing this, so by the moral 'rules' of storytelling he should be punished – and in the assumed identity thriller, he usually is. There is usually a cruel irony in the protagonist's ending in that he is often not punished for his own crimes, but is instead punished for crimes committed by, or wrongly attributed to, the person whose identity he has taken. The protagonist ends up in a worse situation – and may even be killed – because of who they have pretended to be rather than who they really are.

The whole plot hinges on a deception, and so questions of honesty and trust versus duplicity and betrayal are also explored. Aspects of character that are superficial and shallow are compared to those which are deeper and more genuine. Ironically, the protagonist's double-standards mean that he is unable to trust other people and that he reacts violently if someone betrays or cheats him or is merely suspected of doing so.

Romantic relationships are effectively doomed from the beginning. Initially, someone will be attracted to the person he is pretending to be, and he will enjoy their company, but ultimately he will come to realise that they are attracted to his fake persona rather than to him as a genuine person, and he will resent them for this. Sometimes there will be a second potential romantic interest who has glimpsed his true self and *is* attracted to that, but he will reject her because his own lack of respect for his true self means that he cannot possibly be attracted to anyone who is attracted to that worthless self. It is another irony of this type of story that he rejects the one person with whom he could have found genuine happiness and a fulfilling life.

Identity-swap stories have as a theme the fact that although someone can assume a new character and even a new appearance, they are still essentially the same person inside. If you weren't happy being yourself, what makes you think you'll be happy as someone else? You cannot escape from yourself and no matter how hard you try, that self eventually catches up with you. There is also the 'irony of fate' element which says that if you try and escape responsibility for your own actions or crimes, then you could end up paying the price in another way – by being punished for the crimes or actions of someone else. Any story about identity also asks questions about what it is that makes us who we are and which of the parts that make up our identity have genuine value to ourselves and others. There may also be an element of the protagonist becoming 'lost' in his new identity – forgetting who he was or coming to believe his own deception to the extent that he takes risks that he shouldn't.

Iconography

Mirrors, reflections, shadows and other images that suggest a dual self or duplication are often seen in these stories. Changes in appearance – including clothing and hair – to look more like another character are also common. Sometimes there is a significant object or place that the imposter doesn't realise is significant and this risks exposing him. Movements and ways of speaking are imitated. The protagonist is also seen taking pleasure in things he could never afford before – food, drink, cigars, cars, clothes, games or sports. He may also seek to impress people with his wealth in a way that the 'original owner' of the identity would not.

Plot Structure of the Stolen Identity Thriller

Sequence 1
Introduce the protagonist and show how they are disappointed and/or disillusioned with their own life. Show them enviously observing the 'better' life of another individual or group of individuals. The protagonist's situation is presented in such a way that the audience is able to sympathise and/or empathise with them. Often, we share their humiliation or shame which results from poor or unfortunate circumstances. They are an outsider looking in. The audience should also be made aware that the protagonist's situation has reached a point where he or she feels that they have got to do something about it.

The protagonist is not always in a financially poor situation – they may simply feel that their everyday life is futile or boring – they are not committed to any deeply-held beliefs or course of action. Either way, they feel that there has got to be something better out there. And they feel that other people are leading much more thrilling or satisfying lives. In other words, the protagonist is ripe for change – ready for something new.

Sequence 2
Depending on the needs of the story, the major events in sequences two and three can be switched around. Typically sequence two shows a life that the protagonist would like to have and then sequence three shows him or her taking it. But sometimes, the protagonist takes over the identity – as a result of an accident, coincidence, or on a whim – in sequence two, and then learns in sequence three about the life of the other person having taken it over. I'm going to assume the former, typical sequence of events here.

The protagonist learns more about the other person's lifestyle – becoming obsessed by the fact that this life is greatly preferable to their own. Often, we will see contrasts between the other person's circumstances or activities and those of the protagonist. The protagonist may behave like an unseen voyeur, spying on this preferred life and fantasising about it – or they may seek to befriend and get close to this blessed individual, to become part of their charmed circle of acquaintances.

How much emphasis is placed on the protagonist's deteriorating situation and how much is placed on the dreamed-of other life depends on the story being told. *The Talented Mr. Ripley* shows the protagonist spending a great deal of time enjoying his friendship with Dickie Greenleaf. *Dead Ringer,* on the other hand, concentrates more on the protagonist's worsening circumstances. *The Passenger* switches sequences two and three, giving the Jack Nicholson character an opportunity to change identities at the beginning of sequence two – and only later does he become aware of the nature of the life he has assumed.

The end of sequence two, going into the beginning of sequence three, marks the end of Act I and the end of the first quarter (approximately) of the story and is an important turning point. It's a place where the protagonist accepts the challenge or opportunity, making a commitment and performing some action which cannot be undone. Often this involves some form of confrontation. Bette Davis confronts her twin sister and unloads twenty years of unhappiness and resentment. Tom Ripley is mocked by a friend of Dickie's who accuses him of being a freeloader and a peeping tom. The protagonist's situation cannot continue as it is – and so action is taken. The action is usually motivated by envy and/or a desire for revenge. It may be 'revenge' for a specific incident – e.g. stealing the protagonist's lover – or for rejecting and belittling the protagonist. But associated with this will be a lifetime of resentment and feelings of personal inadequacy or disillusionment. Either that or the protagonist's ennui becomes so unbearable that he or she is prepared to do anything.

Sequence 3
This typically involves the death of the person whose identity the protagonist will assume. Either the protagonist kills them or allows them to die, or sees them die in an accident, or discovers them dead in some other circumstance. The rest of the sequence then shows the protagonist dealing with the body and assuming the identity of the dead person. In *The Passenger*, as mentioned above, assuming the dead man's identity occurs in sequence two and sequence three then shows the protagonist discovering whose life he has taken over.

In stories centring on mistaken identity, there often isn't a body – there is a missing person, and the coincidence of the protagonist's arrival at that moment causes people to believe that he or she is that person. Here, sequence one will typically show the protagonist arriving somewhere, perhaps having escaped from an unsatisfactory life. By the end of sequence one, people are assuming that he or she is the person they were expecting – and the protagonist, more or less on a whim, decides to play along. Usually there is something to be gained by allowing the mistake to go uncorrected – even if it is only shelter from a storm or a good meal. The structure of the mistaken identity thriller is more like *The Passenger* than *The Talented Mr. Ripley*. Sequence two then involves the protagonist's first faltering steps in his assumed role which he is, at this point, treating as a bit of a joke. Then by the end of sequence two and into three, he begins to learn the true nature of the person he is pretending to be – and what other people expect of him. This is a turning point where the situation becomes much more serious and can no longer be treated as a joke – he has progressed too far to be able to turn back or deny being the assumed identity.

Initially when the protagonist takes on the new identity things seem to go well. The novelty in itself is exciting and fulfilling. With his new persona, he may meet new people who are attracted to him in a way that they wouldn't have been to his 'old' self. It feels – at this stage – as if the protagonist's needs are being fulfilled.

During sequence three, the protagonist may accidentally encounter someone who will go on to become their romantic co-protagonist.

Sequence 4
Now the protagonist must make a real effort to *be* the person whose identity he or she has assumed. There will be several mistakes and close calls as they slowly discovered who they are expected to be and how they are meant to behave. They also have to negotiate relationships with various other people – some of whom they are meant to know and some who are strangers. And they

will need to avoid anyone who would recognise that they are an impostor. If you are familiar with the 'hero's journey' story model, this corresponds to learning the rules of the 'new world' and discovering allies and opposition.

The protagonist may become aware – or at least receive some hint about – an individual who is potentially a threat to his new life. This may be an investigator who is trying to find either him or the person whose identity he has assumed. Or it may be an old friend or lover – of his 'old' self or of the person he is impersonating. He will need to remain on the look-out for this person in order to stay one step ahead of their investigation. A more paranoid protagonist may only *imagine* that someone is on their trail – a person whose appearance and/or questions are simply a coincidence. The protagonist's feelings of guilt and their need for constant vigilance mean that they cannot fully relax and enjoy their new life.

During sequence four, the protagonist may begin a romantic relationship – or a platonic 'buddy' relationship – with the person they encountered in sequence three. The second encounter may appear to be another coincidental meeting, but may actually have been engineered, either by the protagonist or by the romantic co-protagonist/'buddy'. The forming of this relationship typically occurs before or at the end of sequence four, which is the midpoint of the story.

The midpoint is often a key moment where the protagonist successfully pulls off a major deception, convincing some important individual that he is who he claims to be. This 'victory' usually involves a character who could have exposed the protagonist, so the scene is filled with suspense, leading up to a feeling of intense relief for the protagonist and the audience.

The protagonist's success here in terms of his deception and his relationship mean that sequence five opens on a positive note and typically marks the high-point for the protagonist – after this, things will begin to sour for him and sequence six will involve a rapid decline in his situation that will end at a crisis point.

Sequence 5
This sequence typically concentrates on relationships – the protagonist's relationship with the romantic co-protagonist deepens. Here is where they, perhaps, share their life stories and/or philosophies. The protagonist may even go so far as telling her about his stolen identity – though she may dismiss it as a story designed to impress or intrigue her.

In some stories, the romantic co-protagonist, or perhaps another character, knows (or suspects) that the protagonist isn't who he pretends to be but decides to play along anyway. They may do this because it suits their own purposes, because they are attracted to the protagonist, or just for the fun of it. The romantic co-coprotagonist might have been the wife or lover of the person the protagonist is impersonating and decide not to reveal the deception. Or this character may be lying to the protagonist about their relationship with the person whose identity he has assumed. In stories about identity, no one can be trusted to be who they claim to be!

By this stage of the story, the protagonist has become more confident in his new life and is relishing playing it as a role, like an actor. It is fresh and exciting, and he may surprise himself by brazenly doing things that his 'old' self would never have dreamed of doing. Assuming a new identity has freed him – allowed him to be the person he always dreamed of being. Or so he believes at this point.

There is often a significant challenge or danger to be faced in sequence five, and the protagonist may need the romantic co-protagonist's help to overcome it. The person who has been pursuing the protagonist may be on the point of trapping him – or the old friend or lover (of his old self or his new self) may appear on the scene, risking exposure of his deception. The protagonist must take action to deal with this.

It may be necessary for the protagonist to kill this person, as happens in *The Talented Mr. Ripley*. Or the protagonist may need to pull off a daring escape with his lover's assistance, as he does in *The Passenger*. In *Dead Ringer*, the situation that the protagonist faces is how to sign legal papers with a signature she is unable to forge – and she comes up with a dramatic (and painful!) solution.

Having successfully faced this ordeal, the protagonist often makes his getaway in the literal sense, travelling to a new location or embarking on a road trip. In some stories, including *Dead Ringer,* successfully dealing with the threat means that the protagonist doesn't need to run – they can stay where they are, more secure now in their assumed role.

Towards the end of sequence five, we will probably see the first signs that the protagonist is becoming dissatisfied with his assumed identity. The novelty has worn off, the honeymoon is over, and the reality of the situation is starting to become apparent. This is almost inevitable since the protagonist is essentially the same person they ever were – the change of name and appearance is only superficial.

Sequence 6

Where sequence five showed the protagonist successfully dealing with a major obstacle and ended on an upbeat note, sequence six takes the form of an 'unravelling' as things begin to fall apart, and it typically ends with the protagonist's 'darkest hour.'

The protagonist may quickly discover that life on the run isn't that much fun – and is almost as frustrating as the old life he escaped from. He may also miss some aspects of his old life and begin to regret stealing another identity and burning bridges so that he cannot go back. His growing dissatisfaction makes him unhappy, perhaps even angry, and he may blame circumstances or other people – denying the fact that his unhappiness really stems from internal character flaw or lack.

Sequence six typically features a number of small ironies – and these usually build until the final, ironic climax of the story. In *Dead Ringers*, the protagonist learns that she was due to inherit a large sum of money – it would have allowed her to have the best parts of her old life and this new one, but it is too late now. As things begin to unravel for Tom Ripley, he finds himself forced into assuming his old identity again. The protagonist of *The Passenger* is becoming disillusioned by his new identity – but the romantic co-protagonist encourages him to continue, saying he had been looking for something to commit to, and this is it, he can't give up.

The protagonist may also become dissatisfied with his relationship with the romantic co-protagonist. They were probably initially attracted to the role he was playing – his confident and carefree new identity, and he regarded the relationship as part of the game – something fun to try out, but nothing long-term or serious. But the romantic co-protagonist has come to be important to him – and he may feel guilty about not being honest with them about who he really is. Or he may feel frustrated that this person is in love with his fake self and not his true self. He may try and push them away as a result. Or he may open up to the romantic co-protagonist, admitting who he really is and what he has done, only to have her not believe him or grown angry and leave because he has deceived her. Or he may feel that he *wants* to confess all to her but doesn't have the confidence to do so because he is afraid she will leave when she discovers who/what he really is.

The protagonist may want to abandon his fake identity, may even be thinking about assuming another one, wanting to start over again and try and avoid the mistakes he made this time – wanting to continue his quest for that elusive 'better' life. But he may find himself trapped in his fake identity as a result of not wanting to disappoint the people around him. He is in too deep to escape.

Meanwhile, the opposing forces are closing in. The old friend/lover or investigator that has been pursuing the protagonist discovers some important clue that will bring him or her closer to the target. Often the police are now in pursuit too, as a result of some recent action by the protagonist or some crime committed by the original owner of the identity – that the protagonist may now find himself accused of. The villains who want to obtain the MacGuffin from the protagonist will also be getting closer. All of the different strands of the story will begin to converge as we get closer to the climax in sequence seven.

At the end of sequence six, Tom Ripley has to give up his glamorous life as Dickie Greenleaf, abandon the home he has made for himself, and head off to Venice in a desperate attempt to try and resolve his problems. The protagonist of *Dead Ringer* is confronted by her dead sister's lover who knows she is an imposter. While the protagonist of *The Passenger* is pursued by the police, agents of a foreign government, and his ex-wife, who has just discovered the nature of his deception.

Sequence 7
This sequence forces the protagonist into a confrontation with all of the things that have been chasing him/her – including their own past actions and those of the person they are impersonating. Again, irony plays a part here. The protagonist discovers that the person he/she has been impersonating isn't the person the protagonist thought they were – their life was not the ideal situation he/she had imagined it to be. Often this person was guilty of crimes – perhaps even murder – that the protagonist will now find him/herself held accountable for having assumed the identity of a criminal.

There will usually be some ironic twist in the protagonist's relationship with the romantic co-protagonist. Their relationship is doomed because the lover was attracted to the person the protagonist was pretending to be and is disappointed to discover he/she is not really that person. Or, this person has actually seen beneath the protagonist's façade and loves the *real* version of the protagonist – but the protagonist isn't aware of this and probably wouldn't allow him/herself to believe it if they were. Another possibility is that the romantic co-protagonist also has an assumed identity – they are not who they claimed to be. This may be because they are some sort of 'femme fatale' who has betrayed the hero, or it may be that they have a past of their own that they are trying to escape from.

If the romantic co-protagonist doesn't have an assumed identity, another character may turn out to be a fake – an old friend or lover of the assumed identity may not be who they have claimed; or a 'detective' may not be a genuine detective. Whoever it is that has deceived them, the protagonist isn't really in a position to cry 'foul!'

Given that these thrillers are stories about things that are not what they seem, it is not unusual for a character who was believed to be dead turn out not to be. This can be particularly awkward if the 'not-dead' person turns out to be the person whose identity the protagonist stole. The protagonist may find himself having to kill them to protect his own deception. Or he may arrange for them to be accused of his own recent crimes.

Other twists, as in any thriller, may involve two characters who had no apparent relationship turning out to be partners, lovers, and/or co-conspirators.

At the climax of the story, the protagonist may find him/herself facing a major confrontation or an increasingly intense series of confrontations with different parties.

If someone has discovered – or suspects – the protagonist's deception, they may resort to blackmail or extortion, as happens in *Dead Ringer.* The protagonist may be forced to give up all the wealth that his/her deception has earned them. The blackmailer may coerce the protagonist into carrying out some act – a crime, betrayal, a deception – that he/she wants no part of. The protagonist may have to kill this person – or allow them to die in an accident rather than saving them.

The protagonist's paranoia at this point may be so great that he/she *believes* that someone has uncovered his deception and are now a threat to him, even though they haven't. The protagonist may end up 'dealing with' an innocent person. This person could be the romantic co-protagonist – and someone who genuinely loves him. Or the romantic co-protagonist may have seen through the deception – and actually not care. They love the protagonist no matter what – though the protagonist may still feel that he/she must deal with them as a threat.

In the film version of *The Talented Mr. Ripley,* the protagonist is confronted by the police, who interrogate him, and then by the fiancé of the person whose identity he assumed, who is convinced that Tom Ripley is guilty of murder. Then Ripley's situation seems even blacker as he is confronted by a private detective who claims to have uncovered various bits of evidence missed by the police. This all leads up to an unexpected twist – which I won't reveal – and an instance of past actions catching up with the protagonist and an ironic twist on the romance front. Anthony Minghella's film brings everything together perfectly for a satisfying climax and resolution.

Sequence 8
The final sequence features the aftermath of the previous confrontations – their consequences and the final resolution. There is typically a recognition here by the protagonist that they are 'alone in the dark' again as a result of their own actions. You cannot escape your own demons by assuming someone else's name and appearance – whatever is in your head stays with you. The protagonist may genuinely find themselves changed as a result of their experiences – but they are not a better person in their own eyes or those of the audience. They may have a different life, but it is not a better life. They have lost everything that was good about their old life and gained nothing in exchange. The only way that they could have found genuine happiness and satisfaction would be by being true to themselves – accepting who they were and dealing with their own demons. Having failed to do that, they have not 'earned' a happy ending.

As mentioned previously, there will be some element of irony in the ending and the protagonist's ultimate fate. Typically, they will end up being punished not for their own crimes, but for those attributed to the false identity they stole – either because the 'original owner' of the identity *was* guilty, or because of circumstantial evidence that makes them *appear* to be guilty. The protagonist may have been betrayed, or framed, by someone he thought he could trust – or by the person whose identity he assumed.

The Woman in Jeopardy Thriller

The woman in jeopardy thriller is a 'dark romance' story. Like the 'noir romance,' which we will explore in *Crime Thriller*, it has elements in common with the genre romance. The first two sequences follow almost exactly the 'boy meets girl' formula, except that – from the beginning – there are hints of the darkness to come. There is something not quite right about the handsome hero that the heroine falls for.

Charles Derry, writing about the modern romantic suspense thriller, describes them as stories "... in which a heroine finds herself increasingly certain that her husband is either a killer or a homicidal maniac..." and says that "... the guilt of the husband is never really clear from the beginning (either to the protagonist or to the spectator) ..." The female protagonist effectively acts as a detective as she tries to discover the truth. This means that these stories combine elements of the mystery and the suspense thriller since the protagonist – and the reader – fear that she is in danger and may be killed by her husband, especially if he learns that she is investigating his past activities.

Anne Krentz says of the typical Gothic romance: "Heroines commonly are orphaned, come into a small inheritance, travel to foreign parts, and are employed – sometimes even kidnapped – by the dark, ruthless owners of large, isolated mansions. They often spend a chapter or two 'finding themselves' or establishing their sense of identity, frequently assert their independence in the face of masculine assumptions of authority, and nearly always feel under threat emotionally if not physically from the dominant male in the story." By the end of the story, the heroine "emerges victorious, enriched and with enhanced social status."

In the traditional Gothic romance, as in the stories of Jane Austen, status and independence were closely related to wealth, which usually came to women only through inheritance. A woman with her own income – and by association, social status or 'power' – was much less dependent on her husband and so in a better position to assert her own independence as a person. Women with no money of their own, in a time when women of their class did not or could not work, were in a much more vulnerable position and relied on 'obtaining' a suitable husband to support them. Until then they might find themselves in the position of having to take a position as a companion to a wealthy widow or as governess to the children of a wealthy widower.

In the Gothic romance, heroines are typically 'vulnerable' and heroes are 'brooding.' Heroes, often labelled 'Byronic', are modelled on Jane Austen's Mr. Darcy, Emily Brontë's Heathcliff, and Charlotte Brontë's Edward Rochester. Kate Walker refers to this type of hero as the 'cruel' hero, and says that extra 'emotional punch' is added to a romance "... when the hero appears to be, if not the total villain, then at the very least strongly ambiguous in his attitude to the heroine. He has to remain largely a mystery to her. She doesn't know how he feels about her, or why he is behaving ... unpleasantly, even cruelly towards her."

Anne Krentz's reference above to the heroine 'finding herself' is – or should be – a significant part of the Gothic romance. She may spend a good part of the story afraid of the bullying and unpredictable hero, but she must, ultimately, be able to stand up to him and assert her own independence, as the heroine famously does in *Jane Eyre*. In their book *The Female Hero*, Carol Pearson and Katherine Pope write that "... the traditional love story is about sexuality and autonomy. Many works – especially gothic novels ... focus on the development in the [female] hero of self-command. This means, in practice, that the hero becomes psychologically whole: She learns to balance reason and emotion and to develop the ability not to be emotionally dependent on the man she is to marry."

Other examples include *Dragonwyck,* a 1944 novel by Anya Seton which is an American period drama in the Gothic tradition and was adapted into a film with Vincent Price as the husband in 1946; the Alfred Hitchcock films *Rebecca* (1940), based on the 1938 novel by Daphne Du Maurier, and *Suspicion* (1941) based on the 1932 novel *Before the Fact* by Francis Iles; the 1938 play *Gaslight* by Patrick Hamilton which was filmed in 1940 and 1944; and the 1961 film *The Naked Edge*, based on Max Ehrlich's 1955 novel *First Train to Babylon*. Fritz Lang's 1948 film noir *Secret Beyond the Door*, as its title suggests, is a modern take on the Bluebeard story.

T. Macdonald Skillman in her book *Writing the Thriller* acknowledges that writing a 'woman in jeopardy' story means walking "... a fine line between empowerment and victimization." I would say that you are probably on the wrong side of that line if your heroine does not ultimately attain the 'psychological wholeness' referred to by Pearson and Pope. If your heroine does not stand up to the hero and assert her rights as an independent person, or worse, if she is dependent on another strong male character to rescue her, then you are doing your female protagonist a disservice.

The woman in jeopardy thriller is typically told from the female protagonist's point of view. In a novel that means either the use of first-person narrative – "Last night I dreamt I went to Manderley again..." – third person point of view that is restricted to showing only her actions and the things she sees and which reveals only her thoughts, not those of other characters. In film, it means mainly depicting scenes in which the female protagonist is present, with only a few brooding exterior shots of locations to enhance the atmosphere and to reflect the turmoil of the heroine's inner thoughts. Occasionally, a filmmaker will show scenes in which the heroine is not present – usually to place the audience in a 'superior' position, giving them knowledge of a threat of which the heroine is unaware, and so increase suspense – but generally the story aims to have the audience share the confusion and fear of the main character.

This type of thriller has much in common with the amateur-on-the-run thriller, though the heroine's isolation tends to occur in a single place – a Gothic mansion or its equivalent – and the situation is set up such that she has nowhere to run to and no one she can go to for help. The male hero-villain may have a henchman, butler, or a creepy housekeeper in the tradition of Mrs. Danvers in *Rebecca*. There may also be a sympathetic male character who often secretly loves the heroine but is powerless to rescue or protect her – in some stories this character is killed in the second half of Act II, as the heroine's situation worsens, but in other stories – where the heroine and the hero-villain are not reconciled at the end – this second male lead may be on hand to provide the heroine with a new and less traumatic home life. If I was writing a story today where the heroine ended up with this second male lead character, I would probably have him make a gallant attempt to rescue her but fail, such that the heroine then has to rescue herself and him – I think modern heroines should be responsible for their own rescue.

As mentioned above, with the heroine of a woman in jeopardy thriller, there is a balance to be struck between making her a real, sympathetic (potential) victim and a pathetic individual who is exploited by a dominant male. Suspense, particularly by Hitchcock's definition, requires that the audience is placed in a 'superior' position – they should be aware of dangers that the protagonist does not yet know about. This creates the 'anticipation of something awful' that Hitchcock liked to evoke. But the woman in jeopardy thriller is told or shown almost exclusively – and claustrophobically – from the heroine's point of view, which means that depicting dangers she isn't yet aware of can be tricky.

One way to achieve this 'audience superiority' – or dramatic irony – is to create a heroine who is more naïve and less experienced than the audience. This gives her an excuse for not recognising the warning signs that are obvious to the audience. She trusts the dark, brooding hero when the audience thinks that she shouldn't. And the fact that the heroine is in the grips of a schoolgirlish first romance means that she is less likely – and unwilling – to see any red flags.

In *Rebecca*, the heroine is young and inexperienced, little more than a schoolgirl. While in suspicion, the heroine is a little older but is bookish and has led a very sheltered life with little or no experience of relationships with men. If you find this type of heroine unrealistic, or difficult to empathise with, then the woman in jeopardy thriller probably isn't the right sort of story for you to write. This sort of naïveté and innocence has to be carefully and convincingly evoked – especially for a modern audience. Just making her an ex-nun isn't going to be enough.

The woman in jeopardy thriller also has much in common with the mystery genre, in that there is often some kind of dark mystery at the heart of it: What happened to the first Mrs. De Winter? This mystery, if present, is really only a MacGuffin – an excuse for the heroine to investigate the real mystery of the story: Why does the brooding hero behave in such an unpredictable way?

The enigmatic and occasionally angry or 'cruel' hero is the mystery that the heroine must solve. But in a sense, this is a MacGuffin too – it is not really *his* mystery that she must unravel, but her own. She must discover who *she* is. During the course of the story, she gradually changes from being a victim of circumstance to the master of her own destiny. She grows as a person so that, at some key moment in the story, we recognise that she is no longer simply doing what her husband tells her to do – she is making decisions and controlling the course of the action.

Coupled with this is the development of the heroine's self-confidence and feelings of self-worth. Confidence comes from the experience she has gained as a result of her recent adventures. Self-worth develops as she realises (a) that she has a unique and valuable contribution to make as herself, rather than trying to live up to what she imagines other peoples' expectations to be; and (b) she is able to offer support to her husband when he needs it – she is giving to, rather than just taking from him.

This discovery of her own inner strength typically occurs at exactly the right moment – because that's how stories work! – a moment when we, and she, discovers her husband's inner weakness or vulnerability. He is not the solid, emotionless robot she imagined – he is a human being with his own doubts and fears. This understanding brings the two of them closer together – closer to being equals in terms of both strength/power and emotion/empathy – so that they are able to face the final external ordeal together, as a supportive couple, rather than as frightened, lonely individuals.

An irony of this 'dark romance' is that it presents a very conservative view of marriage and of what a relationship between a man and woman should be. In its traditional form, it depicts a very stereotypical view of male and female roles. There is much more swooning in *Rebecca* than you could expect to get away with in a modern story.

It is not necessary to accept this 1930s model of male-female relationships for a modern woman in jeopardy story – or even to stick to the tradition of heterosexual marriage. Vincent Virga's 1980 Gothic romance novel *Gaywyck* replaces the woman in jeopardy with Robert, a young man with 'soft blond hair, emerald eyes, and porcelain skin.' The title is a reference to Anya Seton's *Dragonwyck*. So the 'woman-in-jeopardy' need not be female; the brooding hero need not be a man. But the *relationship* between two people *is* important. Unlike in many other forms of thriller, the protagonist is not alone – there is always a partner. During a significant part of the central section of the story, the heroine may *feel* that she is alone – and may feel that her brooding husband is the enemy – but their relationship remains central, as it does in the traditional genre romance.

As a final note here, we should probably have an understanding of how the woman in jeopardy thriller differs from the romantic suspense novel. What makes one a sub-genre of the thriller and the other a sub-genre of the romance? It is really a matter of emphasis. In the romance genre, the romance makes up the main plot and the suspense elements make up the external subplot that puts the romance in jeopardy. In the thriller, the external suspense elements constitute the main plot and the romance is the subplot. To put it another way, in the romance there must be a happy ending for the heroine in terms of her relationship with a man – and that man will usually be the brooding hero she has sparred with throughout: if you don't have a happy ever after, you don't have a successful genre romance. But in the thriller, the romance does not have to end happily – the couple may not be reconciled, and the story would still be a successful thriller.

Historical Development

Ann Radcliffe is credited with almost single-handedly creating the Gothic romance with her 1794 novel *The Mysteries of Udolpho*, but stories in which a lone, vulnerable female is trapped in an isolated location with a dangerous and violent husband existed for many years before that. The French folktale *Bluebeard*, which appeared in print in Charles Perrault's retelling in *Histoires ou Contes du Temps Passé* (1697, published in English as *Mother Goose Tales*), is a tale whose origins may date back as far as the sixth century. A young woman is married to a wealthy nobleman, Bluebeard, who takes her to his remote castle. He tells her that she may enter any room in the castle except for a single underground chamber which she must never enter. Or else. Overcome with curiosity, the young woman waits until her husband goes away and then opens the door of the chamber – inside she discovers the corpses of Bluebeard's previous wives. The husband returns unexpectedly and, on discovering what she has done, plans to kill her. It would be wrong for me to give away the ending. Another version of the same story is the French fairy-tale *The White Dove* which has a slightly more pro-active female protagonist.

Ann Radcliffe's Gothic romances are the direct ancestors of the novels of the Brontës, Daphne Du Maurier, and Victoria Holt. The spooky Gothic settings have fallen out of favour in recent times, but the dark atmosphere and jeopardy live on in the Modern Gothic and Romantic Suspense sub-genres.

In cinema, Alfred Hitchcock's *Rebecca* (1940) and *Suspicion* (1941) established the modern model for this type of story, and the plot structures of the two films are very similar.

There are some stories related to the woman-in-jeopardy thriller which I will mention briefly. First is the 'not who she thought he was' story, which combines elements of the stolen identity thriller and the Bluebeard story. In these stories, the heroine finds herself in a relationship with, or married to, a man who she comes to suspect is not the person she thought he was. Either he has a hidden past or he is an impostor. The 1993 romantic drama *Sommersby* is an example – it was based on the 1982 French film *Le Retour de Martin Guerre,* itself based on a real-life case from the 16th century. A number of thrillers have used a similar idea, including the 1963 Audrey Hepburn movie *Charade;* the 1991 film *Deceived;* the legal thriller *High Crimes* (1997) by Joseph Finder, filmed in 2002; and the 2005 film *A History of Violence* based on the graphic novel by John Wagner and Vince Locke.

The 'domestic abuse' thriller takes something that in the Gothic romance was only implied as a threat and makes it overt. Of all the sub-categories of the thriller, this one is the most difficult to handle effectively and sensitively. One example is *Sleeping with the Enemy* a 1987 novel by Nancy Price, filmed in 1991, which tells of a woman who fakes her death to escape from an abusive relationship only to have her husband discover the truth and hunt her down. The film was successful at the box office but fared less well with critics – Roger Ebert said it used the 'old exploitation formula' and it was 'a slasher movie in disguise'. The 2017 film *'Til Death Do Us Part* features a very similar plot, and both films probably owe a debt to the 1949 film noir *Caught,* based on the novel *Wild Calendar* by Libbie Block. Judith Rossner's 1975 bestselling novel *Looking for Mr. Goodbar,* filmed in 1977 and based on a true story, is a bleak portrait of a women's self-destructive behaviour which one psychologist has described as being consistent with Borderline Personality Disorder.

Louisa May Alcott's Gothic suspense novel *A Long Fatal Love Chase,* written in 1866 but not published until 1995, tells of an unhappily-married woman who escapes from her cruel and deceitful husband and attempts to begin a new life – but finds herself pursued by him. It has elements of the 'domestic abuse' and another sub-category, the 'stalker' thriller (see below).

Plot Structure of the Woman in Jeopardy Thriller

Note: The outline below includes significant plot spoilers. If you haven't seen the Hitchcock movies *Rebecca* and *Suspicion,* I would advise watching them *before* reading on.

Sequence 1
The heroine meets the hero. This often happens in the first scene, before we really know anything about either of the characters. Or we may see one of the characters and find out a little about them, and then see them meet the other one. This is more or less identical to the first meeting in any romance story and can go in any one of several ways – they are both instantly attracted to each other; neither is attracted to the other; he is attracted to her, but she is not attracted to him; or she is attracted to him, but he is not attracted to her. The scene can be amusing (*Suspicion*) or tense (*Rebecca*). However it plays out, the two characters should make a distinct impression on each other and on the audience.

In the first three or four minutes of *Rebecca,* we see that Maxim is handsome, brooding, and a little bit scary, while the (unnamed) heroine is school girlish and flighty. In the first three minutes of *Suspicion,* we see that the heroine, Lina, is bookish and reserved, while Johnnie is brash, talkative, and sarcastic. In both cases, the hero gets more screen time and makes a stronger impression – we effectively see him from the point of view of the heroine.

Typically, there is then a second chance encounter where she recognises him or vice versa. In this scene we are introduced to the social world in which the story will take place and we learn something about each of the characters – often in dialogue from a third character. We learn that the heroine is well brought up and somewhat naïve, with little experience in relationships with men. While the hero is charming but either a bit of a cad and a womaniser or brooding and with some sort of dark/tragic secret. The idea is to set up in the mind of the audience that (a) this man is attractive and intriguing, and (b) it would be a mistake for this type of woman to fall in love with that type of man.

By the middle of sequence one, it should also be obvious that there is now some sort of attraction here – mutual or one-sided.

The inexperience of the heroine usually means that it is the hero who makes the first move – unless she makes it accidentally, subconsciously, or gauchely. Either way, he will usually be amused by her and behave in a somewhat condescending manner. But at the same time, he is attracted by her innocence and lack of pretension – he finds her honesty refreshing.

As they begin to spend time together, she will demonstrate her naïveté and lack of experience. And her lack of self-confidence will cause her to comment on the fact that she's not as elegant or sophisticated as the women he usually encounters and that she does not belong to, or feel comfortable in, his social world. She often tells him her life story, revealing the limited extent of her experience and her romantic view of the world. She also typically expresses a sense of dissatisfaction – she longs for a more fulfilling or exciting life, but it is obvious that she will never have that life unless someone pushes or pulls her into it.

Depending on the character of the hero, he will either respect the heroine's innocence, treating her like a child or a delicate china doll, or he will misunderstand it or be frustrated by it and try to surprise her into doing something out of character – usually without success.

Their initial encounters go well, in a first date but no kiss sort of way. She enjoys this because she has stayed, more or less, within her comfort zone – it has been risk-free. But around two-thirds of the way through sequence one there is a less happy moment. The broody hero may become angry because she has accidentally found one of his triggers – a reference to his past trauma that she doesn't yet know anything about. Or the unreliable and caddish hero demonstrates his unreliability or irresponsibility. Either way, the heroine is separated from him for a short time – and this separation makes her very unhappy. This is where we discover how important the relationship has become to her – it has the intensity of a schoolgirl infatuation. This separation may be doubly uncomfortable for her because she may have told other people that she is in a relationship with the hero.

Although it was the hero's decision to separate from her, the heroine blames herself. For not being good enough or for not being as receptive to her advances as he wanted her to be. Her lack of self-confidence and self-worth is such that she is ready to throw herself at him when he returns. Instead of expressing her own unhappiness or disappointment at his having abandoned her or broken his promise to call on her, she showers him with affection and is so grateful for his return that she may apologise for her own behaviour which 'drove' him away.

Sequence 2

Hero and heroine are back together again, but it seems that he does not regard the relationship as being as significant as she does. He still treats her with a mixture of condescension and amusement or condescension and frustration. In *Rebecca*, Maxim grows annoyed when she suggests his interest in her is charitable and that he feels sorry for her. In *Suspicion*, Johnnie returned as if the separation had never happened and continues to take the heroine for granted.

The separation demonstrated to the heroine how strong her feelings for the hero had become, and sequence two will now force her to make a choice: go back to her old life and be alone or give up on her old life and begin a new one with the hero. She will have to make this choice at the end of the sequence. In *Rebecca*, the heroine is about to be whisked off to America by her employer and unhappy at the prospect of being separated from him, she desperately tries to find him so she can say goodbye. In *Suspicion*, hero and heroine sneak away from a party and share a first kiss. In both stories, near the end of sequence two, the hero proposes marriage to the heroine. In both cases, the proposal is unorthodox and catches the heroine unawares. And she feels under pressure to make her decision instantly, for fear of losing the hero again, and permanently.

There is also an acknowledgment that the romance and proposal are not how the heroine imagined it would be. Lina, in *Suspicion*, describes the sort of courtship she expected – something clichéd and very gradual. In *Rebecca*, Maxim describes the clichéd romantic proposal he thinks the heroine expected. This acknowledgment is an attempt to recognise that romantic expectations – those of the heroine and the audience – have not been met, but it also serves as an early warning that the audience recognises but the heroine is only dimly aware of. Reality has not lived up to her fantasy here – does this mean more disappointments lie ahead?

The heroine experiences feelings of guilt arising from deception which accompanied her acceptance of the proposal. The heroine of *Rebecca* conducted her relationship with Maxim behind the back of her employer. While Lina in *Suspicion* elopes with Johnnie, knowing that her father would never approve of their marriage. What should have been a moment in her life to celebrate has become a shabby secret that she must keep to herself. This can't possibly bode well for her future happiness, can it?

The turning point between sequences two and three in both stories is a registry office wedding – a transaction conducted quickly and witnessed by strangers. This is not the white wedding the heroine dreamed of. The honeymoon is passed over very quickly – in *Suspicion* we see only a montage of labels for various romantic destinations pasted onto a trunk; while in *Rebecca* it is hardly referred to at all until sequence four, when the couple watch home movies of their travels.

Sequence 3
This is where the reality of her new situation – the consequences of her decision – are brought home to the heroine. This is where she discovers how her new life will be, now that the honeymoon is over. Hitchcock uses rain as a metaphor to indicate that the future isn't going to be all sunshine: in *Suspicion* it rains when they are in the registry office; in *Rebecca* it rains as they travel up the drive towards Manderley.

In both cases, we see the heroine arriving at her new home – one that the husband has had prepared for them, with no input from her. The house is much grander than the heroine expected – Maxim's home, Manderley, is dark and Gothic; and Johnnie has rented a bright modern home with no expense spared. The heroine is overwhelmed by her new surroundings. Manderley is more unsettling because the whole staff have been assembled to greet the newly-weds, led by the solemn and creepy housekeeper, Mrs. Danvers. In *Suspicion* the only servant is a chirpy cockney maid, Ethel, an unorthodox choice that seems in keeping with Johnnie's avoidance of conformity. Both heroines feel that this is the hero's house and that they are a guest or an interloper. Again, it doesn't live up to the fantasy of her first home as a married woman. The audience sees danger too, in the appearance of the housekeeper and in Johnnie's off-hand attitude towards the bill for refurbishing the house – we get the impression that something is not quite right here.

In terms of the hero's journey story model, the beginning of sequence three – the start of Act II – marks the crossing of a threshold into a new world. In neither of our example stories is the bride carried across the threshold by her new husband – he regards it as no big deal and expects her to just get on with it. This new home – and married life – *is* the heroine's strange new world; a place where she will have to learn the rules and discover who her allies and her enemies might be. The heroine, especially in *Rebecca*, feels lost and doesn't feel that she belongs in this place – she doesn't know how to behave. She doesn't know what her role is and tries to second-guess what people expect of her. Her feelings of inadequacy and lack of confidence are going to make this difficult for her – and her husband's lack of awareness and apparent indifference won't make it any easier.

The hero quickly slips back into his pre-marriage routine, behaving almost like a bachelor, leaving his wife alone to fend for herself as best she can. She had expected continued togetherness but instead finds herself feeling more alone than before she was married – at least back then she had some sort of role and sense of place – now she feels adrift.

The heroine in *Rebecca* does not feel that she is mistress of the house and constantly defers to the servants rather than giving them instructions. And she lives in fear of the vampire-like housekeeper Mrs. Danvers. She feels that she is constantly being compared to the 'first Mrs. De Winter' and found to be inferior to her. All around her are things with Rebecca de Winter's monogram on them. Visitors also comment on how different she is to Rebecca – and everyone assumes she knows the 'whole story' regarding Rebecca's death, but she doesn't because Maxim will never speak of it. She feels like someone trying to feel their way in the dark, trying to avoid setting off unseen traps. Maxim, meanwhile, is still treating her like a child.

Lina, the heroine of *Suspicion,* finds herself in a different sort of situation but feeling equally lost. She learns that Johnnie is broke and has been funding his extravagant lifestyle on borrowed money. He married her in the naïve belief that they would be able to live on her annual allowance from her father – and would borrow against her inheritance if necessary. He is shocked when Lina suggests he should get a job, describing her as a dreamer. She realises that he is like an irresponsible child, unable to take responsibility for his own life, never mind support a wife. Johnnie manages to put her mind at rest, at least temporarily, by telling her that he has received a job offer. But the audience doubts this will be a long-term solution to their financial problems when he admits it was an offer he never dreamed of accepting.

In both of our example stories, we see that married life has not begun well for our heroine and that problems are being stored up for the future. The hero has a secret past that is being kept from the heroine – though she is beginning to piece it together – and already we begin to see the strain on their relationship. Reality has intruded and they are no longer making each other happy – but neither of them wants to admit this.

Sequence 4

This sequence builds to the midpoint where a major revelation or change in circumstances will set the story in the direction of its climax.

In *Suspicion* we meet two new characters who will play significant roles after the midpoint: Johnnie's friend Beaky and Isobel Sedbusk, author of mystery novels. Beaky reveals that Johnnie has been going to the races and betting on horses when Lina thought he had been going off to work every day. Beaky tells her there's no point being angry at Johnnie, it's just the way he is. Again, Johnnie is able to defuse the situation – he reveals he's won £2,000 on the horses. Lina accepts this and the extravagant gifts he brings her, but the audience knows this is only a temporary reprieve: the real problem hasn't really been tackled. There is also a set-up here regarding Beaky's health that will pay-off later. At the midpoint, Lina learns that Johnnie lost his job some weeks ago – and may be prosecuted for the theft of £2,000 if he doesn't pay back the money.

Maxim de Winter's problem in *Rebecca* isn't his attitude to money, it is his feelings for his dead wife. The heroine is aware of this and is slowly coming to understand the nature and extent of this problem. At the beginning of sequence four, she learns there is a cove near the house that he won't visit because it holds bad memories for him. He grows angry when she visits it. The heroine questions Maxim's estate manager and learns more about Rebecca and the circumstances of her death – she comes to know the 'whole story' as everyone else knows it. The heroine tries to be more like Rebecca by ordering a new dress, but Maxim isn't impressed. Instead of explaining that he prefers her to be herself, he is critical and condescending. The heroine wistfully notes that she is such a dull person that no one will ever gossip about her, and this unaccountably makes Maxim angry: Why would she mention gossip? She has no idea why this has upset him so much. She tries to convince him – and herself – that their marriage is a success and that they are both happy, but Maxim is unable to agree with her. The next day he goes away on business. Alone and unhappy, the heroine sees someone at the window in the disused west wing – in Rebecca's room – and discovers the housekeeper, Mrs. Danvers, sneaking around with a man who appears to be a friend of Rebecca's. The midpoint marks the appearance of Jack Favell, Rebecca's cousin – he will play a significant part in the second half of the story.

Sequence 5
In many stories, sequence five concentrates on relationships and marks the deepening of the love between the protagonist and the romantic co-protagonist – the two become closer. In the woman in jeopardy thriller, the opposite is true: during this sequence the two grow further apart and at the end of the sequence there is some event or revelation that highlights how far apart they have drifted.

At the midpoint of *Suspicion*, Lina had discovered that Johnnie had lost his job and been accused of theft. At the beginning of sequence five she is planning to leave him, but her action is postponed when she learns that her father has suffered a fatal heart attack. In his will, she is given the continuance of her small annual income and a painting: Johnny notes the irony of the fact that she would have received much more if she hadn't eloped with him. There is a reconciliation – or at least a temporary truce – and then Johnnie comes up with a get-rich-quick real estate scheme. Lina smiles – this is just Johnnie being Johnnie. When she learns that Beaky is putting up the money for the scheme, she tries to warn him off, afraid that Johnnie will swindle him or at least lose his money. This makes Johnnie angry with her – for the first time – and he tells her not to interfere. By the end of sequence five, Lina has come to suspect that Johnnie intends to murder Beaky for his money. This marks a new low in her feelings for Johnnie – and in what she believes him to be capable of.

In *Rebecca* the heroine learns that Favell was Rebecca's 'favourite cousin' and that Maxim disliked him intensely. He asks the heroine not to tell Maxim that he has visited Manderley. After he's gone, the heroine goes up to Rebecca's bedroom – it has been kept exactly as it was on the night she died. The extent of Mrs. Danvers obsession with Rebecca becomes clear and is extremely unsettling. Later, the heroine orders that Rebecca's things be removed from the morning room, asserting herself for the first time: '*I* am Mrs. De Winter now.' When Maxim returns she persuades him to hold a masquerade ball, like they used to in Rebecca's day, feeling that it will help people accept that she is now mistress of the house. Mrs. Danvers suggests that the heroine base her masquerade costume on one in Maxim's favourite painting in the house, but when she appears in the dress, Maxim is horrified and orders her to take it off. The heroine realises that the housekeeper has deliberately set her up.

In *Rebecca,* sequence five concentrates on the relationship between the heroine and the antagonist, Mrs. Danvers. The housekeeper regards herself as the champion of the first Mrs. De Winter and sets out to sabotage the relationship between the heroine and Maxim – and her plot is a very good one.

In both stories we see the heroine begin to take charge and express her own individuality – and we see her husband react in a way that does not encourage this.

Sequence 6
This sequence, as in most thrillers, presents a rapid unravelling of the protagonist's situation. It ends with a major plot point. Not that in both our example stories, the climax is delayed until the end of sequence seven – there is a mini climax in this sequence and a bigger one in the next.

Suspicion shows Lina suspecting that her husband has driven friend Beaky up to the top of a cliff and killed him. She is able to relax when she learns Beaky is alive and well – but at the end of the sequence, she learns that Beaky has died in suspicious circumstances in Paris and that police are seeking an 'unidentified Englishman' who may have been responsible.

Sequence six in *Rebecca* begins with Mrs. Danvers trying to persuade the heroine to leap to her death, but this is interrupted when a ship runs aground and fires distress flares. Everyone rushed to the beach to try and help. A diver examining the ship discovers the remains of Rebecca's boat on the seabed nearby – and her body is still in it. Maxim tells the heroine what *really* happened on the night of Rebecca's death and reveals the true nature of their 'perfect' relationship. He says that Rebecca has won after all. The heroine refuses to accept this and for the first time takes charge, telling Maxim what he must do and say when questioned about Rebecca's death. No matter what happens, they are in this together.

The two stories take different approaches in their handling of the 'villainy' of the hero. Maxim is revealed to be responsible for Rebecca's death (in the novel it is murder but in the film adaptation it is more of an accident) and the heroine sees this as a good thing – because he didn't really love Rebecca: she is no longer in competition with this paragon for her husband's love. *Suspicion*, as the film's title suggests, is concerned more with what the heroine *believes* could have happened – she suspects that her husband could be a murderer and effectively condemns him on circumstantial evidence. Again, the film's approach to the husband's guilt differs from that of the source novel.

Both of the Hitchcock films differ from the novels on which they are based, in part because of a Hollywood tradition that didn't – at that time – approve of heroes who are not punished for their crimes. The changes in *Rebecca* are less significant than those in *Suspicion*.

Sequence 7
As mentioned above, this sequence builds to a major climax, extending the protagonist's downward spiral and cranking up the suspense. In sequence six, the heroine thought that things couldn't get any worse – in seven they do.

In *Suspicion,* the circumstantial evidence against Johnnie mounts, making it seem certain – at least in Lina's eyes – that he killed Beaky. Johnnie lies to her about where he was at the time of the murder and she learns that the circumstances of the killing mirror those of another true case that Johnnie discussed with mystery writer Isobel Sedbusk. She also discovers that pressure was being put on Johnnie to pay back the £2,000 he stole. Things come to a head when she discovers that (a) Johnnie has been asking about the money he could get from her life insurance policy in the event of her death, and (b) he has been asking Isobel about an untraceable poison. Lina comes to believe that Johnnie plans to poison her and claim on the life insurance policy.

Sequence seven of *Rebecca* is the inquest into Rebecca de Winter's death. Everyone wants to believe that her death was an accident – but there is evidence that the boat was sunk deliberately. The question then becomes whether her death was suicide or murder. Convinced that it must have been murder, Rebecca's 'favourite cousin' Favell tries to blackmail Maxim, saying he has a letter that proves Rebecca didn't kill herself.

By the end of sequence seven, the thing the heroine values most is in danger – Lina fears losing her life and the heroine of *Rebecca* fears that her husband will be sent to the gallows for murder.

Sequence 8

Now we come to the final resolution where we discover whether justice is served and whether the heroine and her husband will live happily ever after. Although the woman in jeopardy thriller is a form of dark romance, we do not necessarily have to end with husband and wife in each other's arms saying, 'I love you.' Ironic and even tragic endings are permissible, as long as they are *satisfying* in terms of the story as a whole. Now is not the time for a surprise or a shock that has not been properly set-up in earlier sequences – that is cheap hack writing and audiences don't like it.

In *Suspicion*, Lina is so convinced that Johnnie will murder her that she flees. In a final confrontation on a clifftop, she learns what *really* happened. As a result, she takes responsibility for her own life and – perhaps more importantly to her – Johnnie takes responsibility for his own actions and will accept the consequences.

In *Rebecca*, Maxim and the others learn Rebecca's final secret – what happened to her on the day before her death. When she learns the truth, Mrs. Danvers performs one final act in memory of the first Mrs. De Winter and Maxim and the heroine are free of her ghost forever.

The Stalker Thriller

The 'stalker' thriller features a protagonist who is the victim of the obsessive interest of another character who has no concept of reasonable behaviour or personal boundaries. In the United States, The Violence Against Women Act of 2005 defines stalking as "engaging in a course of conduct directed at a specific person that would cause a reasonable person to – (a) fear for his or her safety or the safety of others; and, (b) suffer substantial emotional distress."

The actions of a stalker may include repeatedly following the victim or watching them in the manner of a peeping tom or voyeur, sending unwanted gifts or messages, or making telephone calls. The stalker often holds the delusional belief that the victim either loves them – erotomania – or is in need of rescuing ('hero syndrome' or 'saviour complex'). Stalkers – in real life and in fiction – may be male or female. Stalkers tend to obsess about another individual, but occasionally – as in the 2002 film *One Hour Photo* and in *Cape Fear* – target a family. Online social media sites have created a new platform for stalking, an idea explored by the films *Like. Share. Follow.* (2017) and *Ingrid Goes West* (2017).

The Psychology of Stalkers

In their paper 'Study of Stalkers' in *The American Journal of Psychiatry*, Paul E. Mullen et al. identified five types of stalkers:

- *Rejected* – aiming to restart or gain revenge for an ended relationship with an ex-partner, mother, friend, or work colleague. The stalker experienced feelings of loss, frustration, anger, jealousy, vindictiveness and sadness.
- *Intimacy-seeking* – wanting to have an intimate relationship with the target of their unwanted attention. The stalker often holds a delusional belief that their love is reciprocated. Behaviour is consistent with someone who has a romantic infatuation but may include intense jealousy and anger if the victim continually demonstrates indifference to the stalker's advances.
- *Incompetent* – seeking a relationship, and often feeling a sense of entitlement, but lacking the social abilities to successfully begin one. These stalkers are aware that their interest is not reciprocated, and their behaviour is not a full-blown infatuation with an individual, and they often focus on a series of victims in the hope of one day forming a relationship with one of them.
- *Resentful* – deliberately aiming to frighten and distress the victim, either because they have a vendetta against the specific individual, real or imagined, or because they have a general grievance and have chosen a victim at random or as a 'representative' of a target group.
- *Predatory* – preparing for a sexual attack. These stalkers take pleasure in the sense of power stalking gives them, and in 'getting to know' the victim and preparing and rehearsing or fantasising about their intended attack. These stalkers may also have a paraphilia (previously known as sexual perversion and sexual deviation) or sexual fetish.

It is important to note here that when talking about the stalker, we mean something very different to the psychopath. The natures of the disorders which the two suffer – the causes for their dangerous behaviours – are not the same. The psychopath, or sociopath, may suffer from antisocial personality disorder or dissocial personality disorder, and demonstrate an absence of empathy and an absence of, or disregard for, moral beliefs. I have written about psychopaths and their criminal profiling in more detail in *Crime Fiction.*

Personality disorders associated with stalkers include antisocial, borderline, dependent, narcissistic, and paranoid. Mullen et al. also include delusional disorders, erotomania, morbid jealousy, persecution, morbid infatuation, depression, and anxiety disorder as being variously present in the stalkers they examined.

Historical Development

The phenomenon of stalking was initially recognised in the behaviour of the obsessive fans of celebrities before being recognised as more widely applicable, and this is reflected in the movies about stalkers. In *The Fan* (1981), based on the 1977 novel by Bob Randall, Lauren Bacall's character is an actress stalked by an obsessive male fan. Better known is *Play Misty for Me* (1971) in which a radio disc jockey played by Clint Eastwood is stalked by a female fan. Joel Edgerton's 2015 film *The Gift* sees a married couple intimidated by one of the husband's former classmates. *Fear* (1996) has Mark Wahlberg in an early role as the stalker. *Fatal Attraction*, with a screenplay by James Deardon based on his own 1980 short film, was the second-highest-grossing film of 1987 and gave us the phrase 'bunny boiler' for an obsessive and dangerous woman who pursues the lover who spurned her. *Daddy's Gone A-Hunting* (1969) about a young woman stalked by her former lover was directed by Mark Robson, best known for the films *Peyton Place* and *Valley of the Dolls*. Patricia Highsmith's *The Cry of the Owl* – filmed in 2009 and 1987– turns the table on the voyeur, having him become the victim of the woman's ex-fiancé. Or is it the other way around?

Cape Fear (1962) was based on the 1952 novel *The Executioners* by John D. MacDonald and remade by Martin Scorsese in 1991. A lawyer and his family are stalked by a rapist that the lawyer helped to convict.

Plot Structure of the Stalker Thriller

The stalker thriller plot begins with the stalker engaging in behaviour that seems either entirely normal or perhaps a little bit off but essentially benign. It doesn't impact the victim-protagonist's life in a negative way. As the story progresses through the eight sequences, the stalker's behaviour becomes increasingly intense and more and more dangerous. At the same time, the impact of this behaviour on the victim's life becomes greater and greater, disrupting everyday activities and making them feel as if they are under siege.

Like the woman in jeopardy thriller, the stalker thriller is a romance gone wrong – it follows the development of a relationship between two people – but it doesn't end happily ever after. The stalker thriller could also be a 'buddy' movie gone wrong or a student-mentor story gone wrong.

In the archetypal stalker thriller, the stalker becomes obsessed with the victim-protagonist. Initially they believe they are 'in love' with the victim and that this feeling is reciprocated. As it becomes apparent that their love is unrequited, the stalker becomes more unstable and ultimately they reach a point where they want to kill the victim. The stalker wants to punish the victim – seeking revenge for the 'rejection' they have suffered.

The gradual deterioration of the stalker's mental state is an important element in this type of thriller, distinguishing it from the psycho-slasher horror movie. The two best-known stalker movies are *Play Misty for Me* and *Fatal Attraction* – the first is about an obsessive fan seeking a relationship with a media personality and the second is about the one-night stand that won't go away. A third example that I looked at in putting together the structure below was the 1981 film *The Fan*, based on the 1977 novel by Bob Randall, which I chose because – unlike the other two – the 'relationship' between stalker and victim doesn't begin with a sexual encounter, making it much closer to what really happens when obsessive fans stalk actresses, and also it features a male stalker.

Sequence 1
The first sequence introduces the two main characters – stalker and victim – and establishes the nature of the relationship between them. This sequence needs to set-up the everyday life of the victim-protagonist as the audience needs to see the equilibrium that is going to be upset by the actions of the stalker. We also need to see what it is about the victim that attracts the attention of the stalker. In *The Fan*, Lauren Bacall plays a glamorous actress; *Play Misty for Me* has Clint Eastwood as a handsome, smooth-talking late night radio disc jockey; and in *Fatal Attraction*, Michael Douglas is a nice, non-threatening guy with a sense of humour.

There is usually also some characteristic of the protagonist that leads the audience to feel empathy with or sympathy for them – there is something missing in their lives, a lack of some kind, that makes them vulnerable. Loneliness can work – in *Play Misty for Me* David is missing the girlfriend who has walked out on him and in *The Fan*, Sally Ross still loves her ex-husband. Dan in *Fatal Attraction* is a married man with a house, job, and young daughter – and all the responsibilities that go with them – and who is in need of a little excitement.

Establishing the victim-protagonist usually takes up the first fifty to seventy per cent of sequence one. The stalker is typically introduced later in the sequence, serving as a catalyst – a challenge or opportunity that the protagonist must respond to.

In *Play Misty for Me* and *Fatal Attraction*, the male protagonists meet attractive women and have what they believe to be a one-night stand. Neither men seek to deceive the women about it being an ongoing relationship. David meets Evelyn in a bar and thinks he's picked her up, but she is a listener of his show and went to his local bar specifically to meet him. Dan's meeting with the Glenn Close character, Alex, begins with flirting and the question 'are we going to do this?' hanging over them, and it is Alex who decides that they are, and Dan allows himself to be led into temptation. In both stories, there is a question over whether the men 'deserved' what they got after the one-night stand. David is a womaniser who says he'll call but never does and Dan is cheating on the woman he loves. Both use women for sexual gratification – and they assume that their respective sexual partners are in it for the same reason. Taking responsibility for your own actions – and living with the consequences – are themes in both stories.

The Fan is different in that Sally Ross does not invite interaction with Douglas, who is a fan who sends her letters. During sequence one she is barely even aware of his existence – his contact with her is mediated by the secretary,

Belle, who answers her fan mail. In this story we see more of stalker-Douglas and his life – as a form of foreshadowing: this obsessive individual is an approaching storm that will shortly impact on Sally's life.

The transition between sequence one and sequence two in *Play Misty for Me* and *Fatal Attraction* occurs when the protagonist and the stalker have sex. In *The Fan* it is marked by a change in the tone of Douglas's letters, changing from adoring but obsessed to something more intense. Douglas was unhappy with Belle's response to his last letter and tells Miss Ross, 'I think your secretary needs a talking to' – because he's not just a 'cheap, anonymous star-gazer' but is a real friend. Belle reads out his letter, but Sally doesn't listen.

Sequence 2
Here is where we begin to see what the stalker character is *really* like – and that the protagonist has made a mistake in having a relationship with them.

In *Play Misty for Me* and *Fatal Attraction* it is the morning after and the protagonists go back to their daily lives. By the time David gets home, he has virtually forgotten Evelyn. Dan goes home and suffers pangs of guilt, feeling a need to connect with his wife and daughter who are still away. In both cases, the stalker unexpectedly reappears – Evelyn turns up at David's house with groceries, behaving as if she's his long-term girlfriend. Alex phones Dan and says 'What happened? I woke up and you weren't there – I hate that.' Both men make the mistake of agreeing to continue the relationship – in the short term – and this seals their fate, setting up the rest of the story.

This sequence typically includes a reminder to the audience that the protagonist is involved in a long-term relationship. David is happily married. David and Sally Ross are estranged from their respective partners, but still have strong feelings for them. The stalker's behaviour is going to have an impact on this relationship – and the existence of the relationship is going to affect the stalker. In all three of our examples, the protagonist speaks to their partner – Sally banters with ex-husband Jake, Dan telephones his wife, and David meets up with ex-girlfriend Tobie who has just come back to town.

The relationship between stalker-Douglas and victim-Sally in *The Fan* is different in that it is a one-sided love affair. He believes that he is in love with her, but she still isn't really aware of him. We see her life going on as normal and we see more of Douglas's life – seeing how obsessed and unstable he is. His social skills are underdeveloped, and he harbours feelings of resentment towards a co-worker and his boss – and these ultimately get him fired. Douglas's sister visits because the family are concerned about him: he sends her away, claiming he's having dinner with a famous actress – his sister says children play pretend, but it is not appropriate behaviour for adults. Douglas's letters become more intense – he's moved from 'Dear Miss Ross' to 'Dear Sally,' and tells her they will be lovers soon. Secretary Belle tells Sally about this 'raunchy' letter and replies to it saying she won't show his 'tasteless' letter to Miss Ross, and that she won't be replying to any more of his letters. Receiving this, Douglas angrily tears it up.

In *Fatal Attraction* and *Play Misty for Me,* the stalker's behaviour is not as overtly weird at this stage in the story – but they do begin to demonstrate a mean streak. When Dan pretends to have a heart attack, Alex 'punishes' him by saying that her father died of a heart attack, right in front of her, when she was seven years old – but then she pretends she was joking to make him feel bad. They also discuss *Madam Butterfly*, in which a jilted lover commits suicide, another hint of dark things to come. Evelyn demonstrates her darker side when she angrily turns on David's neighbour and curses at him, then turns back and smiles sweetly at David. When she leaves, David says he'll call her sometime and she says he's 'funny' and that they don't need to keep playing 'these games.'

In all three examples, sequence two shows that something about the stalker character is not quite right – that their perception of the relationship with the protagonist (and of the world in general) has an element of fantasy about it. Again, this foreshadows bad times ahead.

Sequence 3
Afraid that the situation is getting away from them, the stalker seeks to assert control by taking decisive action – raising the stakes and moving the story to a new level of weirdness. We are into Act II now, the victim-protagonist has entered a 'strange new world' – one where normal rules of rational behaviour do not apply. This is where the protagonist finally realises how controlling and/or dangerous the stalker character is.

Douglas, in *The Fan*, tries to get a letter to Sally Ross directly, but it still ends up in the hands of her secretary Belle. Frustrated, Douglas finds himself attracted by the display of knives in a shop window. Belle and Sally discuss Douglas's letter – Sally finally becoming properly aware of him. She tells Belle to ignore his letters – 'he's harmless.' Douglas follows Belle when she leaves work, attacks her in the subway, slashing her face.

In *Fatal Attraction*, Dan and Alex are in their last hours of a weekend-long fling. When Dan gets out of bed, saying he's got to go, Alex grows angry. She accuses him of having a good time with no thought for her feelings. He is shocked because he thought they had an understanding. As he's leaving, she apologises and says, 'let's be friends.' He is relieved – until he sees she's slashed her wrists. He bandages them and stays with her – she now has him trapped. When he does finally get home, he has to make it appear that he spent the whole weekend at home. And when his wife returns he says, 'I missed you' and genuinely means it, aware of the terrible mistake he's made. Later, Alex says she wants to see him again, but just as friends; this time he says no. He doesn't realise that it is too late to make a clean break.

Play Misty for Me also features a fake suicide attempt by the stalker, but it doesn't occur until the end of sequence four. Evelyn's behaviour degenerates at a more gradual pace and in a less sensational manner. David tries to avoid her, refusing to take her calls, but she doesn't give up. She lies in wait for him outside the bar and they argue: when two men ask if she needs assistance she turns on them angrily, surprising them and David, and again she then turns and smiles sweetly at David as if nothing has happened. David says he doesn't want to see her again and she says 'Bye. See you later.' When she turns up naked on his doorstep, he has to invite her inside – and again he makes the mistake of allowing her to spend the night. As she leaves he says he'll call her sometime –

he still hasn't learned – and she says Thursday is good for her. She has written their initials on his mirror in lipstick and drawn a heart around it – David looks at it and zips up his pants, a symbolic gesture, but it's too late for that now. When Thursday comes around, Evelyn phones him, demanding to know where he is – he relents and says that he'll be over later, but that they need 'to have a talk.'

Sequence 4
This sequence builds to the midpoint where a major revelation or change in circumstances will set the story in the direction of its climax.

In *Fatal Attraction,* Dan has gone back to his family life and friends. Alex has gone back to her lonely existence and is still thinking about him. She makes phone calls, but he doesn't return them. She calls his home and hangs up if Dan's wife answers. Growing increasingly anxious, Dan agrees to meet Alex. He tells her that 'this has got to stop' and then grows angry, telling her she needs to see a shrink. She says that she isn't trying to hurt him – she loves him. Dan is surprised and shocked by this: she doesn't even know him, they only spent a weekend together. The midpoint revelation occurs when Alex says, 'I'm pregnant.' Initially stunned, Dan says he'll help her and will pay for the abortion. But she says she wants to keep the child – she's happy to be a single parent, it's not going to be a problem – 'You play fair with me, I'll play fair with you.'

Sequence four in *Play Misty for Me* is also a dramatic confrontation between stalker and victim. David tries to convince Evelyn that there's nothing between them, and she says, 'Are you trying to say you don't love me anymore?' He insists he never told her he did, but she says, 'Not in words, maybe, but...' Then Evelyn becomes angry, telling him that he's not dumping her. 'You're not even good in bed,' she yells, 'I just felt sorry for you...' David leaves and she phones to apologise: again her anger has been replaced by sweetness. 'Will I see you tomorrow?' She says she loves him. David is frustrated that he is not able to make her understand. The next day, David spends a romantic afternoon with his girlfriend Tobie – Evelyn watches from the shadows, her face grim. The night Evelyn bursts into David's home, expecting to find him in bed with Tobie – but she's not there. 'Why are you pretending you don't love me?' Evelyn asks. At the midpoint, she goes into his bathroom and slashes her wrists.

In *The Fan,* sequence four is the aftermath of the attack on Sally's secretary, Belle. She is recovering in hospital. Sally is upset by the attack – especially when Douglas writes to her and says he did it because he wanted to get Belle out of the way, so that he and Sally could be together. The police investigate and Sally receives protection. Douglas then attacks a young actor Sally has been working with, sending her a letter saying 'My dearest darling, once more I have proven my love...' He says he's prepared to do it again and again – and he's upset that she hasn't written to acknowledge him. He warns her that there is a limit to his patience – 'I expect a letter tomorrow.' The midpoint occurs with this threat and Sally's acknowledgment of it: 'He's after me now, isn't he?'

Sequence 5

Here we see the victim-protagonist's response to the midpoint. This will lead into sequence six and a rapid unravelling of the protagonist's situation as the stalker becomes increasingly dangerous. Here we also see them trying to be more pro-active, accepting responsibility for their situation and taking action rather than being just a passive victim. In the fifth or sixth sequence we also typically see the protagonist doing what any sensible person would do – going to the police for help. And we see that the police are not able to protect them.

Fatal Attraction's Dan watches his wife and daughter reading together and knows he's put the happiness of his family at risk. He breaks into Alex's apartment, hoping to find some evidence of another lover who could be the father of her child, but he learns only that her father *did* die of a heart attack when she was young. He speaks to a lawyer friend who specialises in family law and learns that his situation 'ain't good.' Alex discovers that Dan has changed his home phone number and swears angrily at the operator who won't give her the new one. Later Dan gets home and finds his wife showing their apartment to a potential buyer – Alex. When he confronts her, she tells him she won't be ignored and wants him to live up to his responsibilities. He calls her lonely and sad. When she threatens to tell his wife, Dan says he'll kill her if she does. Eager to try and escape, Dan moves his family to a new home: when the telephone rings he has a moment of panic, but it is not Alex. Later, Alex vandalises his car and then follows him back to his new house – Dan doesn't know it, but Alex now knows where they live.

Sequence five of *Play Misty for Me* begins with David's doctor friend treating Evelyn's slashed wrists. David stays with her, even though he's supposed to be going out with Tobie. Evelyn has trapped him, like an animal, and he doesn't know how to get out of this situation. The next day, David goes for lunch with a potential employer – Evelyn appears at their table and, thinking the woman is David's lover, is angry and abusive. It ruins David's chances of getting the job.

In *The Fan,* we see the police protection that Sally has been assigned. She tries to give Jake his freedom – he is her *ex*-husband, and she says she has more to give someone than just her problems, she wants to be in a relationship where she can give and not just take. When Sally and her bodyguards are away from her apartment, Douglas breaks in and attacks her maid, slashes a painting of Sally, and trashes her apartment. 'Dearest bitch,' his next letter says, 'see how accessible you are.' He threatens her with sexual violence. Later, Douglas phones Sally and says he wants to make love to her – he doesn't want to have to kill her.

By the end of sequence five, the victim-protagonist has lost control of his or her life – everything is now a reaction to what the stalker is doing. Phone calls make them jumpy; his or her home has been violated and is no longer a sanctuary, and people he or she cares about are in danger of physical or emotional harm, or have already been hurt.

Sequence 6

This sequence typically appears to provide a moment of calm – perhaps even a 'false solution' to the problem – but it is really only a lull in the storm. The worst is yet to come.

In *The Fan,* Sally Ross goes into hiding, leaving the city and going to a beach house. She ignored police advice and continued working in the public eye, believing that her work was all she had. But her insistence on working has caused other people to be harmed, which has caused her to reassess her priorities. Being in the limelight attracted her obsessed fan, Douglas, in the first place; by withdrawing to the isolated beach house, she hopes to protect herself and those she cares about. She is also accepting responsibility for herself, leaving the police and her ex-husband behind. News reports, seen by Douglas, say Sally Ross's whereabouts are unknown. He needs a new plan. He picks up a young man in a bar, kills him and burns the body. He leaves a note for Sally saying suicide was the only way he could 'atone for the pain I have caused you ... Now, my dearest, you are free.' Sally receives the news of her stalker's 'death' from Jake.

Sequence six of *Play Misty for Me* begins with David telling Tobie about Evelyn and her attempted suicide. Meanwhile, David's cleaner goes into his house and sees that it has been trashed. Worse, Evelyn is still there and attacks the cleaner, slashing her with a knife. Police arrest Evelyn and question David about her – but he really doesn't know her at all. Finally free of Evelyn, David and Tobie enjoy a romantic montage to the Roberta Flack song.

Fatal Attraction doesn't allow Dan the same respite. He gets a tape from Alex in which she subjects him to a tirade of abuse and telling him he deserves everything he gets. Dan talks to the police, pretending he's acting for a client, but is told there is little that can be done without proof. The detective also says that the client made his bed and has to lie in it. He warns against taking any action which might provoke Alex into further action – she may have got her desire for 'revenge' out of her system when she trashed his car. Then we see Dan's idyllic home life with his wife and daughter in their new home. Will Alex now leave them alone? Of course not – and a boiling pot on the stove proves the lengths that Alex will go to. After the bunnicide, Dan's wife wants to call the police, but he has something to tell her first: 'I know who did this.' He tells his wife about the affair with Alex – and about her being pregnant. Dan's wife is devastated – and angry. Seeing this upsets their daughter. Dan has ruined everything he cared about.

Until this point in the story, our two male protagonists have compounded the 'crime' of their infidelity by deceiving their respective partners about it. By telling the truth and accepting the consequences of their actions, they have now taken a step towards redeeming themselves.

Sequence 7

This sequence begins with the protagonist's response to the turning point at the end of sequence six and also sets up the final confrontation of the story.

Dan, in *Fatal Attraction,* phones Alex and tells her it's over, he's told his wife. Alex doesn't believe him, so he gives the phone to his wife who says, 'If you ever come near my family again, I'll kill you.' Dan has to move out into a hotel room – he phones his daughter every night, trying to hang on to something of what he had. Alex collects Dan's daughter up from school one day, taking her to a fun fair. Driving around, desperately searching for her daughter, Dan's wife runs into the back of another car. She is injured, but not badly. Dan goes to Alex's apartment and confronts her. They fight and she tries to stab him. Dan disarms her and then leaves. He reports the kidnapping of his daughter to the police and they tell him Alex will be taken in for questioning. It seems as though Dan has finally escaped from the nightmare – but he hasn't.

Believing he is now free of Evelyn, David goes to the Monterey Jazz Festival with Tobie and some friends. Tobie leaves early because she's helping her old roommate move out and a new one, Annabel, move in. Back on air at the radio station, David gets a call from Evelyn – her treatment is complete and she has been released. She says she's moving to Hawaii. David wakes in the night to find Evelyn standing over him with a knife – she plunges it into his pillow, then disappears. The police warn David that she may try to kill him again, and David has to warn Tobie that she's back.

In *The Fan,* Sally believes Douglas is dead and things return to normal. Secretary Belle comes back to work; Sally is about to open in a new musical, and her ex-husband Jake says he wants to get back together with her. All seems well – except that in a dingy hotel somewhere, Douglas is preparing to make his final move on the opening night of Sally's new musical. After the show, everyone goes off to a party and the theatre grows quiet and dark. Sally is in her dressing room, changing for the party. Meanwhile, Douglas is creeping around the empty theatre.

Sequence 8

The original ending of *Fatal Attraction* referred back to *Madame Butterfly* and had Alex commit suicide, cutting her own throat and making it appear that Dan killed her. This was not well-received by test audiences and a new ending was shot in which Alex, having eluded the police, turns up at Dan's home and tries to kill his wife. It takes the efforts of both Dan and his wife to defeat Alex, each saving the other's life, and eventually Dan and his wife appear to be reconciled. I think, given the dramatic and sensational nature of what had gone before, the new dramatic and sensational ending was more appropriate – and it was popular with audiences.

In the final sequence of *The Fan*, Douglas kills two people in the theatre and then confronts Sally. He pursues her through the theatre, alternately seizing and kissing her and hitting her. In a final embrace, Sally manages to overcome him and he dies in her arms. Douglas is left sitting in an audience seat as Sally makes her exit. In voice-over we hear Douglas reading his first fan letter to Miss Ross – a reminder of where this all started and how badly it came unravelled.

Play Misty for Me has David helping the police to find Evelyn: he is at the radio station and they will trace the call when she phones him. David phones Tobie and warns her to lock her doors and not let anyone in – it is good advice, except that Evelyn is already in the house. She ties Tobie up and threatens her with a pair of scissors. Realising where Evelyn is, David drives out to confront her. She subjects David to a prolonged attack with a knife before he finally manages to overcome her.

Alternative Stalker Plots

There is one main variation on the stalker plot in which an obsessive fan *kidnaps* the victim-protagonist rather than simply following them. The two most famous examples are the Robert De Niro and Jerry Lewis film *The King of Comedy* (1982), in which a small-time stand-up comedian makes a bid for stardom by kidnapping his idol and demanding a television spot in lieu of a ransom; and *Misery,* based on the Stephen King novel, in which a novelist's greatest fan rescues him after an accident and holds him hostage until he writes a book resurrecting her favourite character.

Real-life obsessive fans can also offer inspiration for stories. There are stalkers have killed their celebrity victims and there are also people who go around pretending to *be* a celebrity, Stanley Kubrick being a famous victim of this sort of behaviour.

13 | Manhunt – The Chase

The chase is a fundamental part of the thriller in both novels and screenplays. In this chapter we're going to concentrate on a character being chased *on foot*. Although you will find car chases in some thrillers, a character who is being chased on foot seems much more vulnerable than one that is protected within a metal machine. I will write about car chases in the *Crime Thriller* volume in this series because I think they belong more in that genre.

The chase may be one of the earliest stories humans ever told – it is the story of the hunt and it is the story of escaping from the dangerous predator. Escape from predators is still a kind of story we enjoy – it is a fundamental part of *The Predator, Alien, Deep Blue Sea, Jurassic Park* and numerous other stories. And then there are the human predators that hunt other humans. The chase scene or story allows us to vicariously take the place of hunter or hunted, capturing a taste of the exhilaration experienced by our primitive ancestors.

In the *Genre Writer* series we are classifying stories according to their content, but there are other ways to group stories using more general terms that reflect their structure. In his book *20 Master Plots: And How to Build Them* (1993), Ronald B. Tobias defined twenty plot types including quest, revenge, love, temptation and sacrifice. These plots are not specific to any genre – though some are more commonly found in certain genres. Tobias writes about *Pursuit* (as Master Plot #3) and this forms the basis of the thriller genre plot that I am calling the manhunt or chase.

While many thrillers *include* a chase of this kind, there are some stories where the chase forms the whole of the plot. The best-known examples are probably the 1993 film *The Fugitive* starring Harrison Ford and David Morrell's 1972 novel *First Blood*, filmed in 1982 with Sylvester Stallone in the role of John Rambo. Stephen King's *The Running Man* (1982 under the pseudonym Richard Bachman) is a futuristic variation that formed the basis for the 1987 Arnold Schwarzenegger film. All of these were probably inspired, directly or indirectly, by a couple of earlier stories. *Rogue Male* by Geoffrey Household was published in 1939 and filmed by Fritz Lang in 1941 and adapted for television by the BBC in 1976.

Perhaps better known is 'The Most Dangerous Game,' a short story by Richard Connell that was first published in 1924. Also known as 'The Hounds of Zaroff,' it has been filmed a number of times – notably by RKO Pictures in 1932 with Joel McCrae and Leslie Banks in the lead roles. It was also adapted for radio featuring Orson Welles. Countless films, stories, and television episodes have used the idea of humans being hunted as game or for sport. *The Naked Prey* (1965) is a similar tale of 'pursuit and survival' in which a lone white hunter is pursued by the hunters of a tribe in Africa. More famous than all of these are the Warner Bros. cartoons featuring the Road Runner and Wile E. Coyote and the *Tom and Jerry* cartoons produced by Hanna and Barbera for

MGM – proving that the suspense of the chase can also be played for laughs. The very first Road Runner cartoon, incidentally, was called *Fast and Furry-ous* (1949).

The notes below should be helpful whether you want to create a full-length chase thriller or just want to include a chase sequence as part of another type of thriller plot. I have also included a plot template based on a full-length thriller, based on *The Fugitive*.

Hunter or Hunted

If you want your readers or viewers to be caught up in the emotion of a story – and you *do* – then the action has to be presented from the point of view of one of the characters. And that character must be someone whose fate we care about. It is more common for the protagonist to be chased – we want him to escape – and the antagonist to be the chaser – we want his pursuit to fail. Examples of where the hunter is the protagonist tend to fall into the crime thriller subgenre, with detectives hunting criminals being the bulk of them. It is probably also worth noting that the manhunt thriller differs from the detective thriller or the traditional whodunit mystery – both of which, it could be argued, centre on a hunt for a murderer – because the manhunt is literary a physical search or hunt for a person rather than an investigation into that person's actions. Murder or missing person investigations may include elements of the manhunt, but the physical chase is not their primary concern.

In a chase sequence or a short story you can just focus on the actions of the person who is chased – but in a longer story, you will almost certainly need to show some scenes from the escapee's point of view and some from the pursuer's. As we'll see in the chapter on suspense techniques, it is sometimes necessary to make the viewer or reader aware of dangers than the hero does not yet know about, meaning that we cannot always show things from his or her point of view. *The Fugitive* so successfully portrayed pursued and pursuer that Tommy Lee Jones won the Oscar for Best Supporting Actor for his portrayal of Deputy Marshal Sam Gerard and went on to be the protagonist of the spin-off/sequel movie *U.S. Marshals* (1998).

In *The Fugitive* – and in many amateur-on-the-run thrillers – there is a point near the end of sequence three or sequence four (the midpoint) where the hero switches from being the victim and becomes pro-active – he changes from pursued to pursuer, taking the fight to the villain. Richard Kimble (Harrison Ford) in *The Fugitive* remains a fugitive, running from the police and the U.S. Marshals, but at the same time begins his own pursuit/investigation of the real villains. It is a variation of the amateur-on-the-run thriller where the pursuing authorities play a much larger role than the actual villains, who are only really seen in the form of their 'henchman' the one-armed man until quite late in the film. The identity of the villain is hidden such that Kimble has to conduct an investigation in the manner of a murder mystery amateur detective.

Generally speaking, the reason *why* the hero is pursued is a MacGuffin – it is just an excuse to have a chase plot. The conspiracy involving the pharmaceutical company in *The Fugitive* could easily be lifted out and replaced with something else.

Martial Arts and Parkour Movie Sequences

As well as graceful and carefully choreographed fight scenes, martial arts movies have featured chase scenes – and because audiences want to see the artists' physical skills rather than their driving skills, many of these have been chases on foot. *Ong-Bak: The Thai Warrior* (2003, vt. *Ong-Bak: Muay Thai Warrior*) has one of the best examples of these and like many other movies takes its inspiration from one of the best movie martial artists and stuntmen, Jackie Chan. Jackie Chan's movies are filled with inventive extended fight scenes and chases that usually include an element of humour. *Mr. Nice Guy* (1997) has a sequence that takes place in a shopping mall, including the escalators, and in the street beyond that runs for over five minutes. *The Medallion* (2003) has a chase through the streets of Dublin. *Rumble in the Bronx* (1995) sees Chan escaping from a gang, some of whom pursue him on motorcycles. One of my favourites is the chase through the street market in *Miracles* (1989, vt. *Black Dragon* and *The Canton Godfather*). If you've never watched a Jackie Chan film, have a look at *Police Story* (1985) and you'll see a lot of stunt sequences that have served as the inspiration for similar sequences in Hollywood movies.

Parkour (or freerunning) was developed in France and takes its name from *parcours du combatant,* an obstacle course used for military training. It was developed initially by Raymond Belle and then by his son David, who starred in one of the best parkour movies, *District 13* (2004, vt. *Banlieue 13* or *B13*). One of the great things about chase sequences that include parkour moves is that they are filmed live and with no visual effects or wire-work. This tends to give them a more much visceral quality – you really get the sense that someone could misjudge a move and get seriously hurt or even fall to their death. Have a look at some of the following films to see the sort of moves that you could include in your own chase sequences: *Cop Out, Freerunner, Taxi 2, Yamakasi, Beat the World, Brick Mansions, Skills, The Great Challenge,* and *Tracers.*

More Examples

As well as the examples already quoted, here are a few more novels and films worth looking at to see how a chase can be written. When looking at them, note the location(s) used and how the writer utilises them and also see how the pursued character is emotionally, psychologically and/or physically impacted by the action. How does the writer make us *feel* what it is like to run for your life?

There are many novels that feature chase sequences. The best thing to do is choose examples from your own reading that strike you as good examples, and then look at those paragraphs and see how the writer put them together. Here are some more examples – many of which were adapted into movies. *The Night of the Hunter* (1953) by Davis Grubb, inspired by the true story of murderer Harry Powers, and filmed by Charles Laughton in 1955 with Robert Mitchum playing the role of the murderous 'preacher.' *The Warriors* (1965) by Sol Yurick (inspired by Xenophon's *Anabasis* written around 370 BC) and filmed by Walter Hill in 1979. *Deliverance*(1970) by James Dickey, filmed in 1972. *No Country for Old Men* (2005) written by author Cormac McCarthy as a screenplay before he wrote the novel and filmed by Joel and Ethan Coen from their own screenplay in 2007. *Twilight* (2006) by William Gay, a thriller with elements of a Southern Gothic.

Chapter 24 of William Goldman's 1974 conspiracy thriller *The Marathon Man* is a chase sequence. Writer Matt Debenham took it apart and studied it in his 4th December 2013 blog post 'How to Write a Chase Scene The Marathon Man Way.'
http://www.mattdebenham.com/blog/lets-steal-from-this-how-to-write-a-chase-scene-the-marathon-man-way/

Great *movie* chases where the hero is on foot include *Casino Royale* (2006) and the Jason Bourne movie adaptations. *Fast Five* (2011) has a foot chase through a favela. *Point Break* (1991) has a chase scene. *Takers* (2011) has an extended chase on foot. *Seven* (1997) has a dark and moody chase sequence that takes place during a downpour. Guy Ritchie's 2008 movie *RocknRolla* has a chase sequence that makes you feel the pain and exhaustion of the participants. More brutal still is *The Chaser* (2008, original title *Chugyeogja*). Most of these sequences can be found on YouTube or Vimeo by searching for the movie title plus 'chase' – though I would advise you to watch the whole film so that you can see the build-up to, and the aftermath of, the scene rather than just the physical chase out of context. You can also search on Google or YouTube for 'top ten movie foot chases' or 'top ten parkour movies' and see what examples others have listed.

Point of View

You can write a chase scene in a novel from a first-person viewpoint – and in a screenplay, you can describe the action keeping the camera on one character throughout – but I think this limits your options for creating suspense. In the chapter on suspense techniques I talk about this in more detail – but creating suspense often involves revealing something to the audience or reader that one or more of the characters does not know or cannot yet see. To take a simple example, a character runs towards the end of a corridor – suddenly a man appears with a gun. This is an example of surprise or shock – like shouting 'Boo!' – and the effect on the reader lasts a few seconds. We learn of the shock at the same instant as the character who is startled. This can be effective. But you can achieve a more sustained emotional effect – suspense – if the audience *knows* that there is a man with a gun hiding at the end of the corridor. The character does not know and runs towards him – and all the time the audience wants to warn the character that he or she is heading for danger. You can keep this sort of suspense going – creating ebbs and flows as the character heads towards a known (by the audience) danger and then moves away from it before turning back towards it again. This continuing rise and fall of tension is a key aspect of the thriller – and it is difficult to achieve with a first-person narrator. The other negative quality of the first-person narration is that it effectively gives the game away – if the character is telling the story in the past tense, we *know* he survived whatever dangers he is describing to us.

Everything I've just said about first-person narrators is true – but it is also sometimes overstated. An effective writer can use a first-person narrator to do everything that a third-person omniscient viewpoint can do. Can a character describe events that he wasn't present to witness? Yes, he can. Can one character know what another was thinking at a particular moment? Technically, no – but he can imagine what a character was thinking, in the same way that the author writing a third person omniscient viewpoint or even a third person restricted viewpoint can. What's the difference, really? The only risk is that using a 'first-person omniscient' viewpoint will spoil the illusion that the story being told in 'real time' as it unfolds.

In a single scene or series of connected scenes, you would really have to stick to a single first-person narrator. In a full-length chase novel, you can have two (or more) first-person narrators taking turns to tell their side of events. This is not my favourite way of telling or reading a story, but it can be done effectively.

Having said all of that, I think a restricted third-person point of view is a better option for suspense thrillers generally. It allows us to follow the two main characters – hunter and hunted – closely, cutting back and forth to help keep up the pace of the story. You can also cut away to a third character briefly or even add an omniscient aerial view or wide-shot, as long as it is in a separate paragraph or section. Readers are much less likely to be confused by a switch of viewpoint than writers are.

Lee Child writes some of his Jack Reacher novels from a first-person point of view and some from a third. Wikipedia lists the viewpoint in each of the novels and if you want to compare and contrast the two viewpoints, these novels are good examples to look at.

The Risk Involved in Writing Chase Scenes

This is a warning for screenwriters more than novelists and it's something that I hadn't really thought about until I read about it in an article by writer, director and producer John Rogers titled 'Why You Should Never Write Action Scenes For Your Blockbuster Movie.' He quotes an anonymous movie studio executive as saying, "Oh, as soon as I see the action start, I just skip over that writing. Nothing ever happens in an action sequence, and I hate them anyway." Rogers doesn't quote this to show that studio executives are stupid – though I'm sure there are some whose eyes glaze over when they see too much unbroken black text on a page – he's using it as a criticism of writers who write an action scene that has no function within the story other than being an action scene. Action just for the sake of action doesn't belong in a good screenplay. If your chase scene doesn't advance the plot of the movie – if it isn't, first and foremost, an effective scene in its own right – then it shouldn't be there.

The Pursuit Plot

Ronald B. Tobias suggests that part of the appeal of the pursuit story comes from our enjoyment of games like hide-and-seek and 'tag' played as a child. He also points out that in this type of story, *"The tension is greatest at the moment just before it seems capture is inevitable."* The pursued should never get too far ahead of the pursuer because tension is reliant on the proximity of the two characters. The 'inevitable' capture is avoided at the last minute because of some smart move by the pursued or some outside intervention and the pursuit begins again.

Tobias also says that another 'trademark' of the pursuit plot is *confinement*. Suspense is heightened, he says, if the pursued character becomes trapped or confined such that they have 'no place to run.' This makes sense because the main objective of the pursued is to get away, so he – and the audience – are going to because frustrated and agitated if he's stuck somewhere and cannot run away. Especially if the bad guys are closing in. Or if the bad guys are the ones who have trapped him and will return soon to 'deal with' him.

How to Write a Chase Scene or Sequence of Scenes

Here I'm listing fifteen questions to ask yourself when planning to write a chase scene or chase sequence for your story. Many of these are variations on the basic who, what, where, when, why, how questions that apply to any scene in a story. I've also given some clues to the sorts of answers you should be looking for. If the fifteen questions initially seem a bit overwhelming, pick a couple of chase sequences from novels or screenplays that you know, re-read them, and then see how the following questions are answered in those scenes.

1. Who is Being Chased?

This is not just a matter of pointing at a character and saying, 'He is.' There are certain qualities about a particular character that can be used to help determine what goes into – and what doesn't go into – an individual chase scene. In writing any story there are a couple of questions you should always ask yourself. If you have a particular situation in mind, ask: Who is the person least suited to be able to deal successfully with this situation? Or, if you have a particular character in mind, ask: What sort of situation would this person be least likely to deal with successfully? I said in *Plot Basics* that writers have to be sadists – we have to come up with ways to make our characters suffer, and this is an instance where this is especially true.

What qualities about the character would make this chase difficult for them? The more vulnerable we can make our character seem, the more likely the reader or audience is to feel empathy with them. Everyone has been in situations where they feel so tired they can hardly put one foot in front of the other. Or where they have sprained an ankle or cut their foot and can't bear to take another step. We need to evoke these memories and make the reader *feel* what the character is feeling.

Who the main character is will, to some extent, determine the kinds of actions he or she can take during the chase. If they are a martial artist or freerunner, they can make physical moves that your average joe cannot make. And the audience will expect them to use these moves. But there are also issues of personal morality here too – is this character someone who feels comfortable causing physical injury to another person, or even killing them? How the pursued character deals with one or more of his pursuers have to be determined by the sort of person he is. And if the chase is an opening scene, the character's actions here determine how we will perceive the character during the rest of the story. How the character behaves in a scene in Act I may reveal a weakness or opportunity for character development that can be explored during the middle part of the story, so that at the end – when faced with a similar choice – we can see whether the character has 'grown' as a result of his or her experiences. But all actions must be 'in character' no matter what type of scene you are writing.

2. Who is Chasing the Main Character?
Again, this is not just a question of saying, 'The bad guy.' In a chase scene, it must always seem that there is a real possibility of the pursuers catching the pursued – this is what helps to generate the suspense in the scene. And in a thriller it is almost always a good idea to make the protagonist in a scene seem to be an underdog. The bad guys will be stronger or more physically fit than the protagonist; they will have bigger and better weapons, and there will usually be more of them. If the hero of your scene is the one being pursued, ask yourself, 'Who is the worst possible person or group that could be chasing him?' Or if the hero is the one doing the pursuing, ask, 'Who is the worst possible person for him to be chasing?'

In the short-term, you can open the scene with a character running and solely from their reactions we will see that they are running for their life. That someone or something is chasing them – and you can keep the nature of the pursuer a mystery for a little while. But the longer you hold off showing what is coming after them, the more impressive that thing has got to be when you do reveal it.

3. What is at Stake?
What terrible thing will happen to this character if they are caught? Again, another question that writers should always be asking is: What is the worst possible thing that could happen here? Or: What is my character most afraid of? Make sure it is something that most people in the audience would also be afraid of. I've written a separate section on establishing and raising the stakes in your story – apply the techniques from that chapter here.

Often we have seen the pursuers in action before the chase begins – we have seen them do something horrible to someone else and don't want the same thing to happen to the protagonist in the chase scene. But at other times we are thrown straight into the chase with no foreknowledge and had to figure out who is who and what is going on 'on the fly.' There are many films that begin with a chase scene – beginning *in medias res* – to draw the audience into the action before pausing to go back and explain how this situation came about. In such cases visual clues from the actions of the characters involved – physical appearance, how they move, what they do and say – tell us whether the person being pursued is the hero or the villain. The chase scene, like the burglary scene, is one that has built-in tension. No matter who the characters are, we are drawn into the action and quickly come to desire a particular outcome – the bad guy is caught or the good guy escapes. In the short-term, just the chase enough is to establish the stakes – 'getting caught' the immediate terrible fate that awaits the person being chased. That can be enough, to begin with, but later we need to expand on this in terms of the overall stakes within the story.

4. Why is the Chase Taking Place?
There are two things to bear in mind here. First, within the world of the story, what has caused the pursuers to go after the pursued? Second, in terms of the story as a whole, what function does the chase scene serve? How does it further the plot and reveal information about the characters involved? Does it serve to take the hero of the story closer to his ultimate story-objective or is it a setback? The scene must have a purpose beyond the fact that your story needs action at this point. Yes, you can come up with its purpose retrospectively – create an excuse for having this set-piece scene or series of scenes – but it has got to be a valid reason. Bad movies have chase sequences inserted for the sake of having chase sequences, but good movies make them an integral part of the plot. The same is true for novels – readers will start skimming and turning pages if they're faced with action that isn't properly motivated within the context of the story.

The question is, Why does someone want to catch the character who is being pursued? The motivation for the chase should be approached in the same way as the motivation for any other action in the story. Someone wants something. To get something, to keep something, or to take something. To make something happen or to prevent something from happening. To get to a place, stay in a place, or escape from a place. To find something or to hide something. To protect something or to destroy something. To save someone or to kill someone. To meet a deadline. To make a pre-arranged rendezvous. To deliver an item. To prevent an item falling into the 'wrong hands.' Each character or group of characters – pursuer and pursued – will have an overall story-objective or long-term goal and a related shorter term scene goal, which is effectively a stepping stone or staging post on the way to the ultimate goal. The chase must be motivated by something that relates to this longer-term objective. 'Escaping' or 'capturing the fugitive' is a short-term goal that is something important in a larger context. If the escapee has something that the pursuers want to obtain and that thing is fragile, then killing the escapee by blowing them up or running them down won't be an option and this constrains the actions the pursuers can take. But if the objective is just to stop the escapee getting away, then all options are on the table. Or in the armoury.

5. Where is the Chase Taking Place?
The location for your chase is probably the most important choice you have to make here. If people are going to refer to your chase sequence as being memorable, they will refer to it as 'the sewer chase' or 'the fairground chase' or whatever. If you can find (or invent) a location that hasn't been used before and that suits the tone and theme of your story – and if you can utilise it in a way that makes it an *integral* part of the action rather than just a backdrop... you stand a good chance of having created a memorable chase.

There's a question you can ask yourself here – and I'm pretty sure you can guess what it is: What is the worst possible location that you could make your hero run through? How does this location disadvantage the hero and give the bad guys an edge? In what ways is the hero physically, emotionally, or psychologically unsuited for this location?

The decisions you have to make about this location are the same for any setting in your story – but their importance is amplified. Individual locations are very different places at different times of day and not just in terms of daylight versus moonlight. Time of day can determine how many people are around and what kinds of people are around. Are there crowds during the day – shoppers and families? Then is it deserted at night? Are there crowds of teenagers or homeless people after dark? Are some areas closed – gates locked and chained – after dark? Is the car park deserted after the mall has closed? Is the brightly lit supermarket all but deserted? Does the chase take place inside or outside – or in a combination of the two?

The season or time of year should also be considered. Is it a holiday season? Warm weather or cold? Icy? So cold it hurts your lungs when you breathe? So hot and humid that it is impossible to draw breath? Overcast? Foggy? Or dazzling sunlight and blue skies? Shadows or nowhere to hide? Lightning and thunder? Torrential rain forming rivers in the streets or turning the paths to clinging mud? Strong winds that you have to lean against and which whip branches into your face? How does it *feel* to be running in this environment? Can you see or hear who is behind you?

What is the terrain like? Urban? Desert? Farmland? Forest? Is it open and barren or is there cover that you can use to hide for a moment and draw breath? Are you running on tarmac, sand, gravel, mud or something else? Wading through a stream? Avoiding holes in the ground, marsh or quicksand? Are there trees and bushes or other plants? Animals or other inherent dangers? Is the ground littered with trash or other debris? Are there fences and walls that characters have to go over, under, around, or through? Barbed or razor wire? Electric fences? Security cameras? Patrolling guards and/or guard dogs? Searchlights? Is the ground flat or steeply sloped? Smooth or rough? Uneven? Are there stairs? Is there shale or some other surface that threatens to shift or trip the runners? Think in terms of obstacles and other things that could slow a person down. Think about things the pursued character could do to try and slow the pursuers down or to trick them into thinking he has gone a different way. Think of hiding places that the pursued or the pursuers could use. If you're planning on including parkour or martial arts fight moves, think about where they could be staged.

Always try to create specific visual images in what you write – this is true for a screenplay as well as a novel, because you need to make the reader of the screenplay see images in their head before the movie is shot. Whatever location you choose you have to make the reader see things that are specific to that place – and the action of the chase should be such that it makes use of the qualities that are unique to that place.

There are some locations that have been done to death and are too clichéd to be included in a modern thriller as a primary location – glimpses of them in passing are fine, but I wouldn't set my whole chase in or on one. Sewers, fire escapes, and rooftops head this list. Parking garages and subway stations are near the top too. Restaurants and hotel kitchens? Been done – lots of times. Weddings? Seen it. Mardi Gras and street parades including marching bands and cheerleaders? Been there, done that.

Try and think of alternative locations that offer the same opportunities for running, jumping, slips and falls but which we haven't seen numerous times before. If you can't come up with a brand new location, try and use an old one in a fresh way – make the action of the chase different to anything we've seen before. Have your characters be completely at odds or incongruous in the location. Use familiar objects in unexpected ways. Make it look as though you are going to show us the thing we've seen a hundred times before – and then pull the rug out from under us. Readers like to *think* they know what is coming, but they love to be surprised.

6. Which Way Did He Go? – Route Planning
Journeys, like stories, need to be carefully planned. Unfortunately there isn't yet the equivalent of a GPS satellite navigation system for creating chases or other fictional trips, so we'll have to do it the old-fashioned way. Having said that, if you're using a real geographical location, you can use Google Maps and Google Street View to find your way and locate recognisable landmarks. But even then, you're allowed some poetic licence in terms of distances and what place is accessible from which location. You probably have more licence in novels than in movies – almost every movie on IMDb has a 'Goof' entry that says something like 'you can't get to Pottery Barn by turning left off the highway there, you have to go through the underpass and then turn right.' These things matter to some people.

Even if you're using a completely made-up location, it is helpful to have an idea before you begin writing – or before you edit the final draft – of the layout of the land. Sketch a map if it helps. Or use a real place and change the street and place names. At the very least you need to know where your hunted character starts from and where they end up. In between you need to plan out the different types of area they pass through – the mall is next to the street market; the parking garage is under the mall, but can only be entered on the east side, with the exit being on the south side. The road that heads towards the railway line is a dead end for motor vehicles, but there is a footbridge over the lines. The river flows to the west of the mall and curves to the slightly inwards once it passes the old steelworks. If you do just make it up as you go when writing the first draft – which is often the best way to get words on the page – go back and logic-check it afterwards with a sketch map to make sure you haven't written something that is impossible. Most readers won't care, but there will always be someone that knows you said Pottery Barn was north of the mall but you had your hero turn west when he went to buy linens to bind his wounds. Having a basic map blocked out can help you keep your characters orientated and also help you plan the route of, say, one of the villain's people who circles around to head off the villain and lies in ambush near the railway footbridge. The trick, as in most things, is to make the reader believe that you know what you're doing. As long as they don't catch you in a serious mistake, they will trust you on all the rest. Sketch maps can be particularly useful if you have characters circling back to a place they were at before – you may need to know whether the dumpsters were to the right or the left of the fire exit and if there's a street light, which side the darkest shadows will be thrown by a particular object.

Early on in the chase, you need to let the audience know what safe location the hunted person is aiming to reach – and ideally it should be a place that we can *see* in a movie, so that at any point we can tell how near, or far, they are from this goal. This is another way that we can build suspense – will he or won't he escape to safety? He's getting closer – oh, no, now he's been forced into retreat and is further away... If we can also see the route the escapee plans to use, and then see it blocked in some way by enemy forces, we share the escapee's frustration. Obviously, in a novel you have to achieve the same things with a combination of dialogue and description. If you want to have your character running towards a particular landmark – real or imagined – then it may be worth planting that location in the reader's mind *before* the chase begins in earnest. You can mention it in passing as part of your 'establishing shot' scene description – in a novel or a screenplay – and note its approximate location in relation to, say, the shopping mall.

7. What Happened Then? – Sequencing Events

As well as planning out your physical journey, you need to plot out the significant events that happen along the way. Even if the chase is only a single scene, it will have a beginning, a middle, and an end. It is triggered by some sort of inciting incident that presents a challenge that the hunted person and/or the hunter must respond to. What brings hunted and hunter together and sparks off the chase? Each side will have a scene objective – to capture or to escape – and each will face obstacles on the path towards their objective, and each will behave as active opposition to the other: we call this rising action or rising tension. This conflict will build over time to a final climactic event. Each individual scene and sequence of scenes is like a mini story in its own right, each with a three-act structure in miniature.

Once you have decided how the chase begins and how it ends, you can come up with a few interesting events in between, and then place them in ascending order of dramatic – physical and emotional – impact. There will be accident and near-misses. In a long chase there may be a brief pause just after the midpoint of the chase to allow the hunted to catch his or her breath and decide what to do next. They will have tried the obvious actions that anyone would try to get away, they have failed, and now they have to come up with something more creative. You will need to think about those 'obvious choices' and come up with reasons why they don't work. You also need to answer the obvious questions like, Why doesn't he just run to the police? Or, Why doesn't she just scream the place down? And you have to deal with the ever-present cell phone – Why can't they just call for help?

At various points you will need to show how close the pursuers are to the hunted person. Is the gap between them growing or shrinking? And you may need to show the relative positions of different members of the pursuer's team, especially if they're heading off to set-up an ambush somewhere ahead of the hunted person.

At some point during the chase we will see what the bad guys are prepared to do in pursuit of their goal – a demonstration of their ruthlessness. This will also serve to emphasise the danger faced by the protagonist. You will also probably need to have at least one near-miss – the hunted person is actually cornered or caught by one of the hunters. It is a moment of panic and the hunted person has to come up with a way of escaping. This may be the first time that they have to go against their own moral values and deliberately hurt someone. This is where the character discovers what they are capable of in a life or death situation – do they have what it takes? It may also be a point when they switch from being a victim to becoming more proactive – this usually happens at the end of sequence three or at the midpoint/end of sequence four.

After the midpoint of the chase, there may be a brief pause or lull in the action – and then, in the same fashion as in the story as a whole, there will be a rapid decline in the protagonist's fortunes. Things will begin to go wrong and he will systematically lose every advantage or source of comfort or assistance that he had. He will suffer discomfort and then injury. Any weapon or shield he had will be lost. Escape routes will be closed off one by one, until only the riskiest remains. If he had an ally – either with him in the chase zone or outside it providing some kind of help or a potential escape vehicle – that person will be taken from him. They may be captured or killed; they may become so afraid or in such danger that they abandon their post, or they may betray the hunted person and side with the bad guys.

In a long chase, you may give the hunted person a false sense of victory near the end – have them thinking they've got away, only to have the bad guys reappear and closer than ever. Or perhaps the hunted person has walked blindly into a trap or ambush. This is the equivalent of their 'darkest hour' in this scene sequence.

8. What Happened before the Chase?
Where does the chase fit within the context of the overall story? If the chase happens in the middle of the story, it's context may be obvious. But if it occurs as the opening scene, there will come a point where you have to reveal to the audience or reader what happened before. You might do this literally by going back and showing the scene or scenes that occurred a day, a week, or a year earlier, or you may have these earlier events revealed in dialogue, or you may just hint at them and leave the viewer to fill in the blanks – it really depends on how complex and/or how important these earlier events are. And how dramatically they can be portrayed. After a good chase sequence – or action sequence of any kind – you have 'earned' a breathing space where you can present less frenetic activities, but in a thriller you don't want to stop things dead and spend ages on exposition. In a thriller, the less exposition you have the better.

9. Weapons?
One of the questions you have to ask about your hunted character early on is whether they are the sort of person who carries a knife or gun – and knows how to use it. If they are, we need to know if they would shoot it at anyone who is pursuing them, or whether they would only ever use it as a last resort in a life or death situation.

If someone is running away, using a knife or a gun against their pursuers is tricky. They have to stop and turn and aim and fire – during which time the pursuers are getting closer and closer.

Weapons are another area where the hero is usually portrayed as an underdog – he is heavily out-gunned. The bad guys have Uzis and the hero has a pocket knife. Also, it is more fun if we see the hero having to improvise, finding things to use as a weapon or a shield. Heroes are always more ingenious than the bad guys, that's why we love *Macgyver*. Often the hero dodges bullets and doesn't use weapons himself unless he is cornered, stops to take a breather, or reaches the end of the chase scene. Obviously martial arts heroes operate to a different rulebook, but even then the good guy tends to rely on his own hands and feet, improvised use of available props, and his own ingenuity.

10. Breathless Prose – Can You Feel It?
You need to make your reader *feel* what it is like to be on the run and/or what it is like to be pursuing someone. We need to show how it feels physically to run harder and faster than we've ever run before. And we need to show what it feels like to fear for your life. Physically we have to evoke the pounding of feet on the ground, the rapid pumping of the heart, and the harsh rasping of breath. Running makes us sweat – but fear could make it cold sweat. Clothing may be constricting or become soaked with perspiration. Brightly coloured clothes may need to be dirtied down or discarded because they present too much of a target. Remember your high school biology lessons? You never thought that stuff would come in useful. What does adrenaline do to the body? How about that rush of endorphins you get when you exercise hard? How does running on a full stomach make you feel? Does running on an empty stomach make you feel light-headed? What about lack of water? Is it hard to breathe in icy cold air, rain, fog or hot and humid air? What about pollution or dust? What about trying to hide quietly when your breath is wheezing in and out making a noise like a steam engine? What if you lose your glasses or a contact lens? Twist your ankle? Skin a knee or an elbow? Tear your clothes?

There will be little emotional highs when you think you're getting away, quickly replaced by frustration and despair when the enemy reappears behind you, closer than they were before.

Try to involve as many of the senses as you can to allow the reader to share the experience of the hunted person. If the escapee has ducked out of sight and is hiding, we can share in the sounds he hears as he tries to determine if anyone is close by – is that the scuffing of a shoe? A pebble dislodged? Is that a hunter in the bushes or just the breeze stirring the leaves? Have the escapee hold their breath and listen – hopefully the audience will hold their breath too. You can evoke the sense of touch by having the character encounter sharp or prickly things like shards of glass, razor wire, thorns, or splinters; rough surfaces that take the skin off a knuckle or knee; stinging nettles; rope burn; extreme heat or cold; cold water or burning desert sands; walking carefully on spongy rotten stairs or floorboards; balancing on a narrow beam over a steep drop; contending with the buffeting of strong winds; feeling around on a debris-strewn floor for a dropped object; cold water running down the neck or other shiver-inducing sensations; or trying to suppress a sneeze when a cloud of dust is disturbed. All of these things can help the reader feel like they too are in the scene.

You may also be able to evoke certain odours – perhaps the hero catches a whiff of gasoline and realises there is a risk of fire or even an explosion. Or he can smell the cigar or cigarette of one of the villain's men, so knows he is close. The scent of a rotting carcass and the buzzing of flies can be quite disturbing. The smell of smoke in a wooden building might be a spur to action while the scent of freshly cut pine might be a clue to something very different. A familiar smell in the 'wrong' place, or an unfamiliar smell in an ordinary location, may be significant – they may offer a new danger, a possibility of a weapon, or a clue to the conspiracy that is at the heart of the story.

At the same time, you're trying to evoke cocktail of emotions – fear, hope, excitement, disappointment, frustration, gallows humour, elation, and despair. It is that old cliché the emotional rollercoaster ride – and you as the writer have to use all of the techniques in this chapter and elsewhere in the book to orchestrate it.

11. Does It Hurt When I Do This? – Injuries Sustained
Running, jumping, climbing, slipping and falling are physical activities that can potentially injure the hunter or the hunted. That's before we even consider gunshots, knives, or other projectiles being hurled by one side at the other. There are also physical obstacles – moving and stationary – including stairs, doors, glass windows, falling masonry, motor vehicles, and pedestrians. Plus any traps or ambushes that one side has laid for the other. If your characters get through all of this unscathed, your reader or audience is going to feel that they weren't giving it their all. Obviously, comedy chases need comedy injuries, but your standard thriller chase is going to exact some physical toll on those involved. At the very least, the hero's white vest is going to look grey and sweaty and have bloodstains on it. That's a bit of a cliché now. And so is having the hero have to take a moment to sew up his own wounds.

12. What Other Damage is Done?
With a chase or a fight sequence it is not only the participants who are injured. The action may have consequences for other characters – whether innocent bystanders or not-so-innocent observers or colleagues of the hunter or hunted. There is usually property damage too – and the bigger the budget of the movie the more property is likely to be wrecked. Obviously, the chase scene needs to be pitched at a level of emotional and physical damage that is appropriate for its position in the overall story structure. If it is the climactic scene, you can pull out all the stops and make it as big as you want. But if it is somewhere in the middle of the story, it needs to be on a smaller scale than your sequence seven and eight climax. An opening chase can be pretty big as a grabber, but it too shouldn't be bigger than the climactic 'battle' in Act III.

Bear in mind also that the chase isn't just a stand-alone unit of story. Actions or decisions made during the chase should have consequences that affect the way the plot develops later. Delayed consequences are one of the things that helps tie a story together and make it feel less episodic – they help show the reader that the writer didn't just make this stuff up as he went along.

13. What was the Point of All This?
Every scene or sequence of scenes has to achieve some plot purpose – it checks off one of the plot points that you included in your plot outline: 'Hero discovers that Harry Lime isn't dead,' for example, or 'Hero reaches antique shop and discovers the man he met earlier wasn't the owner.' If you are writing an extended chase sequence, it may check off more than one plot point.

14. How Does the Chase End?
The chase ends when the hunted person either escapes, is captured, surrenders, or is killed. He or she may be trapped and the scene may then become a fight to escape; or the hunted character may set a trap to catch the pursuer, disabling or imprisoning that character so they are unable to continue the chase. Either way, the end of the chase will have a climax and resolution, even if it then hooks straight into the next action of the story.

If the hunted person escapes, you need to show *how* they got away. If the hunters capture this character, we need to see how they managed it. Coincidence and luck probably shouldn't play any part in deciding what happens in your story – you're allowed one coincidence as part of your inciting incident, such as your hero being in the wrong place at the wrong time, but after that you should stick to cause and effect. The outcome of an action should come about because of a successful move made by one of the participants or because of a mistake made by one of them. Of course you're allowed to 'cheat' and plant something earlier in the story that will allow the participant to be successful in the chase: it's not really cheating if you've tipped the reader off about the card hidden up your sleeve. Of course, it could be more fun to have the thing you've planted not be where it was planted, or have it not operate in the way expected, or have it completely backfire. You can also plant a red herring early in the chase so that readers think they know how it will be used at the end – and then not use it in that way. This helps avoid predictability and protects you from 'telegraphing' your scene's ending.

You can, if you want to, end the chase with a twist. This could be, as mentioned above, an escape by the hunted person that turns out not to be an escape. Or the hunted person could get to the place or the person they had been aiming for all along and discover that they have been let down or betrayed. Or a person who has doggedly pursued the hunted person (someone who is not the main 'villain') may turn out to be someone who wants to help the hunted person. Or an ally may turn out to be working for the villain. Or the hunted person may discover that they have been duped and put at risk by someone who is using them. Another sort of twist has the hunter or the hunted – perhaps even both? – turn out not to be who we thought they were.

15. What Happens After the Chase?
Most importantly, what are the participants' immediate reactions to what has just happened? Firstly, how do they *feel* – physically and emotionally – about

what they have just experienced? Then, what are their immediate actions? And then, how does the outcome of the chase affect their medium and/or long-term plan? And final, what action do they decide to take next? It will probably be necessary to answer these questions for both the good guy(s) and the bad guy(s).

How to Write a Chase Novel or Screenplay

Here I have provided a template for a pure chase movie – of which there are probably very few. I used *The Fugitive* and David Morrell's *First Blood* as my examples here. *Duel* is another example, told entirely from the point of view of the pursued – and persecuted – driver played by Dennis Weaver. Many other movies are hybrids, mixing this plot with elements of another – *Jaws* is part chase and part monster movie; *The Terminator* is part chase, part technology gone wrong; *Smokey and the Bandit* is part chase, part criminal caper; *Midnight Run, Thelma and Louise, Bonnie & Clyde,* and *Butch Cassidy and the Sundance Kid* are part chase and part buddy movie; *Romancing the Stone* is part chase, part romance; *Halloween* is part chase, part horror movie. There are hundreds of other examples in many different genres – the chase is a very versatile plot.

The basic structure of the chase story looks like this:

Act I: Set-up the hunter, the hunted, and what is at stake for each of them.
Act II: The chase – various twists and turns, reversals and revelations.
Act III: Climax and resolution – the hunted is captured or escapes.

Remember that Act I includes sequences 1 and 2; Act II includes sequences 3 and 5, the midpoint, and sequences 5 and 6; and Act III is made up of sequences 7 and 8. In the following pages are details of what needs to be included in the plot for each of these eight sequences.

Sequence 1
The protagonist is introduced – he has much in common with the hero of an amateur-on-the-run thriller in that he is an amateur who accidentally becomes mixed up in a conspiracy. In the early stages of the story he is effectively a victim of circumstance who, having stumbled on some evidence of the conspiracy, will find himself attracting the interest of the bad guys, who want to prevent him from sharing what he has learned with the authorities.

The protagonist also finds himself the victim of an injustice – accused of a crime he didn't commit. This may have been deliberately set-up by the bad guys as a way of making it impossible for the protagonist to go to the authorities, or it may have been an accidental by-product of actions related to the bad guys' conspiracy. He is usually arrested and taken into custody.

Finally, we need to give the protagonist a very credible reason for going on the run – typically that means that his life has to be in danger. He has to run in order to stay alive – even though it seems to show that he is guilty of the crime of which he has been accused. The protagonist may even find himself 'rescued' by the bad guys or sprung from jail by them and then have to escape and go on the run from them *and* the police.

Things move very rapidly, setting up the protagonist and his basic situation so that by the end of this sequence he is ready to run. The climax of the sequence – the equivalent of the challenge or 'call to adventure' – is an opportunity to escape. Should he stay or should he go?

In *The Fugitive*, Dr. Richard Kimble (Harrison Ford) finds himself arrested, accused of the murder of his own wife, tried, convicted and sentenced to death. As he is transported to prison after the trial, the prisoners on the bus revolt and attack the guards. This results in a dramatic accident and Kimble is presented with an opportunity to escape.

Sequence 2

The protagonist decides to run and escapes from the authorities – he may be assisted by another prisoner of by the villain or one of the villain's men. Depending on the nature of this accomplice, he and the protagonist may part on friendly terms or the protagonist may need to escape from him. Or the protagonist may just have escaped alone – however he gets there, the protagonist begins sequence two alone and on the run.

The escape having been completed successfully, we are now introduced to the main character who will hunt the escapee. We'll call this opponent or antagonist the hunter. He may work for the authorities, or he may work for the villain; he may be the villain's henchman or he could be the main villain himself. His objective is to hunt down and capture – or perhaps kill – the escaped protagonist. We see what sort of person the hunter is – professional, experienced, relentless, self-confident – and see a demonstration of his abilities. This is not someone you want to mess with. He is probably more like a James Bond expert operative – or like the professional assassin in *The Day of the Jackal* – than a robotic bureaucrat. We see that he is a much more competent, ingenious and self-reliant individual than the run of the mill lawmen who are also seeking the escaped protagonist. Compared to this hunter, the protagonist is very much an amateur. How long will he be able to avoid capture?

Meanwhile, the protagonist is still making his escape, trying to put as much space between himself and the authorities as possible. He may have to completely abandon his old life – it is not safe for him to go to any place he has been known to use previously and it is dangerous for him to contact anyone he knows – the police will be watching all of these places and all of these people. At this stage, the protagonist will do the things that any of us might do – changing his clothes and his appearance to reduce the risk of being recognised. If he suffered an injury during his escape he may need to obtain bandages and other supplies. And having been on the run for hours he needs food and drink. He will probably also try and find shelter in a low-budget motel. The protagonist knows that the police will be looking for him and he knows that the bad guys will send someone after him – but he doesn't yet know that a professional hunter is on his trail. At the moment his priorities are meeting his own basic needs and finding somewhere to hide out for a while. Later he will sit down and come up with some sort of plan for what to do next.

The hunter has already picked up the protagonists trail. We see him visiting places that the protagonist has been – getting closer and closer. The protagonist is unaware of the approaching danger until... a near miss. The protagonist's basic survival instincts warn him and he spots the danger just before the hunter spots him or seizes him. He runs. And it is at this point that the chase proper begins.

In *The Fugitive*, faced with the choice of death row or escape, Kimble decides to run. The hunter appears in the form of Deputy U.S. Marshal Sam Gerard (Tommy Lee Jones) and his team, who quickly take charge and organise the hunt for the escaped convict. Kimble makes his way to the nearest hospital where he treats his own injuries, then he steals an ambulance to make his escape.

Sequence 3
We've now crossed from Act I to Act II and the protagonist is in the 'strange new world' – being on the run with a hunter close behind him is his new reality and he has to learn to deal with it. While the protagonist was 'on the run' in sequence two, in the third sequence he is actually 'being chased.' Here the hunter will get the protagonist in his sight for the first time and the hunted will catch his first glimpse of the man (or team) hunting him.

The first half of sequence three is an extended chase – either on foot or in vehicles or using a combination of the two. It may be broken up into a series of chase sequences. Tension mounts as the hunter(s) get(s) closer and closer to the hunted but then, just as capture seems imminent, the protagonist does something smart and slips away. The hunter then proves how good he is by figuring out what the protagonist did and follows. This then leads to the first face-to-face meeting between hunter and hunted, effectively personalising their conflict – they now know each other. And somehow the hunted manages to get away from the hunted.

In *The Fugitive*, Kimble ends sequence two by stealing an ambulance and escaping. Gerard learns about this and gives chase in a helicopter. Kimble is trapped in a road tunnel and law enforcement officers enter from either end, guns drawn, so that it seems his capture is inevitable. But he manages to elude them. Gerard realises that Kimble has gone down a storm drain and the chase continues down in the drains. And this leads to another, even closer call – Gerard corners Kimble and they have their first face-to-face scene. The only way for Kimble to escape is for him to do something unpredictable and crazy. He jumps. This happens round about the middle of sequence three.

This escape gives the hunter a new respect for his prey – the hunted has proved himself to be an ingenious and brave opponent, though there is also a recognition that the hunted is a desperate man who is prepared to take crazy chances to try and elude his pursuers.

The second half of sequence three is less frenetic as hunter and hunted pause to consider what has gone before and to plan their next move. Having lost sight of his prey, the hunter uses the usual methods for reacquiring the target. If the hunted man's escape attempt was particularly dangerous, he may begin by searching for a body, even though he feels that his prey probably survived the attempt. Then hounds are used to try and pick up the scent and helicopters fly low trying to spot him from the air. Typically, night falls and they have to call off the search, saying they will pick up the trail in the morning because 'he won't get far.' Having survived his desperate escape – only just! – the hunted man hides for a while and catches his breath. Having been seen by the hunter, he may decide to change his appearance again. He also has to decide how to try and deal with his situation in the longer term – he can't run forever. He makes a plan. He is typically faced with a dilemma – he can try and get far away, where he will have to live with the constant fear that someone might come and find him; or he can turn and head back towards the most dangerous place – where his trouble all began – and tackle it head-on, in an attempt to finish it once and for all. Or die trying. Of course he's going to choose the do-or-die option. Kimble decides that the only way to deal with his problem is to go back and find the man who really killed his wife.

In *The Fugitive* sequence three ends with a scene that shows Gerard and his team conducting an operation to apprehend a fugitive. The serves to show us more about the hunter's methods and character – but also to raise the stakes for the hunted man, Kimble, by showing us what he's up against now that he's chosen not to head for the hills.

You will probably have noticed how similar this plot is to the amateur-on-the-run structure, but you should also note that the pace of the story is accelerated. The set-up is shorter and the chase begins a whole sequence earlier, and this 'worm that turned' moment when the hero decides to cease being a victim of circumstance and take the fight to the villain occurs at the end of sequence three rather than at the midpoint at the end of sequence four. The chase movie is a speeded-up version of the amateur-on-the-run. Another variation is the expert-on-the-run, but we'll come to that later.

Sequence 4
The fourth sequence is often marked by another change of location as the protagonist moves back into a more dangerous zone – back to where the trouble started for him. The first three sequences often take place in an open, woodland setting and then in the fourth sequence we move to a much more enclosed urban location. Back in the city. Later the story will probably close in even further by moving the chase to the confines of a single building or specific area of the city.

Changing location is a way of adding variety to the story. By the end of sequence three, you have probably exhausted the options for hide-and-seek and chasing in a forest setting. Moving to an urban setting gives you more options – and new dangers – to play with. Also, by moving from open countryside to the confines of a city – and later to the even smaller space of a single building – serves as a metaphor for the hunted man's predicament: the chase is closing in on him and his range of options is becoming narrower and narrower.

Back in the city, the protagonist views it in a new light. It is no longer his home or a place that feels familiar and safe. He now sees it as a place full of hidden dangers and probably more risky than the unknown forest location had seemed to him. He can no longer trust anyone or anything in this place and must be extremely cautious in everything he does. The risk of being recognised is also much greater and there are more police here than out in the open. The once-familiar city is now another 'strange new world' as he has to explore areas of it that he never set foot in before – the dangerous places, ironically, are now those where the dangers are preferable.

To survive, the protagonist may need money. To reach his ultimate goal – proving himself innocent – he may need access to information. He will cautiously contact someone he believes he can trust. That person may refuse to help – either because they are afraid for themselves or because they know they are being watched by the authorities making them a risk to the fugitive. Or that person may readily agree to help – and then later prove to be a traitor who is in cahoots with the conspirators that framed the protagonist. He or she may even turn out to be the lead villain.

Sequence four is more cat and mouse, hide-and-seek stuff than actual chase. It serves as a set-up for the chase that will come later – in sequence six. The hunter's role here is seeking – he learns that the protagonist has returned to the city and must now employ his urban hunting skills rather than his open country ones. Trying to pick up a trail in a city requires different methods – digital tracking via telephones, computers, and security cameras; and interviewing witnesses and informants. His role now becomes more a combination of hardboiled detective and professional assassin, rather than tracker and big game hunter. Is he as skilled in this environment? Sequence four – or the scene at the end of sequence three, or a combination of both – usually gives us proof that the hunter is just as dangerous here, if not more so. We will see an example of his 'soft' skills, using psychology or 'social engineering' to get the information he wants from people and we will probably also see an example of his determination and/or ruthlessness in this urban setting.

The hunter isn't a typical law enforcement officer even when he is an official employee – he is a maverick and a creative thinker. If he's a freelance criminal, a henchman, or the principal villain he is even less likely to be bound by rules and convention. We may see an example of this when the hunter is placed in a situation with a typical 'bureaucrat' – either an official one or a criminal one. He sparks off them and they are both contemptuous and afraid of him. Again, this serves to liven things up and to show the kind of person the protagonist is up against. The hunter will be gathering information about the protagonist – visiting places he went to in his 'old' life and talking to people he interacted with. The hunter is trying to put together the equivalent of a psychological profile of the type created in law enforcement – looking to find patterns of behaviour, favourite places and activities, typical reactions to situations, anything that will enable the hunter to *predict* what the protagonist will do so that he can narrow the search.

The protagonist, either out of habit or because his own investigation requires it, may visit an old haunt or the place where he was employed, putting himself at risk of discovery. He may seek to talk to or even frighten an old acquaintance or colleague, or he may simply be trying to obtain specific bits of information that will – he hopes – lead him to the real guilty party or the leaders of the conspiracy. At this stage, the protagonist may believe he is looking for an individual, a lone gunman, and will only later discover that there is a much larger conspiracy.

People that the protagonist knew before – friends and/or colleagues – may express their own opinions as to his guilt. They may say this to the hunter, to the police, or to the protagonist himself. These statements cannot necessarily be accepted at face value, as the speaker may have his own agenda and may have secrets of his or her own to hide or they may be part of the main conspiracy. They are like witnesses in an old-fashioned whodunit – some of them are unreliable witnesses and one or more of them could be a red herring.

There will be a plot point at the end of sequence four, but it may not have the same significance of the midpoint that we find in other stories – we already had that at the end of sequence three.

In *The Fugitive*, Kimble returns to Chicago. He contacts his lawyer but gets no help there. He does get some money from an old friend and colleague. Kimble then rents an apartment in a very seedy part of town and disguises himself as a janitor so he can enter the hospital where he used to work and look at the patient records in the hope of locating the one-armed man who killed his wife. Gerard and his team, meanwhile, learn that Kimble is back in the city and start questioning people, including the investigating detectives, related to Kimble's case and his wife's murder. People who previously worked with Kimble say that they believe he is innocent – though one of them is a bad guy. At the end of the sequence, the midpoint, there is a police raid on the apartment building where Kimble is living – he is trapped. But this is a false alarm, the police are actually there to arrest a drug dealer. Kimble is relieved – but his relief will be short-lived as this arrest will have consequences for him later.

Sequence 5

In many stories, sequence five concentrates on relationships and provides a glimpse of the sort of ideal life the protagonist could have if he manages to resolve his current situation. It is a glimpse of the prize. In this sequence we may learn more about the protagonist's backstory or we may see a demonstration of the sort of person he is when he is not on the run. But this ideal doesn't last long – a clue or a betrayal by someone leads the hunter to the protagonist's current location. The relative calm of the hide-and-seek phase comes to an end and the chase is about to begin again.

In *The Fugitive,* Kimble manages to obtain a list of suspects – one-armed men who might be the killer he seeks. Positive moment for the hero. The drug dealer arrested at the end of sequence four identifies Kimble as the man living in the apartment downstairs from him and Gerard and his crew search Kimble's place. Negative moment for the hero. In the hospital, Kimble uses his skills as a doctor to save the life of an injured boy. Positive moment for the hero. Gerard tracks Kimble to the hospital and begins questioning staff there. Hero in danger – the hunter is closing in. Kimble begins checking out the suspects on his list – positive action by the hero. Kimble and Gerard end up in the same location and the hunter spots the hunted. Negative moment for the hero – the chase begins again. Somewhere in the middle of this sequence we learn that it is St. Patrick's Day, setting up the location for a chase that will occur in sequence six.

From this, you can see that while sequence four had relatively few swings from positive to negative to positive in terms of the protagonist's fortunes, the pace of change really picks up again in sequence five.

Sequence 6

Sequence six begins with a chase sequence, this time in the urban setting. The protagonist, after a near-miss, manages to outwit his pursuer(s) and get away. Then come several revelations that set up the final act of the story. This sequence doesn't have the usual spiral towards disaster and darkest hour/crisis that we find in other thrillers, because we already had the decline in sequence five and the chase that begins sequence six is the equivalent of the darkest hour moment.

At the end of sequence five in *The Fugitive*, Kimble was spotted by Gerard and the chase began. The chase takes Kimble out through a building, where he outsmarts the authorities by tricking them into slowing down Gerard, and then continues into the middle of the St. Patrick's Day parade through Chicago. By changing his appearance and mingling with the crowd, Kimble is able to get away from his pursuers. Kimble then continues checking out his suspects and finally identifies the one-armed man who murdered Kimble's wife. The man is linked to a pharmaceutical company that was conducting drug trials at the hospital where Kimble was a surgeon. This is a major revelation. Kimble then deliberately draws his pursuers to the one-armed man's home, wanting them to know that this man is part of the conspiracy. Suspecting that the one-armed man has lied to him, Gerard then begins to investigate the people he is connected to. This is a major positive moment for the hero – he has identified the man who killed his wife and he has learned that her death was linked to a larger conspiracy. He now stands a much better chance of proving his own innocence – as long as he isn't captured by Gerard before he can complete his investigation.

Although we can again see some similarities with the amateur-on-the-run thriller here, there are some significant differences too. The innocent on the run learns there is a conspiracy before the midpoint and makes the decision to expose and/or stop it at the midpoint. But in the chase thriller, the hero doesn't discover that his situation is the result of a conspiracy until sequence five. The conspiracy has been a mystery until now for both protagonist and audience.

Sequence 7

We enter Act III, the final two sequences of the story. Now that he is aware of the conspiracy, the protagonist investigates more deeply. He discovers how it was that he came to be mixed up in the whole situation and there are further discoveries and revelations about who was involved and what they were doing. The hunter is investigating the same people and situations as the protagonist, knowing that if he can predict where the investigations will lead the protagonist, he can confront him there and capture him. Meanwhile, the conspirators send their henchman to deal with the protagonist, before he can learn too much and expose them, and the police are hunting the protagonist because he is a fugitive from justice. With all of these forces against him, the protagonist's options become narrower and narrower, and at the same time his investigations are leading him into the heart of the conspiracy. Everything gradually closes in and converges until, in sequence eight, the chase is confined to a single location.

As I mentioned earlier, the conspiracy is just a MacGuffin – an excuse to have a chase plot. In *The Fugitive,* the conspiracy involving the pharmaceutical company serves its purpose, but it is dealt with in a perfunctory manner and is, if we're honest, probably the weakest part of the plot. It serves only to bring hunter, hunted, and lead conspirator/villain together in the final sequence. The location, in this case, is the Chicago Hilton Hotel, where a medical conference is in progress. Before Kimble can get there to confront the villain, he has a final confrontation with the one-armed man on an elevated train. On a positive note, Kimble knocks out the one-armed man and handcuffs him to the train. But on a negative note, Kimble finds himself accused of killing a policeman who was actually shot by the one-armed man. For a second time he finds himself held responsible for this man's killing. Kimble is now on the run from the conspirators, Gerard and the U.S. Marshals, and the Chicago Police Department, who believe he is now a cop-killer. This is another 'darkest hour' for the protagonist.

Sequence 8

Everything converges on a single location, with all of the players brought together for the final chase sequence. Essentially trapped in this place, the protagonist's options are limited and capture or death seem inevitable. At this stage he is prepared to risk everything in an attempt to resolve his situation – if he can't expose the conspiracy, he is effectively dead anyway. The final pieces fall into place and the protagonist knows the whole story about the conspiracy – who did what, when, and why. Of course this makes him all the more dangerous to the conspirators who have no option but to silence the protagonist by killing him. In the final confrontation, the protagonist finds an unlikely ally in the hunter. The hunter too knows the truth about the conspiracy. He has also developed a respect for the protagonist, viewing him as a worthy opponent – they are like soldiers on opposing sides in a war. The hunter's objective hasn't changed – he is still determined to capture the protagonist. If the conspirators get in the way of this mission, the hunter will deal with them. In an ironic way, he becomes the protagonist's protector.

The protagonist ends up playing hide-and-seek with the lead conspirator/villain. Again he's in the underdog position, probably weakened or injured and unarmed. After a dramatic fight sequence and several near-misses, the protagonist outwits the villain who is probably killed in a way that includes an element of poetic justice – dying as a result of his own actions or mistakes, rather than at the hands of the protagonist, who has spent the whole story trying to prove that he is not a killer. That just leaves the final chase between protagonist and hunter. The hunter may try and persuade the protagonist to give himself up – the conspiracy has been exposed, the villain is dead, and the protagonist can now prove he wasn't responsible for the two killings that he has been accused of. Whether or not the protagonist trusts the hunter and surrenders to him will depend on the nature of the two characters, the relationship that has developed between them, and whether the hunter is an employee of the authorities or the bad guys.

Expert on the Run

I mentioned before that *The Fugitive* is an example of a chase story with an innocent amateur in the role of protagonist, but that there is another variation where the fugitive-protagonist is actually an expert. Imagine the hunted man being a James Bond-type, experienced and resourceful. A prime example of this type of story is David Morrell's 1972 novel *First Blood*. This was filmed in 1982 with Sylvester Stallone in the lead role, introducing the character of Rambo to a wider audience. The movie was a faithful adaptation of the novel up until the third act, when things get much more explosive. The Hollywood sequels take the character in a very different direction – being military action-adventure rather than thrillers. I'm going to concentrate on the novel here, which is more thriller-like and has influenced many later writers in the genre.

Sequence 1. Vietnam veteran and drifter Rambo is the victim of an injustice when Sheriff Teasle treats him as hobo and a hippy, literally driving him out of town. Taking exception to this, Rambo walks back into town. We learn something about Rambo's experience and there are hints of the psychological trauma he has suffered – today it would be referred to as post-traumatic stress disorder. It is also obvious that Rambo could be dangerous if pushed. Determined to prove himself the Alpha male, the sheriff arrests Rambo and throws him in jail. Here Rambo is subjected to further humiliations and injustices.

Sequence 2. Opens with a flashback to Rambo's treatment as a prisoner of war. He also remembers his training as a Green Beret and his escape from the Viet Cong. Back in the present, the police continue to humiliate Rambo, until finally he snaps and fights back. Injuring several officers as he escapes, Rambo then rides off naked on a stolen motorcycle. Sheriff Teasle radios his men to pursue the escapee and also phones a friend who has dogs who can track down a fugitive. Rambo uses the motorcycle to take a route that a patrol car cannot follow. After that, he continues to run on foot. With dogs and fellow officers, Teasle pursues Rambo – technically Rambo has now passed out of his jurisdiction, but Teasle doesn't want to give up and hand the chase over to the state police. Finding an old man with a still, Rambo treats him with respect and gets help in return. This ends day one of the story.

Sequence 3. Dawn the next day. Teasle and company wake and the hunt proper begins. A helicopter is brought in. The sound of it overhead reminds Rambo of the Vietnam war. There is a sharp-shooter on the helicopter firing at spots where Rambo might be hiding. The sound of approaching dogs and the near-miss with the helicopter unsettle Rambo. We learn something of Teasle's backstory. The pursuers close behind him on foot, Rambo has another encounter with the helicopter – has to shoot the sharp-shooter and this causes the helicopter to crash. He then picks off all of the hounds except one. Teasle begins to realise what sort of man he has picked a fight with. But he is not prepared to back down.

Sequence 4. Rambo shoots the last dog and their handler. Teasle finally radios the state police, asking for their help, and learns that Rambo was a Green Beret – and a war hero. A storm hits. As the situation gets further out of his control, Teasle grows angry and violent. Rambo considers his own situation – he could run and try to reach Mexico, but that would mean being a fugitive in the U.S. for at least a couple of months while he made the journey. He's also angry because Teasle has turned him into a killer again – and he's worried that perhaps he enjoys it. He decides he'll teach Teasle a lesson – let him know what it is like to be a hunted man. Teasle believes he can outwit Rambo – but all he achieves is the deaths of the last of his men. At the midpoint, the sheriff is in a position where must now face Rambo alone – hunter and hunted.

Sequence 5. Rambo is injured and his internal injuries may be serious, but still he pursues Teasle who is now running. Teasle manages to survive the night and in the morning is picked up by a State Trooper. The National Guard has also arrived and are planning their hunt for Rambo. Rambo's former mentor in the Green Berets, Captain Trautman arrives. He tells Teasle just how good Rambo is at guerrilla warfare – he will be difficult to hunt down. Up in the hills, hidden in an old mine, Rambo wakes – he is injured, feverish and doesn't want to fight anymore, but he knows that escape now will be almost impossible.

Sequence 6. Teasle looks at the men and trucks around him and wishes it was just him and Rambo facing each other. Trautman speaks about how America sends men off to war to kill for their country but doesn't want them when they come back with the smell of death on them. He also knows that Teasle, a Korean war veteran, is much more like Rambo than he wants to admit. Teasle won't admit this or the fact that he pushed Rambo into this situation. Trautman says he will help deal with Rambo – wants the situation to be handled by someone who understands Rambo. The National Guard move in in a line. Instead of retreating, Rambo moves towards them – hides as they pass by within inches of him, unaware of him. But his escape plan doesn't work out and he has to go back up into the hills where he can choose his own site for his last stand.

Sequence 7. Rambo makes it back to his hideout, but the Guardsmen are close behind, opening fire on him. Rambo considers giving himself up, but then realises there may be another way out of the mine. He crawls through narrow spaces filled with bats and beetles and is plunged into total darkness when his torch dies. He considers killing himself, but rallies and makes a final effort to get out of the cave. Teasle, meanwhile, talks to his wife on the phone – she left him recently and says she's not coming back. The sheriff straps on his gun just as the first explosions go off, signalling that Rambo has left the hills and is back in town. Rambo has stolen a police car – the explosions are a distraction, to give him cover to make it across town and to head for freedom.

Sequence 8. Rambo and Teasle in their final showdown. Both are mortally wounded, but Rambo manages to get away. Teasle says he doesn't hate Rambo anymore, just wants to be with him at the end. He seems to regard Rambo as the son he never had.

In its original form, *First Blood* is a tragedy – for both hunter and hunted – and is deeply critical of the hypocrisy connected with the treatment of American soldiers sent to fight abroad. Structurally it has some things in common with the amateur-on-the-run story and the manhunt story. There is a significant reversal at the midpoint where the hunted becomes the hunter. This is a pattern that can be seen in the novels that have been inspired by David Morrell's thriller.

Band on the Run

There is one more variation that I want to mention briefly, which is the chase/hunt thriller where a *group* of people are trying to avoid their pursuers and reach safety. This has elements of the quest, with the group passing through different areas and facing new dangers, and of the disaster story in which a group of people with different personalities and abilities have to work together to survive. One of my favourite examples of this type of film is *The Warriors* (1979) based on the 1965 novel by Sol Yurick.

14 | Bourne, Langdon & Reacher

For this final chapter, I thought it would be helpful to look at how three of the most successful thriller writers have taken the conventions of the genre and adapted them to their own ends. Robert Ludlum's Jason Bourne, Dan Brown's Robert Langdon, and Lee Child's Jack Reacher have each featured in a series of successful novels and made the crossover into big budget movies. Each of these characters is sufficiently well-known as to have their own entries on Wikipedia. What can we learn from the way these characters and plots were created?

Robert Ludlum's Jason Bourne

Robert Ludlum was an American author of twenty-seven novels, mainly suspense and conspiracy thrillers, including the Jason Bourne trilogy. Many of his stories have been adapted for film or television with further adaptations reported as being in development. Ludlum died in 2001 but several of his novels were published posthumously and works featuring his characters have been written by other authors.

The original Jason Bourne trilogy includes *The Bourne Identity* (1980), *The Bourne Supremacy* (1986), and *The Bourne Ultimatum* (1990). Matt Damon played Jason Bourne in movies based on these three novels (in 2002, 2004 and 2007) and has made the role his own, but Bourne was first portrayed by Richard Chamberlain in a 1988 television adaptation. The film series was continued with *The Bourne Legacy* (2007) in which Jeremy Renner played another agent from the same program that had 'created' Bourne. Matt Damon returned to the title role in *Jason Bourne* (2016). The character of Jason Bourne has also appeared in a series of novels – fifteen to date – written by Eric Van Lustbader. The first of these, *The Bourne Legacy* (2004) while having the same title as the fourth film has a different plot and features Bourne as the hero.

The Bourne Identity brings together a number of thriller plot elements. Jason Bourne is suffering from amnesia as the novel opens and is also recovering from physical injuries – these establish him as a sympathetic hero and create a mystery that the reader wants to see him unravel. Who is he and what happened to him? He uncovers several clues that lead him to a bank account, a mysterious organisation, and the name 'Jason Bourne.' These all raise more questions than they answer – especially when Bourne is targeted by killers. The story then uses elements from the amateur-on-the-run thriller, including a female character who is first unwilling hostage and then romantic co-protagonist. Along the way we and Bourne discover that he is not an amateur – he has physical skills and experience that indicate he is some kind of military or espionage professional. Bourne then discovers that he may be a professional assassin who had been engaged to locate and kill rival assassin 'Carlos the Jackal.' But in this story, Bourne's identity has layers within layers like an onion so that we, and he, are never quite sure whether we have finally reached his true self.

We do gradually piece together his past – including his experience as a special forces operative during the Vietnam War and his nihilism after the deaths of those closest to him.

The idea of a highly trained killer created by the military or intelligence services who then goes 'rogue' has fascinated many writers. There is an element of it in David Morrell's *First Blood* and the assassin from the film *In the Line of Fire* is another example. The character of a warrior who is trained to kill during time of war but who then cannot make a life for himself in the everyday world of peace has existed since ancient times. What do we do with our soldiers, assassins, and spies when we don't need them anymore? Patrick McGoohan also explored the fate of a former secret agent in the 1967 television series *The Prisoner*. Jason Bourne is an example of this type of character who, initially, has forgotten that he was such an agent. Even he doesn't know what he is capable of.

Robert Ludlum wove together elements from Cold War espionage stories, mystery, Vietnam military adventure, amnesia and assassination thrillers, and packaged it in a plot that used the amateur-on-the-run or chase thriller structure. This unique blend proved popular with readers in the 1980s and cinema-goers today.

Dan Brown's Robert Langdon

Dan Brown is an American author who has written several stand-alone novels and – to date – five novels featuring protagonist Robert Langdon. *Angels & Demons* (2000), *The Da Vinci Code* (2003), *The Lost Symbol* (2009), *Inferno* (2013), and *Origin* (2017). Three of these were adapted into movies with Tom Hanks in the lead role – *The Da Vinci Code* (2006), *Angels & Demons* (2009), and *Inferno* (2016). *The Da Vinci Code* is reported to have sold over eighty million copies around the world, it was the subject a couple of lawsuits, and there was a great deal of public criticism and debate in religious and artistic circles, creating the sort of publicity that money cannot buy.

Brown brought together a number of things that have always fascinated people – religious conspiracies, codes and symbols, the Knights Templar, the Holy Grail, and the art of Leonardo Da Vinci. He structured his story as the investigation of a mystery, but wrote in short chapters, keeping the action moving and pacing it like a thriller. It opens with the discovery of a body in the Louvre, posed in the manner of Da Vinci's Vitruvian Man, with a pentacle drawn in blood and a coded message beside it. Robert Langdon is called in to assist the investigation as he is a Harvard professor specialising in religious iconography and symbology. He and a police cryptographer work together to discover the meaning of the coded message. They quickly find themselves in the middle of a centuries-old conspiracy centring on the idea that Jesus had a child with Mary Magdalene and that his bloodline has survived into the present day. The plot involves two secret societies, Opus Dei and the Priory of Sion, the latter having once had Da Vinci as its leader.

Although Robert Langdon is an expert in his field and shares many qualities with traditional detectives such as Sherlock Holmes and Hercule Poirot, he is also an amateur and an innocent when it comes to physical danger and adventure: unlike Indiana Jones, he is not a university professor with an action-oriented alter ego. This 'fish out of water' element – giving an amateur a James Bond-style mission – combined with elements of the innocent on the run helps create sympathy for the character. There is also a Bond-style henchman in the form of Silas, an albino Catholic monk, and a variety of European tourist-friendly locations. Dan Brown took the conventions of coded messages from the Cold War espionage thriller and large-scale conspiracy from the political thriller and applied them to theories of religious conspiracy and hidden coded religious messages that had been in circulation since before Da Vinci's time. He put all of this together in a plot that drew on the traditional detective mystery and the innocent on the run thriller.

Lee Child's Jack Reacher

Lee Child is the pseudonym of British author James D. Grant who has written twenty-three thrillers featuring Jack Reacher as of 2018. The first was *Killing Floor* (1997) and two of the novels *One Shot* (2005, the 9th in the series) and *Never Go Back* (2013, 18th in the series) have been adapted into movies with Tom Cruise in the role of Jack Reacher – the films are *Jack Reacher* (2012) and *Jack Reacher: Never Go Back* (2016).

Jack Reacher is described in the novels as being 6 feet 5 inches tall and having scars on his abdomen from a bombing in Beirut in which he was hit by "... a fragment of a Marine sergeant's jawbone." In *Never Go Back* he is said to have "a six-pack like a cobbled city street, a chest like a suit of NFL armor, biceps like basketballs, and subcutaneous fat like Kleenex tissue." As we have seen, many thrillers have an underdog in the lead role, David versus Goliath, but Child deliberately went against that: "I thought, *Suppose the good guy is actually Goliath.*"

Reacher was a major in the United States Military Police Corps and during his thirteen-year military career received a number of medals and a marksmanship trophy. Having left the army, Reacher became a drifter, travelling with little more than a folding toothbrush. He never does laundry - when his chinos and work shirt get dirty, he buys new ones and bins the dirty ones. He doesn't own a car or a cell phone. These quirks help to humanise a character who is built like a superhero. Childs says that Reacher is a wanderer because 'he can't settle into civilian society,' but emphasises that he is mentally stable, avoiding the cliché of the military veteran haunted by his past and suffering PTSD.

Author Michael Connelly has described the Reacher novels as 'postmodern Westerns' – "They're *Shane*. A stranger comes to town and sets things right. Then he leaves town." Child recognises this when he refers to Reacher as a knight-errant.

Lee Child, in an interview with Bryan Curtis, has described them as 'revenge stories' – "Somebody does a very bad thing and Reacher takes revenge." The bad guy, as Curtis points out, is usually a bully: a drug lord, mob boss, terrorist, rogue military officer, or crooked district attorney. Reacher doesn't pick a fight with these people, he just falls into it accidentally after he has stopped to help one of the 'little guys' – a single mom, an elderly librarian, someone wrongly accused, a kidnap victim, or some other character who needs a champion. And when one of the bullies does go up against Reacher, he "... is just *obliterated*," Child says. "That's certainly cathartic for me." And Reacher suffers no angst – having killed five people in the first novel he his asked how he feels and answers, "How do you feel when you put roach powder down?"

Over the course of more than twenty novels, Childs has used a number of variations on thriller plots. Having Reacher as an ex-military policeman allows the author to adapt suspense thriller and hardboiled detective plots to his needs. When I first read *Killing Floor* I was reminded of both *First Blood* and Dashiell Hammett's *Red Harvest* – two stories in which an outsider has a profound impact on a small American town. The laconic first-person narration in that book also made me think of Humphrey Bogart and 'the Man with No Name' from those Sergio Leone Westerns – and that's how I imagined Reacher, a young Clint Eastwood with muscles. The second novel, *Die Trying*, is more like a James Bond adventure in which the villain is the leader of a militia group who wants to create his own nation. In *One Shot* Reacher sets out to prove a former military sniper innocent of murder. But for all their variety, Child says that they are 'the same only different' – the basic template has Reacher come into town and encounter a little guy who is suffering injustice at the hands of a bully and then Reacher obliterates the bully and goes on his way. The appeal of the stories, as Bryan Curtis points out, is that they recognise our everyday frustrations, the anger we feel at being humiliated, and allow us to watch the equivalent of our personal bully or bureaucratic asshole have the snot pounded out of him. That's certainly cathartic for me.

While Jack Reacher appeals as an unapologetic alpha male, there is another side of him that appeals to female readers, as Child explained to Robert Bidinotto: "... Reacher likes strong, realistic women, and he treats women with respect. Reacher is a post-feminist. He doesn't cut them any slack, but also he has no negative preconceptions. If you're a woman, he will be your friend; but if necessary, he will kill you. He doesn't make any gender distinctions."

Bibliography

Listed below are the sources I used when researching this book. They are grouped under broad headings relating to the subject matter of particular chapters, so that all of the material relating to *suspense*, for example, is listed together. As well as the books and websites listed below, I made extensive use of *IMDb (Internet Movie Database)* and *Wikipedia* when researching sub-genres and examples of films and novels.

For fun, you might also want to look at the *TV Tropes* website for their guidelines on creating a thriller title:
https://tvtropes.org/pmwiki/pmwiki.php/Main/MadLibThrillerTitle

And Mikhail 'Koveras' Aristov's random *Thriller Titles Generator* based on the guidelines:
http://legacy.koveras.org/thriller/

General References and Chapters 1, 2 and 5
Amis, Kingsley – *The James Bond Dossier*. Jonathan Cape, 1965.
Baden-Powell, Robert – *My Adventures as a Spy*. C. Arthur Pearson, Ltd, 1915
Barzun, Jacques – 'Meditations on the Literature of Spying,' The Scholar, Spring 1935
Berger, Arthur Asa – *Popular Culture Genres: Theories and Texts*. SAGE Publications Inc., 1992
Brill, Lesley – *The Hitchcock Romance: Love and Irony in Hitchcock's Films*. Princeton University Press, 1988
Buono, Oreste Del and Umberto Eco – *The Bond Affair*, translated by R. A. Downie. Macdonald, 1966
Cawelti, John G. & Bruce A. Rosenberg – *The Spy Story*. University of Chicago Press, 1987
Cobley, Paul – *The American Thriller: Generic Innovation and Social Change in the 1970s*. Palgrave, 2000
Crowdus, Gary (ed.) – *The Political Companion to American Film*. Lakeview Press, 1994
Derry, Charles – *The Suspense Thriller: Films in the Shadow of Alfred Hitchcock*. McFarland & Company, Inc., 1988
Diemert, Brian – *Graham Greene's Thrillers and the 1930s*. McGill-Queen's University Press, 1996
Duncan, Ian – 'Introduction,' in: Stevenson, Robert Louis – *Kidnapped* (Oxford World's Classics). Oxford University Press, 2014
Duns, Jeremy – 'The Secret Origins of James Bond,' *Spywise.net*, (Date? January 2010?) http://www.spywise.net/jamesBond.html
Fitzgerald, Peter (Producer & Director) – *Destination Hitchcock: The Making of North by Northwest*, 2000. Note: DVD extra on *North by Northwest* released in 2000.
Fleming, Ian – 'Bond's Creator on the Thriller.' Originally published in *The Spectator*, 1955. Text retrieved 10/08/2013: http://bondandbeyond.forumotion.com/t151-ian-fleming-on-the-thriller-the-riddle-of-the-sands
Fleming, Ian – 'How to Write a Thriller.' Originally published in *Show*, August 1962. Text retrieved 10/08/2013: http://bondandbeyond.forumotion.com/t151-ian-fleming-on-the-thriller-the-riddle-of-the-sands
Fleming, Ian and Raymond Chandler – 'Ian Fleming and Raymond Chandler in Conversation – The Lost Interview,' *Five Dials*, no. 7 (Date? November 2014?)
Gannon, Michael B. – *Blood, Bedlam, Bullets, and Badguys: A Reader's Guide to Adventure/Suspense Fiction*. Libraries Unlimited, 2004
Harper, Ralph – *The World of the Thriller*. The Johns Hopkins University Press, 1974
Hepburn, Allan – *Intrigue: Espionage and Culture*. Yale University Press, 2005
Hicks, Neill D. – *Writing the Thriller Film: The Terror Within*. Michael Wiese Productions, 2002
Hoffman, Arthur Sullivant – *Fiction Writing Self-Taught: A New Approach*. W. W. Norton & Company, 1939
Johnson, Paul – 'Sex, Snobbery and Sadism,' *The Spectator*, 5th April 1958

Keating, H. R. F. – *Whodunit? : A Guide to Crime, Suspense and Spy Fiction.* Windward (W.H. Smith & Son Ltd.), 1982
Maass, Donald – *Writing the Breakout Novel.* Writer's Digest Books, 2001
Palmer, Jerry – *Thrillers: Genesis and Structure of a Popular Genre.* London: Edward Arnold, 1978
Playboy Magazine – 'Ian Fleming: Playboy Interview,' *Playboy,* December 1964.
Rodell, Marie, F. – *Mystery fiction: Theory and Technique.* Hammond, Hammond & Company, 1954
Rubin, Martin – *Thrillers.* Cambridge University Press, 1989
Snyder, Blake – *Save the Cat Goes to the Movies.* Michael Wiese Productions, 2007
Symons, Julian – *Bloody Murder: From the Detective Story to the Crime Novel – A History.* Papermac, 1992
Tapply, William G. – *The Elements of Mystery Fiction: Writing the Modern Whodunit* (2nd ed.) Poisoned Pen Press, 1995
Truffaut, François – *Hitchcock (Hitchcock/Truffaut).* Simon & Schuster, 1984
Usborne, Richard – *Clubland Heroes: A Nostalgic Study of Some Recurrent Characters in the Romantic Fiction of Dornford Yates, John Buchan and Sapper.* Barrie & Jenkins, 1953.
Wright, Peter and Paul Greengrass – *Spycatcher: The Candid Autobiography of a Senior Intelligence Officer.* Heinemann, 1987.

Conspiracy (Chapter 3)
Barkun, Michael – *A Culture of Conspiracy: Apocalyptic Visions in Contemporary America.* University of California Press, 2003
Berlet, Chip – 'Interview: Michael Barkun,' *New Internationalist Magazine,* September 2004 http://www.publiceye.org/antisemitism/nw_barkun.html
Berlet, Chip – 'Zog Ate My Brains,' *New Internationalist,* October 2004
Nefes, Türkay Salim – 'Political Parties' Perceptions and Uses of Anti-Semitic Conspiracy Theories in Turkey', *The Sociological Review* 61(2), 2013
Walker, Jesse – *The United States of Paranoia: A Conspiracy Theory.* Harper Collins, 2013

Suspense (Chapter 4)
Abbott, H. P. – *The Cambridge Introduction to Narrative.* Cambridge University Press, 2008
Bergman, S. – *Vulnerability of the Protagonist and Suspense in Drama.* (Incomplete, unpublished master's thesis) Indiana University, 1978
Brewer, William F. and Edward H. Lichtenstein – *Stories are to Entertain: A Structural-Affect Theory of Stories.* Centre for the Study of Reading Technical Report No. 265, October 1982
Brewer, William F. and Edward H. Lichtenstein – *Event Schemas, Story Schemas, and Story Grammars.* Centre for the Study of Reading Technical Report No. 197, December 1980
Bryant, J. – 'The Effect of Different Levels of Suspense and the Source of Resolution of Suspense on the Appreciation of Dramatic Presentations.' (Unpublished) University of Massachusetts, 1978(a) [Quoted in Zillmann 1980]
Bryant, J. – 'The Effect of Disposition Toward a Protagonist and of Sex of Viewer on the Appreciation of Dramatic Presentations with Variations in Degree of Suspense and Ultimate Outcome for the Protagonist.' (Unpublished) University of Massachusetts, 1978(b)
Carroll, Noel – 'Toward a Theory of Film Suspense.' *Persistence of Vision* (Summer 1984)
Chatman, Seymour – *Story and Discourse: Narrative Structure in Fiction and Film.* Ithaca: Cornell University Press, 1978
Comsiky, Paul and Jennings Bryant – 'Factors Involved in Generating Suspense.' *Humanities Communication Research* (Vol. 9, September 1982)
Dove, George N. – *Suspense in the Formula Story.* Bowling Green State University Popular Press, 1989
Frome, Jonathan and Aaron Smuts – 'Helpless Spectators.' *TEXT Technology* (Number 1, 2004)
Gerrig, Richard J. – *Experiencing Narrative Worlds: On the Psychological Activities of Reading.* New Haven: Yale University Press, 1993
Gerrig, Richard J. and Allan B. I. Bernardo – 'Readers as Problem-Solvers in the Experience of Suspense,' in: *Poetics* (No. 22, 1994)
Klausner, S. Z. 'Sport Parachuting,' in: *Motivations in Play, Games, and Sports* (ed. R. Slovenko and J. A. Knight) Dpringfield, Charles C Thomas, 1967
Klausner, S. Z. (ed.) *Why Man Takes Chances: Studies in Stress-Seeking.* Anchor Books, 1968

Lehne, Moritz and Stefan Koelsch – 'Toward a General Psychological Model of Tension and Suspense.'
Lehne, Moritz et al. – 'Reading a Suspenseful Literary Text Activates Brain Areas Related to Social Cognition and Predictive Inference.' *PLoS ONE* (6 May 2015)
Loker, Altan – *Film and Suspense: The Use of Free-Floating Anxiety by Hitchcock and Other Cineastes and by Shakespeare to Generate Suspense and Enhance the Illusion of Reality* (2nd ed.). Trafford, 2005
Lüthi, M. – *Das Volksmärchen als Dichtung. Ästhetik und Anthropologie.* Düsseldorf/Köln: Diederichs, 1975 [Quoted in Wulff 1996]
Mag Uidhir, Christy – 'An Eliminativist Theory of Suspense.' *Philosophy and Literature* (35, 2011)
Moriarty, W. D. – *The Function of Suspense in Catharsis.* Ann Arbor: G. Wahr, 1911
O'Neill, Brian – *A Computational Model of Suspense for the Augmentation of Intelligent Story Generation.* A Thesis Presented in Partial Fulfilment of the Requirements for the Degree Doctor of Philosophy in the School of Interactive Computing, Georgia Institute of Technology, December 2013
O'Neill, Brian and Mark Reidl – 'Dramatis: A Computational Model of Suspense,' in: *Proceedings of the Twenty-Eighth AAAI Conference on Artificial Intelligence.* Palo Alto: Association for the Advancement of Artificial Intelligence, 2014
Ortony, Andrew, Gerald L. Clore and Allan Collins – *The Cognitive Structure of Emotions.* Cambridge University Press, 1988
Skulsky, Harold – 'On Being Moved by Fiction.' *The Journal of Aesthetics and Art Criticism* (Vol. 39, 1980)
Smuts, Aaron – 'The Desire-Frustration Theory of Suspense,' in: *The Journal of Aesthetics and Art Criticism* (Vol. 66 No. 3, Summer 2008)
Tan, Ed S. – *Emotion and the Structure of Narrative Film: Film as an Emotion Machine.* Routledge, 1966
Walton, Kendall – *Mimesis as Make-Believe.* Harvard University Press, 1990
Wulff, Hans. J. – 'Suspense and the Influence of Cataphora on Viewers' Expectations,' in: *Suspense: Conceptualizations, Theoretical Analyses, and Empirical Explorations* (ed. Peter Vorderer, Hans J. Wulff & Mike Friedrichsen) Lawrence Erlbaum Associates, 1996
Yanal, Robert J. – 'The Paradox of Suspense.' *British Journal of Aesthetics* (Vol. 36, No. 2, April 1996)
Zillmann, Dolf – 'Anatomy of Suspense,' in: *The Entertainment Functions of Television*, edited by Percy H. Tannenbaum. Hillsdale, Lawrence Erlbaum Associates, 1980
Zillmann, Dolf and J. Bryant – 'Viewer's Moral Sanction of Retribution in the Appreciation of Dramatic Presentations. *Journal of Experimental Social Psychology* (Vol. 11, 1975)
Zillmann, Dolf and J. R. Cantor – 'Affective Responses to the Emotions of a Protagonist.' *Journal of Experimental Social Psychology* (Vol. 13, 1977)

Expert Fiction / Fiction à Substrat Professionnel (Chapter 6)
Genty, Stéphanie – 'Apparent truth and false reality: Michael Crichton and the distancing of scientific discourse,' ASp [Online], 55 | 2009
http://journals.openedition.org/asp/290
Petit, Michel – 'La fiction à substrat professionnel : une autre voie d'accès à l'anglais de spécialité,' ASp [Online], 23-26 | 1999
http://journals.openedition.org/asp/2325

Espionage Thriller (Chapter 7)
Allbeury, Ted – 'Memoirs of an Ex-Spy,' in: *Murder Ink: The Mystery Reader's Companion,* edited by Dillys Winn. Workman Publishing, 1977.
Ambler, Eric – 'Introduction' in: *To Catch a Spy: An Anthology of Favourite Spy Stories.* Fontana/Collins, 1974
Atkins, John – *The British Spy Novel: Styles in Treachery.* John Calder, 1984
Baer, Robert – 'A Dagger to the CIA,' *GQ,* 25th February 2010
https://www.gq.com/story/dagger-to-the-cia
Balachandran, V. – 'True fiction: The best spies are really quite boring,' *The Sunday Guardian*, 28th August 2011. http://www.sunday-guardian.com/analysis/true-fiction-the-best-spies-are-really-quite-boring
Barzun, Jacques – 'Meditations on the Literature of spying,' *The Scholar,* Spring 1965.

https://theamericanscholar.org/meditations-on-the-literature-of-spying
Begoum, F. M. – 'Observations on the Double Agent,' CIA.gov
https://www.cia.gov/library/center-for-the-study-of-intelligence/kent-csi/vol6no1/html/v06i1a05p_0001.htm
Burn, Michael – *The Debatable Land: A Study of the Motives of Spies in Two Ages.* Hamish Hamilton, 1970
Cardwell, John M. 'A Bible Lesson on Spying,' *Studies in Intelligence,* Winter 1978.
http://southerncrossreview.org/44/cia-bible.htm
Denning, Michael – *Cover Stories: Narrative and Ideology in the British Spy Thriller.* Routledge & Kegan Paul, 1987
Emerson, Gloria – 'Graham Greene: Our Man in Antibes,' *Rolling Stone,* 9th March 1978
https://www.rollingstone.com/culture/features/graham-greene-19780309
FBI – 'Twenty-First Century Spies,' *FBI.gov,* 22nd June 2005
https://archives.fbi.gov/archives/news/stories/2005/june/spies_02220
Gardner, John – 'The Espionage Novel,' in: *Whodunit?* Edited by H. R. F. Keating
Goodman, Sam – *British Spy Fiction and the End of Empire.* Routledge, 2015
Hartley, Anthony – 'The Great Game,' *The Spectator,* 30th October 1953.
http://archive.spectator.co.uk/article/30th-october-1953/22/the-great-game
Hopkins, Nick – 'The Libya papers: a glimpse into the world of 21st-century espionage,' *TheGuardian.com,* 9th September 2011
https://www.theguardian.com/world/2011/sep/09/libya-papers-tripoli-mi6-cia
McElroy, Damien – 'Russian Spy Ring Guide: From 21st Century to Cold War Spy Novel,' *Telegraph.co.uk,* 29th June 2010
https://www.telegraph.co.uk/news/worldnews/europe/russia/7861456/Russian-spy-ring-guide-from-21st-Century-to-Cold-War-spy-novel.html
Mendez, Tony – 'Tony's Hollywood Moscow Rules', *SpyMuseum.org*
https://www.spymuseum.org/exhibition-experiences/online-exhibits/argo-exposed/moscow-rules/tonys-hollywood-moscow-rules/
Merry, Bruce – *Anatomy of the Spy Thriller,'* Gill & Macmillan, 1977
Schindler, John R. – 'Friends from the Institute,' *20 Committee,* 29th July 2012
https://20committee.com/2012/07/29/friends-from-the-institute/
Schindler, John R. – 'The Truth About SpyWar and How 21st Century Espionage Really Works,' *Observer.com,* 21st December 2015
http://observer.com/2015/12/the-truth-about-spywar-and-how-21st-century-espionage-really-works/
Scotsman, The – 'Russian spy swap: A Checkpoint Charlie for the 21st century,' *TheScotsman.com,* 9th July 2010
https://www.scotsman.com/news/russian-spy-swap-a-checkpoint-charlie-for-the-21st-century-century-1-816817
Sun Tzu – *The Art of War,* Part 13, The Use of Spies
https://suntzusaid.com/book/13
Talbi, Karim – 'Edward Snowden: A Very 21st Century Spy.' *LiveMint.com,* 7th July 2013.
https://www.livemint.com/Politics/TyDrrk4gVAhyoX9QckrBBJ/Edward-Snowden-A-very-21st-century-spy.html
Wise, David – 'China's Spies are Catching Up,' *The New York Times,* 10th December 2011
https://www.nytimes.com/2011/12/11/opinion/sunday/chinas-spies-are-catching-up.html
Zetter, Kim – 'Tools of Tradecraft: The CIA's Historic Spy Kit,' *Wired.com,* 24th February 2011
https://www.wired.com/2011/02/cia-tools-of-tradecraft/

Political Thriller (Chapter 8)
The United States Department of State publishes an annual report on terrorism – the 2016 report was published in July 2017 and can be found at https://www.state.gov/j/ct/rls/crt/2016/index.htm

Cetti, Robert – *Terrorism in American Cinema: An Analytical Filmography, 1960-2008.* McFarland, 2009
Darlington, Joseph – *British Terrorist Novels of the 1970s.* Palgrave, 2018
Edelman, Rob – 'Politicians in American Cinema,' in: *The Political Companion to American Film,* edited by Gary Crowdus. Lakeview Press, 1994.

Fein, Robert A. and Bryan Vossekuil – 'Assassination in the United States,' *Journal of Forensic Sciences,* Vol.44 No.2, March 1999
Harper, Jim – 'You're Eight Times More Likely to be Killed by a Police Officer than a Terrorist,' Cato Institute, 10th August 2012
https://www.cato.org/blog/youre-eight-times-more-likely-be-killed-police-officer-terrorist
Muzzatti, Stephen – 'Terrorism and Counter-terrorism in Popular Culture in the Post-9/11 Context,' Oxford Research Encyclopedia, Criminology and Criminal Justice, February 2017
http://criminology.oxfordre.com/view/10.1093/acrefore/9780190264079.001.0001/acrefore-9780190264079-e-123
Schaefer, Annette – 'Inside the Terrorist Mind,' *Scientific American,* 1st December 2007
https://www.scientificamerican.com/article/inside-the-terrorist-mind/
Silberman, Robert – 'Political Thrillers,' in: *The Political Companion to American Film,* edited by Gary Crowdus. Lakeview Press, 1994.

Legal Thriller (Chapter 9)

Resources aimed at writers of legal thrillers seem relatively scarce. Much of the information in this chapter has been pieced together from articles in legal and academic journals which were not aimed at writers. Apart from the items listed here, I did find a couple of interesting pieces. Scott Turow wrote for The Guardian newspaper about his working day: https://www.theguardian.com/books/2017/jul/22/scott-turow-my-characters-like-me-find-societys-problems-in-the-law-

And James Grippando has published extracts from his journal under the title 'The Quest: Five or Six (Hundred) Easy Steps to Overnight Success.' It covers the process of writing his first novel, The Pardon, including some of the mistakes he made along the way: http://jamesgrippando.com/for-aspiring-writers

Asimow, Michael – 'Embodiment of Evil: Law Firms in the Movies,' *UCLA Law Review,* vol.48, 2000-2001.
https://papers.ssrn.com/sol3/papers.cfm?abstract_id=270128
Bainbridge, Jason – 'Lawyer as Critic: Analysing the Legal Thriller Through the Works of John Grisham, Erle Stanley Gardner and Harper Lee,' in: *TEXT Special Issue 37: Crime Fiction and the Creative/Critical Nexus,* October 2016.
Beard, Amy S. – 'From Hero to Villain: The Corresponding Evolutions of Model Ethical Codes and the Portrayal of Lawyers in Film,' in: *New York Law School Law Review,* vol. 55, November 2010.
Bergman, Paul and Michael Asimow – *Reel Justice: The Courtroom Goes to the Movies.* Andrews McMeel Publishing, 2006.
Blum, Valerie and Alexandra Rudolph – 'From the Conference Room to the Courtroom: How a Change in Setting Affects Witness Preparation,' *The Jury Expert,* 21(4), 2009. American Society of Trial Consultants, July 2009.
BrettMW – '6 Myths Hollywood Has You Believing About Jury Trials.' *ReelRundown.com,* 8 March 2018.
https://reelrundown.com/misc/6-Myths-Hollywood-Has-You-Believe-About-Jury-Trials
Brust, Richard – 'The 25 Greatest Legal Movies.' www.ABAjournal.com, August 2008
http://www.abajournal.com/magazine/article/the_25_greatest_legal_movies/
Centre for Criminal Justice Advocacy – "a free, nonpartisan, grassroots training resource to assist new lawyers in becoming competent criminal trial practitioners."
http://criminaldefense.homestead.com/index.html
Clover, Carol J. – 'Law and the Order of Popular Culture,' in: *Law in the Domains of Culture,* ed. by Austin Sarat & Thomas R. Kearns. University of Michigan Press, 1998.
Corcos, Christine Alice – 'Legal Fictions: Irony, Storytelling, Truth, and Justice in the Modern Courtroom Drama,' *UALR Law Review,* vol,25, 2003.
https://digitalcommons.law.lsu.edu/faculty_scholarship/253
Cover, Robert – 'Violence and the Word,' *Yale Law Journal* 95, 1986.
Cruess, Sylvia R., Sharon Johnston & Richard L. Cruess (2010) 'Profession: A Working Definition for Medical Educators,' *Teaching and Learning in Medicine,* 16:1, 2004.
Diggs, Terry Kay – 'Through a Glass Darkly,' *ABA Journal* 82, 1996.
Drell, Adrienne – 'Murder They Write,' in: *ABA Journal,* June 1994.
Epting, Chris – 'Author Marcia Clark Goes On the 'Defense',' *HuffingtonPost.com,* 17 May 2016.

https://www.huffingtonpost.com/chris-epting/author-marcia-clark-goes-_b_9995518.html
Gewirtz, Paul – 'Victims and Voyeurs: Two Narrative Problems at the Criminal Trial,' in: *Law's Stories: Narrative and Rhetoric in the Law*, ed. by Peter Brooks. Yale University Press, 1998.
Gillers, Stephen 'Can a Good Lawyer Be a Bad Person,' *Journal of the Institute for the Study of Legal Ethics*, vol. 2, article 14, 1999.
http://scholarlycommons.law.hofstra.edu/jisle/vol2/iss1/14
Haddad, Tonja – 'Silver Tongues on the Silver Screen: Legal Ethics in the Movies," *Nova Law Review*, vol.24 no.2, 2000.
Healy, Jeremiah – 'Writing Legal Thrillers' http://www.jeremiahhealy.com/legalthrillers.html
Kozinski, Alex – 'Criminal Law 2.0,' *Georgetown Legal Journal Annual Review of Criminal Procedure* 44, 2015.
Levine, Paul – 'Legal Thrillers: Trial and (Many) Errors,' *HuffingtonPost.com*, 4th August 2010
https://www.huffingtonpost.com/paul-levine/legal-thrillers-trial-and_b_670856.html
McDowell, James L. – 'From Perry Mason to Primary Colours: Using Fiction to Understand Legal and Political Systems,' *Legal Studies Forum* 24/1, 2000.
McMorrow, Judith A. – 'Law and Lawyers in the U.S.: The Hero-Villain Dichotomy,' in: *Perspectives on American Law*. Peking University Press, 2013.
Menkel-Meadow, Carrie – 'Can They Do That? Legal Ethics in Popular Culture: Of Characters and Acts,' *UCLA Law Review* 48, 2001.
Papke, David Ray – 'Conventional Wisdom: The Courtroom Trial in American Popular Culture,' *Marquette Law Review*, vol.82, iss. 3, Spring 1999.
Pusey, Allen – 'John Grisham on Grappling with Race, the Death Penalty; and Lawyers 'Polluting Their Own Profession' *ABAJournal.com*, 23 September 2011
http://www.abajournal.com/news/article/john_grisham_awarded_inaugural_harper_lee_prize
Robinson, Marlyn – 'Collins to Grisham: A Brief History of the Legal Thriller,' in: *Legal Studies Forum* 21, 1998.
https://tarltonapps.law.utexas.edu/exhibits/lpop/documents/history_legal_thriller.pdf
Robinson, Marlyn – *The Lawyer in Popular Culture: A Bibliography*, Tarlton Law Library, University of Texas, 2006.
https://tarltonapps.law.utexas.edu/exhibits/lpop/documents/bibliography_2011.pdf
Robson, Peter – 'Images of Law in the Fiction of John Grisham' in: John Morrison and Christine Bell (eds.), *Tall Stories: Reading Law and Literature*. Dartmouth Publishing, 1996.
Rosen, Steven O. – 'Ethical Lessons from Courtroom Lawyers in the Movies,' *Aviation Insurance Association Annual Conference,* May 2014.
Rutledge, Andy – 'Design Professionalism.' http://designprofessionalism.com/defining-design-professionalism-1.php
Sauerberg, Lars Ole – *The Legal Thriller from Gardner to Grisham*. Palgrave Macmillan, 2016.
Scherr, Alex and Hillary Farber – 'Popular Culture as a Lens on Legal Professionalism,' 2004
http://digitalcommons.law.uga.edu/fac_artchop/833/
Shapiro, Fred R., and Jane Garry (eds.) – Trial and Error: An Oxford Anthology of Legal Stories. Oxford University Press, 1998.
Shaul, Richard D. – 'Backwoods Barrister,' in: *Michigan History,* November/December 2001.
https://wayback.archive-it.org/418/20061220154411/http://www.michiganhistorymagazine.com/features/discmich/anatomy.pdf
Simonett, John E. – 'The Trial as One of the Performing Arts,' *American Bar Association Journal,* Vol. 52, No. 12 (December 1966).
Turow, Scott – 'Scott Turow Recommends his Favourite Legal Novels,' FiveBooks.com.
https://fivebooks.com/best-books/scott-turow-favourite-legal-novels/
Webb, Sidney and Beatrice – 'The Organization of the Architectural Profession,' *New Statesman,* 21st April 1917.
White, Terry (ed.) – *Justice Denoted: The Legal Thriller in American, British, and Continental Courtroom Literature*. Praeger, 2003
Winters, Larry A. – 'Why Do You Read Legal Thrillers?'
http://manningwolfe.com/why-do-you-read-legal-thrillers/
http://larryawinters.com/

Medical Thriller (Chapter 10)

Cook, Michael – 'Keystroke: The World of the Medical Thriller,' *BioEdge.org*, 2 May 2015. https://www.bioedge.org/bioethics/keystroke-the-world-of-the-medical-thriller/11416

Daley, Yvonne – 'Pulse Fiction,' *Stanford Alumni*, November/December 1997. https://alumni.stanford.edu/get/page/magazine/article/?article_id=42607

Fabrikant, Geraldine – 'Talking Money with Dr. Robin Cook,' in *The New York Times*, 21 January 1996. http://www.nytimes.com/1996/01/21/business/talking-money-with-dr-robin-cook-prescription-real-estate-and-lots-of-it.html

Fernandez, Jasmine and Amrjeet Nayak – 'Structure, Image and Ideas at Play: A Revisitation into the Select Medical Thrillers from a Grotesque Lens.' *Journal of Science, Humanities and Arts*, vol. 3, issue 5, 27 September 2016. https://scholar.google.co.in/scholar?oi=bibs&hl=en&cluster=15373216396183827086

Grbić, Jovana J. – 'Contagion' (review), *www.CEN-online.org*, 12 September 2011. Note: Compares the scientific accuracy of *Contagion* and *Outbreak*.

Hunter, Kathryn Montgomery – *Doctors' Stories: The Narrative Structure of Medical Knowledge*. Princeton University Press, 1991.

Jennes, Gail – 'Dr. Robin Cook Has an Rx for Success,' *People.com*, 6 April 1981. http://people.com/archive/dr-robin-cook-has-an-rx-for-success-a-brain-in-the-bookstores-and-a-beauty-at-home-vol-15-no-13/

Jones, Anne Hudson – 'Literature and Medicine: Narrative Ethics,' in: *The Lancet*, vol. 349, 26 April 1977.

Lewis, Paul – 'Frank Slaughter, Novelist of Medicine, Is Dead at 93,' *The New York Times*, 23 May 2001.

Lyle, D. P. – 'Tess Gerritsen Talks Medical Thrillers,' *The Crime Writer's Forensics Blog*, 29 May 2009. https://writersforensicsblog.wordpress.com/2009/05/29/tess-gerritsen-talks-medical-thrillers/

Lyons, C. J. – 'About CJ,' *CJLyons.net*. https://cjlyons.net/about-cj/

Macdonald, Jay – Interview with Robin Cook, Bookpage.com, September 2001. https://bookpage.com/interviews/8111-robin-cook#.WqrdSujFKMo

McLellan, M. Faith – 'Literature and Medicine: Physician-Writers,' in: *The Lancet*, vol. 349, 22 February 1997.

Palmer, Michael – 'Writing Tips,' *Michael Palmer Official Website*. http://www.michaelpalmerbooks.com/writing-tips/

Sambuchino, Chuck – '6 Rules for Writing a Medical Thriller,' *WritersDigest.com*, 7 March 2014. http://www.writersdigest.com/editor-blogs/guide-to-literary-agents/6-rules-for-writing-a-medical-thriller

Scott, Gale – Interview with Michael Palmer, in: *Physician's Weekly*, vol. XVII, no. 29, 31 July 2000. [Quoted in Charpy]

Scruggs, K. V. – 'Women in Medicine and Other Novelties: An Interview with Author and Physician, Dr. Leonard Goldberg,' *KVScruggs.com*, 2 June 2017. https://kvscruggs.com/2017/06/02/women-in-medicine-and-other-novelties-an-interview-with-author-and-physician-dr-leonard-goldberg/

Seggie, Janet – 'Medicine and the Humanities: Doctors as Artists,' in: *South African Medical Journal*, vol. 104, no. 2, February 2014.

Topol, Eric – '*Coma* Author-Physician on His New Medical Thriller, *Cell*,' *Medscape.com*, 3 February 2014. https://www.medscape.com/viewarticle/819824_4

Wilkens, John – 'UCSD Doctor Writes What He Knows: Medical Thrillers' (interview with Dr. Kelly Parsons), *San Diego Union Tribune*, 3 February 2017. http://www.sandiegouniontribune.com/entertainment/books/sd-et-author-parsons-20170130-story.html

Techno-Thriller (Chapter 11)

Brotherton, Mike – 'Outside the Ghetto and the Ghastly Example of Michael Crichton,' *MikeBrotherton.com*, 3rd July 2008. http://www.mikebrotherton.com/2008/07/03/outside-the-ghetto-and-the-ghastly-example-of-michael-crichton/

Brownlee, John – 'Michael Crichton Fictionalizes Critic as Child Rapist,' *Wired.com*, 20th December 2006
https://www.wired.com/2006/12/michael-crichto/
Cerasini, Marc A. – 'Tom Clancy's Fiction: The Birth of the Techno-Thriller,' in: *The Tom Clancy Companion*, ed. by Martin H. Greenberg.
Clute, John and Peter Nicholls (eds.) – *Encyclopedia of Science Fiction*. Orbit, 1999
Gibson, J. William – 'Redeeming Vietnam: Techno-Thriller Novels of the 1980s,' in: *Cultural Critique*, No.19, The Economies of War (Autumn 1991). http://www.jstor.org/stable/1354313
Grazier, Kevin R. (ed) – *The Science of Michael Crichton: An Unauthorized Exploration into the Real Science Behind the Fictional Worlds of Michael Crichton*. Dallas, TX: BenBella Books Inc., 2008.
Greenberg, Martin H. – 'An Interview with Tom Clancy,' in: *The Tom Clancy Companion*, ed. by Martin H. Greenberg.
Greenberg, Martin H. (ed.) – *The Tom Clancy Companion*. Berkley, 1983.
Jamison, Craig E. (CEJ) – 'Alistair MacLean and *The Satan Bug:* Master Storyteller and the Birth of the Techno-Thriller,' in: *Buried Treasures,* September/October 2011.
http://www.gullcottageonline.com/Buried_Treas.html
LabLit.com – http://www.lablit.com/about – 'dedicated to real laboratory culture and to the portrayal and perceptions of that culture – science, scientists and labs – in fiction, the media and across popular culture.'
Phoenix, Chris – 'Don't Let Crichton's *Prey* Scare You – The Science Isn't Real,' *Nanotech-Now.com*, January 2003.
http://www.nanotech-now.com/Chris-Phoenix/prey-critique.htm
Rogers, Amy – 'Mythbusting Thriller Science: Space Bacteria #1 (Crichton's Andromeda Strain),' *ScienceThrillers.com*, 1st October 2010.
https://www.sciencethrillers.com/2010/mythbusting-space-bacteria-1/
Rogers, Amy – 'What is a Science Thriller?' *ScienceThrillers.com*, 10th June 2011.
https://www.sciencethrillers.com/2011/what-is-a-science-thriller/
Schmidt, Gavin – 'Michael Crichton's State of Confusion,' *RealClimate.org*, 13th December 2004.
http://www.realclimate.org/index.php/archives/2004/12/michael-crichtons-state-of-confusion/
Shapiro, Beth – *How to Clone a Mammoth: The Science of De-Extinction*. Princeton University Press, 2016
Stengler, Erik – 'Beyond the Techno-Thriller: Michael Crichton and Societal Issues in Science and Technology,' in: *Fafnir – Nordic Journal of Science Fiction and Fantasy Research, Volume 2, Issue 3,* 2 (3), 2015. http://eprints.uwe.ac.uk/26408
http://journal.finfar.org/articles/beyond-the-techno-thriller-michael-crichton-and-societal-issues-in-science-and-technology/

Psychological Thriller (Chapter 12)
Baxendale, Sallie – 'Memories Aren't Made of This: Amnesia at the Movies,' British Medical Journal, vol. 329, 18-25 December 2004.
Derry, Charles – *Suspense Thrillers: Films in the Shadow of Alfred Hitchcock*. McFarland & Company, Inc., 2001.
Dieguez, Sebastian and Jean-Marie Annoni – 'Stranger than Fiction: Literary and Clinical Amnesia,' in: J. Bogousslavsky and S. Dieguez (eds.), *Literary Medicine: Brain Disease and Doctors in Novels, Theater, and Film*. Karger AG, 2013.
McLeod, Saul A. – 'Psychology as a Science,' 2008. Retrieved from:
www.simplypsychology.org/science-psychology.html
Pérez-Peña, Richard – 'An Accurate Movie About Amnesia? Forget about It,' *The New York Times*, 2 November 2003.
Pope Jr., H. G., M. B. Poliakoff, M. P. Parker, M. Boynes and J. I. Hudson – 'Is Dissociative Amnesia a Culture-Bound Syndrome? Findings from a Survey of Historical Literature,' *Psychological Medicine* 37(2), February 2007.
Skillman, T. Macdonald – *Writing the Thriller*. Writer's Digest Books, 2001.

The Manhunt / Chase Thriller (Chapter 13)
Benham, Matt – 'How to Write a Chase Scene the *Marathon Man* Way'

http://www.mattdebenham.com/blog/lets-steal-from-this-how-to-write-a-chase-scene-the-marathon-man-way/
Fey, Chrys – 'Writing About: A Foot Chase'
https://writewithfey.blogspot.com/2015/01/writing-about-foot-chase.html
Healy, Ian – 'Types of Action Scenes: The Chase'
http://writebetteraction.ianthealy.com/2011/01/10/10-types-of-action-scenes-the-chase/
Rogers, John – 'Why You Should Never Write action Scenes for Your Blockbuster Movie'
https://io9.gizmodo.com/why-you-should-never-write-action-scenes-into-your-tent-511712234
Tobias, Ronald B. – *20 Master Plots: And How to Build Them*. Writer's Digest Books, 1993.
Write that Scene – 'How to Write a Running Scene' at http://writethatscene.com/running-scene/

Bourne, Langdon & Reacher (Chapter 14)

Beahm, George – *The Jack Reacher Field Manual*. BenBella Books, Inc., 2016
Bidinotto, Robert – 'An Interview with Lee Child,' *Robert Bidinotto: The Vigilante Author,* 13th October 2011.
http://www.bidinotto.com/2011/10/an-interview-with-lee-child-part-1/
Curtis, Bryan – 'The Curious Case of Lee Child.' *Grantland,* 20th December 2012,
http://grantland.com/features/lee-child-jim-grant-jack-reacher/
Martin, Andy – *Reacher Said Nothing: Lee Child and the Making of Make Me.* Transworld, 2015.
Swaim, Robert – 'Audio Interview with Robert Ludlum'
https://web.archive.org/web/20111026182208/http://www.wiredforbooks.org/robertludlum/

Acknowledgments

When I was eleven years old, I wrote in my notebook that I wanted to write stories with the same combination of suspense and macabre humour you find in Alfred Hitchcock movies. I've been trying to do that ever since.

From Jerry Palmer's book *Thrillers: Genesis and Structure of a Popular Genre* I took the concept of professionals versus amateurs and bureaucrats, which helped me figure out how *The 39 Steps* and *Dr. No* could be in the same genre.

Charles Derry's *The Suspense Thriller: Films in the Shadow of Alfred Hitchcock* gave me an understanding of the workings of some of the major thriller sub-genres.

Martin Rubin's *Thrillers* provided the historical context and development of the genre.

John G. Cawelti and Bruce A. Rosenberg's *The Spy Story* helped me understand the differences and similarities between the works of Ian Fleming and John Le Carré, and also provided details of genre iconography and motifs.

For my understanding of the *suspense* on suspense thrillers, I have to thank all of those whose research I drew on for chapter four.

Also by Paul Tomlinson

To find out more about the *Genre Writer* series and to receive additional free writing advice, sign up to the mailing list: **www.paultomlinson.org/signup**

Index

100 Thrills, 5
1920s, 141, 143, 144, 145, 148, 345
1930s, 40, 55, 141, 145, 146, 148, 195, 235, 253, 257, 364
1940s, 141, 149, 163, 164, 166, 177, 257, 330
1950s, 61, 64, 141, 149, 159, 162, 163, 164, 166, 172, 173, 177, 179
1960s, 46, 53, 58, 61, 67, 159, 162, 163, 170, 195, 198, 329
1970s, 195, 228, 254, 255, 257, 306, 309, 314, 330
1980s, 140, 141, 149, 157, 179, 308, 314, 411
1990s, 141
20 Master Plots: And How to Build Them, 384
24, 194
39 Steps, The, see *Thirty-Nine Steps, The*
'39 Ways to Serve and Participate in Jihad', 154
6 Days, 224, 228
'6 Rules for Writing a Medical Thriller', 282
9/11 terrorist attacks, 83
A Stitch in Time, 280
Absolute Power (novel & film), 38
Academy Award, 195, 385
Accused, The, 264
Act I, 10, 12, 13, 23, 97, 101, 130
Act II, 12, 24, 37, 56, 132
Act III, 10, 12, 68, 97, 101, 106, 130
action-adventure, genre, 5, 22, 111, 129, 144, 317, 407
Active Duty, 207
active opposition, 57, 208, 394
Adam's Rib, 261
Adams, John Quincy, 233
adaptability, 15
'Adieu', 341, 343
Admiralty, 176
adrenaline junkies, 95
Adventurer archetype, 18, 19, 95
adversarial nature of courtroom, 238
adverse authority, 250
aerial combat, 313, 317
affect (emotional response), 93, 102, 106, 127
affinity for the hero, 94, 101
African Queen, The, 24
Agnew, Spiro, 192
agony, 100
Air Force One, 224, 228
Airframe, 313
Airport, 312

al-Balawi, Humam Khalil Abu-Mulal, 152
Alcott, Louisa May, 366
Alec Leamas, 151, 159, 160, 161, 162, 171, 173, 174, 175, 180, 185, 186
alibis, 35, 139, 189
Alien, 112, 122, 384
Alien, The, 353
alienation, 36, 55, 140, 141, 148, 150
All the King's Men, 195
All the President's Men, 193, 196, 198, 208, 209-213, 283
All the Year Round, 233
Allbeury, Ted, 156, 157
Allen, Grant, 341
Allende, Salvador, 192
allies, 27, 28, 34, 54, 73, 131, 163, 189, 314
ally, 14, 37, 116, 132, 133, 147
al-Qaeda, 152
altruism, 254
amateur hero, 6, 11, 48, 49, 52, 62, 74, 75, 76
amateur-on-the-run, 5, 7, 11-38, 39, 47, 49, 50, 55, 57, 58, 62, 74, 76, 77, 111, 168, 169, 171, 177, 181, 194, 195, 213, 214, 219, 230, 243, 248, 288, 305, 306, 315, 332, 352, 353, 363, 385, 410, 411
ambassador, 53, 179
Ambler, Eric, 80, 142, 143, 145, 146, 147, 148, 149, 158, 159, 175, 181, 198, 216, 219, 223
American Bar Association, 244, 248, 249, 252, 258
American Bar Association Journal, 244, 263
American Civil War, 280
American Film Institute, 5, 103
American Journal of Psychiatry, The, 374
American Life, An, 158
American Medical Association, 287
American Thriller, The, 283
American War of Independence, 142
Amistad, 233
amnesia, 5, 6, 328, 340, 341, 410, 411
amnesia thrillers, 339-351
Amnesty International, 69
Anabasis, 386
anarchism, 144
anarchy, 309
Anatomy of a Murder, 234, 235
Ancient Greeks, 237, 240, 280, 340

And Justice for All, 249, 263
Andromeda Strain, The, 278, 281, 296, 297, 310, 311, 312, 313
anecdotes, 122, 308
Annoni, Jean-Marie, 341, 342, 343, 344, 345
Anouilh, Jean, 341
antagonism, 12, 14, 18, 23, 33, 58, 210
antagonist, see also villain, 22, 92
anterograde amnesia, 342
Anti-Ballistic Missile Treaty, 192
anticipation, 5, 33, 54, 89, 90, 91, 92, 93, 100, 105, 106, 108, 109, 110, 112, 113, 114, 117, 126, 363
anti-hero, 234
anti-Semitism, 41, 86, 87, 88
Antony and Cleopatra, 194
anxiety, 5, 30, 93, 95, 107, 140
Apocrypha, Bible, 142
appeal of the thriller, 34
Arabesque, 38
Archbishop of Canterbury, 229
archetypal characters, 18, 129, 240, 253
archetypal plots, 7, 132, 375
archetypes, 330
arena, gladiatorial, 243
Argo, 229
Aristotle, 107, 262
Armadale, 234
arousal jag theory, 106
Arrighi, Gianluca, 238
artificial intelligence, 306, 309
As You Desire Me, 341
As You Like It, 351
Ashenden, 80, 138, 145, 159, 166, 176
Asimov, Michael, 242, 246, 253, 254, 255, 256, 257, 259, 263
As-Sālim, Mohammad Bin Ahmad, 154
Assange, Julian, 157, 165
assassination, 28, 80, 84, 155, 192, 196, 198-208
'Assassination in the United States', 198
assassination thriller, 137, 181, 196, 197, 198, 199, 200, 207, 313
assassinations, 5, 22, 28, 29, 80, 83, 86, 138, 147, 162, 178, 182, 190, 191, 192, 193, 194, 195, 196, 197, 198, 199, 200, 213, 411
Assault on Precinct 13, 111
Assignment K, 182

assumed identity, 27, 140
Aston Martin, 66
At Risk, 155
A-Team, The, 66, 91
Athabasca, 311
Atkey, Phil, 157
Atkins, John, 53, 59, 69, 72, 75, 77, 147, 161, 162, 163, 164, 166, 170, 174, 175, 176, 177, 178, 180
atonement, 32
Attending Physician, The, 280
Atticus Finch, 235, 253, 266
attitudes, 55, 58, 95, 161
attorney. See lawyer
audience, 5, 16, 66, 77, 95, 108, 109, 112, 114, 115, 126, 193, 194, 239, 246, 248, 260, 263, 264, 266, 267, 268, 288, 315, 328, 329, 333
audience expectations, 90, 114
audience omniscience. See dramatic irony
audience participation, 108
Austen, Jane, 41, 362
austerity, 26, 62, 64, 150
authorial stakes, 130
authorities, 13, 15, 25, 26, 28, 29, 37, 53, 78, 158, 169, 196, 198, 245
autonomy, 254, 255, 362
Bachman, Richard, 384
backdoor, 173
Background to Danger, 149, 181
bad guys, 12, 37, 51, 53, 57, 69, 114, 190, 231, 233, 248, 308, 332
Bagot, Milicent, 178
Bailey II, Charles W., 215
Bainbridge, Jason, 241
Balchin, Nigel, 341
Baldacci, David, 38
Baldwin, Alec, 317
Balzac, Honoré de, 343, 341
ban. See interdictions
band of brothers, 141
banking, 85, 86, 312
Banks, Leslie, 384
banter, 36, 61
Barker, Clive, 112
Barkun, Michael, 87
barrister. See lawyer
Barzun, Jacques, 140, 143, 144
Battle of Dorking, The, 143, 312
Baxendale, Sallie, 341, 342
Bay of Pigs, 192
BBC, 44, 150, 151, 161, 171, 179, 194, 384
Beat the World, 386
Before I Go to Sleep, 342

Before the Fact, 362
Begoum, F. M., 168
behaviour, 21, 95, 96, 123, 130, 143, 237, 239, 242, 244, 246, 248, 256, 262, 263, 285, 375
behind closed doors, 196, 197
behind enemy lines, 149, 224
beliefs, 14, 16, 20, 31, 34, 52, 85, 87, 96, 97, 102, 141, 142, 146, 159, 165, 173, 246, 309, 329, 353, 374
Bell, Joseph, 280
Bell, Josephine, 280
benevolent conspiracy, 78, 84
Bennett, Alan, 41, 164
Bennett, Charles, 40
Berger, Arthur Asa, 46, 54, 60, 62, 63
Bergman, S., 107, 242, 246, 259, 263
Berlet, Chip, 84, 87
Berlin Wall, 150, 152
Berlyne, Daniel, 106
Bernardo, Allan B. I., 120, 121
Bernstein, Carl, 193, 208, 209, 212, 283
Best Picture, Academy Award, 195
bestseller, 46, 234, 235, 236, 281, 284, 310
betrayal, 14, 21, 24, 29, 30, 60, 73, 76, 80, 86, 128, 140, 141, 142, 147, 148, 160, 162, 163, 164, 165, 166, 167, 168, 169, 173, 174, 176, 177, 194, 259, 354, 398
betrayer, 37
Bible, 59, 142, 245
Bidinotto, Robert, 413
big job, the, 181, 182
Bill of Rights, United States, 238
bin Laden, Osama, 152
Binary, 312, 313
bio-terrorism, 311
Birds of the West Indies, 42
Black Baroness, The, 42
Black Dragon, 386
Black Shrike, The, 311
Black Sunday, 181, 198, 216-219, 223, 306
blackmail, 83, 86, 165, 169, 177, 200, 233, 246
Blake, George, 163, 164
Blind Corner, 40
Blind Flight, 229
Block, Libbie, 366
blockbuster, 172
Blofeld, 51, 57, 121
Blood Run, 281
Bloody Murder, 144
Bluebeard, 362, 365
Blum, Valerie, 244
Blunt, Anthony, 163, 164, 167
boats, 26
Body of Evidence, 249
Bogart, Humphrey, 24, 76, 234, 413
Bogdanovich, Peter, 26
Bolshevik Revolution, 161
bomb, 103, 104, 121
bomb under the table, 103, 105, 109
Bommart, Jean, 341
Bond Affair, The, 46

Bond, James (author), 42
Bond, Larry, 308
Bonnie & Clyde, 399
Boothroyd, Geoffrey, 45
boredom, 52, 160
Boston, Richard, 42
Bounds, Dennis, 234
Bourke, Sean, 164
Bourne Identity, The, 353, 410
Bourne Legacy, The, 410
Bourne Supremacy, The, 410
Bourne Ultimatum, The, 410
brand-names, 45
Breaker Morant, 259
BrettMW, 265
Brewer, William F., 117, 118, 119
bribery, 251
Brick Mansions, 386
Bridge of Sighs, The, 155
briefcase, 27, 66
British Empire, 64, 72, 80, 161, 162, 163, 165, 166, 180
British Intelligence Service, 145
British Medical Journal, 342
British Spy Novel, The, 59
Bronson, Charles, 228
Brontë, Charlotte, 362, 365
Brontë, Emily, 362, 365
Brooks, Mel, 36
Brown, Corale, 164
Brown, Dale, 313
Brown, Dan, 153, 312, 341, 410, 411, 412
Bruneri, Mario, 341, 345
Brust, Richard, 263
Bryan, Michael, 207
Bryant, Jennings, 100, 101, 107
Buchan, John, 9, 10, 11, 26, 38, 40, 41, 58, 75, 80, 143, 144, 145, 157, 163, 181
buddies, 25
buddy movie, 209, 375
Buff, Joe, 313
bug-detectors, 66
Bulldog Drummond, 40, 42, 44, 144
Bulldog Drummond's Baby, 40
Bullets or Ballots, 195
bunny boiler, 375
burden of proof, 238
bureaucracy, 73, 78, 162, 176, 177
bureaucrat, 20, 21, 50, 51, 57, 71, 75, 141, 145, 161, 166, 171, 174, 175, 177
Burgess, Anthony, 176
Burgess, Guy, 163, 164
buried alive, 126
Burke and Hare, 287
burned alive, 126
Burns, Scott Z., 297
burnt-out case, 159, 160
Burton, Richard, 151
Bush, George W., 152, 193, 309
business, 21, 83, 85, 86, 232, 242, 254, 255, 256, 258, 288, 297

Butch Cassidy and the Sundance Kid, 399
buyer's remorse, 96
Byronic heroes, 362
cabal, 22, 84, 88, 158
Caine Mutiny, The, 234, 235
Caine, Michael, 150
Caldwell, John M., 142
Call for the Dead, 150, 151, 167
call to adventure, 10, 12, 97
Cambridge Analytica, 154
Cambridge Spy Ring, 163, 164
Campbell, Joseph, 68, 330
'Can a Good Lawyer Be a Bad Person?', 258
Candidate, The, 195
candle problem, 121
Candyman, 123
Canella, Giulia, 341
Canella, Giulio, 345
Canton Godfather, The, 386
Cape Fear, 375
capers & heists, sub-genre, 6, 352, 399
capitalism, 73, 149
Capra, Frank, 241
Capricorn One, 215
Captain Nemo, 41
Captains Courageous, 341
capture, 12, 15, 26, 27, 28, 29, 42, 44, 49, 56, 68, 71, 79, 95, 142, 167, 178, 229, 395, 398
Cardinal of the Kremlin, The, 309
Carer archetype, 129
Carlos the Jackal, 200, 410
Carmichael, Hoagy, 43
Carpenter, John, 112
Carré, Mathilde, 150
Carroll, Noel, 99, 100, 101, 102
cars, 26, 27, 44, 65, 66, 67, 170, 310
Casablanca, 76, 149
case law, 237, 238, 252
Case of the Velvet Claws, The, 234
Casey, Maud, 341
Casino Royale, 43, 46, 56, 58, 59, 63, 71, 76, 120, 150, 387
casinos, 26, 41, 62, 71, 120, 170
catalyst. See call to adventure
Catch-22, 84
catharsis, 107
Catholicism, 148, 163
Caught, 366
cause and effect, 94, 128, 208, 231, 398
Cawelti, John G., 34, 35, 36, 54, 56, 58, 59, 60, 76, 80, 137, 138, 139, 140, 141, 142, 146, 147, 148, 150, 158, 159, 160, 170, 171, 175, 181, 182
Cell Mates, 164
Cerasini, Marc A., 308, 312, 315
certain failure, 100
chain-reaction, 10
challenge, 12, 57, 97

Chamberlain, Richard, 410
Champlin, Charles, 270
Chan, Jackie, 386
Chandler, Raymond, 44, 79, 148, 150
chaos, 16, 29, 33, 129, 141, 314
Chaplin, Charlie, 54
Chapman Pincher, Henry, 179
chapter headings, 110
character, 7, 11, 15, 18, 19, 21, 43, 45, 46, 49, 53, 54, 67, 99, 101, 109, 110, 115, 116, 119, 123, 132, 142, 150, 171, 253, 263, 328, 353
character defects, 165
character growth, 16, 150
character relationships, 110
character traits, 110, 285
Charade, 366
Charlie Chan, 55
Charlie Muffin, 163
Charpy, Jean-Pierre, 134, 279, 281, 282, 283
chase, 5, 9, 10, 15, 25, 27, 34, 67, 83, 115, 129, 133, 230, 384-399 411
Chaser, The, 387
Chatman, Seymour, 90
Chatte, La, 150
Chayefsky, Paddy, 123
cheating, 56, 71, 113, 233, 257, 398
checkpoints, 150, 170
Chekhov, Anton, 91, 280
cherchez la femme, 167
Chesney, George Tomkyns, 143, 312
chess, 71, 72, 308
Chesterton, G. K., 144, 157
Childers, Erskine, 9, 143, 144, 311
Childs, Lee, 67
China, 153, 154, 155, 192
China Syndrome, The, 215
chivalry, 81, 82, 143
Chopping, Richard, 45
Christie, Agatha, 268
chronological sequence of events, 117, 119
Chugyeogja, 387
Churchill, Winston, 41, 149
CIA, 85, 152, 153, 158, 168, 180, 190, 192, 193, 194, 197, 229, 309, 315, 316, 317
civil law (statutory), 237
civil liberties, 286
civil servants, 51, 52, 138, 162, 179
Clancy, Tom, 137, 154, 305, 307, 308, 309, 310, 311, 312, 315, 316
clandestinity, 17, 18, 20, 33, 34, 35, 36, 139, 146, 148, 151, 158, 159, 160, 169, 171, 175, 209, 313
Clapper, James R., 154
Class Action, 256, 261
claustrophobia, 27, 126

clichés, 23, 26, 27, 62, 77, 82, 91, 99, 114, 115, 122, 127, 129, 172, 196, 209, 244, 392, 397, 412
cliff-hangers, 28, 123
climax, 10, 15, 24, 28, 57, 68, 97, 101, 106, 108, 113, 114, 124, 130, 230, 231, 259, 266, 267, 268, 397, 398
climax, sequence, 13
cloak and dagger, 27, 39, 40, 143, 145, 172
Clore, Gerald L., 98
Close, William T., 283
closing statements, 259, 262, 266
closure, 94, 95, 97, 98, 103
Clover, Carol J., 246, 262, 263, 264, 265
Clubland Heroes, 40, 141, 143, 144, 147, 159, 163, 174
clues, 91, 108, 114, 129, 212, 230, 266, 330, 339
cluster bombs, 155
coaching witnesses, 252
Cobley, Paul, 283
Cobra Event, The, 285
Code of Conduct, Law Society, 248
code of honour, 40, 143
code phrases, 172
codenames, 172
codes and cyphers, 28, 86, 143, 157, 172
codewords, 172
Coen, Joel and Ethan, 386
coercion, 96
cognitions, 95, 96
cognitive dissonance. See dissonance
Cold War, 33, 62, 72, 141, 149, 152, 153, 154, 155, 156, 157, 162, 168, 175, 192, 309, 311, 312, 313, 314, 317, 411, 412
Cold War II, 152, 154
collective unconscious, 330
Collier, Doris Bell, 280
'Collins to Grisham A Brief History of the Legal Thriller', 233
Collins, Allan, 98
Collins, Wilkie, 10, 233, 234, 341
Colonel Sun, 77
colonialism, 64
Coma, 278, 279, 281, 284, 285, 288
Come Tu Mi Vuoi, 341
Comedy of Errors, The, 351
COMINT, 169
Comisky, Paul, 100, 101
commingling, 249
commitment, 16, 18, 21, 24, 31, 32, 52, 75
commitment, lack of, 14, 15, 16, 24, 31, 32, 75, 315
Committee Study of the Central Intelligence Agency's Detention and Interrogation Program, 69
common law, 237, 238
Communism, 34, 76, 85, 147, 148, 149, 150, 152, 161, 164, 167, 168, 173, 255
Compact Oxford English Dictionary, 81

Company, The, 194
competence, 249, 250, 254
competition, 232
computer games, 309
computers, 28, 155, 157, 197
Conan Doyle, Arthur, 280
Condon, Richard, 207
confabulatory amnesia, 343
Confidential Agent, The, 80, 147, 181
confidentiality between lawyer and client, 249
confined spaces, 333
conflict, 20, 72, 85, 93, 95, 97, 98, 101, 110, 124, 127, 141, 142, 148, 159, 173, 191, 192, 238, 239, 243, 247, 262, 394
conflict of interest, 249, 250
'Conflict, Arousal and Curiosity', 106
Connell, Richard, 384
Connery, Sean, 46, 53, 71, 317
Conrad, Joseph, 80, 144, 168, 194
conscience, 20, 69, 76, 147, 148, 180, 286, 316
consequences, 28, 36, 83, 89, 91, 99, 110, 118, 124, 127, 129, 131, 132, 147, 174, 180, 208, 287, 309, 311, 314, 397
Conservative Party, 194
conspiracy, 5, 6, 9, 11, 12, 13, 15, 19, 20, 21, 22, 23, 24, 29, 30, 31, 34, 35, 36, 48, 49, 50, 51, 52, 55, 57, 58, 65, 68, 74, 75, 77, 78, 82, 83-88, 122, 129, 135, 136, 138, 139, 143, 146, 147, 151, 153, 165, 168, 176, 177, 190, 191, 192, 193, 194, 196, 197, 200,208, 209, 212, 213, 215, 216, 219, 230, 232, 233, 242, 246, 278, 284, 288, 296, 329, 385, 387, 397, 411, 412
conspiracy theories, 31, 40, 83, 84, 86, 87, 88, 157, 164, 192, 411
conspiracy thriller, 214
conspirators, 13, 20, 21, 22, 29, 31, 49, 62, 77, 78, 83, 84, 85, 86, 87, 170, 191, 197, 250, 284, 286, 288
Constantine: The Miracle of the Flaming Cross, 280
Constitution, United States, 237, 238
constitutional rights, 247, 258
consumerism, 74
contagion, 306
Contagion, 278, 296, 297
contamination and poisoning, 86
Contemporary Authors, 287
Contraband, 41
'Conventional Wisdom: The Courtroom Trial in American Popular Culture', 244
Conversation, The, 171
convictions, 14, 34

Conway, Simon, 155
Cook, Robin, 134, 278, 279, 281, 284, 287, 288
Coonts, Stephen, 213
Cooper, J. Fenimore, 142
Cop Out, 386
Coppola, Francis Ford, 171
Corcos, Christine Alice, 240, 246, 247, 259, 261, 264, 267
Coriolanus, 194
Cornwell, David John Moore. See Le Carré, John
corporations, 73, 86, 141, 190, 254, 255
corrupt financiers, 34
corruption, 14, 21, 29, 30, 34, 37, 55, 74, 78, 85, 146, 148, 153, 160, 193, 195, 232, 241, 246, 257, 261, 277, 280, 296
Costigan, James, 164
Count of Monte Cristo, The, 10, 352
countdown, see also ticking clock, 110, 121, 122
counter-espionage, 41, 137, 138, 142, 143, 146, 156, 163, 167, 180
counterfeiting, 83, 86
counter-intelligence, 138, 144, 149
courage, 24, 42, 241
courthouse, 244, 245
courtroom, 5, 135, 136, 230-277
Cover Stories, 58, 63, 163
cover-up, 5, 83, 85, 153, 158, 165, 176, 191, 197, 208, 212, 215, 258
Craig, Daniel, 66
CREEP, 212
Crichton, Michael, 280, 281, 283, 296-303, 305, 310, 311, 312, 313, 322-327
Crime Thriller, 5, 59, 182, 189, 199, 278, 328, 352, 361, 384
crime, genre, 5, 189, 281, 329
criminal law, 237
criminal organisations, 86
cross-examination, legal, 239, 245, 259, 264, 265, 276
Crossfire: The Plot That Killed Kennedy, 208
Crouching Beast, The, 53
Cruess, Richard L., 254
Cruess, Sylvia R., 254
Cruise, Tom, 236, 269, 412
Crusader archetype, 18, 32, 34
Cry of the Owl, The, 375
cryptography, 156, 173
Csikszentmihalyi, Mihaly, 94
Cuban Missile Crisis, 192
cults, 85
Culture of Conspiracy, A, 87
Cumberbatch, Benedict, 157

Cumming, Captain Sir Mansfield George Smith, 179
cunning, 145, 248
curiosity, 31, 34, 103, 109, 110, 118, 119
cyber attacks, 154
cyber espionage, 154
cyber spying, 154
cyber terrorism, 154
cyber warfare, 154
cynical mentor, 245
cynicism, 16, 24, 31, 32, 50, 59, 72, 75, 77, 80, 145, 149, 159, 160, 166, 169, 173, 232, 235, 240, 245, 246, 257, 266, 340, 353
Cypher, The (novel), 38
Daddy's Gone A-Hunting, 375
Daily Express, 46
Daily Mail, 40
Dalayrac, Nicolas, 340
Dalton, Timothy, 66
Damon, Matt, 410
Damsgård, Puk, 229
danger, 11, 13, 20, 25, 26, 29, 30, 35, 53, 59, 60, 61, 64, 65, 68, 78, 87, 89, 92, 95, 97, 105, 107, 110, 111, 113, 114, 121, 122, 123, 126, 128, 130, 132, 133, 137, 139, 158, 170, 173, 209, 309, 332, 361, 395, 397
danger zone, 90
Daniel, Frank, 8
Dark Chronicles, The, 155
Dark Crusader, The, 311
Dark Frontier, The, 145, 147
Dark Horse, The, 195
dark web, 157, 173
darkest hour, 24, 48, 56, 68, 106, 186, 395
David versus Goliath, 232, 245, 247, 248, 412
Davies, L. P., 353
Day of the Dolphin, The, 207
Day of the Jackal, The, 181, 196, 197, 198, 199, 200-207
de Gaulle, Charles, 207
De Niro, Robert, 383
Dead Drop, 155
deadline, 10, 21, 24, 28, 121, 122, 182, 391
Deadly Affair, The, 151
Deardon, James, 375
death, 60, 68, 75, 76, 81, 100, 112, 117, 129, 130, 132, 278, 279
death wish, 333
Debenham, Matt, 387
deceit, 54, 143, 243, 280, 351
Deceived, 366
Deception Planners, The, 41
decisions, 12, 14, 16, 51, 87, 96, 127, 131, 133, 174, 179, 180, 186, 235, 243, 244, 248, 251, 262, 266, 267, 287, 397
Declaration of Geneva, 286
deduction, 108
Deep Blue Sea, 384
Deep Sound Channel, 313
Deep Throat, 209
DEFCON3, 192

defection, 163, 164
defence plans. *See* military plans
Defence, Ministry of, 176
defendant, 230, 231, 232, 238, 240, 245, 246, 249, 250, 251, 258, 260, 261, 262, 263, 267, 268, 269, 276
defense and defense counsel, 231, 238, 240, 245, 246, 258, 259, 262
Defoe, Daniel, 10
Deighton, Len, 77, 149, 150, 152, 159, 168, 172, 178, 181, 182
delayed outcome, 94, 100, 101, 111, 121
Delilah, Samson and, 59, 142
Deliverance, 386
demeanour, 244
democracy, 17, 33, 34, 55, 85, 129, 139, 146, 168, 175, 190, 191, 196, 197, 200, 244, 309, 316
Democratic Party, 195
Demon Seed, 305
denial, 96
Denning, Michael, 46, 54, 58, 60, 61, 63, 64, 70, 71, 73, 79, 80, 138, 147, 148, 163, 168, 169, 174
dentist, 90, 93, 126
Department K, 182
Department of Defense, 192
Depp, Johnny, 200
Depression, The, 145, 146
Derry, Charles, 25, 196, 331, 332, 353, 361
DeSalle, Rob, 310
Desert Storm, 308
Designated Survivor, 194
desire versus duty, 127
desired outcomes, 113
desire-frustration theory, 99, 105
detective, 16, 17, 18, 19, 37, 76, 108, 114, 122, 127, 135, 139, 150, 159, 174, 189, 194, 212, 213, 230, 234, 242, 256, 266, 276, 312, 339, 341, 361, 385, 411
Detective, 312
determination, 24, 50
deus ex machina, 107
Devil Rides Out, The, 41
Devil's Advocate, The, 256
Dhamija, Vish, 238
dialogue, 15, 43, 103, 108, 109, 124, 136, 148
Diamonds Are Forever, 55
Dickens, Charles, 233, 341
Dickey, James, 386
dictatorship, 51, 68, 146, 191, 200
Dictionary of National Biography, 77
Die Hard, 122, 198, 224-226, 228, 311
Die Trying, 67, 413
Dieguez, Sebastian, 341, 342, 343, 344, 345
Diggs, Terry Kay, 241
Digital Fortress, 153

dilemma, 63, 107, 120, 127, 133, 160, 171, 173, 239, 269, 284
diplomats, 23
disability, 56
disagreement, 97, 262
disappearing proof, 28
disappointment, 96, 100, 397
disaster movie, 22, 296, 306, 312
disclosure of evidence, 252
discomfort, 96, 104, 106
discovery or exposure, fear of, 16, 17, 24, 27, 34, 68, 126, 132, 170
discovery, of evidence, 252, 255, 260
disease, 278, 296, 297, 306, *See also* outbreaks
disguise, 27, 35, 140, 172, 200, 214
disillusionment, 166
disruption. *See* equilibrium
dissociative fugue, 343
dissonance, 93, 95, 96, 97, 98
distress, 100, 107
district attorney, 234, 240
Dobbs, Michael, 194
Doberman, choking, urban legend, 123
dogma, 161
Dominic, R. B., 280
Domino Killings, The, 353
Domino Principle, The, 353
'Don't let Crichton's Prey scare you – the science isn't real', 310
Don't open that door!, 114, 126
Donne, John, 35, 139
donors, 79
doomed ally, 37
doomed spy, 142, 148
doppelganger, 40
double agent, 23, 141, 150, 155, 158, 159, 167, 168, 352
Doyle, Arthur Conan, 280
Dr. No, 39-82
dragon, 82
Dragons at the Gate, 181
Dragonwyck, 362, 364
dramatic irony, 94, 103, 109, 116
dread, 90
dream interpretation, 330, 333
Dreyfus Affair, 143, 153
Dreyfus, Alfred, 153
drones, 28, 197
drowning, 126
drug-trafficking, 86
Du Maurier, Daphne, 362, 365
dualistic division. *See* Manichaean
due diligence, 249, 251
Duel, 22, 83, 115, 399
Dumas, Alexandre, 10, 194, 352
Duncan, Ian, 10
Duncan, Robert, 181
Duns, Jeremy, 41, 42, 155
Duquesne Spy Ring, 149

duties of a lawyer, 249
Eagle Eye, 38
earthquake, 107
Eastwood, Clint, 197, 199, 200, 208, 313, 316, 375, 413
Ebert, Roger, 366
Ebola, 283
Ebola: A Novel of the First Outbreak by a Doctor Who Was There, 283
Eco, Umberto, 43, 46, 50, 51, 55, 56, 70, 71, 72
Edelman, Rob, 195
Edgerton, Joel, 375
effort, 96
egotism, 242, 287
Ehrlich, Max, 362
Ehrlichman, John, 194
eight-sequence plot model, 7, 8, 11, 12, 13, 47, 70, 182, 188, 270, 271
Eisenhower, Dwight D., 146, 175
electro-convulsive therapy, 333
Elements of Mystery Fiction, The, 124
ELINT, 169
Elizabeth I, 142
Elizabeth II, 164
Elizabethan, 142, 143, 148, 168, 173, 176
Ellin, Stanley, 38
Elliott, Denholm, 151
El-Masri, Khalid, 153
embassy, 53, 228
Emerson, Gloria, 148
emotional experience, 102
emotional response, 5, 6, 7, 95, 102, 105, 108, 109, 112, 117, 125, 127, 128, 209, 266, 282, 331, 343, 362, 387
emotional threat, 129
emotions, 59, 89, 92, 93, 100, 102, 107, 113, 124, 125, 127, 128, 129, 130, 131, 132, 139, 209, 243, 249, 266, 268, 282, 284, 288, 331, 332, 394, 396, 397
empathy, 20, 74, 102, 241, 242, 330, 364, 374, 389
encryption, 157, 173
Encyclopedia of Science Fiction, The, 305, 310, 313
ends justify the means, 248
endurance, 18
enemy above, the, 84
enemy below, the, 84
Enemy Mine, 111
Enemy of the State, 12, 22, 38, 194
enemy outside, the, 84
enemy territory, 137, 146, 169, 181, 182
enemy within, the, 84, 150, 163
Enforcers & Vigilantes, 7
England, 143, 149, 173, 237, 238, 246, 248, 251
England's Peril, 143
Englishman Abroad, An, 164
ennui, 52, 160, 353
entertainment theory, 94

enthusiasm, 106
epidemic, 107
Epitaph for a Spy, 147
equilibrium, 12, 15, 25, 34, 36, 95, 97, 104, 139, 141, 174, 268
eroticism, 61
escape, 11, 12, 13, 15, 17, 26, 28, 29, 34, 61, 65, 95, 110, 112, 120, 121, 147, 164, 170, 242, 313, 351, 353, 354, 384, 385, 391, 394, 395, 398
Espinoza, Juan, 215
espionage, 137, 138, 139, 142, 147, 151, 178, 180
espionage thriller, definition, 145
espionage, sub-genre, 5, 9, 29, 39, 41, 70, 73, 81, 137-189, 191, 195, 305, 308, 309, 311, 313, 314, 317, 352, 411, 412
Essay Concerning Human Understanding, An, 344
Essay on the Dramatic Character of Sir John Falstaff, An, 54
'Ethical Lesson from Courtroom Lawyers in the Movies', 239
ethics, 21, 29, 73, 81, 85, 86, 129, 130, 139, 153, 196, 233, 235, 239, 241, 242, 243, 247, 248, 249, 250, 251, 252, 253, 254, 255, 257, 260, 261, 262, 263, 267, 278, 282, 283, 284, 286, 287, 288
ethics of spying, 175
ethics, legal, 239
ethnicity, 85
Eton, 53, 162
euphoria, 106, 108
Europe, 153
Evening News, The, 312
event order, 117
everyday world. *See* ordinary world
evidence, 15, 18, 22, 26, 30, 35, 86, 87, 92, 189, 208, 230, 237, 247, 248, 249, 250, 251, 252, 257, 259, 260, 262, 263, 264, 265, 267, 276
evidence tampering, 265
evil, 20, 21, 22, 67, 73, 74, 75, 81, 85, 87, 99, 100, 144, 231, 241, 243, 247, 253, 255, 258, 259, 260, 284, 296, 314
Evil Cradling, An, 229
Evil Genius, 234
examination, legal, 239, 245, 259, 263, 264, 265, 266, 267, 269
excessive risk-taking, 333
excitation-transfer theory, 106
excitement, 18, 106, 397
Execution of Charles Horman: An American Sacrifice, The, 215
executioner, 76
Executioners, The, 375
Executive Action, 215
exile, 14, 17, 26, 29, 164
exotic locations, 25, 26, 63
expectation, 93

experiments om human subjects, illegal, 86
expert, 15, 39, 67, 133, 134, 135, 136, 171, 178, 241, 242, 265, 331, 411
expert thriller, 307, 308
'Exploring the Psychology of Interest', 106
exposition, 395
exposure, 14, 15, 27, 29, 111, 126, 132, 137, 140, 158, 172, 351
external conflict, 328
Extreme Measures, 281, 288-296
extrovert, 18
Eye in the Sky, 224
Fabrikant, Geraldine, 284
Face Me When You Walk Away, 164
Face of a Stranger, The, 341
Facebook, 154
faction, 281
failed hero, 147
fairy-tales, 365
fake news, 154
Falkland Islands, 309
falling, fear of, 126
false identity. *See* assumed identity and stolen identity
false imprisonment, 197
Falstaff, 53, 54
family, 32, 36, 58, 129, 132, 133, 141, 232, 315, 316
family values, 316
Fan, The, 375, 376-383
fantasy, genre, 312
Farber, Hillary, 235, 239
far-right politics, 146
Fascism, 141, 145, 146, 149
FASP, 134, 135, 136
Fast and Furry-ous, 385
Fast Five, 387
Fatal Attraction, 375, 376-383
fate of the free world, 129
father-figures, 333
FBI, 149, 180, 192, 193
fear, 18, 20, 30, 56, 64, 78, 85, 90, 98, 100, 105, 106, 107, 111, 126, 128, 129, 132, 140, 149, 150, 162, 170, 171, 177, 232, 244, 278, 279, 296, 310, 314, 332, 351, 361, 396, 397
Fear, 375
Federal Rules of Evidence, 264
fee splitting, 250
Fein, Robert A., 198
fellowship of spies, 175
Female Hero, The, 362
femme fatale, 37, 59, 61, 62
Femme Nikita, La, 353
Fernandez, Jasmine, 278, 279, 285, 287
Festinger, Leon, 95, 96
fetish, 22, 332, 374
Few Good Men, A, 269
'Fiction à Substrat Professionnel', 134
Fiction Writing Self-Taught, 130
field agents, 151, 157, 160, 178, 180
Field, Syd, 12

fifteenth-century, 237
Fifth Amendment, U. S. Constitution, 265, 269
fifth century BC, 142
Fifth Estate, the, 157
Fifth Estate, The (film), 157
Fifth Vial, The, 282
fighter pilots, 52
financial motivation, see also greed, 84
Finder, Joseph, 366
fire service, 52
Firefox, 138, 305, 308, 313, 316-321
Firefox Down, 313
Firm, The, 230, 236, 252, 256, 257
Firmin, Rusty, 228
First Amendment, U.S. Constitution, 193, 197, 260
First Blood, 83, 317, 384, 386-409, 411, 413
first quarter. *See* Quarter 1
First Train to Babylon, 362
First World War, 11, 40, 59, 71, 138, 141, 143, 144, 145, 146, 311, 341, 344
fish out of water, see also outsider, 25, 39, 412
Five Fingers, 229
FiveBooks.com, 255
flashbacks, 331, 333
flaws, character, 21
Fleming, Ian, 26, 39-82, 120, 138, 149, 150, 157, 159, 160, 170, 179, 186
Fleming, Peter, 41, 43, 64
Flight of the Intruder, The, 313
Floodgate, 311
Flow: The Psychology of Optimal Experience, 94
folklore, 22
folktales, 35, 140
Follett, James, 228
Footfalls in Memory, 229
forced compliance, 96
Ford, Harrison, 228, 236, 267, 384, 385
Foreign Correspondent, The, 26, 190
foreign country, 35, 62, 65
Foreign Office, 176, 180
foreigners, 33, 64, 143
Forensic investigation, 7
foreshadowing, 90, 109, 113, 119
forewarning, 103, 104
Formal Opinion on Sexual Relationships with Clients, American Bar Association, 249
formula, 11, 42, 46, 76, 91, 114, 138, 181, 182, 288, 361, 366
Forster, E. M., 208
Forsyth, Frederick, 181, 200, 207
Forty Years On, 41
Foster, Jodie, 264
Fou, Le, 341, 344
four quarters, 13, 46
Fourth Amendment, U.S. Constitution, 239

fourth quarter. *See* Quarter 4
Fowler, Carol, 144
Fox, Edward, 164, 199
France, 72, 150, 153
Frankenstein, 280, 287, 305, 306, 311, 313, 314
fraud, 86
Free Agent, 155
Free World. *See* Western world
freedom of speech and the freedom of the press, 193
Freeman, David, 164
Freeman, R. Austin, 280
Freemantle, Brian, 163, 164
Freemasons, 84, 85
Freerunner, 386
freerunning, 386
French Resistance, 150
French Revolution, 194
Freud, Sigmund and Freudian theory, 330, 331, 332, 333
Friedmann, Litzi, 166
frigidity, 333
From Russia, with Love, 45, 46, 52, 60, 61, 63, 66, 71, 79, 165
From the Hip, 256
frustration, 52, 105, 121, 374, 394, 396, 397
Fu Manchu, 55
Fuchs, Klaus, 163
fugitive, 25
Fugitive, The, 384, 385, 399, 407
fugue state, 343
Funeral in Berlin, 168, 172
Furst, Alan, 149, 155
gadgets, 27, 47, 65, 66, 155, 156, 157, 307, 310
Gallipoli Memories, 145
gallows humour, 36, 397
gambling, 41, 71
Game, Set, and Match trilogy, 152
games, 34, 53, 61, 70, 71, 72, 115, 147, 148, 174, 176, 180, 208, 232, 238, 243, 308, 384
gangsters, 6, 150
Garbo, Greta, 341
Garden of Lies, 341
Gardner, Erle Stanley, 234
Gardner, John, 142, 148, 150, 151, 156
Garrison, Jim, 208
Garry, Jane, 232
Gaslight, 362
Gautier, Leon, 81
Gay, William, 387
Gaywyck, 364
General Medical Council, 287
generosity, 81
genetic engineering, 306
genetically-modified crops, 310
genocide, 83, 86
genre conventions, 5, 6, 7, 9, 11, 13, 15, 114, 136, 151, 158, 190, 195, 198, 230, 240, 284, 308, 317, 410, 412
genre fiction, 6, 7, 115, 175, 178, 191, 309, 316
Genre Writer series, 6, 7, 384
gentleman-heroes, 146

gentlemen's club, 40
Genty, Stéphanie, 135
George Smiley, 19, 138, 150, 151, 159, 160, 161, 162, 167, 169, 176, 177, 178, 180
Gerrig, Richard J., 98, 120, 121
Gerritsen, Tess, 281, 282, 283, 284
Gewirtz, Paul, 232
Ghost, The, 341
Gibson, J. William, 314, 316
Gielgud, John, 145
Gift, The, 375
Gilgamesh, 9
Gillers, Stephen, 258
Giraudoux, Jean, 341, 344
gladiator, 243
glimmer of hope, 101
Go! Go! Go!, 228
goal, see also objective, 20, 21, 29, 33, 34, 83, 86, 89, 95, 99, 120, 125, 127, 128, 130, 131, 133, 238, 391, 394
goal-oriented stories, 125
God Complex, 287
Godfather, The, 36, 117, 141
Godzilla, 307
Goldberg, Leonard S., 281
Golden Gate, The, 311
Goldeneye, 44
Goldfinger, 55, 57, 63, 66, 70, 71, 160
Goldman, William, 208, 209, 387
good guys, 37, 84, 168, 171, 190, 200, 231, 232, 233, 257, 308
Goodbye California, 311
Goodis, David, 341
Goodman, Sam, 140, 151
Google, 43, 135, 156, 197, 387
Google Maps, 393
Google Street View, 393
Google Translate, 135
Gordon, Alex, 38
Gothic, 10, 55, 143, 170, 285, 329, 361, 362, 363, 364, 365, 366, 387
Grady, James, 38, 181, 213
grand jeu, le, 72
Grant, Cary, 16, 23, 26, 53, 54, 115
Grant, Hugh, 281
Grant, James, 412
graverobbers, 287
Gravity, 282
Gray, Simon, 164
Grazier, Kevin R., 310
Great Britain, 34, 40, 41, 54, 62, 64, 72, 73, 79, 143, 146, 150, 153, 154, 159, 162, 163, 164, 167, 169, 173, 175, 177, 178, 180, 181, 191, 234, 238, 309, 314
Great Challenge, The, 386
Great Game, the, 70, 72, 80, 144, 147, 171, 174
Great Game, The (memoir), 72
Great Impersonation, The, 40, 143

Great War in England in 1897, The, 143, 312
great white shark, 112
greater good, the, 24, 33, 168
greed, 68, 73, 148, 162, 198, 242, 247, 287, 288, 297
Greek Memories, 145
Greeks, Ancient, 237, 240, 280, 340
Greenberg, Martin H., 307, 310, 315
Greene, Graham, 38, 80, 145, 146, 147, 148, 150, 158, 159, 160, 169, 170, 175, 181, 182
Greenmantle, 181
Grisham, John, 134, 230, 233, 236, 237, 241, 246, 251, 253, 258, 261
Groundstar Conspiracy, The, 353
group behaviour, 97
Guantanamo Bay, 153
Guardian, The, 200
guilt, 13, 36, 58, 111, 114, 147, 174, 230, 231, 232, 235, 238, 247, 248, 256, 257, 258, 259, 260, 262, 267, 268, 269, 270, 276, 345
Guinness, Alec, 151, 161
Gulino, Paul, 8
gunpowder, 121
Guns of Navarone, The, 311
gunslinger, 57, 232
gut, 18, 19, 108, 266, 267
hacking, 157
Hackman, Gene, 171, 261, 281
Haddad, Tonja, 249, 263
Hague Convention of 1899, 143
Hailey, Arthur, 312
'Hairless Mexican, The', 145
Hall, Adam, 159, 181
Halloween, 112, 399
HALO Trust, 155
Hamilton, Patrick, 362
Hamlet, 54
Hammett, Dashiell, 150, 160, 413
handcuffs, 11, 27
hangman, 93
Hanna and Barbera, 384
hardboiled detective, 5, 37, 58, 59, 76, 79, 80, 148, 149, 150, 159, 160, 241, 256
Harding, Luke, 215
Harpoon, 308
Harris, Thomas, 181, 198, 216, 223
Harrison, Harry, 296
Hartley, Anthony, 144
Harvard Law School, 236
Harvest, 281
Hawks, Howard, 111
head, heart and gut, 18
Healy, Jeremiah, 232, 239
Heart and Science, 234
heavies, 12, 19, 34, 37
hedonism, 74
heightening suspense, 101, 110
Hell in the Pacific, 111

Heller, Joseph, 84
Hellman, Geoffrey T., 42
Hellraiser, 112
helplessness, 94, 104
henchmen, 12, 15, 19, 26, 28, 34, 37, 42, 56, 57, 61, 67, 77, 214, 412
Henissart, Martha, 280
Hepburn, Audrey, 366
Hepburn, Katharine, 24
Herbert, Frank, 311
Hercule Poirot, 18, 53, 150, 411
Heritage of Michael Flaherty, The, 223
hero, 15, 18, 19, 20, 21, 23, 24, 36, 43, 44, 46, 49, 50, 51, 52, 56, 67, 68, 81, 82, 89, 91, 101, 107, 125, 128, 129, 131, 135, 147, 149, 159, 160, 199, 248, 250, 256, 266, 268, 269, 276, 277, 286, 309, 316
hero as victim, the, 181, 182
Hero with a Thousand Faces, The, 330
hero's darkest hour, 15
hero's journey, 68, 330
Hichens, Robert, 243
hide-and-seek, 34
High Anxiety, 36
High Crimes, 366
Highsmith, Patricia, 375
hijack thriller, 224-226
Hinton, S. E., 141
Hippocratic Oath, 286
Hiroshima, 149, 192, 307, 308
Histoires ou Contes du Temps Passé, 365
historical development, of genre / sub-genre, 39, 141, 194, 233, 280, 310, 340, 365, 375
historical fiction, genre, 312
History of Violence, A, 366
Hitchcock, Alfred, 5, 6, 10, 11-38, 40, 58, 80, 89, 102, 103, 104, 105, 109, 114, 115, 122, 140, 145, 164, 168, 190, 243, 330, 331, 332, 333, 362, 363, 365, 366
Hitcher,The, 22
Hitler, Adolf, 146, 149
hoax, 84
Hoffman, Arthur Sullivant, 130, 131
Hoffman, Dustin, 114, 208
Holocaust, 150
Holt, Victoria, 365
Holy Grail, 22, 411
home computing, 309
homeland, 146, 147, 159, 173
homosexuality, 56, 58, 59, 85, 167, 169, 176
Hone, Joseph, 181
honesty, 81
Honourable Schoolboy, The, 151, 160, 172, 176, 178, 180
hook, urban legend, 123
Hoover, J. Edgar, 143
hope, 90, 93, 98, 105, 111, 126, 397
Hopkins, Anthony, 233

Horler, Sidney, 157
Horman, Charles, 215
horror, genre, 5, 10, 22, 67, 94, 106, 112, 126, 284, 296, 313, 329, 375, 399
hospital, 243
hospital, setting, 285
hostage, 15
hostage thriller, 195, 198, 224-229
Hot Zone, The, 283, 297
Hotel, 312
hotels, 26, 41, 44, 62, 170
Hounds of Zaroff, The, 384
House of Cards, 194
House of Cards (novel & film), 38
House of Commons, 177
House on 92nd Street, The, 149
Household Words, 233
Household, Geoffrey, 38, 68, 384
'How to Write a Chase Scene The Marathon Man Way', 387
Howard, Hartley, 182
Human Factor, The, 148, 181, 182
human rights abuses, 69, 85, 139, 165, 286
humiliation, fear of, 111, 127, 129
humility, 287
HUMINT, 169
humour, 26, 36, 53, 77, 103, 109, 111, 114, 129, 282, 285
Hunt for Red October, The, 137, 305, 308, 310, 311, 316-321
Hunter, Stephen, 200
Hussein, Saddam, 152
hypocrisy, 196
Hysteria, 345
Ice Station Zebra, 311
ice-maiden, 115
iconography, 7, 11, 15, 27, 49, 65, 150, 171, 196, 245, 285, 307, 333, 354
idealism, 196, 240, 241, 245, 247, 268
identification with hero, 25, 57, 94, 102, 239
identity, theme, 344
ideology, 33, 68, 139, 140, 149, 161, 162, 164, 165, 173
Iles, Francis, 362
Iliad, 142
illicit love affairs, 35
illness, 56, 278, 332
Illuminati, 85
IMDb, 393
immigration, 87
immoral, 29, 32, 85, 92, 130, 257
immortal characters, 54
impending disaster, 100
imperialism, 63, 73, 85
imprisonment, 29
improvisation, 18, 50, 51, 66, 68, 73, 174, 396
In the Line of Fire, 197, 199, 200, 208, 411
incentives, 100, 287
inciting incident, see also challenge and call to adventure, 57

incompetence, 20, 50, 51, 78, 147, 171, 177, 179
incompetent, stalker type, 374
Indiana Jones, 412
indifference to suffering, 75
industrial espionage, 35, 157
industrial revolution, 306
industrialists, 146, 148, 195
Inferno, 341
ingenuity, 20, 27, 29, 49, 50, 65, 68, 91, 396
Ingrid Goes West, 374
Inherit the Wind, 261, 268
injury, 74, 75, 100, 111, 127, 128, 129, 130, 278, 389
injustice, 17, 30, 81, 102, 130, 231, 232, 238, 247, 258, 266, 413
inner balance, 96
innocence, 11, 12, 14, 20, 22, 23, 26, 28, 37, 50, 60, 74, 75, 78, 107, 115, 139, 147, 158, 173, 174, 230, 231, 233, 235, 238, 240, 247, 249, 252, 258, 259, 260, 262, 265, 276, 288, 344, 364
innocence, presumption of, 258
innuendo, 61
insane asylum, 333
insanity, fear of, 126
instability, 93, 95, 97, 98
integrity, 175, 196, 254
intelligence gathering, 17, 137, 149, 152, 154, 162, 168, 169, 174, 175, 180, 189, 317
intelligence services, 80, 138, 156, 157, 165, 168, 177, 179, 180, 309, 315, 317, 411
Intent to Kill, 207
interdictions, 91
internal conflict, 127, 328
Internal Revenue Service, 193
International Bridges to Justice – Criminal Defense Wiki, 269
International Spy Museum, 156
internet, 154, 157, 172, 309
Interpreter, The, 193, 208
interrogation, 42, 140, 156, 160, 164, 171, 197, 260
interrogatories, legal, 261
intimacy-seeking, stalker type, 374
invasion literature, 312
Invasion of 1910, The, 40, 312
investigative journalist, as hero, 193
investigative journalists, 197
invisibility, 35
Invisible Man, The, 311
Ipcress File, The, 150, 181, 182
iron curtain, 149

irony, 21, 60, 61, 68, 76, 77, 99, 103, 145, 169, 172, 175, 178, 186, 231, 243, 268, 351, 353, 354, 363, 364
irresponsibility, 16, 34
Isani, Shaeda, 134
ISIS Hostage, The, 229
ISIS/Daesh, 152
Islamic fundamentalism, 34
Islamic terrorists, 153, 159, 314
Islamists, radical, 152, 309
Island of Doctor Moreau, The, 311
isolation, 14, 22, 24, 25, 27, 49, 52, 53, 60, 61, 62, 63, 65, 67, 68, 76, 78, 79, 115, 122, 158, 159, 162, 170, 171, 177, 178, 209, 214, 219, 231, 232, 240, 245, 247, 267, 363, 365, 384
Jack Reacher, 67, 388, 410, 412, 413
Jack Reacher: Never Go Back, 412
Jack Ryan, 309, 315, 316, 317
Jackal, The, 198, 199, 200, 207
Jagged Edge, 243, 249, 259, 270, 273-274
James Bond, 5, 6, 19, 26, 28, 35, 39-82, 120, 121, 127, 138, 141, 144, 150, 151, 154, 156, 159, 160, 161, 162, 163, 168, 170, 171, 173, 174, 177, 180, 181, 182, 185, 186, 187, 191, 200, 214, 216, 296, 297, 306, 314, 315, 317, 407, 412, 413
James Bond Dossier, The, 39
'James Bond's Goldenscribes', 46
Jane Eyre, 362
Jardine, Warwick, 157
jargon, 167, 178, 307
Jason Bourne, 353, 387, 410, 411
Jaws, 56, 112, 113, 122, 123, 284, 399
Jennes, Gail, 278, 284
jeopardy, 9, 19, 28, 53, 73, 83, 111, 126, 130, 131, 132, 133, 339, 365
Jesus Christ, 142
Jews, 84, 88, 150
JFK, 208
jingoism. See patriotism
Johnson, Lyndon B., 192
Johnston, Sharon, 254
Jonathan Cape (publisher), 45
Jones, Tommy Lee, 385
Joshua, Biblical character, 142
Journal of Medical Humanities, 279
journalism, 157, 196, 197, 208, 215, 265
journey into fear, 181
Journey into Fear, 147, 181, 182
joust, 238
Judas Iscariot, 142
judge, 76, 86, 234-277
Judgement at Nuremberg, 264
Judith, Biblical character, 142

Julius Caesar, 194
Jumpin' Jack Flash, 36
Jung, Carl and Jungian theory, 330
Jurassic Park, 305, 312, 322-327, 384
jury, 76, 230, 231, 233, 235, 238, 240, 242, 244, 245, 246, 251, 259, 261, 262, 263, 264, 265, 266, 267, 268, 269
jury tampering, 246, 251, 267
justice, 17, 23, 76, 85, 107, 129, 176, 230, 231, 232, 233, 234, 235, 236, 237, 238, 241, 242, 245, 247, 248, 250, 253, 255, 259, 267, 268, 351
Justice Denoted, 240
justifying, 96
Justitia, 237
Kaczynski, Theodore, 144
Kafka, Franz, 190
Kālidāsa, 340
kangaroo courts, 268
Karla Trilogy, 19, 151, 170, 176, 180
Karloff, Boris, 55
Keenan, Brian, 229
'Keeping the Reader on the Edge of His Seat', 112
Kelly, David, 153
Kelly, Grace, 16
Kennedy, Adam, 353
Kennedy, John F., 46, 83, 190, 191, 192, 193, 194, 198, 208, 213, 215
Kennedy, Robert F., 198, 213
KGB, 167, 180
Kidnapped, 10
kidnapping, 20, 23, 28, 58, 83, 86, 197, 229, 252, 383
Killing Floor, 412, 413
Kim, 72, 80, 144
Kim Jong-nam, 80, 155
Kim Jong-un, 155
Kind of Anger, A, 181
King Lear, 54
King of Comedy, The, 383
King, Martin Luther, 198
King, Stephen, 112, 122, 383, 384
Kipling, Rudyard, 72, 80, 144, 341
Kirkbride, Ronald, 164
kitchen sink realism, 123
Klausner, S. Z., 106
kleptomania, 333
Klute, 213
Kneale, Nigel, 296
Knebel, Fletcher, 215
knights, 54, 81, 82, 412
Koelsch, Stefan, 93, 95, 98, 104, 105
Koontz, Dean R., 112
Korsakoff's syndrome, 343
Krentz, Anne, 361, 362
Kubrick, Stanley, 112, 383
Kucherena, Anatoly, 215
Kuhn, Thomas, 330
Kyle, Chris, 200
lack, hero's, 16, 133
Laclos, Choderos de, 341

Lady Chatterley's Lover, 58
Lady Justice, 237
Lambrakis, Grigoris, 207
Lancet, The, 279
'Land Ironclads, The', 311
landmines, 155
Lang, Fritz, 362, 384
language, professional, 136
Larner, Jeremy, 195
Last Days of Alfred Hitchcock, The, 164
Last Juror, The, 237
Lathen, Emma, 280
Latsis, Mary Jane, 280
Law and the Lady, The, 234
law enforcement, 51, 68, 78, 107, 198
law firms, 231, 232, 241, 242, 243, 245, 247, 248, 251, 252, 253, 254, 255, 256, 257, 258
Law Society, 248
law, the, 21, 85, 86, 134, 230-277, 316
lawgiver, 238
Lawrence, D. H., 58
'Lawyer's Story of a Stolen Letter, The', 233
lawyer-hero, 230-277
lawyers, 86, 134, 135, 136, 230-277
lawyer-villain, 230-277
Le Carré, John, 5, 19, 39, 70, 72, 76, 77, 79, 80, 137-189, 317
Le Queux, William, 40, 143, 157, 163, 312
Lee, Christopher, 55
Lee, Harper, 234, 235
left-wing, politics, 147
legal arguments, 240
legal ethics, 235, 239, 246
legal procedures, 237, 240
legal process, 240, 247, 252
legal profession, 230-277
legal system, 31, 35, 85, 135, 136, 230-277, 284
legal technicalities and loopholes, 253
legal thriller, sub-genre, 5, 6, 39, 85, 134, 230-277
legend, see also mythology, 35
Legion of Honour, 143
Legoland Trilogy, 155
Lehman, Ernest, 25, 164
Lehne, Moritz, 93, 95, 98, 104, 105
Leigh, Janet, 114
Leinster, Colin, 223
lesser of two evils, 248
Lethe, 340
letter of the law, 253
Levanter, The, 147, 181, 198, 216, 219-223
Levine, Paul, 239, 269
Lewis, Jerry, 383
Liaisons Dangereuses, Les, 341
licence to kill, 35, 47, 71, 79, 138, 150
Lichtenstein, Edward H., 117, 118, 119
lift shafts, 27

Light of Day, The, 147, 219
Like. Share. Follow, 374
likely vs. unlikely outcomes, 99
limits on advertising, lawyers, 250
Lindley, David, 310
litigation, 236, 253, 255, 256
Little Nikita, 167
Litvinenko, Alexander, 80, 155
Live and Let Die, 55, 63, 64, 79
Living Daylights, The, 66
local guides, 68, 79
locations, see settings and locations
Locke, John, 344
Locke, Vince, 366
logic, 240
Lom, Herbert, 207
loneliness, 111, 158
Long Fatal Love Chase, A, 366
Long John Silver, 53
Long Wait, The, 341
Long, Huey, 195
Looking for Mr. Goodbar, 366
Los Angeles Times, 270
loss of identity, fear of, 126
loss of innocence, 36
Louisiana Purchase, 195
love, 20, 24, 32, 35, 55, 58, 60, 76, 81, 125, 129, 131, 139, 148, 150, 160, 166, 169, 174, 243, 362
Love Story, 284
Lovecraft, H. P., 287
Loyal Spy, A, 155
loyalty, 20, 36, 73, 81, 125, 131, 133, 158, 159, 164, 168, 169, 173
Lucas, George, 330
Luddites, 306
Ludlum, Robert, 410, 411
Lumet, Sidney, 123, 151, 236
Lundegaard, Erik, 193
Lüthi, 91
Lyall, Gavin, 181
Lyle, Doug P., 282
lynch mob, 268
Lyons, C. J., 281
macabre, 36
Macbeth, 54, 103, 194
MacDonald, John D., 375
MacGuffin, 13, 15, 22, 23, 27, 29, 49, 57-58, 168, 190, 194, 199, 309, 311, 345, 385
MacGyver, 66, 91, 396
Machiavelli, 194
MacInnes, Helen, 181
Mackenzie, Compton, 145, 157
MacLean, Alistair, 311
Maclean, Donald, 163, 176
mad dogs, 100
MAD Magazine, 27
Magruder, Jeb, 158
Mahabharata, 340
Maibaum, Richard, 46
Making Movies, 123
male role-models, 315
Maltese Falcon, The, 22
Mamet, David, 236, 242
Man and Wife, 234

man on the run. See amateur on the run
Man Who Knew Too Much, The, 40, 114
Man Who Walked Away, The, 341
Man Who was Thursday, The, 144
Manchurian Candidate, The, 207
Mangin, Anthelme, 341
manhunt, 10, 67, 133, 230, 313, 384, 385
Manhunt (novel & film), 38
manhunts, 6
Manichean ideology, 72, 73
Manicheanism, 73
Manning, Chelsea, 153, 159, 165
Markham, Robert, 77
Markov, Georgi, 80, 155
Markstein, George, 228
Marnie, 333
marriage, 16, 79, 315
Marrs, Jim, 208
Marsollier, Benoît-Joseph, 341
martial arts, 386
Marxism, 166, 167
masculinity, 81, 316, 361
Mask of Dimitrios, The, 147, 149, 181, 219
Mask of Fu Manchu, The, 55
masochistic guilt, 332
Mason, A. E. W., 157
Mason, James, 53, 151, 242
Master of Disguise: My Secret Life in the CIA, 156
Master of Suspense. See Hitchcock, Alfred
Master of the World, 41
Masterman, John, 157
Mata Hari, 59
Maugham, W. Somerset, 80, 138, 145, 148, 155, 157, 159, 166, 176, 179
McCarry, Charles, 158
McCarthy, Cormac, 386
McCarthy, Eugene J., 195
McCarthy, John, 229
McCarthy, Joseph, 150, 153, 192, 255
McCrae, Joel, 384
McDonald, Jay, 278
McGoohan, Patrick, 411
McLellan, M. Faith, 279, 283
McMorrow, Judith A., 238, 247, 250, 258
McNeile, Herman Cyril. See Sapper
Med, The, 313
Medallion, The, 386
medical confidentiality, 286
medical ethics, 278, 283, 284, 286, 287, 288
medical malpractice, 284
medical oath, 284, 288
medical practices, 284
medical procedures, 281, 282, 313
medical profession, 279, 286
medical research, 278, 284, 287, 297
medical slang, 282
medical technology, 310
medical terminology, 281, 282
'Medical Thrillers: Doctored Fiction for Future Doctors?', 279
medical treatment, 287
medical thriller, sub-genre, 5, 10, 39, 85, 134, 278-304, 306, 312
medicine, 21, 35, 85, 86, 134, 135, 278-304
medieval, 81, 143, 238
melodrama, 111, 148
Memento, 342
'Memories Aren't Made of This: Amnesia at the Movies', 342
Mendez, Tony, 156
Menkel-Meadow, Carrie, 241
mental capacity. See ingenuity
mental stress, 96
mental threat, 129
mentor, 15, 49, 79, 132, 133, 136, 245, 246, 375
Mercer, Cecil William. See Yates, Dornford
Merchant of Venice, The, 233
Merle, Robert, 207
messaging apps, 173
MI5, 80, 138, 155, 157, 159, 176, 179, 180
MI6, 154, 158, 176, 178, 179, 180
'Michael Crichton's State of Confusion', 310
Micro, 283
microdots, 172
microfilm, 22, 23, 27, 156
Midnight Plus One, 181
Midnight Run, 399
midpoint, 12, 13, 23, 57, 395
milieu, 7, 171
military, 35, 51, 81, 85, 86, 134, 136, 143, 146, 149, 154, 165, 169, 258, 259, 297, 307, 308, 309, 314, 315
military plans, 11, 86, 137
military secrets, 86
military technology, 310
military techno-thriller, 5, 305, 306, 308, 311, 314, 316
Mine Own Executioner, 341
Minister, the, 179
Ministry of Fear, The, 38, 148, 149
minority rights - see also racism, sexism, and homosexuality, 87
Miracles, 386
Mirage, 345, 346
mirrors, 17, 43
misconduct, lawyers, 250
misdirection, 113
Misery, 122, 383
misogyny, 59
Missing, 215
Missing Person, 341
mission, 33, 39, 41, 62, 65, 78, 133, 137, 139, 141, 147, 148, 151, 174, 181, 182, 186, 187, 189, 199, 200, 214, 216, 224, 228, 229, 243, 296, 297, 412
mission plot, 181, 182, 214
Mission: Impossible, 172
mistaken identity, 5, 27, 104, 328, 351, 352
mistrial, 238, 251
mistrust of allies, 177
Mnemosyne, 340
Model Rules of Professional Conduct, American Bar Association, 248, 257, 258, 261
Modern Gothic, 365
Modiano, Patrick, 341
mole, 137, 151, 152, 167, 169, 174, 180, 182, 186, 188, 189
Molière, 352
money laundering, 83, 86, 151
Moneychangers, The, 312
Monk, William, 341
monologue, 110
monomania, 21
monomyth, 330
monster, 22, 122, 307, 399
Moonraker, 43, 51, 52, 55, 71
Moonstone, The, 234, 341
Moore, Brian, 207
Moore, Roger, 59, 66, 77
morality, 7, 16, 17, 18, 20, 21, 24, 30, 31, 32, 33, 34, 52, 55, 59, 72, 75, 76, 83, 85, 91, 95, 96, 99, 100, 102, 128, 130, 131, 132, 139, 143, 144, 148, 158, 159, 161, 164, 173, 196, 235, 241, 247, 248, 254, 255, 256, 258, 259, 267, 281, 282, 283, 287, 309, 316, 353, 374, 395
Moreau, Abel, 341, 344
Morgann, Maurice, 54
Morphology of the Folktale, 9
Morrell, David, 384, 399, 411
Morrell, Jill, 229
Morton, Ray, 46
Moscow Option, The, 155
Moscow Rules, the, 156
Moses, 142
Most Dangerous Game, The, 384
Mother Goose Tales, 365
motions, legal, 252, 255, 261
motivation, 11, 19, 49, 56, 57, 68, 74, 83, 84, 129, 162, 165, 173, 191, 198, 199, 208, 242, 247, 257, 287, 288, 314, 391
motivation, of assassins, 198
motivation, of spies, 164
motive, 21, 31, 33, 106, 153, 165, 166, 167, 198, 199, 297
Mr. Nice Guy, 386
Mr. Smith Goes to Washington, 190
Mrs. Doubtfire, 351
Mullen, Paul E., 374
murder, 11, 12, 13, 19, 29, 83, 84, 86, 89, 103, 104, 108, 112, 135, 139, 151, 178, 191, 198, 232
Murder of Quality, A, 150, 151, 160
Murder on the Orient Express, 268
Mussolini, 146
My Cousin Vinny, 263, 264
My Silent War, 147
Mycroft Holmes, 178
Mysteries of Udolpho, The, 365
Mysterious Mr. Sabin, 40, 143
mystery, 21, 31, 34, 62, 65, 109, 135, 141, 189
Mystery, 18, 182, 230
Mystery Fiction: Theory and Technique, 123
Mystery of Dr. Fu-Manchu, The, 41
mystery, genre, 5, 9, 10, 17, 18, 33, 108, 117, 118, 120, 124, 135, 138, 139, 141, 151, 174, 181, 182, 188, 189, 199, 209, 230, 233, 242, 276, 278, 280, 332, 352, 361, 364, 385, 411, 412
'Mythbusting Thriller Science: Space Bacteria', 310
mythology, 35, 140, 311
Nagasaki, 149, 192
Naked Edge, The, 362
Naked Prey, The, 384
nanotechnology, 309, 313
nanotech-now.com, 310
Napoleon, 143, 167
Napoleonic Wars, 41
'Narrative Structure in Fleming, The', 46, 50, 70
narratology, 94
national security, 28, 34, 35, 129, 152, 158, 197
National Security Agency, 152
Naval Intelligence, 42
Nayak, Amarjeet, 278, 279, 285, 287
Nazis, 41, 84, 146, 149, 182, 208, 209
Nefes, Türkay Salim, 87
nerve agent, 80, 155, 305, 312
Never Go Back, 412
Never Say Never Again, 66
New Internationalist, 84, 87
New York Times, 42, 192, 193, 215, 234, 235, 236, 280, 281, 342
New Yorker, The, 42
Newman, Bernard, 157, 175
Newman, Paul, 236
News of Devils, 155
Newsday, 193
Nicholas II, 84
Nicholson, Jack, 43, 269
Nick of Time, 200
Night of the Hunter, The, 386
Night Soldiers, 149
Nightfall, 341
Nightmare on Elm Street, A, 123
Nimitz Class, 313
Nina, or The Woman Crazed with Love, 340

Nina, ou La Folle par Amour, 340
Nine Hours to Rama, 207
nineteenth-century, 42, 54, 64, 72, 141, 142, 143, 153, 306, 340, 341
Niven, David, 53
Nixon, Richard, 192, 193, 194
No Country for Old Men, 386
No Name, 234
noir, 37, 59, 361, 362, 366
no-mans-land, 62, 68
non-fiction thriller, 208, 283, 297
Norquist, Roy, 44
North by Northwest, 10, 12, 16, 22, 23, 25, 26, 38
Nothing Lasts Forever, 228, 311
NSA. *See* National Security Agency
nuclear bomb, 310
nuclear weapons, 23, 149, 150, 192, 307, 311
Nunn May, Alan, 163, 165
O'Neill, Brian, 93
Oath of Maimonides, 286
objectivity, 102, 249, 344
obligations, 35, 127, 131, 133, 250
'Observations on the Double Agent', 168
Observer, The, 161, 162, 166, 167, 177
obstacles, 19, 21, 23, 25, 78, 95, 101, 113, 122, 394, 397
Odyssey, 142
Official Secrets Act, Great Britain, 145
oil crisis, 192
Okhranka, 84
Oland, Warner, 55
Old Boy Network, 176
Old Country, The, 164
Old Norse, 237
Oldman, Gary, 151, 161
Olympus Has Fallen, 224, 228
on the run, see also pursuit and chase, 10, 12, 15, 23, 25, 62, 77, 219, 396
On the Trail of the Assassins, 208
One Shot, 412
Ong-Bak: The Thai Warrior, 386
online scammers, 157
Open Secret, 155
opening statements, 259, 262, 263
Operation Eagle Claw, 228
opinions, 95, 110, 265
Oppenheim, E. Phillips, 39, 40, 42, 75, 80, 143, 163
opposition - see also obstacles and villain, 17, 21, 95
Orczy, Baroness, 59, 194
ordinary people, 17, 26, 29, 35, 52, 68, 69, 74, 77, 78, 82, 85, 148, 149, 162, 168, 173, 175, 242, 245, 267

ordinary world, 17, 18, 20, 25, 27, 33, 37, 59, 79, 158, 159
organic amnesia, 341
Organisation Armée Secrète, 207
Organisation, The, 51, 65
Orient Express, 63
Ortony, Andrew, 98
Osteopathic Oath, 286
Othello, 54, 103
Our Man in Havana, 148
Outbreak, 296, 297
outbreaks, 5, 7
outlaws, 141
outsider, 16, 24, 27, 52, 63, 139, 140, 141, 158, 163, 174, 176, 180, 241, 256, 279, 413
Outsider, The, 223
outwitting villain, 17, 67
Overload, 312
overwhelming odds, 100, 241, 248
Oxford Dictionary of Literary Terms, 81
Oxford English Dictionary, The, 328, 331
pace, 10, 12, 77, 247, 388
padded rooms, 333
pain, 100, 126, 127, 128, 332, 387
Pakula, Alan, 213
Palmer, Jerry, 21, 50, 51, 52, 58, 59, 60, 61, 62, 63, 74, 75, 81, 83
Palmer, Michael, 281, 282, 283, 288
Papke, David Ray, 240, 244, 259, 262, 267, 269
Paradine Case, The, 243
paradox of suspense, 98
paralegals, 240
Parallax View, The, 198, 213-14
paralysis, 126
paramedics, 52
paranoia, 20, 30, 31, 32, 140, 177, 190, 193, 213, 309, 329, 331
paranoid personality disorder, 30
paranoid schizophrenia, 30
parcours du combattant, 386
parkour, 386
Paths of Glory, 259
Patient, The, 282
patriarchy, 316
Patriot Games, 309, 316
patriotism, 11, 40, 41, 42, 81, 139, 146, 148, 149, 159, 173, 175
pay-off, of suspense and threats, 113
Pearl Harbor, 192
Pearson, Carol, 362
Pearson, Will, 228
Peck, Gregory, 235
Penn Warren, Robert, 195
Pentagon Papers, 153, 192
people trafficking, 83, 86
Pérez-Peña, Richard, 342
Perils of Pauline, The, 22
perjury, 250

Perowne, Barry, 157
Perrault, Charles, 365
Perry Mason, 230, 234
The Authorship and Reproduction of a Popular Hero, 234
Perry, Anne, 341
persecution, 30, 399
Persian Gulf, 152
personal freedom, theme, 345
personal stakes, 129
personal stakes, increasing, 132
personality, 285
perverting the course of justice, 86
Petit, Michel, 134, 135, 136
Peyton Place, 375
pharmaceutical research, 279, 284
philanthropism, 287
Philby, Kim, 80, 144, 147, 148, 158, 163, 166, 177, 178, 180
philosophy, 161, 242, 315
phobias, 95, 126, 333
Phoenix, Chris, 310
Phoenix, River, 167
phones and cell phones, 28, 157, 173, 197, 310
physical harm, 69, 126, 328
physical stamina, 17, 49, 50, 51, 68, 74
physical threat, 129
physician writer, 280
Physician's Weekly, 288
'Physician-Writers', 279
Pirandello, Luigi, 341
pity, 107
Plague from Space, 296
plants and payoffs, 109
Play Misty for Me, 375, 376-383
Playboy, 42, 44, 45, 53, 58, 59, 60
playwright, 91, 244
pleasure, maximising, 106
Plot Basics, 7, 8, 74, 389
plot conventions, 8
plot device. *See* MacGuffin
plot structure, 6, 7, 11, 12, 13, 70, 108, 181, 189, 197, 208, 209, 213, 259, 345
plotting, story, 13, 51
Poe, Edgar Allan, 102, 233
poetic justice, 21, 76, 91, 268
Poetics, 107
Point Break, 387
Point of Impact, 200
point of view, 16, 116
police, 13, 26, 27, 30, 35, 37, 52, 77, 86, 118, 135, 190, 245, 248, 265
police actions, 309
police procedural, 6, 189
Police Story, 386
political thriller, sub-genre, 5, 39, 85, 137, 138, 152, 181, 190, 191-229, 297, 353, 412
politicians, 34, 51, 85, 86, 174, 190, 195, 196, 244, 246, 308
politics, 21, 34, 35, 71, 72, 73, 86, 134, 146, 162, 190, 192, 193, 195, 196, 246, 315

Pollack, Sydney, 236
polonium, 80, 155
Poodle Springs, 79
pop psychology, 330
Pope, H. G., 340
Pope, Katherine, 362
'Popular Culture as Lens in Legal Professionalism', 239
Popular Culture Genres, 46
popular front, 147
popular justice, 238, 248
pornography, 58, 60, 74
Portia, 233
Post, Melville Davisson, 234
power, 19, 20, 21, 29, 32, 34, 35, 36, 54, 69, 72, 73, 75, 83, 84, 85, 86, 87, 129, 131, 140, 145, 148, 165, 169, 190, 191, 194, 196, 237, 242, 255, 260, 284, 287, 288, 297, 309, 314, 316, 362, 364, 374
Power, 215
Power and the Glory, The, 148
Power of Myth, The, 330
Poyer, David, 313
Pratchett, Terry, 91
precedents, legal, 237, 250
pre-credits sequence, 47, 65
Predator, The, 384
predatory, stalker type, 374
predictability, 109, 398
prediction, 93, 97, 108
prejudice, 87, 162
Preminger, Otto, 235
President Vanishes, The, 194
Preston, Richard, 283, 297
Presumed Innocent, 231, 233, 236, 243, 259, 265, 267, 269, 270, 271-273
presumption of innocence, 238, 252
Prey, 310
Price, Nancy, 366
Price, Vincent, 362
Pringle, Mary Beth, 240, 241
Priollet, Marcel, 341, 343
prior solution removed, 121
PRISM, 152
prison thrillers, 7
Prisoner, The, 411
private detectives. *See* hardboiled detectives
private eyes. *See* hardboiled detectives
proactive, 14, 395
probability, 90, 94, 99, 100, 101, 107
probability of outcomes, 113
probable vs. improbable outcomes, 100
procedural law, 238
professional, 16, 20, 29, 35, 39, 47, 49, 51, 52, 56, 66, 67, 76, 78, 79, 133, 134, 135, 136, 162, 169, 171, 181, 195, 198, 199, 239, 249, 250, 253, 254, 255, 262, 279, 281,

282, 283, 284, 285, 288, 307, 316
professional hero, 6, 39, 48, 49, 50, 51, 52, 55, 56, 57, 58, 59, 61, 62, 68, 74, 75, 76, 78, 79, 82, 134, 151, 315
professional slang, 282
professionally-based fiction, 134
programming, of bureaucrat, 20, 21, 51, 68, 71, 73
Prometheus, 311
Promised Land, 142
proof, 28, 173, 238
propaganda, 268, 312
Propp, Vladimir, 9, 79
prosecution, 238, 244, 245, 246, 252, 258, 259, 262, 265, 266, 267, 276, 277
prosecution, the, 238
prosecutor, 235, 240, 249, 262, 263, 264
protagonist, 100, 107, 146, 240
protagonist, see also hero, 22, 39, 67, 92, 94, 100, 101, 102, 107, 131, 134, 135, 145, 147, 199, 259, 270, 288, 315, 329, 332, 333, 351, 353
protector, from assassin, 199, 200
Protocols of the Learned Elders of Zion, 84
psychiatry, 332
Psycho, 114, 122
psychoanalysis, 5, 328, 330, 331, 332, 333
psychodrama. *See* psychological thriller
psychogenic fugue, 343
psychographics, 154
psychological profiling, 6, 328
psychological thriller, sub-genre, 5, 10, 11, 132, 198, 328, 329, 330, 331
psychological trauma, 69, 332, 339, 341, 343
psychology, 86, 94, 123, 282, 328, 329, 330
psychology of suspense, 34
psychopaths, 328
psycho-traumatic thriller. *See* psychoanalysis thriller
PTSD, 313, 412
public humiliation, fear of, 126
public opinion, 34, 158, 258, 308
public school, 40, 71, 145, 161, 162, 166, 176
Publishers Weekly, 288
Pulitzer Prize, 195, 234, 235
Pulp Fiction, 117
pumpkin, see MacGuffin, 23
punishment, 76, 96, 107, 237, 242, 245, 268, 316
'Purloined Letter, The', 233
pursuers, 11, 27, 389, 390, 391, 394
pursuit, 13, 21, 22, 25, 26, 28, 85, 384, 385, 386, 388, 389, 394
Pusey, Allen, 253

Putin, Vladimir, 152
Puzo, Mario, 117, 141
puzzles, 141
Quaid, Dennis, 246
Quarter 1, 12, 46
Quarter 2, 12, 46
Quarter 3, 12, 47
Quarter 4, 12, 47
Quatermass Experiment, 296
Queensbury, Marquis of, 74, 176
quest, 9
Quest for Karla, The, 176
Question of Attribution, A, 164
Quiet American, The, 148
Quiller Memorandum, The, 160, 181
racism, 41, 55, 56, 85
Radcliffe, Ann, 365
rage, 100, 232
Raid on Entebbe, 198, 224, 228
Raiders of the Lost Ark, 114
Rainmaker, The, 243, 255, 259, 271, 274-275
Raleigh, Sir Walter, 163
Rambo, 316, 317, 384, 386-409
rape, 69
rats, 126, 333
reader expectations, 91
reader manipulation, 124
reader participation, 90, 92
Reagan, Ronald, 308, 309, 310
RealClimate.org, 310
realism, 39, 66, 69, 70, 73, 77, 79, 80, 81, 82, 123, 138, 148, 151, 159, 169, 176, 196, 235, 281, 283, 297, 308, 413
reality TV, 80, 155
reality vs. what *seems* to be, 196
Rear Window, 16, 28
reasonable doubt, 264, 265, 267, 276
reassurance, 231
Rebecca, 362, 363, 364, 365, 366-373
rebellion, 141, 166
rebirth, theme, 344
Recalled to Life, 341
Recognition of Shakuntala, The, 340
Red Harvest, 413
red herrings, 113
Red Storm Rising, 308, 309, 312
'Redeeming Vietnam: Techno-Thriller Novels of the 1980s', 314
redemption, 17, 21, 32, 33, 71, 148, 150, 257
Redford, Robert, 19, 195, 208
Reed, Barry, 236
Reed, Carol, 170
Reel Justice, 259, 263
re-evaluation, 14, 31
referee, judge as, 246
Reilly, Sidney, 179
rejected, stalker type, 374
religion, 21, 32, 72, 81, 85, 139, 142, 148, 150, 168, 173, 180, 198, 411, 412

Rendition, 223
Renner, Jeremy, 410
reparative justice, 237
Republican Party, 212, 309, 315
research laboratory, setting, 285
resentful, stalker type, 374
resentment, 158
Reservoir Dogs, 117
resilience, 50, 69
resolution, 93, 95, 97, 98, 107, 108, 114, 118, 119, 231, 237, 239, 283, 398
responsibilities, 35, 36, 254
restoration of order, 33
restorative justice, 237
Retour de Martin Guerre, Le, 366
retrograde amnesia, 342
revelation, 101, 116, 119, 137, 245
Revenant, Le, 341
revenge, 21, 29, 31, 41, 68, 73, 83, 165, 235, 259, 374, 412
reversing audience expectations, 114
revolution and civil unrest, 35, 83, 86
reward, 19, 60, 96
rhetoric, 240, 243
Richard III, 194
ricin, 80, 155
Riddle of the Sands, The, 9, 144, 311
Riedl, Mark, 93
Right of Way, The, 341
rights, Constitutional, 237
right-wing, 146, 309
Rimington, Stella, 80, 138, 155, 157, 159
Rio Bravo, 111
Riot Act, The, 155
rising tide. *See* deadline and ticking clock
risk, 26, 27, 34, 51, 52, 64, 72, 73, 75, 78, 92, 110, 111, 125, 127, 129, 132, 133, 170, 172, 177, 179, 197, 209, 232, 241, 328, 340, 398
Road Runner, 384
Robin Cook: A Critical Companion, 287
Robin Hood, 53, 141
Robinson Crusoe, 54, 74
Robinson, Leah Ruth, 281
Robinson, Marlyn, 233, 234, 235
Robinson, Patrick, 313
robots, 306, 309
Robson, Mark, 375
Robur the Conqueror, 41
RocknRolla, 387
Rodell, Marie F., 90, 123
Roderick Random, 280
Roger Brook, 41
Rogers, Amy, 310
Rogue Male (film), 38, 68, 384
rogues, 53
Rohmer, Sax, 39, 41, 42, 55
roller coaster rides, 106
Rolling Stone, 148

romance. *See* romantic co-protagonist
romance (genre), 111
Romance of the Three Kingdoms, The, 142
romance, chivalric, 81
romance, genre, 5, 6, 361
Romancing the Stone, 399
Romans, 237
romantic co-protagonist, 11, 12, 14, 15, 18, 19, 20, 21, 23, 24, 25, 30, 34, 36, 49, 52, 57, 58, 60, 61, 62, 79, 125, 169, 243, 249, 276, 280, 284, 288, 331, 332, 333, 354, 410
romantic Suspense, 365
Romm, May E., 332
Rose, Reginald, 228
Rosen, Steven O., 239, 261, 263, 264, 266
Rosenberg, Bruce A., 54, 56, 58, 59, 60, 76, 80, 137, 138, 139, 140, 141, 142, 146, 147, 148, 150, 158, 159, 160, 170, 171, 175, 181, 182
Rosicrucians, 85
Rossner, Judith, 366
Roswell Incident, 83
rubber-ducky, 123
Rubin, Martin, 18
Rudolph, Alexandra, 244
Rules of Evidence, 265, 269
ruling class, 162
Rumble in the Bronx, 386
Rumblefish, 141
Runaway Jury, The, 246, 251, 253, 261
Running Man, The, 384
running out of options, 120
Russia, 72, 152, 153, 154, 155, 161, 164, 167, 175, 176, 314
ruthlessness, 20, 43, 144, 394
Rutledge, Andy, 254
Rye, Daniel, 229
sabotage, 133, 149, 182, 311
Saboteur, 12
sacrifice, 20, 21, 24, 32, 33, 34, 72, 174
sadism, 44, 70, 75, 125, 389
sadness, 100
sailing, 144
Saint, Eva Marie, 23
Sale, Richard, 207
Sambuchino, Chuck, 282
same only different, the, 5, 6, 114, 115, 413
Samson and Delilah, 59, 142
San Kuo, 142
Sánchez, Ilich Ramírez, 200
Sandhurst, 53
Sapper, 40, 41, 42, 144
Sarah Tobias, 264
Satan Bug, The, 311
Sauerberg, Lars Ole, 234
Scales, Prunella, 164
scandal, 43, 153, 154, 193

scapegoats and scapegoating, 84, 87, 146, 258
Scarlet Pimpernel, The, 194
scene goal, 101, 391
Scherr, Alex, 235, 239
Schindler, John R., 152
Schirmer Inheritance, The, 181
Schmidt, Gavin, 310
Schwarzenegger, Arnold, 384
science fiction, genre, 5, 111, 143, 162, 278, 296, 297, 305, 306, 307, 312, 313, 314
Science of Michael Crichton: An Unauthorized Exploration into the Real Science Behind the Fictional Worlds of Michael Crichton, The, 310
ScienceThrillers.com, 310
scorched earth, legal practices, 256
Scorsese, Martin, 375
Scott, Gale, 282, 283, 284, 288
Scott, Ridley, 112, 122
Scott, Walter, 10
Screenwriting The Sequence Approach, 8
ScriptMag, 46
SDI, 309
Sebold, William G., 149
second quarter. See Quarter 2
Second World War, 41, 44, 62, 64, 72, 137, 141, 146, 148, 149, 150, 155, 158, 168, 191, 192, 194, 195, 234, 308, 314
secret agent, 23, 39, 40, 41, 50, 51, 52, 53, 73, 145, 151, 167, 181, 187, 200, 411
secret agent thriller, 39-82, 50, 138
Secret Agent, The, 80, 144, 194
Secret Beyond the Door, 362
secret organisations, 35, 36
'Secret Origins of James Bond, The', 41
secret service, 40, 41, 42, 71, 79, 145, 155, 168, 177, 179, 182, 199
secret societies, 85, 141
secret world, 139, 146, 158, 159, 167
Secretary of State, 173
Seggie, Janet, 283
Seizure, 281
Sela, Owen, 181
self-dealing, 249
self-discovery, 16, 31, 340
self-harm, 333
self-indulgence, 43
selfishness, 21, 32, 33, 34, 68, 73, 74, 85, 248, 297
selflessness, 21, 32, 33, 34, 68, 73, 74, 128, 241, 287
self-obsession, 33
self-reliance, 49, 51, 141
self-sacrifice, 81, 128
self-sufficiency, 15
Selznick, David O., 332

sensation literature, 10, 55
sensations, 18, 106, 397
sense of wonder, 307
sentencing, 267
serial killers, 6, 240, 328
Serling, Rod, 215
Seton, Anya, 362, 364
settings and locations, 7, 11, 15, 25, 26, 49, 56, 61, 62, 63, 67, 91, 133, 169, 243, 244, 284, 285, 392
set-ups and payoffs, 91, 101, 109, 112, 113, 115, 124, 394
Seven, 387
Seven Days in May, 215
sex, 23, 42, 44, 55, 56, 58, 59, 60, 61, 62, 65, 145, 232, 249
sexism, 59, 61
sexual deviancy, 56
sexual encounters. See romantic co-protagonist
sexual tension, 132
sexuality, 56, 169, 362
shadow of a doubt, 238
Shakespeare, William, 35, 54, 103, 139, 194, 233, 351
Shapiro, Fred R., 232
Shattered, 345
Shelley, Mary, 280, 287, 306, 311
Sheppard v. Maxwell, 260
Sherlock Holmes, 18, 45, 52, 53, 54, 116, 178, 280, 411
Shining, The, 112
shock, 34, 103, 104, 109, 112, 117, 126, 276, 387
Shooter, 200
Short Night, The, 164
Shorter Oxford English Dictionary, 167
show trials, 268
Siegfried, 341, 344
Siegfried et le Limousin, 341
Silberman, Robert, 190
Silence of the Lambs, The, 216
Silkwood, 215
Silkwood, Karen, 215
Silvia, Paul J., 106
Simonett, John E., 244
Simple Art of Murder, The, 148
Simpson, O. J., 239
Sinatra, Frank, 207
Singer, Loren, 213
Sister Act, 351
Sisterhood, The, 281
Six Days of the Condor, 38, 181, 213
Sixth Amendment, U.S. Constitution, 258
Sixth Column, The, 41
skiing, 67
Skillman, T. Macdonald, 362
Skills, 386
Skulsky, Harold, 98, 101
skydivers, 106
Skyfall, 154
Sladen, N. St. Barbe, 40
slang, professional, 136
slasher movie, 328, 366
Slaughter, Frank G., 280
slavery, 83, 86
sleeper agents, 167

Sleeping with the Enemy, 366
slum tourism, 64
Smiley versus Karla, 176
Smiley's People, 151, 176, 178
Smith, Lane, 263
Smith, Will, 12
Smokey and the Bandit, 399
smoking, 95, 96
Smollett, Tobias, 280
Smuts, Aaron, 98, 99, 105
snakes, 100, 126, 333
Snare of the Hunter, 181
Sneakers, 157
Snelling, O. F., 40
snipers, 200
snobbery and violence, 41, 42, 44, 150
Snowden, 215
Snowden Files, The, 215
Snowden, Edward, 153, 155, 159, 165, 216
Snyder, Blake, 212
social change, 196
social debasement, 100
social engineering, 157
social identity, 344
social media, 154, 251
social relatedness, theme, 344
social roles, 141, 258
socialism, 146, 164, 166, 167
societal stakes, 129
societal stakes, increasing, 131
Sociological Review, The, 86
sociology, 86
solicitor. See lawyer
Solicitor's Code of Conduct, 252
Some Other Rainbow, 229
Somewhere in the Night, 344, 345
Sommersby, 366
Song of Treason, 155
sophistication, 25
South African Medical Journal, 283
Southern Gothic, 387
Soviet Union, 62, 72, 73, 149, 153, 156, 159, 161, 163, 164, 165, 167, 175, 192, 309, 313, 314
Spain, 153
Speed, 228
Spellbound, 330, 331, 333
spiders, 126, 333
Spielberg, Steven, 22, 83, 112, 114, 122
spies, doomed, 142
spies, motivation of, 164
Spillane, Mickey, 61, 341
spirit of the law, 253
spontaneity, 20
sports, 47, 71, 176, 232, 384
Springing of George Blake, The, 164
spy, 19, 52, 137, 138, 139, 142, 143, 147, 152, 181, 194
spy gadgets, 65, 66, 156
spy goes over, the, 181
Spy of Napoleon, A, 59
Spy Out The Land, 155

Spy Story, The, 34, 76, 137, 158, 181
spy thriller, see secret agent thriller and espionage thriller
Spy vs. Spy, 27
Spy Who Came in from the Cold, The, 72, 137-189
Spy Who Loved Me, The, 72
Spy Who Sat and Waited, The, 165, 167
spycraft, 156
spy-fi, 305
spymaster, 72, 139, 142, 151, 155, 176, 180, 308
stage, 244
stakes, 23, 29, 34, 84, 93, 94, 99, 101, 105, 111, 122, 125-133, 190, 232, 233, 239, 246, 260, 266, 390
stakes, raising the, 130
stalker thriller, 5, 22, 328, 366, 374-383
stalkers, 198, 329, 373, 374-383
Stallone, Sylvester, 384
star chambers, 268
Star Wars, 67, 330
Star Wars anti-missile project, 309
State of Fear, 310, 313
state secrets, 165, 265
statutes, legal, 237, 238
statutory law, 237
steganography, 172
Steinberg, Sybil, 288
Steinhauer, Olen, 155
step-mothers, 333
stereotypes, 115
Stevenson, Robert Louis, 10, 280, 287, 311
Stewart, Bill, 215
Stewart, James, 16
Stimson, Henry, 143
stock characters, 115
Stock, Jon, 155
stoicism, 128
stolen identity thriller, 5, 27, 83, 86, 111, 328, 351-361, 365
Stone, Oliver, 208, 216
Stookey, Lorena Laura, 287, 288
story literacy, 91
story question, 101
Stout, Rex, 194
straitjackets, 333
Strange Case of Dr. Jekyll and Mr. Hyde, 10, 280, 287, 311
Strange Conflict, 42
Strangers on a Train, 89, 124
Strategic Defense Initiative, 309
Street Lawyer, The, 253, 258
stress, 87, 106, 131
Strong Medicine, 312
'Study of Stalkers', 374
subconscious, 332
subjectivity, 94, 243
submarine, 66, 311, 317
submarine commander, 136
subpoena, 261
Suddenly, 207
Suez Crisis, 162
suffering, 56, 75, 90, 100, 126, 127, 128, 169, 268
suffocation, 126
suicide, 152, 198

suicide bombing, 86
Sun Tzu, 142
Sunday Times, 45
superhero, 47, 69
superior position. *See* dramatic irony
supernatural, 22
support team, 68
surgeon, 136
Surgeon, The, 281
surprise, 26, 34, 104, 110, 114, 115, 118, 119, 266, 276, 277, 387
surveillance, 28, 152, 153, 156, 171, 172, 193, 197
survival, 17, 21, 28, 30, 32, 33, 34, 66, 67, 68, 74, 83, 92, 95, 100, 104, 108, 147, 296, 384
Suspect, 246, 263
suspense, 5, 6, 9, 11, 18, 23, 26, 34, 53, 54, 59, 65, 67, 78, 83, 89-124, 126, 127, 133, 135, 170, 190, 200, 209, 212, 213, 230, 233, 241, 244, 260, 266, 276, 351, 363, 385, 387, 388, 390, 394
Suspense Thriller, The, 25, 196, 331
suspense, definition, 92
suspense, techniques for creating, 108
suspense, techniques for increasing, 121
suspense, time-dependence of, 93
Suspicion, 249, 362, 365, 366
suspicions, 30, 64
Sutherland, Kiefer, 194
Suvorin, A. S., 280
sweatshops, law firms, 256
symbolism, 7, 20, 23, 82, 132, 162, 170, 171, 172, 255, 285, 328, 330, 332, 333
Symons, Julian, 144, 145
sympathy, 20, 74, 98, 101, 102, 127, 128, 241, 242, 247, 264, 316, 330
sympathy vs. empathy, 102

taboo, 59
tag, 34
tailing, 172
Taken on Trust, 229
Takers, 387
Tale of Two Cities, A, 341
talisman, 22
Tall Target, The, 207
Tapply, William G., 124
Tarantino, Quentin, 117
tarantulas, 100
target, of assassin, 199, 200
Tartuffe, or The Impostor, 352
Taxi 2, 386
technical terms, 136, 244
technicality, legal, 238, 239, 241
technocrat, 307
technology as weapon, 305, 306
technology gone wrong, 5, 6, 305, 306, 307, 312, 313, 314, 322, 399
technology is the solution, 305

technology misused, 305
techno-thriller, subgenre, 5, 134, 137, 138, 149, 173, 278, 305-327, 399
temptress, 58, 59
tension, 5, 34, 36, 37, 92, 93, 95, 97, 105, 107, 108, 114, 126, 130, 132, 159, 169, 235, 387, 388, 390, 394
Tepper, Leopold, 72
Terminal Man, The, 281, 312, 313
Terminator, The, 115, 399
terrible fate, 126, 127, 128, 129, 390
terror, 89, 104, 106, 112, 152
terrorism, 5, 6, 64, 144, 152, 153, 154, 155, 173, 191, 216, 219, 228, 229, 283, 311, 312, 313
terrorism thriller, 137, 147, 181, 191, 195, 198, 216-224, 313
Terrorist Surveillance Program, 152
Testament, The, 253
testimony, 234, 239, 244, 261, 263, 265, 266, 277
That None Should Die, 280
Thatcher, Margaret, 309
theatre sets, 244
Their Trade is Treachery, 179
Thelma and Louise, 399
theme park, 307, 322
themes, 7, 11, 15, 17, 20, 22, 29, 32, 34, 35, 37, 49, 54, 72, 148, 169, 171, 173, 178, 194, 195, 196, 231, 239, 242, 247, 257, 259, 280, 283, 284, 286, 288, 306, 308, 313, 314, 328, 329, 332, 344, 351, 353, 354, 391
Theory of Cognitive Dissonance, A, 95
There's Something About Mary, 104
thieves, 53
Thinker archetype, 18, 19, 20, 129
Third Day, The, 344, 345
Third Man, The, 148, 170, 179
third quarter. *See* Quarter 3
Thirty-Nine Steps, The, 6, 9, 10, 11, 12, 38, 40, 58
This Gun for Hire, 147, 149
Thomas, Craig, 138, 313, 316
Thorp, Roderick, 228, 311
threats, 25, 65, 104, 110, 129, 147, 251, 316
Three Couriers, The, 145
Three Days of the Condor, 12, 19, 38, 213
Three Musketeers, The, 194
three-act structure, 7, 8, 11, 12, 13
thrill seekers, 95
thriller, definition, 9

Thrillers, 21, 50, 83, 215, 236, 313
Thrilling Cities, 63
Thunderball, 51, 75
ticking clock, 10, 21, 28, 87, 100, 126
Til Death Do Us Part, 366
time frame, 10
Time magazine, 236
Time of the Octopus, The, 215
Time to Kill, A, 236
time-bombs, 100
Tinker, Tailor, Soldier, Spy, 137-189
Tiptoe Boys, The, 228
Titanic, 209
to catch a spy, 181
To Catch a Spy, 142, 181, 182
To Kill a Mockingbird, 234, 235, 241, 253, 266
To Live and Die in L.A., 253
To the Devil... a Daughter, 41
Tobias, Ronald B., 384, 388, 389
Tom and Jerry, 384
Tom Clancy's Net Force, 154
tone, 7, 11, 15, 36, 42, 49, 76, 77, 145, 151, 177, 178, 391
'Tony's Hollywood Moscow Rules', 156
'Tools of Tradecraft: The CIA's Historic Spy Kit', 156
Tootsie, 114, 351
Top Secret, 172
Topkapi, 147, 219
Topol, Eric J., 284
torture, 19, 28, 42, 44, 51, 56, 60, 65, 68-70, 75, 76, 83, 86, 100, 127, 128, 140, 182, 197, 229
tourism, 26, 61, 62-65, 67, 71, 74, 170
Tourist, The, 155
Towering Inferno, The, 306
Tracers, 386
tradecraft, 155, 156, 172, 178
tragedy, 21, 36, 94, 99, 100, 102, 107, 108, 147, 175, 178, 186, 309, 351
trains, 26, 170, 171
traitors, 17, 20, 49, 133, 137, 138, 139, 144, 145, 151, 159, 162, 163, 165, 173, 174, 176, 186
Tramp, The, 54
Transplant, 281
transport, 25, 26, 170
Traveller without Luggage, The, 341
Traver, Robert, 234, 235
treachery, 73, 148
treason, 176, 192
trespassing, 64
'Trial as One of the Performing Arts, The', 244
trial by media, 260
trial, courtroom, 230-277
tribunals, 268
Trickster, 140, 141, 352
triple agent, 168
Truffaut, Francois, 11
Trump, Donald, 154, 309

trust, 11, 14, 20, 21, 23, 24, 29, 30, 32, 33, 37, 57, 58, 60, 61, 62, 73, 76, 78, 86, 103, 110, 140, 147, 150, 153, 158, 163, 169, 171, 174, 176, 178, 196, 242, 250, 279, 316, 329, 339, 354
truth, 17, 82, 108, 133, 176, 230, 232, 238, 242, 245, 247, 248, 263, 266, 276, 361
Turow, Scott, 231, 233, 236, 255, 269, 270
Twelfth Night, 351
Twelve Angry Men, 246, 261, 267
twentieth-century, 41, 42, 55, 60, 73, 77, 141, 142, 150, 153, 191, 233
Twenty Thousand Leagues Under the Sea, 311
twenty-first-century, 141, 152
Twilight, 387
U.S. Marshals, 385
UCLA, 8
UFO conspiracy theory, 85
Ultimate Punishment: A Lawyer's Reflections on Dealing with the Death Penalty, 236
umbrella, 27, 80, 155
Unabomber, 144
unattainable women, 79
uncertainty, 93, 94, 97, 98, 99, 101, 105, 133
Under Fire, 215
Under Pressure, 311
Under Siege, 223, 224, 228
Under Western Eyes, 80, 168
undercover agent, 144
undercover cop, 6, 352
underdog, 100, 241, 242, 248, 390, 396, 412
underworld, 35, 68, 169, 296, 340
unethical behaviour, 247
ungentlemanly behaviour, 69, 71, 143, 153, 179
unhappy child, 333
United Kingdom, 153
United States of America, 142, 146, 149, 150, 152, 153, 154, 157, 163, 173, 175, 176, 177, 180, 191, 192, 193, 194, 195, 196, 237, 238, 246, 248, 250, 251, 252, 254, 258, 309, 314, 315, 316
United States of Paranoia, The, 84
University of Mississippi, 236
unjustly accused. *See* innocent
unresolved situations, 93, 94, 97
unseen world, 35
Unthinkable, 224
upper-class, 53
upper-class heroes, 40, 41, 53, 63, 144, 145
Usborne, Richard, 40, 144
Usual Suspects, The, 117
utopia, 306, 307
Valley of the Dolls, 375

vampire, 122
vanity, 166, 242, 287, 288
Vassall, John, 176
ventilation ducts, 27
verdict, 259, 267
Verdict, The, 236, 242, 253, 257
verisimilitude, 63, 66, 136, 172, 308
Verne, Jules, 41, 311
Vertigo, 333
Vesper Lynd, 43
Veuves Blanches, Les, 341
vice, 24, 32, 42
victim, 12, 13, 22, 50, 69, 70, 75, 93, 110, 131, 132, 181, 198, 199, 236, 315, 329, 332, 395
victimisation, 107, 288
Victorian era, 9, 10, 55, 143
Victory of Conscience, The, 341
Vietnam, 192, 309, 314
Vietnam War, 192, 193, 314
viewpoint, 17, 20, 114, 116, 199, 387, 388
vigilance, 15, 60
vigilantism, 65, 76, 79, 107, 248
villain, 15, 17, 19, 20, 21, 22, 23, 24, 34, 41, 42, 44, 49, 51, 52, 55, 56, 57, 60, 61, 62, 65, 67, 68, 74, 75, 83, 85, 86, 89, 114, 120, 124, 128, 132, 143, 145, 148, 155, 162, 163, 174, 191, 209, 215, 241, 242, 250, 266, 276, 286, 287, 296, 332, 362
villain's lair, 12, 25, 67, 68
Vimeo, 387
violence, 61, 67, 68, 74, 75, 86, 111, 112, 113, 132, 148, 191, 232, 252
Violence Against Women Act, The, 373
Virga, Vincent, 364
virtue, 24, 32, 42, 81, 91, 171, 237
Vital Signs, 288
vivisectionists, 287
vocabulary, 136
vodka martini, 62
Voelker, John D., 235
Vogler, Christopher, 68, 330
voir dire, jury selection process, 251, 261
voodoo, 42
Vossekuil, Bryan, 198

Voyageur sans Baggage, Le, 341
voyeurism, 28, 35, 60, 140
Wagner, John, 366
Wahlberg, Mark, 375
Waite, Terry, 229
Walker, Jesse, 84
Walker, Robert, 89
Walsingham, Sir Francis, 142
want, character objective, 33
War in the Air, The, 311
war of attrition, between lawyers, 252
war on terror, 34, 141, 151, 152, 175, 193, 309
war, genre, 5, 143, 148, 155, 163, 191, 305, 308, 309, 311
Ward, Arthur Henry Sarsfield. *See* Rohmer, Sax
wargames, 308, 317
WarGames, 157
Warren Commission, 192, 208
Warrior archetype, 15, 18, 19, 52, 56, 62, 129, 142, 316, 411
Warrior code, 316
Warriors, The, 141, 386, 409
Warwick, Francis, 157
Washington Masquerade, The, 195
Washington Merry-Go-Round, 195
Washington Post, 208
Washington: Behind Closed Doors, 194
watchmen, 173, 248
Watergate, 85, 153, 158, 191, 193, 194, 197, 208, 209-213, 232, 255, 283, 309
Watson, Steven J., 342
wealth, 21, 29, 34, 41, 45, 125, 237, 314
wealthy industrialists, 85
weapons, 5 , 25, 27, 42, 45, 66, 67, 86, 91, 120, 121, 133, 146, 147, 151, 152, 156, 192, 200, 296, 305, 306, 308, 309, 314, 396, 397
weapons inspector, 153
weapons of mass destruction, 153
Weaver, Dennis, 22, 116, 399
Weaver, Sigourney, 122
Webb, Beatrice, 254
Webb, Sidney, 254

weenie, see MacGuffin, 22
Welles, Orson, 170, 384
Wells, H. G., 311
West Wing, The, 194
Western world, 34, 73, 146, 149, 154, 168, 175, 191, 286, 316
Western, genre, 5, 111, 232
Westworld, 305, 312, 322
whatdunit, 330
Wheatley, Dennis, 41, 42, 45, 157
Wheels, 312
Where Eagles Dare, 311
whistle-blower, 153, 165, 215, 258
White Dove, The, 365
White House Down, 224, 228
White Windows, The, 341, 343
White, Terry, 240, 241, 255
Who Dares Wins, 198, 224, 226-228
who watches the watchmen, 165
whodunit, 139, 151, 159, 209, 212, 230, 330, 331, 332, 385, *See also* murder mystery
whores, 142
whydunit, 212
Widmark, Richard, 264
WikiLeaks, 153, 157, 165
Wikipedia, 43, 66, 121, 152, 156, 178, 179, 180, 280, 388, 410
Wild Calendar, 366
wildlife documentary, 89
Wile E. Coyote, 384
Williams, John, 112
Williams, Valentine, 53
Willis, Bruce, 122, 200, 228
Wilson, H. W., 312
Wilson, Harold, 177
Winter Kills, 207
Winters, Larry A., 232, 241
Wintringham, David, 280
Wired.com, 156
wisdom, 233, 243, 314
witch-hunts, Communist, 85, 153, 255
witness, 13, 50, 78, 101, 105, 170, 189, 212, 213, 230, 235, 239, 244, 245, 250, 251, 252, 257, 260,
261, 262, 264, 265, 266, 269, 271, 276, 277
Witness for the Prosecution, 259
witness intimidation, 251
Wolpert, Stanley, 207
woman in jeopardy, 5, 11, 328, 329, 361, 362, 363, 364, 365, 375
Woman in White, The, 233
women in jeopardy, 6
women-in-jeopardy, 22
Woodward, Bob, 193, 208, 209, 212, 223, 283
working class, 53
World Health Organisation, 30
World Medical Association, 286
World of Espionage, The, 175
World Set Free, The, 311
World Trade Centre, 83
World War III, 308, 309
worldview, 73, 162
worry. *See* anxiety
Wouk, Herman, 234
Wright Campbell, R., 166, 167
wristwatches, 66
Writer's Journey, The, 68, 330
writing process, 44
Writing the Thriller, 362
wrong man. *See* amateur on the run
wrongly accused. *See* innocent
Wulff, Hans J., 90, 91, 92
xenophobia, 33
Xenophon, 386
X-Files, The, 31, 196, 209
Xin Zhu, 155
Yalta Boulevard sequence, the, 155
Yamakasi, 386
Yanal, Robert J., 98, 99, 101
Yapp, Malcolm, 72
Yates, Dornford, 40, 41, 42, 144
Young, Terence, 53
YouTube, 67, 103, 387
Yurick, Sol, 386
Z, 207
Zetter, Kim, 156
Zillmann, Dolf, 100, 102, 106, 107, 108
'Zog Ate My Brains', 84, 87
Zombie movies, 162

Made in the USA
Las Vegas, NV
26 August 2023